# The dBASE® Language Handbook

The DATA BASED ADVISOR® Series
Lance A. Leventhal., Ph.D., Series Director

# The dBASE® Language Handbook

Quicksilver®, Clipper®, dBXL®, dBASE® III, dBASE® III Plus, dBASE® IV, and FoxBASE+®


David M. Kalman
Editor-in-Chief, DATA BASED ADVISOR®



Microtrend™ Books

**TRADEMARKS**
Clipper is a trademark of Nantucket Corp.
dBASE is a registered trademark of Ashton-Tate
dBXL is a trademark of WordTech Systems, Inc.
FoxBASE+ is a registered trademark of Fox Software
Quicksilver is a trademark licensed to WordTech Systems, Inc. by Quicksilver Software, Inc.
Ventura Publisher is a registered trademark of Xerox Corp.



**ISBN 0-915391-30-9**

**Library of Congress Card Catalog Number: 89-42977**

Microtrend Books
165 Vallecitos de Oro
San Marcos, CA 92069

Cover design by Lorri Maida
Interior design by Dave Morgan, Slawson Communications, Inc.,
and DATA BASED ADVISOR®
Edited by Lance A. Leventhal, Ph.D., San Diego, CA

Printed in the United States
10 9 8 7 6 5 4 3 2 1

# CONTENTS

## SECTION 2-COMMAND REFERENCE *(continued)*

## SECTION 2-COMMAND REFERENCE *(continued)*

## SECTION 2-COMMAND REFERENCE *(continued)*

## SECTION 2-COMMAND REFERENCE *(continued)*

## SECTION 2-COMMAND REFERENCE *(continued)*

## SECTION 2-COMMAND REFERENCE *(continued)*

## SECTION 2-COMMAND REFERENCE *(continued)*

## SECTION 2-COMMAND REFERENCE *(continued)*



## SECTION 3-FUNCTION REFERENCE

## SECTION 3—FUNCTION REFERENCE *(continued)*

## SECTION 3—FUNCTION REFERENCE *(continued)*

## SECTION 3—FUNCTION REFERENCE *(continued)*

## SECTION 3—FUNCTION REFERENCE *(continued)*

## SECTION 3—FUNCTION REFERENCE *(continued)*

# ABOUT THE AUTHOR

David M. Kalman is Editor-in-Chief of *Data Based Advisor,* the leading magazine for PC database managment systems users. Since 1983, he has followed the evolution of the dBASE language through its many stages and variations. He has spoken at major dBASE meetings, forums, and conferences, and has commented on the dBASE scene in his monthly "Editor's File" column. He has also written major dBASE applications both for resale and for use at the magazine.

Mr. Kalman also operates Kalman Communications, a sole proprietorship that provides technical publications, information, and computer solutions to the business community. He has extensive experience in graphic arts production, typographic design, and technical communications.

Kalman received a B.A. from the University of California, San Diego, where he specialized in literature, language, and education.

# ABOUT THE SERIES EDITOR

Lance A. Leventhal is the author of 25 books, including *80386 Programming Guide, 68000 Assembly Language Programming, 6502 Assembly Language Programming*, and *Microcomputer Experimentation with the IBM PC*. His books have sold over 1,000,000 copies and have been translated into many foreign languages. He has also helped develop microprocessor-based systems and has served as a consultant for Disney, Intel, NASA, NCR, and Rockwell.

Dr. Leventhal served as Series Editor on Personal Computing for Prentice-Hall and as Technical Editor for the Society for Computer Simulation. He has lectured throughout the United States on microprocessors for IEEE, IEEE Computer Society, and other groups.

Dr. Leventhal's background includes affiliations with Linkabit Corporation, Intelcom Rad Tech, Naval Electronics Laboratory Center, and Harry Diamond Laboratories. He received a B.A. degree from Washington University (St. Louis, Missouri) and M.S. and Ph.D. degrees from the University of California, San Diego. He is a member of the AAAI, ACM, ASEE, IEEE, IEEE Computer Society, and SCS.

# FOREWORD

## by C. Wayne Ratliff, inventor of dBASE

When David Kalman asked me to write this foreword, I thought back to 1975. That was when I first needed a database and a language to help track statistics so that I could win the office football pool. Not even in my wildest dreams did I imagine that one day an entire industry would grow up around my language.

At the time, while working at the Jet Propulsion Laboratory in Pasadena, I chanced on a Univac 1108 database program called JPLDIS. As I later learned, it was based on an earlier program, Retrieve, a middle 1960's product of Tymshare Corporation, While reading the JPLDIS manual, I decided that a scaled-down version would fit on my IMSAI 8080, a 48K (eventually) PTDOS computer built from a kit.

JPLDIS was a command driven, primitive language intended for interactive use on printing terminals. It was developed long before the modern era of video displays. As I implemented its commands, I realized that the language needed programming constructs and desperately needed the ability to use a CRT terminal. Implementing these features was the first step on the path that led from JPLDIS to Vulcan and finally to dBASE.

Each time that I, or a friend, wrote a Vulcan application, we found we needed more commands to address specific requirements. Although I tried to keep the language clean and pure, syntactic ambiguities occasionally crept in. Many of today's dBASE language problems are the result of the Vulcan-dBASE evolutionary path.

Languages that are fully designed before implementation are low in ambiguity and often low in value. Evolutionary languages, on the other hand, more closely match users' needs. Unfortunately, these languages always develop some baroque features. Esperanto, for example, is a carefully designed language that is completely regular and syntactically elegant. But it remains largely unused, whereas English, an eclectic and diversified evolutionary language, has become the world standard.

The emergence of many vendors was an unexpected development in the evolution of the dBASE language. Compatible compilers and interpreters provided new features to enhance their appeal in a competitive marketplace. The proliferation of dBASE variations accelerated the evolution of the language tremendously. Vendors essentially campaign with new features, and the end users vote with their dollars. The wide acceptance of dBASE as well as the need for standardization has led to the proposed IEEE 1192 standard.

This book is especially important in documenting current dBASE dialects. The multiplicity of divergent implementations has created an obvious need for a comprehensive, cohesive guide. David Kalman's book fulfills this need.

C. Wayne Ratliff

# PREFACE

## WHAT IS dBASE®?

In personal computing circles, programmers and application developers have given the term "dBASE" two meanings. The first is widely known: "dBASE" refers to Ashton-Tate's dBASE II, dBASE III, dBASE III PLUS, or dBASE IV database management systems. The second meaning is the programming language built into Ashton-Tate's systems. This "dBASE" language lets programmers create powerful applications for business, engineering, finance, government, the professions, and the sciences. It has a rich vocabulary of commands and functions for handling input/output, designing user interfaces, printing reports, and doing calculations.

The distinction between "dBASE" the product and "dBASE" the programming language is significant because several vendors offer compatible interpreters and compilers. They are dialects of the language, much like the many dialects of BASIC that have emerged over the years. Vendors include Fox Software, developer of FoxBASE+ and FoxBASE+/Mac; Nantucket Corp., developer of Clipper and McMax; and WordTech Systems, developer of Quicksilver and dBXL. Other companies, such as VersaSoft Corp., Paperback Software International, and Ratliff Software Production, Inc. also produce dBASE-like systems.

The dialects have become popular because of the demand for:

- Faster-running and more reliable applications
- Applications on different kinds of computers and in different software environments
- More functions and improved productivity for developers
- Source code security
- No runtime royalties for applications
- Lower-cost development systems

This book covers major dBASE-compatible language products for PC/MS-DOS, specifically Clipper, dBASE III PLUS, dBASE IV, dBXL, FoxBASE+, and Quicksilver. These products share a command set, with minor variations. Plus, each has its own special commands and functions. The book contains a complete command and function reference. Each definition includes detailed explanations and practical examples of the Ashton-Tate implementations. Then, variations among the dialects follow, also with practical examples. Commands and functions unique to dialects have their own entries. Appendixes cover character codes, special features of the dialects, and other reference material.

## WHO NEEDS THIS BOOK?

"The dBASE Language Handbook" offers concise explanations and realistic examples of dBASE commands and functions. Programmers, analysts, applications developers, consultants, students, teachers, managers, users of dBASE-compatible systems, and software developers and vendors will find it handy for quick reference or in-depth study. It can serve as a convenient supplement or alternative to the standard manuals.

Foremost, "The dBASE Language Handbook" offers a single reference for programmers and end users who sell, support, or work with several dBASE-compatible products. I know from personal experience that many people do this. Some programmers prototype applications in dBASE III PLUS or dBASE IV, then compile them with Quicksilver or Clipper. Consultants, analysts, and managers often must deal with a variety of hardware and software. For example, FoxBASE+ runs under Xenix and on the Macintosh. Clipper runs on Wang computers and other non-IBM systems. Quicksilver also runs on generic MS-DOS systems. By providing a single, cohesive reference, "The dBASE Language Handbook" eases the problem of developing, maintaining, supporting, and using multiple products.

Until now, users of Clipper, dBXL, FoxBASE+, and Quicksilver have had only their product manuals to help them. They often have a difficult time recognizing differences from standard dBASE III PLUS or dBASE IV features. The Handbook serves as a secondary reference that clearly indicates new features and incompatibilities in the various systems.

"The dBASE Language Handbook" will also help those who are considering or evaluating compatible products. They can see examples of the features provided by Clipper, Quicksilver, and other products. They can also determine the effort required to make their programs run under another system.

"The dBASE Language Handbook" is a programming language reference. As such, it focuses on programming commands and functions—the elements of the language that make dBASE resemble BASIC, C, or Pascal. Detailed examples illustrate commands and functions so programmers can apply them to their own applications effectively. When a command or function appears in one system but not another, I describe ways to simulate the missing feature. For commands and functions that are superfluous or obsolete, I offer complete references while pointing out superior alternatives.

## WHAT ABOUT THE FUTURE?

As software developers produce new versions and new products, the dBASE language will change. I expect to update "The dBASE Language Handbook" regularly. I welcome your comments and suggestions for future editions.

# ACKNOWLEDGEMENTS

I thank my editor and series director, Dr. Lance Leventhal, for both his consummate editing skill and his moral support. In those moments when I saw nothing amusing in dBASE, he pointed out FKLABEL( ), the function you cannot discuss in mixed company.

Many thanks to Russ Freeland for the CALL( )/CCALL entries, and to George F. Goley, IV for his encouragement and sage advice on FoxBASE+.

I also owe gratitude to numerous individuals at Ashton-Tate, Fox Software, Nantucket, and WordTech Systems. I will certainly never run out of floppy disks.

Special thanks to the *Data Based Advisor* editorial team—Dian Schaffhauser, David Kodama, and Jewel Nelson—for their constant encouragement and support.

Thanks to my production editor, David Morgan, and the staff of Slawson Communications for making this book possible.

Finally, thanks to my parents Emily and Jack, for *everything* else.

# SECTION 1

## OVERVIEW OF THE dBASE® LANGUAGE DIALECTS

## USING THE COMMAND AND FUNCTION REFERENCE

## dBASE® LANGUAGE OPERATORS

# OVERVIEW OF THE dBASE® LANGUAGE DIALECTS

## dBASE IV, Version 1.0 — Ashton-Tate

Provides interactive database management by entering commands at the dot prompt, or by using the Control Center menu system. The Control Center provides automatic generation of reports, forms, queries, and applications.

The programming language lets users automate database management applications. It includes commands and functions for storing and manipulating data, designing forms, and generating reports. dBASE IV runs dBASE III PLUS applications with little or no modification. It supports multiuser applications on local area networks.

dBASE IV also supports relational database management through either interactive or embedded SQL. You can type SQL statements at the dot prompt, or include them in dBASE language programs.

Purchasers of the Developers Edition can distribute applications under the dBASE IV unlimited runtime license. Multiuser applications require a LAN PACK key disk at the workstation.

## dBASE III PLUS, Version 1.1 — Ashton-Tate

Provides interactive database management by entering commands at the dot prompt, or by using the dBASE Assistant. The Assistant provides menus for most database management functions.

The programming language lets users automate database management applications. It includes commands and functions for storing and manipulating data, designing forms, and generating reports.

Distributing dBASE III PLUS applications requires paid runtime licenses from Ashton-Tate. Multiuser applications require a LAN PACK key disk at the workstation.

## Clipper, Summer 1987 Version — Nantucket Corp.

Compiles applications into executable programs (extension EXE). Clipper has no interactive database management features, but it comes with an interactive debugger (DEBUG.OBJ) for developing applications.

Clipper offers a superset of the dBASE III PLUS programming language. Notable features include user defined functions, light bar menus, memo functions, array functions, and DOS-level file input/output. Clipper's open architecture allows the linking of object modules written in C or assembly language.

Clipper supports multiuser applications on local area networks. Applications may be freely distributed without runtime license fees.

## dBXL, Version 1.2 — WordTech Systems

Provides interactive database management by entering commands at the interactive prompt, or with the INTRO mode. INTRO provides an easy to use prompt system for novices.

dBXL's language is a superset of dBASE III PLUS. Most dBASE III PLUS programs run without modification.

The language includes the standard dBASE III PLUS commands and functions. The extended features include windowing, graphing, arrays, user defined functions, and DOS interrupt level commands and functions.

Distribution of dBXL applications requires additional copies of dBXL, or compilation with Quicksilver.

## FoxBASE+, Version 2.0 — Fox Software

Provides interactive database management by entering commands at the dot prompt.

The FoxBASE+ language is a superset of dBASE III PLUS. dBASE III PLUS programs run without modification, but much faster.

The language includes the standard dBASE III PLUS commands and functions. Extended features include user defined functions, system information functions, light bar menus, and arrays. A multiuser version is available.

Distribution of runtime applications requires the purchase of a runtime license. Unlimited licenses are available.

## Quicksilver, Version 1.2 — WordTech Systems

Compiles applications into executable programs (extension EXE). Quicksilver has no interactive database management features; however, its companion product, dBXL, is highly compatible (sold separately). Quicksilver includes an interactive debugger for application development.

Quicksilver's language is a superset of dBASE III PLUS. Most programs run without modification.

The language includes the standard dBASE III PLUS commands and functions. The extended features include windowing, graphing, arrays, DOS interrupt level commands and functions, and user defined functions. Quicksilver allows direct linking of object modules written in C or assembly language.

Quicksilver offers comprehensive multiuser capabilities, based on the NetworkerPlus module (sold separately). Applications may be distributed freely without runtime licensing.

## Contact information

Ashton-Tate
20101 Hamilton Avenue
Torrance, Calif. 90502-1319
(213) 329-8000

Fox Software
118 W. South Boundary
Perrysburg, Ohio 43551
(419) 874-0162

Nantucket Corp.
12555 West Jefferson Blvd.
Los Angeles, Calif. 90066
(650) 257-4125

WordTech Systems, Inc.
P.O. Box 1747
Orinda, Calif. 94563
(415) 254-0900

# USING THE COMMAND AND FUNCTION REFERENCE

The reference section is divided into command and function entries. Each entry has some or all of the following material:

- COMMAND OR FUNCTION NAME
- DIALECTS
- RETURN VALUE (functions only)
- SYNTAX
- DEFINITION
- RECOMMENDED USE
- EXAMPLE
- SPECIAL USES
- LIMITS AND WARNINGS
- VARIATIONS
- CROSS REFERENCE TO RELATED COMMANDS AND FUNCTIONS

At the top of the page, the keyword indicates the command or function. Keywords are the basis for alphabetizing the references.

*Dialects* lists the database systems that contain the command or function.

Function entries indicate the data type of the *return value.*

The *syntax notation* shows the command or function, its options, and its arguments in an abbreviated form. The notation uses the following symbols:

| | |
|---|---|
| [] | Contains optional arguments. (Do not type the brackets). |
| <> | Contains an argument. (Do not type the brackets). |
| ( ) | Delimits function arguments. (You must type the parentheses). |

a/b — Either a or b

<exp> — Expression with a data type determined by context.

<exp1>,.....n — Contains from 1 to n expressions in a list; expressions are separated by commas and are limited in length to 254 characters. The list may contain different data types, depending on context.

<expN> — Numeric expression (decimal integer). May include the digits 0 through 9, a negative sign, and a decimal point; or scientific notation (except Clipper) in the form xe+y (10 to the yth power times x).

For example, 5e+4 equals 10 to the 4th powertimes 5, or 50,000.

<expC> — Character expression.

<expD> — Date expression, in the form mm/dd/yyyy.

<expF> — Floating point numeric. IEEE 754 real floating point (dBASE IV only).

<expL> — Logical expression, evaluating to true or false; or a logical constant in the form .T., .t., .F., or .f. (period delimiters are required).

<N> — Numeric constant.

Note that expressions may consist of literal strings, numeric or logical constants, literal dates delimited with braces (dBASE IV only), or fields and memory variables that contain data of these types.

Occasionally, descriptions appear instead of the terse <exp> notation. For example, the RUN command has the argument <operating system command> instead of <expC>. Other such descriptions include:

<comment> — Text embedded in a program. See commands NOTE, *, and &&.

<condition> — Logical expression evaluating to true or false. Same as <expL>

<coord> — Screen coordinate, consisting of a row and column number.

<expression list> — Expressions in a list separated by commas; sometimes specified as <exp1>,.....n.

<statement> — Any valid dBASE command or function.

The descriptions make the notation more readable.

Keywords appear in upper case.

A *definition* follows, summarizing the function or command. The definition also explains any special notation in the syntax listing. *Unless otherwise noted, definitions refer to dBASE III PLUS usage.* Syntactic or semantic variations in the other dialects (including dBASE IV) use dBASE III PLUS as a baseline since it is the standard subset of them all. Commands or functions unique to a dialect have their own entries.

After the definition, the recommended use describes a useful context and gives *examples.*

Program examples follow these conventions:

- Keywords appear in uppercase.
- Memory variables, fields, and command options appear in lowercase.
- Program control structures are indented two spaces.
- Program output appears in boldface.

Note that dBASE is not sensitive to case or indentation. These conventions simply make program logic easier to follow.

To enter and run programs, you must use an editor that produces an ASCII file. Most word processors have a program editing mode, or can export to an ASCII file. Most specialized program editors produce only ASCII files. You can also use the editors built into dBASE III PLUS, dBASE IV, dBXL, and FoxBASE+. Use the command MODIFY COMMAND to begin editing.

Type the program listings exactly as shown. If a database is required, use the CREATE command to create it. Program listings generally illustrate a single command, and therefore may not represent a complete operation. Code fragments that are not complete programs may show lines marked by an asterisk that represent other commands or modules you must add. Program fragments may also name databases that are not described in detail.

Following the examples, *Special Uses* describes unexpected or innovative usage. *Limits and Warnings* highlights potential problems.

*Variations* describes how commands or functions work in other dialects where they differ from dBASE III PLUS.

## A Typical Command:

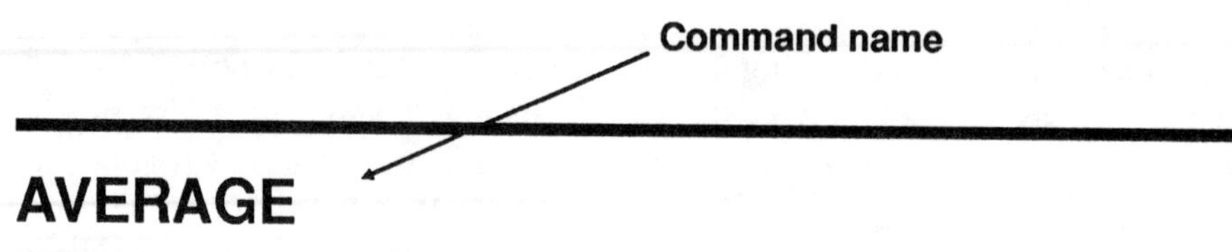


# AVERAGE

### DIALECTS

Clipper, dBASE III PLUS, dBASE IV, dBXL, FoxBASE+, and Quicksilver.

**Supported dialects**

### SYNTAX:

AVERAGE [<expression list>][<scope>]
[FOR/WHILE <condition>]
[TO <memory variable list>]

*See Glossary for definitions of <scope> and <condition>*

### DEFINITION:

Computes arithmetic mean of numeric expressions. Uses all fields, or the <expression list> you specify. Averages all records unless you specify a condition with FOR or WHILE. The results may go to a memory variable list. In dBASE III PLUS, dBASE IV, FoxBASE+, and dBXL, displays on the screen when SET TALK is ON.

**Example 1**—A regional sales office must determine the average mileage logged by traveling representatives. From the database file MILELOG, average MILES can be calculated FOR a particular SELLER.

**dBASE program file**

```
SET TALK on
* Database file MILELOG contains mileage
* information for sales representatives.
USE milelog
* MILES and SELLER are fields in MILELOG.
AVERAGE miles FOR seller = "James"
32 records averaged
MILES
201
```

**Program or command output in bold type**

**Example 2**—In the same sales office, the manager wants a printed mileage report. To produce it, the AVERAGE miles must be saved in a memory variable that can be either printed or stored in another database.

```
SET TALK off
USE milelog
* Store the average of MILES in memory variable AMILES.
AVERAGE miles FOR seller = "James" TO amiles
* You can now print AMILES, or store it in another database.
SET DEVICE TO PRINT
@ 10,10 SAY "A = age miles" + STR(amiles,4,2)
SET DEVICE TO SCREEN
USE summary
REPLACE avemiles WITH amiles
```

## VARIATIONS:

**Clipper, Quicksilver:** AVERAGE requires an expression list and a memory variable list. For example:

```
AVERAGE sales,profits TO sale_ave,prof_ave
```

puts the average of SALES in memory variable SALE_AVE, and the average of PROFITS in PROF_AVE.

**dBASE IV:** You can send AVERAGE results to an existing one-dimensional array. They fill it starting with the first element until there are no more results, or no more elements. Leftover elements retain their previous values.

In this example, JAN, FEB, MAR, and APR contain sales figures for a major corporation. The array RESULTS[] has four elements, one for each field:

```
PUBLIC results
DECLARE results[4]
USE sales
AVERAGE jan,feb,mar,apr TO ARRAY results
DISPLAY MEMORY
RESULTS       pub  A   [6]
     [1]        elem  N              3409040.92  (3409040.920000000000)
     [2]        elem  N                30923.33  (30923.33000000000000)
     [3]        elem  N                23456.23  (23456.23000000000000)
     [4]        elem  N               323423.55  (323423.5500000000000)
```

The dBASE IV CALCULATE command can also do AVERAGEs with its AVG( ) option.

Cross reference

## SEE ALSO:

Commands CALCULATE, DECLARE, and SET TALK ON.

# dBASE® LANGUAGE OPERATORS

**Arithmetic and string (in order of increasing precedence):**

| | |
|---|---|
| +, - | plus, minus |
| **, ^ | exponentiation |
| *, / | multiplication, division |
| +, - | addition, subtraction, or string concatenation |
| % | modulus (Clipper only) |
| ( ) | grouping numbers (Clipper only) |

**Comparison (no precedence):**

| | |
|---|---|
| < | less than |
| <= | less than or equal to |
| = | equal to |
| >= | greater than or equal to |
| > | greater than |
| <>, # | not equal to |
| $ | substring (a$b is true if a is a substring of b) |
| == | Exact equality (similar to using = with SET EXACT ON) (Clipper and FoxBASE+ only) |

**Logical (in order of increasing precedence):**

| | |
|---|---|
| .NOT., ! | logical not |
| .AND. | logical and |
| .OR. | logical or |
| != | logical not equal |
| ( ) | logical grouping |

**String operators:**

| | |
|---|---|
| + | string concatenation |
| - | string concatenation moving trailing blanks from first string to end of second |
| { } | convert string to date (dBASE IV only) |

**Operator precedence in evaluating expressions is (descending order):**

1) Within parentheses
2) Mathematical and string (as specified)
3) Comparison
4) Logical (as specified)

Evaluation is left to right if not otherwise specified.

**Data types**

| | |
|---|---|
| C | Character |
| D | Date |
| F | IEEE 754 real floating point (dBASE IV only) |
| L | Logical |
| M | Memo (long text) |
| N | Numeric (decimal integer) |

## SEE ALSO:

Commands SET EXACT and STORE; function & (macro).

# SECTION 2

## dBASE® LANGUAGE COMMANDS

# &&

## DIALECTS:

Clipper, dBASE III PLUS, dBASE IV, dBXL, FoxBASE+, and Quicksilver.

## SYNTAX:

[<statement>] && [<comment or note>]

## DEFINITION:

Lets you add program notes to the end of an executable program statement. Text after && is ignored at runtime.

A double ampersand may also start a comment line.

## RECOMMENDED USE:

Notes are invaluable for maintaining programs. They act as reminders, and let you keep track of changes. Use && to put notes in a program's margin.

**Example**—A manufacturing control program contains notes describing what it is doing.

```
DO WHILE enter          && ENTER is true when user wants to add record.
  mspace = SPACE(10)    && Create variable to hold user response.
  * <More statements>
ENDDO
```

See command NOTE for another example.

## LIMITS/WARNINGS:

A semicolon at the end of a note continues it onto the next line. Be careful—if you put a command on the next line, dBASE ignores it. (The semicolon is the dBASE line continuation character).

Program notes can slow the execution of dBASE III PLUS and dBXL programs. Such slowing is negligible unless you use extensive notes between commands, or within DO WHILE loops that parse them repeatedly.

The compilers strip program notes from their runtime modules.

## VARIATIONS:

**Clipper:** Does not treat a semicolon in a note as a continuation character.

**dBXL, Quicksilver:** Treats text to the right of &&\ as an executable statement.

This lets you put dBXL-specific or Quicksilver-specific statements in programs running on other systems. For example, Clipper, dBASE III PLUS, dBASE IV, and FoxBASE+ treat

```
&&\ DOSINT mvar
```

as a program note. You must enable this feature in dBXL by putting COMMENT=ON in CONFIG.XL.

You can disable this feature by using the -\ option when compiling your application. Quicksilver will then ignore statements after the &&\.

## SEE ALSO:

Commands * and NOTE; Appendix 2, "Sensing the Environment."

# *

## DIALECTS:
Clipper, dBASE III PLUS, dBASE IV, dBXL, FoxBASE+, and Quicksilver.

## SYNTAX:
* <program note or comment>

## DEFINITION:
Marks a program line as non-executable, that is, a note or comment.

Same as NOTE.

## SEE ALSO:
Commands && and NOTE.

# *QSOFF...*QSON

## DIALECTS:

Quicksilver only.

## SYNTAX:

*QSOFF
<statements>.
*QSON

## DEFINITION:

Causes program statements to be disregarded.

*QSOFF directs Quicksilver to ignore subsequent text. *QSON resumes normal execution.

Other systems treat *QSOFF and *QSON as program notes.

## RECOMMENDED USE:

Normally, Quicksilver cannot compile unsupported commands such as EDIT and BROWSE, even if they are "hidden" by the special memory variables XQUICKS or XNATIVE, or in conditional structures that never execute. However, *QSOFF and *QSON let you compile and run applications containing unsupported commands.

**Example**—A program designed for both dBXL and Quicksilver includes two routines for editing a file. Running under dBXL, it uses the BROWSE command. Compiled with Quicksilver, it uses memory variables to GET data (Quicksilver doesn't have BROWSE). *QSOFF and *QSON hide the BROWSE statement from the compiler.

```
PUBLIC xquicks
IF xquicks
   @ 10,10 SAY "Description   " GET descrip
   @ 11,10 SAY "Serial number" GET serial
   READ
ELSE
  *QSOFF
  BROWSE
  *QSON
ENDIF
```

## SEE ALSO:

Commands &&, *, and NOTE; Appendix 2, "Sensing the Environment."

# !/RUN

## DIALECTS:
Clipper, dBASE III PLUS, dBASE IV, dBXL, FoxBASE+, and Quicksilver.

## SYNTAX:
!/RUN <operating system command>/<external program>

## DEFINITION:
Executes a single operating system command from within a program. Same as RUN.

## SEE ALSO:
Command RUN.

# ?/??

## DIALECTS:
Clipper, dBASE III PLUS, dBASE IV, dBXL, FoxBASE+, and Quicksilver.

## SYNTAX:
?[?] <exp1>[,<exp2>,<exp3>,...]

## DEFINITION:
? evaluates expressions and expression lists and displays their values on the next line. ?? displays them on the same line. ? alone displays or prints a blank line.

## DEFAULT:
? directs output to the screen. To direct it to a printer as well, use SET PRINT ON. To direct it to the printer only, use SET PRINT ON and SET CONSOLE OFF.

## RECOMMENDED USE:
In the interactive mode, use ? to evaluate numeric, string, and date expressions. It also evaluates functions that give environment and database information.

In programs, use ? to produce simple list-oriented reports.

## SPECIAL USE:
CHR(7) is the ASCII character that rings the system bell, producing a short "beep." Use ?? CHR(7) in programs to ring the bell without moving the display up a line. This is useful for warnings and prompts.

## EXAMPLES:
**Example 1**—SORTing a database file requires free disk space up to three times the file's size. From the interactive prompt, use ? and DISKSPACE( ) to find out how much space is available. The result appears on the next line.

```
. ? DISKSPACE()
9877504
```

**Example 2**—A towing company must generate lists of vehicles towed and stored for major clients (such as the port authority and the police department). The following program gathers data from file MAINTOW and prints it using ?. The example shows several uses of ? to evaluate and display expressions.

```
USE maintow
SET CONSOLE off         && Turn off screen output.
SET PRINT on            && Turn on printer output.
* Data items with different types must be converted to the same type
* to be concatenated. DTOC() converts MTODAY from date to character.
? "DATE: " + DTOC(mtoday)
* Memory variable GETCLIENT holds the name of the client passed from
* a calling program. The macro function (&) evaluates GETCLIENT
* within a string.
? "VEHICLES TOWED and STORED FOR &getclient"
? "-----------------------------------------"
DO WHILE .NOT. EOF()     && Continue until End of File.
  * Print only records for which field ASSIGNOR equals GETCLIENT.
  IF UPPER(assignor) = getclient
    ? "     Owner: " + SUBSTR(reg_fname,1,1),reg_lname
    ? "  Vehicle: " + year,make,model,tag_state,tag_num
    ? "       VIN: " + vin_num
    ? " Tow date: " + DTOC(tow_date)
  ENDIF
  ?
  SKIP                   && Move to the next record.
ENDDO
?? CHR(7)
? "**End of VEHICLES TOWED and STORED FOR &getclient **"
EJECT                    && Eject the paper.
SET PRINT off
SET CONSOLE on
```

## VARIATIONS:

**dBASE IV:** The ?/?? command has the four options PICTURE, FUNCTION, STYLE, and AT in the form:

?/?? [<expression 1>] [PICTURE <format>]
    [FUNCTION <format>] [AT <expN>] [STYLE <font number>]]
    [,<expression 2>...]

The AT option lets you specify the column at which to print the expression.

The STYLE option lets you control printed output by specifying bold, italic, underline, superscript, and subscript. You can also specify fonts 1 through 5 as defined in your CONFIG.DB file.

The STYLE option depends on the installed printer driver. If it does not support a font, the output prints normally.

Use the STYLE option to change fonts for individual data items. For example, to print a report heading in boldface at column 15, use the following:

```
rpthead = "Marigold Software Corp. Annual Report"
? rpthead STYLE "B" AT 15
```

To change a document's overall typestyle, use the system variables _pscode and _pecode. To change blocks of text within a document, use ???.

The PICTURE and FUNCTION options let you use templates and functions to format output. PICTURE lets you use templates and functions together, in the form:

? <exp> PICTURE "@<function> <template>"

FUNCTION allows only a function, in the form:

? <exp> FUNCTION "<function>"

With ?/??, you can use all templates available in the @...SAY command. However, there are only eight valid functions.

## Functions for use with Numeric Data

### $

Displays numbers with a floating currency symbol (a dollar sign by default). SET CURRENCY RIGHT makes the symbol appear on the right. SET CURRENCY LEFT (the default) makes it appear on the left.

```
amount = 844.33
? amount FUNCTION "L"
        $844.33
```

### B

Left justifies numeric data.

```
? daysleft PICTURE "@B"   && or ? daysleft FUNCTION "B"
22
```

### L

Displays numbers with leading zeros.

```
amount = 844.33
? amount FUNCTION "L"
000000000000000844.33
```

## Functions for Long Character Fields (data exceeds the PICTURE template).

### H<expN>

Should format a character string to fit horizontally within length <N>, but doesn't work in dBASE IV version 1.0.

### V<expN>

Formats a character string to fit within length <expN>. It wraps text to subsequent lines if it exceeds the width, creating a vertical column.

```
mstring = "Please enter your name and address in the space below"
? mstring FUNCTION "@V10"
Please
enter your
name and
address in
the space
below
```

## Functions for Short Character Fields (data does not exceed template).

### J

Right justifies text within a field. Overrides the _alignment system variable.

```
mprompt1 = "Name: "
mprompt2 = "Address: "
mprompt3 = "City: "
* The ! template converts characters to uppercase.
? mprompt1 PICTURE "@J !!!!!!!!!!!!!!!!!!!!!!!!!!!!!!"
? mprompt2 PICTURE "@J !!!!!!!!!!!!!!!!!!!!!!!!!!!!!!"
? mprompt3 PICTURE "@J !!!!!!!!!!!!!!!!!!!!!!!!!!!!!!"
                         NAME:
                      ADDRESS:
                         CITY:
```

### T

Removes leading and trailing blanks from a field.

```
mname = "    Household Construction Corp.   "
? mname FUNCTION "T"
Household Construction Corp.
```

## Functions for both Numeric and Short Character Fields

**I**

Centers numeric or character data within a field. Use it in reports to produce centered columns. Overrides the _alignment system variable.

With character data:

```
USE companies
? cname1 PICTURE "@I XXXXXXXXXXXXXXXXXXXXXXXXXXXXXX"
? cname2 PICTURE "@I XXXXXXXXXXXXXXXXXXXXXXXXXXXXXX"
? cname3 PICTURE "@I XXXXXXXXXXXXXXXXXXXXXXXXXXXXXX"

     IBM International
          Xerox
   Compaq Computer Corp.
```

With numeric data:

```
USE sales
? jan FUNCTION "I"
? feb FUNCTION "I"
? mar FUNCTION "I"

     9837.22
      33.00
     422.00
```

## SEE ALSO:

Commands @, ???, SET CONSOLE, SET DEVICE, SET PRINT, and SET SPACE.

# ???

## DIALECTS:

dBASE IV only.

## SYNTAX:

??? <expC>

## DEFINITION:

Sends control codes to the printer without changing the row and column position (PROW( ) and PCOL( )).

??? ignores the installed printer driver.

??? also prints text.

You can send control codes to the printer in three ways: 1) use CHR( ) to send ASCII characters directly; 2) use control code brace delimiters to send mnemonic codes or ASCII characters; 3) combine ASCII characters with letters using either CHR( ) or brace delimiters.

Control codes vary with printer model and brand. See your printer's manual listing.

Control character specifiers can be arguments of the ??? command. You can use either the mnemonic specifier or its ASCII value, for example "{CTRL-R}" or "{18}". You must enclose the specifier in quotation marks.

The number in each column is the ASCII value. The form in braces is the specifier. Some codes have alternate specifiers (separated by /). Use only one.

| | | | | | |
|---|---|---|---|---|---|
| 0 | {NULL}/{CTRL-@} | 11 | {CTRL-K} | 22 | {CTRL-V} |
| 1 | {CTRL-A} | 12 | {CTRL-L} | 23 | {CTRL-W} |
| 2 | {CTRL-B} | 13 | {RETURN}/{CTRL-M} | 24 | {CTRL-X} |
| 3 | {CTRL-C} | 14 | {CTRL-N} | 25 | {CTRL-Y} |
| 4 | {CTRL-D} | 15 | {CTRL-O} | 26 | {CTRL-Z} |
| 5 | {CTRL-E} | 16 | {CTRL-P} | 27 | {ESC}/{ESCAPE}/{CTRL-[} |
| 6 | {CTRL-F} | 17 | {CTRL-Q} | 28 | {CTRL-\} |
| 7 | {BELL}/{CTRL-G} | 18 | {CTRL-R} | 29 | {CTRL-]} |
| 8 | {BACKSPACE}/{CTRL-H} | 19 | {CTRL-S} | 30 | {CTRL-^} |
| 9 | {TAB}/{CTRL-I} | 20 | {CTRL-T} | 31 | {CTRL-_} |
| 10 | {LINEFEED}/{CTRL-J} | 21 | {CTRL-U} | 127 | {DEL}/{DELETE} |

## RECOMMENDED USE:

Use ??? to change typestyles for blocks of text within a report, and to change global characteristics such as page length and linespace. Also use it to access printer capabilities not supported by the driver.

There are three other ways to control print characteristics: the STYLE options of the ? and ?? commands, the system variables _pecode and _pscode, and the CHR( ) function. Use _pecode and _pscode with the PRINTJOB command to control entire reports. Use ?...STYLE to change typestyles for individual lines. Use CHR( ) as an alternative to the STYLE option to embed control codes in character strings.

**Example**—An accounts receivable program prints invoices using several typestyles. The heading prints in expanded mode, the detail in compressed double strike, and the notices at the end in emphasized pica.

```
* Control codes for Epson printers.
SET CONSOLE off
SET PRINT on
??? "{CTRL-N}"+"Invoice " + DTOC(DATE())  && Turns on expanded mode.
??? "{CTRL-O}"                            && Turns on compressed mode.
?
?
?  "Service  " + STR(service,9,2)  AT 01
?? "Mileage  " + STR(mileage,9,2)  AT 40
?  "Materials" + STR(material,9,2) AT 01
?? "Hourly   " + STR(hourly,9,2)   AT 40
?  "Postage  " + STR(postage,9,2)  AT 01
?? "Freight  " + STR(freight,9,2)  AT 40
?  "Labor    " + STR(labor,9,2)    AT 01
?? "Meals    " + STR(meals,9,2)    AT 40
?  "Travel   " + STR(travel,9,2)   AT 01
?? "TOTAL    " + TRANSFORM(mtotal,"@$ ###,###.##") AT 40
?
??? "{CTRL-R}{ESC}E"     && Cancels compressed mode/turns on emphasized.
?
? "Your account is now 120 days past due. Please remit today."
? "If you have any questions, please call our toll free hotline."
?
* Cancel emphasized mode. You could also have used the
*   ASCII characters "{27}F" or CHR(27)+"F".
??? "{ESC}F"
?
SET PRINT off
SET CONSOLE on
```

**Example**—A programmer creates custom drivers that the user can install for a particular printer. Each one consists of a set of memory variables containing ASCII characters.

```
empha_on =  CHR(27) + "E"    && Turn emphasized on.
empha_off = CHR(27) + "F"    && Turn emphasized off.
exp_on =    CHR(27) + "W1"   && Turn expanded on.
exp_off =   CHR(27) + "W1"   && Turn expanded off.
```

The driver is saved in a memory file (SAVE TO epson), then later restored with the command "RESTORE FROM epson".

In a report, the program uses the restored variables with the ??? command:

```
??? exp_on    && Turn emphasized on.
? "Kalman Communications Annual Report"
* <More text>.
??? exp_off
```

## SEE ALSO:

Commands ?, @...SAY, PRINTJOB, SET DEVICE, and SET PRINT; function CHR( ).

## DIALECTS:

Clipper, dBASE III PLUS, dBASE IV, dBXL, FoxBASE+, and Quicksilver.

## SYNTAX:

@ <coord> [[SAY <exp> [PICTURE <format>] [FUNCTION <format>]]
[[GET <exp> [PICTURE <format>]] RANGE <expN1>,<expN2>] / [CLEAR]]

## DEFINITION:

@ ("AT") indicates position <coord> on the screen or on a printout. It places output (SAYs) on the screen or on printed reports, and input fields (GETs) on the screen.

<coord> represents a coordinate pair, R and C, where R is the row (0 to 24 from top to bottom), and C is the column (0 to 79 from left to right). For printed reports, ranges are limited to the page size.

## DEFAULT:

@ directs output to the screen, unless you redirect it with the SET DEVICE command.

## OPTIONS:

### @ <coord>

@ <coord> alone clears the line to the right of <coord>. For example;

```
@ 10,9
```

clears line 10 to the right of column 9.

### @ <coord> **SAY <exp>**

Evaluates and displays an expression. For example;

```
@ 5,10 SAY "Please enter today's date: "
```

displays the message "Please enter today's date: " starting at line 5, column 10.

### @ <coord> SAY <exp> **PICTURE <format>**

The PICTURE option formats the SAY output with templates and functions. A PICTURE can add attributes such as commas, dollar signs, and plus signs. It can also manipulate date formats, scroll fields, and do case conversion.

### @ <coord> SAY <exp> **FUNCTION <format> PICTURE <format>**<br>GET<exp> **FUNCTION <format> PICTURE <format>**

FUNCTION provides an alternate way to specify functions in SAYs and GETs. Within a PICTURE <format>, you can use both templates and functions to format SAYs and GETs. FUNCTION lets you separate function codes and templates into separate clauses for more flexibility and greater readability. FUNCTIONs do not require the @ symbol.

### @ <coord> SAY <exp> PICTURE <format> **GET <exp> PICTURE <format>**

GET displays an expression (field, memory variable, or array element). When you issue READ after GETs, the cursor returns to the first GET to allow the user to edit the field or variable. The GET appears one space after the SAY expression on the same line.

A PICTURE associated with a GET formats both input and output. As you edit the GET field with a PICTURE, the data you enter assumes the specified format.

## PICTURES

A PICTURE consists of a character string containing function or template codes. The character string may be a literal, a character memory variable or field, or some other character expression.

Functions consist of the @ symbol and function codes. Templates consist of string literals and template codes. A PICTURE must be of character type.

(If you use the FUNCTION keyword, the @ symbol is unnecessary).

Both function and template codes appear below.

## FUNCTIONS

Functions operate on an entire SAY or GET. They can be combined.

### Function Codes that Work Only with Character Data

**!**

Allows any character and converts letters to uppercase. Used with SAY and GET statements.

```
make = "Chevrolet"
@ 22,25 SAY make PICTURE "@!"
CHEVROLET
```

### A

Allows letters only (no spaces or other characters). Used only with GET statements.

```
lookup = SPACE(20)
@ 13,22 GET lookup PICTURE "@A"
READ
BaldersonPeteM
```

### R

Displays literal characters in the template, but does not save them in the field. Used only with GET statements.

```
mphone = SPACE(12)
@ 09,15 SAY "Phone: " GET mphone PICTURE "@R 999-999-9999"
READ
619-555-1222

? mphone
6195551212
```

In all systems except dBXL, when a literal is the last character of an @R template, it is truncated as follows:

```
SET DELIMITERS on
mvar = SPACE(6)
@ 01,10 SAY "Enter id number" GET mvar PICTURE "@R (999999)"
READ
          :(      :
```

To avoid this problem, add a space to the GET variable.

### S<n>

Limits a character GET display to <n> characters and scrolls wider input horizontally. In scrolling, the previous characters move to the left and out of view. By moving the cursor, you can see <n> characters at a time. S<n> affects only the display, not the input string. In this example, the user enters a vehicle identification number longer than the defined width of 10. Although only the last 10 characters show, the memory variable VIN_NUM contains the complete string.

```
vin_num = SPACE(50)
@ 01,01 SAY "Vehicle ID: " GET vin_num PICTURE "@S10"
READ
3838XXXZZZ

? vin_num
2XD28283XX983838XXXZZZ
```

## Function Codes that Work With Date and Character Data

### D

Displays dates in MM/DD/YY format (American date format). Used with SAY and GET statements.

```
enddate = SPACE(8)
@ 22,03 SAY "Ending date: " GET enddate PICTURE "@D"
READ
08/23/87
```

### E

Displays dates in DD/MM/YY format (European date format). Used with SAY and GET statements.

Without PICTURE:

```
begin = DATE()
@ 24,01 SAY "Starting date: " GET begin
READ
09/29/87
```

With PICTURE:

```
@ 24,01 SAY "Starting date: " GET begin PICTURE "@E"
READ
29/09/87
```

## Function Codes that Work Only With Numeric Data

### (

Displays negative numbers inside parentheses. Used only with SAY statements.

```
@ 10,10 SAY -283.22 PICTURE "@("
( 283.22)
```

### B

Left justifies numeric data. Used with GET and SAY statements.
Without PICTURE:

```
daysleft = 22
@ 10,00 SAY daysleft
            22
```

With PICTURE:

```
@ 10,00 SAY daysleft PICTURE "@B"
22
```

### C

Displays CR (credit) after a positive number. Used only with SAY statements.

```
@ 22,01 SAY 9828.44 PICTURE "@C"
9828.44 CR
```

### X

Displays DB (debit) after a negative number. Used only with SAY statements.

```
@ 10,10 SAY -83207 PICTURE "@X"
83207 DB
```

### Z

Displays blank field instead of zero. Used with GET and SAY statements.

Without PICTURE:

```
quantity = 0
@ 02,05 SAY quantity
                   0
```

With PICTURE:

```
@ 02,05 SAY quantity PICTURE "@Z"
```

Now you see it, now you don't!

## TEMPLATES

Template characters operate on the character or number in the exact corresponding position of a GET or SAY. Different characters may appear in the same PICTURE.

### Templates that Work Only With Character Data

### !

Converts letters to uppercase. Does not affect other characters. Used with GET and SAY statements.

```
@ 23,10 SAY "Press space bar" PICTURE "!!!!!!!!!!!!!!!"
PRESS SPACE BAR
```

### A

Allows letters only. Used only with GET statements.

```
partcode = SPACE(10)
@ 11,60 SAY partcode PICTURE "999AAAAA9A"
124BdEFI5Z
```

### L

Makes characters appear as logical data. Allows only the letters "T", "t", "F", "f", "Y", "y", "N", and "n". Used only with GET statements.

```
continue = " "
@ 10,10 SAY "Continue? " GET continue PICTURE "L"
READ
Y
```

### N

Allows letters and numbers. Used only with GET statements.

```
partcode = SPACE(10)
@ 11,60 SAY partcode PICTURE "NNNNNNNNNN"
1A399CCDDR
```

### X

Allows any character. Used with GET and SAY statements.

```
partcode = SPACE(10)
@ 11,60 GET partcode PICTURE "999AXXXA9A"
151D4ZmD2D
```

## Templates that Work with Character and Numeric Data

### #

Allows only numbers, spaces, signs, and decimal points. Used only with GET statements.

```
cashflow = SPACE(10)
@ 03,03 SAY "Enter cash flow: " GET cashflow PICTURE "##########"
READ
-964573821
```

### 9

Allows only numbers for character data. Allows numbers and signs for numeric data. Used only with GET statements.

```
ssn = SPACE(11)
@ 08,02 SAY "Social Security No.: " GET ssn PICTURE "999-99-9999"
READ
001-974-2938
```

## Templates that Work with Character and Logical Data

### Y

Allows only logical "Y", "y", "N", and "n", representing logical .T. and .F. Converts y and n to uppercase. Used with GET and SAY statements.

```
continue = .t.
@ 05,04 SAY "Do you want to proceed? " GET continue PICTURE "Y"
READ
Y
```

## Templates that Work Only with Numeric Data

### $

Displays the currency symbol (dollar signs) in place of leading zeroes. Used with GET and SAY. Used in reports to highlight totals.

```
@ 06,21 SAY 27477 PICTURE "$$$$$$$$"
$$$27477
```

**Note:** FoxBASE+ prints only a single floating dollar sign.

### *

Displays asterisks in place of leading zeroes. Used with GET and SAY. A common application is in check printing to make amounts difficult to change.

```
@ 06,21 SAY 27477 PICTURE "********"
***27477
```

### .

Marks decimal point position. Decimal remains fixed during a READ. Used with GET and SAY.

```
@ 06,21 SAY 27477 PICTURE "99999.99"
27477.00
```

If you use a PICTURE to GET a number with decimal places, you must include the decimal point in the template.

### ,

Inserts a comma if number extends left far enough. Used with GET and SAY.

```
@ 06,21 SAY 8327477 PICTURE "9,999,999.99"
8,327,477.00
```

## PICTURE Tips:

Non-template characters used in a PICTURE appear within the field at their specified positions. In a GET, the cursor skips over them, preventing the user from editing them. For example, when formatting a telephone number, you may use parentheses and hyphens in the template. When the user edits the formatted GET, the cursor skips over those characters.

```
mphone = SPACE(12)
@ 09,04 "Enter phone: " GET mphone PICTURE "(999)999-9999"
READ
(   )    -
```

When you enter a telephone number, it looks like this:

```
(619)555-1212
```

If you specify the "R" function, non-template characters appear in the GET, but are not stored in the variable, as follows:

```
@ 09,04 "Enter phone: " GET mphone PICTURE "@R (999)999-9999"
READ
(   )    -
```

The telephone number appears formatted on the screen, but the actual variable or field appears like this:

```
6195551212
```

### Combining Function Codes and Templates

When combining function codes and templates in a <format>, function codes appear first. A space indicates the end of the function code and the beginning of a template. For example, using the Z function, the following PICTURE displays a numeric value as all blanks if its value is zero. Template code 9, together with literal commas, displays the number in a standard form:

```
testno = 2948383
@ 10,10 SAY testno PICTURE "@Z 99,999,999.99"
2,948,383.00
```

### @ <coord> SAY <exp> PICTURE <format> GET <variable> PICTURE <format> RANGE <expN1>,<expN2>

RANGE defines the high and low date or numeric values the user may enter into a GET. For example,

```
items = 0
@ 05,05 SAY "Enter number of items: " GET items RANGE 0,99
READ
```

displays the message and allows a number in the range from 0 to 99. The following checks a range of dates:

```
today = CTOD('  /  /  ')
@ 05,05 SAY "Date: " GET today RANGE CTOD('01/01/86'),CTOD('12/30/87')
READ
```

In all systems other than dBASE IV, you must use the CTOD( ) (character-to-date) function for constant dates in a RANGE. In dBASE IV, you can use the brace delimiters ({ }) to indicate a date. Invalid input produces a message on line 0 unless you SET SCOREBOARD OFF. The user can then reenter the value. In a RANGE option, you may omit either the upper or lower boundary. However, the comma must be there. For example, the command:

```
@ 05,05 SAY "Enter date: " GET today RANGE ,CTOD('12/30/87')
```

prompts the user to enter a date no later than 12/30/87. In dBASE IV, the equivalent statement would be:

```
@ 05,05 SAY "Enter date: " GET today RANGE ,{12/30/87}
```

**Note:** Pressing ENTER before modifying a RANGE-checked variable circumvents the RANGE check. So does pressing ESCape. Both thus allow storage of an invalid default value. The solution to this problem is to assign a default value that falls within the range, or to validate the data after the read.

### @ <coord> CLEAR

Erases the screen from the indicated coordinate to the lower right corner. Note: you can substitute the CLEAR option of the @ command for CLEAR itself. For example, issuing CLEAR in a user defined function cancels active GETs. @ 0,0 CLEAR erases the screen, but leaves GETs intact.

### @ <coord> CLEAR TO <coord2>

Erases a box on the screen from <coord> at the top left corner to <coord2> at the bottom right corner.

### @ <coord> TO <coord2> [DOUBLE]

Draws a single line box on the screen with the top left corner at <coord> and the bottom right corner at <coord2>. The result is a horizontal line if the rows are the same and a vertical line if the columns are the same. For example, @ 10,10 to 10,30 draws a horizontal line on row 10. Specify DOUBLE for a double line box.

## RECOMMENDED USE:

Use @ in programs to design input screens and format reports. The PICTURE and RANGE options provide the first line of defense in data validation.

**Example**—A human resource information system (HRIS) uses @ to present carefully laid-out, reliable data entry screens. The @ command displays text, prompts, and boxes. The careful use of PICTURE functions and templates prevents entry of erroneous data.

```
STORE SPACE(20) TO lastname,address,city
state = SPACE(2)
zip = SPACE(10)
DO WHILE .t.
  SET COLOR TO /w      && Highlight prompt with black on white display.
  @ 06,02 SAY " ENTER EMPLOYEE INFORMATION..."
  SET COLOR TO w
  * Leave SAYs outside DO WHILE to prevent flickering during loop.
  @ 07,01 TO 13,40        && Draw single line box around input area.
  * Function converts all letters to upper case.
  @ 08,02 SAY " Last name: " GET lastname PICTURE "@!"
  @ 09,02 SAY "   Address: " GET address
  @ 10,02 SAY "      City: " GET city
  * Template converts two letters to upper case.
  @ 11,02 SAY "     State: " GET state PICTURE "!!"
  * Template allows numbers, spaces and signs. Hyphen is literal.
  @ 12,02 SAY "Postalcode: " GET pcode PICTURE "99999-9999"
  READ
  complete = .F.
  * Get LOGICAL response using "Y" and "N" instead of "T" and "F"
  @ 14,02 SAY "Is information complete? (Y/N)" GET complete PICTURE "Y"
  READ
  IF complete
    CLEAR
    * <replace statements>
    EXIT
  ENDIF
ENDDO
```

## LIMITS/WARNINGS:

@ can display output on the screen anywhere and in any order. However, printers require you to print linearly, from the top to the bottom of the page. Printing at a previous coordinate causes a page eject.

dBASE III PLUS, dBASE IV, and FoxBASE+ reserve line 0 to display status information. To use it in programs, first issue the command SET SCOREBOARD OFF.

## VARIATIONS:

**Clipper:** Does not allow the FUNCTION option of @...SAY.

**Clipper, dBASE IV, dBXL, FoxBASE+, Quicksilver:**

@ <coord> SAY <exp> GET <variable> PICTURE <format> VALID <condition>

The VALID option prevents the user from exiting a GET until he or she provides a valid entry.

Pressing ESC before modifying the <variable> terminates the GET without validation. The <variable> retains its original value, even if it would not satisfy <condition>. Also, ESCape terminates the GET, restoring the default value, regardless of its validity.

The example below requires the user to enter "A", "B", or "C":

```
response = " "
@ 05,05 SAY "Your Choice? (A/B/C) (Y/N) " ;
        GET response PICTURE "!" VALID (response $"ABC")
READ
```

Think of the statement as meaning "Get a memory variable called RESPONSE containing a letter "A," "B," or "C". PICTURE "!" forces uppercase. The dollar sign operator ($) means "contained in." The VALID expression enforces the proper entry.

The VALID expression may also include internal functions and user defined functions, as long as they RETURN a value of .T. or .F.. User defined functions must not CLEAR the screen, CLEAR GETS, or issue a READ command.

dBASE III PLUS and early versions of dBXL (before version 1.2) do not have a VALID clause; however, you can simulate it with a DO WHILE loop. The code below prompts the user for an answer of "A", "B", or "C". If RESPONSE does not contain one of those letters, the loop repeats. Unfortunately, this technique allows only one GET at a time:

```
* Initialize RESPONSE variable.
response = " "
* Display prompt outside of loop to prevent flickering.
@ 05,05 SAY "Your Choice? (A/B/C) "
* "Do while RESPONSE does not contain A, B, or C."
DO WHILE .NOT. response $ "ABC"
  * Template converts letter to uppercase.
  @ 05,19 GET response PICTURE "!"
  READ
ENDDO
```

**Clipper, FoxBASE+:**

@ <coord> PROMPT <exp> [MESSAGE <exp>]

Produces "bounce bar" menu prompts activated by the MENU TO command. See MENU TO.

### @ <coord1>,<coord2> BOX [<expC>]

Draws a box from <coord1> at the top left corner to <coord2> at the bottom right. <expC> may contain up to nine characters, one for each corner, each side, and the background. This form of the @ command draws a single line if you do not specify <expC>. The following command draws a box from coordinate 10,10 to 15,30 using the numbers 1 through 8 in the box frame, and 9 as a background character. (The numbers are examples to guide an actual design).

```
@ 10,10,15,30 BOX "123456789"
```

This command produces the following image:

```
122222222222222222223
899999999999999999994
899999999999999999994
899999999999999999994
899999999999999999994
766666666666666666665
```

**dBASE III PLUS:** FUNCTION must precede PICTURE when you use them together.

**dBASE IV:**

@ <coord> [[SAY <exp> [PICTURE <format>] [FUNCTION <format>]]
 [GET <exp> [[OPEN] WINDOW <window name>]
 [PICTURE <format>] [FUNCTION <format>]
 [RANGE <expN1>,<expN2>] [VALID <condition>] [ERROR <expC>]]
 [WHEN <condition>] [DEFAULT <exp>] [MESSAGE <expC>]
 [COLOR [<standard>][,<enhanced>]]]

dBASE IV provides several additional options for SAYs and GETs:

**COLOR**—Designates the color for SAYs and GETs, temporarily overriding the SET COLOR command. <standard> affects the SAY colors. <enhanced> affects the GET colors.

You can specify either attribute or both. If you specify only <enhanced>, use a comma to indicate no <standard> attribute as follows:

```
@ 10,10 SAY "Enter last name: " GET lname COLOR ,GR+/b
```

See SET COLOR for more information on color attributes.

**DEFAULT <exp>**—An expression containing the initial value of the GET field. The expression must match the field's data type. DEFAULT is valid only in a format file when you are APPENDing records.

**ERROR <expC>**—A character expression to display when the VALID condition is not satisfied. It overrides the internal error message.

**FUNCTION <format>**—Lets you specify PICTURE formatting functions without using the @ sign as in the PICTURE <format> clause. See PICTURE for more information.

**MESSAGE <expC>**—Displays a message when the user places the cursor on the associated GET. With SET STATUS ON, the message appears centered on line 24. With SET STATUS OFF, it appears on the right side of line 0. If you SET SCOREBOARD and STATUS OFF, the MESSAGE will not appear.

**WINDOW <window name>**—Specifies the window to open when the user presses Ctrl-Home to edit a memo field. Without this option, memo editing defaults to the window defined by SET WINDOW, or to the full-screen if there is no SET WINDOW. The specified window must be in memory.

**OPEN WINDOW <window name>**—Same as WINDOW above, except it does not require the user to press Ctrl-Home to open the window. The window opens as soon as the READ executes. Note: the window may overlap other active GETs and other windows.

**PICTURE <@format>/FUNCTION <format>**—dBASE IV recognizes several PICTURE function codes besides the standard ones in dBASE III PLUS.

### dBASE IV PICTURE/FUNCTION Codes

#### ^ (exponent symbol)

Converts numbers to scientific notation. Accepts either type N or type F numeric input. A number in scientific notation has the format:

S.###0...E+###

If the value is negative, S is a minus sign. If it is positive, the sign is omitted. The #s represent significant digits. The value is padded with zeros to align the notation properly. The number of zeroes before the E depends on whether the value comes from a field or a memory variable. If from a field with no decimal places, the number is its length plus one. If the field has decimal places, the number is its length. If the value is from a memory variable, the number is 20.

For example, the memory variable MTOTAL has a value of 5,753.23. The ^ function converts it to scientific notation:

```
mtotal = 5753.23
@ 01,01 SAY mtotal PICTURE "@^"
.575323000000000E+4
```

### $

Displays a currency symbol in front of a number. Works in both GETs and SAYs. Works in GETs only if you SET CURRENCY LEFT (the default). You can change the currency symbol using the command SET CURRENCY. You can change the separators (usually commas) using SET SEPARATOR, and you can change the decimal point with SET POINT.

**Programming tip:** Use the $ function with a template:

```
mtotal = 38383
@ 10,10 SAY mtotal PICTURE "@$ 999,999.99"
$38,383.00
```

### M

Lets the user scroll through a list by pressing the space bar. To make a selection, the user then presses Enter. For example, an office management program lets the operator select a department by scrolling through a list and pressing Enter.

```
mresp = space(20)
@ 10,10 SAY "Enter department" GET mresp ;
PICTURE "@M Advertising,Editorial,Software,Marketing,General,Production"
READ
? mresp
Advertising
```

### I

Centers numeric data within a field. Valid in GETs and SAYs. Used in reports to center columns of numbers.

```
USE sales
@ 01,01 SAY jan PICTURE "@I"
@ 02,01 SAY feb PICTURE "@I"
@ 03,01 SAY mar PICTURE "@I"
```

This produces the following results:

```
     9837.22
      33.00
     422.00
```

**J**

Right justifies character data in a field.

```
message = "WARNING"
@15,00 SAY message PICTURE "@J !!!!!!!!!!!!!!!!!!!!!!!!!!!"
                   WARNING
```

**L**

Inserts leading zeroes. Only valid with numeric data in SAYs, for example:

```
subtotal = 5677
@ 23,25 SAY subtotal PICTURE "@L 999,999.99"
05,677.00
```

**T**

Removes leading and trailing blanks from a field.

**RANGE**—Same as the standard dBASE III PLUS RANGE clause.

**VALID <condition>**—Same as the Clipper, dBXL, FoxBASE+, or Quicksilver VALID clause.

**WHEN <condition>**—Lets you edit the associated GET when <condition> is true (.T.). Without a WHEN clause, you can edit all active GETs (the default). Use WHEN to exclude GETs under certain conditions. The GET appears, but the cursor skips over it. For example, use WHEN to establish user levels in an application. You may assign a clerk a level of 5 and a manager a level of 9. (You can define a PUBLIC memory variable called USERLEVEL containing the value). When you have a field that only the manager can change, use the command:

```
* <More GETs>.
@ 08,02 SAY "Department code: " GET dcode WHEN userlevel = 9
* <More GETs>.
READ
```

By making it easy to add field security, WHEN lets you avoid dBASE IV's cumbersome internal security system.

**Example**—A collections management program stores client names, addresses, and amounts due and past due. A data entry screen uses many @...SAY options to display and edit data.

```
CLEAR
DEFINE WINDOW swindow FROM 10,01 TO 23,79
SET STATUS ON

* Get NAME. Do not allow blank field. Display SAY in inverse video.
@ 01,01 SAY "Enter name: " GET name PICTURE "@!" ;
        VALID LEN(TRIM(name))>0 ERROR "Name must not be blank" COLOR n+/w
```

```
@ 02,01 SAY "Address   : " GET address
@ 03,01 SAY "City      : " GET city
* Display scrolling STATE field. Message appears at bottom of screen.
@ 04,01 SAY "State     : " GET state PICTURE "@M CA,MA,VA,VT,MT" ;
        MESSAGE "Press space bar to see more states"
@ 05,01 SAY "Zipcode   : " GET postalcode PICTURE "@!"
@ 06,01 SAY "Telephone : " GET telephone PICTURE "(999) 999-9999"
* Center output.
@ 07,01 SAY "Amount due: " GET amount PICTURE "@I"
* Allow editing only when AMOUNT > 100
@ 08,01 SAY "Past due  : " GET pastdue PICTURE "@I" WHEN amount > 100
* Edit memo field SALESMEM in window SWINDOW.
@ 09,01 SAY "Notes     : " GET salesmem WINDOW swindow
READ
```

## @ <coord> TO <coord2> **[DOUBLE/PANEL/<border definition>] [COLOR <color attribute>]**

dBASE IV offers three new border options: PANEL, <border>, and COLOR.

**PANEL** creates a solid bar border.

**<color attribute>** lets you define the border's foreground and background colors. It does not affect the colors inside. If you use the PANEL option, only the foreground color takes effect. See SET COLOR for more information.

**<border definition>** lets you define the sides and corners of the border individually. The definition consists of up to eight keyboard characters or ASCII decimal values in a list, as follows:

```
SET BORDER TO <t>,<b>,<l>,<r>,<tl>,<tr>,<bl>,<br>
```

```
tl_____t_____tr        tl = top left          bl = bottom left
|             |        t  = top               b  = bottom
l             r        tr = top right         br = bottom right
|             |        l = left
bl_____b_____br        r = right
```

If you specify only one character, the entire border consists of it.

You must delimit keyboard characters, but not ASCII values, with quotation marks.

The border defined here overrides the one defined by the SET BORDER command.

To draw a single-line yellow border on a blue background from 10,10 to 20,30, use the command:

```
@ 10,10 TO 20,30 COLOR GR+/B
```

To draw a border of asterisks, use the command:

```
@ 10,10 TO 20,30 "*"
```

The following statement draws a border using ASCII characters 176 and 178.

```
@ 10,10 TO 20,30  178,178,178,178,176,176,176,176
```

See command SET BORDER for more information.

### @ <coord1> FILL TO <coord2> [COLOR <color attribute>]

Lets you change the standard foreground and background colors of a screen region. Existing text appears in the new setting. Subsequent screen output to the region reverts to the previous setting.

See SET COLOR for more information on color attributes.

The region is a rectangle starting at <coord1> and extending to <coord2>

If you omit the COLOR option, @...FILL TO clears the specified region like the @...CLEAR TO command.

To make the region from 5,5 to 23,35 yellow on blue, use the following command:

```
@ 5,5 FILL TO 23,35 COLOR GR+/B
```

## dBXL, Quicksilver:

### @ <coord> SAY <exp> GET <exp> PICTURE <format> VALID <condition> [HELP <expC>]

The HELP option displays the message in <expC> when the user presses F1 while editing the corresponding GET variable. The message may be up to 254 characters long. By default, it appears in the upper right corner of the screen. You can change the location with the SET USERHELP TO command. To disable HELP messages, SET USERHELP OFF.

**Example**—A car rental customer wants a particular compact model for a week. The clerk, unable to remember the exact model code, presses F1 to produce a list on the screen.

```
* Create End of Line character to produce multi-line messages
* within a string.
eol = CHR(13) + CHR(10)
* Store the message in a memory variable.
STORE "E—Economy  S-Subcompact " + eol + ;
```

```
      "C—Compact  M-Midsize " + eol + ;
      "L—Luxury   F—Sport " + eol + eol +;
      "Press SPACE BAR to continue" TO codestring
* <statements>
CLEAR
@ 08,10 SAY "Press F1 for more information"
carcode = " "
@ 10,10 SAY "Enter car code: " GET carcode PICTURE "!" HELP codestring
READ
```

**FoxBASE+:**

@ <coord> SAY <exp> PICTURE <format> FUNCTION <format>
GET <exp> PICTURE <format> FUNCTION <format>

FUNCTION provides an alternate way to specify functions in GETs and SAYs. Within a PICTURE <format>, you can use both templates and function codes to format GETs and SAYs. FUNCTION lets you separate function codes and templates into separate clauses for more flexibility and greater readability.

## SEE ALSO:

Commands ?/??, ???, APPEND, MENU TO, SET BORDER, SET COLOR, SET CURRENCY, SET POINT, SET SEPARATOR, and SET WINDOW; function TRANSFORM( ).

# ACCEPT

## DIALECTS:
Clipper, dBASE III PLUS, dBASE IV, dBXL, FoxBASE+, and Quicksilver.

## SYNTAX:
ACCEPT [<prompt>] TO <memory variable>

## DEFINITION:
Lets the user enter character data into a memory variable. If the variable does not exist, it is created automatically. If the user just presses the Enter key without entering anything, the memory variable takes the value ASCII 0 (a null string). These features can cause errors if you misspell a name or accidentally press Enter before typing a value.

## DEFAULT:
ACCEPT lets the user enter up to 254 characters on the next available line. It does not display an input field.

## OPTIONS:
ACCEPT displays an optional prompt you define as a character variable or as a string delimited by single or double quotation marks.

## RECOMMENDED USE:
ACCEPT is helpful in simple tasks that do not require sophisticated error trapping or data validation. Validation is difficult, as ACCEPT does not allow PICTURE functions or templates.

**Example**—A secretary must search indexed files to find names in an appointment database. Rather than typing:

```
. SEEK "Robertson"
. EDIT
```

the secretary writes a simple program to ACCEPT the name to SEEK:

```
* FINDNAME.PRG
* Create NAMESEEK for use as a condition in the DO WHILE.
nameseek = SPACE(15)
```

```
* ReDO the DO WHILE as long as NAMESEEK is not "QUIT."
DO WHILE nameseek # "QUIT"
  CLEAR
  ACCEPT "Enter name to find or type 'QUIT': " TO nameseek
  SEEK trim(nameseek)          && Trim function strips trailing blanks.
  IF FOUND()                   && If the name exists, then EDIT.
    EDIT
  ELSE
    WAIT "Name not found"      && If name not found, pause.
  ENDIF
ENDDO
```

## SPECIAL USES:

If your Clipper, dBASE IV, dBXL, or FoxBASE+ program branches to a user defined function in a VALID clause, issuing a CLEAR, CLEAR GETS, or another READ clears previously active GETs. As ACCEPT does not require a READ, you may put it in user defined functions to do interactive input.

## LIMITS/WARNINGS:

ACCEPT does not strictly control input length. Programs using it should allow for a maximum length string of 254 characters in dBASE III PLUS, dBASE IV, dBXL, and Quicksilver, and 255 in Clipper and FoxBASE+.

## SEE ALSO:

Commands INPUT, READ, and STORE.

# ACTIVATE MENU

## DIALECTS:

dBASE IV only.

## SYNTAX:

ACTIVATE MENU <menu name> [PAD <pad name>]

## DEFINITION:

Activates a defined pad menu.

By default, pad menus appear as horizontal lists on line 0. You move the cursor with the left and right arrow keys, making selections with the Enter key.

When activated, the pad menu covers existing text. To deactivate it, press ESC or issue the DEACTIVATE MENU command. The previous text then reappears.

## OPTIONS:

By default, the cursor starts on the first DEFINEd PAD. You can change the starting point with the PAD <pad name> option.

## RECOMMENDED USE:

Use ACTIVATE MENU after you first DEFINE MENU, DEFINE PADs, and specify ON SELECTIONs.

**Example**—A library management application displays a bar menu with selections for searching and updating records. After the menu is defined, the program ACTIVATEs MENU.

```
DEFINE MENU library
DEFINE PAD sell OF library PROMPT "Search for titles"
DEFINE PAD sel2 OF library PROMPT "Record Updates"
ON SELECTION PAD sell OF library DO tsearch
ON SELECTION PAD sel2 OF library DO rec_up
ACTIVATE MENU library

PROCEDURE tsearch
* <statements>

PROCEDURE rec_up
* <statements>.
```

## SEE ALSO:

Commands ACTIVATE POPUP, ACTIVATE WINDOW, DEACTIVATE, DEFINE MENU, ON PAD, and SHOW MENU; functions MENU( ), PAD( ), and PROMPT( ).

# ACTIVATE POPUP

## DIALECTS:

dBASE IV only.

## SYNTAX:

ACTIVATE POPUP <popup name>

DEFINITION:

Activates a defined popup menu.

By default, a popup menu appears as a vertical list in a window. You move the cursor with the up and down arrow keys, and make selections with the Enter key.

When activated, the popup menu covers existing text. To deactivate it, press Esc, issue the DEACTIVATE MENU command, or ACTIVATE another POPUP.

## RECOMMENDED USE:

Use ACTIVATE POPUP after you first DEFINE POPUP, DEFINE BARs, and specify ON SELECTIONs.

**Example**—A menu in an anthropological application offers several choices for maintaining information on ancient artifacts. The program uses ACTIVATE POPUP to display popup menus.

```
DEFINE POPUP digs FROM 15,01 TO 20,25
DEFINE BAR 1 OF digs PROMPT "Add new artifact"
DEFINE BAR 2 OF digs PROMPT "Search for artifacts"
DEFINE BAR 3 OF digs PROMPT "Exit"
ON SELECTION POPUP digs DO msub1
ACTIVATE POPUP digs

PROCEDURE msub1
mchoice = BAR()
DO CASE
  CASE mchoice = 1
    * <DO art_add>.
  CASE mchoice = 2
    * <DO serch_art>.
  CASE mchoice = 3
    DEACTIVATE POPUP
ENDCASE
RETURN
```

## SEE ALSO:

Commands ACTIVATE MENU, ACTIVATE WINDOW, DEACTIVATE, DEFINE MENU, ON PAD, and SHOW MENU; functions MENU( ), PAD( ), and PROMPT( ).

# ACTIVATE SCREEN

## DIALECTS:
dBASE IV only.

## SYNTAX:
ACTIVATE SCREEN

## DEFINITION:
Disables the active window, restoring output to the full screen. The window's image remains. You can then CLEAR it or overwrite it with text.

You may recall the window, or activate another one with the ACTIVATE WINDOW command.

Unlike the DEACTIVATE WINDOW command, ACTIVATE SCREEN does not erase the window.

## RECOMMENDED USE:
Use ACTIVATE SCREEN when alternating between full screen output and window output, if you want the inactive window's image to remain.

**Example**—An accounting program displays a popup help message in a window. The program switches from the full screen mode to the help window, then back to the full screen using ACTIVATE SCREEN. The program uses ACTIVATE SCREEN instead of DEACTIVATE WINDOW so the help window stays in view during full screen operations.

```
DEFINE WINDOW mhelp FROM 2,50 TO 15,79

DEFINE MENU acct
DEFINE PAD acctp1 OF acct PROMPT "End of month"
DEFINE PAD acctp2 OF acct PROMPT "Close quarter"
DEFINE PAD acctp3 OF acct PROMPT "Help"
ON SELECTION PAD acctp1 OF acct DO eom
ON SELECTION PAD acctp2 OF acct DO eoq
ON SELECTION PAD acctp3 OF acct DO mhelp
ACTIVATE MENU acct

PROCEDURE mhelp
*
ACTIVATE WINDOW mhelp
```

```
TEXT

  This menu offers batch
  selections for closing
  months, quarters, and years

ENDTEXT
ACTIVATE SCREEN
RETURN
```

## SEE ALSO:

Commands ACTIVATE WINDOW and DEFINE WINDOW.

# ACTIVATE WINDOW

## DIALECTS:
dBASE IV only.

## SYNTAX:
ACTIVATE WINDOW <window name list>/ALL

## DEFINITION:
Activates a defined window. Subsequent program output appears there.

The <window name list> consists of windows already defined in memory. You may define up to 20 windows.

Although you can specify a list of windows, only the last one becomes active. The others flash on the screen in order, overlaying their predecessors.

If you specify ALL, all windows in memory flash on the screen in the order in which they were defined. The last window defined becomes active.

When activated, a window covers existing text and windows. To deactivate a window, issue the DEACTIVATE WINDOW command, or ACTIVATE another window "on top" of it. When you DEACTIVATE a WINDOW, the previous text and windows reappear.

## RECOMMENDED USE:
DEFINE all your windows in advance, then ACTIVATE them in subroutines as needed.

**Example**—A political campaign management system displays user help screens in windows. The use of windows makes it easy to display help information without disturbing the underlying program screen. The MAIN popup calls PROCEDURE MACTION. When the user presses F3, the ON KEY F3 command executes the help procedure instead. The help procedure ACTIVATEs WINDOWs and displays help text.

```
* Define windows.
DEFINE WINDOW help1 FROM 02,03 TO 10,79
DEFINE WINDOW help2 FROM 17,01 TO 23,60

* When user presses F3, DO procedure THELP with bar and popup values.
```

```
ON KEY F3 DO thelp WITH BAR(),POPUP()
DEFINE POPUP main FROM 10,15 TO 18,35
DEFINE BAR 1 OF main PROMPT "Add records"
DEFINE BAR 2 OF main PROMPT "Delete records"
DEFINE BAR 3 OF main PROMPT "Dirty tricks"
DEFINE BAR 4 OF main PROMPT "Exit"
ON SELECTION POPUP main DO maction    && Do PROCEDURE MACTION.
ACTIVATE popup MAIN
ON KEY                                && Disable ON KEY when done.

PROCEDURE maction                     && Main action procedure.
mbar = BAR()
DO CASE
  CASE mbar = 1
   * <Add records>.
  CASE mbar = 2
   * <Delete records>.
  CASE mbar = 3
   * <Do dirty tricks program>.
  CASE mbar = 4
   DEACTIVATE POPUP
ENDCASE
RETURN

PROCEDURE thelp                       && Main help procedure.
PARAMETERS mbar,mpop
DO CASE
  CASE mbar = 1 .AND. mpop = "MAIN"
    ACTIVATE WINDOW help1             && Activate defined window HELP1.
    @ 03,04 SAY "To add records you need the following information:"
    @ 04,04 SAY "  Local delegate names, addresses, telephone numbers"
    @ 05,04 SAY "Press any key to continue"
    WAIT ""                           && Pauses screen with no message.
    DEACTIVATE WINDOW help1
  CASE mbar = 2 .AND. mpop = "MAIN"
    ACTIVATE WINDOW help2             && Activate defined window HELP2.
    @ 01,04 SAY "Deleted records are only marked for deletion."
    @ 02,04 SAY "You can recall them later if necessary."
    @ 03,04 SAY "Press any key to continue"
    WAIT ""
    DEACTIVATE WINDOW help2           && Pauses screen with no message.
  * <More CASEs>.
ENDCASE
RETURN
```

## SEE ALSO:

Commands ACTIVATE MENU, ACTIVATE POPUP, DEACTIVATE, DEFINE MENU, DEFINE WINDOW, ON PAD, RESTORE WINDOW, and SAVE WINDOW; functions MENU( ), PAD( ), and PROMPT( ).

# APPEND

## DIALECTS:

Clipper, dBASE III PLUS, dBASE IV, dBXL, FoxBASE+, and Quicksilver.

## SYNTAX:

APPEND [BLANK]

## DEFINITION:

Adds a new record to the end of a database. Opens a full screen with field name prompts for it. APPEND's primary use is for adding records interactively. Programs use the BLANK option instead.

After you enter data into a record, APPEND displays a new empty record. APPENDing ends:

1) if the user immediately presses PgDn or Ctrl-C;

2) if the user keeps pressing Enter until the cursor passes through the empty record;

3) if the user presses Enter before entering data in the first field.

You can also end APPENDing by pressing Ctrl-W, Ctrl-Q, or ESCape. Ctrl-W saves the current record, the others do not.

## OPTIONS:

APPEND BLANK adds a blank record to the end of the database in use.

## RECOMMENDED USE:

Use APPEND interactively. If you activate a format file, the full screen APPEND assumes its characteristics.

In a program, use APPEND BLANK to add a record to a database. I recommend the following procedure:

1) Edit the data in memory variables

2) USE (open) the file

3) APPEND BLANK

4) REPLACE edited memory variables in the new blank record

5) Close the file.

The user can edit the data completely before saving it in the database file. The file need only be open briefly. This lessens the danger of a power loss or computer error damaging or destroying data. This is like unbagging your groceries first, then putting them all in your refrigerator at once, rather than leaving the door open for a long time.

**Example**—A reliable dBASE program opens a database file only long enough to extract or replace data. In this example, the program prompts the user when the data in variables MLAST and MFIRST is ready to be APPENDed. Only when the user finishes does the program open the database file and APPEND BLANK.

```
* Create memory variables MLAST and MFIRST with lengths of
* 20 and 15, respectively.
mlast = SPACE(20)
mfirst = SPACE(15)
DO WHILE .t.
  @ 10,01 SAY "LAST NAME : " GET mlast      && Edit the variables
  @ 11,01 SAY "FIRST NAME: " GET mfirst     &&  with the READ command.
  READ
  * Get a logical response (Y/N) and store it in a variable DONE.
  done = .f.                                && Initialize DONE to false.
  @ 17,01 SAY "Are you done? (Y/N) " GET done PICTURE "Y"
  READ
  * If done editing MLAST and MFIRST, open the file long enough
  *  to APPEND BLANK and REPLACE edited data.
  IF done                                   && If DONE = .T.
    USE testfile INDEX testfile
    APPEND BLANK
    REPLACE last WITH mlast, first WITH mfirst
    USE
  ENDIF
ENDDO
```

## LIMITS/WARNINGS:

**dBASE III PLUS:** After APPENDing to a shared database on a network, the record count is not updated until you move the pointer. To avoid errors, issue GO RECNO( ) immediately.

## VARIATIONS:

**Clipper:** APPEND requires BLANK. With SET EXCLUSIVE OFF (multiuser mode), Clipper tries to APPEND and automatically locks the new blank record. The NETERR( ) function returns true (.T.) if another user has already locked the file or tries to APPEND BLANK at the same time.

**dBASE IV:** To speed execution, dBASE IV does not immediately write its data buffers to disk. The directory listing of the active database may not reflect recent changes until you close the file. You can force immediate writing of data by issuing the command SET AUTOSAVE ON. It makes dBASE IV write the data after every record is added.

**dBXL, Quicksilver:** APPEND AUTOMEM appends a record and gives each field the value of the memory variable with the same name. If you have not initialized any variables, APPEND adds a blank record.

APPEND AUTOMEM is equivalent to APPEND BLANK followed by REPLACE commands to initialize the fields. However, APPEND AUTOMEM is faster because it only updates the database file and indexes once.

APPEND BLANK and REPLACE both update the database file and open index files.

**Quicksilver:** APPEND must always include either BLANK or AUTOMEM.

## SEE ALSO:

Commands CLEAR AUTOMEM, INSERT, REPLACE, and STORE.

# APPEND FROM

## DIALECTS:

Clipper, dBASE III PLUS, dBASE IV, dBXL, FoxBASE+, and Quicksilver.

## SYNTAX:

APPEND FROM <file> [FOR <condition>] [TYPE <file_type>]

## DEFINITION:

Adds records to the database in use from another database. Only APPENDs records in the FROM database for which the expression is true. If no expression is specified, APPENDs all records. Note: APPEND FROM only appends fields with the same names.

If fields in the FROM database are larger than corresponding ones in the target database, APPEND FROM truncates them to fit. It replaces numeric data with asterisks.

## DEFAULT:

APPEND FROM assumes that the FROM database is a dBASE database file unless you specify otherwise with the FILE option. APPEND FROM appends all records unless you specify an expression.

## OPTIONS:

APPEND FROM can append records selectively using a logical expression that applies to the FROM database. For example, you could APPEND FROM a file for all records in which STATE equals "CA."

## RECOMMENDED USE:

When running applications programs with many daily transactions, one often prefers to accept new data in a batch mode. The idea is to save it in files, and later update a main database using APPEND FROM. This approach is useful because:

- It eliminates slow index updates on a large main file.
- It protects the main file from corruption, as it is opened only once a day.

**Example**—A telemarketing company qualifies leads and enters them into two 20,000 record databases. Rather than open and close the two databases repeatedly, new leads go into a temporary file. At the end of the day, records are APPENDed from the temporary file into the main files.

```
* Open main file 1 with active indexes.
USE mainfile1 INDEX leadname,leadzip,leadco
* Add data from temporary file, but only for California leads.
APPEND FROM tempfile FOR state = "CA"
* Open main file 2 with active indexes.
USE mainfile2 INDEX leadname,leadzip,leadco
* Add data from temporary file for all states except California.
APPEND FROM tempfile FOR state # "CA"
```

## LIMITS/WARNINGS:

**dBASE III PLUS, dBASE IV:** APPEND FROM <file> FOR DELETED( ) does not work.

## SPECIAL USES:

The dBASE language lets you APPEND FROM other types of files. You can thus import data from applications such as spreadsheets and word processors. If the FROM <file> is not a DBF file, choose the TYPE option from the following:

**DBASEII**
Ashton-Tate dBASE II database.
dBASE IV only.

**DELIMITED [WITH <delimiter>/BLANK]**
Delimited format file
Clipper, dBASE III PLUS, dBASE IV, dBXL, FoxBASE+, and Quicksilver.

**DIF**
VisiCalc™ spreadsheet format.
dBASE III PLUS, dBASE IV, and dBXL.

**FW2**
Ashton-Tate Framework database or spreadsheet.
dBASE IV only.

**RPD**
Ashton-Tate RapidFile database.
dBASE IV only.

**SDF**
System Data Format
Clipper, dBASE III PLUS, dBASE IV, dBXL, FoxBASE+, and Quicksilver.

**SYLK**
Multiplan™ spreadsheet format.
dBASE III PLUS, dBASE IV, and dBXL.

**WK1**
Lotus 1-2-3 release 2.x.
dBASE IV only.

**WKS**
Lotus 1-2-3 release 1.A spreadsheet format.
dBASE III PLUS, dBASE IV, and dBXL.

dBASE III PLUS and dBASE IV have an IMPORT command for creating dBASE files from foreign formats.

## VARIATIONS:

**dBASE IV:** The APPEND FROM ? option displays a list of available databases.

dBASE IV also allows the form:

APPEND FROM ARRAY **<array name> FOR <condition>**

The ARRAY option adds an array to a database. Each row becomes a record, and each column a field. (In ARRAY[x,y], x is the row, y the column.)

The first column in the array becomes the first field in the record, the second column becomes the second field, and so on, until there are no more fields or no more array columns. APPEND FROM ARRAY ignores excess columns. Excess fields remain empty.

Elements in the array must have the same data types as the target database fields.

**Example**—To protect its database from damage due to power losses, a sales contact program opens CONTACT.DBF only long enough to update it. The program first stores data in an array, opens the database, APPENDs FROM ARRAY, and then closes the database.

```
DECLARE mrec[1,5]         ** One row, five columns/one record, five fields,
mrec[1,1] = SPACE(30)     **    could also be represented as mrec[5]
mrec[1,2] = SPACE(30)
mrec[1,3] = "San Diego           "
mrec[1,4] = "CA"
mrec[1,5] = "     "

@ 01,01 SAY "Enter name:     " GET mrec[1,1]
```

```
@ 02,01 SAY "Enter address: " GET mrec[1,2]
@ 03,01 SAY "Enter city:    " GET mrec[1,3]
@ 04,01 SAY "Enter state:   " GET mrec[1,4]
@ 05,01 SAY "Enter zipcode: " GET mrec[1,5]
READ
USE contacts
APPEND FROM ARRAY mrec
USE
```

The FOR <condition> option appends only rows matching the condition. The condition is evaluated before each row is appended; however, dBASE IV associates the data in the array with its target field! For example, you can issue

```
APPEND FROM ARRAY mrec FOR name = "SMITH"
```

where NAME is the field corresponding to the array column.

APPEND FROM ARRAY is similar to FoxBASE+'s GATHER command.

**FoxBASE+:**

APPEND FROM <file> **[FIELDS <fieldlist>]**
[FOR <condition>] [TYPE <file type>]

An optional FIELDS list APPENDs only a subset of fields. The field list must be chosen from the currently selected database.

**Example**—An accountant uses a FIELDS list to APPEND only sales and tax data FROM a daily transaction file into a yearly file.

```
USE yearacct
APPEND FROM daily FIELDS totsales,salestax
108 Records added
```

## SEE ALSO:

Commands COPY TO, DECLARE, GATHER, IMPORT, and SCATTER.

# APPEND MEMO

## DIALECTS:
dBASE IV only.

## SYNTAX:
APPEND MEMO <memofield name> FROM <filename> [OVERWRITE]

## DEFINITION:
Adds a text file to a memo field in the current record.

APPEND MEMO appends the text file unless you specify the OVERWRITE option. OVERWRITE erases the old text first.

Unless you specify an extension for the filename, APPEND MEMO assumes TXT.

**Example**—A building inspector uses a word processor on a portable computer to take notes about building sites. Back at the office, a tracking program uses APPEND MEMO to add the notes to a memo field F_NOTES. Previous notes are preserved.

```
USE inspects
site = "1091MAIN"
SEEK site
APPEND MEMO f_notes FROM A:\NOTE6_10        && Memo field F_NOTES,
                                            &&  external file NOTE6_10.TXT
```

## LIMITS/WARNINGS:
Imported text files must be in ASCII format. You can use the dBASE IV internal editor (MODIFY COMMAND/FILE) or other text editors that produce ASCII files.

## SEE ALSO:
Commands APPEND, APPEND FROM, COPY MEMO, and MODIFY COMMAND/FILE.

# ASSIST

## DIALECTS:
dBASE III PLUS and dBASE IV.

## SYNTAX:
ASSIST

## DEFINITION:
Makes the interactive modes of dBASE III PLUS and dBASE IV switch from command line control to menu control. The menu control mode in dBASE III PLUS is called "The dBASE Assistant." In dBASE IV, it is "The Control Center."

ASSIST is not intended for programs.

## VARIATIONS:
The menu mode of dBXL is called "INTRO." The dBXL INTRO command is equivalent to ASSIST.

## SEE ALSO:
Command INTRO.

# AVERAGE

## DIALECTS:

Clipper, dBASE III PLUS, dBASE IV, dBXL, FoxBASE+, and Quicksilver.

## SYNTAX:

AVERAGE [expression list] [<scope>] [FOR/WHILE <condition>]
[TO <memory variable list>]

## DEFINITION:

Computes the arithmetic mean of numeric expressions. Uses all fields or the <expression list> you specify. Averages all records unless you specify a condition with FOR or WHILE. The results may go to a memory variable list. In dBASE III PLUS, dBASE IV, dBXL, and FoxBASE+, displays on the screen when SET TALK is ON.

**Example 1**—A regional sales office must determine the average mileage logged by traveling representatives. From the database file MILELOG, average MILES can be calculated FOR a particular SELLER.

```
SET TALK on
* Database file MILELOG contains mileage information for sales reps.
USE milelog
* MILES and SELLER are fields in MILELOG.
AVERAGE miles FOR seller = "James"

32 records averaged
MILES
201
```

**Example 2**—In the same sales office, the manager wants a printed mileage report. To produce it, the AVERAGE miles must be saved in a memory variable that can be either printed or stored in another database.

```
SET TALK off
USE milelog
* Store the average of MILES in memory variable AMILES.
AVERAGE miles FOR seller = "James" TO amiles
* You can now print AMILES, or store it in another database.
SET DEVICE TO PRINT
@ 10,10 SAY "Average miles" + STR(amiles,4,2)
SET DEVICE TO SCREEN
USE summary
REPLACE avemiles WITH amiles
```

## VARIATIONS:

**Clipper, Quicksilver:** AVERAGE requires an expression list and a memory variable list. For example:

```
AVERAGE sales,profits TO sale_ave,prof_ave
```

puts the average of SALES in memory variable SALE_AVE, and the average of PROFITS in PROF_AVE.

**dBASE IV:** You can send AVERAGE results to an existing one-dimensional array. They fill it, starting with the first element, until there are no more results or no more elements. Leftover elements retain their previous values.

In this example, JAN, FEB, MAR, and APR contain sales figures for a major corporation. The array RESULTS[] has four elements, one for each field:

```
PUBLIC results
DECLARE results[4]
USE sales
AVERAGE jan,feb,mar,apr TO ARRAY results
DISPLAY MEMORY
RESULTS      pub  A   [6]
     [1]        elem  N                    3409040.92  (3409040.920000000000)
     [2]        elem  N                      30923.33  (30923.33000000000000)
     [3]        elem  N                      23456.23  (23456.23000000000000)
     [4]        elem  N                     323423.55  (323423.5500000000000)
```

The dBASE IV CALCULATE command can also do AVERAGEs with its AVG( ) option.

## SEE ALSO:

Commands CALCULATE, DECLARE, and SET TALK ON.

# BEGIN SEQUENCE...

## DIALECTS:

Clipper only.

## SYNTAX:

BEGIN SEQUENCE...
<statements>
[BREAK]
<statements>
END

## DEFINITION:

A control structure for handling errors locally within a procedure. When an error or exception occurs, issue the BREAK statement to transfer control to the statement immediately following the END.

BEGIN SEQUENCE resembles DO WHILE...[EXIT]...ENDDO and IF...ENDIF, except that it does not repeat, and it does not depend on a condition. Also, unlike DO WHILE and IF, a SEQUENCE can be terminated from a subprogram with the BREAK command.

## RECOMMENDED USE:

You can use BEGIN SEQUENCE with Clipper's error system (ERRORSYS.PRG) to BREAK for certain types of runtime errors. Runtime errors call functions which, in turn, RETURN true (.T.) or false (.F.). Most error functions QUIT Clipper when they RETURN (.F.). A value of true retries the operation that caused the error.

**Example**—A file routine USEs a file on drive A. If the user inserts the wrong disk, the program calls the OPEN_ERROR function which in turn BREAKs to the END of the current SEQUENCE.

```
* ACCOUNTS.PRG
*
CLEAR
BEGIN SEQUENCE
  @ 0 ,0 SAY "Insert disk in drive A and press SPACE BAR"
  WAIT ""
  USE a:accounts              && Use file that does not exist.
```

```
  LIST name
  * <more database statements>
END
* <resume program without open file>
FUNCTION open_error           && Modified by David Kalman
PARAM name, line, info, model, _1
*
SET DEVICE TO screen
@ 00,00 SAY "File not found, change disks and retry? (Y/N)"
INKEY(0)
DO WHILE .NOT. CHR(LASTKEY()) $ "YyNn"
  INKEY(0)
END
@ 00,00
IF .NOT. CHR(LASTKEY()) $ "Yy"
  BREAK
END
@ 00,00 SAY "Insert new disk in drive A and press SPACE BAR"
WAIT ""
@ 00,00
RETURN .T.
```

## SEE ALSO:

Command ON ERROR; functions DOSERROR( ) and FERROR( ).

# BEGIN/END TRANSACTION

## DIALECTS:

dBASE IV only.

## SYNTAX:

```
BEGIN TRANSACTION [<path name>]
    * <Database operations>.
END TRANSACTION
```

## DEFINITION:

Treats a series of database operations as a logical unit which you can undo when an error occurs. Such a series, or transaction, may involve several database files.

The ROLLBACK command "undoes" changes made to the databases during the transaction.

To provide this undo capability, BEGIN TRANSACTION sets an integrity flag in the database file header and creates a log file duplicating the pre-transaction data.

When true, the integrity flag indicates that the transaction was interrupted, leaving the database in a state of change. You can test the flag with the ISMARKED( ) function.

On single user systems, the transaction log file is called TRANSLOG.LOG. To store it in a directory other than the current one, you can specify a path name in the BEGIN TRANSACTION command. On local area networks, the transaction log file takes the name of the workstation (<workstation name>.LOG). This lets the system administrator determine which station initiated a transaction on shared databases.

A successful END TRANSACTION resets the integrity flag to false and erases the transaction log file.

The BEGIN TRANSACTION and END TRANSACTION must be in the same procedure. You may not nest transactions. One must end before another begins. All files and records locked during the transaction remain locked until the END TRANSACTION. During the transaction, the UNLOCK command has no effect. END TRANSACTION releases all file and record locks issued during the transaction.

## Transaction Commands:

The transaction log records commands that change data or create new database files or indexes. Some commands are not allowed in transactions (they cause an error message).

| Database Commands Always Recorded in the Transaction Log | Database Commands Allowed if They Do Not Overwrite or Close Existing Files | Prohibited Commands |
|---|---|---|
| APPEND | COPY TO | CLEAR ALL |
| BROWSE | CREATE | CLOSE ALL/DATABASE/INDEX |
| CHANGE | IMPORT FROM | DELETE FILE |
| DELETE | INDEX TO | ERASE |
| EDIT | JOIN TO | INSERT |
| RECALL | SET CATALOG TO | MODIFY STRUCTURE |
| REPLACE | SORT TO | PACK |
| UPDATE | TOTAL TO | RENAME |
| | | ZAP |

## RECOMMENDED USE:

Use BEGIN TRANSACTION and END TRANSACTION to ensure data integrity when a transaction cannot be successfully completed. Transactions may fail if another user has locked a file or record, the power fails, or a disk drive is not ready. Transaction processing is especially useful for updating interdependent files. For example, a general ledger program might update six master database files from a transaction file. If five updates succeed, but the last one fails, the entire transaction is invalid. ROLLBACK can recover the five updated databases.

**Example**—An invoicing system updates tax tables and transaction files with new tax rates. The procedure uses an ON ERROR routine to trap transaction errors. If an operation fails, the user can RETRY the operation or ROLLBACK.

```
SET REPROCESS TO 20          && Set RETRY counter to 20.
ON ERROR DO trans_err        && If error occurs, DO PROCEDURE trans_err.
*
BEGIN TRANSACTION F:\log         && Begin logging in F:\log subdirectory
USE taxtable INDEX taxdex  IN 1  && File contains state tax information.
* Update file using new tax rate.
REPLACE ALL statetx WITH (.065*statetx) + statetx
USE acctbills IN 2                 && File contains current billing.
* Update file using new tax rate.
REPLACE ALL mtotal WITH subtotal*.065
END TRANSACTION                && Reset integrity flag; delete log file.
ON ERROR                       && Turn off ON ERROR handler.
IF COMPLETED()                 && TRUE if transaction is successful.
  @ 23,01 SAY "Your transaction is completed."
```

```
ENDIF
CLEAR
*

PROCEDURE trans_err
@ 22,01 CLEAR TO 24,70      && Clear rectangle.
@ 22,01 TO 24,70 DOUBLE     && Draw box.
mretry = .f.
* Prompt user to retry.
@ 23,03 SAY "Your transaction has failed. Try operation again? " ;
        GET mretry PICTURE "Y"
READ
IF mretry                   && TRUE if user answers "Y".
  RETRY                     && RETURNs to line that failed,
                            && and reexecutes it.
ELSE
  @ 23,03 CLEAR TO 23,69
  @ 23,03 SAY "Recovering databases."
  ROLLBACK                  && Recover transaction databases.
  @ 22,01 TO 24,70
  IF ROLLBACK()            && TRUE if ROLLBACK succeeds.
    @ 23,03 SAY "Rollback successful"
  ENDIF
ENDIF
RETURN
```

## LIMITS/WARNINGS:

Because they are disk intensive, transaction logging and recovery reduce processing speed significantly. Also, they require disk space nearly four times the cumulative total of all files included in a transaction.

For sensitive data, you should make file backups before beginning a transaction. On single user systems, file backups will often be easier and more efficient than transaction logging.

## MULTIUSER TIP:

On local area networks, store all transaction log files in a common subdirectory. This will simplify recovery for each workstation in the event of a power loss.

## SEE ALSO:

Commands RESET, RETRY, ROLLBACK, and UNLOCK; functions COMPLETED( ), FLOCK( ), ISMARKED( ), LOCK( ), and ROLLBACK( ).

# BREAK

## DIALECTS:
Clipper, dBXL, and Quicksilver.

## DEFINITION:
Ends execution of a BEGIN SEQUENCE...END SEQUENCE structure in Clipper.

Ends execution of a FOR...NEXT loop in dBXL and Quicksilver.

## SEE ALSO:
Commands BEGIN SEQUENCE...END SEQUENCE and FOR...NEXT.

# BROWSE

## DIALECTS:

dBASE III PLUS, dBASE IV, dBXL, and FoxBASE+.

## SYNTAX:

BROWSE [FIELDS <field list>] [LOCK <expN>] [FREEZE <field>]
    [NOFOLLOW] [NOMENU] [NOAPPEND] [WIDTH <expN>]

## DEFINITION:

Allows easy interactive editing and adding of records. It opens up a full screen edit/add mode with several menu options. The options vary among dBASE III PLUS, dBASE IV, dBXL, and FoxBASE+. BROWSE allows editing of all fields. Because it is an interactive command, Clipper and Quicksilver do not have it.

## DEFAULT:

BROWSE selects all fields unless you specify a field list.

## OPTIONS:

**BROWSE [FIELDS <field list>]:** Limits the BROWSE mode to the specified fields. Default is all fields.

**BROWSE [FREEZE <field>]:** Allows changes to only one field on the screen. All fields are still displayed.

**BROWSE [LOCK <exp>]:** Specifies contiguous fields on the left side of the screen that do not move when you pan the display.

**BROWSE [NOAPPEND]:** Prevents the user from adding records to the file.

**BROWSE [NOFOLLOW]:** Makes the record pointer stay at its original location. When you use index files and change a key field, BROWSE normally repositions the record pointer. For example, suppose you want to change 10 records in a database file indexed on a date. When you BROWSE through the file, records having the same date are together. If you change a date, the record (and the pointer) will be repositioned. Use NOFOLLOW if you want to continue working on records with the original date.

**BROWSE [NOMENU]:**
*dBASE III PLUS:* Prevents display of the menu bar (Top, Bottom, Record No., Lock, Freeze, and Find).

*dBASE IV:* Prevents display of the menu bar (Records, Fields, Go To, and Exit).

*FoxBASE+:* Prevents the user from accessing the cursor movement key menu. Allows access to menu bar.

*dBXL:* Not available.

**BROWSE [WIDTH <expN>]:** Limits the number of characters displayed for any field (between 4 and 99 characters). You can scroll the field horizontally with the arrow keys.

## VARIATIONS:

**dBASE III PLUS:** Does not allow browsing of MEMO fields.

**dBASE IV:** Displays the STATUS bar, even when BROWSEing in a window.

Allows browseing of MEMO fields.

Pressing F2 switches from BROWSE mode to EDIT mode. The PICTUREs and VALID clauses from an active format file remain in effect.

dBASE IV also offers five new options:

*COMPRESS:* Squeezes two more lines of data on the screen by removing some blank lines. The normal mode shows 17 lines of data. The COMPRESSed mode shows 19.

*FORMAT:* Uses the @...SAY command options in the active format file. For example, you can use PICTUREs, FUNCTIONs, RANGEs, and VALID clauses defined for each field in the BROWSE. The screen positioning of the @...SAY is disabled; the data remains in the standard BROWSE table format.

*NOCLEAR:* Leaves data on the screen after exiting the BROWSE. The screen clears by default.

*NOEDIT:* Restricts the user from changing the data on the screen. The user can still delete with Ctrl-U.

*NOINIT:* Uses the options specified in the previous BROWSE command. (If you repeat a lengthy BROWSE command, you only have to type most of it once).

*WINDOW <window name>:* Specifies a defined window in which to open the BROWSE. When you exit, the window automatically deactivates (it remains in memory, but is erased from the screen). When the window is erased, the underlying text reappears.

*FIELDS:* In addition to setting a field list, you can SET read-only fields, calculated fields, and field widths, in the form:

BROWSE...FIELDS <fieldname> / [/R][/<column width>] /
<calculated fieldname> ...

Read-only fields are fields you want to prevent the user from editing. Note that the slash (/) is a literal character you must enter with the R. To limit the field list to ARTICLE, AUTHOR, and PAY, while specifying PAY as read-only, use the command:

```
BROWSE FIELDS article, author, PAY /R
```

To limit the width of ARTICLE to 10 characters, use the command:

```
BROWSE FIELDS article /10, author, PAY /R
```

To make a field read-only and limit it to 10 characters, put the options together without any spaces between them:

```
BROWSE FIELDS article /10/R, author, PAY /R
```

A calculated field is the result of a valid dBASE expression. The <calculated fieldname> is a memory variable containing the expression. In BROWSE, calculated fields change on the screen as you edit fields involved in their expressions. In EDIT, the calculated field doesn't change until you move off the record.

**Example**—An invoice program in a towing company uses a calculated field MTOTAL to display the amount due. The program defines MTOTAL as the sum of MILES, PARTS, and LABOR.

```
USE invoice
BROWSE FIELDS miles, parts, labor, mtotal = miles + parts + labor, inv_num
```

Because you can use any valid expression in a calculated field, you can go far beyond simple mathematics and do things such as include the time, date, diskspace, and record count as part of the fields list.

You can also use user defined functions in calculated fields. This lets you do complex computations without cluttering the BROWSE command. In the interactive mode, just call your user defined function from the calculated field expression, then SET PROCEDURE TO the program file containing your UDFs. In programs, simply add the user defined function to the end of a program file. Unfortunately, this can slow BROWSE down to a crawl.

**Example**—An aircraft repair shop has an invoice with over 15 items. To compute the total efficiently, the programmer puts the formula in a user defined function.

```
USE invoice
SET FIELDS to miles, parts, labor, mtotal = REPAIR(), inv_num


FUNCTION repair
*
RETURN subtotal = miles + parts + labor + pickup + insur + postage + ;
           handling + driver + hookup + overhed + expenses + tools + ;
           license + fuel + phone + oil
* End of REPAIR
```

**FoxBASE+:** Allows browsing of MEMO fields. The NOMODIFY option prevents the user from changing the data.

## SEE ALSO:

Commands ASSIST and INTRO.

# CALCULATE

## DIALECTS:
dBASE IV only.

## SYNTAX:
CALCULATE [<scope>]
AVG(<expN>) / CNT( ) / MAX(<exp>) / MIN(<exp>) /
NPV(<rate>,<flows>,<initial>) / STD(<expN>) /
SUM(<expN>) / VAR(<expN>)
[FOR <condition>] [<WHILE>]
[TO <memory variable list>/ARRAY <array name>]

## DEFINITION:
Computes financial and statistical functions in one pass through a database file.

It supports eight functions that operate on records limited by <scope>, FOR <condition>, and WHILE <condition>.

CALCULATE produces at least one result. If you do not specify a target memory variable or array, the result appears on the screen when TALK is SET ON. Its data type depends on the function.

The <memory variable list> corresponds to the list of functions. The first result goes in the first memory variable, the second result in the second variable, and so on. The number of functions and memory variables must agree.

A target array must be one-dimensional. dBASE IV permits more elements than there are results. However, you cannot have more results than elements.

## DEFAULT:
If you do not use a scope or condition, CALCULATE processes all records.

## OPTIONS:
CALCULATE supports the following functions:

**AVG(<expN>)** **Returns numeric**

Computes the arithmetic mean of <expN>. <expN> is the fieldname, or an expression involving the fieldname.

**CNT( )** **Returns numeric**

Counts the number of records CALCULATEd (limited by <scope> and FOR/WHILE <condition>).

**MAX(<exp>)** **Returns numeric, date, or character.**

Returns the largest value in a field. <exp> can be a numeric, date, or character field.

**MIN(<exp>)** **Returns numeric, date, or character.**

Returns the smallest value in a field. <exp> can be a numeric, date, or character field.

**NPV(<rate>,<flows>,[<initial>])** **Returns numeric**

Computes the Net Present Value of a field. <rate> is the discount rate. <flows> is the numeric field containing periodic cash flow values (both positive and negative). <initial> is the initial investment or a negative number representing cash outflow.

**STD(<expN>)** **Returns type F numeric**

Computes the standard deviation of a field (the square root of the variance). <expN> is the fieldname, or an expression involving the fieldname.

**SUM(<expN>)** **Returns numeric**

SUMs the specified field. <expN> is the fieldname, or an expression involving the fieldname.

**VAR(<expN>)** **Returns type F numeric**

Computes the variance of a field. <expN> is the fieldname, or an expression involving the fieldname.

## RECOMMENDED USE:

Use CALCULATE in financial and statistical applications. A single CALCULATE command can replace several other dBASE commands, reducing the amount of coding and increasing execution speed. For example, in dBASE III PLUS, you need two commands to compute average income in Massachusetts, requiring two passes through the file:

```
COUNT FOR state = "MA" TO statect
AVERAGE ALL income FOR state = "MA" TO income
```

dBASE IV requires only one command:

```
CALCULATE FOR state = "MA" CNT() AVG(income) TO statect,income
```

The more functions you use, the greater the benefits of using CALCULATE.

**Example**—An analysis program uses CALCULATE to compute the average accounts receivables over twelve months, counting only ones with sales over $10,000. CALCULATE also determines the maximum, minimum, and standard deviation for those months. The results go to an array RESULTS.

```
. DECLARE RESULTS[5]
. CALCULATE CNT(), AVG(rcv), MAX(rcv), MIN(rcv), STD(rcv) ;
            TO ARRAY RESULTS FOR rcv > 10000

   CNT()       AVG(rcv)       MAX(rcv)       MIN(rcv)       STD(rcv)
       3          49556          54556          44556        4082.48
   3 records

. DISPLAY MEMORY

        User Memory Variables

RESULTS       pub   A  [5]
   [1]        elem  N                      3  (3.000000000000000000)
   [2]        elem  N                  49556  (49556.00000000000000)
   [3]        elem  N                  54556  (54556.00000000000000)
   [4]        elem  N                  44556  (44556.00000000000000)
   [5]        elem  F                4082.48  (4082.482904638630316)
```

Other parts of the analysis program use more sophisticated expressions in the CALCULATE command. For example, one query averages sales from separate regional divisions:

```
. CALCULATE AVG(ne_sales+sw_sales) TO regional
. ? regional
54223
```

In some computations, the program ignores empty fields by averaging FOR fields with values greater than zero.

```
. CALCULATE AVG(ne_sales+sw_sales) FOR ne_sales > 0 .AND. ;
            se_sales > 0 TO regional
. ? regional
45002
```

CALCULATE duplicates other dBASE commands such as AVERAGE, COUNT, and SUM. However, CALCULATE's MAX( ) and MIN( ) functions differ from the standalone MAX( ) and MIN( ) functions. The standalone MIN( ) and MAX( ) compute the greater or lesser of two values.

## SEE ALSO:

Commands AVERAGE, COUNT, and SUM; functions MAX( ) and MIN( ).

# [C]CALL

## DIALECTS:
Clipper, dBASE III PLUS, dBASE IV, dBXL, FoxBASE+, and Quicksilver.

## SYNTAX:
[C]CALL <module> [WITH <exp>[,<exp>,<exp>,...]]

## DEFINITION:
Executes a routine written in another language (typically assembly language or C).

In dBASE III PLUS, dBASE IV, dBXL, FoxBASE+, and Quicksilver, the routine is a binary program file (extension BIN) previously placed in memory with the LOAD command. In Clipper, routines must be in Intel 8086 relocatable object file format (extension OBJ). You include them in your applications by making them available at link time.
Quicksilver supports both BIN and OBJ methods with CALL (BIN) and CCALL (OBJ). CCALL is the same as Clipper's CALL. You can only use it with the native code optimizer (QS.EXE). It does not work in the d-code mode.

## OPTIONS:
WITH allows rapid parameter passing between dBASE language applications and subroutines written in other languages. The addresses of parameters are passed to the subroutines. In dBASE III PLUS, dBXL, FoxBASE+, and Quicksilver CALL, you may pass only one parameter at a time. Furthermore, it must be either a memory variable or a literal string. In Clipper and in Quicksilver's CCALL, you can pass multiple parameters of most types.

No parameter type checking is done, and the actual address of a memory variable is passed to the BIN routine. Using this scheme, you may not lengthen the passed parameter without corrupting memory.

For information on dBASE IV's CALL, see Variations.

## PARAMETER PASSING CONVENTIONS:
To call binary program files (extension BIN), you must pass the parameter's address in the DS (segment) and BX (offset) register pair. In dBASE III PLUS, the byte at DS:[BX-1] contains the variable's length. However, FoxBASE+ does

not implement the "length byte," and other systems don't use it consistently. We suggest you avoid using it altogether.

Clipper's CALL and Quicksilver's CCALL pass parameter addresses in standard C format on the stack (see Example 2). You can CALL (CCALL) C library routines (large model) in this way. The C library's segment classes for code segment, data segment, and so on, must match those used in the dBASE compiler's library—Lattice C libraries should work with pre-Summer '87 Clipper or Quicksilver, but you must use Microsoft libraries with Clipper Summer '87 and later releases. Do not use C functions that dynamically allocate memory using library routines, such as malloc( ).

In addition to its C parameter-passing conventions, Clipper also passes the first parameter's address in the DX:BX register pair. Most other implementations use DS:BX.

## LIMITS/WARNINGS:

Do not insert a null byte into a character parameter. The variable will appear to be truncated at the point of the insertion. (Typically, dBASE and C character strings end in a null byte.)

BIN routines must not have any segment fixups (much like COM files) and cannot be more than 32K in size. Maintain all data space within the module's code space. Be sure to preserve register values on entry (especially segment registers and the stack pointer).

CALLed modules must take full responsibility for changes they make to memory variables in most implementations. Since internal storage formats vary, each dialect has slightly different rules. (In dBASE III PLUS, lengthening a passed parameter corrupts memory).

## RECOMMENDED USE:

Use CALL and CCALL to extend your applications to do anything a low-level language can do, such as:

- get information about the runtime enviroment,
- control hardware directly,
- process files in ways not provided in the language,
- add functions for memory variable manipulation.

Writing your own assembly language and C routines requires great programming skill. If you are inexperienced, you can use pre-written CALLable subroutines as long as you follow their instructions carefully.

**Example 1**—PRTSC.ASM—BIN/OBJ routine to print the screen (no check for printer not ready):

```
OBJ EQU 1                          ;Change this to 0 for BIN format
PROG SEGMENT PUBLIC 'PROG'         ; if using the Lattice C compiler,
                                   ; for Microsoft C, use 'CODE'
PUBLIC PRTSC
 PRTSC PROC FAR
      INT 5                   ;Call BIOS routine to print the screen.
      RET                     ;Far return to system.
PRTSC ENDP
IF OBJ                        ;If linked into compiled application,
                              ; don't use a label after END directive.
        END
ENDIF
END PRTSC                     ;BIN code requires label after END.
```

To use PRTSC.ASM in OBJ format, assemble it with the Microsoft Macro Assembler (MASM) as follows:

```
MASM PRTSC;
```

Then, if you need a BIN routine, use LINK to create an intermediate EXE file:

```
LINK PRTSC;
```

To create the final BIN file, use the EXE2BIN utility:

```
EXE2BIN PRTSC;
```

**Example 2**—DIREXIST.ASM is an assembly language routine that verifies the existence of DOS subdirectories on any drive. It prevents errors when trying to create or use files. For example, we could test for the existence of a subdirectory on different disk drives. If it is not on A, check B, C, and so on. Here is the assembly language code for DIREXIST.ASM:

```
OBJ EQU 0  ;make it 1 for OBJ code, will insert appropriate instructions
MYPROG SEGMENT BYTE PUBLIC 'PROG'
      assume cs:codeseg
PUBLIC DIREXIST
DIREXIST PROC FAR
START:
IF OBJ  ;---------- To produce more generic code, we make DS:BX
        ;---------- point to the passed parameter in any case
```

```
        push bp                         ;Save BP before setting
        mov  cp,sp                      ;  it up as the frame pointer.
        mov  ds,[bp+8]                  ;BP+8 has word segment
        mov  bx,[bp+6]                  ;BP+6 has word offset
 ENDIF
        mov  dx,bx                      ;Move the offset of memory
                                        ;variable into DX
        mov  ah,4eh                     ;  to set up DOS function
                                        ;  call "find first."
        mov  cx,18d                     ;Look for file with directory
                                        ;  attribute (it will find hidden
                                        ;  subdirectories, by the way).
        int  21h                        ;Call DOS.
        jnc  found                      ;Carry not set, must have found it.
        mov  byte ptr ds:[bx],' '       ;Move in a space if not found.
found:
IF OBJ
        pop  bp
ENDIF
        RET                             ;Back to dBASE or other system.
DIREXIST  ENDP
MYPROG  ENDS
IF OBJ
        END
ELSE
        END  START
```

To create DIREXIST.BIN, type:

```
MASM DIREXIST;
LINK DIREXIST;
EXE2BIN DIREXIST;
```

To link into Clipper or Quicksilver applications (CCALL for Quicksilver), change OBJ EQU 0 to OBJ EQU 1 and type:

```
MASM DIREXIST;
```

You can CALL DIREXIST from a dBASE language program as follows:

```
PUBLIC clipper
subdir = 'C:\work'  && Check for existence of
                    &&   subdirectory "work" on drive C.
IF .NOT. clipper    && If not Clipper (or QS CCALL),
   LOAD direxist    &&   use LOAD and CALL format (BIN file).
ENDIF
CALL direxist WITH subdir
```

If C:\work does NOT exist, DIREXIST sets the ASCII value of SUBDIR to 32 (a blank). Test for this with the statement:

```
IF ASC(subdir) = 32
    * your error routine
ENDIF
```

If C:\work exists, SUBDIR does not change.

## VARIATIONS:

**dBASE IV:** CALL converts parameters to ASCII format. It accepts up to seven parameters, which may be memory variables or fields of any type (but not arrays). The CALL( ) function lets you use BIN routines within such command constructs as REPLACE ALL...WITH and COUNT FOR, thus giving them some of the power of user defined functions.

In dBASE IV, you may modify a field or memory variable in a BIN routine, as long as you do not lengthen it or change its type. If you lengthen a parameter, dBASE IV truncates it to the original length. This does not corrupt memory as in dBASE III PLUS. dBASE IV passes the address of a pointer table in ES and DI, as well as the first parameter's address in DS and BX (for compatibility with dBASE III PLUS). The number of parameters is passed in CX. ES:DI points to a (null-terminated) table of doubleword pointers to the "translated" parameters, each of which is stored in a 255-byte scratch buffer. Since dBASE IV allows almost any type of expression to be passed, you can easily prevent a BIN routine from changing a memory variable or field by enclosing it in parentheses. For example:

```
CALL litebar WITH mchoice
```

allows LITEBAR to change memory variable "mchoice", whereas

```
CALL litebar WITH (mchoice)
```

passes only a copy of the variable.

**Example 3**—OUTP.ASM—dBASE IV-specific routine to send a value to a specified output port using multiple parameters:

```
page 66,132
name outp

Comment $------------------------------------------------
        Example of a simple BIN routine that uses dBASE IV's
        multiple-parameter-passing convention.  Sends a value
        to the specified port.
        Syntax:
        LOAD outp
```

```
        CALL outp WITH <port>,<value>
        * Port and value can be numeric memory variables,
        *   ASCII text numerics, or immediate values.
        Use the following commands to make a BIN routine from OUTP.ASM:
        masm outp;
        link outp;
        exe2bin outp;
        del outp.exe
        ---------------------------------------------------------------$

ARGCOUNT EQU cx                         ;argument count is passed in cx
CODESEG SEGMENT PUBLIC 'CODE'
outp    PROC FAR
        ASSUME CS:CODESEG,ES:nothing,DS:nothing,SS:nothing
        cmp  ARGCOUNT,2                 ;two arguments?
        jne  do_nada                    ;no, don't do anything
        push ds                         ;save ds
        push si                         ;and si
        lds  si,es:[di]                 ;load ds:si with first pointer
        call atoi                       ;trans. to binary number in ax
        mov  dx,ax                      ;first param goes in dx for OUT
        add  di,4                       ;move to next parameter
        lds  si,es:[di]                 ;load ds:si again
        call atoi                       ;translate into ax
        out  dx,ax                      ;send value to port
        pop  si                         ;restore si,ds
        pop  ds
do_nada:
        RET                             ;return to dBASE IV

outp ENDP
comment $-------------------------------------------------------------*
*                                                                     *
*                         procedure atoi                              *
*                                                                     *
*    -Makes ASCII int pointed to by DS:SI into integer in AX-         *
*                                                                     *
*                    ignore overflow and sign                         *
*                                                                     *
* --------------------------------------------------------------------$
atoi    PROC
        push bx                         ;save bx,cx,dx
        push cx
        push dx
        xor  ax,ax                      ;clear accumulator
        mov  bx,10                      ;set radix
        xor  ch,ch                      ;clear ch for adds
skipspaces:
        cmp  byte ptr ds:[si],' '       ;pointing at space?
        jne  accumulate                 ;no, go on
        inc  si                         ;else look at next
```

```
        jmp  skipspaces
accumulate:
        mov  cl,ds:[si]                  ;move in next digit
        cmp  cl,'0'                      ;is it numeric?
        jl   done                        ;if not, we're done
        cmp  cl,'9'                      ;check high end
        ja   done
        sub  cl,'0'                      ;if numeric, make it binary
        mul  bx                          ;shift ax left (decimal)
        add  ax,cx                       ;add in new digit
        inc  si                          ;look at next loop
        jmp  accumulate
done:
        pop  dx
        pop  cx                          ;restore dx,cb,bx
        pop  bx
        RET
atoi    ENDP

CODESEG ENDS

END     outp
```

## SEE ALSO:

Commands LOAD and RUN; function CALL( ).

# CANCEL

## DIALECTS:

Clipper, dBASE III PLUS, dBASE IV, dBXL, FoxBASE+, and Quicksilver.

## SYNTAX:

CANCEL

## DEFINITION:

Stops execution of a program file and closes all open program files. Clears all private memory variables and returns control to the interactive mode without closing database files.

## RECOMMENDED USE:

Use CANCEL to end program execution in dBASE III PLUS, dBASE IV, dBXL, and FoxBASE+ without closing database files. Many dBASE users employ both programs and interactive commands. CANCEL leaves database files available for interactive use. (Clipper and Quicksilver close all files and return control to the operating system).

**Example**—Financial counselors use a program to project investment returns. Occasionally they want to compute a SUM or AVERAGE that is not in the menu. CANCELling the program allows them to access the open database files directly. A selection in the menu CANCELs program execution, but leaves the active files open.

```
* Create logical variable RESPONSE with a value of .F. (false).
response = .F.
* The PICTURE "Y" displays the logical variable as Y or N.
@ 10,10 SAY "End the program? (Y/N)"  GET response PICTURE "Y"
READ
IF response    && If RESPONSE is true (.T.)...
  CANCEL
ENDIF
```

This example issues the prompt "End the program? (Y/N)". The answer, "Y" or "N", goes in memory variable RESPONSE. The IF statement evaluates RESPONSE. If it is true, the program CANCELs.

## SPECIAL USES:

If you SUSPEND program execution, you cannot edit the open program files using the MODIFY COMMAND editor. Issue CANCEL to end the SUSPENDed mode before trying to edit a program.

## VARIATIONS:

**dBXL:** CANCEL returns control to the XL prompt and clears all memory variables.

**Clipper, Quicksilver:** CANCEL returns control to the operating system.

**FoxBASE+:** In the Runtime version, control returns to the operating system. In the development version, control returns to the interactive mode. CANCEL releases all private memory variables.

## SEE ALSO:

Commands RETURN and QUIT.

# CASE

## DIALECTS:
Clipper, dBASE III PLUS, dBASE IV, dBXL, FoxBASE+, and Quicksilver.

## SYNTAX:
CASE <condition>

## DEFINITION:
Indicates a branching point in a program when <condition> evaluates to true (.T.). CASE is part of a DO CASE structure.

## SEE ALSO:
Command DO CASE for more information.

# CD

## DIALECTS:
dBXL only.

## SYNTAX:
CD [<path>]

## DEFINITION:
Changes the MS-DOS/PC-DOS directory to the specified <path>.

<path> consists of a valid drive letter and directory.

If the path specifies a drive other than the current one, CD changes the directory, but not the drive.

CD without a path displays the current directory and drive.

CD works like the MS-DOS/PC-DOS CD or CHDIR commands.

## RECOMMENDED USE:
Use CD from dBXL's interactive mode to navigate through file directories. It is not necessary in programs since you can control directory access with the commands SET DBF, SET NDX, and SET PATH.

**Example**—Working in dBXL's interactive mode, Samuel in accounting browses directories looking for the accounts receivable database.

```
SET PROMPT TO ". "      && Change to standard dot prompt.
. CD \DBXL\AR
. DIR AR*.DBF
```

## SEE ALSO:
Commands SET DBF, SET DEFAULT, SET NDX, and SET PATH.

# CHANGE/EDIT

## DIALECTS:

dBASE III PLUS, dBASE IV, dBXL, and FoxBASE+.

## SYNTAX:

CHANGE [scope] [FIELDS <field list>] [WHILE <condition>] [FOR <condition>]

## DEFINITION:

Allows full-screen editing of fields in the database in use.

## DEFAULT:

Displays all fields unless otherwise specified in the FIELDS option. Selects all records unless otherwise specified by SCOPE, FOR, or WHILE conditions.

CHANGE is the same as EDIT.

## RECOMMENDED USE:

Use CHANGE in the interactive mode of dBASE III PLUS, dBASE IV, dBXL, and FoxBASE+. You can include it in programs; however, it does not allow enough control over the user's actions for sophisticated applications. For example, CHANGE lets users modify the database directly.

**Example 1**—A legal secretary wants to quickly change one client's address in a database file. From the dBASE dot prompt, he or she uses CHANGE to initiate full-screen editing.

```
. USE clients
. CHANGE FOR lname = "Marvin"
```

The screen now appears as follows:

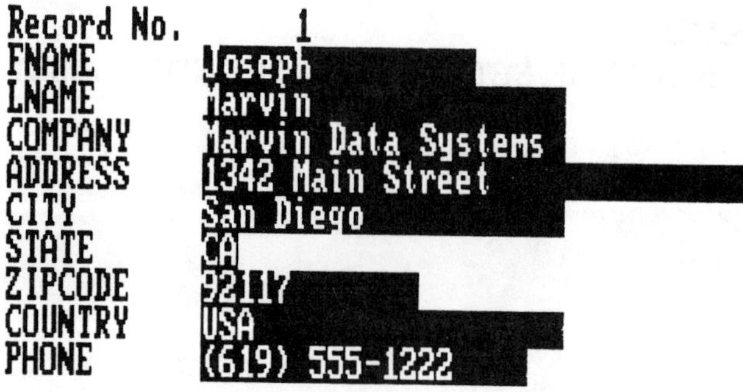

## VARIATIONS:

**Clipper:** The interactive editing utility, DBU, lets you change database records.

**dBASE IV:** Pressing F10 invokes a bar menu that lets you control CHANGE operations such as Undo Change, Add New Records, Mark Record for Deletion, Blank Record, Lock Record, and Follow Record to New Position. The F10 menu also lets you move through the database by record number or do simple searches. CHANGE has several more command line options, in the form:

CHANGE [NOINIT] [NOFOLLOW] [NOAPPEND] [NOMENU] [NOEDIT] [NODELETE][NOCLEAR] [<record number>]

*NOAPPEND:* Stops the user from adding records.

*NOCLEAR:* Leaves data on the screen after exiting the CHANGE. The screen clears by default.

*NODELETE:* Stops the user from deleting records with Ctrl-U.

*NOEDIT:* Stops the user from changing the data on the screen. The user can still delete with Ctrl-U.

*NOFOLLOW:* Changing a key field in an indexed database moves the changed record to a new position in the index. By default, the record pointer follows the moved record. NOFOLLOW leaves the pointer in its original position. The next record after the original position becomes the current record. This lets you CHANGE sequentially, without jumping around the database.

*NOINIT:* Uses the options specified in the previous CHANGE command. (If you have long repetitive CHANGE commands, you only have to type the options once).

*NOMENU:* Stops the user from invoking the CHANGE/EDIT bar menu by pressing the F10 key.

*<record number>:* Starts the CHANGE at the specified record number, and lets the user access all other records.

*Warning:* <record number> alone is easily confused with a scope that uses a record number. To restrict CHANGE to a single record, use CHANGE RECORD <record number>, using the "RECORD" keyword.

*Networking Notes:* On a network, the status bar indicates the locking condition, as follows (in the lefthand column):

| Message | Cause |
|---|---|
| Exclusive use | (USE <filename> EXCLUSIVE) |
| File locked | (Automatic, FLOCK()) |
| Read only | (PROTECT) |
| Record locked | (Automatic, LOCK( ), RLOCK( ), or Ctrl-O interactively) |
| Record unlocked | (Automatic, UNLOCK) |

On a network, when you press a key to update a record, CHANGE automatically tries to lock the record and related ones. If the lock succeeds, dBASE IV rereads the record from disk to determine whether another user has changed it since you first displayed it. If so, the new data appears with the prompt, "Data in record has changed." You can press Esc to cancel CHANGE, unlocking the record. If you press any other letter or number key, CHANGE proceeds.

## SEE ALSO:

Commands BROWSE, EDIT, and SET AUTOSAVE.

# CLEAR

## DIALECTS:

Clipper, dBASE III PLUS, dBASE IV, dBXL, FoxBASE+, and Quicksilver.

## SYNTAX:

CLEAR

## DEFINITION:

Erases the screen, releases all pending GET statements, and puts the cursor in the upper left corner. You can clear parts of the screen with the @ <coord> CLEAR statement. (See @ <coord> CLEAR).

## RECOMMENDED USE:

Use CLEAR to erase the screen before displaying menus or reports.

**Example**—A programmer uses CLEAR at the beginning of every application as part of a general "housekeeping" routine that resets the program environment.

```
* HOUSE.PRG
SET SAFETY OFF
SET TALK off
SET SCOREBOARD off
SET UNIQUE on
CLEAR ALL
CLEAR
```

## LIMITS/WARNINGS:

Because CLEAR releases pending GETs, don't use it in procedures or user defined functions while GETs are active. For example, avoid CLEAR in procedures initiated with Clipper's SET KEY command or in Clipper, FoxBASE+, or Quicksilver user defined functions called from a VALID clause (see @...SAY...GET). If you must CLEAR the screen in these situations, use @ 0,0 CLEAR or, in Clipper, CLEAR SCREEN.

## VARIATIONS:

**Clipper:** The SCREEN option clears the screen without releasing pending GETs. It lets you CLEAR the screen in SET KEY procedures or in user defined functions called from the VALID clause of the @...SAY...GET command.

**dBASE IV:** If you have an active window, CLEAR erases only its contents. The border and the full screen surrounding it remain intact. You must enter the full-screen mode to CLEAR the entire screen by first DEACTIVATing, CLEARing, or RELEASing the window. You can also ACTIVATE SCREEN to select the full-screen mode.

**dBXL, Quicksilver:**

CLEAR [CHARACTER "<expC>"]

The CHARACTER option fills the screen with the leftmost character of <expC>. For example, CLEAR CHARACTER "*" fills the background with asterisks. dBXL and Quicksilver have special windowing commands and functions that are enhanced by using the CHARACTER option.

This option helps you simulate "desktop" user interfaces (such as Apple Macintosh, the GEM operating system, and Microsoft Windows) by defining backgrounds with a single command.

Also, if you have an active window, CLEAR erases only its contents. The frame and the screen surrounding it remain intact. To clear the screen, you must select the full screen mode as follows:

```
WSELECT 0
CLEAR
```

## SEE ALSO:

Command @...CLEAR TO.

# CLEAR ALL

## DIALECTS:

Clipper, dBASE III PLUS, dBASE IV, dBXL, FoxBASE+, and Quicksilver.

## SYNTAX:

CLEAR ALL

## DEFINITION:

Releases all memory variables and arrays, closes open database files and all set relations, and selects work area 1 (the default). It also closes all related index files, format files, and memo files, and rejects all current @...GET commands. CLEAR ALL does not close PROCEDURE files.

## RECOMMENDED USE:

Use CLEAR ALL as the first command in a main program. It assures a clean work environment and avoids corrupting open files from a previous application.

**Example**—A library application consists of 20 program files. The main one, called LIB.PRG, calls the others. CLEAR ALL at the beginning of LIB.PRG assures that previous programs do not leave active variables or open files.

```
* LIB.PRG
CLEAR ALL
SET TALK off
SET ECHO off
```

## VARIATIONS:

**dBASE IV:** Also removes MENUS and POPUPS from memory.

## SEE ALSO:

Commands CLEAR MENUS, CLEAR POPUPS, CLEAR WINDOWS, CLOSE DATABASES, CLOSE PROCEDURE, and RELEASE.

# CLEAR AUTOMEM

## DIALECTS:

dBXL and Quicksilver.

## SYNTAX:

CLEAR AUTOMEM

## DEFINITION:

Creates a set of memory variables for an open database with the same names as the field names (AUTOMEM variables). CLEAR AUTOMEM overwrites existing memory variables with the same names.

## RECOMMENDED USE:

Use CLEAR AUTOMEM to create new AUTOMEM variables within a DO WHILE loop during data entry. This clears AUTOMEM variables with the same names used in the previous record. You can also use CLEAR AUTOMEM in the interactive mode, from the XL prompt.

**Example**—A data entry module initializes 42 AUTOMEM variables with CLEAR AUTOMEM. After adding a new record (with APPEND AUTOMEM), issue CLEAR AUTOMEM to reset the AUTOMEM variables.

```
SET TALK off
response = "Y"
USE mainentr
DO WHILE response # "N"
  CLEAR
  CLEAR AUTOMEM
  * <42 @...SAY...GETs>
  READ
  APPEND AUTOMEM
  @ 10,10 SAY "Add more records? (Y/N) " GET response PICTURE "!"
  READ
ENDDO
```

Without CLEAR AUTOMEM, this example would require 42 memory variable declarations, an APPEND BLANK, and 42 REPLACEs.

## VARIATIONS:

**FoxBASE+:** SCATTER...TO <array> stores fields from the current record in an array.

## SEE ALSO:

Commands CLEAR, GATHER, and SCATTER.

# CLEAR FIELDS

## DIALECTS:

dBASE III PLUS, dBASE IV, dBXL, FoxBASE+, and Quicksilver.

## SYNTAX:

CLEAR FIELDS

## DEFINITION:

Releases field lists created with the SET FIELDS TO <field list> command. It releases fields set in all work areas.

If there is no SET FIELDS TO <field list>, CLEAR FIELDS has no effect.

## RECOMMENDED USE:

The SET FIELDS command limits the fields available to LIST, DISPLAY, EDIT, etc. CLEAR FIELDS restores ALL FIELDS. SET FIELDS and CLEAR FIELDS are intended for interactive use.

**Example**—A large inventory file contains four fields. A clerk wants to work with only two of them without having the others cluttering the screen. He uses the SET FIELDS command to select the fields he wants. He later issues CLEAR FIELDS to restore the field list.

```
. USE invent
. LIST
Record#  PARTNO     QUANT      DESC                 UNITCOST
      1  0383           1      Widget                   2.95
. SET FIELDS TO partno,quant
. LIST
Record#  PARTNO      QUANT
      1  0383            1
. CLEAR FIELDS
. LIST
Record#  PARTNO     QUANT      DESC                 UNITCOST
      1  0383           1      Widget                   2.95
```

In this example, the user selects fields PARTNO and QUANT from file INVENT. A LIST shows only the selected fields. After issuing CLEAR FIELDS, the LIST once again shows all fields.

## SEE ALSO:

Command SET FIELDS.

# CLEAR GETS

## DIALECTS:

Clipper, dBASE III PLUS, dBASE IV, dBXL, FoxBASE+, and Quicksilver.

## SYNTAX:

CLEAR GETS

## DEFINITION:

Cancels all pending GET statements. It does not erase the screen as CLEAR does.

## RECOMMENDED USE:

You can use GETs to display data, and then issue a READ conditionally to edit. However, there is a limit on the number of GETs you can use before issuing the next READ, CLEAR, or CLEAR ALL.

**Example**—An editing module of a real estate application displays a record with GETs. It asks the user whether to EDIT or continue to the next record. If the user chooses to EDIT, the program executes a READ. Otherwise, the program executes a CLEAR GETS before proceeding to the next record.

```
USE property
DO WHILE .t.
  CLEAR
  * 1) Initialize memory variables from PROPERTY.
  * 2) @...SAY...GET memory variables.
  * Use WAIT instead of @...SAY...GET...READ because READ
  * activates all GETs.
  WAIT "(E)dit (C)ontinue (R)eturn? (E/C/R)" TO response
  DO CASE
    CASE UPPER(response) = "E"     && If RESPONSE is E, READ.
      READ
      * <REPLACE memory variables into PROPERTY>.
      * If RESPONSE is C, CLEAR GETS and move to next record.
    CASE UPPER(response) = "C"
      CLEAR GETS
      SKIP
    CASE UPPER(response) = "R"     && If RESPONSE is R, RETURN.
      RETURN
  ENDCASE
ENDDO
```

## SEE ALSO:

Commands CLEAR, CLEAR ALL, and GET.

# CLEAR KEY

## DIALECTS:
dBXL and Quicksilver.

## SYNTAX:
CLEAR KEY

## DEFINITION:
Clears the typeahead buffer. Same as CLEAR TYPEAHEAD in dBASE III PLUS and dBASE IV.

## SEE ALSO:
Command CLEAR TYPEAHEAD.

# CLEAR MEMORY

## DIALECTS:

Clipper, dBASE III PLUS, dBASE IV, dBXL, FoxBASE+, and Quicksilver.

## SYNTAX:

CLEAR MEMORY

## DEFINITION:

Releases all memory variables. It differs from RELEASE ALL in that it releases public variables as well as private ones.

## SEE ALSO:

Command CLEAR ALL.

# CLEAR MENUS

## DIALECTS:
dBASE IV only.

## SYNTAX:
CLEAR MENUS

## DEFINITION:
Erases all bar menus and removes them from memory.

## RECOMMENDED USE:
Use CLEAR MENUS to clear the screen and reclaim memory space for more menus.

**Example**—A subroutine DEFINEs and ACTIVATEs several menus. Before returning to the calling program, it issues CLEAR MENUS.

```
CLEAR MENUS
RETURN
```

## SEE ALSO:
Commands CLEAR POPUPS and CLEAR WINDOWS.

# CLEAR POPUPS

## DIALECTS:

dBASE IV only.

## SYNTAX:

CLEAR POPUPS

## DEFINITION:

Erases all popup menus and removes them from memory.

Clears all ON SELECTION commands.

## RECOMMENDED USE:

Use CLEAR POPUPS to clear the screen and reclaim memory space for more popups.

**Example**—A subroutine DEFINEs and ACTIVATEs several popups. Before returning to the calling program, it issues CLEAR POPUPS.

```
CLEAR POPUPS
RETURN
```

## SEE ALSO:

Commands CLEAR MENUS and CLEAR WINDOWS.

# CLEAR PROGRAM

## DIALECTS:
FoxBASE+ only.

## SYNTAX:
CLEAR PROGRAM

## DEFINITION:
Clears the FoxBASE+ program buffer.

## RECOMMENDED USE:
FoxBASE+ executes programs using a buffering system to improve performance. Entire command files (PRGs) are loaded into memory. During development, if you edit with an external editor, issue CLEAR PROGRAM before DOing the new program. Otherwise, the old program remains in the buffer and will execute.

Also use CLEAR PROGRAM when editing a procedure file, even if you use the internal FoxBASE+ editor MODIFY COMMAND.

## SEE ALSO:
Commands CLOSE PROCEDURE, DO, and MODIFY COMMAND.

# CLEAR TYPEAHEAD

## DIALECTS:

Clipper, dBASE III PLUS, dBASE IV, dBXL, FoxBASE+, and Quicksilver.

## SYNTAX:

CLEAR TYPEAHEAD

## DEFINITION:

Empties the keyboard typeahead buffer.

## RECOMMENDED USE:

Use CLEAR TYPEAHEAD to prevent a program user from entering data before viewing a screen prompt.

**Example**—A critical menu selection decides whether to delete 10 years' data in a communicable disease tracking application. Normally, an impatient operator can enter a response before the actual prompt appears. To prevent this, the programmer includes CLEAR TYPEAHEAD before all critical prompts.

```
CLEAR TYPEAHEAD
response = " "
@ 10,05 SAY "Delete data for last 10 years? (Y/N) "
DO WHILE .NOT. response $ "YN"
  @ 10,42 GET response PICTURE "!"
  READ
ENDDO
```

## VARIATIONS:

**Clipper:** CLEAR TYPEAHEAD not available in versions before Summer '87. To clear the keyboard buffer in earlier versions, use the KEYBOARD command with a null value:

```
KEYBOARD ""
```

**dBXL, Quicksilver:** CLEAR KEY is the same as CLEAR TYPEAHEAD.

## SEE ALSO:

Commands CLEAR KEY, KEYBOARD, and SET TYPEAHEAD TO.

# CLEAR WINDOWS

## DIALECTS:
dBASE IV only.

## SYNTAX:
CLEAR WINDOWS

## DEFINITION:
Erases all windows and removes their definitions from memory.

Restores full-screen operation and reveals text previously covered by windows.

## RECOMMENDED USE:
Use CLEAR WINDOWS as a quick way to clear the screen and reclaim memory space for more windows. If you want to save window definitions, use the command SAVE WINDOWS. You can later use RESTORE WINDOWS to reload them into memory.

## SEE ALSO:
Commands CLEAR MENUS, CLEAR POPUPS, RESTORE WINDOWS, and SAVE WINDOWS.

# CLOSE

## DIALECTS:

Clipper, dBASE III PLUS, dBASE IV, dBXL, FoxBASE+, and Quicksilver.

## SYNTAX:

CLOSE [ALTERNATE/DATABASES/FORMAT/INDEX/PROCEDURE]/ALL

## DEFINITION:

Closes alternate, database, format, index, and procedure files.

## OPTIONS:

### CLOSE ALL

Closes all files without releasing memory variables.

### CLOSE ALTERNATE

Closes an alternate file.

### CLOSE DATABASES

Closes all database, index, and format files.

### CLOSE FORMAT

Closes an open format file in the currently selected work area.

### CLOSE INDEX

Closes open indexes in the currently selected work area.

### CLOSE PROCEDURE

Closes a procedure file.

## VARIATIONS:

**dBASE III PLUS, FoxBASE+, and Quicksilver:** When you CLOSE ALL from an open procedure file, the procedure remains open. You cannot issue CLOSE PROCEDURE from within an open procedure file.

**dBASE IV:** You may issue CLOSE ALL from an open procedure file.

**dBXL:** CLOSE ALL causes a syntax error when issued from a procedure file. The problem is that it tries to close the open procedure, giving the error message "File is in use." Similarly, you cannot issue CLOSE PROCEDURE from within an open procedure file.

CLOSE UDF closes a user defined function file. Opened by the command SET UDF TO <filename>, a function file may contain up to 32 user defined functions. SET UDF TO <filename> closes the previous function file before opening the new one. SET UDF TO without a filename also closes the user defined function file. CLOSE UDF is not available in Quicksilver.

## SEE ALSO:

Commands CLEAR ALL, INDEX, RELEASE, SET ALTERNATE, SET PROCEDURE, SET UDF TO, and USE.

# COMMIT

## DIALECTS:
Clipper only.

## SYNTAX:
COMMIT

## DEFINITION:
Writes all active data buffers to disk without affecting record pointers or closing open database files.

## RECOMMENDED USE:
When you add or edit records, new data stays in memory buffers until you close the file or until the buffers are full. If the computer loses power during data entry, data in the buffers is lost. Issuing COMMIT after adding or changing a record protects the new data.

In multiuser applications, COMMIT ensures that changes to a database are reflected immediately, providing a higher degree of concurrency control. Without COMMIT, data needed by other users may remain in buffers unnecessarily.

## LIMITS/WARNINGS:
Do not use COMMIT after issuing PACK/ZAP. This combination of commands in a multiuser application could corrupt the database.

## SEE ALSO:
Commands FLUSH and SET AUTOSAVE.

# COMPILE

## DIALECTS:
dBASE IV only.

## SYNTAX:
COMPILE <filename>

## DEFINITION:
Converts a source program into an executable tokenized form. COMPILE also checks syntax. If it detects an error, it stops and you must fix the program before recompiling.

COMPILE converts only one program at a time.

The target file has an extension of DBO. Source programs are ASCII files.

DOing an uncompiled program will automatically COMPILE it.

With SET DEVELOPMENT ON, DO compares the PRG file with the DBO file. If the PRG file's time and date are later, DO <filename> recompiles the PRG file, then executes it.

Using the internal MODIFY COMMAND editor to change a program erases the associated DBO file. With SET DEVELOPMENT ON, the next time you run the program, DO <filename> recompiles it, thus avoiding the possibility of running an old version.

## DEFAULT:
COMPILE looks for a file with a PRG extension, unless you specify otherwise.

COMPILE looks in the default directory for the specified file.

## RECOMMENDED USE:
You must COMPILE all source files before executing them. Even if you are not ready to run a program, COMPILE does a quick syntax check and finds most obvious errors.

## LIMITS/WARNINGS:

Be sure to give source programs unique names. Otherwise, you might overwrite existing DBO files without warning.

dBASE III PLUS does not recognize dBASE IV-compiled programs.

The compiler optimizes program speed by evaluating constants at compile time.

*Note:* Source files may have extensions FRG (generated report form), FMT (format), LBG (generated label), PRG (program), PRS (SQL program), QBE (query file), and UPD (update query).

## SEE ALSO:

Commands DO, MODIFY COMMAND, and SET DEVELOPMENT.

# CONTINUE

## DIALECTS:

Clipper, dBASE III PLUS, dBASE IV, dBXL, FoxBASE+, and Quicksilver.

## SYNTAX:

CONTINUE

## DEFINITION:

Causes a record-by-record search to continue, using the conditions in the previous LOCATE command.

When the search finds a matching record, it positions the record pointer there. CONTINUE reexecutes the LOCATE, starting at the next record. If the search fails, the record pointer ends up at the end of the LOCATE scope, or at the End of File (EOF), whichever comes first.

CONTINUE only works on the database in the active work area. Distinct CONTINUEs can operate independently in different work areas.

**Example**—A career placement agency must find all Brodericks in a client database. Because there are no indexes, the secretary uses LOCATE instead of SEEK or FIND. After finding the first match, the secretary issues the CONTINUE command to continue the search, starting with the next record.

```
. USE mainfile
. LOCATE FOR lname = "Broderick"
Record = 5
. ? lname
Broderick
. CONTINUE
Record=122
. ? lname
Broderick
. CONTINUE
End of LOCATE scope
```

## SEE ALSO:

Command LOCATE.

# CONVERT

## DIALECTS:
dBASE IV only.

## SYNTAX:
CONVERT [TO <expN>]

## DEFINITION:
Adds a internal field called _DBASELOCK to an open database file in the current work area. In multiuser applications, _DBASELOCK contains information about record and file locks.

<expN> is the length of _DBASELOCK, ranging from 8 to 24 characters. If you do not specify its value, the default is 16 characters.

CONVERT makes a backup of the original database file with a CVT extension.

## RECOMMENDED USE:
Use CONVERT to prepare databases for multiuser applications that use CHANGE( ) and LKSYS( ). These functions tell you who has locked a record or file, when it was locked, and whether it has been changed. You must also CONVERT databases to use SET REFRESH. SET REFRESH updates a user's BROWSE or EDIT screen when another user changes the data being displayed. The _DBASELOCK field holds the data that makes these multiuser features possible.

The counter that indicates whether a record was CHANGEd occupies the first two bytes of _DBASELOCK. The TIME indicator (returned by LKSYS(3)) occupies the next three bytes. The DATE indicator (returned by LKSYS(4)) occupies the next three. The LOGIN NAME (returned by LKSYS(5)) occupies the remainder. If you CONVERT TO 24 (the maximum length of _DBASE-LOCK( )), the login takes the last 16. If you CONVERT TO 16 (the default), the login name takes the last eight. If you CONVERT TO 8, the login name is not stored.

The CHANGE( ) indicator, the time, and the date are in hexadecimal format. The login name is a character representation.

**Example**—To prepare a multiuser application, the programmer CONVERTs database files. For small databases (under 10,000 records), the programmer specifies the full 24 characters. However, to save disk space, the programmer specifies only 16 characters for files over 10,000 records.

```
USE mainsales
CONVERT          && Default to 16. Creates MAINSALES.CVT backup file.
USE subsales
CONVERT TO 24    && Also creates SUBSALES.CVT backup file.
```

## LIMITS/WARNINGS:

You cannot view _DBASELOCK directly. Instead, you must use the functions CHANGE( ) and LKSYS( ) to return its value. _DBASELOCK appears in the file structure; you can delete it. However, you cannot add it through CREATE/MODIFY STRUCTURE.

## SEE ALSO:

Command SET REFRESH; functions CHANGE( ), LKSYS( ), LOCK( ), and RLOCK( ).

# COPY

## DIALECTS:

Clipper, dBASE III PLUS, dBASE IV, dBXL, FoxBASE+, and Quicksilver.

## SYNTAX:

COPY TO <new file> [<scope>] [FIELDS <field list>] [FOR <condition>] [WHILE <condition>] [TYPE] <file type>]

## DEFINITION:

COPY TO moves data in the active database to a new file. The output file can be a different type, such as DELIMITED ASCII or Standard Data Format (SDF). dBASE III PLUS and dBASE IV can also produce files in DIF, SYLK, and WKS formats. Additionally, dBASE IV can produce dBASE II, Framework II, and RapidFile files.

## DEFAULT:

Unless you specify a scope, or a FOR or WHILE condition, COPY copies all records. Unless you specify a different file TYPE, it creates another dBASE III PLUS or dBASE IV database file (DBF). Unless you specify a FIELDS list, it copies all fields.

COPY copies memo fields only when the target is a dBASE III PLUS or dBASE IV database file.

## OPTIONS:

The TYPE <file type> option converts COPY output to file formats other than dBASE III PLUS or dBASE IV. The other TYPEs are:

**DBASEII**
Ashton-Tate dBASE II database. dBASE IV only.

**DELIMITED [WITH <delimiter>/BLANK]**
Delimited format file
Clipper, dBASE III PLUS, dBASE IV, dBXL, FoxBASE+, and Quicksilver.

**DIF**
VisiCalc™ spreadsheet format.
dBASE III PLUS, dBASE IV, and dBXL.

**FW2**
Ashton-Tate Framework database or spreadsheet.
dBASE IV only.

**RPD**
Ashton-Tate RapidFile database.
dBASE IV only.

**SDF**
System Data Format
Clipper, dBASE III PLUS, dBASE IV, dBXL, FoxBASE+, and Quicksilver.

**SYLK**
Multiplan™ spreadsheet format.
dBASE III PLUS, dBASE IV, and dBXL.

**WKS**
Lotus 1-2-3 release 1.A spreadsheet format.
dBASE III PLUS, dBASE IV, and dBXL.

The dBASE III PLUS/dBASE IV EXPORT command creates pfs:File files.

## RECOMMENDED USE:

Use COPY TO to create files containing query results. By putting selected records in another file, you can manipulate data and create reports without considering irrelevant records.

**Example**—An inventory application uses several report programs to format data in different ways (e.g., one program lists parts sorted by number, another by product category). To choose and organize records for a report, each program could include data selection commands. However, it is easier to select data in a separate program and COPY the selected records TO a summary file. When the search criteria changes, the report programs need not be modified.

```
USE inventl
COPY TO repfile FOR category = "KITCHEN"
USE repfile
SORT ON partno TO partno
DO reportl
```

In this example, COPY examines records from REPFILE for the category "KITCHEN." Only records meeting this criteria go into REPFILE, a temporary database that the program overwrites every time it executes.

## LIMITS/WARNINGS:

**dBASE III PLUS, dBASE IV, dBXL, and FoxBASE+:** Do not use the letters A through J or M as database file names to COPY TO. Clipper and Quicksilver do not have this restriction.

Only FoxBASE+ allows ALIAS-> designators in the COPY TO FIELDS option. This lets you COPY FIELDS from an unselected database.

In dBASE III PLUS and dBASE IV, you must first SET RELATION INTO the unselected database, then use the alias-> designator in the SET FIELDS command. You can then COPY TO with a FIELD list without alias designators, as follows:

```
USE file1 INDEX key                   && KEY is index name and key field name.
SELECT 2
USE file2
SET RELATION TO key INTO file1
SET FIELDS TO file1->partnum, key     && PARTNUM is a field in FILE1.
COPY TO temp FIELDS partnum, key      && Field names must be unique, or only
                                      &&  those in the current file will COPY.
```

## VARIATIONS:

**dBASE IV:** You can send data to an array with

COPY TO ARRAY <array name> [FIELDS <field list>] [<scope>]
    [FOR <condition>] [WHILE <condition>]

The ARRAY option adds the contents of an open database to an existing array. Each record in the database becomes an array row. Each field becomes an array column. (In ARRAY[x,y], x is the row, and y the column.)

The first field in the record becomes the first column in the array. The second field becomes the second column, and so on, until there are no more fields or no more columns. COPY TO ARRAY ignores excess columns or fields.

The first record in the database becomes the first row in the array. The second record becomes the second row, and so on, until there are no more records or no more rows.

All data copied from a database to an array is subject to <scope>, FOR, WHILE, and <field list> conditions. The first field or record is the first matching these conditions if specified.

Elements in the target array must have the same data types as the database fields.

**Example**—Database defaults are stored in a database. To protect the database from damage due to power losses, a sales contact program opens CONTACT.DBF only long enough to COPY its contents to an array. The program first opens the database, COPYs TO ARRAY, then closes the database.

```
DECLARE mrec[5]
USE contacts
GOTO 10
COPY TO ARRAY mrec NEXT 1       && Copy only current record.
USE
@ 01,01 SAY "Enter name:     " GET mrec[1,1]
@ 02,01 SAY "Enter address:  " GET mrec[1,2]
@ 03,01 SAY "Enter city:     " GET mrec[1,3]
@ 04,01 SAY "Enter state:    " GET mrec[1,4]
@ 05,01 SAY "Enter zipcode:  " GET mrec[1,5]
READ
```

**FoxBASE+:** Allows alias-> designators in the COPY TO FIELDS <field list>. This lets you COPY fields from unselected work areas.

Can read, but not directly modify, dBASE II and FoxBASE database files. You can use COPY to convert dBASE II and FoxBASE files to dBASE III PLUS files.

## SEE ALSO:

Commands APPEND FROM, COPY FILE, EXPORT, GATHER, and SCATTER.

# COPY FILE

## DIALECTS:

Clipper, dBASE III PLUS, dBASE IV, dBXL, FoxBASE+, and Quicksilver.

## SYNTAX:

COPY FILE <file1> TO <file2>

## DEFINITION:

Duplicates a closed file. You must specify extensions for both files. You may also specify drive designators and DOS path names.

## RECOMMENDED USE:

COPY FILE works like the DOS COPY command. Use it to create archival backups.

**Example**—A finance company requires floppy disk backups every evening. The system administrator issues the COPY FILE command for drive A.

```
. COPY FILE pastdue.prg TO a:pastdue.prg
1222 bytes copied
```

## LIMITS/WARNINGS:

**dBASE III PLUS, dBASE IV, dBXL, and FoxBASE+:** Do not use the letters A through J or M as database file names.

## VARIATIONS:

**Clipper:** COPY FILE copies from the default drive and directory (set by SET DEFAULT and SET PATH).

**dBASE IV:** COPY FILE copies from the default directory established by the SET PATH command or the PATH set in the CONFIG.DB file.

## SEE ALSO:

Commands COPY and SET PATH.

# COPY INDEXES

## DIALECTS:
dBASE IV only.

## SYNTAX:
COPY INDEXES <file list> [TO <MDX filename>]

## DEFINITION:
Copies index files (extension NDX) into a multiple index file (extension MDX), creating a TAG in the target MDX for each index.

The original index file is unchanged.

To use COPY INDEXES, you must first USE a database and activate the indexes to be copied.

## DEFAULT:
If you do not specify a target MDX file with the TO option, COPY INDEXES adds the TAGs to the production multiple index file.

If no such file exists, COPY INDEXES creates one with the same name as the database.

## OPTIONS:
You can specify a target MDX file with the TO <MDX filename> option. If it does not exist, COPY INDEXES creates it and gives it the specified name.

## LIMITS:
Multiple index files are limited to 47 TAGs. However, you can only use COPY INDEXES on 10 indexes at a time, since that is the open index limit.

## RECOMMENDED USE:
Use COPY INDEXES to convert dBASE III PLUS applications to dBASE IV.

**Example**—A dBASE III PLUS property management application uses four index files with a main file called TENANTS. The programmer uses COPY INDEXES to convert to a dBASE IV production multiple index file. The TO option is not required, since COPY INDEXES creates the production index with the same name as the database.

```
USE tenants INDEX rents,duedates,balance,deposits
COPY INDEXES rents,duedates,balance,deposits
```

To COPY INDEXES to an existing multiple index file, the command would be:

```
COPY INDEXES rents,duedates,balance,deposits TO prop_mdx
```

## SEE ALSO:

Commands COPY TAG, INDEX, and SET INDEX; functions MDX( ) and NDX( ).

# COPY MEMO

dBASE IV only.

## SYNTAX:

COPY MEMO <memo name> TO <filename> [ADDITIVE]

## DEFINITION:

Copies text from the current record's memo field to a text file. If the file already exists, COPY MEMO erases it.

If SET SAFETY is ON, dBASE IV prompts the user before erasing the file.

Drive and path designators are optional.

You can specify a memo field in an unselected work area by using the ALIAS-> designator with the fieldname. You can also copy a memo field from another work area if it is part of the current SET FIELDS list.

## DEFAULTS:

The target file defaults to a TXT extension.

## OPTIONS:

You can append the current memo field to an existing text file with the ADDITIVE option.

## RECOMMENDED USE:

**Example**—A law office management program stores case notes in memo fields. At the end of the month, the program generates a log file containing all case notes.

```
USE legal
DO WHILE end_date < {02/08/89} .AND. .NOT. EOF()
  COPY MEMO c_notes TO feblog ADDITIVE
  SKIP
ENDDO
```

The program produces a text file called FEBLOG.TXT.

## SEE ALSO:

Command APPEND MEMO; functions MEMLINES( ), MLCOUNT( ), and MLINE( ).

# COPY STRUCTURE

## DIALECTS:

Clipper, dBASE III PLUS, dBASE IV, dBXL, FoxBASE+, and Quicksilver.

## SYNTAX:

COPY STRUCTURE TO <filename> [FIELDS <field list>]

## DEFINITION:

Copies the active database's structure to a new file, a database file (extension DBF) with no records.

## DEFAULT:

All fields, unless limited by the FIELDS option.

## RECOMMENDED USE:

Use COPY STRUCTURE to create new empty databases from existing databases. If some field definitions differ, you can then use MODIFY STRUCTURE to change the structure.

**Example**—A programmer must create a new database file for a towing company application under development. To avoid the tedious definition process, the programmer copies the structure of an existing file.

```
. USE vehicles
. LIST STRUCTURE
Structure for database: C:vehicle.dbf
Number of data records:       104
Date of last update   : 05/17/87
Field  Field Name  Type        Width    Dec
    1  MAKE        Character      10
    2  MODEL       Character      10
    3  MILEAGE     Numeric        10
    4  COST        Numeric        10
** Total **                       41

. COPY STRUCTURE TO veh2 FIELDS make,model
. USE veh2
. LIST STRUCTURE
Structure for database: C:subfile.dbf
  Number of data records:       0
  Date of last update   : 05/17/87
```

```
Field  Field Name  Type        Width    Dec
    1  MAKE        Character      10
    2  MODEL       Character      10
** Total **                       21
```

## SPECIAL USE:

You can use COPY STRUCTURE to regain disk space from database files. In some cases, dBASE files from which records have been DELETEd and PACKed, or ZAPped, do not relinquish their disk space. To reclaim disk space fully, proceed as follows:

1) COPY STRUCTURE of the active database to a temporary file.

2) USE the temporary file.

3) APPEND FROM the original file.

4) DELETE the original file with the DELETE FILE command.

5) RENAME the temporary file to the name of the original file.

## SEE ALSO:

Command COPY TO <file> STRUCTURE EXTENDED.

# COPY...STRUCTURE EXTENDED

## DIALECTS:

Clipper, dBASE III PLUS, dBASE IV, dBXL, FoxBASE+, and Quicksilver.

## SYNTAX:

COPY TO <filename> STRUCTURE EXTENDED

## DEFINITION:

Creates a new database that contains information about the currently active database's structure. The new database contains a record for every field in the original. It has the following structure:

```
1 FIELD_NAME  Character   10
2 FIELD_TYPE  Character    1
3 FIELD_LEN   Numeric      3
4 FIELD_DEC   Numeric      3
```

## RECOMMENDED USE

Use COPY TO as the first step in creating new database files under program control. First, create a STRUCTURE EXTENDED file with the COPY TO command. Then modify its contents using EDIT, REPLACE, etc.. Next, create a new database file with the modified structure using the CREATE FROM command.

**Example**—A programmer uses similar database files in several applications. Rather than CREATE each file from scratch, he or she copies the STRUCTURE EXTENDED, then EDITs the resulting file. To modify the applications, the programmer need only reedit the STRUCTURE EXTENDED file before regenerating the database files.

```
. USE receipts
. DISPLAY STRUCTURE
Structure for database: C:receipts.dbf
Number of data records:      104
Date of last update    : 05/17/87
Field  Field Name  Type        Width    Dec
    1  NAME        Character      10
    2  ADDRESS     Character      10
    3  PRETAX      Numeric        10
    4  POSTTAX     Numeric        10
** Total **                       41
```

```
. COPY TO rec_extnd STRUCTURE EXTENDED
. LIST
Record#  FIELD_NAME FIELD_TYPE FIELD_LEN FIELD_DEC
      1  NAME       C                 10         0
      2  ADDRESS    C                 10         0
      3  PRETAX     N                 10         0
      4  POSTTAX    N                 10         0
```

REC_EXTND contains a record for each field in RECEIPTS. Each record can be treated like any other dBASE record. It can be EDITed, REPLACEd, etc. In this example, the programmer changes NAME to FIRSTNAME and adds 2 decimal places to PRETAX.

```
. LIST
Record#  FIELD_NAME FIELD_TYPE FIELD_LEN FIELD_DEC
      1  FIRSTNAME  C                 10         0
      2  ADDRESS    C                 10         0
      3  PRETAX     N                 10         2
      4  POSTTAX    N                 10         0
```

Using CREATE FROM, the programmer then generates a new database containing the changes:

```
. CREATE new_rec FROM rec_extd
. DISPLAY STRUCTURE
Structure for database: C:new_rec.dbf
Number of data records:      0
Date of last update    : 08/19/87
Field  Field Name  Type        Width    Dec
    1  FIRSTNAME   Character      10
    2  ADDRESS     Character      10
    3  PRETAX      Numeric        10      2
    4  POSTTAX     Numeric        10
** Total **                       43
```

## SEE ALSO:

Commands CREATE, CREATE FROM, and MODIFY STRUCTURE.

# COPY TAG

## DIALECTS:
dBASE IV only.

## SYNTAX:
COPY TAG <tag name> [OF <MDX filename>] TO <NDX filename>

## DEFINITION:
Copies a multiple index file TAG into an index file (extension NDX).

The MDX file is unchanged.

To use COPY TAG, you must first USE a database and activate the MDX from which to copy.

## OPTIONS:
If you have more than one open MDX file, OF <MDX filename> specifies the one you want.

## DEFAULT:
Without the OF option, COPY TAG copies TAGs from the open MDX.

## RECOMMENDED USE:
Use COPY TAG to create dBASE III PLUS-compatible indexes from the dBASE IV-specific MDX format.

**Example**—A dBASE IV parcel tracking system uses a file PARCELS and two multiple index files PARCMDX and TRACKER. PARCMDX has four TAGs: SHIPDATE, RECVDATE, COST, and WEIGHT. To use the PARCELS file and PARCMDX with dBASE III PLUS, the programmer copies the TAGs to a dBASE III PLUS-compatible index file (NDX).

```
USE parcels INDEX tracker,parcmdx
*
COPY TAG shipdate OF parcmdx TO shipdate
100% indexed                 92 Records indexed
COPY TAG recvdate OF parcmdx TO recvdate
100% indexed                 92 Records indexed
```

```
COPY TAG cost OF parcmdx TO cost
100% indexed                    92 Records indexed
COPY TAG weight OF parcmdx TO weight
100% indexed                    92 Records indexed
```

## SEE ALSO:

Commands COPY TAG, INDEX, and SET INDEX; functions MDX( ) and NDX( ).

# COUNT

## DIALECTS:
Clipper, dBASE III PLUS, dBASE IV, dBXL, FoxBASE+, and Quicksilver.

## SYNTAX:
COUNT [<scope>] [WHILE <condition>] [FOR <condition>]
    [TO <memory variable>]

## DEFINITION:
Counts the number of records within the given scope for which the expression is true. The count appears on the screen when you SET TALK ON. With SET TALK OFF, you must use a TO <memory variable> clause.

## DEFAULT:
All records if no scope, WHILE, or FOR is given.

## OPTIONS:
TO <memory variable> puts the result in a numeric memory variable.

## RECOMMENDED USE:
Use COUNT to determine how many records meet a specified condition.

**Example**—A demographics application analyzes the purchasing habits of mailorder customers. COUNT determines how many live in the state of Washington and earn over $50,000. The number counted is stored in memory variable QUALIFY.

```
. USE customers
. COUNT FOR state = "WA" .AND. income > 50000 TO qualify
. ? qualify
455
```

## VARIATIONS:
**Clipper, Quicksilver:** The COUNT result must go to a memory variable with the TO <memory variable> clause.

## SEE ALSO:
Commands AVERAGE, CALCULATE, SET TALK, and SUM; function RECCOUNT( ).

# CREATE

## DIALECTS:

dBASE III PLUS, dBASE IV, dBXL, and FoxBASE+.

## SYNTAX:

CREATE [<filename>]

## DEFINITION:

Starts an interactive program to define the structure of a new database.

If you don't supply a filename, a prompt asks for one. Prompts then ask for the name, type, length, and number of decimals for each field. You end the process by pressing the Enter key when the cursor is at the last empty input field. At that point, a prompt asks:

```
Do you wish to add data now?
```

Answering (Y)es puts dBASE in the APPEND mode. Answering (N)o restores the interactive prompt or continues to the next line in a program.

Change the structure of existing files with MODIFY STRUCTURE.

## RECOMMENDED USE:

Use CREATE to generate new database files. When creating several similar files, you can often save time by copying the first one's structure, then modifying it with MODIFY STRUCTURE.

**Example**—A large university grading application uses 10 database files. Four are nearly identical. To save time, CREATE one file, then copy its structure to others that you can modify later.

```
. CREATE freshman
```

The following screen appears. You enter the specifications for the FRESHMAN file.

```
Layout   Organize   Append   Go To   Exit                              5:30:08 pm

                                                         Bytes remaining:   3816
| Num | Field Name | Field Type | Width | Dec | Index |
|  1  | LNAME      | Character  |  30   |     |   N   |
|  2  | FNAME      | Character  |  20   |     |   N   |
|  3  | ADDRESS    | Character  |  30   |     |   N   |
|  4  | CITY       | Character  |  20   |     |   N   |
|  5  | STATE      | Character  |   2   |     |   N   |
|  6  | CODE       | Character  |  12   |     |   N   |
|  7  | PHONE      | Character  |  12   |     |   N   |
|  8  | AMOUNT     | Numeric    |  10   |  2  |   N   |
|  9  | STUDENTID  | Character  |  10   |     |   N   |
| 10  | COUNTRY    | Character  |  20   |     |   N   |
| 11  | ENTERED    | Date       |   8   |     |   N   |
| 12  | STU_NOTES  | Memo       |  10   |     |   N   |
| 13  |            | Character  |       |     |   N   |

Database D:\dbase\FRESHMAN        Field 13/13
          Enter the field name.  Insert/Delete field:Ctrl-N/Ctrl-U
Field names begin with a letter and may contain letters, digits and underscores
```

When you finish specifying the new file, press Enter. You will be asked if you want to enter data. If you say no, control passes back to the interactive mode. Now, to duplicate the file structure, do the following:

```
COPY STRUCTURE to soph
COPY STRUCTURE to junior
COPY STRUCTURE to senior
```

You can now use MODIFY STRUCTURE to change the three new files SOPH, JUNIOR, and SENIOR. Perhaps, for example, SENIOR has added fields for GRADUATING, EXPECTED DATE OF GRADUATION, and SENIOR HONORS.

## LIMITS/WARNINGS:

**dBASE III PLUS, dBASE IV, dBXL, FoxBASE+:** Do not use the letters A through J or M as database filenames. They are reserved for ALIAS names.

## VARIATIONS:

**Clipper, Quicksilver:** No built-in interactive file creation screen. However, both provide stand-alone utility programs for file creation.

**Clipper:** CREATE <file> produces an empty STRUCTURE EXTENDED file. (See COPY TO <file> EXTENDED). From it, you can then create other database files with the CREATE FROM command.

## SEE ALSO:

Commands CREATE FROM and MODIFY STRUCTURE.

# CREATE...FROM

## DIALECTS:

Clipper, dBASE III PLUS, dBASE IV, dBXL, FoxBASE+, and Quicksilver.

## SYNTAX:

CREATE <file> FROM <structure extended file>

## DEFINITION:

Produces a new database file using a structure in a STRUCTURE EXTENDED file.

## RECOMMENDED USE:

Use CREATE FROM to build temporary database files for storing intermediate calculations or for modifying database structures under program control.

## SPECIAL USE:

In Clipper, the CREATE <file> command produces an empty STRUCTURE EXTENDED file. You may CREATE FROM it under program control to generate all databases for an application. You can thus deliver an application program to clients as a single executable (EXE) file.

A trick in dBASE III PLUS and dBASE IV lets you achieve the same effect as Clipper's CREATE FROM. The SET CATALOG command CREATEs a database file without user interaction. It thus lets you create a database file and immediately COPY its STRUCTURE EXTENDED. The new file can serve as the basis for all other database files in an application. The procedure is:

```
* dBASE III PLUS example.
* When creating a new catalog, prompts for a "catalog title."
SET TITLE OFF           && SET TITLE OFF disables the prompt.
SET CATALOG TO origin   && Creates ORIGIN.CAT (a database file).
SET CATALOG TO          && Close the CATALOG file.
USE origin.cat          && Catalog assigns a CAT ext. instead of DBF.
COPY STRUCTURE EXTENDED TO base_ext
USE base_ext
DISPLAY STRUCTURE
```

```
Structure for database: C:\BASE_EXT.DBF
  Number of data records:           5
  Date of last update   :    09/23/87
     1 FIELD_NAME  Character     10
     2 FIELD_TYPE  Character      1
     3 FIELD_LEN   Numeric        3
     4 FIELD_DEC   Numeric        3
 ** Total **                     18
```

dBASE IV has an additional field FIELD_IDX for the index indicator.

You can now modify the STRUCTURE EXTENDED file and generate new database files using CREATE FROM.

## SEE ALSO:

Commands COPY STRUCTURE EXTENDED, CREATE, MODIFY STRUCTURE, and SET CATALOG.

# CREATE GRAPH

## DIALECTS:
dBXL only.

## SYNTAX:
CREATE/MODIFY GRAPH <filename>

## DEFINITION:
Starts an interactive program for defining bar graphs, line graphs, pie charts, regression lines, scatter plots, and step graphs. CREATE GRAPH uses up to 40 records from the current database.

Graph definitions are stored in graph format files (extension GRF). The data remains in the database file. You may use a GRF file with another database, as long as it contains the same fields as the original. dBXL GRF files are compatible with Quicksilver.

On systems with the Enhanced Graphics Adapter (EGA), you can define color graphs. Systems with the Color Graphics Adapter (CGA) or Hercules card are limited to monochrome graphs with cross-hatching.

The GRAPH FORM command displays graph format files.

CREATE graph also lets you store graphs in formats for Aldus Pagemaker (PCX), PC Paintbrush (PCX), and Xerox's Ventura Publisher (IMG).

You can use the printer defined by dBXL's SET GRAPHPRINT command or Quicksilver's INSTALL program. Supported printers are:

- Epson FX (or LX86)
- Epson MX/IBM Graphics Printer (the default)
- Hewlett Packard LaserJet
- Okidata dot matrix

The manual also lists an HPGL Plotter option, but it does not work.

## RECOMMENDED USE:
Use CREATE GRAPH with GRAPH FORM to display simple business graphs. The graph format file (GRF) defines the graph type, titles, expressions, and color, but the plotting conforms to the open database.

**Example**—An accountant wants to display a bar graph comparing 1988 and 1989 expenses. To do this, she opens the associated database and issues CREATE GRAPH.

```
* Database contains three fields, MONTH (C,12), PAY1988 (N,8,2),
*   and PAY189 (N,8,2).
USE expenses
CREATE GRAPH expgraph
```

The accountant then defines the graph in the following steps:

1) Choose graph TYPE: BAR GRAPH:

```
dBXL GRAPH
 Type      Values      Titles      Display      Quit
Choose graph format.

 Pie Chart
 Bar Graph
 Step Graph
 Line Graph
 Scatter Plot
 Regress Line
```

| Type : Bar Graph | | | | | |
|---|---|---|---|---|---|
| X Field | Y Field1 | Y Field2 | Y Field3 | Y Field4 | Y Field5 |
| SUBSTR(mont | pay1988 | pay1989 | | | |

```
GRAPH     |<D:>|EXPENSES.DBF     |1/12
Draw a bar graph.
```

2) Enter X and Y axis values:

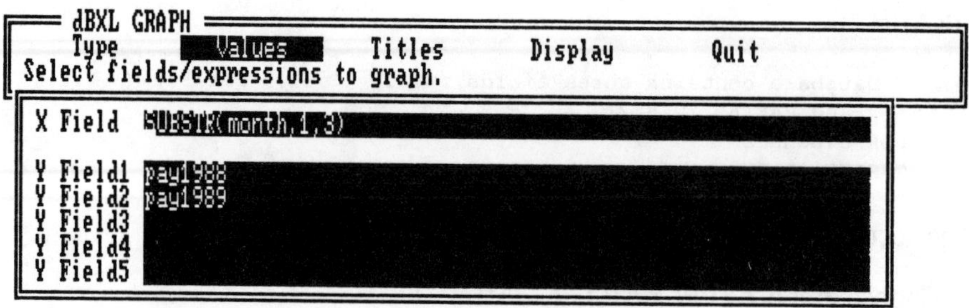


| Type : Bar Graph | | | | | |
|---|---|---|---|---|---|
| X Field | Y Field1 | Y Field2 | Y Field3 | Y Field4 | Y Field5 |
| SUBSTR(mont | pay1988 | pay1989 | | | |

GRAPH <D:> EXPENSES.DBF 1/12
Enter a CHARACTER or NUMERIC expression to graph on the x-axis.

3) Enter graph titles:

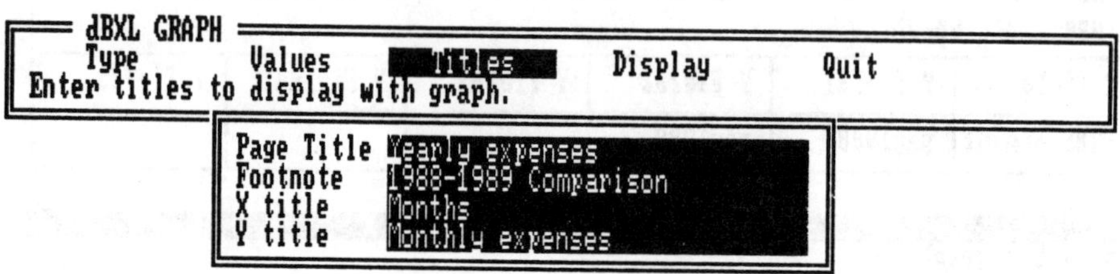


| Type : Bar Graph | | | | | |
|---|---|---|---|---|---|
| X Field | Y Field1 | Y Field2 | Y Field3 | Y Field4 | Y Field5 |
| SUBSTR(mont | pay1988 | pay1989 | | | |

GRAPH <D:> EXPENSES.DBF 1/12
Enter a page title to be displayed on the top of the graph.

4) Choose output options:

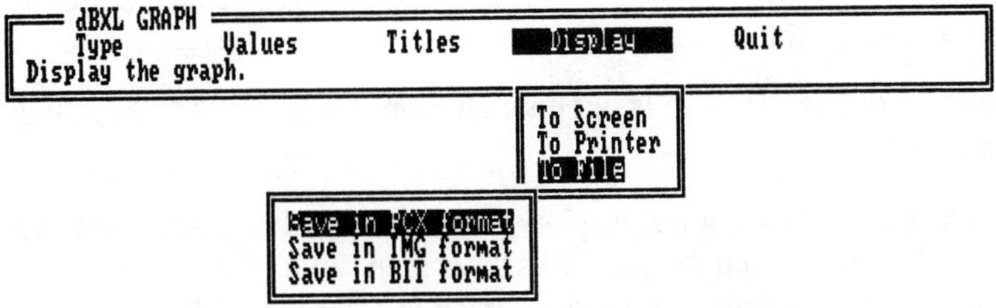


| Type : Bar Graph | | | | | |
|---|---|---|---|---|---|
| X Field | Y Field1 | Y Field2 | Y Field3 | Y Field4 | Y Field5 |
| SUBSTR(mont | pay1988 | pay1989 | | | |

Save the graph in PC Paintbrush (TM) PCX format.

After she saves the graph, it is ready for display with the command

```
GRAPH FORM expgraph
```

The graph appears as follows:

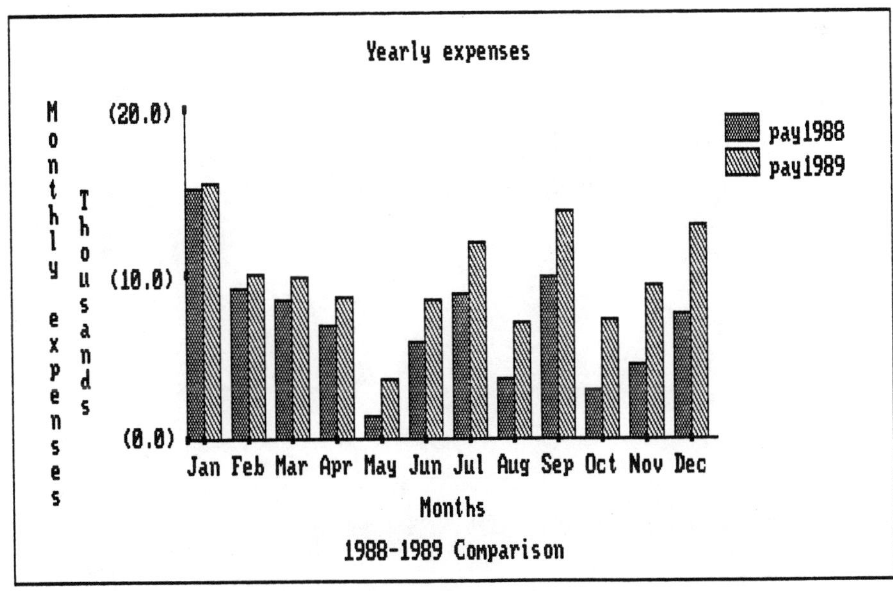

## LIMITS/WARNINGS:

CREATE GRAPH requires a Hercules, IBM Color, or IBM Enhanced Graphics Adapter (or compatible).

X axis labels overlap if there is not enough room. To avoid this, keep them as short as possible.

dBXL and Quicksilver do not display graphs within the active window. The screen blanks briefly, then the graph fills the screen. When the user presses a key, the graph disappears and the previous screen is erased as well. To preserve it, issue WSAVE before displaying the graph, then WRESTORE after.

## VARIATIONS:

**Quicksilver:** The standalone program MODIGRF.EXE creates graph forms compatible with Quicksilver. Quicksilver can use graphs generated by dBXL.

## SEE ALSO:

Commands GRAPH FORM, RESTORE GRAPH, and SET GRAPHPRINT.

# CREATE COMMAND/LABEL/REPORT/ QUERY/SCREEN/VIEW

## DIALECTS:

dBASE III PLUS, dBASE IV, dBXL, and FoxBASE+.

## SYNTAX:

CREATE/MODIFY LABEL/REPORT/QUERY/SCREEN/VIEW
MODIFY COMMAND

## DEFINITION:

These are utility programs designed for interactive use. Support for them varies from product to product, as follows:

**dBASE III PLUS:**
CREATE LABEL/REPORT/QUERY/SCREEN/VIEW FROM ENVIRONMENT

**dBASE IV:**
CREATE LABEL/REPORT/QUERY/SCREEN/VIEW/VIEW FROM ENVIRONMENT

**dBXL:**
CREATE LABEL/REPORT/QUERY/FILE/COMMAND/VIEW FROM ENVIRONMENT

**FoxBASE+:**
CREATE LABEL/REPORT

Clipper has separate interactive utility programs for creating LABELS and REPORTS. The Quicksilver manual recommends that programmers create LABEL and REPORT forms in advance with dBASE III PLUS. See REPORT FORM and LABEL FORM.

## OPTIONS:

### CREATE COMMAND [<filename>]

Invokes dBXL's text editor. Files have a default extension of PRG.

**CREATE FILE [<filename>]**
Invokes dBXL's text editor.

**CREATE LABEL [<filename>]**
Automates mailing label generation. Allows saving and reusing of label forms.

**CREATE QUERY [<filename>]**
dBASE III PLUS, dBASE IV, and dBXL offer interactive prompting for sophisticated searches on a database. You can save complex queries for reuse.

**CREATE REPORT [<filename>]**
The dBASE III PLUS, dBXL, and FoxBASE+ internal report generators provide simple summary reports without programming. dBASE IV provides more powerful reports.

**CREATE SCREEN [<filename>]**
Starts an interactive forms design program. It lets you define input forms with boxes, lines, database views, and custom typestyles.

**CREATE VIEW [<filename>]**
Creates a special file (extension VUE) in which you define databases, indexes, active relations, filters, and open format files. Restoring the VUE file with SET VIEW TO <filename> establishes the dBASE working environment.

**CREATE VIEW FROM ENVIRONMENT [<filename>]**
Creates a view (extension VUE) file containing information on open database files and their work areas, formats, indexes, relations, set fields, and filter conditions.

Issuing CREATE VIEW FROM ENVIRONMENT is like taking a snapshot of the dBASE working environment. When you finish a work session, use it to preserve the current environment. Start the next session with SET VIEW TO the VUE file.

**MODIFY COMMAND [<filename>]**
Starts the internal program editor. Gives files a default extension of PRG.

## SEE ALSO:

Commands LABEL FORM, MODIFY COMMAND/FILE REPORT FORM, SET CATALOG, SET FIELDS, SET INDEX, SET RELATION, and SET VIEW.

# DEACTIVATE MENU/POPUP/WINDOW

## DIALECTS:
dBASE IV only.

## SYNTAX:
DEACTIVATE MENU/POPUP
DEACTIVATE <window name list>/ALL

## DEFINITION:
Deactivates and erases a menu, popup, window, or group of windows.

These objects remain in memory for later reactivation. To remove them from memory, use RELEASE MENUS/POPUPS/WINDOWS or CLEAR MENUS/POPUPS/ WINDOWS.

Text covered by menus, popups, and windows is restored upon deactivation. When you DEACTIVATE WINDOW, the previously active window (if there is one) becomes active again. DEACTIVATing all windows restores full-screen mode.

DEACTIVATE MENU and DEACTIVATE POPUP are not valid from the dot prompt, since no menu or popup can be active.

DEACTIVATion of a MENU or POPUP does not interrupt or terminate program execution. Control returns to the line after the menu or popup was activated.

## OPTIONS:
You can DEACTIVATE multiple windows by using a list or by specifying ALL.

## RECOMMENDED USE:
Use DEACTIVATE MENU and DEACTIVATE POPUP from an ON SELECTION PAD or ON SELECTION POPUP statement. The DEACTIVATE commands have the same effect as pressing ESC.

**Example 1**—An automobile parts inventory menu offers three choices. The last one is "Return," which deactivates the POPUP.

```
DEFINE POPUP parts FROM 01,01 To 05,25
DEFINE BAR 1 OF parts PROMPT "Stock report"
DEFINE BAR 2 OF parts PROMPT "Product search"
DEFINE BAR 3 OF parts PROMPT "Return to previous menu"
```

```
ON SELECTION POPUP parts DO mchoice
ACTIVATE POPUP parts

PROCEDURE mchoice
msel = BAR()
DO CASE
  CASE msel = 1
    * <Do stock procedure>.
  CASE msel = 2
    * <Do search procedure>.
  CASE msel = 3
    * End execution of popup
    DEACTIVATE POPUP
ENDCASE
```

If you display the POPUP under a MENU PAD (using ON PAD), control returns to the MENU when you DEACTIVATE POPUP. In this situation, DEACTIVATE POPUP does not appear to work because the ON PAD immediately reactivates the POPUP. To deactivate the POPUP and its controlling MENU, use DEACTIVATE MENU.

**Example 2**—The inventory program from Example 1 uses DEFINE MENU to list user selections. The last choice on every MENU is "Exit."

```
DEFINE MENU refill
DEFINE PAD sel1 OF refill PROMPT "List stock numbers for refill" AT 0,0
DEFINE PAD sel2 OF refill PROMPT "Exit" AT 0,50
ON SELECTION PAD sel1 OF refill DO rquery
ON SELECTION PAD sel2 OF refill DO mexit
ACTIVATE MENU refill

PROCEDURE rquery
DISPLAY part,qty FOR qty < 5
RETURN

PROCEDURE mexit
DEACTIVATE MENU
RETURN
```

**Example 3**—The inventory system from Examples 1 and 2 uses ten windows to display information. They are called WIN1 through WIN10. The program deactivates them by name.

```
DEACTIVATE win1,win7,win9
```

Before exiting to the dot prompt, the inventory system DEACTIVATEs ALL windows.

```
DEACTIVATE WINDOW ALL
```

*Warning:* Avoid the temptation to use DEACTIVATE ALL WINDOW instead of DEACTIVATE WINDOW ALL. While most dBASE syntax is flexible, this command is not.

## SEE ALSO:

Commands ACTIVATE MENU, ACTIVATE POPUP, CLEAR MENUS/POPUPS/ WINDOWS, DEFINE MENU, DEFINE POPUP, and RELEASE MENUS/POPUPS/WINDOWS; functions BAR( ), MENU( ), PAD( ), and PROMPT( ).

# DEBUG

## DIALECTS:

dBASE IV only.

## SYNTAX:

DEBUG <fileame> [WITH <parameter list>]

## DEFINITION:

Executes the specified program or procedure under the control of the interactive debugger.

The debugger lets you analyze a program while it runs (see the figure below for a typical screen). You can set breakpoints, display the results of expressions, edit the program, or execute it a line at a time.

The debugger has debugger, display, breakpoint, and edit windows. The debugger window shows work areas, open files, active procedures, and the current line number. The edit window shows the program lines as they execute. Pressing E lets you edit them. The breakpoint window lets you use the LINENO( ) function to set breakpoints (see function LINENO( ) for an example). The display window lets you specify expressions to trace as values change in the program.

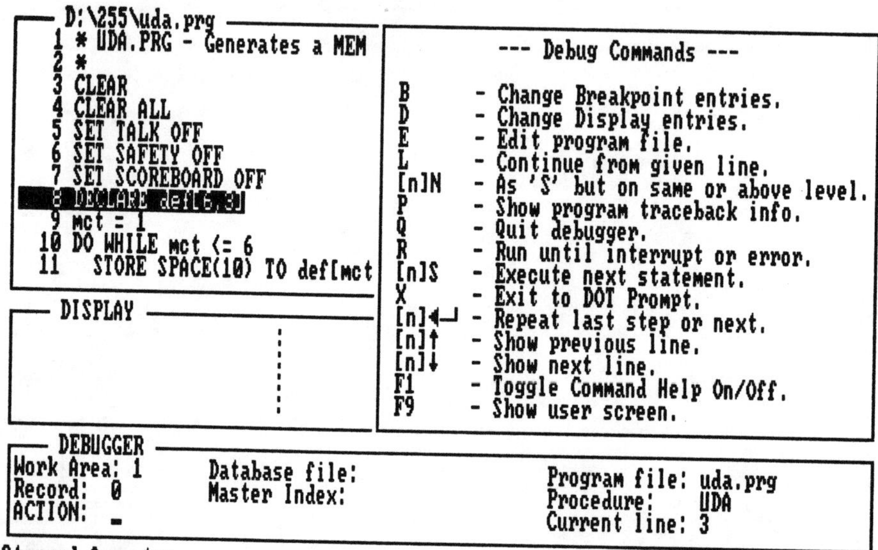
D:\255\uda.prg
1 * UDA.PRG - Generates a MEM
2 *
3 CLEAR
4 CLEAR ALL
5 SET TALK OFF
6 SET SAFETY OFF
7 SET SCOREBOARD OFF
9 mct = 1
10 DO WHILE mct <= 6
11 STORE SPACE(10) TO def[mct
DISPLAY
--- Debug Commands ---
B - Change Breakpoint entries.
D - Change Display entries.
E - Edit program file.
L - Continue from given line.
[n]N - As 'S' but on same or above level.
P - Show program traceback info.
Q - Quit debugger.
R - Run until interrupt or error.
[n]S - Execute next statement.
X - Exit to DOT Prompt.
[n]◄┘ - Repeat last step or next.
[n]↑ - Show previous line.
[n]↓ - Show next line.
F1 - Toggle Command Help On/Off.
F9 - Show user screen.
DEBUGGER
Work Area: 1
Record: 0
ACTION:
Database file:
Master Index:
Program file: uda.prg
Procedure: UDA
Current line: 3
Stopped for step.

## RECOMMENDED USE:

Use the debugger to fix program syntax and logic errors, and to optimize program performance. Quite often, watching a program's execution can point out inefficiencies such as lines that execute unnecessarily.
You can display the debugger's command list by pressing F1. The list overlaps the breakpoint window.

## VARIATIONS:

**Clipper:** The interactive debugger is in a linkable object module called DEBUG.OBJ. The ALTD( ) function activates it.

**dBASE III PLUS, dBXL, FoxBASE+:** Use SET DEBUG, SET ECHO, SET STEP, and SET TALK to debug programs.

**Quicksilver:** You can select the interactive debugger (called dB Debugger) at compile time with the -G switch.

## SEE ALSO:

Commands SET DEBUG, SET ECHO, SET STEP, and SET TALK; functions ALTD( ), LINENO( ), and PROGRAM( ).

# DECLARE

## DIALECTS:

Clipper and dBASE IV.

## SYNTAX:

DECLARE <array name>[<expN1>,<expN2>]] [,<array list>]

**Note:** The outer square brackets around expN1,expN2 are literals. They must be included in the DECLARE statement.

## DEFINITION:

Activates an array of <expN1> rows and <expN2> columns. For example, you would DECLARE an array NAME with five rows as follows:

```
DECLARE name[5]
```

Clipper allows only one dimension. dBASE IV allows two. You would DECLARE a dBASE IV array with five rows and 2 columns as follows:

```
DECLARE names[5,2]
```

Array elements can be referenced by the array name and a number (subscript) representing its relative position. Subscripts start at 1.

The data type in an element is determined by the last STORE made to it. Before values are STOREd in an array, all elements are false (.F.).

Arrays use only one memory variable name. When you LIST MEMORY, they appear with type "A".

Two-dimensional arrays can be DECLAREd and accessed with 1 or 2 subscripts.

## OPTIONS:

You may DECLARE several arrays at once. For example:

```
DECLARE week[7],year[12]
```

creates two arrays, week and year, with seven and 12 elements, respectively.

## RECOMMENDED USE:

Use DECLARE to store lookup data for quick access, or to load and unload data from databases. You can also use arrays to accept the results of the AVERAGE and CALCULATE commands.

**Example 1**—A dBASE IV editing program copies data from a database to an array using the COPY TO ARRAY command. The database contains five fields and 10 records.

```
SET TALK ON
DECLARE mdata[10,5]
USE trans
COPY TO ARRAY mdata
10 Records Copied
```

**Example 2**—A Clipper programmer designs files with numbered field names. He or she can then initialize memory variables in a DO WHILE loop by incrementing a counter, replacing many STORE or equal sign declarations. As the counter increases, the elements of the array are assigned the values of the corresponding numbered fields. You can then edit the array and REPLACE the data back into the file using the same incrementing technique. This program adds a new record to a form letter generating program. Each field is one line in the letter.

```
DECLARE mline[23]          && Declare an array of 23 elements.
USE letters                && LETTERS file has fields LINE1 through LINE23.
APPEND BLANK               && Add a record.
FOR counter = 1 TO 23
  * As counter increments, array MLINE and field LINE increment.
  * Create a string version of counter and remove leading blanks.
  scnter = LTRIM(STR(counter,2,0))
  * The & expands SCNTER, forming field names LINE1, LINE2, LINE3, etc.
  STORE line&scnter TO mline[counter]
NEXT counter
```

Now array MLINE contains 23 elements, each representing a blank field in the new database record. To edit it, increment GETs in a DO WHILE or FOR NEXT loop. This is the equivalent of 23 @...SAY...GET statements:

```
FOR counter = 1 TO 23
  @ counter,1 GET mline[counter]
  NEXT counter
  READ
```

After editing is completed, the program can REPLACE the values in the same way:

```
FOR counter = 1 TO 23
  scnter = LTRIM(STR(counter,2,0))
  REPLACE line&scnter WITH mline[counter]
  NEXT counter
```

See APPEND FROM ARRAY, AVERAGE, and COPY TO ARRAY for more examples.

## VARIATIONS:

**Clipper:** Limited to one-dimensional arrays. You may use PUBLIC <memory variable/array list> or PRIVATE <memory variable/array list> instead of DECLARE to create arrays, reducing the number of lines of code. Also note that LEN(<arrayname>) returns the number of elements in the array.

**dBASE IV:** Has two-dimensional arrays.

**FoxBASE+:** The DIMENSION command provides multidimensional array capability.

## LIMITS:

**Clipper:** Arrays must have at least one element and may have up to 4096. Ones DECLAREd with fewer or more elements default to 1 or 4096, respectively.

**dBASE IV:** Arrays may have up to 1023 elements, depending on the amount of available memory.

## SEE ALSO:

Commands APPEND FROM ARRAY, COPY TO ARRAY, DIMENSION, FOR...NEXT, GATHER, PRIVATE, PUBLIC, and SCATTER; functions ADIR( ), AFILL( ), AINS( ), ADEL( ), LEN( ), and TYPE( ).

# DEFINE BAR

## DIALECTS:

dBASE IV only.

## SYNTAX:

DEFINE BAR <bar number> OF <popup name> PROMPT <expC>
[MESSAGE <expC>][SKIP [FOR <condition>] [NOSPACE]]

## DEFINITION:

Defines a selection item in a popup menu. You must DEFINE POPUP before using DEFINE BAR.

<bar number> is the relative number in the selection list. It must be an integer. Omitting it leaves a blank line in the popup menu. Specifying an existing BAR number overwrites the BAR.

POPUP BARs scroll vertically when there are more BARs than available lines in the popup.

<popup name> is the name of a defined popup. It may be up to 10 characters long.

PROMPT <expC> is the text that appears in the menu. It is truncated if it exceeds the window's width.

## OPTIONS:

MESSAGE <expC> is text that appears centered on line 24 when the user moves the cursor to the associated BAR. The message overwrites any message defined in the POPUP command.

SKIP lets you display an item in the menu without letting the user select it with the cursor. In addition, you can specify a SKIP FOR <condition> clause that deactivates the BAR when a condition is true (.T.). For example, you may SKIP a BAR that says "Move to next record" when the pointer is at the end-of-file, as follows:

```
DEFINE BAR 1 OF main PROMPT "Move to next record" SKIP FOR EOF()
```

## RECOMMENDED USE:

Use DEFINE BAR after first DEFINEing a POPUP. The sequence for using POPUP menus is as follows:

1. DEFINE the POPUP.
2. DEFINE its BARs.
3. ACTIVATE it.
4. Specify an action when the user makes a selection with the ON SELECTION POPUP command.

**Example**—A popup menu appears in a genealogy program.

```
DEFINE POPUP tree1 FROM 15,01 TO 20,35
DEFINE BAR 1 OF tree1 PROMPT "Trace maternal" ;
                      MESSAGE "Show mother 20 generations"
DEFINE BAR 2 OF tree1 PROMPT "Trace paternal"
* If update file doesn't exist, then disallow selection.
DEFINE BAR 3 OF tree1 PROMPT "Update files" SKIP FOR .NOT. FILE("trans")
DEFINE BAR 4 OF tree1 PROMPT "Exit"
ON SELECTION POPUP tree1 DO msub1
*
* <More statements>.
ACTIVATE POPUP tree1
```

## LIMITS/WARNINGS:

You may not DEFINE BAR if you use the FIELD, FILES, or STRUCTURE options of the DEFINE POPUP command. These options predefine the BARs.

A popup must have at least one BAR.

The number of BARs is limited only by the amount of available memory; however, popups with several hundred BARs execute slowly.

## SEE ALSO:

Commands ACTIVATE POPUP, DEFINE POPUP, and ON SELECTION POPUP; functions BAR( ) and PROMPT( ).

# DEFINE BOX

## DIALECTS:

dBASE IV only.

## SYNTAX:

DEFINE BOX FROM <col1> TO <col2> HEIGHT <expN> [AT LINE <line>]
[SINGLE/DOUBLE/<border definition>]

## DEFINITION:

Prints boxes in reports.

<col1> is the starting (left) column. <col2> is the right column. Column values can range from 0 (far left) to 255.

HEIGHT <expN> is the depth of the box in lines (rows). Its value is relative to the top of the box. It can range from 1 to 32767.

Boxes appear only around text printed with ?/?? statements. DEFINE BOX does not work with @...SAYs and SET DEVICE TO PRINT. You must use SET PRINT ON instead.

## OPTIONS:

You can specify the box's starting line with AT LINE <line>.

You can specify a SINGLE or DOUBLE line border. Or you can define a border with a string. SINGLE is the default.

The <border definition> lets you define the sides and corners of the border individually. The definition consists of up to eight keyboard or ASCII characters in a list organized as follows:

```
<t>,<b>,<l>,<r>,<tl>,<tr>,<bl>,<br>
```

```
tl______t______tr        tl = top left        bl = bottom left
|              |         t  = top             b  = bottom
l              r         tr = top right       br = bottom right
|              |         l = left
bl______b______br        r = right
```

BOX <border definitions> are the same as in SET BORDER, except that you cannot DEFINE an entire BOX with one character. (SET BORDER TO "$"

defines the entire box as dollar signs; DEFINE BOX..."$" defines only the top as dollar signs).

See command SET BORDER for details on border definitions.

## RECOMMENDED USE:

Use DEFINE BOX to embellish printed reports. (The dBASE IV report generator uses it extensively).

Because most printers do not permit reverse line positioning, you cannot use @ <coord> TO <coord> to print a box, then reverse to print text. To avoid this limitation, DEFINE BOX prints part of the box with each line of text output.

**Example**—A magazine editor keeps article information in a database. To highlight parts of a weekly report, the editor uses DEFINE BOX.

```
USE articles
SET PRINT ON
?
DEFINE BOX FROM 0 TO 70 HEIGHT 11 DOUBLE
?
?
?? "ARTICLE" AT 2
?? ARTICLE AT 12
?
?? "AUTHOR" AT 2
?? AUTHOR AT 12
?
?? "RECEIVED" AT 2
?? RECEIVED PICTURE "Y" AT 12
?
?? "PAGES" AT 2
?? PAGES PICTURE "99.99" AT 12
?
?? "COLUMNS" AT 2
?? COLUMNS PICTURE "9" AT 12
?
?? "DEPT" AT 2
?? DEPT AT 12
?
?? "PAY" AT 2
?? PAY PICTURE "9,999.99" AT 12
?
?
?
SET PRINT OFF EJECT
```

A typical report appears as follows (formatted for an Epson LX-80):

```
+-------------------------------------------------------------+
:                                                             :
: ARTICLE  THE BEES OF SOUTH AMERICA                          :
: AUTHOR   WALLINGHAM                                         :
: RECEIVED N                                                  :
: PAGES     10.25                                             :
: COLUMNS  2                                                  :
: DEPT     INSECT LIFE                                        :
: PAY       1,543.88                                          :
:                                                             :
+-------------------------------------------------------------+
```

You can define your own border characters with the <border definition>. For example, to print a border of dollar signs, use the command:

```
DEFINE BOX FROM 0 TO 75 HEIGHT 11 "$","$","$","$","$","$","$","$"
```

## LIMITS/WARNINGS:

The appearance of printed boxes depends on your printer. ASCII graphics characters (non-keyboard characters) such as SINGLE and DOUBLE lines may be simulated with keyboard characters. Some boxes may be garbled. If so, check whether system variable _pdriver has the correct value (e.g., _pdriver= "LX80.PR2" for an Epson LX-80).

## SEE ALSO:

Commands @...TO and SET BORDER.

# DEFINE MENU

## DIALECTS:
dBASE IV only.

## SYNTAX:
DEFINE MENU <menu name> [MESSAGE <expC>]

## DEFINITION:
Initializes a horizontal PAD menu.

To use a PAD menu, you must follow these steps:

1. DEFINE the MENU
2. DEFINE the PADs (selections)
3. Define what happens when the cursor moves to a PAD with ON SELECTION PAD or ON PAD
4. ACTIVATE the MENU.

DEFINE MENU gives the menu a name, and provides an optional message that appears centered on line 24 when you ACTIVATE MENU. If you give individual PADs messages in the DEFINE PAD command, they supersede the menu message.

To erase a menu, but leave it in memory, use DEACTIVATE MENU. To remove a menu from memory, use RELEASE MENUS.

## RECOMMENDED USE:
Use DEFINE MENU and DEFINE PAD in the same procedure to make the program easier to read. Then ACTIVATE or DEACTIVATE the menu from other procedures when necessary.

**Example**—An inventory program displays a pad menu with selections for updating records. The first step in creating a menu is DEFINE MENU. Another procedure later ACTIVATEs MENU.

```
PROCEDURE defmenu1
*
DEFINE MENU parts
DEFINE PAD sel1 OF parts PROMPT "Search for titles"
```

```
DEFINE PAD sel2 OF parts PROMPT "Record Updates"
ON SELECTION PAD sel1 OF parts DO tsearch     && Do search module.
ON SELECTION PAD sel2 OF parts DO rec_up      && Do update module.
* end of procedure
```

## SEE ALSO:

Commands ACTIVATE MENU, DEACTIVATE MENU, DEFINE PAD, ON PAD, ON SELECTION PAD, and RELEASE; functions MENU( ) and PAD( ).

# DEFINE PAD

## DIALECTS:

dBASE IV only.

## SYNTAX:

DEFINE PAD <pad name> OF <menu name> PROMPT <expC>
  [AT <coord>] [MESSAGE <expC>]

## DEFINITION:

Defines a single selection item (a pad) in a pad menu.

In an activated menu, the user can press the left and right arrow keys to move the cursor bar. The ON SELECTION PAD and ON PAD commands determine whether the user can press Enter to make a selection or whether a POPUP appears immediately.

To use a PAD menu, you must follow these steps:

1. DEFINE the MENU.
2. DEFINE the PADs.
3. Define what happens when the cursor moves to a PAD with ON SELECTION PAD or ON PAD.
4. ACTIVATE the MENU.

To DEFINE PAD, you must first DEFINE MENU <menu name>. If there is no such menu, dBASE reports an error.

You may use up to 10 characters in the <pad name>. It may not begin with a number.

The PROMPT is the text that appears in the menu selection. Moving the cursor bar to the PROMPT highlights it. The maximum length is 79 characters.

By default, menus appear on line 0. Because dBASE IV places the prompts end-to-end, their total length may not exceed the screen's width.

## OPTIONS:

AT <coord> lets you place prompts anywhere on the screen. For example,

```
DEFINE PAD sell OF master PROMPT "Enter name" AT 2,4
```

places the pad on row 2, starting in column 4.

If you use the AT option, prompts may overlap.

You can define a MESSAGE of up to 79 characters to appear when the cursor bar touches the pad. It is centered on line 24, overwriting the message in the DEFINE MENU command.

## RECOMMENDED USE:

When you DEFINE PAD, give it a name related to its action or to its position in the menu.

**Example**—An farm management program has a menu with two pads, GRAINYIELD and AVGPRICE.

```
DEFINE MENU farm1     &&Old MacDonald had an agribusiness
DEFINE PAD grainyield OF farm1 PROMPT "Grain yield report" AT 2,1 ;
  MESSAGE "A listing of this month's yields"
DEFINE PAD avgprice OF farm1 PROMPT "Average grain prices" AT 2,30 ;
  MESSAGE "A listing of the average grain prices at local markets"
ON SELECTION PAD grainyield OF farm1 DO gr_rpt    && Print grain report.
ON SELECTION PAD avgprice OF farm1 DO price_rpt   && Print price report.
*
* <Statements>.
ACTIVATE MENU farm1
```

## LIMITS/WARNINGS:

By default (without the AT <coord> option), pad menus appear on line 0, conflicting with the SCOREBOARD display, including the Caps, Ins, and Del status. To avoid this conflict, SET SCOREBOARD OFF when using pad menus on line 0.

## SEE ALSO:

Commands ACTIVATE MENU, DEFINE MENU, ON PAD, ON SELECTION PAD, and SET SCOREBOARD; functions MENU( ) and PAD( ).

# DEFINE POPUP

## DIALECTS:

dBASE IV only.

## SYNTAX:

DEFINE POPUP <popup name> FROM <coord> [TO <coord>]
    [PROMPT FIELD <field name>/PROMPT FILES [LIKE <pattern>]]
    [PROMPT STRUCTURE] [MESSAGE <expC>]

## DEFINITION:

Adds a popup menu definition to memory. It remains inactive until you ACTIVATE POPUP.

Popup menus display prompts vertically within a single line box. The user makes a selection by moving the cursor bar to a prompt and pressing Enter.

To create popup menus, you first DEFINE POPUP, DEFINE its BARs, and then ACTIVATE POPUP. (You do not have to DEFINE BARs if you use the FIELD, FILES, or STRUCTURE options). Use DEACTIVATE POPUP to erase popups from the screen and leave them in memory. Use RELEASE POPUPS to erase popups and remove them from memory.

<popup name> is the name of a defined popup. If it already exists, the new definition overwrites it. The name may be up to 10 characters long.

<coord> is the top left <row>,<column> position of the popup's border. The lower right corner is set automatically to accommodate the longest prompt.

## OPTIONS:

You can specify the lower right corner of the popup border with TO <coord>. With the status bar on (SET STATUS ON), the popup border may extend to row 21, column 79. With the bar off, it may extend to row 24. (You may define the border to row 24 at any time; however, its validity depends on the status bar at the time you ACTIVATE POPUP).

Prompts wider than the border are truncated.

MESSAGE <expC> is text that appears centered on line 24 when you ACTIVATE the POPUP. MESSAGEs specified in the DEFINE BAR command overwrite it.

The PROMPT FIELD, PROMPT FILES, and PROMPT STRUCTURE options let you easily create "pick lists" of field data, files, and field names, respectively. If you use one of these options, you may not DEFINE BARs for the popup.

The PROMPT FIELD <fieldname> lets you use the values in a database as prompts for the popup.

The PROMPT FILES option defines all filenames in the current directory as prompts. If you use the PROMPT FILES LIKE <pattern> option, you can limit the file selection to those matching <pattern>. The pattern may include a drive and pathname; however, once the popup is activated, the user may branch throughout the file directories. There is no apparent way to restrict the user from browsing directories.

The PROMPT STRUCTURE option defines fieldnames from the open database as prompts.

## RECOMMENDED USE:

DEFINE POPUP is the first step in creating a popup menu. If you do not use the PROMPT FIELD, PROMPT FILES, or PROMPT STRUCTURE options, you must then DEFINE BARs. The next step, ON SELECTION POPUP, specifies a command to execute when the user makes a selection. You can use this to DO a procedure. In the procedure, use BAR( ) to determine which popup BAR the user selected.

**Example 1**—A simple popup menu appears in a membership program.

```
DEFINE POPUP members FROM 15,01 TO 20,35
DEFINE BAR 1 OF members PROMPT "Renewals list"
DEFINE BAR 2 OF members PROMPT "Members past due"
DEFINE BAR 3 OF members PROMPT "Membership report"
ON SELECTION POPUP members DO maction
*
* <More statements>.
ACTIVATE POPUP members

PROCEDURE maction
mbar = BAR()
DO CASE
  CASE mbar = 1
    DO renewals
```

```
  CASE mbar = 2
    DO expires
  CASE mbar = 3
    DO memreport
ENDCASE
RETURN
```

**Example 2**—An advertising sales program attaches POPUP menus to PAD menus with the command ON PAD ACTIVATE <popup>. When the user moves the cursor to a menu PAD, the associated POPUP appears automatically.

```
SET SCOREBOARD OFF
CLEAR
*
DEFINE MENU master
DEFINE PAD sel1 OF master PROMPT "File updates"
DEFINE PAD sel2 OF master PROMPT "Reports"
DEFINE PAD sel3 OF master PROMPT "Reindex"
ON PAD sel1 OF master ACTIVATE POPUP fupdate
ON PAD sel2 OF master ACTIVATE POPUP freport
ON PAD sel3 OF master ACTIVATE POPUP freindex

DEFINE POPUP fupdate FROM 1,1
DEFINE POPUP freport FROM 1,15
DEFINE POPUP freindex FROM 1,30
DEFINE BAR 1 OF fupdate PROMPT "Add records"
DEFINE BAR 2 OF fupdate PROMPT "Edit records"
DEFINE BAR 3 OF fupdate PROMPT "Delete records"
DEFINE BAR 1 OF freport PROMPT "List sales"
DEFINE BAR 2 OF freport PROMPT "List commissions"
DEFINE BAR 3 OF freport PROMPT "List salaries"
DEFINE BAR 1 OF freindex PROMPT "Reindex all files"
DEFINE BAR 2 OF freindex PROMPT "Reindex master files"
*
ACTIVATE MENU master
```

This program produces the following menu:

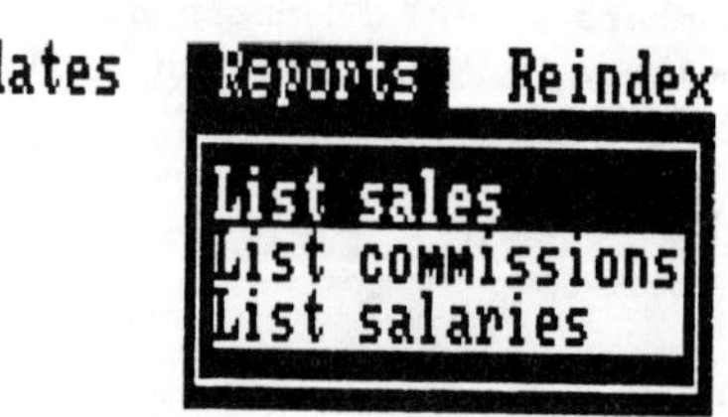

**Example 3**—A query program lets users choose a database file and then a field from a popup menu. The program then DISPLAYs the chosen fields.

```
SET SCOREBOARD OFF          && Disable to avoid overwriting on line 0.
CLEAR

PROCEDURE dbfpop
DEFINE POPUP dbfs FROM 1,1 TO 15,20 PROMPT FILES LIKE *.DBF
ON SELECTION POPUP dbfs DO dbf_use
ACTIVATE POPUP dbfs
*
DEFINE POPUP query FROM 1,1 TO 15,20 PROMPT STRUCTURE
ON SELECTION POPUP query DO qprocess
ACTIVATE POPUP query
* end of procedure

PROCEDURE dbf_use
mfile = PROMPT()            && PROMPT() returns the value of the prompt,
USE (mfile)                 &&   in this case, a filename.
DEACTIVATE POPUP
RETURN
* end of procedure

PROCEDURE qprocess
CLEAR                       && BAR() returns the BAR number selected.
search = FIELD(BAR())       &&   It can then be used as an argument
DISPLAY ALL &search         &&   in the FIELD() function to get the
WAIT                        &&   fieldname from the number.
CLEAR
RETURN
* end of procedure
```

## LIMITS/WARNINGS:

You may not DEFINE BAR if you use the FIELD, FILES, or STRUCTURE options of the DEFINE POPUP command. These options predefine the BARs.

A popup must have at least one BAR.

The number of BARs is limited only by the amount of available memory; however, popups with several hundred BARs execute slowly.

## SEE ALSO:

Commands ACTIVATE POPUP, DEACTIVATE POPUP, ON SELECTION POPUP, RELEASE, and SHOW POPUP; functions BAR( ) and PROMPT( ).

# DEFINE WINDOW

## DIALECTS:

dBASE IV only.

## SYNTAX:

DEFINE WINDOW <window name> FROM <coord1> TO <coord2>
[DOUBLE/PANEL/NONE/<border definition>]
[COLOR [<standard>][,<enhanced>][,<frame>]]

## DEFINITION:

Creates a window definition. You can then activate the window with the ACTIVATE WINDOW command. All subsequent output goes to the active window.

You can define up to 20 windows, then switch among them with ACTIVATE WINDOW.

DEACTIVATE WINDOW erases the window, but leaves it in memory. RELEASE WINDOW erases the window, and removes its definition from memory. Both DEACTIVATE WINDOW and RELEASE WINDOW restore the underlying text. CLEAR ALL also erases the window and removes it from memory.

<window name> is up to 10 characters long. It may not begin with a number. If you define a new window with the same name, it overwrites the old one.

<coord1> is the screen coordinate of the upper left corner of the window border. <coord2> is the lower right. The coordinate range is 0,0 to 23,79 when the status bar is off (SET STATUS OFF), and 0,0 to 20,79 when it is on. (The status bar setting is relevant when you ACTIVATE WINDOW, rather than when you DEFINE WINDOW).

## OPTIONS:

DOUBLE specifies a double line border instead of the default single line.

PANEL specifies an inverse video border (ASCII character 219).

NONE specifies a window with no border.

<border definition> lets you define the border's sides and corners. It consists of up to eight keyboard or ASCII characters organized as follows:

```
<t>,<b>,<l>,<r>,<tl>,<tr>,<bl>,<br>
```

where:

```
t = top                 tl = top left
b = bottom              tr = top right
l = left                bl = bottom left
r = right               br = bottom right
```

You may omit any character inside the list by leaving its comma in place. You must omit extra commas from the end of the list. Only parts of the border you specify will be redefined, unless you specify only the first character. In that case, it forms the entire border.

The COLOR option lets you change the color of the window's contents and border. See SET COLOR for valid codes.

## RECOMMENDED USE:

Use windows to display reports, menus, or help screens without disturbing the underlying text. Also use them to BROWSE data and edit memo fields.

**Example 1**—A legal program lets clerks enter case briefs into a memo field. After DEFINEing WINDOW, the program use the SET WINDOW OF MEMO command to set the default memo-editing window. When the clerk moves the cursor to a memo field and presses Ctrl-Home, the memo editor opens in the defined window.

```
* ASCII character 168 prints as an upside-down question mark. The window
* has yellow on blue standard text, red on white enhanced text, and
* a black on white border.
DEFINE WINDOW brief FROM 02,03 TO 10,79 168 COLOR gr+/b,r/w,n/w
SET WINDOW OF MEMO TO brief
```

**Example 2**—A library program defines two windows. One displays the author, title, and pages, another displays an abstract. The windows appear simultaneously, but only one is actually active. This program demonstrates switching among windows and the full screen (with the ACTIVATE SCREEN command).

```
DEFINE WINDOW source FROM 01,01 TO 07,48
DEFINE WINDOW abstract FROM 01,50 TO 21,79
USE source
DO WHILE .t.
  ACTIVATE WINDOW source
  ?
  ? "AUTHOR: " + author AT 2         && Data type C, length 30.
  ? "TITLE:  " + title  AT 2         && Data type C, length 30.
  ? "PAGES:  " + STR(pages,3,0) AT 2  && Data type N, length 3.
```

```
    ?
    ACTIVATE WINDOW abstract
    ? nmemo                               && Data type MEMO.
    ACTIVATE SCREEN                       && Activates full screen mode.
    mview = .f.
    @ 23,01 SAY "View another? " GET mview PICTURE "Y"
    READ
    IF .NOT. mview
      RELEASE WINDOWS source, abstract    && Erase windows and remove
                                          &&    from memory.
      RETURN
    ENDIF
    SKIP
    IF EOF()
      ?? CHR(7)
      SKIP -1
    ENDIF
ENDDO
```

## LIMITS/WARNINGS:

Some ASCII characters display correctly on the screen, but may not print correctly. Do not use ASCII characters 7, 8, 10, 12, 13, 27, or 127 in <border definition>.

## SEE ALSO:

Commands ACTIVATE SCREEN, ACTIVATE WINDOW, CLEAR WINDOWS, DEACTIVATE WINDOW, RESTORE WINDOW, SAVE WINDOW, SET BORDER, SET COLOR, and SET WINDOW OF MEMO.

# DELETE

## DIALECTS:

Clipper, dBASE III PLUS, dBASE IV, dBXL, FoxBASE+, and Quicksilver.

## SYNTAX:

DELETE [<scope>] [WHILE <condition>] [FOR <condition>]

## DEFINITION:

Marks records to be removed from the active database. Physical removal does not occur until you issue the PACK command. DELETE ALL/PACK does not reclaim the disk space occupied by MEMO fields. ZAP is similar, but it is faster and does reclaim MEMO field space.

SET DELETED ON hides deleted records.

RECALL removes deletion marks. It restores records marked for deletion since the last time you PACKed the database.

## DEFAULT:

DELETE marks the current record for deletion, unless you select records using a scope, WHILE, or FOR clause. When you use a scope or other condition with DELETE, the record pointer moves to the next record after the scope is exhausted.

## RECOMMENDED USE:

Use DELETE and PACK to purge database files of unwanted records. If your application has large files, frequent PACKs may not be practical. Instead, SET DELETED ON to hide DELETEd records until you have time to PACK. DELETE alone does not move the record pointer.

**Example 1**—A hotel reservation system consistently overbooks rooms by 20 percent. At the end of every week, the administrator purges "no-shows" from the file with the DELETE command.

```
USE reserves
* SHOW is a logical field which, if true, indicates that
* a reservation was fulfilled.
DELETE ALL FOR .NOT. SHOW
    36 records deleted
PACK
    120 records copied
```

In this example, 36 reservations went unfulfilled out of a total of 156.

## VARIATIONS:

**dBASE III PLUS, dBASE IV, dBXL, FoxBASE+:** SET TALK ON echoes the number of records deleted. Also, deleted records appear with "del" at the top of the screen when SET SCOREBOARD is ON, or on the STATUS BAR when editing. When LISTing or DISPLAYing a database, deleted records have an asterisk ahead of the first field.

**Example 2**—A LIST of unfulfilled hotel reservations from the previous example (before PACKing the database) shows deleted records with an asterisk preceding the first field.

```
. LIST
Record#  NAME          ADDRESS                 STATE
      1 *Jones         122 Main Street          CA
      2  Johnson       14 Arizona Ave.          MA
      3 *Edwards       P.O. Box 2222            CA
      4  Rowlands      24 Pennsylvania Ave.     VA
```

## SEE ALSO:

Commands PACK, RECALL, SET DELETED, and SET SCOREBOARD; function DELETED( ).

# DELETE FILE

## DIALECTS:
Clipper, dBASE III PLUS, dBASE IV, dBXL, FoxBASE+, and Quicksilver.

## SYNTAX:
DELETE FILE <filename>

## DEFINITION:
DELETE FILE deletes a file specified by a full filename and extension. The file cannot be in USE. You may use disk drive designators and paths, but not wildcard characters such as * and ?.

In dBASE III PLUS and dBASE IV, the command

```
DELETE FILE ?
```

displays a menu of files created by the SET CATALOG command. Deleted files are then removed from the active CATALOG.

## RECOMMENDED USE:
DELETE FILE removes files permanently.

**Example**—An antique store program copies the month's database files on a floppy disk, then erases them from the hard disk to make room for new files.

```
COPY FILE oldsales.dbf TO A:augsales.dbf
DELETE FILE oldsales.dbf
File has been deleted
```

## SEE ALSO:
Commands COPY FILE and SET CATALOG.

# DELETE TAG

## DIALECTS:

dBASE IV only.

## SYNTAX:

DELETE TAG <tag1> [OF <MDX filename>][, <tag2> [OF <MDX filename>...47]] / <NDX filename1>, [<NDX filename2>...10]

## DEFINITION:

Erases TAGs from a multiple index file (extension MDX) or closes index files (extension NDX).

DELETE TAG has two functions: it can either erase TAGs from an MDX file or close index files (NDX).

DELETEing a TAG reclaims its disk space.

If you DELETE the last TAG, DELETE TAG erases the MDX file.

### Erasing MDX TAGs

If you don't use the OF <MDX filename> option, DELETE TAG affects the first open MDX (in most cases, the production MDX file).

Use the OF <MDX filename> option when you have more than one MDX file open with duplicate TAGs.

### Closing indexes

If you use index filenames instead of TAGs, DELETE TAG closes them. It does not erase them.

Whereas SET INDEX TO without arguments closes all index files, DELETE TAG lets you close individual TAGs. All TAGs in the active MDX file move up to fill in the closed TAG, changing the order.

## RECOMMENDED USE:

Use DELETE TAG to remove unused TAGs from an MDX file. Keep as few TAGs in the MDX as possible, since it can grow rapidly. Also, the REINDEX command reindexes every TAG. With a large database and many TAGs, a REINDEX could take hours!

**Example**—Through months of continuous use, the production MDX file of a SALES database becomes cluttered with unused TAGs. To erase them, the programmer issues DELETE TAG from the dot prompt.

```
. DISPLAY STATUS
Currently Selected Database:
Select area:  1, Database in Use: D:\DBASE\SALES.DBF   Alias: SALES
Production   MDX file:  D:\DBASE\SALES.MDX
           Index TAG:      JAN  Key: jan
           Index TAG:      FEB  Key: feb
           Index TAG:      MAR  Key: mar
    Master Index TAG:      APR  Key: apr

. DELETE TAG jan,feb
. DISPLAY STATUS
Currently Selected Database:
Select area:  1, Database in Use: D:\DBASE\SALES.DBF   Alias: SALES
Production   MDX file:  D:\DBASE\SALES.MDX
    Master Index TAG:      APR  Key: apr
           Index TAG:      MAR  Key: mar
```

To DELETE a TAG called JUN from MTOTALS.MDX, use the command:

```
. DELETE TAG jun OF MTOTALS
```

## SEE ALSO:

Commands COPY TAG, INDEX, SET INDEX, and SET ORDER; functions MDX( ), NDX( ), TAG( ), and ORDER( ).

# DIMENSION

## DIALECTS:

dBXL, FoxBASE+, and Quicksilver.

## SYNTAX:

**FoxBASE+:** DIMENSION <array name> (<expN1>[,<expN2>])[,<array list>]

(Allows one or two dimensions. You must include the parentheses in the command).

**dBXL/Quicksilver:** Use brackets ([]) instead of parentheses. Allows up to 255 dimensions.

## DEFINITION:

DIMENSION activates memory variable arrays of mixed data types. You can reference an element by the array name, and a number (subscript) representing its relative position. Subscripts begin at 1.

The STORE command assigns values to the entire array, or to individual elements. The data type in an element is determined by the last STORE made to it. Before values are STOREd in an array, all elements are false (.F.).

An array uses one memory variable name. When you LIST MEMORY, arrays appear with data type "A".

You can DIMENSION a list of arrays in one command as in:

```
DIMENSION main(2,5),sub(3,10),sub2(4,10)
```

## VARIATIONS:

**dBXL/Quicksilver:** DIMENSION uses brackets ([]) around its subscripts, There can be (theoretically) up to 254 subscripts, specified as follows:

DIMENSION <array name> [<expN1>[,<expN2>][,<expN3>]....[,<expN255>] [,<array list>]

You will exhaust memory space, or reach the maximum command line length, before reaching the array dimension limit.

An array can have at most 254 elements.

**FoxBASE+:** DIMENSION uses parentheses around its subscripts. Arrays can have one or two subscripts.

An array can contain no more than 3,600 elements. Each element occupies at least 18 bytes of storage.

## RECOMMENDED USE:

Use DIMENSION to hold structured data in memory. This is useful for data driven menus and lookup tables.

**Example 1**—A FoxBASE+ program stores menu items in database files. Each item consists of a user prompt and a subroutine name MACTION that indicates the subroutine to execute.

```
CLEAR                        && CLEAR the screen.
mrow = 2                     && Upper left coordinates for menu box.
mcol = 2                     &&   You could pass these as PARAMETERS to
                             &&   the menu routine.
USE menu                     && Use DBF with fields
                             && MSELECT (char,30) and MACTION (char,10).

mrec = RECCOUNT()            && Record count is the # of array elements.
DIMENSION smenu(mrec,2)      && DIMENSION array with element
                             &&   for each record.

* Array building routine.
ctr = 1                                 && Start a counter.
DO WHILE ctr <= mrec                    && Repeat until CTR equals MREC.
  STORE mselect TO smenu(ctr,1)         && Put field MSELECT into
                                        &&   element CTR,1.
  STORE maction TO smenu(ctr,2)         && Put field MACTION into
                                        &&   element CTR,2.
  SKIP                                  && SKIP to next record.
  ctr = ctr + 1                         && Add 1 to CTR.
ENDDO

* Menu building routine.
@ mrow,mcol-1 TO mrow+mrec+1, mcol+30        && Draw BOX around menu
                                             &&   coordinates.
ctr = 1                                      && Repeat DO WHILE process,
DO WHILE ctr <= mrec                         &&   taking data from array,
 @ mrow+ctr,mcol PROMPT smenu(ctr,1)         &&   then use data as
                                             &&   menu PROMPTs.
  ctr = ctr + 1
ENDDO
MENU TO mresponse                            && Activate @...PROMPT
                                             &&   menu, store selection
                                             &&   to MRESPONSE.
mdo = smenu(mresponse,2)                     && Store subroutine name
                                             &&   in MDO.
DO &mdo                                      && Execute subroutine.
```

When retrieving data from a database file, the SCATTER command automatically DIMENSIONs an array and stores the contents of the current record in it. You can edit the array using @...SAY...GETs, then use the GATHER command to reload the database record. This is similar to the dBXL and Quicksilver AUTOMEM capability.

**Example 2**—An edit routine in a library management system lets the librarian change book descriptions. To edit a record, the program SCATTERs the current values into an array. The librarian then edits the data. When done, he or she saves it. The program GATHERs the array back into the current record.

```
USE booklist
GOTO 5
SCATTER FIELDS title,desc,isbn TO listedit
CLEAR
* LISTEDIT is the name of the array. In this application,
*  the arrays have only one dimension.
@ 01,01 SAY "Title: " GET listedit(1)
@ 02,01 SAY " Desc: " GET listedit(2)
@ 03,01 SAY " ISBN: " GET listedit(3)
READ
GATHER FROM listedit FIELDS title,desc,isbn
```

## VARIATIONS:

**Clipper:** Has one dimensional arrays using DECLARE instead of DIMENSION.

**dBASE IV:** Has two dimensional arrays using DECLARE instead of DIMENSION.

## SEE ALSO:

Commands APPEND FROM ARRAY, COPY TO ARRAY, DECLARE, GATHER, and SCATTER.

# DIR/DIRECTORY

## DIALECTS:

Clipper, dBASE III PLUS, dBASE IV, dBXL, FoxBASE+, and Quicksilver.

## SYNTAX:

DIR [[ON] <drive:><path>] [[LIKE [<pattern>] [TO PRINT]

## DEFINITION:

DIR (DIRECTORY) displays information about files located on the designated disk drive. DIR alone displays the record count, the last update, and the file size in bytes for all database files (DBF). With a <pattern> (asterisks and question marks), DIR can show files of all types.

Changes in the DIRECTORY record count are not recorded until the listed file is closed.

## DEFAULT:

DIR displays a directory listing. The TO PRINT option also produces a printed version.

## RECOMMENDED USE:

Use DIR to get detailed information about database files in the specified directory. With a <pattern>, DIR acts much like the MS-DOS DIR command.

**Example 1**—A magazine publisher wants to find the latest payroll information stored on drive C. She issues the DIR command and sees filenames, record counts, dates of last update, and file sizes in bytes.

```
. DIR C:
Database Files    # Records    Last Update     Size
ACCTSRCV.DBF             48    11/17/87        1106
PAYRLL.DBF                6    10/15/87         132
PAYRLL2.DBF              11    12/15/87         329
INVENT.DBF                3    11/16/87         146

   1713 bytes in     4 files.
11333632 bytes remaining on drive.
```

**Example 2**—Using DIR with a <pattern>, the publisher searches for program files on the current drive. The TO PRINT option produces a printed directory.

```
. DIR *.prg TO PRINT
POST.PRG            CALL.PRG            INVENT.PRG

     380 bytes in      3 files.
11331584 bytes remaining on drive.
```

## VARIATIONS:

**Clipper:** Use the ADIR( ) function to store directory information in arrays. You can then create sophisticated file selection and maintenance menus. The ON and LIKE options are not available.

**dBASE IV:** You can display a directory with a POPUP menu using the DEFINE POPUP...FILES command.

If you SET AUTOSAVE ON, dBASE IV will update the directory after every change, even if the file is not closed. Otherwise, it updates the directory only when you close the file.

**dBXL/Quicksilver:** Unlike dBASE III PLUS and FoxBASE+, dBXL and Quicksilver update the directory record count after a change, even if the file is not closed. Also, only the command DIR is valid, not the word DIRECTORY. The ON and LIKE options are not available.

**FoxBASE+:** ON and LIKE options not available.

## SEE ALSO:

Commands DEFINE POPUP and DISPLAY/LIST FILES; function ADIR( ).

# DISPLAY

## DIALECTS:

Clipper, dBASE III PLUS, dBASE IV, dBXL, FoxBASE+, and Quicksilver.

## SYNTAX:

DISPLAY [<scope>] [[FIELDS] <expression list>] [WHILE <condition>]
    [FOR <condition>] [OFF] [TO PRINT]

## DEFINITION:

Selects records in a database file for viewing on the screen or for printing. If you DISPLAY many records, dBASE III PLUS, dBASE IV, and FoxBASE+ show only 20 at a time, prompting you to "Press any key to continue..." for every screen.

## DEFAULT:

Shows the current record, unless you specify a scope or other condition with a FOR or WHILE clause.

Shows all fields, except memo fields, unless you specify otherwise with the FIELDS expression. You must name memo fields explicitly. When displaying them, the text width defaults to 50 characters. Use the SET MEMOWIDTH command to change it.

Sends output to the screen, unless you add TO PRINT. It sends output to the printer and to the screen.

## OPTIONS:

Normally, the record number precedes each line displayed. OFF omits record numbers.

## RECOMMENDED USE:

Use DISPLAY to query unindexed files in which many records may satisfy the selection criteria.

**Example 1**—An employment agency wants to DISPLAY all applicants with M.S. degrees. The database file SCI_APPS contains employment applications for positions in scientific research.

```
. USE sci_apps
. DISPLAY lname,fname,degree,area FOR degree="MS"

Record#  lname        fname        degree area
     11  Robinson     Stuart       MS     Electrical Engineering
     28  Martinez     Jorge        MS     Environmental Sciences
     37  Marzo        Elaine       MS     Computer Science
     49  Elgin        Robin        MS     Oceanography
```

## VARIATIONS:

**Clipper:** DISPLAY requires a field list and does not include field name headings with the data. The TO FILE <filename> option sends the output to a text file.

**Example 2**—Sending DISPLAY output to a text file called MSFILE.

```
USE sci_apps
DISPLAY ALL lname,area FOR degree = "MS" TO FILE msfile
```

**Clipper,Quicksilver:** No automatic pause after 20 records. The following program simulates the effect.

**Example 3**—You can simulate a DISPLAY pause with a brief program.

```
USE sci_apps
yourpres = " "
* Displaying 10 records at a time. The loop repeats when the user
*   presses any key except X or until the end of file is reached.
DO WHILE UPPER(yourpres) #"X" .AND. .NOT. EOF()
  DISPLAY NEXT 10
  WAIT 'Press SPACE BAR to continue, or X to exit' TO yourpres
ENDDO
```

**dBASE III PLUS, dBASE IV, dBXL, and FoxBASE+:** SET HEADING OFF omits the field names.

**dBASE IV:** The TO FILE <filename> option sends the output to a text file.

## SEE ALSO:

Commands LIST, SET HEADING, SET MARGIN, and SET MEMOWIDTH.

# DISPLAY FILES

## DIALECTS:

dBASE III PLUS, dBASE IV, dBXL, FoxBASE+, and Quicksilver.

## SYNTAX:

DISPLAY FILES [ON <drive/dir>] [LIKE <pattern>] [TO PRINT]

## DEFINITION:

Lists names of files on the specified disk drive and directory.

## DEFAULT:

Unless you specify a <pattern>, DISPLAY FILES shows only database files (extension DBF), their sizes, and the dates when they were last changed. If you do not specify a drive or directory, DISPLAY FILES shows files in the current directory.

## OPTIONS:

DISPLAY FILES LIKE <pattern> displays files that match the pattern.

TO PRINT sends output to the screen and the printer.

## EXAMPLES:

**Example 1**—A user wants to reindex database files but cannot remember the filenames.

```
. DISPLAY FILES ON C:
Database Files    # Records    Last Update     Size
JKDPOLIC.DBF              6    02/06/88        1229
TEMP.DBF                  3    02/06/88         775
SCI_APPS.DBF              5    02/06/88         457

   2461 bytes in      3 files.
9330688 bytes remaining on drive.
```

**Example 2**—After reindexing, the user wants to make a note in a text file called NDXNOTE.TXT. He verifies the name by displaying all filenames that end with ".TXT".

```
. DISPLAY FILES LIKE *.TXT
MV.TXT                 BIZ.TXT                OP.TXT                 ACCT.TXT
NDXNOTE.TXT

  383488 bytes in      5 files.
9330688 bytes remaining on drive.
```

## SPECIAL USES:

DISPLAY FILES can determine whether a database file (extension DBF) is in the dBASE III PLUS format. An unrecognized filetype will appear with the message "Not a dBASE III PLUS file" (or dBXL, dBASE IV, FoxBASE+, etc.). A dBASE II file will appear with an identifying message.

## VARIATIONS:

**Clipper:** Use DIR instead.

**dBASE IV:** The TO FILE <filename> option sends output to the specified text file and gives it a TXT extension.

## SEE ALSO:

Commands DIR/DIRECTORY and LIST FILES; function FILE( ).

# DISPLAY HISTORY

## DIALECTS:
dBASE III PLUS, dBASE IV, dBXL, and FoxBASE+.

## SYNTAX:
DISPLAY HISTORY [LAST <expN>] [TO PRINT]

## DEFINITION:
Shows the latest commands in order, with the most recently executed ones at the bottom.

## DEFAULT:
The buffer size defaults to 20 commands. You can change this number with the command SET HISTORY TO.

SET HISTORY OFF prevents the storage of commands. SET DOHISTORY ON includes commands issued from a program.

## OPTIONS:
TO PRINT sends output to the screen and to the printer.

LAST <expN> shows only the latest <expN> commands.

## VARIATIONS:
**dBASE IV:** The TO FILE <filename> option sends output to a file with a TXT extension.

## SEE ALSO:
Commands LIST HISTORY, SET DOHISTORY, and SET HISTORY.

# DISPLAY MEMORY

## DIALECTS:

dBASE III PLUS, dBASE IV, dBXL, FoxBASE+, and Quicksilver.

## SYNTAX:

DISPLAY MEMORY [TO PRINT]

## DEFINITION:

Displays information about active memory variables. dBASE III PLUS, dBASE IV, dBXL, and FoxBASE+ show name, type, size, and status (public or private) of active memory variables, plus the number of variables, the number of additional variables available, the number of bytes used, and the number of bytes still available for memory variables.

## OPTIONS:

TO PRINT sends output to the screen and to the printer.

## RECOMMENDED USE:

Use DISPLAY MEMORY during debugging to display active memory variables. You may put it at strategic points in your program during debugging, or you may SUSPEND execution to view memory variables. CANCELling program execution releases memory variables defined within the program.

**Example 1**—During debugging, a manual check of a billing program discovers an incorrect amount on an invoice. An inspection of the memory variables shows that variable SALESTAX has an incorrect value.

```
. DISPLAY MEMORY
AMT          pub   N        19292.22  (      19292.22000000)
LNAME        pub   C  "Sevrinson"
LOOKUP       pub   L  .F.
SALESTAX     pub   N            0.08  (          0.08000000)
    4 variables defined,       31 bytes used
  252 variables available,   5969 bytes available
```

## VARIATIONS:

**dBASE IV:** Shows active memory variables, arrays, system memory variables, menu, pad, popup, and window definitions. It also shows memory variable and runtime symbol space allocation and the amount of available memory in bytes.

The TO FILE <filename> option sends output to a text file with a TXT extension.

**FoxBASE+:** Shows active arrays and screen memory variables created with the SAVE SCREEN TO command.

**Example 2**—DISPLAYing MEMORY in FoxBASE+. Note the variable names, their scopes (PUBLIC or PRIVATE), their types, and their values. The types shown here include numeric, character, array, date, and screen. Note that TARRAY uses only one memory variable name, but has many elements. The elements do not count toward the number of variables defined.

```
. DISPLAY MEMORY
X           Pub   N       192929  (     192929.00000000)
NAME        Pub   C  "Johnson"
TARRAY      Pub   A
  (   1,   1)     L  .F.
  (   1,   2)     L  .F.
MDATE       Pub   D  08/23/87
OPEN_SCR    Pub   S
    5 variables defined,        14 bytes used
  251 variables available,    5986 bytes available
```

**Quicksilver:** Also shows the states of environmental variables, and memory variable names, types, and contents, plus whether they are public or private.

## SEE ALSO:

Commands LIST, LIST MEMORY, PRIVATE, PUBLIC, and STORE.

# DISPLAY STATUS

## DIALECTS:

dBASE III PLUS, dBASE IV, dBXL, and FoxBASE+.

## SYNTAX:

DISPLAY STATUS [TO PRINT]

## DEFINITION:

Displays general information about open database files, function key assignments, and the state of SET commands.

dBASE III PLUS displays the following status information:

Database filename, drive, directory
Open alternate file
Current work area number and alias
Active relations
Open index filenames and keys
Open memo filenames
Active filters
Open format files
Loaded modules
Margin settings
Active work area
Current file path
ON KEY command settings
Default disk drive
Print destination
Open procedure file
Settings for SET commands
DEVICE selection (SCREEN or PRINT)
Function key assignments

The following SET commands also appear:

```
Press any key to continue...

ALTERNATE  - OFF  DELETED    - OFF   FIXED      - OFF  SAFETY     - OFF
BELL       - ON   DELIMITERS - OFF   HEADING    - ON   SCOREBOARD - ON
CARRY      - OFF  DEVICE     - SCRN  HELP       - OFF  STATUS     - OFF
CATALOG    - OFF  DOHISTORY  - OFF   HISTORY    - ON   STEP       - OFF
CENTURY    - OFF  ECHO       - OFF   INTENSITY  - ON   TALK       - ON
CONFIRM    - OFF  ESCAPE     - ON    MENU       - OFF  TITLE      - ON
CONSOLE    - ON   EXACT      - OFF   PRINT      - OFF  UNIQUE     - OFF
DEBUG      - OFF  FIELDS     - OFF

Programmable function keys:
F2  - assist;
F3  - list;
F4  - dir;
F5  - display structure;
F6  - display status;
F7  - display memory;
F8  - display;
F9  - append;
F10 - edit;
```

## OPTIONS:

TO PRINT sends output to both the printer and the screen.

## VARIATIONS:

**dBASE IV:** The option TO FILE <filename> sends output to a text file with a TXT extension. DISPLAY also shows current reprocess count, refresh count, currency symbol, delimiter symbol, and complete NDX/MDX information, including filenames, TAGs, and key expressions. The following SET commands also appear:

```
Press any key to continue...
Number of files open =    8
Current work area =    4
   Delimiters are '&' and '&'
Currency: $

ALTERNATE  - OFF  DELIMITERS - ON   FIELDS    - OFF  PRINT      - OFF
AUTOSAVE   - OFF  DESIGN     - ON   FIXED     - OFF  SAFETY     - ON
BELL       - ON   DEVELOP    - ON   HEADING   - ON   SCOREBOARD - ON
CARRY      - OFF  DEVICE     - SCRN HELP      - ON   SPACE      - ON
CATALOG    - OFF  ECHO       - OFF  HISTORY   - ON   SQL        - OFF
CENTURY    - OFF  EMACRO     - OFF  INSTRUCT  - OFF  STATUS     - OFF
CONFIRM    - OFF  ENCRYPTION - ON   INTENSITY - ON   STEP       - OFF
CONSOLE    - ON   ESCAPE     - ON   LOCK      - ON   TALK       - ON
DEBUG      - OFF  EXACT      - OFF  MENU      - ON   TITLE      - ON
DELETED    - OFF  EXCLUSIVE  - ON   NEAR      - OFF  TRAP       - OFF

Programmable function keys:
F2       - assist;
F3       - list;
F4       - dir;
F5       - display structure;
F6       - display status;
Press any key to continue..._
```

On a local area network, locked files and records also appear.

Files created with the DISTINCT option of the SQL SELECT command appear as read-only.

**dBXL:** Also shows:

Prompt setting
Margin
Decimals

**FoxBASE+:** Also shows:

Current processor
Margin, Decimals, Memowidth, Typeahead, and History settings
Date format

## SEE ALSO:

Commands DIR, DISPLAY FILES, LIST STATUS, SAVE STATUS, and SET; functions ALIAS( ), FILE( ), MEMORY( ), NDX( ), ORDER( ), OS( ), PROGRAM( ), and TAG( ).

# DISPLAY STRUCTURE

## DIALECTS:
dBASE III PLUS, dBASE IV, dBXL, FoxBASE+, and Quicksilver.

## SYNTAX:
DISPLAY STRUCTURE [TO PRINT]

## DEFINITION:
Shows the database name, number of records, date of last update, number of bytes per record, and fields of each record for the active database. Also shows each field's name, number, length, and type.

DISPLAY STRUCTURE prints until the screen is full. It then prompts the user to press a key to continue the display.

## OPTIONS:
TO PRINT sends output to the printer as well.

## RECOMMENDED USE:
Use DISPLAY STRUCTURE during interactive use of dBASE III PLUS, dBASE IV, dBXL, or FoxBASE+ to review a file structure.

**Example**—A police department maintains a dBASE IV database of local law enforcement agencies. The key field for the production MDX file is AG_ZIP. DISPLAY STRUCTURE shows the structure of the main file:

```
. USE jkdpolic
. DISPLAY STRUCTURE
Structure for database: C:\MAIN.DBF
Number of data records:       180
Date of last update    : 02/09/88
Field  Field Name  Type         Width     Dec      Index
    1  OURCOUNTY   Character        1
    2  AGENCY      Character       30
    3  AG_ADRES    Character       20
    4  AG_CITY     Character       15
    5  AG_STATE    Character        2
    6  AG_ZIP      Character       10                  Y
    7  AG_PHONE    Character       12
```

```
      8  AG_PERSON   Character     30
      9  AG_COMNT    Character     30
  ** Total **                     151
```

**dBASE IV:** Also shows which fields are tags in the production MDX file.

## SEE ALSO:

Commands COPY STRUCTURE, CREATE, LIST STRUCTURE, and MODIFY STRUCTURE.

# DISPLAY USERS

## DIALECTS:
dBASE IV only.

## SYNTAX:
DISPLAY USERS

## DEFINITION:
Shows the assigned workstation names of users logged in on a local area network.

The workstation data is stored in a file called LOGIN.DB in the default directory.

If two stations have the same name, it appears only once in the list.

The listing pauses when the screen is full. You can then press a key to continue. The LIST USERS command scrolls the listing non-stop.

If there are no users on the system, nothing appears.

## RECOMMENDED USE:
Use DISPLAY USERS to monitor multiuser applications. This is helpful when doing system maintenance, backups, or other operations that might affect other users. Workstations are often hundreds of feet apart, and sometimes at different sites. It's better to DISPLAY USERS than run a marathon to find out who's on the system. Arbitrarily shutting down the system without notification is likely to lead to an old-fashioned lynch mob.

## SEE ALSO:
Commands DISPLAY and DISPLAY STATUS; functions NETNAME( ) and NETWORK( ).

# DO

## DIALECTS:

Clipper, dBASE III PLUS, dBASE IV, dBXL, FoxBASE+, and Quicksilver.

## SYNTAX:

DO <filename>/<procedure name> [WITH <parameter list>]

## DEFINITION:

Executes a program file or a procedure. It allows the passing of parameters in a list. If one exists, the program file or procedure must contain a PARAMETERS <parameter list> as its first statement. A parameter may be any valid expression. The number of parameters in the PARAMETERS statement must match the number of arguments in the DO...WITH statement.

The program file name may include a drive designator. It must include an extension if it is not PRG.

When the program file or procedure is complete, control returns to the caller or to the keyboard in the interactive mode.

**Example 1**—A publishing company wants to compute the weekly gross pay of its employees. The program E_PAY.PRG computes it based on parameters passed from another program.

```
* E_PAY.PRG
* Computes an employee's pay
* Hours and rate are numeric memory variables
PARAMETERS hours,rate
tot_pay = hours * rate     && Multiply HOURS times RATE and
                           &&  store the value in TOT_PAY
? tot_pay
```

For an employee making $5.00 per hour for 20 hours, the parameters 20 and 5.00 are passed to E_PAY.PRG as follows:

```
* Execute E_PAY with a parameter list corresponding to
*  its PARAMETER statement.
DO e_pay WITH 20,5.00
```

The result goes in memory variable TOT_PAY:

```
      100.00
```

## LIMITS/WARNINGS:

**dBASE III PLUS, dBASE IV, and dBXL:** Consider a program file executed with a DO as one open file. They also consider an open procedure file containing a collection of programs as one open file.

The number of open files can increase quickly, so procedure files can help you keep within system limits.

The systems have varying limits on recursive DO commands (programs DOing themselves). Recursive programming can be a powerful technique; however, nesting levels are limited.

**dBXL:** Limit of 25 DO <filename> statements in a program.

## VARIATIONS:

**dBASE IV:** All program files should have unique names. Do not rename DBO files, since they will no longer correspond to their source PRG files.

If a program has not been compiled, DO automatically compiles it into an object file (extension DBO) and then executes it. dBASE IV follows a specified search order when you issue the DO command. It searches for:

1. A procedure in the open, executing DBO file.
2. A procedure in SET PROCEDURE TO file.
3. A procedure in other open DBO files.
4. A DBO file.
5. A PRG file
6. A PRS file (SQL file).

If SET DEVELOPMENT is ON, DO automatically recompiles a program if it has been edited since the last time it was compiled.

## SEE ALSO:

Commands CANCEL, COMPILE, PARAMETERS, PRIVATE, PUBLIC, SET DEVELOPMENT, and SET PROCEDURE.

# DO CASE...CASE...OTHERWISE...ENDCASE

## DIALECTS:

Clipper, dBASE III PLUS, dBASE IV, dBXL, FoxBASE+, and Quicksilver.

## SYNTAX:

```
DO CASE
  CASE <expL_1>
    <statements>
  [CASE <expL_N>
    <statements>]
  [OTHERWISE
    <statements>]
ENDCASE
```

## DEFINITION:

DO CASE starts a decisionmaking structure that selects an action to execute from a list. It selects the first one for which the given expression is true (.T.).

If an expression is true, the computer executes all subsequent statements until it reaches a CASE, OTHERWISE, or ENDCASE. If the expression is false, the computer evaluates the next CASE expression.

If no expression is true, the computer executes the OTHERWISE statement. The ENDCASE statement marks the end of the CASE structure. If there is no OTHERWISE statement, the computer executes the statement immediately following ENDCASE.

## RECOMMENDED USE:

Use the CASE structure in menu systems to analyze users' responses to prompts.

**Example 1**—A program that moves through database records examines users' input with a CASE structure to determine the proper action. Pressing "F" skips forward a record. "B" skips backward a record. "D" deletes the current record. "R" returns control to the calling program. If the user enters an invalid letter, the OTHERWISE statement executes, alerting the user to the mistake.

```
CLEAR
USE acct_feb
DO WHILE .t.          && Perpetual DO WHILE loop (condition always true).
```

```
@ 05,10 say "(F)orward one record"
@ 06,10 say "(B)ack one record"
@ 07,10 say "(D)elete record"
@ 08,10 say "(R)eturn to previous menu"
choice = " "
@ 10,10 SAY "Your Choice? (F/B/D/R) " GET choice PICTURE "!"
READ
DO CASE
  CASE choice = "F"
    IF .NOT. EOF()
      SKIP
    ENDIF
    IF EOF()
      SKIP-1
    ENDIF
  CASE choice = "B"
    IF .NOT. BOF()
      SKIP-1
    ENDIF
  CASE choice = "D"
    DELETE              && Delete current record.
  CASE choice = "R"
    USE
    RETURN
  OTHERWISE
    WAIT "INVALID ENTRY, PRESS A KEY TO CONTINUE"
    @ 24,00
ENDCASE
@ 24,00 SAY RECNO()
ENDDO
```

*NOTE:* The CASE structure is like an IF/ELSE/ENDIF structure, but it allows more than two alternatives.

You may nest CASE statements, as long as you terminate each DO CASE properly with an ENDCASE. The allowed levels of nesting vary among systems. Clipper allows up to 63 levels. dBASE III PLUS, dBASE IV, and FoxBASE+ allow an unspecified number. dBXL allows up to 20, and Quicksilver up to 39.

## VARIATIONS:

**Clipper:** The ELSEIF statement makes IF...ENDIF structures work like DO CASE...ENDCASE.

## SEE ALSO:

Commands IF, ELSEIF, and ENDIF.

# DO WHILE...ENDDO

## DIALECTS:

Clipper, dBASE III PLUS, dBASE IV, dBXL, FoxBASE+, and Quicksilver.

## SYNTAX:

```
DO WHILE <condition>
  <statements>
  [LOOP]
  <statements>
  [EXIT]
  <statements>
ENDDO
```

## DEFINITION:

The paired DO WHILE... ENDDO commands repeat program statements located between them as long as the <condition> is true.

We call the DO WHILE...ENDDO structure a "control structure" because it regulates program flow.

ENDDO terminates the DO WHILE.

DO WHILE...ENDDO statements may be nested.

DO WHILE makes the computer do the following:

1. Evaluate the condition.
2. Exit if the condition is false.
3. Execute the statements up to ENDDO.
4. Return to step 1.

Note that the computer never executes the statements if the condition is false initially.

## OPTIONS:

LOOP returns control to the beginning of the DO WHILE/ENDDO. The computer does not execute any commands following it.

EXIT ends execution of the DO WHILE, and passes control to the statement immediately following ENDDO.

**Example 1**—A menu in an accounting program prompts the user for input. As the menu is in a DO WHILE/ENDDO loop, it repeats until the user tells it to EXIT. Within the main loop, a smaller loop repeats a GET and a READ until the user enters a valid character.

```
* Set DO WHILE expression to logical true. This expression stays true.
* The only ways to leave the loop are with EXIT, CANCEL, RETURN, or QUIT.
DO WHILE .t.
  @ 10,10 SAY "A. Print end of month report"
  @ 11,10 SAY "B. Print end of year report"
  @ 12,10 SAY "X. Leave this menu"
  * This DO WHILE repeats the prompt and the GET/READ until the user
  * enters A, B, or X, making the expression true.
  action = " "
  DO WHILE .NOT. action$"ABX" && Repeat until ACTION contains A,B, or X.
    @ 14,10 SAY "Your choice? (1-3) " GET action PICTURE "!"
    READ
  ENDDO
  DO CASE
    CASE action = "A"
      DO eom_rpt      && Execute subroutine EOM_RPT.
    CASE action = "B"
      DO eoy_rpt      && Execute subroutine EOY_RPT.
      * When user enters "X," the DO WHILE loop terminates and control
      * passes to the first command immediately following ENDDO.
    CASE action = "X"
      EXIT
  ENDCASE
ENDDO
? "This statement executes upon EXIT"
```

## VARIATIONS:

**dBASE III PLUS, dBXL, and FoxBASE+:** Macros in a DO WHILE statement are not reevaluated during iterations. Therefore, you cannot redefine the macro value within the loop. Clipper, dBASE IV, and Quicksilver reevaluate macros in the DO WHILE statement.

**Example 2**—In designing a modular reporting program, a programmer stores the DO WHILE <condition> in a variable, then uses the macro (&) to evaluate it. If the user redefines the <condition> within the DO WHILE loop, Clipper, dBASE IV, and Quicksilver reevaluate it.

```
mcondit = "LNAME = 'SMITH'"       && Store a condition in MCONDIT.
*
DO WHILE &mcondit                 && Evaluate MCONDIT with a macro.
  *
  * <Report statements>
  *
  SKIP
  * Get new condition from user
  newcond = .F.
  @ 23,03 SAY "Enter a new condition? " GET newcond PICT "Y"
  READ
  IF newcond
    mcondit = "POSTCODE = '92116'"
  ENDIF
ENDDO
```

## SEE ALSO:

Command FOR...NEXT; function &.

# DOS

## DIALECTS:

dBXL only.

## SYNTAX:

DOS

## DEFINITION:

Stops execution of dBXL and displays a DOS prompt. You can then enter DOS commands and run external programs. The only limitation is available memory. To return to dBXL, type EXIT.

## RECOMMENDED USE:

Use DOS to run external programs that interact with dBXL data files or incidental programs such as text editors, directory utilities, or other applications.

## VARIATIONS:

You can simulate the DOS command in systems other than dBXL. To do so, use the RUN command to execute a batch file that loads COMMAND.COM. Include the following command in your program:

```
RUN DOS.BAT
```

Place the following DOS batch file in the search path:

```
:DOS.BAT – shell to DOS – this batch file is used
:  only to change the DOS prompt, otherwise you can just RUN COMMAND
PROMPT Type EXIT to return to dBASE $_$n$g
:Give a normal prompt with our message above it
COMMAND
:Preceding line just loads COMMAND.COM–must be found on DOS PATH
```

## SEE ALSO:

Commands !/RUN.

# DOSINT

## DIALECTS:

dBXL and Quicksilver.

## SYNTAX:

DOSINT <expN>, [<memory variable list>]

## DEFINITION:

Allows direct execution of DOS and BIOS interrupts.

<expN> is the interrupt number.

You may pass up to six numeric memory variable parameters. Their values are placed in the microprocessor's registers before executing the specified interrupt, and the register values are copied back into the memory variables afterward.

## RECOMMENDED USE:

Only programmers who are familiar with DOS and BIOS interrupts should use DOSINT. Direct access to hardware, low-level file I/O, and other low-level functions could cause an application to fail or corrupt its environment.

Memory variable parameters are loaded into the following registers (in order): AX, BX, CX, DX, SI, and DI. Interrupts that use SI and DI usually require addresses to be placed in them. As this is difficult to do, SI and DI are seldom used.

Only order is important in the memory variable parameter list, not the names of the variables. DOSINT copies values into registers according to the number of parameters passed. For instance, if you pass only one parameter, it goes in AX. If you pass two, they go in AX and BX, respectively, and so on.

To load only AX and DX, you must supply dummy values for BX and CX (see Example 2). Only 16-bit registers may be specified, although you can use MOD( ) to separate out the low byte (AL, BL, CL, or DL) and subtract to find the high byte value (AH, BH, CH, or DH).

The HTOI( ) and ITOH( ) functions (hexadecimal to decimal conversion and vice versa) are useful for setting initial register values and examining return values (see Example 2). The BITSET( ) function is also useful for examining return values (see Example 3).

**Example 1**—When an error occurs in a financial application, the program automatically prints the screen using DOSINT in an ON ERROR routine.

On IBM and compatible PCs, BIOS interrupt 5 prints the screen just as if the user had pressed the PrtSc key. Note that the interrupt routine does no error checking. Before calling it, you should check printer readiness with the PRINTER( ) function.

```
* PRTSC.PRG - Print the screen.

* <error-checking statements>
DOSINT 5     && Prints the screen in most situations, but does
             &&   no error checking.
```

**Example 2**—To determine which disk drives are valid on the system, use DOS function calls 0eh and 19h. Function 0eh selects a drive as the default. Function 19h determines the current drive, and also returns the top "selectable" drive which is set up with the CONFIG.SYS "lastdrive" parameter (defaults to E in DOS 3).

```
* VALDRIVE.PRG
valdrives = ""          && Store null in valid drive string.
abyte     = 256         && Largest value stored in one byte,
                        &&   plus 1 for MOD().
doscall   = HTOI("21")
cur_disk  = HTOI("1900")           && AX=1900h = current disk DOS call.
sel_drive = HTOI("0E00")           && AX=0e00h = select drive DOS call.

axreg = cur_disk
DOSINT doscall,axreg               && call DOS (get current drive)
init_drive = MOD(axreg,abyte)      && MOD() removes AH value,
                                   &&  reports current drive from AL.

* Now setup for first "drive select" call, which returns the
* "top" drive letter (from CONFIG.SYS) in AL as a fringe benefit.

axreg = sel_drive
dxreg = 0                          && Select A: first, DL=0.
STORE 0 to bxreg,cxreg             && Store dummy parameters.
DOSINT doscall,axreg,bxreg,cxreg,dxreg
top_drive = MOD(axreg,abyte)-1     && Save top drive number.

DO WHILE dxreg <= top_drive
  axreg = cur_disk                 && Find out what default is now.
  DOSINT doscall,axreg             && Make DOS function call.
  IF MOD(axreg,abyte) = dxreg      && If they match, add to string.
```

```
    valdrives = valdrives + CHR(dxreg+65)      && CHR(0+65)="A", etc.
  ENDIF
  dxreg = dxreg + 1                 && Test next drive.
  axreg = sel_drive
  DOSINT doscall,axreg,bxreg,cxreg,dxreg
ENDDO

dxreg = init_drive                  && Cleanup,
axreg = sel_drive                   && select original drive.
DOSINT doscall,axreg,bxreg,cxreg,dxreg
? "Valid drives: "+valdrives+"...CONFIG.SYS top end is: "+;
          CHR(top_drive+65)
WAIT ''
```

**Example 3**—Widely distributed programs must adapt to different hardware configurations. By using DOSINT to check system equipment, you can can avoid subjecting end users to tedious installation programs.

This example uses BIOS interrupt 11 hex to determine what equipment is installed. Information is returned in the AX register. The BITSET( ) function is used to extract bits from it.

```
* EQUIP.PRG - Use DOSINT to check equipment using BIOS interrupt 11h.
* (see your system's hardware reference manual for details)

ax = 0                   && Initialize variable AX as numeric.

DOSINT HTOI("11"),ax     && Get configuration with BIOS call.

IF BITSET(ax,0)
  IF BITSET(ax,6)
    diskettes = '2'
  ELSE
    diskettes = '1'
  ENDIF
ELSE
  diskettes = "none"
ENDIF

IF BITSET(ax,4)
  IF BITSET(ax,5)
    videomode = "80x25 monochrome"
  ELSE
    videomode = "40x25 color"
  ENDIF
ELSE
  videomode = "80x25 color"
ENDIF
  rs232 = 0
IF BITSET(ax,9)
```

```
  rs232 = rs232 + 1
ENDIF
IF BITSET(ax,10)
   rs232 = rs232 + rs232 + 2
ENDIF
IF BITSET(ax,11)
   rs232 = rs232 + 4
ENDIF
rs232 = LTRIM(STR(rs232))       && Convert to string value.

printers = 0
IF BITSET(ax,14)
   printers = printers + 1
ENDIF
IF BITSET(ax,15)
   printers = printers + 2
ENDIF
printers = LTRIM(STR(printers)) && Convert to string value

? "Diskettes on the system = " + diskettes
? "Initial video mode = " + videomode
? "Number of RS232 ports = " + rs232
? "Number of printer ports = " + printers
WAIT
RETURN
```

## SEE ALSO:

Functions BITSET( ), IN( ), and OUT( ).

# DOWNSCROLL

## DIALECTS:

dBXL and Quicksilver.

## SYNTAX:

DOWNSCROLL <expn>

## DEFINITION:

Moves the current screen or window area down <expN> lines. If <expN> is a negative number or 0, the screen does not move.

If you move the text off the screen or window area, it will be erased.

## RECOMMENDED USE:

Use DOWNSCROLL with UPSCROLL to provide scrollable help screens or lookup windows.

**Example**—An invoicing application requires the entry of a customer account number for each invoice. If the operator forgets a number, he or she can look it up in a scrollable help window.

```
* HELPWIN.PRG
WSET WINDOW acctlook TO 10,01,23,40    && Create window specification.
WSELECT 1                              && Select window area.
WUSE acctlook                          && Use acctlook window.
USE sales
keypress = 0
? "Account number"                && List account numbers.
LIST accounts
DO WHILE keypress # 32            && DO WHILE user does not press space bar.
  keypress = INKEY()              && Store INKEY() to KEYPRESS variable.
  DO CASE
    CASE keypress = 5             && If user presses up arrow,
      UPSCROLL 1                  &&   scroll up 1.
    CASE keypress = 24            && If user presses down arrow,
      DOWNSCROLL 1                &&   scroll down 1.
  ENDCASE
ENDDO
```

## SEE ALSO:

Commands UPSCROLL, WSELECT, WSET WINDOW, and WUSE.

# EDIT

## DIALECTS:
dBASE III PLUS, dBASE IV, dBXL, and FoxBASE+.

## SYNTAX:
EDIT [scope] [FIELDS <field list>] [WHILE <condition>] [FOR <condition>]

## DEFINITION:
Allows full-screen editing of fields in the database in use.

## DEFAULT:
Displays all fields unless otherwise specified in the FIELDS option. Selects all records unless otherwise specified by SCOPE, FOR, or WHILE conditions.

EDIT is the same as CHANGE.

## SEE ALSO:
Command CHANGE.

# EJECT

## DIALECTS:

Clipper, dBASE III PLUS, dBASE IV, dBXL, FoxBASE+, and Quicksilver.

## SYNTAX:

Sends the printer a form feed character (ASCII 12), advancing the paper one page. Refer to your printer's manual to change the number of lines per page.

EJECT resets the printer to the top of the new page (row 0, column 0).

**Note:** Be sure the printer is ready before issuing EJECT. It does not require SET PRINT ON or SET DEVICE TO PRINT.

## SEE ALSO:

Commands ENDPRINTJOB, PRINTJOB, SET DEVICE, and SET PRINT; functions PCOL( ) and PROW( ).

# ENDPRINTJOB

## DIALECTS:
dBASE IV only.

## SYNTAX:
ENDPRINTJOB

## DEFINITION:
Marks the end of a PRINTJOB construct. See PRINTJOB for more information.

## SEE ALSO:
Commands ON PAGE, PRINTJOB, and SET PRINT.

# ENDTEXT

## DIALECTS:

Clipper, dBASE III PLUS, dBASE IV, dBXL, FoxBASE+, and Quicksilver.

## SYNTAX:

TEXT
<Unformatted text>
ENDTEXT

## DEFINITION:

Marks the end of an unformatted text block set off by the TEXT command. See TEXT for more information.

ENDTEXT has no function alone.

## SEE ALSO:

Command TEXT.

# END TRANSACTION

## DIALECTS:
dBASE IV only.

## SYNTAX:
```
BEGIN TRANSACTION
  * <Database operations>.
END TRANSACTION
```

## DEFINITION:
Terminates transaction logging initiated by the BEGIN TRANSACTION command.

## SEE ALSO:
Commands BEGIN TRANSACTION, RESET, RETRY, and ROLLBACK; functions COMPLETED( ), ISMARKED( ), and ROLLBACK( ).

# ELSE

## DIALECTS:
Clipper, dBASE III PLUS, dBASE IV, dBXL, FoxBASE+, and Quicksilver.

## SYNTAX:
ELSE

## DEFINITION:
Indicates an alternate course of execution when an IF <condition> is false.

## SEE ALSO:
Command IF.

# ELSEIF

## DIALECTS:

Clipper only.

## SYNTAX:

IF <condition>
  * <statements>

  .
ELSEIF <condition>
  * <statements>

  .
ELSEIF <condition>
  * <statements>
ENDIF

## DEFINITION:

Evaluates multiple conditions in an IF...ENDIF, much like a CASE statement in a DO CASE structure.

If the first IF <condition> is false, the first ELSEIF <condition> to evaluate true executes. Afterward, program control continues with the first statement after the matched ENDIF.

## RECOMMENDED USE:

Use IF...ELSEIF instead of DO CASE...ENDCASE. It simplifies coding by reducing the number of statements by one. Use ELSE to indicate an exception (instead of OTHERWISE in the CASE structure).

**Example 1**—A program examines users' input with an IF...ELSEIF structure to determine the proper action. Pressing "F" skips forward a record. "B" skips backward. "D" deletes the current record. "R" returns control to the calling program. If the user enters an invalid letter, the LOOP statement after the ELSE returns control to the menu that got the user's response.

```
DO WHILE .t.
  * <GET user's response.>
  *
  IF choice = "F"
```

```
    * <code to move forward.>
  ELSEIF choice = "B"
    * <code to move backward.>
  ELSEIF choice = "D"
    * <code to delete.>
  ELSEIF choice = "R"
    RETURN
  ELSE
    @ 23,01 SAY "Invalid selection, please re-enter"
  ENDIF
ENDDO
```

## SEE ALSO:

Commands CASE, DO CASE, ENDIF, and IF; function IIF( ).

# END

## DIALECTS:
Clipper only.

## SYNTAX:
END

## DEFINITION:
Marks the end of a DO CASE, DO WHILE, or IF structure. This is an abbreviated version of ENDCASE, ENDDO, and ENDIF.

## RECOMMENDED USE:
END is a convenient command for terminating control structures; however, using it makes them less readable.

## SEE ALSO:
Commands DO CASE, DO WHILE, ENDCASE, ENDDO, ENDIF, and IF.

# ENDCASE

## DIALECTS:
Clipper, dBASE III PLUS, dBASE IV, dBXL, FoxBASE+, and Quicksilver.

## SYNTAX:
ENDCASE

## DEFINITION:
Ends a DO CASE structure.

## SEE ALSO:
Commands DO CASE and END.

# ENDDO

## DIALECTS:
Clipper, dBASE III PLUS, dBASE IV, dBXL, FoxBASE+, and Quicksilver.

## SYNTAX:
ENDDO

## DEFINITION:
Ends a DO WHILE structure.

## VARIATIONS:
**Clipper:** You can substitute END.

## SEE ALSO:
Commands DO WHILE and END.

# ENDIF

## DIALECTS:
Clipper, dBASE III PLUS, dBASE IV, dBXL, FoxBASE+, and Quicksilver.

## SYNTAX:
ENDIF

## DEFINITION:
Ends an IF structure.

## VARIATIONS:
**Clipper:** You can substitute END.

## SEE ALSO:
Commands END and IF.

# ENDSCAN

## DIALECTS:
dBASE IV only.

## SYNTAX:
ENDSCAN

## DEFINITION:
Ends a SCAN structure.

## SEE ALSO:
Commands DO WHILE, END, and SCAN.

# ERASE

## DIALECTS:
Clipper, dBASE III PLUS, dBASE IV, dBXL, FoxBASE+, and Quicksilver.

## SYNTAX:
ERASE <filename>

## DEFINITION:
Same as DELETE FILE.

## SEE ALSO:
Command DELETE FILE.

# EXIT

## DIALECTS:
Clipper, dBASE III PLUS, dBASE IV, dBXL, FoxBASE+, and Quicksilver.

## SYNTAX:
EXIT

## DEFINITION:
Terminates a DO WHILE/ENDDO loop, passing program control to the first statement following the ENDDO.

## VARIATION:
**Clipper:** Also terminates a FOR...NEXT loop.

**dBASE IV:** Also terminates a SCAN...ENDSCAN loop.

**dBXL:** Also terminates a FOR...NEXT loop. When used with FOR...NEXT, EXIT is the same as BREAK.

## SEE ALSO:
Commands BREAK, DO WHILE, FOR...NEXT, and SCAN.

# EXPORT

## DIALECTS:
dBASE III PLUS, dBASE IV, dBXL, and Quicksilver.

## SYNTAX:
EXPORT TO <filename> [TYPE] PFS *(dBASE III PLUS)*

EXPORT TO <filename> [TYPE] PFS/DBASEII/FW2/RPD *(dBASE IV)*
[FIELDS <field list>] [<scope>][FOR <condition>] [WHILE <condition>]

EXPORT TO <filename> TYPE VENTURA *(dBXL/Quicksilver)*

## DEFINITION:
Copies the open database file to a foreign format.

## DEFAULT:
Unless you limit the scope or provide a condition, EXPORT TO copies all records to the new file.

## OPTIONS:
**PFS (dBASE III PLUS and dBASE IV)**
Creates a pfs:File data file (pfs:File is a product of Software Publishing, Inc.). EXPORT TO copies files in indexed order if an index file is in use. It also exports the screen form of an open format file.

**DBASEII (dBASE IV only)**
Creates a dBASE II (Ashton-Tate) database and gives it a DB2 extension.

**FW2 (dBASE IV only)**
Creates a Framework II (Ashton-Tate) database frame.

**RPD (dBASE IV only)**
Creates a Rapidfile (Ashton-Tate) database with a RPD extension.

**VENTURA (dBXL and Quicksilver)**
Creates a file for Xerox's Ventura Publisher. If you do not provide an extension, it defaults to TAG. Copies all fields except memos. Records in the TAG file have the format:

@<fieldname> = <field contents>

The <field contents> are not delimited.

From Ventura Publisher, open the TAG file as a WordStar file.

## LIMITS/WARNINGS:

You can use a format file (extension FMT) for EXPORTing to PFS:File. If you don't use one, the default APPEND or EDIT screen becomes the PFS:File screen format.

Format files to be EXPORTed may not have more than 200 @ commands. The form must also be limited to screen rows 0 through 20.

With SET SAFETY ON, EXPORT prompts the user before overwriting files.

## SEE ALSO:

Commands COPY TO, IMPORT, SET FORMAT, and SET SAFETY.

# EXTERNAL

## DIALECTS:
Clipper only.

## SYNTAX:
EXTERNAL <procedure list>

## DEFINITION:
Declares the names of undefined procedures for the linker. This lets you execute procedures in overlay files using a procedure name stored in a memory variable.

Overlay files reduce the memory requirements of Clipper applications by segmenting them. Application segments load into memory only when required. Putting a procedure name in a memory variable and executing it with a macro leaves the name unknown to the linker.

EXTERNAL solves this problem by declaring undefined procedure names. You can then execute procedures in overlay files using a filename stored in a memory variable.

**Example**—A programmer writes a program to execute procedures based on certain conditions. Rather than write a CASE structure, she uses a single DO statement and passes the procedure name to it in a memory variable. Because she does not explicitly reference the procedure name in the DO statement, she must declare EXTERNAL any procedures located in overlays. Note that Clipper allows parentheses around filenames in lieu of the macro (&) symbol.

```
* At start of program, declare three procedures EXTERNAL.
EXTERNAL totcalc,subcalc,salestax
** <statements>
** Program stores a procedure name in memory variable RUNPROC.
DO (runproc)
```

## SEE ALSO:
Command DO.

# FIND

## DIALECTS:

Clipper, dBASE III PLUS, dBASE IV, dBXL, FoxBASE+, and Quicksilver.

## SYNTAX:

FIND <character string>/<expN>

## DEFINITION:

Does a fast search in an indexed database file using a character string or numeric argument. The argument corresponds only to the index key value. FIND does not work on unindexed fields.

FIND finds only the first matching record.

If the search succeeds, the record pointer points to the record, and FOUND( ) returns true (.T.). If the search fails, the pointer moves to the End of File and FOUND( ) returns false (.F.).

Note that FOUND( ) does not always work properly in dBASE III PLUS and FoxBASE+. Instead, you should use EOF( ) to test for the end-of-file. If EOF( ) is true, the FIND did not succeed.

## RECOMMENDED USE:

Use FIND in applications requiring rapid retrieval. Even in files containing thousands of records, FIND takes only a few seconds.

**Example 1**—A customer service agent handles consumer complaints. When someone calls, the agent searches for his or her last name with FIND. To minimize errors, the program assumes that the operator will enter the name in uppercase.

```
. USE complaints INDEX con_lname
. FIND "GRISWOLD"
. ? FOUND()
.T.
. EDIT
```

If the search fails and TALK is SET ON, dBASE III PLUS and FoxBASE+ display the terse, ungrammatical message "No Find." dBXL displays the more proper "Key not found." dBASE IV reports "Find not successful."

FIND does not require delimiters on character string searches; however, the character expression begins with the first non-blank character. If your search string contains leading blanks, you must use delimiters. You must also use them if the string begins with a delimiter, such as a single or double quotation mark.

You can use memory variables in FIND arguments. When using a character variable, you must use the macro (&) function. If the argument contains leading blanks, enclose the & and the memory variable in quotation marks.

**Example 2**—In the same customer service application as Example 1, a program GETs the last name in a memory variable. The variable is then used with the FIND command using a macro (&).

```
USE complaints INDEX con_lname
* Create memory variable SRCH_NAME in which to GET last name.
srch_name = SPACE(15)
* PICTURE function "@!" forces uppercase.
@ 10,10 SAY "Enter last name to find: " GET srch_name PICTURE "@!"
READ
* Requires the macro function when FINDing a memory variable.
FIND &srch_lname
* If search succeeds, display record on screen.
* <more statements>
```

FIND can also search for partial keys, starting with the leftmost character. In this respect, it conforms to the rules of SET EXACT ON/OFF. When SET EXACT is OFF, a partial match counts as FOUND. When SET EXACT is ON, the search argument and the index key must match character for character.

**Example 3**—The customer service agent does not remember how to spell WILTENBACHER (or is it WILTINBOCHER or perhaps WILTUNBECKER). He enters only the first part of the name—a partial key. Note that EXACT cannot be SET ON when doing partial key searches.

```
. USE complaints INDEX con_lname
. SET EXACT off
. FIND WILT
. ? FOUND()
.T.
. EDIT
```

Note that the first "WILT" in the index could also be WILTON, WILTOWSKI, WILT, or WILTCHER.

SEEK is like FIND, except that its search argument may be any valid expression of type numeric, character, or date. SEEK also requires the delimiting of characters with single quotation marks, double quotation marks, or square brackets. You do not have to delimit memory variables.

## VARIATIONS:

**dBASE IV:** If you SET NEAR ON, an unsuccessful FIND moves the pointer to the record with the next highest key value. If there is no higher key value, the pointer moves to the end-of-file.

## LIMITS/WARNINGS:

FIND is a carryover from dBASE II included in later versions for compatibility.

## SEE ALSO:

Commands SEEK, SET NEAR, and SET SOFTSEEK; functions EOF( ) and FOUND( ).

# FLUSH

## DIALECTS:

dBXL, FoxBASE+, and Quicksilver.

## SYNTAX:

FLUSH

## DEFINITION:

Writes all active database file buffers to disk without closing the open files.

To improve performance, changes and additions are retained in memory buffers. They are stored on disk only when you issue a command, such as USE, CLOSE DATABASES, or CLOSE, that closes the database file, or when the buffer becomes full.

The drawback to keeping data in memory is the risk of power loss or computer error. Either problem causes the loss of data retained in the buffers.

FLUSH does not affect record pointers, open indexes, or format files.

## VARIATIONS:

**Clipper:** COMMIT is similar to FLUSH.

**dBASE IV:** To protect data, SET AUTOSAVE ON writes data at regular intervals.

## SEE ALSO:

Commands CLOSE DATA, COMMIT, SET AUTOSAVE, and USE.

# FOR

## DIALECTS:

Clipper, dBXL, and Quicksilver.

## SYNTAX:

```
FOR <numeric memory variable> = <expN> TO <expN> [STEP <expN>]
   <statements>
   [BREAK]                    (dBXL/Quicksilver)
   [EXIT]                     (Clipper/dBXL)
   <statements>
   NEXT [<memory variable>]
```

## DEFINITION:

Repeats statements while incrementing or decrementing a memory variable through a numeric range. FOR...NEXT creates the specified memory variable itself. The computer repeats the statements between FOR and NEXT until it exhausts the range.

## OPTIONS:

STEP steps the variable by a value other than 1.

BREAK or EXIT ends the FOR...NEXT before the specified range is exhausted. Control passes to the statement following the NEXT statement.

To improve readability, you can put the memory variable's name after NEXT. This does not affect execution.

## RECOMMENDED USE:

FOR...NEXT replaces DO WHILE...ENDDO in cases where the loop executes a fixed number of times. Use FOR...NEXT in any application where you would use a counter. It is especially helpful in manipulating arrays.

**Example 1**—A Clipper program scans a database file, storing part numbers in an array called PART for later use in a menu. The program loads the array by incrementing a FOR...NEXT counter, SKIPping a record in each pass. If the record pointer reaches the end-of-file before the counter expires, the EXIT option cancels the FOR...NEXT, passing control to the statement after NEXT.

```
USE invent INDEX invdex      && Open accounts database.
DECLARE part[23]             && Declare array PART.
  FOR ctr = 1 TO 23          && Stop counting at 23.
  part[ctr] = partno         && Load data from each record until
  SKIP                       &&    array is full.
  IF eof()                   && If end of file, end array loading.
    EXIT
  ENDIF
NEXT
```

FOR...NEXT works just like its namesake in BASIC.

## VARIATIONS:

**Clipper:** The EXIT option ends execution of FOR...NEXT.

**dBXL:** Both BREAK and EXIT end execution of FOR...NEXT. You can also use BREAK to terminate a DO...ENDDO loop.

**Quicksilver:** BREAK ends execution of FOR...NEXT.

## SEE ALSO:

Commands DECLARE, DIMENSION, DO WHILE, and EXIT.

# FUNCTION

## DIALECTS:

Clipper, dBASE IV, dBXL, and Quicksilver.

## SYNTAX:

FUNCTION <user defined function name>
 [PARAMETERS <expression list>]
 <statements>
RETURN <exp>

## DEFINITION:

Marks the beginning of a user defined function (UDF), a procedure that returns a value.

Call UDFs with the standard function syntax <function name>( ). For example, to call a UDF with the name MSTRING, use the statement:

```
? MSTRING()
```

You can use an optional PARAMETERS statement to pass values to the function. Put parameters inside parentheses in a list, as in the following example:

```
? MSTRING(p1,p2,p3)
```

Memory variables are passed by value, not by reference. Therefore, changing a parameter does not change the variable after a return to the caller.

## RECOMMENDED USE:

Write user defined functions for repetitive operations that return values. They increase readability by reducing the amount of code in the main program. They also save development time since you can reuse them in many applications.

**Example 1**—A programmer designs several reports for a financial application. Each one has an uppercase, centered heading. Rather than repeat the centering code, the programmer writes a user defined function UPCTR( ).

UPCTR( ) accepts two arguments, a string (STG) and the length in which to center it (LNG). Subtracting the length of STG from LNG and dividing by two produces the starting position of the centered string. STUFF( ) then inserts STG into a blank string with length LNG at the computed starting position. UPPER( ) converts the result to uppercase.

```
FUNCTION upctr
* Syntax: UPCTR(<expC>,<expN>)
* Return <expC> centered in a line with a length <expN>.
PARAMETERS stg,lng
*
RETURN UPPER(SUBS(STUFF(SPACE(lng),(lng-(LEN(stg)))/2,len(stg),stg),1,lng))
```

To display a report heading in Clipper using CENTER( ), use the following statements:

```
mheading = "Babbitt Corporation Sales Report"
@ 01,00 SAY UPCTR(mheading,80)
                    Babbitt Corporation Sales Report
```

**Example 2**—User defined functions can help maintain compatibility between implementations of dBASE. dBASE IV's SEEK( ) function searches for an expression and returns true if found and false if not. It replaces several statements, making the code more concise. It also lets you SEEK( ) from a VALID clause. You can simulate it with a Clipper, dBXL, FoxBASE+, or Quicksilver user defined function called MSEEK( ):

```
FUNCTION mseek               && Make a PROCEDURE in FoxBASE+.
PARAMETERS mexp,malias
oldalias = STR(SELECT())     && Save original work area.
SELECT &malias               && SELECT new work area.
SEEK mexp                    && SEEK search expression.
isfound = FOUND()            && Save FOUND() value after a SEEK since a
SELECT &oldalias             &&   subsequent change in areas will
                             &&   reset it.
RETURN isfound               && Return .T. or .F.
```

See SEEK( ) for more examples.

UDFs are also useful in the interactive modes of dBASE IV, dBXL, or Fox-BASE+. From the dot prompt, you can use them to analyze data. For example, you may have a UDF "library" file of financial functions. To make them available in dBASE IV or FoxBASE+, SET PROCEDURE TO <filename>. In dBXL, SET UDF TO <filename>.

## VARIATIONS:

**Clipper:** A UDF that begins a line acts like a command. For example, a UDF BOXDRAW( ) clears a box on the screen and draws a double line border around it. It returns a null string to satisfy the RETURN <exp> requirement.

```
FUNCTION boxdraw
PARAMETERS tr,tc,br,bc    && Top row,top column,bottom row,bottom column
@ tr,tc CLEAR TO br,bc
@ tr,tc TO br,bc DOUBLE
RETURN ""
```

You can call BOXDRAW( ) like a command, as in

```
BOXDRAW(5,5,10,20)
```

Clipper lets you pass a parameter by reference, instead of by value, in two ways:

- Precede it with @ in the parameter list.
- Pass an array element.

See the command PARAMETERS for more information.

Clipper lets user defined functions appear nearly anywhere an internal function can appear. For example, you can use one in an index key. However, be sure the function is available whenever the index is updated. The UDF becomes part of the internal index key.

**Example 3**—Clipper doesn't display record numbers when indexing. The following user defined function in an index key (character type only) compensates for the omission. You must set a logical flag YESDEX = .t. to indicate that you are creating an index. Otherwise, the record number will appear whenever the index is used.

```
FUNCTION ixnum
IF yesdex              && Check to see if indexing. If so, then
  @ 1,1 SAY RECNO()    &&   display record number.
ENDIF                  &&
RETURN ""              && Return null value. Doesn't affect index order.
```

To use IXNUM, create the index as follows:

```
USE prospects                 && Sample database.
yesdex = .t.                  && Set flag to indicate indexing.
* Index on character string key plus the IXNUM function.
INDEX ON names+IXNUM() TO namedex
```

When indexing, the record number will appear at 1,1. As long as you do not set the logical flag YESDEX to true (.T.), it will not appear on subsequent index updates. Remember to include IXNUM in all applications using the indexes it creates.

**dBASE IV:** You can put user defined functions in a program file or PROCEDURE file. In a program, user defined functions go at the end. Statements after a FUNCTION...RETURN, except for other PROCEDUREs and FUNCTIONs, will never execute.

You may execute a user defined function in the current program file, or in the active PROCEDURE file. From a subroutine, you may also execute a FUNCTION located in a calling program.

dBASE IV searches places for the named function in the following order:

1. Currently executing object file (extension DBO).
2. Procedure file opened with SET PROCEDURE TO.
3. Another open calling object file starting with the most recently opened.

dBASE IV prohibits the following commands in user defined functions:

& (macro)

| | | | | |
|---|---|---|---|---|
| APPEND | DISPLAY | LABEL | SAVE | TOTAL |
| AVERAGE | EDIT | LIST | SET CATALOG TO | UPDATE |
| BROWSE | EXPORT | LOAD | SET FIELDS TO | ZAP |
| CHANGE | HELP | LOGOUT | SET FILTER TO | |
| COPY | IMPORT | MODIFY | SET ORDER TO | |
| CREATE | INDEX | PACK | SET RELATION TO | |
| DELETE | INPUT | PROCEDURE | SET VIEW TO | |
| DIR | INSERT | REINDEX | SORT | |
| DIRECTORY | JOIN | REPORT | SUM | |

**dBXL:** You must put user defined functions in a separate function file, then SET UDF TO <function filename>. A file may contain up to 32 functions.

**FoxBASE+:** User defined functions do not use the word FUNCTION. Instead, a UDF can be a PROCEDURE or program, provided it RETURNs a value. UDFs count toward the limit of 128 procedures per procedure file.

User defined functions are limited to:

?/?? statements
Arguments of DISPLAY and LIST commands
Control statements
STORE and REPLACE statements
@...SAY...VALID clauses

**Quicksilver:** You must put user defined functions in a separate function file, then SET UDF TO <function filename>. A file may contain up to 127 functions, and you may have an unlimited number of files. Defining function names with more than eight characters causes a runtime error.

When creating memory variables in user defined functions, first declare them PRIVATE to avoid overwriting variables in the calling program.

## LIMITS/WARNINGS:

User defined functions cannot have the same names as internal commands or functions.

If you change the states of open databases in user defined functions, be sure to restore them before RETURNing.

## SEE ALSO

Commands PARAMETERS, PROCEDURE, SET PROCEDURE, and SET UDF; function SEEK ( ).

# GATHER

## DIALECTS:

FoxBASE+ only.

## SYNTAX:

GATHER FROM <array> [FIELDS <field list>]

## DEFINITION:

Transfers the contents of a memory variable array into the current database record.

Elements in the array fill the fields sequentially.

GATHER defaults to all fields if you do not specify a field list.

If you specify a field list, the first element goes into the first field, the second element goes into the second field, etc., until the specified fields are filled or the array is exhausted.

Note that GATHER ignores memo fields.

## RECOMMENDED USE:

Use GATHER to reduce the amount of programming required to initialize arrays.

SCATTER works with GATHER. SCATTER moves data from the current record of the active database to an array.

Together, they provide a simple way to edit database records in memory without making explicit declarations for each field.

**Example**—In dBASE III PLUS, moving data from a record to memory variables requires that you initialize a variable for each field. A record with 40 fields requires 40 STORE or = statements. After changing the variables, you must then REPLACE each one into its original field. SCATTER and GATHER reduce the amount of code by eliminating these steps.

```
* Without SCATTER and GATHER.
USE acctnames
* Initialize memory variables
mname = name
maddress = address
mcity = city
```

```
mstate = state
mzip = zip
* Edit memory variables with GET.
@ 05,01 SAY "    Name: " GET mname
@ 06,01 SAY "Address: " GET maddress
@ 07,01 SAY "    City: " GET mcity
@ 08,01 SAY "   State: " GET mstate
@ 09,01 SAY "     Zip: " GET mzip
READ
REPLACE name WITH mname,address WITH maddress,city WITH mcity,;
        state WITH mstate,zip WITH mzip
```

Use SCATTER and GATHER to simplify the code by eliminating memory variable assignments:

```
USE acctnames
SCATTER TO acctedit     && Initialize array.
* Edit array.
@ 05,01 SAY "    Name: " GET acctedit(1)
@ 06,01 SAY "Address: " GET acctedit(2)
@ 07,01 SAY "    City: " GET acctedit(3)
@ 08,01 SAY "   State: " GET acctedit(4)
@ 09,01 SAY "     Zip: " GET acctedit(5)
READ
GATHER FROM acctedit    && Write array back to record.
```

The benefit of this technique increases with the number of fields.

## VARIATIONS:

**dBASE IV:** COPY TO ARRAY is similar to SCATTER; however, dBASE IV has no equivalent to GATHER. (APPEND FROM ARRAY adds a record with the contents of the specified array).

**dBXL, Quicksilver:** The REPLACE AUTOMEM command is similar to GATHER.

## SEE ALSO:

Commands APPEND FROM ARRAY, COPY TO ARRAY, DIMENSION, REPLACE, and SCATTER.

# GENERATE

## DIALECTS:
dBXL and Quicksilver.

## SYNTAX:
GENERATE [<expN>]

## DEFINITION:
Adds records to the current database and fills them with random data. GENERATE does not affect existing records.

<expN> ranges from 1 to 1 billion, subject to the database size limit of 2 billion bytes.

If you issue GENERATE without an argument, dBXL asks for the number of records.

## RECOMMENDED USE:
Use GENERATE to create sample databases for debugging applications.

**Example**—To test a data entry screen and a report module, a programmer GENERATEs 1000 records. The sample data fills each field, making it easy to find alignment problems in reports and data entry screens.

```
USE maillist
GENERATE 1000
DISPLAY name, city, state
Record#    NAME                       CITY             STATE
     14    wMFNbctiePiyufMwSdiNHEsav  tJbIHengGcwocgZ  WL
```

## SEE ALSO:
Command APPEND BLANK; functions RECCOUNT( ) and RECNO( ).

# GET

## DIALECTS:
Clipper, dBASE III PLUS, dBASE IV, dBXL, FoxBASE+, and Quicksilver.

## DEFINITION:
Displays a variable, and accepts input when activated with the READ command. Works with the @ command.

## SEE ALSO:
Command @...GET.

# GO

## DIALECTS:

Clipper, dBASE III PLUS, dBASE IV, dBXL, FoxBASE+, and Quicksilver.

## SYNTAX:

GO[TO] TOP/BOTTOM/<expN>

## DEFINITION:

Moves the record pointer. GO and GOTO are synonyms. If <expN>'s value is a valid record number, the pointer moves to it. Otherwise, the error message "Record is out of Range" appears.

*Note:* GOTO can access deleted records hidden by the SET DELETED ON command or by a filter.

GOTO TOP moves the pointer to the first record in the database. GOTO BOTTOM moves it to the last record. When an index file is in use, TOP is the record with the lowest key value and BOTTOM the one with the highest.

**Note:** In all systems except Clipper, a number or numeric expression alone on the command line indicates a record number to GOTO.

## RECOMMENDED USE:

GO can rapidly traverse a database using the TOP and BOTTOM options.

**Example**—In a database of company employees indexed on last name, GOTO TOP moves the pointer to the record with the lowest key value— "Adams." GOTO BOTTOM moves the pointer with the highest key value— "Zoeller." In an unindexed file, TOP is record 1 and BOTTOM is the last record.

```
. USE employ INDEX emplname
. GOTO TOP
. ? lname
Adams
. ? RECNO()
223
. GOTO BOTTOM
. ? lname
Zoeller
. ? RECNO()
9
```

## VARIATIONS:

**dBASE IV:** The option IN <alias> lets you GOTO a record in an unselected database. <alias> is the actual database name or its full alias.

## SEE ALSO:

Commands SET DELETED and SET FILTER.

# GRAPH FORM

## DIALECTS:

dBXL and Quicksilver.

## SYNTAX:

GRAPH FORM <file1> [<scope>] [WHILE <condition>] [FOR <condition>]
[HATCH] [TO PRINT] [TO FILE <file2> [IMAGE/PAINT]]

## DEFINITION:

Processes the current database file and graphs its data based on the graph format file <file1>. Graph types include bar graphs, line graphs, pie charts, regression lines, scatter plots, and step graphs.

GRAPH FORM uses the first 40 records in the current database unless you limit records with a <scope>, WHILE, or FOR clause.

<file1> is the graph format (extension GRF) file defined with dBXL's CREATE/MODIFY GRAPH command or Quicksilver's MODIGRF.EXE program.

GRAPH FORM can display up to 40 records.

You can use the same graph format file with different databases, as long as they contain all the fields used in the graph.

## OPTIONS:

<scope>, WHILE, and FOR limit the records to display.

HATCH determines whether enclosed parts of a graph have cross-hatching. It only works on computers with Enhanced Graphics Adapter (EGA) cards. Omit it when using color to represent parts of a graph. You can define colors when you create or modify a graph. Color is only available on EGA systems.

Because color graphs are not available on CGA or Hercules systems, cross-hatching always appears, and the HATCH option has no effect.

TO FILE <file2> lets you save the graph image, like a snapshot, in a form that you can restore later with RESTORE GRAPH. The new file has a BIT extension. RESTORE GRAPH simply redisplays the graph image without processing data.

You do not need to open a database, and execution is much faster than with GRAPH FORM.

TO FILE <file2> IMAGE saves the graph in a Xerox Ventura Publisher format (extension IMG).

TO FILE <file2> PAINT saves the graph in a PC Paintbrush/Aldus Pagemaker format (extension PCX).

The TO PRINT option prints the graph. To use a printer other than the default (IBM Graphics Printer), you must first select it with the SET GRAPHPRINT command or Quicksilver's INSTALL program. The supported printers are:

- Epson FX (or LX86)
- Epson MX/IBM Graphics Printer (the default)
- Hewlett Packard LaserJet
- Okidata dot matrix

The manual also lists an HPGL Plotter option, but it does not work.

## RECOMMENDED USE:

Use GRAPH FORM to display simple business graphs based on live data. The graph format file defines the graph type, titles, expressions, and color, but the plotting conforms to the open database.

Also use GRAPH FORM to export graphs for use in desktop publishing or graphics software such as Aldus Pagemaker, PC Paintbrush, and Xerox Ventura Publisher.

**Example**—A pie chart shows a company's growth percentage. Database file GAINS contains five years' worth of quarterly data. GRAPH FORM displays the chart for each year, processing four records at a time.

```
USE gains
DO WHILE .NOT. EOF()
  GRAPH FORM gaingraf NEXT 4
  SKIP
ENDDO
```

The 1989 graph appears as follows:

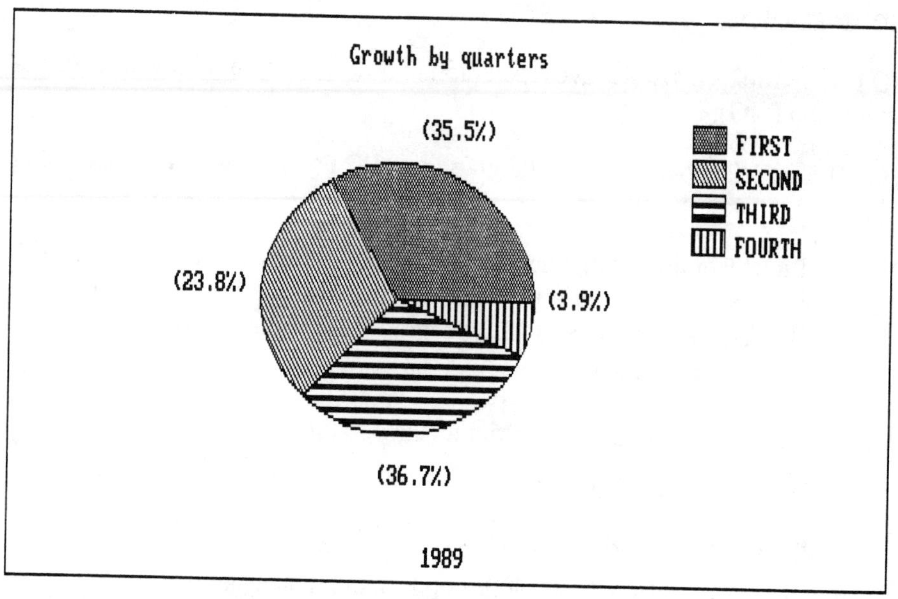


To export a graph to Ventura Publisher, the program issues

```
GRAPH FORM gaingraf NEXT 4 TO FILE IMAGE
```

To export a graph to Aldus' PageMaker, the program issues

```
GRAPH FORM gaingraf NEXT 4 TO FILE PAINT
```

## LIMITS/WARNINGS:

dBXL and Quicksilver do not display graphs within the active window. The screen blanks briefly, then the graph fills it. When the user presses a key, the graph disappears and the previous screen is erased as well. To preserve the previous screen, issue WSAVE before displaying the graph. To restore the previous screen, issue WRESTORE afterward.

## SEE ALSO:

Commands CREATE GRAPH, RESTORE GRAPH, SET GRAPHPRINT, WRESTORE, and WSAVE.

# HELP

## DIALECTS:
dBASE III PLUS, dBASE IV, dBXL, and FoxBASE+.

## SYNTAX:
HELP [keyword]

## DEFINITION:
Displays a help screen or menu.

## VARIATIONS:
dBASE III PLUS, dBASE IV, dBXL, and FoxBASE+ provide information about specific commands or topics, specified by [keyword]. HELP alone displays generalized help menus.

dBASE III PLUS, dBASE IV, and dBXL have interactive modes with help screens. To invoke them, type ASSIST (dBASE III PLUS and dBASE IV) or INTRO (dBXL).

## SEE ALSO:
Commands ASSIST, INTRO, and SET FUNCTION TO.

# IF...ELSE...ENDIF

## DIALECTS:

Clipper, dBASE III PLUS, dBASE IV, dBXL, FoxBASE+, and Quicksilver.

## SYNTAX:

IF <condition>
  <statements>
[ELSE
  <statements>]
ENDIF

## DEFINITION:

Evaluates an expression and does one of two actions, depending on whether the condition is true or false.

If it is true, the computer executes the statements following IF until it encounters an ELSE or ENDIF. Control then passes to the statement immediately following ENDIF.

If the condition is false, the computer executes the statements following the ELSE until it encounters an ENDIF. Again, control passes to the statement immediately following ENDIF. If no ELSE exists, control passes to the statement immediately following ENDIF.

You can nest IF/ENDIF constructs as long as each IF has a matching ENDIF. ELSEs go with the most recent unsatisfied IF.

## RECOMMENDED USE:

Use IF/ELSE/ENDIF to make "either/or" decisions in programs. When choosing among more than two decisions, a DO CASE structure is more convenient and easier to understand, and requires less programming.

**Example 1**—A sales application computes invoice totals depending on whether payment is to be cash or credit. Cash sales earn a 3% discount. Cash sales over $1000 earn an extra 3% discount. IF/ELSE/ENDIF determines the total discount.

```
IF method = "CASH"
  IF sale_amt > 1000
    subtotal = sale_amt - (sale_amt * .06)
```

```
  ELSE
      subtotal = sale_amt - (sale_amt * .03)
  ENDIF
ELSE
  subtotal = sale_amt
ENDIF
total = subtotal + (subtotal * salestax)
```

## WARNINGS/SPECIAL CASES:

IF/ELSE/ENDIF works only in programs. In the interactive mode, use the IIF( ) (immediate IF) function to emulate it. IIF( ) performs either/or decisionmaking on one line.

In the previous example, you could replace the lines:

```
IF sale_amt > 1000
  subtotal = sale_amt - (sale_amt * .06)
ELSE
  subtotal = sale_amt - (sale_amt * .03)
ENDIF
```

with a single line using IIF( ):

```
    subtotal = sale_amt - (sale_amt * IIF(sale_amt > 1000,.06,.03))
```

IIF( ) tests SALE_AMT. If it exceeds 1000, a discount of .06 applies. Otherwise, a discount of .03 applies.

Using IIF( ) results in fewer program lines and faster execution; however, the code is somewhat more difficult to understand.

## VARIATIONS:

**Clipper:** The ELSEIF structure lets you specify several alternatives within an IF...ENDIF structure. ELSEIF has the form:

```
IF <condition>
  <statements>
[ELSEIF]
  <statements>
[ELSEIF]
  <statements>
[ELSE]
ENDIF
```

IF...ELSEIF...ENDIF is the same as the DO CASE structure. The IF statement is like the first CASE, ELSEIFs act like subsequent CASEs, and ELSE acts like the OTHERWISE option.

```
DO WHILE .t.
   CLEAR
   resp = " "
   @ 10,01 SAY "Print (L)abels (I)nvoices (R)eminders (L/I/R)" ;
           GET resp PICTURE "!"
   READ
   IF resp = "L"
      DO labels
   ELSEIF resp = "I"
      DO invoices
   ELSEIF resp = "R"
      DO reminders
   ELSE
     ?? CHR(7)
     @ 24,03 SAY "Invalid key, try again."
     WAIT ""
   ENDIF
ENDDO
```

## SEE ALSO:

Commands DO CASE and ELSEIF; function IIF( ).

# IMPORT

## DIALECTS:
dBASE III PLUS and dBASE IV.

## SYNTAX:
IMPORT FROM <filename> [TYPE] PFS *(dBASE III PLUS)*

IMPORT FROM <filename> [TYPE] PFS/DBASEII
/FW2/RPD/WK1 *(dBASE IV)*

## DEFINITION:
Creates a database file (extension DBF) from a foreign file format.

The new file has the same name as the original (with a DBF extension added). If a catalog is open, the new file is added to it. When importing from a PFS format, dBASE III PLUS automatically creates FORMAT (extension FMT) and VIEW (extension VUE) files. dBASE IV creates just a FORMAT file. These files are added to the open catalog as well.

## DEFAULT:
IMPORT copies all records from the source file.

## OPTIONS:
### DBASEII
Imports a dBASE II (Ashton-Tate) database, and gives it a DB2 extension.

### FW2
Imports an Ashton-Tate Framework II (extension FW2) file.

### PFS
Imports a pfs:File data file (Software Publishing, Inc.) and creates a matching format file (extension FMT).

### RPD
Imports an Ashton-Tate Rapidfile database (extension RPD).

### WK1
Imports a Lotus 1-2-3 Release 2.x worksheet (extension WK1).

## RECOMMENDED USE:

Use IMPORT to get data from another application.

**Example**—Becky uses Lotus 1-2-3 Release 2.0 to manage data. To use the data in a dBASE report, she IMPORTs it in the WK1 format.

```
. IMPORT FROM payroll TYPE WK1
15 records added
```

## LIMITS/WARNINGS:

The file you import must not exceed the dBASE limits of 255 fields per form and 254 characters per field.

## SEE ALSO:

Commands APPEND FROM, COPY, EXPORT, and SET FORMAT.

# INDEX

## DIALECTS:

Clipper, dBASE III PLUS, dBASE IV, dBXL, FoxBASE+, and Quicksilver.

## SYNTAX:

INDEX [ON <exp> TO <filename> [UNIQUE]]

## DEFINITION:

Reorders the database in the current work area in numeric, character, or date order, according to a key expression. It does not alter the records in the database physically. Instead, INDEX creates a separate index file with references, or "pointers," to the key fields in the database file that make it appear to be rearranged physically.

An index key expression usually consists of a field, parts of a field, or combinations of fields in the active database file (See *Special Uses* for exceptions). You can combine any fields using the + or - operators. You can combine numeric and date fields using the STR( ) (string conversion) and DTOC( ) (date conversion) functions. Mixing data types in a key expression causes a "Data type mismatch" error.

The index file actually contains the key value and number of each record in its associated database file. The index file becomes active as soon as it is created. The index order is maintained as long as the index is active, or made active prior to changes to the database. You can reactivate the index file with the command:

```
SET INDEX TO <filelist>
```

or by USEing a database file with indexes as follows:

```
USE <database file> INDEX <filelist>
```

In both cases, the <filelist> may include up to seven names. When several index files are active, all are updated when their associated key fields are changed; however, the index order corresponds only to the first one in the list. We call it the *primary index.*

The index name must be a legal DOS filename.

If you SET TALK ON in dBASE III PLUS, dBASE IV, dBXL, or FoxBASE+, a counter showing the INDEX's progress appears. SET ODOMETER TO <expN> controls how often the counter is updated (except in dBXL).

## DEFAULT:

If you enter INDEX alone, dBASE III PLUS, dBASE IV, and dBXL prompt for a key expression and destination filename.

## OPTIONS:

UNIQUE makes the index include only the first of a group of records with duplicate keys. It works the same as the SET UNIQUE ON command. Records with duplicate keys remain in the database, but they are effectively hidden from most operations. If you recreate the index without the UNIQUE option, or if you USE the database file without the index, the records with duplicate keys appear as usual.

## RECOMMENDED USE:

Use an index file when doing searches with the FIND and SEEK commands. They let you do rapid searches for key expressions. Also, use index files to group data within a file. For example, in a file indexed on a date, all records with the same date stay together.

Create indexes with the UNIQUE option to hide duplicate records. To remove them from a database file permanently, first INDEX the file with the UNIQUE option (or SET UNIQUE ON). Then COPY the file to a temporary database file. Because UNIQUE hides duplicate records, COPY copies only the visible, unique records. Delete your original database and rename the temporary file to its name. Don't forget to reindex the new file.

**Example 1**—Creating an index using UNIQUE to hide records with duplicate keys. To save mailing costs, a promotions director wants to send only one flyer to each household. Because many families have the same last name, the index key also includes the address. The combination ensures unique records.

```
USE employ
LIST lname,address
Record #  lname       address
       1  Smith       189 S. Windsor Dr.
       2  Adams       237 Charleston Ave.
       3  Randall     88 Morena Blvd.
       4  Randall     88 Morena Blvd.
       5  Bailey      3101 S. Pedro St.
       6  Adams       8 Main St.
INDEX ON lname + address TO lnamedex UNIQUE
100% indexed         5 records indexed
LIST lname,address
Record #  lname       address
       2  Adams       237 Charleston Ave.
       6  Adams       8 Main St.
       5  Bailey      3101 S. Pedro St.
       3  Randall     88 Morena Blvd.
       1  Smith       189 S. Windsor Dr.
```

Note that before indexing, two records contain LNAME "Adams" and two contain "Randall." Because ADDRESS is part of the key expression, after indexing with UNIQUE, only one "Randall" appears, but two "Adams" remain.

**Example 2**—By indexing on compound keys, files can appear in groups and subgroups. A transaction file in a sales application records buyers and the amounts of their purchases. The sales manager wants to view the data in NAME order, with the amount purchased appearing in descending order, within NAME.

*Note:* To arrange a list in descending order, you must subtract AMOUNT from a number higher than any other in the database.

Because AMOUNT and NAME are different data types, the elements must be converted to a common type. The STR( ) function converts AMOUNT to character type.

```
. USE employ
. INDEX ON name + STR(99999-amount,7,2) TO empdex
100% indexed           9 Records indexed
. LIST name,amount
Record#  name         amount
      8  Hobek        145.32
      2  Hobek          2.23
      5  Rosner       999.44
      6  Rosner       383.00
      3  Rosner        33.00
      4  Rosner        23.99
      1  Sherman     2222.20
      7  Sherman        1.22
```

STR(amount,7,2) specifies a total length of seven digits (including the decimal point), with two decimal places.

## SPECIAL USES:

Index keys can contain any valid expression, including functions, memory variables, and fields from other open databases (using the ALIAS -> operator). However, the index order will not change unless the expression includes a field, or part of a field, from the selected database. Also, the index will not be properly updated if data in the unselected database is changed.

Indexing on a date field that has been converted to a character string does not produce true date order. INDEX treats a date converted with DTOC( ) like any other string. Indexing in true date order requires reordering of the date string itself, i.e., year, month, and day (YYMMDD). You can do this with the SUBSTR( ) (substring) function. The index expression is

```
. INDEX ON SUBSTR(DTOC(today),7,2) + SUBSTR(DTOC(today),4,2) + ;
          SUBSTR(DTOC(today),1,2) TO empdex
100% indexed            8 Records indexed
. LIST today
Record#  TODAY
      6  03/25/84
      1  02/18/85
      2  02/11/86
      4  02/13/86
      7  03/16/86
      5  04/16/86
      8  02/17/87
      3  01/12/88
```

Clipper, dBASE IV, dBXL, FoxBASE+, and Quicksilver have other methods of indexing on dates. See *Variations* below.

Key expressions may not involve logical or MEMO fields. However, you can simulate an index on a logical field by using the IIF( ) function to check the key field.

**Example 3**—An airline application marks passengers true (.T.) for smoking, and false for non-smoking. To group passengers by smoking preference, you must simulate an index on a logical field.

In this example, IIF( ) evaluates SMOKING. If it is true, IIF( ) assigns 1 to the index key. If false, it assigns 2. The result is a binary (2 element) numeric index, 1 representing true and 2 false.

```
. USE testfile
. LIST smoking
Record#  smoking
      1  .T.
      2  .F.
      3  .F.
      4  .T.
      5  .F.
. INDEX ON IIF(smoking,1,2)
. LIST smoking
Record#  smoking
      1  .T.
      4  .T.
      2  .F.
      3  .F.
      5  .F.
```

Index expressions may involve functions, such as string and date conversion functions. Clipper, dBXL, and Quicksilver even allow user defined functions

(UDFs) in index expressions. If you create an index using a UDF, it must be available whenever you open that index. If not, the index will be unusable.

## LIMITS/WARNINGS:

TRIM( ) causes problems in index expressions because it reduces an empty field to length 0, creating a null index key.

You can avoid this situation by padding the expression with spaces to the length of the untrimmed fields.

**Example 4**—A magazine for car aficionados maintains a list of classic roadsters in CARS.DBF. The goal is to SEEK a car in the database without worrying about trailing blanks in the index key. To achieve this, the managing editor creates an index on the TRIM( ) of three fields, permitting SEEKs for keys like "FORD, THUNDERBIRD,57".

```
Field        Fieldname  Type         Width
1            MAKE       Character     15
2            MODEL      Character     15
3            YEAR       Character      2
```

```
INDEX ON SUBSTR(TRIM(make) + TRIM(model) + TRIM(year) +;
              SPACE(32),1,32) TO car_ntx
```

The SUBSTR( ) function treats the compound key as a single string. The SPACE( ) function pads the key to the untrimmed length of the fields.

## VARIATIONS:

Blank date fields are handled inconsistently. When indexed on a date field, dBASE III PLUS, dBASE IV, and dBXL put blanks at the end. Clipper, FoxBASE+, and Quicksilver put them at the beginning.

**Clipper:** In versions before Summer '87, the current UNIQUE setting affects all open index files regardless of their UNIQUE status at creation. This error was fixed in Summer '87.

**Clipper, dBASE IV, dBXL, Quicksilver:** The DTOS( ) function (date-to-string) lets you index on dates as character strings in true date order as follows:

```
* mdate is a field
INDEX ON DTOS(mdate) TO datedex
```

This produces an index in ascending date order, in the form YYYYMMDD.

**dBASE IV:** The INDEX command also supports multiple index (MDX) format, with the syntax:

```
INDEX ON TAG <tag name> [OF <MDX filename>] [UNIQUE] [DESCENDING]
```

A multiple index file is a collection of indexes in a single DOS file. Each index has a TAG, a name of up to ten characters. TAGs follow the naming conventions for memory variables.

A database can also have a *production* multiple index file. This is an MDX with the database's name that automatically becomes active when you USE the database. If you erase a production MDX file, dBASE IV issues a warning the next time you USE the associated database file. You can then cancel the USE, or reset the production MDX flag in the database header.

If you INDEX with a TAG, but do not specify an MDX name with the OF option, INDEX checks for a production MDX. If one exists, INDEX adds the new TAG to it. If not, INDEX creates one and adds the TAG.

If you use the OF <MDX filename> option and the specified MDX file does not exist, INDEX creates a new one. If the MDX exists, but is not open, INDEX opens it.

INDEX creates separate NDX files if you do not use the TAG option.

Indexes default to ASCENDING order. When you use multiple index files, you can specify DESCENDING order. Note that the DESCENDING option applies to the entire key expression. A compound expression cannot combine DESCENDING and ASCENDING keys. NDX format indexes do not support the DESCENDING option.

The UNIQUE option works the same for MDX files as for NDX files.

**Example**—An order entry program tracks machine parts. For reporting, it creates two TAGs in a multiple index file, using ORDERED and PARTNUM.

```
USE parts
* Create TAG on part number.
INDEX ON partnum TAG partnum        && If no production MDX exists,
                                    &&    one will be created.
* Create TAG on descending order date.
INDEX ON ordered TAG ordered DESCENDING
```

A third TAG is created in a second MDX file, TRANS_MDX, using the part NAME:

```
INDEX ON name TAG name OF trans_mdx
```

**dBXL/Quicksilver:** WordTech recommends avoiding TRIM( ) in index key expressions.

**FoxBASE+:** An optional numeric argument (1) in the DTOC( ) function permits direct date indexing, as follows:

```
* mdate is a field
INDEX ON DTOC(mdate,1) TO datedex
```

This produces an index in ascending date order, in the form YYYYMMDD.

In multiuser applications, you must have exclusive use of a database before INDEXing.

Quicksilver allows the index status to be displayed, but only when selected as a library-installed option.

## INDEX COMPATIBILITY:

**Clipper:** Default indexes have an NTX extension. They are not compatible with dBASE III PLUS index files. You can specify compatible (NDX) indexes by linking NDX.OBJ (on the system disk) to your application.

**dBASE III PLUS:** Creates index files with an NDX extension.

**dBXL and Quicksilver:** Both use dBASE III PLUS compatible indexes; however, WordTech notes some differences between the two in evaluating numeric keys. To avoid discrepancies, convert numeric keys to character using the STR( ) function.

**FoxBASE+:** Indexes have an IDX extension. They are not compatible with dBASE III PLUS index files. However, when FoxBASE+ detects a dBASE III PLUS index, it automatically builds a matching index in its own format.

## SEE ALSO:

Commands REINDEX, SET INDEX TO, SET ODOMETER, SET ORDER, SET UNIQUE, SORT, and USE; functions DTOS( ), NDX( ), MDX( ), SPACE( ), SUBSTR( ), TAG( ), and TRIM( ).

# INPUT

## DIALECTS:

Clipper, dBASE III PLUS, dBASE IV, dBXL, FoxBASE+, and Quicksilver.

## SYNTAX:

INPUT [<expC>] TO <memory variable>

## DEFINITION:

Prompts the user to enter data into a memory variable. The data may be any valid expression, and its type determines the variable's type.

All character data must be delimited with double quotation marks, single quotation marks, or square brackets.

Numeric data does not require delimiters.

To terminate data entry, press the Enter key. If the user presses Enter without entering any data, the INPUT command repeats.

## OPTIONS:

PROMPT displays a message. If the prompt is a character string, you must surround it with square brackets, single quotation marks, or double quotation marks. If it is a memory variable, do not use delimiters.

Without the PROMPT option, only the cursor appears on the screen.

## RECOMMENDED USE:

Use INPUT to gather data for simple applications that do not require validation.

**Example 1**—A school administrator uses INPUT when computing students' grade point averages.

```
* Capture the grade for each class.
INPUT "Enter the grade for Math 2A: " to math2A
INPUT "Enter the grade for Chem 1C: " TO chem1C
INPUT "Enter the grade for Microbiology: "  TO micro
INPUT "Total number of courses: " TO courses
gpa = (math2A + chem1C + micro) / courses
? "Grade point average is: " + STR(gpa,4,2)
```

On the screen, the output from this program would appear as follows (with the user's input):

```
Enter the grade for Math 2A: 3
Enter the grade for Chem 1C: 3.33
Enter the grade for Microbiology: 2
Total number of courses: 3
Grade point average is: 2.78
```

*Note:* INPUT is like ACCEPT. However, ACCEPT allows only character data, whereas INPUT accepts any valid expression.

## SEE ALSO:

Command ACCEPT.

# INSERT

## DIALECTS:

dBASE III PLUS, dBASE IV, dBXL, FoxBASE+, and Quicksilver.

## SYNTAX:

INSERT [BEFORE] [BLANK]

## DEFINITION:

Adds a record to the active database file just after the current record.

After you INSERT a record, the computer displays it for full-screen data entry. If you SET CARRY ON, the display has the contents of the preceding record.

To enter data into a memo field, place the cursor on the memo label and press Ctrl-PgDn. To save the memo, press Ctrl-End. Press ESC to exit and abandon changes.

INSERT works like APPEND on an indexed file.

## OPTIONS:

BEFORE puts the new record ahead of the current one. For example, if the pointer is at record 99 when you issue INSERT BEFORE, the new record becomes record 99, the old 99 becomes record 100, and all succeeding records have their numbers increase by 1.

BLANK adds a new record, but does not open it for full-screen editing.

## RECOMMENDED USE:

Use INSERT primarily during interactive use of dBASE III PLUS, dBASE IV, FoxBASE+, or dBXL. You can use INSERT BLANK in programs, but it works only with unindexed files (with an active index, a new blank record immediately changes position).

## VARIATIONS:

**dBXL, Quicksilver:** INSERT AUTOMEM sets the fields to the values of the corresponding AUTOMEM variables (they have the same names as fields in the current database). When there are no variables, INSERT AUTOMEM inserts a blank record. The BEFORE option works with either AUTOMEM or BLANK.

**Quicksilver:** Requires either the BLANK or the AUTOMEM option.

## SEE ALSO:

Commands APPEND and SET CARRY ON.

# INTRO

## DIALECTS:
dBXL only.

## SYNTAX:
INTRO

## DEFINITION:
Starts the menu help system, providing an interactive user interface.

INTRO works like ASSIST in dBASE III PLUS.

## SEE ALSO:
Commands ASSIST and HELP.

# JOIN

## DIALECTS:

Clipper, dBASE III PLUS, dBASE IV, dBXL, FoxBASE+, and Quicksilver.

## SYNTAX:

JOIN WITH <alias> TO <filename> FOR <condition> [FIELDS <field list>]

## DEFINITION:

Merges selected records from two databases to create a third database. Using an expression, such as ACCOUNTNO = "A2347" or AMOUNT = 1259.99, the JOIN command tests conditions in both database files. It creates a record in the new file for every combination of records for which the expression is true.

JOIN pairs every record in the active database file with every record of another open file. For example, given an expression that is true for all records, every record in file TEST1 will JOIN with every record in file TEST2. If TEST1 and TEST2 each contain 100 records, their JOIN file will contain 10,000 records.

In dBASE III PLUS and dBASE IV, JOIN causes a catalog to be updated if SET CATALOG is ON.

## OPTIONS:

A FIELD <field list> limits the fields put in the new JOIN file. Without it, the JOIN file contains everything except memo fields from both database files. (A field list defined by the SET FIELDS command also limits the fields put in the new JOIN file.)

The FIELD list may contain any type of field except memo.

In the FIELD list, you must use ALIAS->fieldname to refer to a field in the unselected database with a duplicate fieldname.

## RECOMMENDED USE:

To use JOIN, open a database file in the selected work area, and another in an unselected work area. To refer to fields from the unselected area, use the syntax:

```
ALIAS->fieldname
```

Use JOIN to merge databases that have records related by a key field, such as an account number or identification number.

**Example 1**—A hardware store manager wants to list power tools and the customers who have bought them. As is common in multi-file applications, different types of data are stored in separate files. This is useful for storage efficiency and performance; however, it can make reporting difficult. Tool information is in TOOLS.DBF. Customer transactions are in SALES.DBF. In both files, field PARTNO identifies the tool. By JOINing for PARTNO in SALES equal to PARTNO in TOOLS, the manager creates a summary file. He or she can then produce the desired report with a simple LIST command.

```
. USE tools
. LIST
Record#  TOOL                  PARTNO
      1  B&D Electric Drill    1001
      2  Band Saw              1111
      3  Chain Saw             3222
      4  Table Saw             3331
      5  Drill Press           5455

. SELECT 2
. USE sales
. LIST
Record#  CUSTOMER           AMOUNT PARTNO
      1  Barnard            122.77 1111
      2  Hawkins            888.76 1001
      3  Jimenez            211.22 3331
      4  King               283.33 5455
      5  Sanchez           2838.00 3222

. SELECT 1
. JOIN WITH sales TO history FOR partno = sales->partno
 5 records joined
. USE history
. LIST
Record#  TOOL                 PARTNO CUSTOMER          AMOUNT
      1  B&D Electric Drill    1001   Hawkins           888.76
      2  Band Saw              1111   Barnard           122.77
      3  Chain Saw             3222   Sanchez          2838.00
      4  Table Saw             3331   Jimenez           211.22
      5  Drill Press           5455   King              283.33
```

## LIMITS/WARNINGS:

Use JOIN carefully. A simple JOIN of two 100-record database files could create a file with 10,000 records. JOIN is an extremely time-consuming activity, and it could create a file larger than your computer's disk storage capacity.

In practice, you can ensure reasonable file size only by not using JOIN on large files.

JOIN begins with the first record in the active database and evaluates the expression for every record in the second database. It then moves to the next record in the active database, and so on. The process continues until the computer reaches the end of the active file.

JOIN can also easily exceed a database's field limits. When no field list is specified, JOIN first merges fields from the first database. It then starts selecting fields from the second database.

## SEE ALSO:

Command SELECT and SET RELATION.

# KEYBOARD

## DIALECTS:

Clipper, dBXL, FoxBASE+, and Quicksilver.

## SYNTAX:

KEYBOARD <expC>

## DEFINITION:

Inserts the specified character expression into the keyboard buffer. For example, the command

```
KEYBOARD "A" + CHR(13) + "C" + CHR(13)
```

puts the letters "A" and "C" into the keyboard buffer, each followed by a carriage return.

## RECOMMENDED USE:

Use KEYBOARD to automate menu selections or to create self-running demonstration programs. In effect, you can write programs that control other programs through the keyboard (like keyboard macro programs such as ProKey and SmartKey).

**Example 1**—An applications developer sells a demonstration version of a real estate program. The KEYBOARD command automates menu selections so the prospective buyer can watch the program execute. The command

```
KEYBOARD "1" + CHR(13) + "1" + CHR(13) + "D"
```

selects option 1 from the first program menu, option 2 from the second program menu, and selection "D" from the third program menu.

## SPECIAL USES:

**Clipper (pre-Summer '87 versions):** You can use KEYBOARD to emulate CLEAR TYPEAHEAD by inserting a null string. Use the command

```
KEYBOARD ""
```

to clear the buffer before a READ and a GET to keep the user from entering data before reading the prompt. CLEAR TYPEAHEAD was added to Clipper Summer '87.

You can also use KEYBOARD to complete a GET with data from a HELP or SETKEY procedure. In Clipper, pressing F1 from a GET executes a procedure HELP. The SETKEY command designates a "hot key" the user can press to execute any procedure. In the HELP or SETKEY procedure, you can display a menu and KEYBOARD an item into the current GET.

**Example 2**—A data entry screen in a sales application lets the user press F1 to display customer names. The user can then move the cursor to a name and press Enter to complete the current GET with the name.

```
* ENTRY.PRG—Main data entry screen
CLEAR
CLEAR ALL
SET TALK off
PUBLIC inhelp       && Set flag INHELP to prevent HELP from calling itself.
mcust = SPACE(30)
@ 10,32 SAY "Enter customer" GET mcust
* <More GETs>.
READ


PROCEDURE help
PARAMETERS p1,p2,p3  && Parameters automatically sent, but not used here.

IF inhelp         && INHELP is true only if user presses F1 while HELP is
  RETURN          &&   already executing. If true, RETURN to previous level.
ENDIF             &&   (Recursive calls to HELP cause memory errors).
inhelp = .t.      && Set INHELP to true. (Will be reset before RETURNing).
oldalias= STR(SELECT())              && Save work area number.
SELECT 9                             && SELECT an unused work area.
USE custfile                         && File contains menu data.
ctr = 1
DO WHILE ctr < 10 .AND..NOT.EOF()    && Repeat 10 times or until
                                     &&   end-of-file.
  @ ctr,1 PROMPT customer            && Display PROMPT for each record.
  SKIP                               && SKIP to next record.
  ctr = ctr + 1                      && Increase counter.
ENDDO
MENU TO choice                       && Activate PROMPT menu and get result.
IF choice # 0         && If CHOICE is 0, do not KEYBOARD anything.
  GO choice           && GOTO record number matching CHOICE.
  KEYBOARD author     && KEYBOARD author field.
ENDIF
@ 0,0 CLEAR TO 11,31  && Clear display area.
USE                   && Close the database.
SELECT &oldalias      && Restore original work area.
inhelp = .f.          && Reset INHELP flag to false.
RETURN                && RETURN to data entry screen.
```

In dBXL and Quicksilver, the HELP option of the @...SAY...GET command can execute a user defined function. When entering data, the user can press F1 to open a help window containing a "pick list." KEYBOARD puts the user's selection into the current GET.

```
* ENTRY.PRG—Main data entry screen
CLEAR
CLEAR ALL
SET TALK off
SET UDF TO ufuncs
SET USERHELP TO 1,1,20,40 DOUBLE
mcust = SPACE(30)
@ 10,32 SAY "Enter customer " GET mcust HELP MHELP()
*  <More GETs>.
READ

* UFUNCS.PRG—User defined function file.
FUNCTION mhelp
USE custfile             && Contains a field CUSTOMER, character, 30.
DO WHILE recno() < 5
  ? STR(RECNO(),1,0) + " " + customer
  SKIP
ENDDO
INPUT "Enter a number " TO choice
GOTO choice
KEYBOARD " " + customer   && KEYBOARD customer field.
USE                       && Close the database.
RETURN ""                 && RETURN to data entry screen.
```

## LIMITS/WARNINGS:

**dBXL, Quicksilver:** When you KEYBOARD a string from a USERHELP window, the first character is truncated. (It is used to close the window). To solve this problem, add a blank to the beginning of strings KEYBOARDed from a USERHELP window, as follows:

```
customer = "Kalman Communications"
KEYBOARD " " + customer
```

or

```
KEYBOARD " Kalman Communications"
```

## SEE ALSO:

Commands @...PROMPT, CLEAR KEY, CLEAR TYPEAHEAD, and SET KEY.

# LABEL FORM

## DIALECTS:

Clipper, dBASE III PLUS, dBASE IV, dBXL, FoxBASE+, and Quicksilver.

## SYNTAX:

LABEL FORM <filename>/? [SAMPLE] [WHILE <condition>] [FOR <condition>]
[TO PRINT/TO FILE <filename>]

## DEFINITION:

Displays or prints mailing labels from the active database file using a special template file created by the CREATE/MODIFY LABEL command.

## DEFAULT:

Without any options, LABEL FORM displays labels on the screen for all records in the database. Use the <scope>, WHILE, and FOR options to select records.

## OPTIONS:

TO PRINT prints labels. TO FILE <filename> saves them in an ASCII text file. The file's extension is TXT unless you specify otherwise.

SAMPLE prints one label so the user can check and adjust alignments.

? presents a menu of available label forms.

## RECOMMENDED USE:

LABEL FORM provides an easy to use, but limited, label printing capability. Sophisticated applications that involve repeating labels or multiple-across labels must be programmed.

**Example**—Print labels from file CLIENTS with label file CLABELS. STATE is a field in CLIENTS. Print labels for which the STATE field is "CA" in the NEXT 10 records.

```
USE clients
LABEL FORM clabels SAMPLE NEXT 10 FOR state = "CA" TO PRINT
```

## VARIATIONS:

**dBASE IV:** LABEL FORM searches first for a file with an LBO extension (a compiled label form), then LBG (a generated form), then LBL (source form).

If you have installed a printer driver other than ASCII.DPR, the TO FILE option produces a file with a TXT extension. (Text files created for a printer driver have a PRT extension and may contain escape codes for special print attributes.)

When you first CREATE or MODIFY LABEL, dBASE IV creates an LBL file and an LBG file. When you print labels with LABEL FORM, dBASE IV compiles the LBG file into an LBO file and runs the LBO file.

## SEE ALSO:

Commands CREATE/MODIFY LABEL.

# LIST

## DIALECTS:

Clipper, dBASE III PLUS, dBASE IV, dBXL, FoxBASE+, and Quicksilver.

## SYNTAX:

LIST [OFF] [<scope>] [<expression list>] [WHILE <condition>]
    [FOR <condition>] [OFF] [TO PRINT]

## DEFINITION:

Selects records in a database file for viewing on the screen or for printing. It works like DISPLAY, except that it does not pause when the screen is full. To pause a LIST, type Ctrl-S. To cancel it, press ESCape. Press any other key to continue.

You must SET ESCAPE ON to pause or cancel a list.

## DEFAULTS:

Shows all fields, except memos, unless otherwise specified in the expression list. You must name memo fields explicitly. When LISTing them, the text width defaults to 50 characters. Use the SET MEMOWIDTH command to change it.

Displays all records unless you specify a <scope>, FOR, or WHILE clause.

## OPTIONS:

The expression list may contain field names and expressions separated by commas, or concatenated with plus and minus signs. Using commas lets you LIST fields of different data types because each expression is independent. Using plus or minus signs to concatenate creates a single expression within which data types must agree.

Use <scope>, the FOR clause, and the WHILE clause to select records to LIST.

OFF omits record numbers at the start of each line.

## RECOMMENDED USE:

Use LIST with scopes and conditions to formulate database queries.

**Example**—An employment agency wants to LIST all applicants with B.A. degrees. The database file APLCANT contains employment applications for positions in literary research. The TO PRINT option prints the listing.

```
. USE aplcant
. LIST lname,fname,degree,area FOR degree = "BA" TO PRINT
Record#   lname          fname           degree area
     13   Salinger       James           BA     Modern British Fiction
     29   Blackmoor      Susan           BA     Shakespearean Drama
     36   Edelstein      Edward          BA     Walt Whitman
     52   D'Gregorio     Alfredo         BA     Middle English Studies
```

## VARIATIONS:

**Clipper:** Requires a field list. Clipper does not display the field names with the data. The TO FILE option sends the results to a text file.

**Clipper, dBXL, FoxBASE+, Quicksilver:** SET ESCAPE OFF does not deactivate Ctrl-S (pause).

**dBASE III PLUS/dBASE IV/dBXL/FoxBASE+:** SET HEADING OFF omits the field names.

**dBASE IV:** The TO FILE <filename> option sends results to a text file with a TXT extension.

## SEE ALSO:

Commands DISPLAY, SET HEADING, and SET MEMOWIDTH.

# LIST FILES

## DIALECTS:

Clipper, dBASE III PLUS, dBASE IV, dBXL, FoxBASE+, and Quicksilver.

## SYNTAX:

LIST FILES [ON <drive/dir>] [LIKE <skeleton>] [TO PRINT]

## DEFINITION:

Lists names of files on the specified disk drive and directory. Same as DISPLAY FILES, except that it does not pause when the screen fills.

## VARIATIONS:

**dBASE IV:** The TO FILE <filename> option sends output to a text file with a TXT extension.

## SEE ALSO:

Commands DIR/DIRECTORY and DISPLAY FILES.

# LIST HISTORY

## DIALECTS:
dBASE III PLUS, dBASE IV, dBXL, and FoxBASE+.

## SYNTAX:
LIST HISTORY [LAST <expN>] [TO PRINT]

## DEFINITION:
Shows the latest commands in order, with the most recently executed ones at the bottom. Same as DISPLAY HISTORY, except that it does not pause when the screen fills.

## VARIATION:
**dBASE IV:** The TO FILE <filename> option sends output to a text file with a TXT extension.

## SEE ALSO:
Commands DISPLAY HISTORY, SET DOHISTORY, and SET HISTORY.

# LIST MEMORY

## DIALECTS:
dBASE III PLUS, dBASE IV, dBXL, FoxBASE+, and Quicksilver.

## SYNTAX:
LIST MEMORY [TO PRINT]

## DEFINITION:
Displays information about active memory variables. Same as DISPLAY MEMORY, except that it does not pause when the screen fills.

## VARIATION:
**dBASE IV:** The TO FILE <filename> option sends output to a text file with a TXT extension.

## SEE ALSO:
Command DISPLAY MEMORY.

# LIST STATUS

## DIALECTS:
dBASE III PLUS, dBASE IV, dBXL, FoxBASE+, and Quicksilver.

## SYNTAX:
LIST STATUS [TO PRINT]

## DEFINITION:
Displays general status information such as open database files, function key assignments, and the state of SET commands. Same as DISPLAY STATUS, except that it does not pause when the screen fills.

## VARIATION:
**dBASE IV:** The TO FILE <filename> option sends output to a text file with a TXT extension.

## SEE ALSO:
Command DISPLAY STATUS.

# LIST STRUCTURE

## DIALECTS:
dBASE III PLUS, dBASE IV, dBXL, FoxBASE+, and Quicksilver.

## SYNTAX:
LIST STRUCTURE [TO PRINT]

## DEFINITION:
Shows the database name, number of records, date of last update, number of bytes per record, and fields of each record for the active database. Same as DISPLAY STRUCTURE, except that it does not pause when the screen fills.

## VARIATION:
**dBASE IV:** The TO FILE <filename> option sends output to a text file with a TXT extension. The IN <alias> option lets you LIST the STRUCTURE of an unselected database.

## SEE ALSO:
Command DISPLAY STRUCTURE.

# LIST USERS

## DIALECTS:
dBASE IV only.

## SYNTAX:
LIST USERS

## DEFINITION:
Shows workstations currently logged into dBASE IV on a local area network.

Same as DISPLAY USERS, except that it does not pause when the screen fills.

## SEE ALSO:
Command DISPLAY USERS; functions NETNAME( ) and NETWORK( )

# LOAD

## DIALECTS:
dBASE III PLUS, dBASE IV, dBXL, FoxBASE+, and Quicksilver.

## SYNTAX:
LOAD <filename>

## DEFINITION:
Puts a binary program (extension BIN) in memory for CALL to execute. The use of assembly language binary programs allows advanced programmers to access operating system functions and hardware operations that the dBASE language does not support. For example, they can check the system for valid disk drives, determine whether communications ports are available, or identify the type of display.

You can remove binary programs from memory with the RELEASE MODULE <module name> command.

## VARIATIONS:
**Clipper:** Lets you link external programs.

**dBASE III PLUS, FoxBASE+:** Limit of 16 binary programs.

**dBXL, Quicksilver:** Limit of 10 binary programs.

## SEE ALSO:
Commands CALL/CCALL and RELEASE MODULE.

# LOGOUT

## DIALECTS:

dBASE IV only.

## SYNTAX:

LOGOUT

## DEFINITION:

Ends a user's session and presents a security login screen for the next user.

LOGOUT resets dBASE IV to its startup condition. It clears the screen, clears memory, and closes all files. It then presents the login screen, which asks for group name, user name, and password.

You must first define login security with the PROTECT command. Otherwise LOGOUT resets dBASE IV to its startup condition and returns you to the dot prompt.

## RECOMMENDED USE:

Use LOGOUT when a new user takes over at a workstation or to change workgroups during a session.

## SEE ALSO:

Commands PROTECT and SET ENCRYPTION; functions ACCESS( ) and USER( ).

# LOOP

## DIALECTS:
Clipper, dBASE III PLUS, dBASE IV, dBXL, FoxBASE+, and Quicksilver.

## SYNTAX:
LOOP

## DESCRIPTION:
Returns program control to the top of DO WHILE... ENDDO loop.

## VARIATIONS:
**dBASE IV:** LOOP also works with SCAN...ENDSCAN.

## SEE ALSO:
Commands DO WHILE and SCAN...ENDSCAN.

# MENU TO

## DIALECTS:

Clipper and FoxBASE+.

## SYNTAX:

MENU TO <memory variable> [MESSAGE <expC>]

## DEFINITION:

Creates a "bounce bar" menu that lets users point to selections with a highlighted cursor bar. They can make choices from the menu by moving the bar to a prompt with the arrow keys, and then pressing the Enter, PgUp, or PgDn keys. Alternatively, pressing the first character of a selection will highlight and select it.

MENU TO requires a series of @PROMPT commands. It invokes the menu, allowing the cursor to move between PROMPTs. Upon selection, MENU TO stores the PROMPT's relative number in a memory variable. You can then use the number in a CASE expression.

Pressing ESCape stores 0 in the memory variable. You can use this as an alternate exit condition.

## OPTIONS:

When the menu bar moves to a prompt, you can display an associated MESSAGE. The MESSAGE option prints a character string on the line specified in the SET MESSAGE TO command (the default is line 24, column 0).

## RECOMMENDED USE:

Use the MENU TO command to provide menus that require minimal typing skill. Users find such menus friendly and easy to use.

**Example**—A payroll program contains a menu with four options. By moving the cursor bar with the arrow keys, the bookkeeper can make selections easily. When he or she presses Enter, the relative number of the prompt is saved in the variable ACTION. The first prompt stores 1 in ACTION, the second 2, etc. The DO CASE structure evaluates ACTION and does the appropriate program. Selecting prompt 4, EXIT TO MAIN MENU, stores 4 in ACTION and

RETURNs control to the previous menu. Pressing the ESCape key has the same effect except that it stores 0 in ACTION.

```
SET MESSAGE TO 1    && Display optional prompt message
@ 05,10 PROMPT "Maintenance Menu " MESSAGE "Reindex files"
@ 06,10 PROMPT "Query Menu       " MESSAGE "Ask questions"
@ 07,10 PROMPT "Post Payroll     " MESSAGE "Update main database"
@ 09,10 PROMPT "Exit to Main Menu" MESSAGE "Return to start point"
MENU TO action
DO CASE
  CASE action = 1       && User selected first prompt.
    DO maint
  CASE action = 2       && User selected second prompt.
    DO query
  CASE action = 3       && User selected third prompt.
    DO post
  CASE action = 0 .OR. action = 4   && Exit program on 0 (ESC) or 4.
  RETURN
ENDCASE
```

## LIMITS:

The number of PROMPTs cannot exceed 32; however, you can nest them to allow more selections.

## VARIATIONS:

**Clipper:** The cursor bar stops at the top and bottom of the menu by default; however, you can SET WRAP ON to make it "wrap" between them.

**Clipper:** Pressing F1 from a MENU TO menu executes a help procedure or program HELP and sends it three parameters: the calling program or procedure name, the line number in the caller, and the MENU TO variable name. This lets you write context sensitive help programs. Pressing F1 from an active GET...READ also calls HELP and sends the same parameters.

**FoxBASE+** Cursor bar always "wraps" between the top and bottom prompts.

## SEE ALSO:

Commands @...GET, @...PROMPT, PARAMETERS, and SET MESSAGE.

# MODIFY

## DIALECTS:
dBASE III PLUS, dBASE IV, dBXL, and FoxBASE+.

## SYNTAX:
MODIFY LABEL <label form>
MODIFY QUERY <query file>
MODIFY REPORT <report form>
MODIFY SCREEN <screen file>
MODIFY STRUCTURE <filename>
MODIFY VIEW <view file>

## DEFINITION:
Invokes interactive programs to change label forms, query files, report forms, screen files, database files, and view files.

See the corresponding CREATE commands for more details.

## SEE ALSO:
Commands CREATE and CREATE COMMAND/LABEL/QUERY/REPORT/SCREEN/VIEW.

# MODIFY COMMAND

## DIALECTS:

dBASE III PLUS, dBASE IV, dBXL, and FoxBASE+.

## SYNTAX:

MODIFY COMMAND/FILE <filename>

## DEFINITION:

Calls up the full-screen program editor. If the file does not exist, MODIFY COMMAND creates it. If it exists, MODIFY COMMAND displays it for editing.

If you do not specify an extension, MODIFY COMMAND assumes PRG (that is, a dBASE command file).

MODIFY COMMAND uses WordStar-like Ctrl-key combinations and cursor keys to navigate through and manipulate text. Ctrl-W or Ctrl-End exits and saves changes. ESC or Ctrl-Q exits without saving changes. F1 toggles the help menu.

You may substitute a word processor or other text editor by modifying the CONFIG file. Add the following line to the dBASE III PLUS or dBASE IV CONFIG.DB file, the FoxBASE+ CONFIG.FX file, or the dBXL CONFIG.XL file:

```
TEDIT=<external word processor>
```

For example, to use WordStar to edit programs, enter:

```
TEDIT=WS
```

Do not put quotation marks around the word processor's name. You can specify any word processor or text editor that produces ASCII text files, as long as enough memory is available to run it.

## LIMITS/WARNINGS:

**Note:** You cannot edit memo fields with MODIFY COMMAND. Use the CHANGE or EDIT commands, move the cursor to the memo field, and press Ctrl-PgUp to begin editing.

MODIFY COMMAND has an annoying 68 character word wrap feature that cannot be disabled.

## VARIATIONS:

**dBASE III PLUS:** The largest file you can edit is 5K bytes, unless you specify an external word processor. This restriction militates against using the internal text editor. You will get a warning message if a file exceeds the limit, but only after the file is loaded and susceptible to damage.

**dBASE IV:** After editing a program, MODIFY COMMAND automatically erases its associated object file (extension DBO). The next time you DO the edited program, dBASE IV creates a new object file.

If you replace the MODIFY COMMAND editor with an external editor, you must then manually delete related DBO files, or SET DEVELOPMENT ON. With SET DEVELOPMENT ON, the next time you DO <program>, dBASE IV compares the dates of the PRG and DBO file. If the PRG file is newer, dBASE will recompile it, producing a new DBO file. You can also SET DEVELOPMENT in the CONFIG.DB file with the statement:

```
DEVELOPMENT = ON
```

MODIFY COMMAND files are limited to 32 megabytes, effectively removing all restrictions.

MODIFY COMMAND operates in the active window; however, you can specify an alternate window with the syntax:

MODIFY COMMAND/FILE <filename> WINDOW <window name>

An error message appears if the window does not exist.

**dBXL:** CREATE COMMAND is the same as MODIFY COMMAND, except that it assumes you are creating a new program. CREATE FILE is also similar, except that it does not assume a default extension of PRG.

The MODIFY COMMAND editor offers menu prompting, plus access to disk and environment information using the F1 key. It is also more reliable. It only loads a file if there is enough room in memory to accommodate it safely. If a file is too big, an error message appears before it is loaded. You can execute a program statement by putting the cursor on it and pressing Alt-E. Control returns to the editor afterward.

**FoxBASE+:** MAXMEM in the CONFIG.FX file sets the maximum file size. Like dBASE III PLUS, FoxBASE+ does not protect oversized files from inadvertent damage. An error message appears stating that "data may be lost," but this does not prevent the damaged file from being saved on disk. When you see the message, you must either continue, knowing that a portion of your program may be lost, or abandon the file without saving it.

## SEE ALSO:

Commands CHANGE/EDIT, COMPILE, CREATE, CREATE COMMAND, CREATE FILE, RUN, and SET DEVELOPMENT.

# MODIFY FILE

## DIALECTS:

dBXL only.

## SYNTAX:

MODIFY/CREATE FILE <filename>

## DEFINITION:

Creates or changes ASCII text files. Same as MODIFY COMMAND.

## SEE ALSO:

Command MODIFY COMMAND.

# MODIFY GRAPH

## DIALECTS:
dBXL only.

## SYNTAX:
MODIFY/CREATE GRAPH <filename>

## DEFINITION:
Starts an interactive program for defining pie charts, bar graphs, step graphs, line graphs, scatter plots, and regression lines. Same as CREATE GRAPH.

## SEE ALSO:
Command CREATE GRAPH.

# MOVE WINDOW

## DIALECTS:

dBASE IV only.

## SYNTAX:

MOVE WINDOW <window name> TO <row>,<col> /
BY <relative row>,<relative col>

## DEFINITION:

Moves a window to a new position.

You can move the specified window to exact coordinates with the TO <row>,<col> option. You can move it relative to its position with the BY <row>,<col> option. For example, TO 01,01 moves the window's top left corner to coordinate 01,01. BY 01,01 moves the window's top left corner down one row and right one column.

If the window is active, MOVE WINDOW makes it seem to jump across the screen. If the window is in memory, but not active, it appears in the new position the next time you ACTIVATE it.

The new coordinates remain associated with the specified window until you change them again, or DEACTIVATE the WINDOW.

The BY option may use negative row and column numbers. Both the TO and BY <row>,<col> ranges depend on the window's size. Windows may not extend beyond the screen boundary.

## RECOMMENDED USE:

Use MOVE WINDOW to animate screen displays without DEACTIVATing and ACTIVATing windows.

**Example**—The greeting message of an accounting program moves around the screen to catch the user's attention.

```
DEFINE WINDOW greeting FROM 4,5 TO 10,60
ACTIVATE WINDOW greeting
@ 2,2 SAY "Welcome to Account Tracker"
ctr = 1
DO WHILE ctr <= 5
```

```
  MOVE WINDOW greeting BY ctr,1      && Each time CTR increases by 1, the
  ctr = ctr + 1                      &&   window moves down one row.
ENDDO
ctr = 1
DO WHILE ctr => -5
  MOVE WINDOW greeting BY ctr,1      && Each time CTR decreases by 1, the
  ctr = ctr - 1                      &&   window moves up one row.
ENDDO
MOVE WINDOW greeting TO 5,5          && Finally, move window directly to 5,5.
ACTIVATE SCREEN                      && Select the full screen.
```

## SEE ALSO:

Commands ACTIVATE SCREEN, ACTIVATE WINDOW, DEFINE WINDOW, RESTORE WINDOW, and SAVE WINDOW.

# NOTE/*/&&

## DIALECTS:

Clipper, dBASE III PLUS, dBASE IV, dBXL, FoxBASE+, and Quicksilver.

## SYNTAX:

NOTE [<text>]

or

* [<text>]

or

[<statement>] && [<text>]

## DEFINITION:

Lets you add program documentation or notes to programs. Any form will do at the beginning of a line. You may use only && to put text after a statement; the program statement must come first.

## RECOMMENDED USE:

Notes and documentation are invaluable for maintaining programs. With time, you will surely forget what program segments and procedures do. Notes act as reminders, and let you track changes.

Also, you can use asterisks to make programs more legible by using them to delineate sections.

**Example**—Part of a scrolling program that illustrates different ways to add notes. Use whichever form seems most legible and sensible.

```
* PAGE.PRG—A PROGRAM FOR SCROLLING THROUGH RECORDS
*           IN A NAME AND ADDRESS DATABASE FILE
NOTE - PROGRAM UPDATED 7/3/87
CLEAR
USE NAMES  && CONTAINS MEMBERSHIP INFORMATION.
@ 10,10 SAY "NAME: "
@ 11,10 SAY "ADDRESS: "
*
DO WHILE .T.
  @ 10,16 SAY NAME          && SHOW FULL NAME
  @ 11,16 SAY ADDRESS
  ACTion = " "
  @ 12,10 SAY "(F)wd (B)wd (R)eturn? (F/B/R) " GET action PICT "!"
  READ
  * <More statements>.   *
```

## LIMITS/WARNINGS:

A semicolon at the end of a line continues the note onto the next line. Be careful—if you put a valid command on the next line, dBASE ignores it. (The semicolon is the line continuation character).

Notes can slow the execution of dBASE III PLUS and dBXL programs. Such slowing is negligible unless you use extensive notes between commands, or within DO WHILE loops that parse them repeatedly.

Clipper, dBASE IV, FoxBASE+, and Quicksilver strip program notes from their runtime modules.

## VARIATIONS:

**Clipper:** The semicolon does not continue a note onto the next line.

**dBXL/Quicksilver:** *\ indicates a comment in Clipper, dBASE III PLUS, dBASE IV, and FoxBASE+, but is a valid command in Quicksilver and dBXL. It lets programmers include Quicksilver- and dBXL-specific commands in programs that will be run with other systems.

The Quicksilver compiler option -\ turns off the special handling of *\. Quicksilver then treats *\ as a comment.

Add the statement COMMENT=ON to the dBXL configuration file (CONFIG.XL) to turn off the special handling of *\. dBXL then treats *\ as a comment.

**Quicksilver:** The commands *QSOFF and *QSON let you compile and run applications that contain unsupported commands. All text between *QSOFF and *QSON is ignored. For example:

```
IF xquicks
  @ 10,10 SAY "Description  " GET descrip
  @ 11,10 SAY "Serial number" GET serial
  READ
ELSE
  *QSOFF
  BROWSE
  *QSON
ENDIF
```

lets you include the BROWSE statement in a Quicksilver program.

The other systems treat *QSOFF and *QSON like program notes.

## SEE ALSO:

Commands *, &&, and PUBLIC.

# ON ERROR/ON ESCAPE/ON KEY

## DIALECTS:

Clipper (except ON KEY), dBASE III PLUS, dBASE IV, dBXL, FoxBASE+, and Quicksilver.

## SYNTAX:

ON ERROR [<command>]
ON ESCAPE [<command>]
ON KEY [<command>]

## DEFINITION:

Execute a command on a condition. ERROR refers to DBMS errors, such as "Syntax error" or "File Not Found." ON ERROR does not detect operating system or hardware errors. ESCAPE refers to a press of the ESC key. KEY refers to a press of any key. ON's common use is to cause a branch to another program or procedure using the DO command.

ON remains active until you specify another ON with the same condition. You can check which ON statements are active with the DISPLAY STATUS command. To deactivate an ON command, issue ON ERROR, ON ESCAPE, or ON KEY by itself. You can also disable ON ESCAPE with SET ESCAPE OFF.

## RECOMMENDED USE:

With ON KEY, a command that is executing when a key is pressed, such as COPY, LOCATE, or SORT, will finish before the program stops.

When using ON KEY, be sure to clear the keyboard buffer with an INKEY( ) or a READ in the program to which you branch. Failure to do so may cause ON KEY to repeat indefinitely when a key is pressed. Some commands, such as ON KEY WAIT TO <memory variable>, clear the keyboard buffer automatically. The WAIT TO clears the KEY and STOREs its value in the specified memory variable.

When using ON ERROR, note that IFs and DO WHILEs are not re-evaluated upon return to the erroneous program.

The three ON commands may be active simultaneously. ON ESCAPE takes precedence over ON KEY. That is, pressing the ESCape key makes the computer execute its command. When ESCAPE is SET OFF and ON KEY is active, the ESCape key acts like any other key and ON KEY will detect it.

**Example 1**—An error condition can sometimes damage or destroy data. A programmer may prefer to be notified when an error occurs, rather than have a user try to correct it. In this example, ON ERROR executes a generic error-handling procedure that tells the user what has happened.

```
* MAIN.PRG
CLEAR
ON ERROR DO gen_err     && GEN_ERR is a program that lets user
                        &&   exit without damaging data files.
USE lmain               && Try to use a file that does not exist.
@ 10,10 SAY "************ AGED RECEIVABLES ************"
@ 11,10 SAY "*                                        *"
** <more statements>

* GEN_ERR.PRG
CLEAR
ON ERROR   && Disable succeeding ON ERRORs to avoid repeating GEN_ERR.
@ 10,10 SAY "The program has run into a little trouble."
@ 11,10 SAY "Please notify the programmer that an error exists."
@ 12,10 SAY "Exiting now until the problem can be determined."
CLEAR ALL
CANCEL
```

**Example 2**—Programmers often use ESCape as a convenient way to exit a menu. ON ESCAPE lets the programmer execute a command with the ESCape key, without SETting ESCAPE OFF. In this example, ESC stores "R" in the variable ACTION, and returns control to the main menu.

```
* MAINMENU.PRG
* The ESC key stores the character "R" in memory variable ACTION.
CLEAR
ON ESCAPE action = "R"
action = " "
@ 1,1 SAY "<N>ew record"
@ 2,1 SAY "<E>dit record"
@ 3,1 SAY "<R>eturn to main menu"
@ 5,1 SAY "Your Choice (N/E/R)? " GET action pict "!"
READ
* When memory variable ACTION equals "R", the program executes RETURN.
DO CASE
  CASE action = "N"
    DO newrec
  CASE action = "E"
    DO edrec
  CASE action = "R"
    RETURN
ENDCASE
```

**Example 3**—ON KEY is useful for interrupting an automated process such as a print job. It lets the user pause the job to adjust paper, load labels, etc. In this example, the program lists records on the printer. When the user presses a key, procedure PAUSE pauses the program and prompts for a response of (R)esume or (Q)uit. If you select "R", the listing resumes with the next record.

```
* LISTREC.PRG
* Show a list of records, or jump to a particular record
* under program control. Processing is interrupted when a key
* is pressed. This is commonly used to interrupt print routines.
SET TALK on
SET PROCEDURE TO mainproc
USE prospects
ON KEY DO pause     && When a key is pressed, do procedure PAUSE.
SET PRINT on
DO WHILE .NOT. eof()
  ? lastname        && Display last name.
  SKIP              && Move ahead one record.
ENDDO
ON KEY              && Clear ON KEY after use.
SET PRINT off


* MAINPROC.PRG
PROCEDURE pause
SET PRINT off
CLEAR
* Clear the keypress so procedure JUMP does not repeat.
? INKEY()
response = " "
DO WHILE .not. response$"RQ"
  @ 10,10 SAY "(R)esume or (Q)uit" GET response PICTURE "!"
  READ
ENDDO
IF response = "R"
  SET PRINT on
  RETURN
ELSE
  CLEAR ALL
  CANCEL
ENDIF
```

## VARIATIONS:

Unfortunately, no two implementations of ON KEY are alike.

**Clipper:** ON KEY not available.

**dBASE IV:** ON KEY can detect specific keystrokes with the syntax

ON KEY LABEL <key>

where <key> is a specific key.

ON KEY lets you redefine many keys simultaneously.

Use the following key labels:

| | |
|---|---|
| F1 - F10 | PGUP |
| CTRL-F1 - CTRL-F10 | DEL |
| ALT-F1 - ALT-F10 | BACKSPACE |
| ALT-A - ALT-Z | TAB |
| CTRL-A- CTRL-Z | BACKTAB |
| LEFTARROW | CTRL-LEFTARROW |
| DNARROW | CTRL-RIGHTARROW |
| UPARROW | CTRL-HOME |
| RIGHTARROW | CTRL-END |
| HOME | CTRL-PGUP |
| END | CTRL-PGDN |
| PGDN | |

You can specify other keys with their labels. Labels are not case sensitive. Do not use quotation marks. Typical examples are:

```
ON KEY LABEL CTRL-A CLEAR
ON KEY LABEL DNARROW SKIP
ON KEY LABEL X DO BACKUP
```

**dBXL:** ON KEY can detect a specific keystroke. The syntax is:

ON KEY <key> <command>

where <key> is a specific key. Specify function keys with the letter F and the key number (e.g., F9). Do not put quotation marks around function key labels. Specify control keys with the caret symbol (^) and the key letter (e.g., ON KEY ^C DO BACKUP). Do not use quotation marks. You can also specify key values as two-byte hardware-specific scan codes. The dBXL manual indicates that you can specify other keys as literal strings, such as "X" or "Y". This does not work.

**FoxBASE+:** A variation of ON KEY lets you specify a particular key:

ON KEY = <expN> <command>

<expN> is either:

1) the ASCII value of a printable character, or

2) the IBM PC-specific scan code assigned to the control key plus 256.

*NOTE:* Unlike the other systems, FoxBASE+ does not save the keystroke that activates ON KEY in the keyboard buffer; therefore, it is unnecessary to clear the buffer with INKEY( ) or READ.

**Quicksilver:** You may specify a particular key to activate ON KEY as follows:

ON KEY ["<key>"] [<command>]

"<key>" is a string constant containing the key's letter or number. Specify function keys with F and the key number without quotation marks, for example, ON KEY F2. Specify control key sequences with the caret symbol (^) and a letter or number (e.g., ON KEY "^C" DO BACKUP) with quotation marks. Note: ON KEY assignments are case sensitive. Quicksilver and dBXL differ on this command.

## SEE ALSO:

Command SET KEY; function INKEY( ).

# ON EVENT

## DIALECTS:

Quicksilver only.

## SYNTAX:

ON EVENT [<command>]

## DEFINITION:

Executes a command on the condition specified in SET EVENT. ON EVENT checks continuously for the condition while the application is doing other operations.

<command> is any valid Quicksilver command.

ON EVENT with no <command> argument turns ON EVENT off.

## RECOMMENDED USE:

Use ON EVENT and SET EVENT to monitor the clock, keyboard, serial ports, and other system devices. You can also use it to simply monitor conditions within your application, such as EOF( ) or LASTNAME = "Smith."

**Example**—A scheduling application uses ON EVENT to remind users of important appointments. By monitoring the system clock, the application can display a message and ring the bell at a specific time of day.

```
* APPT.PRG—Appointment scheduler.
WSET WINDOW evnt TO 1,1,20,60 DOUBLE
SET EVENT TO TIME()="15:30:00"   && 3:30 p.m.
ON EVENT DO reminder
* <Statements>.
* End of program.

* REMINDER.PRG
oldselect = WSELECT()           && Save old window area.
WSELECT 98                      && Select any unused window area.
WUSE evnt
?? + CHR(7) + CHR(7) + CHR(7) + CHR(7)
@ 10,05 SAY "Don't forget your appointment at: " + TIME()
@ 11,05 SAY "Press a key to continue"
WAIT ""
WCLOSE
WSELECT oldselect               && Restore previous window area.
RETURN
```

With ON EVENT and SET EVENT, you can use binary programs (extension BIN) to monitor system devices, such as a modem. For example, WordTech provides two programs CHECKCOM.BIN and GETCOM.BIN. CHECKCOM monitors serial port COM1 for input. When it detects an incoming character, GETCOM captures it and saves it in the file XMODEM.RCV. Use these commands as follows:

```
LOAD GETCOM
SET EVENT TO FILE CHECKCOM
ON EVENT CALL GETCOM
```

See SET EVENT for another example.

## LIMITS/WARNINGS:

Writing binary programs for use with ON EVENT and SET EVENT requires advanced programming skills.

Quicksilver continuously executes SET EVENT between other commands and during wait states. To avoid noticeable slowing of your application, make your logical expressions and binary programs as short and efficient as possible.

## SEE ALSO:

Commands LOAD and SET EVENT.

# ON PAD

## DIALECTS:

dBASE IV only.

## SYNTAX:

ON PAD <pad name> OF <menu name> [ACTIVATE POPUP <popup name>]

## DEFINITION:

Activates a POPUP when you move the cursor bar to the specified menu PAD. The PAD is from an active menu created with the DEFINE MENU command.

When a popup appears, you can use the up and down arrow keys to move among its BARs. You can then select a BAR by pressing Enter.

ON PAD without the ACTIVATE POPUP option disables the specified PAD.

## RECOMMENDED USE:

Use ON PAD to associate a popup menu with a bar menu's selection. As the user moves the cursor from pad to pad, the associated popups appear.

**Example**—An inventory program uses a bar menu with the prompts "Inventory," "Operator," and "Exit." The ON PAD command associates POPUP INVENT with the "Inventory" selection and POPUP OPERATOR with the "Operator" selection.

```
CLEAR
SET SCOREBOARD OFF                    && Disable line 0 status messages
DEFINE MENU master
DEFINE PAD sel1 OF master PROMPT "Inventory"
DEFINE PAD sel2 OF master PROMPT "Operator"
DEFINE PAD sel3 OF master PROMPT "Exit"

DEFINE POPUP invent FROM 02,01 TO 10,20
DEFINE BAR 1 OF invent PROMPT "Add new items"
DEFINE BAR 2 OF invent PROMPT "Edit items"
DEFINE BAR 3 OF invent PROMPT "Reports"

DEFINE POPUP operator FROM 02,22 TO 10,42
DEFINE BAR 1 OF operator PROMPT "Add new operator"
DEFINE BAR 2 OF operator PROMPT "Delete operator"
DEFINE BAR 3 OF operator PROMPT "Usage Reports"
```

```
ON PAD sel1 OF MASTER ACTIVATE POPUP invent
ON PAD sel2 OF MASTER ACTIVATE POPUP operator
ON SELECTION PAD sel3 OF MASTER RETURN
ACTIVATE MENU master
```

This program produces the following menu:

Inventory menu Operator menu Exit

## LIMITS/WARNINGS:

Do not confuse ON PAD with ON SELECTION PAD. ON SELECTION PAD requires you to press Enter to make a PAD selection, whereas ON PAD requires only that you move the cursor to a PAD.

A PAD can have only one ON PAD or ON SELECTION PAD command.

## SEE ALSO:

Commands DEFINE BAR, DEFINE MENU, DEFINE PAD, DEFINE POPUP, ON SELECTION PAD, and SET SCOREBOARD.

# ON PAGE

## DIALECTS:

dBASE IV only.

## SYNTAX:

ON PAGE [AT LINE <expN> <command>]

## DEFINITION:

Executes a command when a PRINTJOB reaches the specified line number. It is typically used to print report headers and footers.

ON PAGE monitors the system memory variable _plineno. When it determines that _plineno has reached <expN>, it executes the <command>.

ON PAGE with no argument disables the previous setting.

ON PAGE works only within an active PRINTJOB...ENDPRINT.

## RECOMMENDED USE:

Use ON PAGE to execute header and footer procedures that print titles, page numbers, dates, and other data.

**Example**—An application managing a database of accredited universities uses PRINTJOB and ON PAGE to control output. Search results print on 40-line custom forms, with page footers.

```
mregion = "NORTHEAST"              && User enters region to search.
_peject = "NONE"                   && Disable page ejects.
_plength = 40                      && Set page length to 40 lines.
_pageno=1                          && Set page number to 1.
USE colleges
ON PAGE AT LINE 37 DO footer       && When at line 37, DO FOOTER procedure.
SET PRINT on
PRINTJOB                           && Begin printjob.
  DO WHILE .NOT. EOF()
    ? school,city,state,specialty
    SKIP
  ENDDO
ENDPRINT
SET PRINT off
PROCEDURE footer
?
? _pageno PICTURE [999] AT 05, "Region Search: "+mregion " AT 30
?
?
RETURN
```

## SPECIAL USE:

You can also use ON PAGE with LIST and DISPLAY.

REPORT FORMs do not require ON PAGE, since they have "built-in" headers and footers.

## LIMITS/WARNINGS:

Be sure to avoid running your footers over the page break. For example, if page length is 50 (_plength=50), and you specify ON PAGE AT LINE 48 DO footer, the footer should not have more than two lines. The third line will print on the next page.

## SEE ALSO:

Commands ?/??, LIST, PRINTJOB, PROCEDURE, REPORT FORM, SET PRINT, and SET PRINTER.

# ON READERROR

## DIALECTS:
dBASE IV only.

## SYNTAX:
ON READERROR [<command>]

## DEFINITION:
Executes a command when the user enters invalid data in an input field. Such data includes invalid dates and RANGEs, and unsatisfied VALID clauses of the @...SAY...GET command.

ON READERROR alone resets error handling to the default messages.

ON READERROR overrides the @...SAY...GET ERROR clause.

## RECOMMENDED USE:
Use ON READERROR to execute custom error handling routines for data entry screens. Use it as an alternative to the @...SAY...GET ERROR clause when you want to execute several statements in response to an error.

Also, ON READERROR does not force the user to press the space bar to recover from unsatisfied VALID, invalid RANGE, and invalid DATE errors. The user can reenter continuously until the input criteria are satisfied.

**Example**—An inventory system data entry screen uses ON READERROR to DO an error-handling procedure. The VARREAD( ) function tells the procedure which memory variable is active.

```
CLEAR
SET TALK OFF
ON READERROR DO rerror
qty = 0
desc = SPACE(20)
@ 10,10 SAY "Enter quantity:    " GET qty RANGE 0,9
@ 11,10 SAY "Enter description: " GET desc VALID LEN(TRIM(desc))>0
* <More GETs>.
READ
* <More statements>.
```

```
PROCEDURE rerror
mvar = VARREAD()          && VARREAD() returns the name of the active
*                         &&   memory variable.
DO CASE
  CASE mvar = "QTY"
    ?? CHR(7)             && Ring the bell.
    SET COLOR TO R*       && Change color of message.
    msg = "If there are more than 9 items to enter, go to Menu 1A."
  CASE mvar = "DESC"
    SET COLOR TO B+       && Change color of message.
    msg = "Please don't leave the description blank!"
  * <More cases>.
  *
ENDCASE
@ 23,00
@ 23,01 SAY msg
SET COLOR TO
RETURN
```

## SEE ALSO:

Commands @...SAY and READ; function VARREAD( ).

# ON SELECTION PAD

## DIALECTS:

dBASE IV only.

## SYNTAX:

ON SELECTION PAD <pad name> OF <menu name> [<command>]

## DEFINITION:

Executes a command when the user presses Enter to make a pad menu selection.

You create pad menus with the DEFINE MENU command. You define PADs with DEFINE PAD.

ON SELECTION PAD <pad name> OF <menu name> without a command deactivates the specified PAD.

## RECOMMENDED USE:

When you make a menu selection, program control branches to the <command> you specify (usually DO procedure or DO program). When the procedure, program, or command finishes, control returns to the menu. In this respect, the pad menu has a built-in DO WHILE and DO CASE mechanism.

**Example**—An inventory program uses a pad menu to do control procedures. When the user moves the cursor and makes a selection by pressing Enter, the ON SELECTION PAD commands execute the appropriate command or procedure.

```
SET SCOREBOARD OFF
CLEAR
USE parts        && Has two fields, PART (character), and QTY (numeric).
DEFINE MENU mparts
DEFINE PAD sel1 OF mparts PROMPT "Stock numbers for refill" AT 0,0
DEFINE PAD sel2 OF mparts PROMPT "Overstock" AT 0,30
DEFINE PAD sel3 OF mparts PROMPT "Exit" AT 0,50
ON SELECTION PAD sel1 OF mparts DO rquery
ON SELECTION PAD sel2 OF mparts DO oquery
ON SELECTION PAD sel3 OF mparts DEACTIVATE MENU
ACTIVATE MENU mparts
USE

PROCEDURE rquery                 && Sample query program.
DISPLAY part,qty FOR qty < 5
WAIT
CLEAR
RETURN
```

```
PROCEDURE oquery                   && Sample query program.
DISPLAY part,qty FOR qty > 100
WAIT
CLEAR
RETURN
```

When you have several menus, use the functions MENU( ) and PAD( ) to determine which one selected a procedure. See MENU( ) and PAD( ) for more information.

## LIMITS/WARNINGS:

Don't confuse ON SELECTION PAD with ON PAD. ON PAD executes a command as soon as the cursor touches the specified PAD. With ON SELECTION PAD, the user must press Enter. ON PAD is typically used to display popup menus as the user moves the cursor.

## SEE ALSO:

Commands DEFINE MENU, DEFINE PAD, ON PAD, and PROCEDURE; functions MENU( ), PAD( ), and PROMPT( ).

# ON SELECTION POPUP

## DIALECTS:
dBASE IV only.

## SYNTAX:
ON SELECTION POPUP <popup name> /ALL [<command>]

## DEFINITION:
Executes a command when a user presses Enter to make a POPUP menu selection. ON SELECTION POPUP executes the command when the user presses any selection. The command is typically a procedure or subroutine.

The subroutine must determine which BAR the user selected with the BAR( ) function.

## RECOMMENDED USE:
Use ON SELECTION POPUP after you DEFINE POPUP and before you ACTIVATE POPUP. Use BAR( ) to get the user's menu selection. You can then execute a CASE or use the result as the argument of another function.

**Example 1**—An educational program uses popup menus. When the user makes a selection, the program uses the bar number to execute the appropriate CASE. Each CASE executes a subroutine.

```
DEFINE POPUP educ FROM 03,05 TO 15,30
DEFINE BAR 1 OF educ PROMPT "Display students"
DEFINE BAR 2 OF educ PROMPT "Change student data"
DEFINE BAR 3 OF educ PROMPT "Delete Students"
ON SELECTION POPUP educ DO pcase    && Execute PROCEDURE pcase.
ACTIVATE POPUP educ

PROCEDURE pcase
pbar = BAR()                        && Store BAR() in a variable.
DO CASE
  CASE pbar = 1
    * <do display program>
  CASE pbar = 2
    * <do change program>
  CASE pbar = 3
    * <delete students>
ENDCASE
```

If you have multiple POPUPS, use the POPUP( ) function to identify the active one.

**Example 2**—An auto parts inventory program has a procedure containing a CASE structure that is called by two different POPUPs. To identify the calling POPUP, the procedure uses the POPUP( ) function.

```
DEFINE POPUP autos FROM 01,01 TO 10,30
DEFINE BAR 1 OF autos PROMPT "Search for pistons"
DEFINE BAR 2 OF autos PROMPT "Search for brakes"
DEFINE BAR 3 OF autos PROMPT "Transmissions parts"
ON SELECTION POPUP autos DO acase
ACTIVATE POPUP autos
DEFINE POPUP amaint FROM 11,01 TO 20,30
* <Define more bar statements>.
*

PROCEDURE acase
mbar = BAR()
popcall = POPUP()              && Get name of calling popup.
DO CASE
  CASE mbar = 1 .AND. popcall = "AUTOS"
    * <Search for pistons>.
  CASE mbar = 2 .AND. popcall = "AUTOS"
    * <Search for brakes>.
  CASE mbar = 3 .AND. popcall = "AUTOS"
    * <Transmission parts>.
  CASE mbar = 1 .AND. popcall = "AMAINT"
    *
  CASE mbar = 2 .AND. popcall = "AMAINT"
    *
ENDCASE
```

## SEE ALSO:

Commands ACTIVATE POPUP, DEFINE BAR, DEFINE POPUP, and ON SELECTION PAD; functions MENU( ), PAD( ), and PROMPT( ).

# OTHERWISE

## DIALECTS:
Clipper, dBASE III PLUS, dBASE IV, dBXL, FoxBASE+, and Quicksilver.

## SYNTAX:
OTHERWISE

## DEFINITION:
Indicates an alternative action in a CASE structure when no CASE applies.

## VARIATIONS:
**Clipper:** The ELSE statement in an IF...ELSEIF...ENDIF structure is equivalent to OTHERWISE.

## SEE ALSO:
Commands DO CASE and ELSE.

# OUT

## DIALECTS:
dBXL and Quicksilver.

## SYNTAX:
OUT <port#, expN>

## DESCRIPTION:
Sends a single numeric value to a specified output port (device) such as the speaker. OUT lets advanced programmers control hardware features not otherwise accessible in the dBASE language.

All values must be decimal, not hexadecimal, octal, or binary.

## RECOMMENDED USE:
OUT is for advanced programmers who need access to functions dBASE does not support. Possible applications include telephone dialers, graphics displays, and sound generation.

**Example**—Routine for generating tones as signals or prompts. This is an alternative to using CHR(7) to produce a beep.

```
* ENDTONE.PRG
* Generates tones as signals or prompts
SET TALK OFF
CLEAR
* Save original speaker status using IN() function
ostat = IN(97)
snum = 5
DO WHILE snum > 0
  * Designate speaker frequency in decimal
  OUT 66,151            && Speaker controller is port 66
  OUT 66,snum
  newstat = (INT(IN(97)/4)) * 4 + 3
  OUT 97,newstat        && System speaker is port 97
  snum = snum - 1
ENDDO
OUT 97,ostat
```

## WARNINGS/LIMITS:
Port numbers vary with computer makes, models, and configurations. See the DOS Technical Reference and your computer's technical reference manual for

the numbers and valid expressions. IBM PC and PS/2 assignments are in Norton, P. and R. Wilton, *Programmer's Guide to the IBM PC and PS/2*, (Microsoft Press, Redmond, WA, 1989).

## SEE ALSO:

Command DOSINT; functions IN( ) and TONE( ).

# PACK

## DIALECTS:

Clipper, dBASE III PLUS, dBASE IV, dBXL, FoxBASE+, and Quicksilver.

## SYNTAX:

PACK

## DEFINITION:

Purges deleted records from the active database file. The records may no longer be RECALLed. PACK automatically rebuilds all open index files.

When the PACK is completed, the pointer moves to the first record in the file or in the index.

## RECOMMENDED USE:

Although you may hide deleted records with SET DELETED ON, file sizes increase and processing speed degrades as their number increases. PACK removes them from the file permanently and reclaims used disk space.

**Example**—A simple name and address application contains two deleted records, 3 and 4 (marked by asterisks). PACK removes them from the active database file, and automatically rebuilds the open index file NAMEDEX.

```
. USE names INDEX namedex
. LIST
Record#  NAME                  ADDRESS
      2  Adams, Rollie         3333 Normal Street
      4 *Josephs, Robert       456 Edwards
      1  Ralphson, Ralph       222 Main Street
      5  Stanley, Stan         5 Old Mill
      3 *Zoohaus, Bernard      333 South Adams
. PACK
       3 records copied
Rebuilding index - C:name.ndx
  100% indexed            3 Records indexed
. LIST
Record#  NAME                  ADDRESS
      2  Adams, Rollie         3333 Normal Street
      1  Ralphson, Ralph       222 Main Street
      3  Stanley, Stan         5 Old Mill
```

## SEE ALSO:

Commands DELETE, RECALL, and ZAP.

# PARAMETERS

## DIALECTS:

Clipper, dBASE III PLUS, dBASE IV, dBXL, FoxBASE+, and Quicksilver.

## SYNTAX:

PARAMETERS <parameter list>

## DEFINITION:

A parameter is a data item sent by a calling program to a subprogram. PARAMETERS is the subprogram command that receives the items and gives them local variable names. The calling program passes the parameters with the command

```
DO <program or procedure> WITH <expression list>
```

The list may include any valid expressions separated by commas. You can pass constants, fields, memory variables, or the result of any function or operation.

In programs, PARAMETERS must be the first executable command. In procedures, it must be the first executable command after the PROCEDURE statement.

Changing the value of a passed memory variable in the subprogram (except in a user defined function) changes the value in the calling program. We refer to this as *call by reference.*

In contrast, when you use a fieldname in an expression list, changing its value in the subprogram does not change its value in the database. We refer to this as *call by value.* You must use the REPLACE command to update the database field.

Clipper, dBASE IV, dBXL, FoxBASE+, and Quicksilver allow parameter passing to user defined functions using the syntax:

```
? FUNCTION(parameter1,parameter2,...)
```

By default, memory variable parameters are passed to user defined functions by *value*, instead of by reference. See *Variations* for exceptions.

The number of parameters sent and received must agree.

## RECOMMENDED USE:

Use parameter passing to transfer data to a subroutine. The PARAMETERS statement clarifies which data items a subroutine needs.

Parameter passing is useful in writing modular applications. It lets you write and test subprograms separately, then pass data to them in a structured way.

**Example 1**—A calling program passes data to a search subprogram. MAINFIND.PRG requests a file name and a last name to search. It passes the user's response to SUBFIND.PRG which opens the specified file and does a SEEK. If the name is found, MAINFIND DISPLAYs the record.

```
* MAINFIND.PRG
CLEAR
ACCEPT "Enter file name:      " TO mfile    && Request a file name.
ACCEPT "Last name to search: " TO msearch  && Request name to search.
DO subseek WITH mfile,msearch

* SUBSEEK.PRG, search subprogram.
* Accept data from MAINFIND and store it in two local variables.
PARAMETERS rfile,rsearch
*
* Assume the DBF and INDEX files have the same name. Use the
* macro function to use the file name within the memory variable.
USE &rfile INDEX &rfile
SEEK rsearch     && Do a rapid search for the last name.
IF FOUND()
  DISPLAY lname,fname,company,ssn
ELSE
  ? "Name not found. Press SPACE BAR to continue"
  WAIT ""
ENDIF
```

**Example 2**—User defined functions pass data as function arguments that are received in PARAMETERS. A box drawing function accepts five parameters (two screen coordinate pairs, and a single character, "S" or "D", for single or double lines).

```
BOX(1,2,20,30,"D")

FUNCTION BOX
PARAMETERS r1,c1,r2,c2,char
PRIVATE mchar
mchar = (char="D")
IF mchar                          && If MCHAR is true, make DOUBLE lines.
  @ r1,c1 TO r2,c2 DOUBLE
ELSE
  @ r1,c1 TO r2,c2
ENDIF
RETURN ""
```

## LIMITS/WARNINGS:

If you intend to change a passed memory variable in a procedure and don't want the original to change, save it under another name.

## VARIATIONS:

**Clipper:** Agreement in the numbers of parameters sent and received is not required. The PCOUNT( ) function indicates how many parameters were passed.

You may specify character parameters on the DOS command line. Strings or character expressions (strings in quotation marks) must be separated by spaces, in the form

C> <program name> p1 p2 p3

For example, to run a program called INVENTRY with parameters for PARTNAME and PARTNO, issue the command

```
C> INVENTRY screwdriver 1243
```

Clipper lets you pass a parameter to a function by reference by preceding its name with @, as in

FUNCTION(@memvar)

By default, Clipper passes array elements to user defined functions by reference.

For example, a user defined function CONVERT( ) converts U.S. dollars to Canadian dollars. The numeric variable AMOUNT is passed by reference. As a result, changing the receiving parameter FAMOUNT changes AMOUNT.

```
amount = 4562.22
? CONVERT(@amount)
? amount                    && Result is 5292.18


FUNCTION convert
PARAMETERS famount
*
famount = famount * 1.16
RETURN famount
```

**dBASE III PLUS:** User defined functions not available.

**Quicksilver:** The compiler reserves 6K bytes of memory for command line parameters, limiting their number to approximately 42. Note that Quicksilver uses Environmental Variables to handle command line arguments.

## SEE ALSO:

Commands DO, FUNCTION, PROCEDURE, and RETURN; function PCOUNT( ).

# PLAY MACRO

## DIALECTS:

dBASE IV only.

## SYNTAX:

PLAY MACRO <macro name>

## DEFINITION:

Replays a macro, a series of recorded keystrokes.

Macros recorded in the current work session remain in memory until you QUIT. You can save them with SAVE MACROS, then later RESTORE MACROS.

## RECOMMENDED USE:

You can record keystrokes entered in the interactive mode. Later, you can replay them (the *macro*) to automate repetitive operations. You begin recording, end recording, and playback with the macro menu, accessed by pressing SHIFT-F10. You can also replay macros by typing a macro key (an Alt-function key combination followed by a letter), or by using the command PLAY MACRO. Use PLAY MACRO when executing a macro from a dBASE program.

**Example**—While generating reports from the dot prompt, Arthur records the keystrokes in a macro. He later wants to use a dBASE program to replay the keystrokes, so he saves them in a macro file.

```
* <Begin recording from SHIFT-F10 menu>.
. CLEAR
. CLEAR ALL
. USE grades INDEX student,class
. LIST ALL grades FOR grades ="A" .AND. class = "6" TO PRINT
. USE
. CLEAR
* <End recording and give macro the name GRADERPT>.
. SAVE MACROS TO macpupil
. QUIT
```

The program later RESTOREs the MACRO file, then issues PLAY MACRO to repeat the earlier procedure.

```
* RPT.PRG
RESTORE MACROS FROM macpupil
PLAY MACRO graderpt
* <More program statements>.
```

## LIMITS/WARNINGS:

Macro files can contain up to 35 macros.

RESTORE MACROS erases macros in memory with the same names as ones in the macro file.

Do not use the extension MAC for macro files, since it conflicts with the extension used by dBASE IV's applications generator.

PLAY MACRO, RESTORE MACROS, and SAVE MACROS have nothing to do with the macro function (&).

## SEE ALSO:

Commands RESTORE MACROS and SAVE MACROS.

# PRINTJOB...ENDPRINTJOB

## DIALECTS:

dBASE IV only.

## SYNTAX:

PRINTJOB
<statements>
ENDPRINTJOB

## DEFINITION:

Identifies a program section as a report, invoking the print controls set in the system memory variables. PRINTJOB also enables ON PAGE, the command that defines report headers and footers.

PRINTJOB...ENDPRINT is valid only in programs.

PRINTJOB does the following:

- Sends the printer control codes defined in the _pscode (print start) system variable.
- Checks _peject. If it contains "BEFORE" or "BOTH", dBASE IV sends a page eject.
- Resets _pcolno, the print head column counter, to 0.
- Activates _plineno, the line number counter.
- Activates ON PAGE. ON PAGE monitors the line count, executing a command when it reaches the number defined by the programmer.

ENDPRINTJOB does the following:

- Sends the print codes defined in the _pecode (print end) system memory variable.
- Checks _peject again. If it contains "AFTER" or "BOTH", dBASE IV sends a page eject.
- Checks _pcopies (number of copies to print). If it is greater than 1, the PRINTJOB repeats until all copies are printed.
- Resets _plineno and deactivates ON PAGE.

## RECOMMENDED USE:

Use PRINTJOB...ENDPRINTJOB to print list-oriented reports. Otherwise, they are difficult to format since they print in a stream and page breaks are not explicit. Commands such as ?/?? and LIST produce list-oriented reports.

**Example 1**—A library management system uses PRINTJOB to control output. Book search results print on 12-line custom forms, with page footers.

```
msubject = "SCIENCE"              && User enters subject to search.
_peject = "AFTER"                 && Issue eject after printing.
_plength = 12                     && Set page length to 12 lines.
SET HEADING off                   && Omit field headings in LIST command.
 _pageno=1                        && Set page number to 1.
ON PAGE AT LINE 09 DO footer      && When at line 09, DO FOOTER procedure.
PRINTJOB                          && Begin printjob.
  LIST ALL title,author FOR subject=msubject
ENDPRINTJOB
PROCEDURE footer
?
? _pageno PICTURE [999] AT 01, "Library Search: "+msubject " AT 40
?
?
RETURN
```

## SPECIAL USE:

PRINTJOB is not necessary when using REPORT FORM, as it is built into the command.

## LIMITS/WARNINGS:

You cannot nest PRINTJOBs.

For more precise control over reports, avoid the EJECT command. EJECT depends on the printer's page length setting, not the report's line count. Instead, keep tight control over line count and do page breaks with the ? command. For example, if you have 50-line reports, and 60-line paper, feed the printer ten lines for a page break instead of an EJECT.

## SEE ALSO:

Commands ?/??, LIST, ON PAGE, REPORT FORM, SET PRINT, and SET PRINTER.

# PRIVATE

## DIALECTS:

Clipper, dBASE III PLUS, dBASE IV, dBXL, FoxBASE+, and Quicksilver.

## SYNTAX:

PRIVATE <memory variable list>/[ALL [LIKE/EXCEPT <pattern>]]

## DEFINITION:

Lets you create memory variables in a subprogram with the same names as PUBLIC variables or ones declared in the calling program.

PRIVATE does not create the specified memory variables. After declaring variables PRIVATE, you must still initialize them with STORE or =.

PRIVATE hides the previous variables until the subprogram terminates. Then, PRIVATE variables are released automatically, leaving previous ones with the same names intact.

LISTing MEMORY from within a program displays both PUBLIC and PRIVATE variables. When they have the same names, the PUBLIC ones are listed as "Hidden," and the PRIVATE ones show the name of the program that created them.

## OPTIONS:

You can declare variables PRIVATE in groups, using ALL LIKE <pattern> and ALL EXCEPT <pattern>, where <pattern> is a string using asterisks and question marks as "wildcards."

## RECOMMENDED USE:

PRIVATE is particularly useful for building programs from subroutines. You do not have to worry about conflicting variable names.

**Example 1**—Often, programmers build libraries of subroutines to use in many applications. To write subroutines that will not conflict with other applications, the programmer declares memory variables PRIVATE. In this example, program MAINACCT calls program NEW_RPT, a subroutine that prints data in columnar format. NEW_RPT uses PRIVATE variables to avoid conflict with its caller.

```
* MAINACCT.PRG
* Declare printer setup codes in main application.
PUBLIC bold_on,bold_off
* Store printer control codes in memory variables.
bold_on = chr(27) + chr(69)  && Epson FX-80 setup codes.
bold_off = chr(27) + chr(70)
** <more statements>
DO new_rpt                   && Execute subroutine NEW_RPT.
* BOLD_ON and BOLD_OFF return to original PUBLIC value.
* <more statements>

* NEW_RPT.PRG
PRIVATE bold_on,bold_off
bold_on = CHR(27) + CHR(77)   && Change codes for a different type style.
bold_off = CHR(27) + CHR(80)
** <print a report>
RETURN                        && Return to MAINACCT.PRG.
```

## SPECIAL USE:

Always declare variables in user defined functions PRIVATE. This prevents name conflicts with existing variables.

## VARIATIONS:

**Clipper:** The memory variable list may also contain arrays. Declaring a PRIVATE array creates it with the specified number of elements. All elements are initially false. For example, the following statement creates two memory variables and an array with nine elements:

```
PRIVATE mdate, muser, rptarray[9]
```

**dBXL:** Trying to declare a PRIVATE variable from the interactive prompt fails, producing the message, "Only valid in program files."

## SEE ALSO:

Commands DO and PUBLIC.

# PROCEDURE

## DIALECTS:

Clipper, dBASE III PLUS, dBASE IV, dBXL, FoxBASE+, and Quicksilver.

## SYNTAX:

PROCEDURE <procedure name>

## DEFINITION:

Marks the beginning of a program within a procedure file. A procedure file consists of a program, or collection of programs, in a single file. It is loaded into memory using the command SET PROCEDURE TO.

Procedures are executed like any program using the command DO <program name>. If a procedure file containing the designated program is active, it will be executed. Procedures take precedence over programs. If one has the same name as a program, it is executed and the program is ignored.

## RECOMMENDED USE:

Using PROCEDUREs improves program performance and allows larger applications. Because the procedures, or information about them, are pre-loaded into memory, they are executed instantaneously. Otherwise, issuing the DO <program name> command causes dBASE III PLUS, dBASE IV, dBXL, or FoxBASE+ to search the disk for the designated program. It then loads from disk and executes, all with slight delays. You will notice longer delays in large applications with many disk files.

Also, PROCEDUREs allow more open files. A procedure file containing many programs counts as only one open file. You can thus use more programs without exceeding system limitations.

**Example**—An airline maintenance program stores commonly used subroutines in a procedure file MAINPROC. Upon starting up a maintenance logging module, the program SETs PROCEDURE TO MAINPROC, then executes PROCEDURE chekdate to confirm the system date. With the date confirmed, the program prompts the user to enter the weekly log update disk created off site.

```
* AIRLINE.PRG
SET PROCEDURE TO mainproc
DO chekdate       && Procedure to verify system date.
DO l_update       && Procedure alerts user to insert disk to update log.

* MAINPROC.PRG
* Contains two procedures, CHEKDATE and LUPDATE
*
PROCEDURE chekdate
PUBLIC mdate
mdate = DATE()
@ 10,10 SAY "Press ENTER key to verify today's date: " GET mdate
READ
CLEAR
*
*
PROCEDURE l_update
@ 22,01 SAY "Insert log update disk in drive A and shut drive door."
@ 23,01 SAY "Press SPACE BAR when ready to update."
* When user presses a key, open AIR_LOG database with active index
* LOG_DEX. Check for the existence of the file on drive A. If the
* update file exists, APPEND records from A into the main database.
WAIT ""
USE air_log INDEX log_dex
IF FILE("A:L_UPDATE.DBF")
  APPEND FROM A:l_update
  USE
ELSE
  * If file L_UPDATE is missing, generate error message with a beep.
  @ 22,00 CLEAR
  ?? CHR(7)         && Ring the bell.
  @ 22,01 SAY "Update file missing from drive A"
  @ 23,01 SAY "Notify technical support at (555) 555-2222."
  WAIT
ENDIF
```

## Optimization

In all systems except Quicksilver, a procedure file can open itself as shown here:

```
* MAINPROC.PRG                && Main procedure file.
SET PROCEDURE TO mainproc     && Set procedure to itself.
DO greeting                   && Do the first procedure in MAINPROC.
PROCEDURE greeting            && First procedure shows main menu.
CLEAR
@ 2,15 SAY "Easy Accounting Main Menu"
* <more statements>
*
PROCEDURE g_ledger
* <more statements>
```

This lets you put an entire application in a single program file that you can load as a procedure file.

## VARIATIONS:

**Clipper:** You may include PROCEDUREs in any program in an application without the SET PROCEDURE TO command. However, if a program file contains procedures and is not referenced by a DO <program name> elsewhere in the application, you must use SET PROCEDURE TO <program name> to locate the procedures at compile time. Clipper does not limit the number of procedures.

**dBASE III PLUS:** Allows up to 32 procedures per procedure file.

**dBASE IV:** All PROCEDUREs must end with a RETURN statement.

dBASE IV lets you put procedures in any program without a SET PROCEDURE command. To do this, put them at the end of the program file. Statements after a PROCEDURE...RETURN, except for other PROCEDUREs and FUNCTIONs, will never execute.

dBASE IV allows 1,170 procedures per file (limited by available memory).

For best performance and the fewest object files, put as many procedures as possible in the main program file.

If a program file contains procedures and is not referenced by a DO <program name> elsewhere in the application, dBASE IV cannot find it. You must use SET PROCEDURE TO <program name> to locate the procedures at runtime.

You may DO a procedure in the current program file, or in the active PROCEDURE file. From a subroutine, you may also DO a procedure located in a calling program.

dBASE IV searches areas for the procedure in the following order:

1. Currently executing object file (extension DBO).
2. Open procedure file using SET PROCEDURE TO.
3. Another open calling object file, starting with the most recently opened.
4. Object file with the same name as the procedure.
5. Program file (extension PRG) with the same name as the procedure.
6. SQL program file (extension PRS) with the procedure name.

dBASE IV compiles program files before executing them.

*Warning:* dBASE IV will not execute a program on disk with the same name as an active procedure. The procedure always takes precedence.

When you put PROCEDUREs in a program file, dBASE IV treats it as the "default" procedure. The program name is the PROCEDURE name. The program statements up to the first PROCEDURE or FUNCTION become part of the default procedure.

**dBXL:** Allows up to 32 procedures per procedure file.

**FoxBASE+:** Allows up to 128 procedures per procedure file. Fox Software highly recommends using procedures to improve performance. The company provides a utility FOXBIND which collects programs from disk into a procedure file. It inserts the PROCEDURE <filename> declarations automatically.

**Quicksilver:** Allows up to 32 procedures per procedure file. PROCEDURE names cannot exceed eight characters. The PROCEDURE statement must be the first command in the file. This prevents procedure files from calling themselves as in dBASE III PLUS, dBASE IV, dBXL, and FoxBASE+. Using procedures has no performance advantage.

## SEE ALSO:

Commands DO, FUNCTION, RETURN, and SET PROCEDURE TO.

# PROTECT

## DIALECTS:
dBASE IV only.

## SYNTAX:
PROTECT

## DEFINITION:
Invokes the security setup program.

PROTECT offers three levels of security:

1. Login security: Limits access to dBASE IV.
2. Field- and file-level security: Limits who can view or change data.
3. Encryption: Prevents unauthorized users from reading data from within dBASE IV or from the system level.

Once you PROTECT, all users must enter a login name and password upon startup. Issuing the LOGOUT command ends a user's session and presents a login screen for the next user.

If you use SQL, you must add the login name SQLDBA (SQL database administrator) to the PROTECT system. From SQL, you then use the GRANT command to make SQLDBA the system administrator. SQL's GRANT and REVOKE rely on login names defined in PROTECT.

## RECOMMENDED USE:
PROTECT helps database administrators prevent unauthorized access to sensitive data. The combination of login security, access security, and encryption deters (or at least discourages) snooping and unauthorized updating.

Login security limits access to dBASE IV. To define it, assign a user name, password, a group name, and an access level from 1 (highest) to 8 (lowest) to each user. The access level is used in field and file access security.

Access security gives certain fields and files a minimum security level. You define users' security levels when you add them to PROTECT. File privileges include READ, UPDATE (edit), EXTEND (add), and DELETE. Field privileges include FULL, R/O (read-only), and NONE.

When you assign access levels to a file, PROTECT automatically creates an encrypted version of it and gives it a CRP extension. To secure the system, the system administrator must erase the original database file and rename the encrypted file with a DBF extension.

PROTECT requires a login name, password, group name, and access level. Full name is optional.

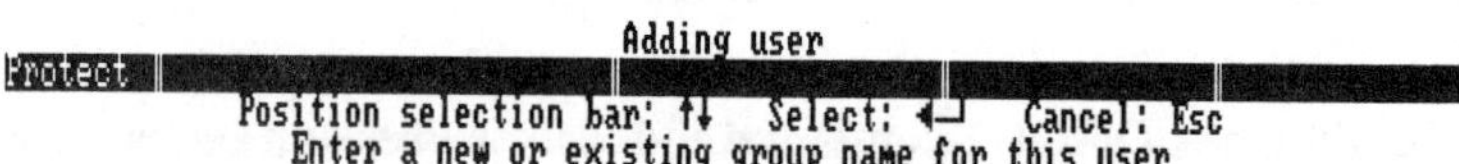


File access levels are numbers from 1 (highest) to 8 (lowest).

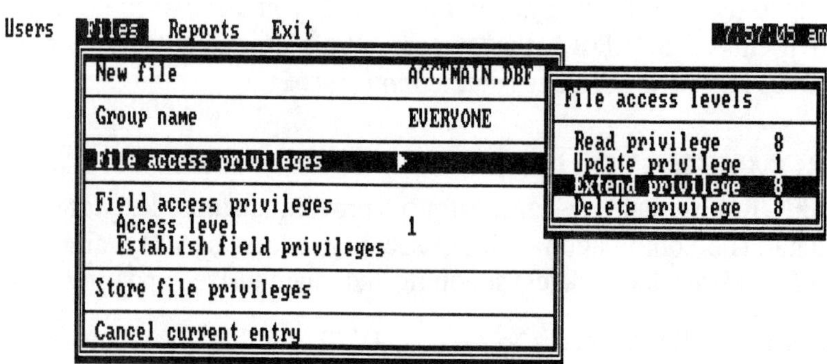


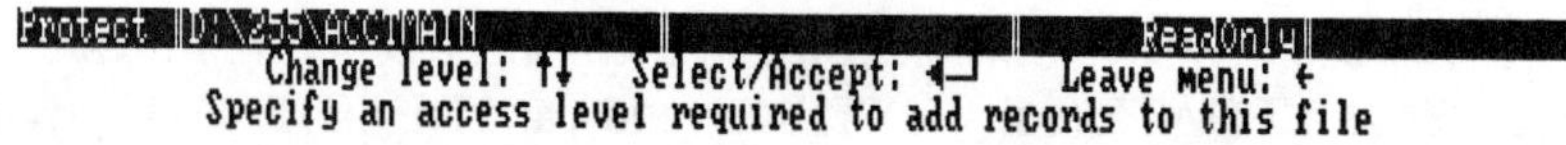

You can designate field access levels of R/O (read-only), FULL, and NONE.

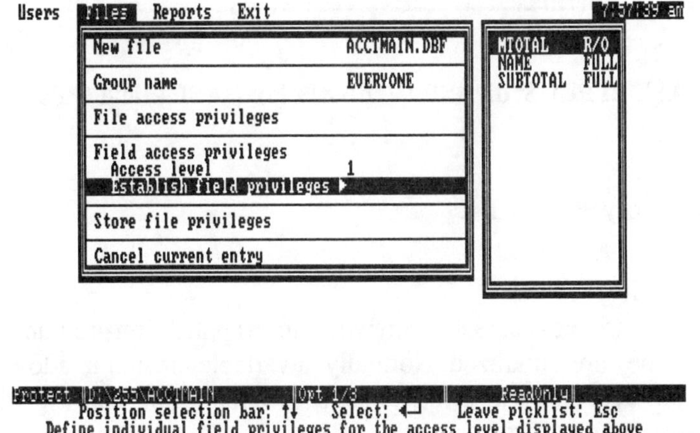


When working with encrypted files, commands that copy data such as COPY, JOIN, and TOTAL create encrypted files with SET ENCRYPTION ON. INDEXes or REINDEXes on encrypted files create encrypted indexes.

## LIMITS/WARNINGS:

Login security without encryption is inadequate. The user can simply rename the DBSYSTEM.DB file before running dBASE IV, disabling the login process. After QUITting, or during the session, the user can then restore DBSYSTEM.DB, leaving no trace of the unauthorized access.

dBASE IV stores encrypted password information in an encrypted file called DBSYSTEM.DB. Keep this file in the directory where dBASE IV is installed. Erasing it destroys all security definitions. As a precaution, you should print the definitions from the Reports menu in PROTECT. If you forget the system administrator's password, you will not be able to recover your encrypted data.

There is no way to prevent an unauthorized user from PROTECTing an unprotected system.

You may not MODIFY the STRUCTURE of encrypted files.

## SEE ALSO:

Commands LOGOUT and SET ENCRYPTION; functions ACCESS( ) and USER( ).

# PUBLIC

## DIALECTS:

Clipper, dBASE III PLUS, dBASE IV, dBXL, FoxBASE+, and Quicksilver.

## SYNTAX:

PUBLIC <memory variable list>

## DEFINITION:

Makes memory variables accessible anywhere in an application program, regardless of where they are initialized. Normally, a variable created in a lower level program is not accessible in a higher level program. You can use PUBLIC memory variables anywhere.

To create PUBLIC memory variables, first declare them PUBLIC, then give them values. The variables are initially all false (.F.).

You can temporarily hide PUBLIC memory variables in a subroutine by declaring PRIVATE variables with the same names. When control returns to the caller, the PRIVATE variables release automatically, leaving the PUBLIC ones intact.

Declaring an existing variable as PUBLIC causes a syntax error.

## RECOMMENDED USE:

Use PUBLIC memory variables to make data available to all subroutines in an application.

**Example**—A bibliographic database application searches for books using a subroutine. When it FINDs a book, it stores the TITLE, ISBN, and PUBLISHER information in PUBLIC variables. On return to the caller, these variables are available for display or printing.

```
* BIBLIO.PRG
* BOOKFIND is a subroutine that FINDs the requested book.
mfind = SPACE(20)
@ 10,10 SAY "Enter book title to find: " GET mfind PICTURE "@!"
READ
* Title to find passed to BOOKFIND through PARAMETER mfind.
DO bookfind WITH trim(mfind)
@ 10,05 SAY "     TITLE:" + mtitle
@ 11,05 SAY "      ISBN:" + misbn
```

```
@ 12,05 SAY " PUBLISHER:" + mpub
* <more statements>

* BOOKFIND.PRG
PARAMETERS mfind
PUBLIC mtitle,misbn,mpub
* Use bibliographic database and title index.
USE bibmain INDEX bibtitle
FIND &mfind
* If found, store field contents in PUBLIC variables.
IF FOUND()
  mtitle = title
  misbn = isbn
  mpub = pub
ELSE
  * If not found, display message and pause.
  @ 10,10 SAY "Not found."
  WAIT
ENDIF
```

## SPECIAL USES:

When you SAVE variables in a memory file, they are always PUBLIC when RESTOREd at the interactive prompt. When RESTOREd in a program, they are always PRIVATE. To restore PUBLIC variables from a memory file, declare them PUBLIC, then RESTORE FROM <memory file> ADDITIVE.

## VARIATIONS:

Variables that you declare PUBLIC are of type logical until you assign them values. The default is usually false. A few special variables default to true to allow programmers to identify the system in use. See PUBLIC CLIPPER/FOX/XNATIVE/XQUICKS.

**Clipper:** The memory variable list may contain arrays. Declaring a PUBLIC array creates it with the specified number of elements. All elements are initially false. For example, the following statement creates two memory variables and an array with nine elements:

```
PUBLIC mdate, muser, rptarray[9]
```

**dBASE IV:** You can also declare arrays PUBLIC with the command

```
PUBLIC <array name>([<expN1>[,<expN2>])
    [,<array name>(<expN>[,<expN]),...]
```

You cannot declare arrays and memory variables PUBLIC on the same line. Note that the brackets surrounding <expN1>,<expN2> are literals you must include in the command.

**FoxBASE+:** A special form creates one or two dimensional arrays:

PUBLIC <array name>(<expN1>[,<expN2>])
    [,<array name>(<expN>[,<expN>]),...]

Note that the parentheses surrounding <expN1>,<expN2> are literals you must include in the command.

For example, to create the arrays STATES and ZIPS, with 10 and 22 elements respectively, use

```
PUBLIC states(2,5),zips(2,11)
```

## SEE ALSO:

Commands DECLARE, DIMENSION, DO, PRIVATE, PUBLIC CLIPPER/FOX/XNATIVE/XQUICKS, RESTORE, and SAVE.

# PUBLIC CLIPPER/FOX/XNATIVE/XQUICKS

## DIALECTS:

Clipper, FoxBASE+, and Quicksilver.

## SYNTAX:

PUBLIC CLIPPER/FOX/XNATIVE/XQUICKS

## DEFINITION:

Declares a memory variable with a value of true to allow programs to detect the Clipper, FoxBASE+, or Quicksilver environment. All other variables start out false.

CLIPPER refers to the Clipper compiler, FOX to FoxBASE+, XNATIVE to the Quicksilver native code optimizer, and XQUICKS to the Quicksilver intermediate d-code mode.

## RECOMMENDED USE:

PUBLIC variables that initialize as true allow programmers to run system-specific program code on other dBASE-language systems. For example, you may be developing code interactively or using tools meant for a specific environment. By checking the status of the PUBLIC variables, you can determine which system is running.

**Example 1**—Including a Clipper-specific user defined function in a dBASE III PLUS, dBASE IV, dBXL, FoxBASE+, or Quicksilver program.

```
* DISPLAY.PRG
*
* <statements>
PUBLIC CLIPPER
IF CLIPPER                  && If true, execute a user defined function.
  ? STATE(12222)
ELSE
  DO STATE WITH "12222"     && If false, execute a procedure.
ENDIF
```

**Example 2**—A programmer prototypes a Quicksilver application using dBASE III PLUS. Because some functions are unique to Quicksilver, the program checks the environment with XQUICKS. UPPER.PRG converts all customer names to upper and lower case. If the environment is Quicksilver, UPPER uses the handy

PROPER( ) function. If the environment is dBASE III PLUS, a procedure does the conversion.

```
* UPPER.PRG *
PUBLIC xquicks,xnative
USE acctview INDEX viewdex
* If XQUICKS is true, use the QBROWSE subroutine.
IF xquicks
  REPLACE ALL customer with PROPER(customer)
ELSE
  * If dBASE III PLUS, use a custom procedure called UPLOW.
  DO uplow WITH customer
ENDIF
```

dBASE IV allows you to hide unsupported functions but not commands. Programs with unsupported commands will not compile.

## LIMITS/WARNINGS:

**Clipper, dBASE IV, FoxBASE+, and Quicksilver:** All try to compile unsupported commands, even if they are "hidden" by an IF CLIPPER/FOX/XQUICKS statement. Clipper and FoxBASE+ generate error messages, but produce programs that run. Quicksilver compiles only trivial unsupported commands (such as SET TALK), but refuses to compile commands such as EDIT and BROWSE. dBASE IV will not compile programs with unsupported commands. Both Quicksilver and dBASE IV will compilc programs with unsupported functions since they assume they are user defined.

You can compile and link the following program in Clipper but not in Quicksilver.

```
PUBLIC xquicks,clipper
IF xquicks .OR. clipper
 DO browprog
ELSE
  BROWSE
ENDIF
```

## SEE ALSO:

Command PUBLIC; Appendix 2, "Sensing the Environment."

# QUIT

## DIALECTS:
Clipper, dBASE III PLUS, dBASE IV, dBXL, FoxBASE+, and Quicksilver.

## SYNTAX:
QUIT

## DEFINITION:
Ends a dBASE III PLUS, dBASE IV, dBXL, or FoxBASE+ session and exits a Clipper or Quicksilver program. Closes all open files. QUIT always returns control to the operating system.

## SEE ALSO:
Commands EXIT and RETURN.

# READ

## DIALECTS:

Clipper, dBASE III PLUS, dBASE IV, dBXL, FoxBASE+, and Quicksilver.

## SYNTAX:

READ [SAVE]

## DEFINITION:

Lets you edit memory variables or fields that an @...GET statement has displayed on the screen. With READ, all @...GET statements issued since the last READ, CLEAR, CLEAR GETS, or CLEAR ALL can be edited in a full-screen mode. New values you enter replace the old values. When you select a format file using SET FORMAT TO, READ activates its @...GET statements.

READ uses the same editing conventions as other full-screen editing commands, such as APPEND or EDIT.

## OPTIONS:

Normally, READ clears GETs once editing is completed. The SAVE option preserves them, making them available for the next READ. The data from the previous GETs appears for editing. This is convenient for repetitive entries. To release SAVEd GETs, use CLEAR GETS.

## RECOMMENDED USE:

Although READ allows direct editing of fields stored in GETs, you should not generally use it in programs. Direct editing does not let the program validate data before the user saves it.

In a program, store fields in memory variables with similar names, then use @...GETs to edit and validate the variables.

When the user is satisfied with changes to a record, REPLACE the fields with the corresponding memory variables. To add a new record, use the command APPEND BLANK before REPLACE.

**Example**—A subroutine in a sales application edits a database. It opens the file SALES, then initializes memory variables from the fields. The program then

GETs the variables for editing. Only when the user indicates that he or she is done editing does the program REPLACE the original fields with the new data.

```
* MADDRESS, MCITY, and MSTATE are memory variables.
* ADDRESS, CITY, and STATE are fields.
SET TALK off
CLEAR
USE sales
maddress = address
mcity = city
mstate = state
DO WHILE .t.
  @ 06,02 SAY "Address: " GET maddress
  @ 07,02 SAY "City:    " GET mcity
  @ 08,02 SAY "State:   " GET mstate
  READ
  finish = " "   && Create variable FINISH to hold user's response.
  @ 14,10 SAY "<S>ave or <C>ancel? (S/C)"
  * Force uppercase response with the PICTURE "!" statement.
  @ 15,10 SAY "Press any other key to re-edit" GET finish PICTURE "!"
  READ
  IF mstate = "  "   && Validation code checks whether MCITY is blank.
    @ 24,10 SAY "State must not be blank."  && If blank, redo.
    LOOP
  ENDIF
  * <More validation code>
  DO CASE
    CASE finish = "S"  && If user presses "S", then REPLACE data.
      @ 23,01 SAY "Saving"
      * Use APPEND BLANK here to create a new record.
      REPLACE address with maddress,city with mcity,state with mstate
      RETURN
      * If user presses "C", exit DO WHILE and proceed to first
      *  statement after the ENDDO.
    CASE finish = "C"
      CLEAR
      EXIT
  ENDCASE
ENDDO
```

## VARIATIONS:

**Clipper:** Pressing F1 from a GET...READ automatically sends three parameters to a help routine HELP.PRG, if it exists. The parameters are the caller's name, the line number in the caller, and the GET variable name. This lets you write context sensitive help programs. Pressing F1 from an @...PROMPT...MENU TO also calls HELP.PRG and sends the same parameters.

## SEE ALSO:

Commands APPEND BLANK, CLEAR GETS, and REPLACE.

# RECALL

## DIALECTS:

Clipper, dBASE III PLUS, dBASE IV, dBXL, FoxBASE+, and Quicksilver.

## SYNTAX:

RECALL [<scope>] [WHILE <condition>] [FOR <condition>]

## DEFINITION:

Removes deletion marks from records in the active database file.

## DEFAULT:

RECALL with no options recalls only the current record. You can RECALL multiple records with a scope, WHILE, or FOR condition. Sample <scopes> include RECALL RECORD <n>, RECALL NEXT 10, and RECALL ALL.

## RECOMMENDED USE:

Records marked for deletion are not physically purged from the database file until you issue a PACK or ZAP command. Therefore, you may use DELETE to temporarily hide records when SET DELETED is ON. When you finish querying, reporting, listing, etc., restore DELETED records with the RECALL command.

**Example**—A hotel marks group reservations with a special field. At the end of each week, the system administrator purges old reservations with DELETE after saving them in a backup file. However, one time, due to a calendar mixup, the administrator accidentally removes next week's reservations. Fortunately, they are gone but not forgotten. All the administrator must do is RECALL ALL, then start over.

Note that GROUP is a logical field which, if true, indicates that a reservation was made at a group rate.

```
. USE reserves
. DELETE ALL GROUP
  36 records deleted
. RECALL ALL
  36 records recalled
```

(Large sigh of relief at this point!)

## LIMITS/WARNINGS:

If you SET DELETED ON, deleted records become invisible in the active database and RECALL generally has no effect. However, if you move the record pointer directly to an invisible record using GOTO, or if the pointer remains on a record you have just deleted, RECALL alone or RECALL with a "NEXT <n>" scope will restore it. RECALL will ignore all other invisible deleted records.

Note that you cannot RECALL records removed from the database file with the PACK or ZAP commands.

## SEE ALSO:

Commands DELETE, PACK, and SET DELETED.

# REINDEX

## DIALECTS:
Clipper, dBASE III PLUS, dBASE IV, dBXL, FoxBASE+, and Quicksilver.

## SYNTAX:
REINDEX

## DEFINITION:
Rebuilds all active indexes associated with the open database file. The keys and the UNIQUE specifications (see SET UNIQUE) remain the same as when you first created the index.

## RECOMMENDED USE:
In rare situations involving physical damage to a disk, index files can become corrupted and REINDEX cannot rebuild them. If this concerns you, always rebuild indexes from scratch using the INDEX command. INDEX also makes programs easier to understand since the key and the UNIQUE option are explicit.

REINDEX is useful for rebuilding indexes in the interactive mode.

To use REINDEX in multiuser applications, you must open the database file for exclusive use.

## VARIATIONS:
**dBASE IV:** REINDEX also rebuilds multiple index files (extension MDX) in the current work area.

## SEE ALSO:
Commands INDEX, SET INDEX TO, SET ORDER, SET UNIQUE, and USE; functions KEY( ), MDX( ), and NDX( ).

# RELEASE

## DIALECTS:

Clipper, dBASE III PLUS, dBASE IV, dBXL, FoxBASE+, and Quicksilver.

## SYNTAX:

RELEASE <memory variable list> / <ALL [LIKE/EXCEPT attern>]

## DEFINITION:

Erases variables from memory.

## RECOMMENDED USE:

All systems limit the number of memory variables, making it good practice to erase unnecessary ones. By using a list or pattern, you can RELEASE groups at one time.

**Example**—In an airline ticket application, the programmer uses rigid naming conventions to identify memory variables. Variables with three-character names are passenger names. Ones starting with Z are printer control strings. Ones starting with T are temporary variables for intermediate calculations.

```
* Releasing variables with names three characters long.
* Three-character variables contain passenger names.
RELEASE ALL LIKE ???
* Releasing variables with names starting with T.
* T variables are temporaries for arithmetic subtotals.
RELEASE ALL LIKE T*
* Releasing variables in a list.
RELEASE name,address,city
* Releasing all variables except those starting with Z. The Z
* variables contain printer control strings which must remain intact.
RELEASE ALL EXCEPT z*
```

## VARIATIONS:

**dBXL, Quicksilver:** RELEASE AUTOMEM clears all AUTOMEM variables from memory.

## SEE ALSO:

Commands CLEAR, CLEAR MEMORY, RELEASE MENUS/POPUPS/WINDOW, RELEASE MODULES, and STORE.

# RELEASE MENUS/POPUPS/WINDOW

## DIALECTS:

dBASE IV only.

## SYNTAX:

RELEASE MENUS <menu name list>/POPUPS <popup name list>/
WINDOW <window name list>

## DEFINITION:

Erases the specified bar menus, popup menus, or windows from the screen and from memory.

Active bar menus, popup menus, or windows are deactivated if they are named in the list. RELEASE also clears active ON SELECTION and ON PAD commands.

If no list appears, all specified objects are affected.

Erasing a window causes the text it covers to reappear on the screen.

## SEE ALSO:

Commands ACTIVATE, DEACTIVATE, DEFINE MENU, DEFINE POPUP, DEFINE WINDOW, RESTORE WINDOW, and WRELEASE.

# RELEASE MODULE

## DIALECTS:
dBASE III PLUS, dBASE IV, dBXL, FoxBASE+, and Quicksilver.

## SYNTAX:
RELEASE MODULE <module name>

## DEFINITION:
Removes a LOADed assembly language module from memory. The name has no extension.

## RECOMMENDED USE:
Because of limitations on the number of LOADed modules, it is often desirable to RELEASE one to make room for another.

Use the DISPLAY STATUS command to list the LOADed assembly language modules.

## SEE ALSO:
Commands DISPLAY STATUS and LOAD.

# RENAME

## DIALECTS:

Clipper, dBASE III PLUS, dBASE IV, dBXL, FoxBASE+, and Quicksilver.

## SYNTAX:

RENAME <filename1> TO <filename2>

## DEFINITION:

Changes a disk file's name. You must specify extensions explicitly. For files not on the default drive, you must use explicit drive designations. You cannot rename a file to an existing name (that is, you must delete the old file first), and you cannot rename an open file.

## RECOMMENDED USE:

Use RENAME to change a file's name to make it easier to remember or compatible with other names.

**Example**—A secretary renames files to reflect their purposes. A word processing document named JAMES.TXT contains a letter to Ralph James. The secretary renames the file with an LTR extension to identify it.

```
. RENAME james.txt TO james.ltr
```

By specifying the drive designation, the secretary RENAMEs files on other drives.

```
. RENAME C:sales.dbf TO prospect.dbf
```

RENAME does not allow pattern matching "wildcards" using * and ?.

## SEE ALSO:

Commands COPY FILE and DIR/DIRECTORY.

# REPLACE

## DIALECTS:

Clipper, dBASE III PLUS, dBASE IV, dBXL, FoxBASE+, and Quicksilver.

## SYNTAX:

REPLACE [<scope>] <field> WITH <expl>[, <field> WITH <exp2>...]
[WHILE <condition>] [FOR <condition>]

## DEFINITION:

Replaces the specified field or fields with the values of the specified expressions. Without any scope or conditions, REPLACE affects only the current record. It acts on multiple records when used with a scope, WHILE, or FOR clause.

You can only REPLACE data into fields of the same type. REPLACE automatically truncates character data that is longer than the target field.

You can REPLACE fields in any open database file. To apply it to an unselected work area, use the form ALIAS->FIELD.

## RECOMMENDED USE:

REPLACE is the primary way to change data under program control (you can also GET a field directly).

**Example 1**—An accounts receivable program uses REPLACE with string and numeric expressions to add a $10 fee to past due accounts with NET 30 terms. The first REPLACE statement replaces the field PAST_DUE with PAST_DUE + 10. The REPLACEment only occurs in records for which TERMS is "NET30". The second REPLACE changes TERMS in the same records to "NET15."

```
. USE ar_main
. LIST FOR TERMS = "NET30"
Record#  TERMS       PAST_DUE CLIENT
      1  NET30          43.00 ACME SOCKS
      9  NET30         454.00 MATSON LAW
. REPLACE ALL past_due WITH past_due + 10 FOR terms = "NET30"
   2 Records replaced.
. LIST FOR terms = "NET30"
Record#  TERMS       PAST_DUE CLIENT
      1  NET30          53.00 ACME SOCKS
      9  NET30         464.00 MATSON LAW
```

```
. REPLACE ALL terms WITH "NET15" FOR terms = "NET30"
  2 Records replaced.

. LIST FOR terms = "NET15"
 Record#  TERMS          PAST_DUE CLIENT
       1  NET15             53.00 ACME SOCKS
       9  NET15            464.00 MATSON LAW
```

**Example 2**—While working in one area, you can REPLACE data in another. AR_MAIN is in area 1. The SELECTed database, AR_SUB, is in area 2. The bookkeeper REPLACEs data from area 2 into the unselected database in area 1 using the ALIAS->FIELDNAME method. AR_MAIN contains amounts past due from 60 to 90 days. AR_SUB contains amounts past due over 90 days. Each month, the bookkeeper must REPLACE the OVER90 amount in AR_SUB with the PAST_DUE_60 amount in AR_MAIN.

```
SELECT 1
USE ar_main
LOCATE FOR acctno = "122"    && Locate account 122
SELECT 2
USE ar_sub

LOCATE FOR acctno = "122"    && Locate account 122
* REPLACE field OVER90 in AR_SUB with field PAST_DUE_60 in AR_MAIN.
REPLACE ar_sub->over90 with ar_main->past_due_60.
 1 Record replaced.
```

## LIMITS/WARNINGS:

REPLACing into a key field with open indexes updates them automatically. Note that when you REPLACE with a scope, WHILE, or FOR clause, all records may not be REPLACEd properly. As multiple replacements update the index, the record pointer moves to the record's new position. REPLACE continues to execute sequentially starting there. This could miss some records entirely, and REPLACE others multiple times.

## VARIATIONS:

The handling of numeric overflow varies among the systems.

*Clipper:* A numeric overflow interrupts program execution, or calls the programmer-defined error handler if it is installed. Clipper does not support scientific notation, nor does it replace overflow fields with asterisks.

*dBASE III PLUS, dBASE IV, dBXL, and FoxBASE+:* All truncate decimals, and convert large numbers to scientific notation. This causes a loss of precision.

dBASE III PLUS, dBASE IV, and FoxBASE+ also replace extremely large numbers with asterisks.

*Quicksilver:* Replaces the overflow with 0.00, but does not interrupt program execution.

**dBASE IV:** The ADDITIVE option lets you append character strings to a memo field, in the form:

```
REPLACE <field> WITH <expC> ADDITIVE
```

You can only REPLACE one field at a time when using ADDITIVE.

**dBXL, Quicksilver:** An AUTOMEM option simplifies the REPLACE command:

REPLACE [<scope>] <field> WITH <exp1>[,<field> WITH <exp2>...]
[WHILE <condition>] [FOR <condition>] | [AUTOMEM]

The AUTOMEM option replaces fields with AUTOMEM variables (created by STORE AUTOMEM).

## SEE ALSO:

Commands @...GET, CHANGE, EDIT, SELECT, SET INDEX, SET ORDER, and STORE.

# REPORT FORM

## DIALECTS:

Clipper, dBASE III PLUS, dBASE IV, dBXL, FoxBASE+, and Quicksilver.

## SYNTAX:

REPORT FORM <filename> [<scope>] [WHILE <condition>]
    [FOR <condition>] [PLAIN] [HEADING <expC>] [NOEJECT]
    [TO PRINT] [TO FILE <filename> [SUMMARY]

## DEFINITION:

Generates a report using a form created by the dBASE III PLUS, dBASE IV, dBXL, or FoxBASE+ report generators (CREATE/MODIFY REPORT), or by the Clipper report generator.

## DEFAULT:

Unless you send output to the printer or to a text file, REPORT FORM only displays it on the screen.

REPORT FORM assumes that the FORM file has an extension of FRM unless specified otherwise.

REPORT FORM uses all records unless you limit the <scope> or provide a FOR or WHILE <condition>.

## OPTIONS:

TO PRINT sends the report to the printer. TO FILE <filename> sends it to the screen and to a text file. The text file is given a TXT extension.

Other options include PLAIN, HEADING, NOEJECT, and SUMMARY. Normally, REPORT FORM ejects a sheet from the printer before beginning the REPORT. NOEJECT prevents this and begins the report on the current page. HEADING puts a message at the top of each page. The HEADING string must be delimited. PLAIN disables the standard page number and date, as well as any HEADING that has been SET.

SUMMARY provides only group total and subtotal reports. The group detail is omitted.

If you define group subtotals, you must INDEX or SORT the database on the grouping field.

## VARIATIONS:

**Clipper:** Can use existing REPORT FORMS, but cannot create new ones. It has a stand alone report generator for creating report forms. The SUMMARY option is not available.

**dBASE IV:** Automatically locks the database file in multiuser operations.

**Quicksilver:** Can use existing REPORT FORMS, but provides no way to create them. The SUMMARY option is not available.

## LIMITS/WARNINGS/SPECIAL USES:

A semicolon in a report column causes a carriage return/line feed.

**dBASE III PLUS:** A REPORT FORM defined with the Plain Page option locks up the computer when immediately rerun with the HEADING, NOEJECT, or SUMMARY options. To avoid this bug, issue any DISPLAY command between REPORT FORMs. In programs, you can hide DISPLAY's output with SET CONSOLE OFF as follows:

```
REPORT FORM file1
SET CONSOLE off
DISPLAY 1
SET CONSOLE on
REPORT FORM file1 NOEJECT
```

## SEE ALSO:

Commands CREATE REPORT and MODIFY REPORT.

# RESET

## DIALECTS:

dBASE IV only.

## SYNTAX:

RESET [IN ALIAS <alias name>]

## DEFINITION:

Sets the integrity tag in a database file to false (.F.).

BEGIN TRANSACTION makes the integrity tag true, indicating that the database file is in a state of change. If the transaction ends due to an error or power loss, the tag remains true. The ISMARKED( ) function returns its value.

## RECOMMENDED USE:

First use ISMARKED( ) after error recovery to check the database files. If ISMARKED( ) is true, you must either RESET the integrity tag or ROLLBACK the transaction. Use RESET if the ROLLBACK fails, or to simply ignore the tag.

**Example**—A user inadvertently pulls the computer's plug during a transaction, leaving the integrity tag set true. Upon restarting, the program can recover by attempting a ROLLBACK or by resetting the integrity tag with RESET.

```
USE sales EXCLUSIVE
IF ISMARKED()
  mreset = " "
  @ 24,03 SAY DBF() + " has been in an incomplete transaction. "+;
          "Do you wish to I)GNORE or R)OLLBACK" ;
          GET mreset VALID "IR"$mreset
  IF mreset="I"
    RESET
  ELSE
    ROLLBACK
  ENDIF
ENDIF
```

## LIMITS/WARNINGS:

RESETting the integrity tag accepts possibly bad data.

RESET requires exclusive use of a file.

## SEE ALSO:

Commands BEGIN TRANSACTION, END TRANSACTION, and ROLLBACK; functions COMPLETED( ), ISMARKED( ), and ROLLBACK( ).

# RESTORE

## DIALECTS:
Clipper, dBASE III PLUS, dBASE IV, dBXL, FoxBASE+, and Quicksilver.

## SYNTAX:
RESTORE FROM <filename> [ADDITIVE]

## DEFINITION:
Retrieves variables previously SAVEd in a memory file (MEM extension). Erases existing variables.

Memory files are specialized disk files for memory variables.

Note that within programs, all RESTOREd memory variables are PRIVATE unless you first declare them PUBLIC and RESTORE them with the ADDITIVE option. In the interactive mode, all RESTOREd memory variables are PUBLIC.

## OPTIONS:
ADDITIVE preserves existing memory variables. Ones with the same names as RESTOREd variables are redefined.

## RECOMMENDED USE:
A common use of memory files is to hold printer control codes. Depending on which printer the user selects, an application can RESTORE the corresponding codes. Generally, use memory files only to store data that would otherwise fit in a single database record.

**Example**—A multiuser application tracks development costs of computer programs. Because programmers have different printers, custom control codes are necessary. Before printing, each user selects the printer to install.

```
CLEAR
* Display choices.
@ 03,03 SAY "Select a printer"
@ 04,03 SAY "1. Mannesmann Tally"
@ 05,03 SAY "2. Epson FX85"
@ 06,03 SAY "3. Diablo 630"
@ 07,03 SAY "4. LaserWriter II"
response = 0   && GET response in a RANGE of 1 to 4.
```

```
@ 09,03 SAY "Your Choice? (1-4) GET response RANGE 1,4
READ
DO CASE          &&  RESTORE FROM the appropriate memory file.
  CASE response = 1
    RESTORE FROM mann ADDITIVE
  CASE response = 2
    RESTORE FROM epfx85 ADDITIVE
  CASE response = 3
    RESTORE FROM di630 ADDITIVE
  CASE response = 4
    RESTORE FROM laserII ADDITIVE
ENDCASE
```

## VARIATIONS:

**Quicksilver:** The EXCLUSIVE option allows only one user access to a memory file at a time. When a user RESTOREs FROM <filename> EXCLUSIVE, no other user can access the file. Only when the original user writes changes back to the disk with the SAVE command will the memory file become available. RESTORE FROM EXCLUSIVE resembles a file lock. The original user can edit the memory file with confidence that no one else has altered it.

## SEE ALSO:

Commands PRIVATE, PUBLIC, and SAVE.

# RESTORE GRAPH

## DIALECTS:

dBXL and Quicksilver.

## SYNTAX:

RESTORE GRAPH [FROM <filename>] / ? / <pattern> [PAINT] [TO PRINT]

## DEFINITION:

Displays a graph image saved in the BIT or PC Paintbrush/Aldus Pagemaker (PCX) format.

You specify these formats when you create, modify, or display the graph.

BIT and PCX formats are graph pictures. They do not process live data as do graph format files (GRF).

The user must press a key to erase the current graph.

## DEFAULT:

RESTORE GRAPH assumes that <filename> is in BIT format, with a BIT extension.

## OPTIONS:

The PAINT option RESTOREs GRAPHs from a PC Paintbrush or Pagemaker format (PCX).

The TO PRINT option prints the graph. To use a printer other than the default (IBM Graphics Printer), you must first select it with the SET GRAPHPRINT command or Quicksilver's INSTALL program. The supported printers are

- Epson FX (or LX86)
- Epson MX/IBM Graphics Printer (the default)
- Hewlett Packard LaserJet
- Okidata dot matrix

The manual also lists an HPGL Plotter option, but it does not work.

**dBXL:** RESTORE GRAPH ? displays a menu of available BIT or PCX files. You can select one by moving the cursor and pressing Return. RESTORE

GRAPH <pattern> lets you use wildcard characters (* and ?) to limit the filename selections in the menu.

## RECOMMENDED USE:

Use RESTORE GRAPH to display static graphs in BIT or PCX format. These displays do not process data, but are simply "snapshots" of live graphs. Because there is no disk access, RESTORE GRAPH is much faster than GRAPH FORM.

**Example**—An application displays financial data from the past five years. Because the old data is static, the graphs are generated in BIT format.

```
* TOTSALES.BIT contains total monthly sales over five years.
RESTORE GRAPH FROM totsales
```

The graph appears as follows:

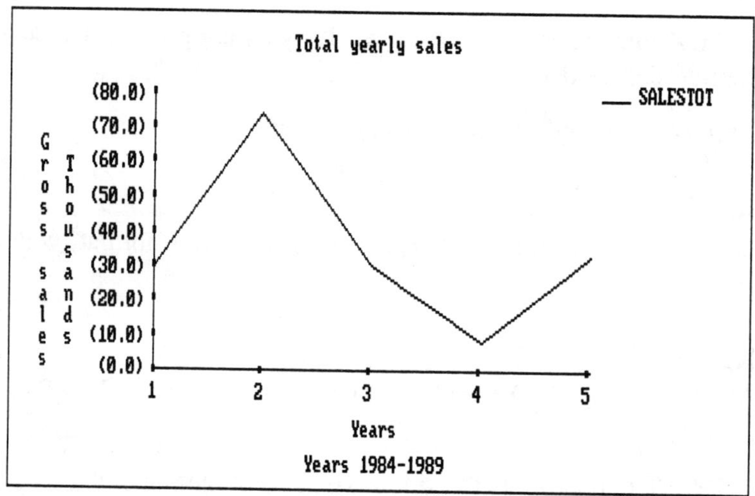


You can restore images in PCX format with the PAINT option:

```
RESTORE GRAPH FROM volume PAINT
```

## LIMITS/WARNINGS:

RESTORE GRAPH cannot display graphs in Ventura Publisher (IMG) format.

RESTORE GRAPH requires a Hercules, IBM Color, or IBM Enhanced Graphics Adapter (or compatible).

dBXL and Quicksilver do not display graphs within the active window. The screen blanks briefly, then the graph fills the screen. When the user presses a key, the graph disappears and the previous screen is erased as well. To preserve it, issue WSAVE before displaying the graph, then WRESTORE after.

## VARIATIONS:

**Quicksilver:** ? and <pattern> options not available. FROM <filename> is not optional.

## SEE ALSO:

Commands CREATE/MODIFY GRAPH, GRAPH FORM, and SET GRAPHPRINT.

# RESTORE MACROS

## DIALECTS:

dBASE IV only.

## SYNTAX:

RESTORE MACROS FROM <macro filename>

## DEFINITION:

Loads keyboard macros from a macro file into memory.

Macros execute from memory and are erased when you QUIT. However, you can save them on disk with SAVE MACROS, then later RESTORE MACROS.

The macro file has a default extension of MCR unless specified otherwise.

## RECOMMENDED USE:

dBASE IV lets you record keystrokes entered in the interactive mode. Later, you can replay them (the macro) to automate repetitive operations. You can begin recording, end recording, and playback with the macro menu, which you access by pressing SHIFT-F10.

**Example**—Every morning, Sandra checks the parts inventory. She USEs the file and types her query. After several weeks, she decides to automate the process with a macro.

```
* <Begin recording from SHIFT-F10 menu>.
. CLEAR
. CLEAR ALL
. USE parts INDEX mparts,qty
. LIST ALL parts FOR qty < 5 .AND. orders > 2 TO PRINT
. USE
. CLEAR
* <End recording from SHIFT-F10 menu and give macro a name>.
. SAVE MACROS TO macsave
. QUIT
```

The next day, Sandra restores the macro and executes it.

```
. RESTORE MACROS FROM macsave
* <Execute macro from SHIFT-F10 menu, with Alt-F10 key, or
*    with the PLAY MACROS command>.
```

## LIMITS/WARNINGS:

Macro files may contain up to 35 macros.

RESTORE MACROS erases macros in memory with the same names as ones in the macro file.

Do not use the extension MAC for macro files, since it conflicts with the extension used by dBASE IV's applications generator.

RESTORE MACROS and SAVE MACROS have no connection with the macro function (&).

## SEE ALSO:

Commands PLAY MACROS and SAVE MACROS.

# RESTORE SCREEN

## DIALECTS:

Clipper and FoxBASE+.

## SYNTAX:

RESTORE SCREEN [FROM <memory variable>]

## DEFINITION:

Restores a screen image saved with the SAVE SCREEN command.

Without the FROM option, RESTORE SCREEN restores the image placed in the screen buffer. RESTORE SCREEN FROM <memory variable> retrieves a screen image placed in a memory variable by SAVE SCREEN. Like other memory variables, screen variables can be saved on disk using the SAVE TO command. They appear with type "S" when you LIST MEMORY. Screen memory variables occupy 4K bytes.

## RECOMMENDED USE:

RESTORE SCREEN restores images very quickly, making them flash on the screen. This is useful for animating the display and creating windowed menus.

**Example**—Use RESTORE SCREEN to restore a screen after displaying help messages or lookup windows.

```
CLEAR
* Screen display with boxes, gets, @/SAYs, etc.
* <statements>
yname = space(10)
@ 12,10 SAY "Enter id number or 'L' for lookup table" GET yname
READ
* <User requests lookup assistance>
SAVE SCREEN
* <Do lookup subprogram>
DO SLOOK
* Return to screen display
RESTORE SCREEN
* <more statements>
```

## SEE ALSO:

Commands LIST MEMORY, SAVE, and SAVE SCREEN.

# RESTORE STATUS

## DIALECTS:
dBXL only.

## SYNTAX:
RESTORE STATUS FROM <filename>

## DEFINITION:
Reinstates environment settings saved on disk with the SAVE STATUS command.

The file holding STATUS information has a SET extension.

RESTORE STATUS restores the following environment settings:

| | | | | |
|---|---|---|---|---|
| ALTERNATE ON/OFF | DATE | ECHO | INTENSITY | RETRACE |
| ALTERNATE <file> | DEBUG | ESCAPE | MARGIN | SAFETY |
| BELL | DECIMALS | EXACT | MEMOWIDTH | SCOREBOARD |
| CARRY | DEFAULT | FIELDS | ODOMETER | STATUS |
| CENTURY | DELIMITERS | FIXED | OOPS | STEP |
| COLOR | DELIMITERS TO | HEADINGS | PATH | TALK |
| CONFIRM | DEVICE | HELP | PRINT | TITLE |
| CONSOLE | DOHISTORY | HISTORY | PROMPT | UNIQUE |

## SEE ALSO:
Commands DISPLAY STATUS and SAVE STATUS.

# RESTORE WINDOW

## DIALECTS:

dBASE IV only.

## SYNTAX:

RESTORE WINDOW <window name list>/ALL FROM <filename>

## DEFINITION:

Loads window definitions into memory from a file created by SAVE WINDOW.

Windows already in memory are overwritten if you RESTORE WINDOWs with the same names.

You can RESTORE some or ALL windows from a definition file. If you RESTORE WINDOW using a list, the window order does not matter.

## DEFAULT:

The window definition file has a default extension of WIN.

## RECOMMENDED USE:

Use RESTORE WINDOW and SAVE WINDOW to create application window "libraries." Rather than redefine windows, define them once, then RESTORE them as needed.

**Example**—An accounting system uses standardized windows to simplify development and maintenance. A "library" contains all the definitions.

```
RESTORE WINDOW mbrowse, mmaint FROM winlib
DISPLAY MEMORY
              Logical Window Definition
Window         From      To          Size
MBROWSE        5,5       10,20          44 bytes
MMAINT         10,10     20,50         956 bytes
```

## SEE ALSO:

Commands ACTIVATE WINDOW, DEFINE WINDOW, DISPLAY MEMORY, and SAVE WINDOW.

# RESUME

## DIALECTS:
dBASE III PLUS, dBASE IV, dBXL, and FoxBASE+.

## SYNTAX:
RESUME

## DEFINITION:
Continues execution of a program paused by the SUSPEND command. The program resumes on the line following the one on which it stopped.

## RECOMMENDED USE:
Use SUSPEND and RESUME to debug program files with an interpreter. When you SUSPEND a program, you may perform database operations, change memory variables, and change environment settings, such as SET ECHO or SET TALK.

## SEE ALSO:
Command SUSPEND.

# RETRY

## DIALECTS:

dBASE III PLUS, dBASE IV, dBXL, FoxBASE+, and Quicksilver.

## SYNTAX:

RETRY

## DEFINITION:

Returns control to the caller from a subprogram, and re-executes the line that called it.

RETRY releases memory variables created by the subprogram, closes files opened there, and clears the ERROR( ) function.

RETRY works like RETURN, except that RETURN goes back to the next line in the caller, rather than the same line.

## RECOMMENDED USE:

Use RETRY together with ON ERROR to repeat the command that caused an error after it is corrected. For example, suppose you write a program to update a database from floppy disks, but you forget which disk contains the file you need. You can use RETRY to repeat the subprogram until you find the proper file or give up. You should have labeled your disks better. (You could also check for the existence of the database first with the FILE( ) function).

Note that dBXL's error codes differ from those of FoxBASE+, dBASE III PLUS, and dBASE IV.

**Example**—A building inspection application uses portable computers in the field to track dangerous construction sites. Each week, disks are brought in from the field to update a main database on a desktop computer. MUPDATE.PRG appends data from the floppy disk. If the file SUBDBF is not found on drive A, program CHEKFILE.PRG executes, using the ERROR( ) function code as a parameter. CHEKFILE prompts the user to either RETRY the disk read or ignore the error.

```
* MUPDATE.PRG
ON ERROR DO chekfile WITH ERROR()
CLEAR
@ 04,00 SAY "Insert update disk in drive A"
```

```
WAIT
USE maindbf
SET TALK ON
APPEND FROM A:subdbf
SET TALK OFF

* CHEKFILE.PRG
PARAMETERS problem
* dBXL error code is 28
IF problem = 1
  ?? chr(7)
  @ 20,00 SAY "Specified database file not found. "
  @ 21,00 SAY "Change disks and press 'R' to RETRY "
  @ 22,00 SAY "or any other key to ignore"
  WAIT TO action
  IF action$"rR"
    RETRY     && Return to mupdate, re-execute APPEND FROM A:subdbf
  ELSE
    RETURN    && Return to mupdate and continue with SET TALK OFF
  ENDIF
ENDIF
```

## VARIATIONS:

**Quicksilver:** To use the RETRY command, use the -O option of the QS optimizer.

## SEE ALSO:

Commands ON ERROR, PARAMETERS, and RETURN; function ERROR( ).

# RETURN

## DIALECTS:

Clipper, dBASE III PLUS, dBASE IV, dBXL, FoxBASE+, and Quicksilver.

## SYNTAX:

RETURN [TO MASTER]

## DEFINITION:

Ends program execution and returns control to the caller. In the highest level program, RETURN passes control to the interactive prompt in dBASE III PLUS, dBASE IV, dBXL, and FoxBASE+, or to the operating system in Clipper and Quicksilver.

RETURN releases all PRIVATE memory variables. When used in dBASE III PLUS, dBASE IV, dBXL, and FoxBASE+ programs, it closes the program file. When used in procedures, it does not.

When RETURNing to a program, control passes to the next line (RETRY executes the last line). Like RETRY, RETURN clears the ERROR( ) function.

## OPTIONS:

RETURN TO MASTER is a shortcut that returns control to the highest-level calling program from anywhere. Its main use is to deal with errors, such as missing files or disk full conditions.

## RECOMMENDED USE:

Avoid using RETURN TO MASTER other than in error-handling routines. To keep program modules orderly, control should pass to and from subroutines one level at a time.

**Example**—A video store checkout system executes a program called TRAP.PRG when an error occurs (as specified in the ON ERROR command). Rather than RETURN control to the program that caused the error, RETURN TO MASTER passes control to the highest level program. In this example, a menu selection in VIDMAIN executes VIDSUB. An error in VIDSUB (File not found) executes TRAP. TRAP gives the user the choice to RETRY, or return to the main menu using RETURN TO MASTER.

```
* VIDMAIN.PRG contains main menu for video store application.
ON ERROR DO trap        && When error occurs, run TRAP.PRG.
* <menu selections 1-5>
DO CASE
  CASE action = 1
    DO vidsub
    * <other cases>

* VIDSUB.PRG run video store weekly sales report.
USE tapefile      && Assume tapefile has been damaged or erased.
* <print report>
* When report is finished, RETURN to caller.
RETURN

* TRAP.PRG
@ 23,03 SAY MESSAGE()  && MESSAGE() function describes the error.
response = "?"
DO WHILE .not. response $ "RE"
  @ 24,03 SAY "(R)etry or (E)xit? (R/E) " GET response PICTURE "!"
  READ
ENDDO
IF response = "R"    && RETRY command is common in multiuser
  @ 23,00 CLEAR      &&  systems to access locked files.
  RETRY
ELSE
  RETURN TO MASTER  && Return to VIDMAIN.PRG.
ENDIF
```

## VARIATIONS:

**Clipper:** TO MASTER not available.

**Clipper, dBASE IV, dBXL, FoxBASE+, and Quicksilver:** RETURN can return a value from a user defined function with the form

RETURN <exp>

User defined functions must RETURN a value. The value replaces the function expression in the caller.

Except for the expression, RETURN <exp> acts like a standard RETURN.

Use RETURN <exp> to return a memory variable or literal value to the caller. (You cannot RETURN anything with the TO MASTER option.)

**Example**—A user defined function in a mailing list program (Clipper, dBASE IV, dBXL, FoxBASE+, or Quicksilver) spells out state abbreviations. The function LSTATE( ) accepts a two letter abbreviation as a parameter. It then searches for the abbreviation and its associated state name. If a match is found, LSTATE( ) RETURNs the full state name. If no match is found, it RETURNs "NOT FOUND."

```
FUNCTION lstate         && Use FUNCTION in dBASE IV, Clipper, dBXL,
                        &&   Quicksilver.
* PROCEDURE lstate      && Use PROCEDURE in FoxBASE+.
PARAMETER fstate
PRIVATE warea,retstate
SELECT 7
USE states INDEX states
SEEK fstate
IF FOUND()
  retstate = TRIM(sname)
ELSE
  retstate = "NOT FOUND"
ENDIF
SELECT 2
RETURN retstate
```

If RETURNing a value is inappropriate (for example, in a function that displays a menu or list), simply return a null string with

```
RETURN ""
```

**dBASE III PLUS:** RETURN <exp> not available.

## SEE ALSO:

Commands PRIVATE, PUBLIC, and RETRY; function ERROR( ).

# ROLLBACK

## DIALECTS:
dBASE IV only.

## SYNTAX:
ROLLBACK [<database filename>]

## DEFINITION:
Reverses changes made to database records during a transaction. If you create database files or indexes, ROLLBACK erases them.

ROLLBACK affects all changed databases in the open transaction.

ROLLBACK restores data from the transaction log file to reverse the open transaction. After a ROLLBACK, the transaction log file remains open, awaiting the next BEGIN TRANSACTION.

If the transaction log file is unreadable or nonexistent, the ROLLBACK may fail. The ROLLBACK( ) function reports whether the ROLLBACK command succeeded.

## OPTIONS:
You can use ROLLBACK with a database filename as an argument to reset the file's integrity tag and erase the transaction log file.

## RECOMMENDED USE:
Use BEGIN TRANSACTION and END TRANSACTION to ensure data integrity when a transaction cannot be successfully completed. Transactions may fail if another user has locked a file or record, the power fails, or a disk drive is not ready. If the transaction fails, use ROLLBACK to reverse changes made to the open databases.

**Example**—A library database uses transaction processing to update overdue book lists in a batch process. If another user has a record locked, the ON ERROR command executes ROLLBACK to reverse the update.

```
USE biblio INDEX mbib IN 1
ON ERROR ROLLBACK
BEGIN TRANSACTION
REPLACE ALL onloan WITH "out" FOR due > DATE()
END TRANSACTION
ON ERROR
```

See BEGIN TRANSACTION and the ROLLBACK( ) function for more examples.

## LIMITS/WARNINGS:

For sensitive data, you should make file backups before beginning a transaction. On single user systems, file backups will often be easier and more efficient than transaction logging.

## SEE ALSO:

Commands RESET and RETRY; functions COMPLETED( ), ISMARKED( ), and ROLLBACK( ).

# RUN/!

## DIALECTS:

Clipper, dBASE III PLUS, dBASE IV, dBXL, FoxBASE+, and Quicksilver.

## SYNTAX:

RUN <OS command>/<external program>

## DEFINITION:

Executes operating system commands or other applications from within a program. Preserves the entire environment, including open files, record pointers, and filter conditions.

## RECOMMENDED USE:

You can RUN programs written in any language to read and manipulate dBASE files.

You can also use RUN to execute incidental programs not directly related to your application.

**Example 1**—A menu selection in an inventory management system lets the user temporarily exit to DOS to run external programs. The RUN command executes a batch file that loads COMMAND.COM, giving the user full access to DOS. The colons indicate DOS comments.

```
RUN DOS.BAT
:DOS.BAT - DOS shell - this batch file simply
: changes the DOS prompt, otherwise you can just
: RUN COMMAND
PROMPT Type EXIT to return to dBASE $_$n$g
:give a normal prompt with our message above it
COMMAND
:preceding line just loads the DOS command processor COMMAND.COM
```

**Example 2**—An option in the inventory system from Example 1 does file backups using an external program. RUN executes BACKUP, sending it parameters stored in the memory variable OPTION.

```
DO CASE
  CASE method = "daily"              && Daily backup parameters
    options = "C:\DBASE\*.DBF A: /M"
```

```
  CASE method = "weekly"          && Weekly backup parameters
    options = "C:\ A: /S/M"
  CASE method = "complete"
    options = "C:\ A: /S"         && Backup entire hard disk
ENDCASE
RUN BACKUP &options               && Execute BACKUP with defined options
```

**Example 3**—To return information from an external program to a dBASE application, you can either 1) have the external program write the information in a dBASE format file (typically of type .MEM or .DBF), or 2) redirect program output to an ASCII file and APPEND...SDF into a database file.

For example, an external communications program captures data from an on-line information service and stores it in an ASCII file ONLINE.TMP. To import the data into a dBASE application, the programmer creates a database CAPTURE.DBF, with one long character field CAPINFO. The program first USEs CAPTURE, then issues the command APPEND FROM ONLINE.TMP SDF to move the ASCII text into CAPTURE.DBF. The program can then manipulate the captured data just like any other data.

```
USE CAPTURE                    && open DBF file
APPEND FROM online.tmp SDF     && and append from flat ASCII file
```

## LIMITS/WARNINGS:

Your computer must have sufficient memory for the external program to execute.

In dBASE III PLUS, each time a RUN command is executed, available memory may shrink slightly. If you RUN enough times, you will eventually run out of memory!

The program you RUN must not stay resident in memory. (For example, avoid loading memory resident DOS programs such as Borland's SideKick and SuperKey from within your application). Your computer may lock up when you exit.

In MS/PC-DOS, RUN executes COMMAND.COM. For it to work, it must find COMMAND.COM using the DOS COMSPEC environment variable.

If you change COMSPEC using the DOS SET command, whatever program you specify will be loaded instead of COMMAND.COM. Be careful when changing COMSPEC; systems also use it to load text editors for program files and memo fields (when external programs are designated).

Note that you cannot change COMSPEC using RUN SET COMSPEC=<shellname>. RUN loads another copy of COMMAND.COM (or whatever shell COMSPEC specifies) and passes it a copy of the current environment. Changes to environment variables will affect only the copy. To change environment variables for access from within an application, issue SET commands within your startup batch file. To change environment variables during a command you RUN, use a batch file that first SETs the desired environment (see Example 1).

## SEE ALSO:

Commands !, APPEND FROM, CALL, and DOS.

# SAVE

## DIALECTS:

Clipper, dBASE III PLUS, dBASE IV, dBXL, FoxBASE+, and Quicksilver.

## SYNTAX:

SAVE TO <filename> [ALL LIKE/EXCEPT <pattern>]

## DEFINITION:

Stores memory variables in a disk file. The file, called a *memory file*, has a default extension of MEM. It can later be LOADed into memory with the RESTORE command.

Saves files on the default drive unless you specify otherwise.

## OPTIONS:

You can save groups of memory variables using the ALL LIKE <pattern> and ALL EXCEPT <pattern> options. A pattern is a character string containing asterisks and question marks that serve as "wildcard" characters.

## RECOMMENDED USE:

Use SAVE TO to retain system data such as printer control codes and video attributes. Generally, data that requires only a single record in a database can be SAVEd in a memory file. Data that must be edited, reported on, or shared on a network is best stored in a database.

**Example**—An application that tracks cars in a repossession agency has several workstations on a local area network. An installation program for each station determines the monitor type (monochrome or color) and SAVEs a memory file containing the video attributes.

The application running on each workstation uses the saved memory variables as video attribute defaults.

```
IF ISCOLOR()            && ISCOLOR function is true if monitor is color.
  * Red/White for regular text; White/Red for highlights; White border.
  vstandrd = "R/W,W/R,W"
  venhance = "W*/R"     && Blinking white on red.
ELSE
  * Bright white, with underlined highlighted areas.
  vstandrd = "w+,U"
ENDIF
* Save memory variables starting with V in file VIDEO.
SAVE TO video ALL LIKE v*
```

When an application starts, it retrieves the variables stored in the memory file. LIST MEMORY shows the variable VSTANDRD containing the video attribute for monochrome monitors.

```
RESTORE FROM video
LIST MEMORY
 VSTANDRD     pub    C   "w+,U"
    1 variables defined,          6 bytes used
    255 variables available,   5994 bytes available
```

The application can then use VSTANDRD as an argument in the SET COLOR command, as follows:

```
SET COLOR TO &vstandrd
```

## VARIATIONS:

**Quicksilver:** Allows SAVE with no argument. This form corresponds to the multiuser command RESTORE FROM <filename> EXCLUSIVE. RESTORE FROM <filename> EXCLUSIVE allows a user to open a memory file while preventing access by other users. The original user must issue SAVE to release the file.

SAVE TO <filename> also exists, but does not release the memory file from EXCLUSIVE use.

## SEE ALSO:

Commands RESTORE, STORE, and USE.

# SAVE MACROS

## DIALECTS:
dBASE IV only.

## SYNTAX:
SAVE MACROS TO <macro filename>

## DEFINITION:
Saves keyboard macros from memory in a macro file.

Macros execute from memory and are erased when you QUIT. However, you can save them on disk with SAVE MACROS, then later RESTORE MACROS.

## DEFAULT:
The macro file has a default extension of MCR.

## RECOMMENDED USE:
dBASE IV lets you record keystrokes entered in the interactive mode. Later, you can replay them (the macro) to automate repetitive operations. You can begin recording, end recording, and playback from the macro menu, accessed by pressing SHIFT-F10. You can also replay macros with the PLAY MACROS command, or by typing a macro key combination (an Alt-key/macro name combination).

**Example**—Ron prints several sales reports every day. Tired of reentering commands, he SAVEs MACROS in a macro file, then later RESTOREs them.

```
* <Begin recording from SHIFT-F10 menu>.
. CLEAR
. SET DELETED OFF
. SET EXACT OFF
. USE sales INDEX sales,month
. COPY TO salestemp FOR sales > 0 .and. today = DATE()
. USE salestemp
. INDEX ON sales TO salesdex
* <Do report program>.
. USE
. DELETE FILE salesdex.ndx
. DELETE FILE salestemp.dbf
. CLEAR
```

```
* <End recording from SHIFT-F10 menu and give macro a name>.
. SAVE MACROS TO mac_rpt
. QUIT
```

The next day, Ron restores the macro and executes it.

```
. RESTORE MACROS FROM mac_rpt
* <Execute macro from SHIFT-F10 menu, with Alt-F10 key, or
*    with the PLAY MACROS command>.
```

## LIMITS/WARNINGS:

Macro files can contain up to 35 macros.

Do not use the extension MAC for macro files, since it conflicts with the extension used by dBASE IV's applications generator.

RESTORE MACROS and SAVE MACROS have no connection with the macro function (&).

## SEE ALSO:

Commands PLAY MACROS and RESTORE MACROS.

# SAVE SCREEN

## DIALECTS:

Clipper and FoxBASE+.

## SYNTAX:

SAVE SCREEN [TO <memory variable>]

## DEFINITION:

Stores the current screen image in a buffer or in a memory variable that can be SAVEd, and then RESTOREd later. To redisplay a SAVEd screen, use the RESTORE SCREEN command.

If you SAVE SCREEN to a nonexistent memory variable, one is created automatically. When you LIST MEMORY in FoxBASE+, screen memory variables appear with data type "S".

Like other variables, saved screens can be stored in MEM files with SAVE TO.

## RECOMMENDED USE:

The SAVE/RESTORE SCREEN commands provide very fast screen displays. Use them in procedures or user defined functions to avoid disturbing the calling program. Also use SAVE/RESTORE SCREEN to flash images on the screen, rather than drawing them line-by-line.

**Example**—A payroll program displays a menu, SAVEs the SCREEN, and does a subroutine selected by the user. Upon return, the program issues RESTORE SCREEN to redisplay the menu.

```
* <Display main menu>
* Save the screen in memory variable MAINMENU.
SAVE SCREEN TO mainmenu
* <Do subroutines>
RESTORE SCREEN from mainmenu
```

## LIMITS/WARNINGS:

**Clipper and FoxBASE+:** Screens saved in MEM files are not compatible.

## VARIATIONS:

Screens saved in memory variables occupy approximately 4K bytes of memory. FoxBASE+ allocates the 4K from the memory variable pool.

## SEE ALSO:

Command RESTORE SCREEN and SAVE TO.

# SAVE STATUS

## DIALECTS:
dBXL only.

## SYNTAX:
SAVE STATUS TO <filename>

## DEFINITION:
Stores system attributes in a disk file.

SAVE STATUS saves the following environment settings:

| | | | | |
|---|---|---|---|---|
| ALTERNATE ON/OFF | DATE | ECHO | INTENSITY | RETRACE |
| ALTERNATE <file> | DEBUG | ESCAPE | MARGIN | SAFETY |
| BELL | DECIMALS | EXACT | MEMOWIDTH | SCOREBOARD |
| CARRY | DEFAULT | FIELDS | ODOMETER | STATUS |
| CENTURY | DELIMITERS | FIXED | OOPS | STEP |
| COLOR | DELIMITERS TO | HEADINGS | PATH | TALK |
| CONFIRM | DEVICE | HELP | PRINT | TITLE |
| CONSOLE | DOHISTORY | HISTORY | PROMPT | UNIQUE |

## DEFAULT:
The STATUS file has a default extension of SET.

## SEE ALSO:
Commands DISPLAY STATUS, RESTORE STATUS, and SET VIEW.

# SAVE WINDOW

## DIALECTS:
dBASE IV only.

## SYNTAX:
SAVE WINDOW <window name list>/ALL TO <filename>

## DEFINITION:
Copies window definitions from memory to a disk file that you can later RESTORE.

If a file of the same name already exists, SAVE WINDOW overwrites it.

You can SAVE some or ALL windows from memory. The order of the names has no effect.

## DEFAULT:
The window definition file has a default extension of WIN unless specified otherwise.

## RECOMMENDED USE:
Use SAVE WINDOW and RESTORE WINDOW to create application window "libraries." Rather than redefine windows throughout an application, define and SAVE them once, then RESTORE them as needed.

**Example**—An inventory system uses standardized windows to simplify program maintenance. A "library" contains all the definitions.

```
DEFINE WINDOW mmaint FROM 10,10 TO 20,50 COLOR GR+/B
DEFINE WINDOW mbrowse FROM 2,5 TO 10,30 DOUBLE
* <Define more windows>.
*
SAVE WINDOW ALL TO winlib
```

To save only selected windows, use a list as follows:

```
SAVE WINDOW mmaint, mbrowse TO winlib
```

## SEE ALSO:
Commands ACTIVATE WINDOW, DEFINE WINDOW, RESTORE, and SAVE WINDOW.

# SCAN...ENDSCAN

## DIALECTS:
dBASE IV only.

## SYNTAX:
SCAN [<scope>] [FOR <condition>] [WHILE <condition>]
 [<statements>]
 [LOOP]
 [<statements>]
 [EXIT]
 [<statements>]
ENDSCAN

## DEFINITION:
Repeats the program statements in-between while skipping through database records.

SCAN...ENDSCAN processes records for the specified <scope> or <condition>, or until reaching the end-of-file.

## DEFAULT:
Processes all records unless you limit it with a <scope> or <condition>.

## OPTIONS:
LOOP returns control to the beginning of the structure. The computer does not execute any commands after it.

EXIT ends execution of the SCAN, and returns control to the statement immediately following ENDSCAN.

## RECOMMENDED USE:
Think of SCAN...ENDSCAN as a DO WHILE...ENDDO loop designed strictly for processing records. SCAN...ENDSCAN automatically skips through the file, executing statements within the loop when the conditions are met. This simplifies the logic for processing records, and reduces the number of statements required.

**Example**—A financial program analyzes data, then executes a subroutine to graph it. dBASE III PLUS requires the following:

```
USE plotdata
LOCATE FOR entered = DATE()
DO WHILE FOUND() .AND. .NOT. EOF()
  DO bargraf WITH pctplus,netplus,issue
  CONTINUE
ENDDO
```

dBASE IV's SCAN...ENDSCAN simplifies the code, eliminating LOCATE, CONTINUE, and the test for end-of-file, as shown:

```
USE plotdata
SCAN FOR entered = DATE()
  DO bargraf WITH pctplus,netplus,issue
ENDSCAN
```

The programmer enhances the SCAN loop with a printer check and a scope of 100 records. If PRINT( ) returns false (.F.), the user is prompted to turn on the printer and press "R" to retry. If INKEY(0) does not return 114 (r) or 82 (R), the loop EXITs. Otherwise, LOOP returns control to the top of the loop, and checks the printer again. If it is ready, the check routine is skipped, and the BARGRAF subroutine executes.

```
USE plotdata
SCAN NEXT 100 FOR entered = DATE()
  IF .NOT. PRINT()
    @ 01,01 SAY "Turn printer on and press 'R' to retry. "+;
                "Press any other key to cancel"
    IF .NOT. (INKEY(0) = 114 .or. INKEY(0) = 82)
      EXIT
    ELSE
      LOOP
    ENDIF
  ENDIF
  DO bargraf WITH pctplus,netplus,issue
ENDSCAN
```

## SPECIAL USES:

To speed up processing, first INDEX the file on the expression from the FOR <condition>. Then SEEK <condition> and SCAN WHILE <condition>. This eliminates the processing of unnecessary records. Modify the previous example as follows:

```
INDEX ON entered TO enterdex
*
*
```

```
USE plotdata INDEX enterdex
SEEK date()
SCAN WHILE entered = DATE()
  DO bargraf WITH pctplus,netplus,issue
ENDSCAN
```

## LIMITS/WARNINGS:

SCAN...ENDSCAN does not optimize searches on indexed databases.

## SEE ALSO:

Commands CONTINUE, DO WHILE...ENDDO, FOR...NEXT, and LOCATE.

# SCATTER

## DIALECTS:

FoxBASE+ only.

## SYNTAX:

SCATTER [FIELDS <field list>] TO <array>

## DEFINITION:

Transfers the contents of the current database record into a memory variable array. If the array does not exist, SCATTER creates it. Fields in the record are loaded into the array, starting with the first one specified, and filling array elements sequentially. SCATTER defaults to all fields if you do not specify a field list.

Note that SCATTER ignores memo fields.

## RECOMMENDED USE:

Use SCATTER to reduce the amount of programming required to initialize arrays.

SCATTER works with GATHER. GATHER moves data from an array into the current record of the active database.

Together, they provide a simple way to edit database records in memory without making explicit declarations for each field.

**Example**—In dBASE III PLUS, moving data from a record to memory variables requires that you initialize a variable for each field. A record with 30 fields requires 30 STORE or = statements. After changing the memory variables, each variable must then be REPLACEd into its original field. SCATTER eliminates many program lines by initializing an array containing the field values of the current record.

```
* Without SCATTER and GATHER.
CLEAR
USE acctnames
* Initialize memory variables
mname = name
maddress = address
mcity = city
```

```
mstate = state
mzip = zip
* Edit memory variables with GET.
@ 05,01 SAY "    Name: " GET mname
@ 06,01 SAY "Address: " GET maddress
@ 07,01 SAY "    City: " GET mcity
@ 08,01 SAY "   State: " GET mstate
@ 09,01 SAY "     Zip: " GET mzip
READ
REPLACE name WITH mname,address WITH maddress,city WITH mcity,;
        state WITH mstate,zip WITH mzip
```

Use SCATTER and GATHER to simplify the code by eliminating memory variable assignments:

```
CLEAR
USE acctnames
SCATTER TO acctedit    && Initialize array.
* Edit array.
@ 05,01 SAY "    Name: " GET acctedit(1)
@ 06,01 SAY "Address: " GET acctedit(2)
@ 07,01 SAY "    City: " GET acctedit(3)
@ 08,01 SAY "   State: " GET acctedit(4)
@ 09,01 SAY "     Zip: " GET acctedit(5)
READ
GATHER FROM acctedit    && Write array back to record.
```

The benefit of this technique increases with the number of fields.

## VARIATIONS:

**dBXL, Quicksilver:** The STORE AUTOMEM command is similar to SCATTER.

**dBASE IV:** COPY TO ARRAY is similar to SCATTER; however, dBASE IV has no equivalent to GATHER. (APPEND FROM ARRAY adds a record with the contents of the specified array).

## SEE ALSO:

Commands APPEND FROM ARRAY, COPY TO ARRAY, DIMENSION, and GATHER.

# SEEK

## DIALECTS:

Clipper, dBASE III PLUS, dBASE IV, dBXL, FoxBASE+, and Quicksilver.

## SYNTAX:

SEEK <expression>

## DEFINITION:

Searches an indexed database for the first match between the expression and the index key. If one is found, the record pointer stops there. The FOUND( ) function returns true (.T.). If no match is found, FOUND( ) returns false (.F.). If TALK is SET ON, a message reports that the record was not found.

SEEK can use any valid expression. You must enclose string expressions inside delimiters.

SEEK can search for partial matches, but only starting with the first character. SET EXACT must be OFF.

SEEK is case sensitive.

SEEK with a memory variable does not require the macro function (&), as does the closely related FIND command.

SEEK is similar to FIND. However, SEEK offers more flexibility because its argument can be any valid expression.

## RECOMMENDED USE:

SEEK provides the fastest dBASE search method. Use it in applications requiring rapid retrieval of information. Typical examples are point of sale and customer service applications where people call for account information.

**Example**—The customer service department of a magazine handles hundreds of inquiries every month. When a customer calls with a problem, the information goes into a database so that its resolution can be traced. If the customer calls back, SEEK instantly finds his or her record.

SUBSEEK.PRG prompts the operator for the customer's last name. It goes into variable LNAME, which is then used in the SEEK. If FOUND, subroutine

SDISPLAY presents the data. If not FOUND, the operator can enter a new name, or exit.

```
* SUBSEEK.PRG finds subscriber and display data.
USE subdata INDEX lnamedex    && Indexed on LNAME.
DO WHILE .t.
  lname = SPACE(15)           && Create variable to hold last name
  * PICTURE "@!" forces all uppercase
  @ 05,10 SAY "Enter subscriber's last name: " GET lname PICTURE "@!"
  @ 06,10 SAY "Leave blank to exit"
  READ
  IF lname = "  "
    RETURN
  ENDIF
  SEEK TRIM(lname)             && TRIM removes trailing blanks.
  IF FOUND()                   && If the record is FOUND,
    DO sdisplay                &&  do subroutine that displays data.
  ENDIF                        && If not FOUND, go back to top of loop,
ENDDO                          &&  and redo user prompt.
```

## VARIATIONS:

**Clipper:** If you SET SOFTSEEK ON, an unsuccessful SEEK moves the pointer to the record with the next highest index key value, instead of to the end-of-file. This lets you search for "next closest" matches.

**dBASE IV:** If you SET NEAR ON, an unsuccessful SEEK moves the pointer to the record with the next highest index key value, instead of to the end-of-file. This lets you search for "next closest" matches.

The dBASE IV SEEK( ) function seeks a specified value and returns true if it is found.

## SEE ALSO:

Commands FIND, INDEX, SET NEAR, and SET SOFTSEEK; functions FOUND( ), LOOKUP( ), and SEEK( ).

# SELECT

## DIALECTS:

Clipper, dBASE III PLUS, dBASE IV, dBXL, FoxBASE+, and Quicksilver.

## SYNTAX:

SELECT <work area>/<alias>

## DEFINITION:

Chooses a work area. Areas are designated by the numbers 1 through 10, the letters A through J, or by the alias or name of a database file open in them.

## DEFAULT:

If you open a file without selecting a work area, the area number defaults to 1.

## RECOMMENDED USE:

All systems except Clipper provide up to ten independent work areas in which to open database files, associated indexes, and format files. In this way, you can open multiple files simultaneously, and you can gather data from each by changing areas or by designating fields with their aliases in the form ALIAS->FIELDNAME.

Most commands that affect the file in the active work area do not affect database files in other work areas. For example, COPY, DISPLAY, LIST, and USE all act on the active database file. The record pointers of files in other work areas do not move. In contrast, SET RELATION TO relates records in one open file to records in another, across work areas. CLOSE DATABASES and CLEAR ALL close all open database files.

**Example**—A general ledger application opens files in three separate work areas and includes data from all of them in an aged receivables report. ACCTCURR contains current receivables. ACCTPAST contains past due accounts. ACCOUNTS contains client information.

```
SELECT 1
USE acctcurr DISPLAY
Record#  ITEM   ACOUNTNO  AMOUNT    PAST    PDATE
      1  1410   1237      1222.00   0       12/22/88
```

```
SELECT 2
USE acctpast ALIAS owedfile
DISPLAY
Record#   ITEM   ACOUNTNO  AMOUNT COMMENT            PAST  PDATE
      1  1238   1237       350.94 Six month payment  30   09/22/87
```

```
SELECT c
USE ACCOUNTS
DISPLAY
Record#  LASTNAME   ADDRESS           CITY     STATE  ACOUNTNO
      1  Lowdon     1414 S. Malden Ralson    VA      1237
```

To obtain data from separate work areas, specify a field in an unselected area using the syntax ALIAS->FIELDNAME. In this example, the receivables report displays the account information from ACCOUNT, and the history from ACCTCURR and ACCTPAST, without changing work areas.

```
SELECT c
SET DEVICE TO print
@ 06,05 SAY "ACCOUNT NAME: " + lastname
@ 07,05 SAY "ACCOUNT NUM.: " + acountno
@ 08,05 SAY "ADDRESS: " + TRIM(address) + ", " + TRIM(city) + ", " + state
@ 09,05 SAY "--------------------------------------------------------------"
@ 10,05 SAY "ITEM: " + acctcurr->item + " AMT: " +;
        STR(acctcurr->amount,7,2) + "  DATE DUE: " + DTOC(acctcurr->pdate)
@ 11,05 SAY ""
@ 12,05 SAY "ITEM: " + owedfile->item + " AMT: " +;
        STR(owedfile->amount,7,2) + "  DATE DUE: " + DTOC(owedfile->pdate)
@ 13,05 SAY "--------------------------------------------------------------"
```

This program fragment prints the following report:

```
ACCOUNT NAME: Lowdon
ACCOUNT NUM.: 1237
ADDRESS: 1414 S. Malden Street, Ralston, VA
---------------------------------------------------
ITEM: 1410 AMT: 1222.00  DATE DUE: 12/22/88
---------------------------------------------------
ITEM: 1238 AMT:  350.94  DATE DUE: 09/22/87
---------------------------------------------------
```

## LIMITS/WARNINGS:

Although you can open different files simultaneously, you cannot open a single file in more than one area at a time.

Note that memory variables are not allocated by work area, only files.

## VARIATIONS:

Note that the number of open files is limited, and varies among the systems.

**Clipper:** Work areas may be designated 0 through 254. The first ten may be designated by the letters A through J.

**Clipper, FoxBASE+:** SELECT 0 selects the first available (unused) work area. It is useful for creating general purpose subroutines that do not conflict with other programs.

**dBASE III PLUS:** Allows work area M as well as A through J. The letters are reserved words; do not use them as field names or memory variable names. If you need a memory variable "A," call it "AA" instead.

Also note that dBASE III PLUS reserves work area 10 for an open catalog. Opening a catalog will automatically close a file open in area 10.

**dBASE IV:** You can define work areas A through J. These letters are reserved words.

Also note that dBASE IV reserves work area 10 for an open catalog. Opening a catalog will automatically close a file open in area 10.

You can open a database file in another work area without first SELECTing it, with the command:

```
USE <filename> IN <work area>
```

Many functions can operate on other work areas by using the area alias as an argument as in the end-of-file function:

```
? EOF("main")
.T.
```

**FoxBASE+:** Many functions can operate on other work areas by using the area number as an argument as in the end-of-file function:

```
? EOF(1)
.T.
```

## SEE ALSO:

Commands SET CATALOG, SET RELATION, and USE; function EOF( ).

# SET

## DIALECTS:
dBASE III PLUS, dBASE IV, dBXL, and FoxBASE+.

## SYNTAX:
SET

## DEFINITION:
Displays a menu for controlling system attributes. Designed for interactive use, it is available only in the interpreters dBASE III PLUS, dBASE IV, dBXL, and FoxBASE+. Avoid SET in programs because it allows the end user to tamper with the program's working environment.

Attributes controlled in the SET menu include:

- SET options (CONSOLE, DEVICE, TALK, DEVICE)
- Screen colors and other screen attributes
- Function key assignments
- Default disk drives
- Open ALTERNATE, INDEX, or FORMAT files
- Margins
- Decimals
- Date

## RECOMMENDED USE:
Use the SET command in the interactive mode. In programs, all SET menu selections have command equivalents.

## VARIATIONS:
The menu formats and options vary slightly among dBASE III PLUS, dBASE IV, dBXL, and FoxBASE+.

## SEE ALSO:
Command DISPLAY/LIST STATUS, RESTORE STATUS, and SAVE STATUS; function SET( ).

# SET ALTERNATE

## DIALECTS:

Clipper, dBASE III PLUS, dBASE IV, dBXL, FoxBASE+, and Quicksilver.

## SYNTAX:

SET ALTERNATE TO [<filename>]
SET ALTERNATE ON/OFF

## DEFINITION:

Redirects line-oriented screen output to an ASCII text file. The file is given an extension of TXT and can be edited with most word processors.

Operations which do direct screen positioning, such as @ ... SAY, EDIT and BROWSE, are not redirected. Commands that produce line-oriented output include DISPLAY, LIST, and ?.

SET ALTERNATE TO <filename> overwrites an existing file with the same name. It does not respect the SAFETY setting.

## RECOMMENDED USE:

The SET ALTERNATE command consists of two parts:

1. SET ALTERNATE TO [<filename>]
2. SET ALTERNATE ON/OFF

SET ALTERNATE TO <filename> creates and opens the text file. It overwrites an existing file with the same name.

Then, when you SET ALTERNATE ON, output goes to the specified text file. If you SET ALTERNATE OFF and then ON again, output is added to the open ALTERNATE file. To close the file, use SET ALTERNATE TO with no argument, or CLOSE ALTERNATE.

Note that dBASE III PLUS, dBASE IV, dBXL, and FoxBASE+ redirect keyboard input, as well as screen output, to the alternate file.

SET ALTERNATE does not affect the screen's appearance.

**Example**—A condominium timeshare sales program generates sales reports. Rather than printing them, it puts them in text files for merging with word processing documents.

The SALES file contains end of month figures. The program SETs ALTERNATE TO endmonth. After SETting ALTERNATE ON, the LIST command chooses all accounts in California and displays sales amounts. The program then USEs an EXPENSE file and LISTs the California sales representatives' mileage. This report is added to the file ENDMONTH.

```
USE sales           && Create end of month sales report in a text file.
SET ALTERNATE TO endmonth
SET ALTERNATE on
LIST ALL acct_name,amount FOR state = "CA"    && Sample query
SET ALTERNATE off
USE expenses
SET ALTERNATE on    && Add expense information to sales report.
LIST ALL mileage FOR state = "CA"
CLOSE ALTERNATE
```

## LIMITS/WARNINGS:

dBASE III PLUS: SETting ALTERNATE TO an existing filename causes an error. To avoid it, erase the file first as in:

```
mfile = "TEMP.TXT"
ERASE &mfile
SET ALTERNATE TO &mfile
```

## VARIATIONS:

**Clipper, FoxBASE+:** You can redirect @...SAYs to a text file by specifying a filename instead of a printer, as in SET PRINTER TO ENDMONTH. When you SET DEVICE TO PRINT, all @...SAY output goes to the file ENDMONTH. No extension is given.

**dBASE IV:** The ADDITIVE option appends to a text file with the form:

SET ALTERNATE TO <filename> ADDITIVE

Without ADDITIVE, SET ALTERNATE TO <filename> overwrites an existing file with the same name.

**dBXL, Quicksilver:** You can redirect @...SAYs to a text file using the command SET DEVICE TO ALTERNATE. The other two SET ALTERNATE commands are also necessary. First, SET DEVICE TO ALTERNATE, then SET ALTERNATE TO <filename>. Finally, SET ALTERNATE ON.

## SEE ALSO:

Command CLOSE ALTERNATE, SET DEVICE, and SET PRINTER.

# SET AUTOLOCK

## DIALECTS:
Quicksilver only.

## SYNTAX:
SET AUTOLOCK ON/OFF

## DEFINITION:
Toggles Quicksilver's automatic record locking mode for multiuser operation on a network.

With SET AUTOLOCK ON, a REPLACE or READ on a single record automatically locks it. With SET AUTOLOCK OFF, you must issue an explicit RLOCK( ).

When you SET AUTOLOCK ON, trying to REPLACE or READ a locked record causes an error. Use the ON NETERROR command to trap failed locking attempts.

## DEFAULT:
OFF

## RECOMMENDED USE:
SET AUTOLOCK ON simplifies multiuser programming by eliminating explicit record locking.

SET AUTOLOCK OFF to maintain dBASE III PLUS-compatibility.

**Example**—A multiuser inventory program uses SET AUTOLOCK ON to eliminate explicit record locking.

```
SET EXCLUSIVE off
SET AUTOLOCK on
ON ERROR DO trapfail          && TRAPFAIL contains a RETRY command
                              &&  to reexecute READ if AUTOLOCK fails.
USE invent INDEX invdex
SEEK "8245"
STORE AUTOMEM
@ 10,10 SAY "Description"
@ 10,22 GET desc
@ 11,10 SAY "Quantity"
@ 11,22 GET qty
@ 12,10 SAY "Price"
@ 12,22 GET price
```

```
READ
REPLACE AUTOMEM
```

## LIMITS/WARNINGS:

You must use Quicksilver's -O compiler option to use ON ERROR.

## SEE ALSO:

Functions FLOCK( ) and RLOCK( ).

# SET AUTOSAVE

## DIALECTS:

dBASE IV only.

## SYNTAX

SET AUTOSAVE ON/OFF

## DEFINITION:

Determines whether a disk write occurs after each update to a database record. With AUTOSAVE OFF, records are written when the internal buffer is full. This makes processing faster but increases the chance of a power loss damaging data.

SET AUTOSAVE ON forces a disk write after each update.

## DEFAULT:

OFF

## VARIATIONS:

**Clipper:** Use COMMIT or SKIP 0 to force a disk write.

**dBASE III PLUS, dBXL, and Quicksilver:** Write data to disk immediately.

**FoxBASE+:** Use FLUSH to force a disk write.

## SEE ALSO:

Commands COMMIT, FLUSH, and SKIP.

# SET BELL

## DIALECTS:
Clipper, dBASE III PLUS, dBASE IV, dBXL, FoxBASE+, and Quicksilver.

## SYNTAX:
SET BELL ON/OFF

## DEFINITION:
Toggles the computer bell ON or OFF during data entry. The BELL normally rings when you enter invalid data or reach the end of a field.

## DEFAULT:
ON. SET BELL does not affect rings programmed using the command

```
? CHR(7)
```

## RECOMMENDED USE:
SET BELL OFF to eliminate the annoying bell when entering data into a GET.

## VARIATIONS:
**Clipper:** You can specify the logical expressions (.T.) or (.F.) to indicate ON or OFF in the SET command. Enclose the logical value in parentheses.

Clipper's TONE( ) function lets you create musical sounds. What could be more fun than a musical database?

**dBASE IV:** You can change the bell's tone and length by supplying a frequency and duration with the command:

```
SET BELL TO [<frequency>,<duration>]
```

Frequency is a value ranging from 19 to 10,000 inclusive. The duration can be from 1 to 20 seconds.

Whenever the bell sounds, it has the tone and duration of the last SET BELL command.

To set the bell for a high pitched tone lasting 5 seconds, use the command

```
SET BELL TO 7500,5
```

The following user defined function simplifies the use of SET BELL:

```
FUNCTION tone
PARAMETERS freq,dura
*
SET BELL TO freq,dura
?? CHR(7)
RETURN ""
```

To get maximum speed, TONE( ) has no error checking.

## SEE ALSO:

Functions CHR( ) and TONE( ).

# SET BLOCKSIZE

## DIALECTS:
dBASE IV only.

## SYNTAX:
SET BLOCKSIZE TO <expN>

## DEFINITION:
Changes the disk storage block size of memo fields and multiple index files (extension MDX). The block size is 512 times <expN>, where <expN> is between 1 and 32.

Existing memo fields retain their block sizes. New ones created with CREATE, COPY, or MODIFY STRUCTURE have the new block size.

## DEFAULT:
1

## RECOMMENDED USE:
Even if you enter only one character in a memo field, dBASE IV allocates space for an entire block. If you generally enter short memos or index small files, you will greatly reduce disk storage requirements by specifying a small block size.

For large memo fields, defining a larger block size improves performance for formatting and printing. However, at the same time, dBASE IV takes slightly longer to open and save the memo.

**Example**—An architect stores design notes in memo fields. Since the notes are generally only one or two lines, the architect issues the command

```
. SET BLOCKSIZE TO 1
```

You can SET BLOCKSIZE with the BLOCKSIZE parameter in the CONFIG.DB file, in the form

BLOCKSIZE=<expN>

## LIMITS/WARNINGS:
To maintain compatibility with dBASE III PLUS, SET BLOCKSIZE TO 1 (the default).

# SET BORDER

## DIALECTS:

dBASE IV only.

## SYNTAX:

SET BORDER TO [SINGLE/DOUBLE/NONE/PANEL/<border definition>]

## DEFINITION:

Changes the default window and popup borders, and boxes created by the @...TO command.

## OPTIONS:

The <border definition> lets you define each side and corner individually. The definition consists of up to eight keyboard characters or ASCII characters in a list representing parts of the border, as follows:

```
SET BORDER TO <t>,<b>,<l>,<r>,<tl>,<tr>,<bl>,<br>

tl______t______tr      t = top          tl = top left
|               |      b = bottom       tr = top right
l               r      l = left         bl = bottom left
|               |      r = right        br = bottom right
bl______b______br
```

You may omit any characters in the list by leaving their commas in place. You must omit extra commas from the end. Only parts of the border you specify will be redefined, unless you specify just the first character. In that case, it makes up the entire border.

A SINGLE-line border is the default. (Equivalent to SET BORDER TO 196,196,179,179,218,191,192,217).

DOUBLE creates a double line border. (Equivalent to SET BORDER TO 205,205,186,186,201,187,200,188).

NONE omits the border.

PANEL creates a solid bar border. (Equivalent to SET BORDER TO 219).

## RECOMMENDED USE:

Use SET BORDER to change the default border. Windows and popups can override the default without changing it.

**Example**—An invoicing application prints a border with dollar signs, just to remind recipients of the subject under consideration.

```
SET BORDER TO "$"
@ 10,10 TO 15,30
$$$$$$$$$$$$$$$$$$$$$
$                   $
$                   $
$                   $
$                   $
$$$$$$$$$$$$$$$$$$$$$
```

To redefine only the top, bottom, and sides of a border, leaving the corners as dollar signs, the programmer uses the ASCII characters for single lines.

```
SET BORDER TO 196,196,179,179
```

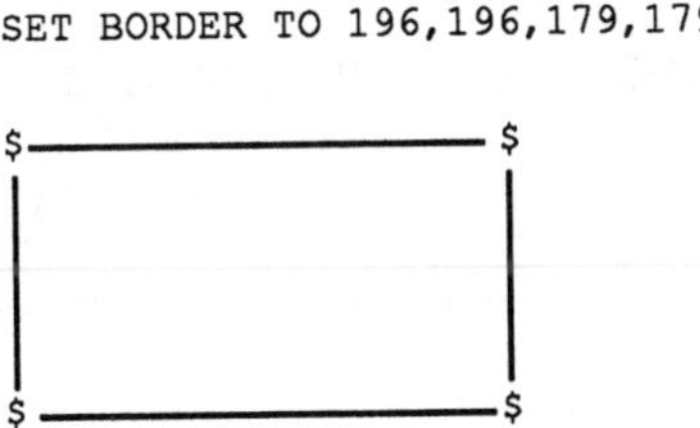

To restore the default single line, the programmer issues SET BORDER TO by itself.

## LIMITS/WARNINGS:

Do not use ASCII characters 7, 8, 10, 12, 13, 27, and 127 in <border definitions>. They may interfere with print drivers.

## SEE ALSO:

Commands @...TO, DEFINE POPUP, and DEFINE WINDOW.

# SET CARRY

## DIALECTS:
dBASE III PLUS, dBASE IV, dBXL, and FoxBASE+.

## SYNTAX:
SET CARRY ON/OFF

## DEFINITION:
Determines whether data from the previous record is copied to the one newly added by APPEND, BROWSE, or INSERT. SET CARRY ON is helpful when data items (such as state, country, telephone area code, or industry type) remain unchanged over many records. You need not reenter them each time.

SET CARRY does not affect INSERT BLANK or APPEND BLANK.

## DEFAULT:
OFF

## VARIATIONS:
**dBASE IV:** Allows a list of fields to be copied, as follows:

```
SET CARRY TO <field list> [ADDITIVE]
```

This form of SET CARRY automatically SETs CARRY ON. The ADDITIVE option lets you add fields to the list. For example, to just carry default values for state, zipcode, and dialing prefix, issue the command

```
SET CARRY TO state,zip,prefix
```

To add entry date to the list, use the command

```
SET CARRY TO entdate ADDITIVE
```

SET CARRY TO <field list> ignores the SET FIELDS command.

## SEE ALSO:
Commands APPEND and INSERT.

# SET CATALOG

## DIALECTS:

dBASE III PLUS and dBASE IV.

## SYNTAX:

SET CATALOG ON/OFF
SET CATALOG TO [<filename>]>/?

## DEFINITION:

SET CATALOG keeps a record of open files. It helps organize related files for users who work primarily in the interactive mode. (In programs, the required files are explicit.)

SET CATALOG is an interactive command. It has no use in programs.

## RECOMMENDED USE:

Use SET CATALOG to organize groups of files. For example, if you work interactively with payroll data and accounts receivable data, you could maintain two catalogs. Each simply presents a list of logically grouped files.

When you SET CATALOG ON, and SET CATALOG TO <filename>, any new files you use are added to the catalog. If no catalog exists, one is created. You are then asked for a title, if SET TITLE is ON. If this is the first catalog to be created, dBASE III PLUS and dBASE IV automatically generate a master catalog, which keeps track of all other catalogs.

The command SET CATALOG TO ? lists all catalogs.

Whenever you create a new catalog or open an existing one, SET CATALOG is automatically set ON.

The catalog file is a standard dBASE database file, except that it has an extension of CAT. It has the following structure:

```
Field  Field Name  Type       Width    Dec
   1  PATH        Character    70
   2  FILE_NAME   Character    12
   3  ALIAS       Character     8
   4  TYPE        Character     3
   5  TITLE       Character    80
   6  CODE        Numeric       3
   7  TAG         Character     4
** Total **                   181
```

The catalog maintains a record of files associated with open database files. The following commands update the catalog automatically:

COPY STRUCTURE
COPY STRUCTURE EXTENDED
COPY TO
CREATE
CREATE FROM
CREATE/MODIFY LABEL
CREATE/MODIFY QUERY
CREATE/MODIFY REPORT
CREATE/MODIFY SCREEN
CREATE/MODIFY VIEW
IMPORT FROM
INDEX
JOIN
SET FILTER TO
SET FORMAT
SET VIEW
SORT
TOTAL
USE

If dBASE III PLUS or dBASE IV finds the name of an affected database file in the catalog, and SET TITLE is ON, the user is prompted for a file title.

If the user deletes files listed in the catalog, but SET CATALOG is OFF, dBASE will update the catalog the next time it is opened.

## SPECIAL USES:

SET CATALOG TO <filename> is the only dBASE III PLUS or dBASE IV command that can create a database file under program control. (The CATALOG file itself is a database file, despite its CAT extension). This means programmers can create a catalog file, COPY its STRUCTURE EXTENDED, and then create any other database file with CREATE FROM. See CREATE FROM and COPY STRUCTURE for more information.

## LIMITS/WARNINGS:

Work area 10 is reserved for the open catalog.

## SEE ALSO:

Commands COPY and SET TITLE.

# SET CENTURY

## DIALECTS:

Clipper, dBASE III PLUS, dBASE IV, dBXL, FoxBASE+, and Quicksilver.

## SYNTAX:

SET CENTURY ON/OFF

## DEFINITION:

Allows the input of four-digit years in date fields. Normally, only the last two digits are read and twentieth century dates are assumed.

Although four digit years appear, SET CENTURY ON does not affect the storage size of date fields since dates are stored internally as numbers. Non-twentieth century date values retain the correct century, even if you SET CENTURY OFF.

## DEFAULT:

OFF

## VARIATIONS:

**Clipper:** You can specify the logical expressions (.T.) or (.F.) to indicate ON or OFF in the SET command. Enclose the logical value in parentheses.

## SEE ALSO:

Command SET DATE; functions DATE( ) and YEAR( ).

# SET CLEAR

## DIALECTS:
FoxBASE+ only.

## SYNTAX:
SET CLEAR ON/OFF

## DEFINITION:
Determines whether the commands SET FORMAT TO and QUIT clear the screen.

By SETting CLEAR OFF, programmers can lay format file screens over background screens, simulating windowing. In addition, you can leave messages on the screen even after issuing QUIT.

## DEFAULT:
ON

## SEE ALSO:
Commands CLEAR, SET FORMAT, and QUIT.

# SET CLOCK

## DIALECTS:
dBASE IV only.

## SYNTAX:
SET CLOCK ON/OFF
[SET CLOCK TO [<coord>]]

## DEFINITION:
SET CLOCK ON displays a clock based on the system time. It shows hours, minutes, seconds, and am or pm. The display is 11 characters wide.

The display format is controlled by the command SET HOURS TO 12/24. The 12-hour format is the default.

SET CLOCK TO <coord> displays the clock at a different coordinate. The default is 0,69.

SET CLOCK TO with no coordinates returns the clock to its default position.

SET CLOCK OFF deactivates the clock, but does not erase the screen.

## DEFAULT:
OFF

## RECOMMENDED USE:
Display the system clock as a convenience to users.

**Example**—A large bakery takes orders by telephone. The order entry program displays the time in the lower right corner of the screen.

```
SET CLOCK TO 24,68
```

The clock appears as:

```
2:06:07 pm
```

## LIMITS/WARNINGS:

Be sure to put the clock in an unused part of the screen; otherwise, it covers other screen output, including SAYs and GETs.

## SEE ALSO:

Function TIME( ).

# SET COLOR

## DIALECTS:
dBASE III PLUS, dBASE IV, dBXL, FoxBASE+, and Quicksilver.

## SYNTAX:
SET COLOR ON/OFF

## DEFINITION:
Switches between color and monochrome displays on systems that have both.

When you SET COLOR ON, you may change screen colors with the SET COLOR TO command. If you SET COLOR OFF, the SET COLOR TO command changes other screen attributes such as underline and inverse video.

## DEFAULT:
Display used when you started the program.

## SEE ALSO:
Command SET COLOR TO.

# SET COLOR TO

## DIALECTS:

Clipper, dBASE III PLUS, dBASE IV, dBXL, FoxBASE+, and Quicksilver.

## SYNTAX:

SET COLOR TO [[<standard>][,<enhanced>][,<border>][,<background>]]

## DEFINITION:

Changes the screen colors or video attributes. <standard> refers to normal text display. <enhanced> refers to error message and input field display. Specify both <standard> and <enhanced> as foreground and background colors separated by a slash. Specify colors by codes from the tables below. <border> refers to the screen perimeter. Use the <background> setting on computers that allow only one background color for both standard and enhanced displays.

Note that you cannot set background and border attributes on monochrome monitors.

## RECOMMENDED USE:

Use colors and video attributes to highlight user prompts and error messages.

**Example**—Set standard text to red on blue, and enhanced text to white on green, with a green border.

```
SET COLOR TO R/B,W/G,G
```

The default setting for both color and monochrome is white letters on a black background with a black border. Highlighted or enhanced displays appear in black on a white background.

| COLOR | LETTER CODE | COLOR | LETTER CODE |
|---|---|---|---|
| Black | N or blank | Green | G |
| Blank | X | Inverse | I |
| Blinking | * | Magenta | RB |
| Bold | + | Red | R |
| Blue | B | Underline | U |
| Brown | GR | White | W |
| Cyan | BG | | |

**Monochrome only attributes**

| | | | |
|---|---|---|---|
| Black | N | Underline | U |
| Blank | X | White | W |
| Inverse | I | | |

Attributes can also make colors blink or appear in high intensity. High intensity makes colors brighter and lighter in hue. To make them blink, use the letter code with an asterisk (*) as in SET COLOR TO B*. To make colors high intensity, use the plus sign (+), as in SET COLOR TO B+.

**Example 1**—Set standard text to yellow on blue, and enhanced text to white on green, with a green border.

```
SET COLOR TO GR+/B,W/G,G
```

Yellow is not on the chart, but you can create it with high intensity brown. You can create grey with N+.

The ability to use color attributes varies among computer systems. Some allow different background colors for standard and enhanced text areas as in the examples above. Others allow only one background color. In this case, set the <standard> and <enhanced> texts without a background (no slash), then set a <border> and a single <background> color.

**Example 2**—Set standard text to yellow, enhanced text to white, and border and background to green.

```
SET COLOR TO GR+,W,G,G
```

When setting colors, note that you need not specify everything. If you omit an attribute from a SET COLOR TO command, it simply keeps its current setting. Use a comma to mark an omitted option. For example, the command SET COLOR TO ,,R changes the border to red.

## LIMITS/WARNINGS:

SET COLOR TO's effects may vary from one computer to another. Some monochrome monitors, for example, automatically translate colors into contrasting shades of green or amber, depending on the screen color. Such displays are called *composite monitors*. They respond to SET COLOR TO commands like color monitors. When you use conventional color combinations on composite displays, the screen may become unreadable because of a lack of contrast. Popular computers with composite displays include Compaq's Deskpro series.

## VARIATIONS:

**Clipper:** Allows the English spelling COLOUR.

Clipper has an additional color attribute, <unselected>, in the form

SET COLOR TO [[<standard>][,<enhanced>][,<border>]
[,<background>][,<unselected>]]

When you specify an unselected color, the current GET (the one the cursor is touching) appears in the enhanced color, whereas other GETs appear in the unselected color.

High intensity and blink are available only for foreground text. You may also specify colors by number, except when you are using the ANSI terminal support program (ANSI.OBJ on the System Disk).

**Clipper, dBXL, FoxBASE+, and Quicksilver:** Also recognize numerical codes.

| COLOR | NUMBER | LETTER CODE |
|---|---|---|
| Black | 0 | N |
| Blue | 1 | B |
| Green | 2 | G |
| Cyan | 3 | BG |
| Red | 4 | R |
| Magenta | 5 | RB |
| Brown | 6 | GR |
| White | 7 | W |
| Blank | | X |

**dBASE IV:** You can change colors for specific display areas with the command SET COLOR OF BOX/FIELDS/HIGHLIGHT/MESSAGES/NORMAL/TITLES TO [<attribute>]. This version of SET COLOR controls colors in applications and in the development system, including the Query-by-Example, Applications Generator, Report Writer, Text Editor, and Forms Generator modules.

The following list shows the screen areas affected by SET COLOR OF, grouped by keyword. (This list is limited to screen areas relevant to dBASE programs.)

**ALERT:**

Clock
Line 23 status bar
Borders on help box
Selected button in error and help boxes

**BOX:**

Menu, list, and prompt box borders

**FIELDS:**

Prompt box data entry areas
BROWSE mode's selected field
Available GET fields

**HIGHLIGHT:**

Highlighted menu, list, and prompt box choices
Information box borders and interiors
Selected boxes

**MESSAGES:**

Bright help box text
Unselected, bright prompt box, error, and help box buttons
Message line messages
Unselected, available menu and list choices
Navigation line messages
Error, help, and prompt box interiors

**NORMAL:**

Window borders
Calculated field expressions
@...SAY output
Unselected fields in BROWSE
Uncolored box borders drawn with @...TO.

**TITLES:**

LIST and BROWSE field headings
BROWSE table borders
Help box titles
Underlined help text

**dBXL and Quicksilver:** The CHARACTER option defines a background character to be displayed within the border where no text has been entered. After the usual color command (on the same line), add the option

[CHARACTER "<background character>"]

For example, the following command sets the dBXL screen to high intensity white with a background filled with the letter "X":

```
SET COLOR TO W+ CHARACTER "X"
```

When used with dBXL or Quicksilver windows, the background character feature can produce interesting graphical displays. Note that the CHARACTER option requires at least one other color attribute in the string.

**SEE ALSO:**

Commands SET DISPLAY and SET INTENSITY; functions ISCOLOR( ) and SETCOLOR( ).

# SET CONFIRM

## DIALECTS:

Clipper, dBASE III PLUS, dBASE IV, dBXL, FoxBASE+, and Quicksilver.

## SYNTAX:

SET CONFIRM ON/OFF

## DEFINITION:

Determines whether the user must press Enter (Return) when entering data into an input field. The field may be a database field, or a memory variable edited using the @...SAY...GET command.

With SET CONFIRM OFF, the cursor automatically moves to the next input field when it reaches the end of one. With SET CONFIRM ON, the operator must confirm each input field by pressing the Enter key. Ctrl-C, Ctrl-W, PgUp, and PgDn also confirm and save the entry, then exit. Pressing ESC exits, abandoning changes made to the current variable or field. Ctrl-Q works like ESC in all systems except Clipper. Clipper ignores Ctrl-Q.

## DEFAULT:

OFF

## RECOMMENDED USE:

Use SET CONFIRM ON to prevent operators from "overflowing" input fields. Forcing confirmations also improves the accuracy of data entry.

## VARIATIONS:

**Clipper:** You can specify the logical expressions (.T.) or (.F.) to indicate ON or OFF in the SET command. Enclose the logical value in parentheses.

## SEE ALSO:

Commands @ and SET BELL.

# SET CONSOLE

## DIALECTS:

Clipper, dBASE III PLUS, dBASE IV, dBXL, FoxBASE+, and Quicksilver.

## SYNTAX:

SET CONSOLE ON/OFF

## DEFINITION:

Determines whether messages, reports, listings, etc., appear on the screen. SET CONSOLE OFF suppresses screen output, except for error messages and ones displayed using the @...SAY...GET command. SET DEVICE controls @...SAY output.

With SET CONSOLE OFF, programs can record keyboard input using the WAIT, ACCEPT, or INPUT commands; however, neither the prompting message nor the input will appear on the screen.

## DEFAULT:

ON

## RECOMMENDED USE:

Use SET CONSOLE OFF to suppress the screen display when you print reports using the TO PRINT option or the SET PRINT ON command.

**Example**—A real estate program prints lists of contact names. The programmer uses LIST with the TO PRINT option, but first SETs CONSOLE OFF to prevent the output from going to the screen. When the LIST ends, SET CONSOLE ON restores screen output.

```
USE propsects
CLEAR
@ 10,10 SAY "Now printing a list of qualified prospects..."
SET CONSOLE off
LIST lastname TO PRINT
SET CONSOLE ON
```

In this example, LASTNAME values appear on the printer, but not on the screen.

## LIMITS/WARNINGS:

SET CONSOLE OFF is only valid in programs. It has no effect in the interactive mode.

## VARIATIONS:

**Clipper:** You can specify logical expressions (.T.) or (.F.) to indicate ON or OFF in the SET command. Enclose the logical value in parentheses.

## SEE ALSO:

Command SET DEVICE.

# SET CURRENCY

## DIALECTS:

dBASE IV only.

## SYNTAX:

SET CURRENCY TO [<expC>]
SET CURRENCY LEFT/RIGHT

## DEFINITION:

Controls the currency symbol in PICTURE and FUNCTION numeric output.

SET CURRENCY TO [<expC>] replaces the default dollar sign with a string of up to nine characters.

You continue to specify dollar signs in PICTUREs and FUNCTIONs, but they display as the new string.

SET CURRENCY TO with no argument returns the current currency symbol.

SET CURRENCY LEFT/RIGHT controls the side of the number on which the symbol appears. The default is LEFT.

## RECOMMENDED USE:

Use SET CURRENCY in applications dealing with international funds or specialized units.

**Example**—A program converts dollars to Japanese yen. The programmer uses SET CURRENCY TO change the currency symbol to YEN, then SETs CURRENCY TO RIGHT.

```
SET CURRENCY TO " YEN "
SET CURRENCY RIGHT
mconvert = 87372.22
? mconvert PICTURE "@$"
87372.22 YEN
```

## LIMITS/WARNINGS:

If you specify a word as a currency symbol, leave a space before the first letter, as in

```
SET CURRENCY TO " YEN"
```

Otherwise, the PICTURE "@$" will repeat the first character of the word if there is room in the template, as follows:

```
SET CURRENCY LEFT
SET CURRENCY TO "YEN"
mconvert = 87372.22
? mconvert PICTURE "@$"
YYYYYYYYYYEN87372.22
```

You may use non-printing ASCII characters as currency symbols (for example, CHR(155) is a cents sign). The symbols appear on the screen properly, but won't print on most printers.

## SEE ALSO:

Commands @...SAY, SET POINT, and SET SEPARATOR.

# SET CURSOR

## DIALECTS:

Clipper only.

## SYNTAX:

SET CURSOR ON/OFF

## DEFINITION:

Turns the cursor on or off.

## DEFAULT:

ON

## RECOMMENDED USE:

SET CURSOR OFF when creating graphic displays, menus, or other screens that do not require a cursor.

**Example**—A legal application uses MEMOEDIT( ) to view a brief without editing. To eliminate the distraction of a blinking cursor, the programmer turns it off.

```
CLEAR
tfile = MEMOREAD("brief")
SET CURSOR off
@ 0,0 SAY "Press ESC to exit"
@ 1,0 TO 21,61
MEMOEDIT(tfile,2,1,20,60,.F.)
SET CURSOR on
```

## LIMITS/WARNINGS:

If you SET CURSOR OFF, remember to restore it with SET CURSOR ON. Otherwise, the cursor will remain off after you exit from Clipper.This will make your word processor somewhat difficult to use.

## SEE ALSO:

Command SET CURSORMOVE.

# SET CURSORMOVE

## DIALECTS:

dBXL and Quicksilver.

## SYNTAX:

SET CURSORMOVE ON/OFF

## DEFINITION:

Controls the position of the cursor while the screen is being updated.

SET CURSORMOVE OFF keeps the cursor in the top left corner while the screen is being updated. SET CURSORMOVE ON makes the cursor follow each character as it is displayed.

## DEFAULT:

OFF

## RECOMMENDED USE:

SET CURSORMOVE OFF makes screen updates faster and neater. Use it to display information screens or reports. However, users rely on the cursor to identify input fields and prompts. SET CURSORMOVE ON whenever user input is required.

## SEE ALSO:

Command SET CURSOR.

# SET DATE

## DIALECTS:
Clipper, dBASE III PLUS, dBASE IV, dBXL, FoxBASE+, and Quicksilver.

## SYNTAX:
SET DATE AMERICAN/ANSI/BRITISH/FRENCH/GERMAN/ITALIAN

## DEFINITION:
Sets the convention used for displaying dates.

The formats are:

| | | |
|---|---|---|
| AMERICAN | MM/DD/YY | (month/day/year) |
| ANSI | YY.MM.DD | |
| BRITISH | DD/MM/YY | |
| FRENCH | DD/MM/YY | |
| GERMAN | DD.MM.YY | |
| ITALIAN | DD-MM-YY | |

All date type memory variables and fields must be entered using the active SET DATE format. The format does not affect internal storage.

SET CENTURY ON makes the dates appear with a four-digit year instead of two digits.

## DEFAULT:
AMERICAN (MM/DD/YY, with two digits each).

## VARIATIONS:
**dBASE IV:** Allows five additional formats: DMY, JAPAN, MDY, USA, and YMD.

| | | |
|---|---|---|
| DMY | dd/mm/yy | (same as BRITISH/FRENCH) |
| JAPAN | yy/mm/dd | (same as YMD) |
| MDY | mm/dd/yy | (same as AMERICAN) |
| USA | mm-dd-yy | |
| YMD | yy/mm/dd | (same as JAPAN) |

Allows an optional TO keyword, as follows:

SET DATE TO <format>

instead of simply SET DATE <format>.

**SEE ALSO:**
Command SET CENTURY; function DATE( ).

# SET DBF

## DIALECTS:
dBXL and Quicksilver.

## SYNTAX:
SET DBF TO <path>

## DEFINITION:
Tells dBXL and Quicksilver which drive and directory contain database files. The <path> specification can include a drive designator and a path name terminated by a backslash (\).

Regardless of the DBF setting, DIR displays files in the current directory only.

## DEFAULT:
Without SET DBF, dBXL and Quicksilver search for database files in the current directory and in ones specified by the SET PATH command.

## RECOMMENDED USE:
SET DBF and SET NDX let you store database files and index files in their own directories. This makes file storage more manageable. It also lets you address specific sets of database and index files by directory.

**Example**—A genealogy application maintains index files in directory C:\GDEX. It uses database files in C:\GFILES. The application uses SET DBF and SET NDX to find its files.

```
SET NDX TO C:\GDEX\
SET DBF TO C:\GFILES\
```

## SEE ALSO:
Command SET NDX.

# SET DEBUG

## DIALECTS:

dBASE III PLUS, dBASE IV, dBXL, and FoxBASE+.

## SYNTAX:

SET DEBUG ON/OFF

## DEFINITION:

Prints a line-by-line history of a program's execution when SET ECHO is ON. With SET DEBUG OFF, SET ECHO ON simply displays program lines.

## DEFAULT:

OFF

## RECOMMENDED USE:

Use SET DEBUG to find errors in a program's execution.

**Example**—Crash! An order tracking program in a large warehouse comes to an unexpected halt. To document the problem, the programmer SETs DEBUG ON and reruns the program. Again it fails. The programmer then compares the DEBUG output with the program source code and notices that the program branched to the wrong subroutine during data entry. The operator had apparently entered an "O" instead of a zero, and poor data validation did not trap it. But who cares if the last order of Christmas stockings arrives on December 26th instead of December 24th?

## SEE ALSO:

Commands DEBUG, SET ECHO, SET STEP, and SET TALK.

# SET DECIMALS

## DIALECTS:

Clipper, dBASE III PLUS, dBASE IV, dBXL, FoxBASE+, and Quicksilver.

## SYNTAX:

SET DECIMALS TO <expN>

## DEFINITION:

Determines how many decimal places appear in mathematical functions such as EXP( ), LOG( ), and SQRT( ) and in calculations such as division and exponentiation.
SET DECIMALS rounds trailing decimals to accommodate the setting.

When SET FIXED is ON, the SET DECIMALS command affects all numeric displays. When it is OFF, decimals are determined as follows:

- In multiplication and divison, the number of places is the sum of the numbers for all values involved.
- For other calculations, the number of places is the maximum in any value.

SET DECIMALS and SET FIXED control only how numbers are displayed. Internally, numbers retain their full values.

## DEFAULT:

2

## RECOMMENDED USE:

Use SET DECIMALS to align numeric results in screens and reports.

**Example 1**—A program computes college grade point averages. The commands SET DECIMALS TO 3 and SET FIXED ON rounds the results to three places. (SET DECIMALS is ignored when you SET FIXED OFF).

```
SET DECIMALS TO 3
SET FIXED ON
STORE 2.3568 TO gradepoint
2.357
SET FIXED OFF
? gradepoint
2.3568
```

**Example 2**—An engineering application displays the actual number of decimal places in each value. SET FIXED OFF causes SET DECIMAL to be ignored.

```
SET FIXED OFF
? 1.000002 * 4.000005
4.000013000010
? 1.000002 + 4.000005
5.000007
```

## VARIATIONS:

**dBASE IV:** SET FIXED is not functional. SET DECIMALS alone determines and activates the specified number of places.

## SEE ALSO:

Command SET FIXED; function ROUND( ).

# SET DEFAULT

## DIALECTS:

Clipper, dBASE III PLUS, dBASE IV, dBXL, FoxBASE+, and Quicksilver.

## SYNTAX:

SET DEFAULT TO [<drive designator>]

## DEFINITION:

Specifies the disk drive for data and program files. <drive designator> is a letter representing a valid drive. No colon is needed. For example, to change the default disk drive to A, use the command

```
SET DEFAULT TO A
```

Valid drives include both physical drives and logical drives defined in memory (using a RAM disk program). On some computers, drive designators are valid even if they don't exist (to allow you to add them later). For example, if you have only drives A and C and you SET DEFAULT TO E, the program may not indicate that E does not exist. A directory listing of E will show no files.

## DEFAULT:

SET DEFAULT TO with no <drive designator> sets the default drive to the one on which the work session began.

## RECOMMENDED USE:

Use SET DEFAULT to specify the *primary* drive on which to search for files. Use SET PATH to specify additional drives and paths to search.

## LIMITS/WARNINGS:

dBASE does a poor job of validating drive designators. It allows single digits, single letters, character strings, etc., regardless of whether they mean anything. If you use a character string to designate a drive, dBASE takes the first character. It ignores trailing letters or digits. Completely meaningless designators, such as numbers or signs, restore the original default drive. So type carefully.

## VARIATIONS:

**Clipper:** SET DEFAULT TO compiles without error, but it does nothing at runtime. Clipper provides complete drive and path support for individual commands and through the SET PATH command.

**dBXL:** SET DBF and SET NDX specify where dBXL searches for databases and index files, respectively.

**FoxBASE+:** Produces a syntax error if you specify a nonexistent drive. FoxBASE+ loads program files into a memory buffer to improve execution speed. If you change the default drive using SET DEFAULT, the program in the memory buffer will still execute until you issue CLEAR PROGRAM.

**Quicksilver:** SET DBF and SET NDX specify where Quicksilver searches for databases and index files, respectively.

## SEE ALSO:

Commands CD, DIR, SET DBF, SET NDX, and SET PATH.

# SET DELETED

## DIALECTS:
Clipper, dBASE III PLUS, dBASE IV, dBXL, FoxBASE+, and Quicksilver.

## SYNTAX:
SET DELETED ON/OFF

## DEFINITION:
Controls whether records marked for deletion remain visible. With SET DELETED ON, they are ignored. With SET DELETED OFF, they appear in the file with an asterisk when LISTed, DISPLAYed, or BROWSED, or with the word DEL in the full-screen edit mode.

Even when hidden with SET DELETED ON, deleted records retain their positions in the database file. The record pointer simply skips over them in most operations. This does not affect operations that move the pointer directly to a particular record. You can access deleted records with the GO <record number> command, or the SCOPE options NEXT <n> or RECORD.

## DEFAULT:
OFF

## RECOMMENDED USE:
SET DELETED ON makes it unnecessary to waste time PACKing a large file after each deletion.

**Example 1**—An inventory system tracks quantities of pet food in a dockside warehouse. During a day ITEMs may be deleted if deliveries are cancelled. Rather than DELETE and PACK each time, the programmer uses SET DELETED ON to hide deleted records until the end of the week.

```
USE petfood
LIST
Record#  ITEM
      1  Corn mash
      2 *Beef byproducts
      3  Seed mix
      4 *Nutriseed
      5  Fish mulch
      6  Aardvark chow
```

```
SET DELETED ON
LIST Record#  ITEM
      1  Corn mash
      3  Seed mix
      5  Fish mulch
      6  Aardvark chow
```

**Example 2**—In the same warehouse inventory system, the programmer avoids the use of GOTO to move the record pointer. Even with SET DELETED ON, GOTO moves the pointer to deleted records, producing unexpected results.

```
 . GOTO 2
 . ? ITEM
Beef byproducts
 . LIST NEXT 2
Record#  ITEM
      2 *Beef byproducts
      3  Seed mix
```

## LIMITS/WARNINGS:

The commands INDEX and REINDEX disregard SET DELETED. They always include all records.

## VARIATIONS:

**Clipper:** You can use the logical expressions (.T.) or (.F.) to mean ON or OFF in the SET command. Enclose the logical value in parentheses.

## SEE ALSO:

Commands DELETE, PACK, and RECALL; function DELETED( ).

# SET DELIMITERS

## DIALECTS:

Clipper, dBASE III PLUS, dBASE IV, dBXL, FoxBASE+, and Quicksilver.

## SYNTAX:

SET DELIMITERS ON/OFF
SET DELIMITERS TO [<expC>/DEFAULT]

## DEFINITION:

SET DELIMITERS ON/OFF determines whether delimiters appear. They are marking characters that enclose entry areas during full-screen editing, thus clearly indicating the beginning and end.

SET DELIMITERS TO lets you change the delimiters to any pair of characters.

<expC> must evaluate to either one or two characters. If there is only one, it will be both the left and right delimiter. If there are two, the first is the left delimiter, and the second the right. Delimiters may be non-keyboard ASCII characters specified with the CHR( ) function.

If you use a literal string for <expC>, you must surround it with quotation marks.

## DEFAULTS:

DELIMITERS are normally set OFF. If they are set ON, the default delimiters are colons.

## RECOMMENDED USE:

Use delimiters to clearly mark input fields.

**Example 1**—To improve the speed and accuracy of data entry, the programmer SETs DELIMITERS ON. When the program GETs data from the user, the input field appears delimited by colons.

```
SET DELIMITERS on
STORE SPACE(10) TO name
@ 10,10 SAY "Enter name " GET name
* <more @...SAY...GETs>
READ
Enter name :_         :
```

**Example 2**—Using parentheses as delimiters.

```
SET DELIMITERS on
SET DELIMITERS TO "()"
STORE SPACE(10) TO name
@ 10,10 SAY "Enter name " GET name
READ
Enter name (_          )
```

**Example 3**—Using arrow symbols (ASCII 16 and 17) as delimiters.

```
SET DELIMITERS on
SET DELIMITERS TO CHR(16)+CHR(17)
STORE SPACE(10) TO name
@ 10,10 SAY "Enter name " GET name
READ

Enter name ►_          ◄
```

## VARIATIONS:

**Clipper:** You can use the logical expressions (.T.) or (.F.) to mean ON or OFF in the SET command. Enclose the logical value in parentheses.

**FoxBASE+:** DEFAULT is not optional in the SET DELIMITERS TO command. To restore the colon delimiter, use SET DELIMITERS TO DEFAULT.

## SEE ALSO:

Command @...SAY...GET; function CHR( ).

# SET DESIGN

## DIALECTS:

dBASE IV only.

## SYNTAX:

SET DESIGN ON/OFF

## DEFINITION:

Controls access to the design mode.

SET DESIGN OFF restricts end users from creating or modifying database structures, and creating reports, applications, queries, and other dBASE IV objects.

By default, pressing SHIFT-F2 from an EDIT or BROWSE screen brings up the design mode. SET DESIGN OFF disables SHIFT-F2.

## RECOMMENDED USE:

SET DESIGN OFF lets developers provide limited use of dBASE IV to end users, without the risk of corrupting applications.

**Example**—A programmer creates a quick application for sales personnel. To save time, he uses BROWSE to let them edit files. To prevent them from pressing SHIFT-F2 to escape from BROWSE to the design mode, he issues SET DESIGN OFF.

```
SET DESIGN on
BROWSE NODELETE     && Do not let users delete records.
SET DESIGN ON
```

## LIMITS/WARNINGS:

SET DESIGN does not restrict users from tampering with the PROTECT system.

## SEE ALSO:

Commands BROWSE and EDIT.

# SET DEVICE

## DIALECTS

Clipper, dBASE III PLUS, dBASE IV, dBXL, FoxBASE+, and Quicksilver.

## SYNTAX:

SET DEVICE TO PRINT/SCREEN

## DEFINITION:

Lets you choose whether @...SAY commands are sent to the screen or the printer.

## DEFAULT:

SCREEN

## OPTIONS:

SET DEVICE TO PRINT sends output only to the printer. SET DEVICE TO SCREEN sends output only to the screen.

## RECOMMENDED USE:

Use SET DEVICE TO PRINT to print reports formatted with @...SAYs. A similar command, SET PRINT ON, sends only list-oriented output to the printer.

**Example**—AdTrack 2.0 tracks magazine advertising sales. The program prints contracts using SET DEVICE TO PRINT.

```
SET DEVICE TO PRINT            && Begin printing.
@ 05,10 SAY "Modern Cycling Magazine Advertising Contract"
@ 10,05 SAY "Under this agreement, you " + trim(ad_name)
* <more @...SAY statements>
SET DEVICE TO SCREEN           && End printing.
```

## LIMITS/WARNINGS:

Of course, the screen and the printer differ in many ways. SCREEN coordinates are limited to 25 lines and 80 columns. Paper allows a wider range of positions. With SET DEVICE TO SCREEN, the command

```
@ 50,10 SAY "This is line 50"
```

produces a syntax error. The same command works correctly with SET DEVICE TO PRINT.

Another difference between SCREEN and PRINT is the ordering of @...SAYs. Because most printers do not allow reverse line feeds, @...SAYs must be printed from the top left to the bottom right of the page. (On the screen, the order doesn't matter). If a printed @...SAY has a lower value than its predecessor, the page will eject. Quicksilver has a SET FEED OFF command that prevents this.

## VARIATIONS:

**Clipper, FoxBASE+:** You can send @...SAYs to a text file with SET PRINTER TO <filename>, and SET DEVICE TO PRINT.

**dBASE IV:** You can send @...SAYs to a text file with SET DEVICE TO FILE <filename>. The file is given a TXT extension.

**Example**—A chemical company saves test results in word processing documents. The results are produced with @...SAYs redirected to a text file with SET DEVICE TO FILE RESULTS. RESULTS.TXT is the target file.

```
SET DEVICE TO FILE results
* <@...SAYs and other statements>.
SET DEVICE TO SCREEN
```

**dBXL:** An ALTERNATE option lets you redirect @...SAYs to a text file with

```
SET DEVICE TO ALTERNATE
```

This command works in conjunction with SET ALTERNATE TO and SET ALTERNATE ON.

**Example**—A government agency includes dBXL reports in word processing documents. To redirect @...SAY output to a text file, the program opens an ALTERNATE file that can later be edited by a word processor.

```
SET ALTERNATE TO taxbills
SET ALTERNATE on
SET DEVICE TO ALTERNATE
* <more @...SAYs and other statements>
CLOSE ALTERNATE
```

In this example, the report goes into the text file TAXBILLS.TXT.

## SEE ALSO:

Commands @, SET ALTERNATE, SET FEED, SET PRINT, and SET PRINTER.

# SET DISPLAY

## DIALECTS:
dBASE IV only.

## SYNTAX:
SET DISPLAY TO MONO/COLOR/EGA25/EGA43/MONO43

## DEFINITION:
Selects the type of graphics display card in your computer.

If you specify a type not supported by your graphics card, SET DISPLAY has no effect.

## DEFAULT:
Specified by user during installation.

## RECOMMENDED USE:
Use SET DISPLAY to switch between 25- and 43-line displays. You can also use it to switch display modes if your graphics card supports multiple modes.

**Example**—Before switching to a full screen BROWSE mode, a program uses SET DISPLAY TO EGA43. The 43-line display mode lets the user view nearly twice as much data on a single screen.

```
SET DISPLAY TO EGA43
BROWSE
SET DISPLAY TO EGA25
```

## SEE ALSO:
Commands SET and SET COLOR; function ISCOLOR( ).

# SET DOHISTORY

### DIALECTS:
dBXL, dBASE III PLUS, and FoxBASE+.

### SYNTAX:
SET DOHISTORY ON/OFF

### DEFINITION:
Determines whether dBXL, dBASE III PLUS, and FoxBASE+ record program file commands in a special memory area called the *history buffer*.

When you SET DOHISTORY ON, programs are recorded so you can later trace their execution and make temporary changes.

### DEFAULT:
OFF

### RECOMMENDED USE:
DISPLAY/LIST HISTORY lets you easily test and debug program commands. You can even edit them in the history buffer; however, the changes do not go into the program file.

### LIMITS/WARNINGS:
SET DOHISTORY ON slows program execution significantly.

**dBASE IV:** SET DOHISTORY is valid, but has no effect.

### SEE ALSO:
Commands DISPLAY HISTORY, SET DEBUG, SET ECHO, SET HISTORY, SET STEP, and SUSPEND.

# SET ECHO

## DIALECTS:

dBASE III PLUS, dBASE IV, dBXL, and FoxBASE+.

## SYNTAX:

SET ECHO ON/OFF

## DEFINITION:

Controls whether to display program command lines as they are executed. When SET ON, this powerful debugging command displays command lines while the program runs. If you first SET DEBUG ON, the program lines are sent to the printer rather than the screen.

## DEFAULT:

OFF

## RECOMMENDED USE:

By using SET ECHO ON together with SET STEP ON and SET TALK ON, you can see each line as it executes, plus the value of any expressions, variables, or fields that are evaluated.

## LIMITS/WARNINGS:

SET ECHO ON displays program lines on the screen simultaneously with other screen output. The results can be hard to follow because of overwriting. If you cannot follow the display, put plenty of paper in your printer and SET DEBUG ON.

## SEE ALSO:

Commands DEBUG, SET DEBUG, SET STEP, SET TALK, and SET TRAP.

# SET EDITOR

## DIALECTS:
dBXL and Quicksilver.

## SYNTAX:
SET EDITOR TO "<filename>"

## DEFINITION:
Specifies an external word processor or text editor for editing memo fields in Quicksilver, and both memo fields and programs in dBXL.

## DEFAULT:
Quicksilver's or dBXL's internal editor.

## RECOMMENDED USE:
**Example**—A fast, programmable text editor such as QEDIT from SemWare, Inc. is often preferable to the internal editor. A sales management system uses QEDIT as specified by SET EDITOR.

```
* MAINSALE.PRG
SET EDITOR TO "QEDIT"     && Select text editor QEDIT.
USE sales                 && Use a file with a memo field NMEMO.
SET FORMAT TO screenfmt   && Open a format file SCREENFMT.
READ

* SALESFMT.FMT
@ 1,1 GET nmemo      && GET the memo field NMEMO in the format file.
```

The last statement in the example presents the memo field NMEMO for editing. Pressing Ctrl-PgUp or Ctrl-PgDn invokes the text editor, loading a file NMEMO.TMP. This temporary file is written into the memo field and then deleted.

## VARIATIONS:
You can specify external word processors or text editors in CONFIG files for dBASE III PLUS, dBASE IV, dBXL, FoxBASE+, and Quicksilver with the TEDIT and WP statements. For example

```
TEDIT=QE
```

runs the external editor QE when you issue MODIFY COMMAND. The WP statement changes the memo editor.

## SEE ALSO:
Command MODIFY COMMAND; function MEMOEDIT( ).

# SET ENCRYPTION

## DIALECTS:
dBASE IV only.

## SYNTAX:
SET ENCRYPTION ON/OFF

## DEFINITION:
Determines whether dBASE IV encrypts database files created by COPY, JOIN, and TOTAL. If the PROTECT security system is not installed, SET ENCRYPTION has no effect.

If you use the PROTECT security system to login to dBASE IV and SET ENCRYPTION ON, database files created with COPY, JOIN, and TOTAL are encrypted. Only users with sufficient access rights can read them.

The new file retains the source file's access and authorization requirements as established by the system administrator in the PROTECT system.

To decrypt a file, SET ENCRYPT OFF, then COPY it.

To encrypt a file defined by CREATE, first CREATE it, then grant access privileges for it in the PROTECT system.

## DEFAULT:
ON

## RECOMMENDED USE:
SET ENCRYPTION OFF to circumvent the default encryption when COPYing, JOINing, or TOTALling databases. For SET ENCRYPTION to have any effect, the PROTECT system must be installed.

**Example**—A commodities trading program uses encrypted master databases, yet lets users create unencrypted summary files. To protect the confidentiality of the data, all COPYing, TOTALling, and JOINing is strictly controlled. SET FIELDS is handy for restricting fields to COPY.

```
USE secrets                         && File has access level of 5.
SET ENCRYPTION off
SET FIELDS to code,refnum
COPY TO temp FOR code = "1484"      && TEMP.DBF is unencrypted.
SET ENCRYPTION on
```

## LIMITS/WARNINGS:

You cannot COPY <filename> TO TYPE <filetype> to convert encrypted databases to foreign files (e.g., COPY TO <filename> TYPE WK1).

You cannot JOIN encrypted and unencrypted files.

MODIFY STRUCTURE and COPY STRUCTURE EXTENDED require unencrypted files. You must first SET ENCRYPTION OFF, then modify the unencrypted structure.

Since you cannot change administrative GROUPs in a program, encrypted files in an application must have the same group name (defined in PROTECT).

## SEE ALSO:

Commands PROTECT and SET FIELDS; functions ACCESS( ) and USER( ).

# SET ESCAPE

## DIALECTS:

Clipper, dBASE III PLUS, dBASE IV, dBXL, FoxBASE+, and Quicksilver.

## SYNTAX:

SET ESCAPE ON/OFF

## DEFINITION:

Controls the ESC key's effect on program execution. SET ESCAPE ON means that pressing ESC interrupts execution. SET ESCAPE OFF lets INKEY( ) read ESC just like any other key.

In the interactive mode with SET ESCAPE ON, pressing the ESC key during an operation causes the message *****INTERRUPTED***** to appear. Control returns to the prompt.

For example, pressing ESC during execution of ACCOUNTS.PRG causes the following message to appear:

```
*** INTERRUPTED ***
Called from - C:accounts.prg
Cancel, Ignore, or Suspend? (C, I, or S) Cancel
Do cancelled
```

Choosing "C" cancels program execution and closes the program file. Ignore resumes execution as if the ESC key hadn't been pressed. Suspend interrupts execution temporarily. Control returns to the interactive prompt from which you can then perform other database tasks. When finished, issue the RESUME command. Program execution will continue from where it left off.

## DEFAULT:

ON

## RECOMMENDED USE:

Use SET ESCAPE OFF in programs to be run by novices. It reduces the chance of someone accidentally causing an exit to the prompt. This is particularly a problem on IBM PCs and compatibles where ESC is just left of the 1 key and just above the Tab key.

## VARIATIONS:

**Clipper:** Uses the key combination Alt-C to break program execution. In versions prior to Summer '87, SET ESCAPE OFF disabled Alt-C. In Summer '87, use the SETCANCEL( ) function instead.

Also in Clipper, SET ESCAPE ON allows the ESC key to terminate a GET...READ, bypassing any VALID clause. With SET ESCAPE OFF, ESC will not terminate the READ. You can then use SET KEY to process the ESC key within the read, assigning it to another action.

Clipper lets you use the logical expressions (.T.) or (.F.) to mean ON or OFF in the SET command. Enclose the logical value in parentheses.

**dBXL:** The FIX option lets you edit the current program line before resuming execution.

## SEE ALSO:

Commands ON ERROR, ON ESCAPE, and ON KEY; functions INKEY( ), READKEY( ), and SETCANCEL( ).

# SET EXACT

## DIALECTS:
Clipper, dBASE III PLUS, dBASE IV, dBXL, FoxBASE+, and Quicksilver.

## SYNTAX:
SET EXACT ON/OFF

## DEFINITION:
Determines how to compare two character strings. When EXACT is ON, two strings are equal only if every character matches.

SET EXACT ON ignores trailing blanks in string comparisons.

SET EXACT OFF causes strings to be compared starting with the leftmost character and moving right. The comparison continues to the end of the string on the right of the relational operator (=<>#). In other words, if the string on the right is an abbreviation of the one on the left, they match.

## DEFAULT:
OFF

## RECOMMENDED USE:
Use SET EXACT ON for searches requiring an EXACT match.

**Example**—A demographic database uses SET EXACT ON to ensure that a search produces the correct result. Normally, you can search for a partial key. This creates problems in a large database. For example, suppose you LIST ALL FOR LASTNAME = "JACOBS". Not only do you get JACOBS, but you also get JACOBSON, JACOBSEN, JACOBSSON, etc. SET EXACT OFF gives you only records with an EXACT match.

```
* EXACT is set off by default.
USE leads
LIST ALL lastname FOR lastname = "JACOBS"
Record #    lastname
       2    JACOBSSON
      27    JACOBSEN
      66    JACOBS
      88    JACOBSON
```

With SET EXACT OFF, the righthand string can be an abbreviation of the lefthand string.

```
? "JACOBSON" = "JACOBS"
.T.
```

With SET EXACT ON, the strings must match exactly.

```
? "JACOBSON" = "JACOBS"
.F.
? "JACOBS" = "JACOBS"
.T.
```

## LIMITS/WARNINGS:

SET EXACT ON ignores trailing blanks. For example, the following strings evaluate as equal.

```
SET EXACT on
? "Johnson   " = "Johnson"
.T.
? "Johnson   " = "Johnson"
.T.
```

To check for exact equality, add a character to each string as follows:

```
? "Johnson" + "." = "Johnson   " + "."
.F.
```

## VARIATIONS:

**Clipper:** You can use the logical expressions (.T.) or (.F.) to mean ON or OFF in the SET command. Enclose the logical value in parentheses.

**Clipper, FoxBASE+:** The double equal sign operator (==) in logical equations indicates EXACT equality. It acts as though SET EXACT is ON, regardless of the actual setting. Unlike SET EXACT ON, however, the double equal sign does not ignore trailing blanks as shown:

```
? "Johnson   " == "Johnson"
.F.
? "Johnson   " == "Johnson"
.F.
```

**Clipper:** The double equal sign operator applies to both numbers and strings. Clipper sometimes evaluates two numbers as being equal when, in fact, the 15th or 16th decimal places are not. The double equal sign assures that they will evaluate as equal, since it uses only 12 decimal places.

**FoxBASE+:** The double equal sign operator applies only to strings.

## SEE ALSO:

Commands FIND, LOCATE, and SEEK.

# SET EXCLUSIVE

## DIALECTS:

Clipper, dBASE III PLUS, dBASE IV, FoxBASE+, and Quicksilver.

## SYNTAX:

SET EXCLUSIVE ON/OFF

## DEFINITION:

Determines whether database files are opened in a shared or reserved mode.

On a network, SET EXCLUSIVE ON reserves database files for the user who opens them. They may not be shared.

SET EXCLUSIVE OFF allows shared database files.

Changing the EXCLUSIVE setting does not affect previously opened files.

## DEFAULT:

ON

On single user systems, SET EXCLUSIVE OFF is ignored.

## RECOMMENDED USE:

Issue SET EXCLUSIVE OFF at the beginning of an application to allow file sharing on a local area network. You can also use SET EXCLUSIVE at specific points in a program. However, it does not affect files that are already open.

## LIMITS/WARNINGS:

Although SET EXCLUSIVE OFF lets many users access the same files on a network, the programmer must use appropriate file and record locks to maintain data integrity.

## VARIATIONS:

**Clipper:** You can use the logical expressions (.T.) or (.F.) to mean ON or OFF in the SET command. Enclose the logical value in parentheses.

## SEE ALSO:

Command USE EXCLUSIVE; functions FLOCK( ) and RLOCK( ).

# SET FEED

## DIALECTS:

dBXL and Quicksilver.

## SYNTAX:

SET FEED ON/OFF

## DEFINITION:

Controls page ejects when printing with SET DEVICE TO PRINT. SET FEED OFF prevents the page from advancing and sets the current line to zero. The line coordinate to print on is then calculated relative to the new line zero.

Normally, printing at a line coordinate below its predecessor causes the printer to advance automatically to the top of the next page. The line counter is then set to 0.

## DEFAULT:

ON

## RECOMMENDED USE:

Use SET FEED OFF to print on non-standard forms such as continuous form Rolodex® cards, or invoices. By disabling automatic page ejects, it gives programmers complete line-by-line printing control.

**Example 1**—A software company prints employee identification cards on non-standard forms. SET FEED OFF prevents automatic page ejects.

```
SET DEVICE TO PRINT
SET FEED off                    && Turn off page ejects.
@ 05,10 SAY "Name: "            && Print on line 5.
@ 06,10 SAY "SSN:"              && Print on line 6.
@ 02,10 SAY "*EMPLOYEE*"        && Print two lines below last line.
```

The printed output looks like this:

```
Name:
 SSN:

 *EMPLOYEE*
```

With SET FEED OFF, printing on line 2 after printing on line 6 indicates a coordinate two lines below line 6. With SET FEED ON, a page eject would occur and the word "*EMPLOYEE*" would appear at the top of the next page.

## VARIATIONS:

**dBASE IV:** You can control page ejects with the _PEJECT system variable. Its options are AFTER, BEFORE, BOTH, or NONE.

## SEE ALSO:

Commands PRINTJOB and SET DEVICE TO PRINT; functions PCOL( ) and PROW( ).

# SET FIELDS

## DIALECTS:
dBASE III PLUS, dBASE IV, dBXL, and FoxBASE+.

## SYNTAX:
SET FIELDS ON/OFF
SET FIELDS TO [ list>/ALL]

## DEFINITION:
Controls whether all or selected fields are accessible in database files.

SET FIELDS ON activates the field list in the SET FIELDS TO [<field list>/ALL] command.

SET FIELDS TO <field list> specifies which fields to access in database files. Specify fields by names separated by commas. Select fields in unselected work areas with ALIAS->FIELDNAME.

SET FIELDS TO <field list> automatically invokes SET FIELDS ON. You can switch the SET FIELDS TO <field list> ON or OFF with SET FIELDS ON/OFF.

Subsequent SET FIELDS TO [<field list>] commands add the specified fields to the active field list.

SET FIELDS TO by itself removes all fields from the field list of the active database. SET FIELDS TO ALL restores all fields.

If you LIST or DISPLAY STRUCTURE, fields in the active list are marked with the right angle bracket >.

## DEFAULT:
OFF, making all fields accessible.

## RECOMMENDED USE:
When used interactively, SET FIELDS provides a focused view of your data quickly and easily.

In programs, however, there is a tradeoff between ease and control. When using SET FIELDS, conflicts can easily arise with FILTERs and RELATIONS if a key field is not specified. To limit the fields the end user sees, use FORMAT files and commands with explicit field lists. For example, instead of:

```
SET FIELDS TO LNAME,ADDRESS
LIST
```

use the command

```
LIST LNAME,ADDRESS
```

As a result, valid fieldnames will not be ambiguous, giving you better control over your program.

**Note:** dBASE IV's SET FIELDS command has other options that make it more useful in programs. See *Variations.*

**Example 1**—An airline personnel database contains information about active pilots. The personnel manager, wanting to view and edit only lastname and age information, uses SET FIELDS TO LNAME,AGE to limit the display.

```
. USE pilots
. LIST
Record# LNAME       AGE CITY         STATE ADDRESS     NMEMO
      1 Ralphson    30  Boston       MA    12 Elm Ln.  Memo
      2 Johnson     22  San Diego    CA    22 Main St  Memo

. SET FIELDS TO lname,age
. LIST
Record#  LNAME       AGE
      1  Ralphson    30
      2  Johnson     22
```

You can see which fields are SET by listing the structure. Specified fields appear with a right angle bracket:

```
. LIST STRUCTURE
    Structure for database: C:\ACCT\SALES.DBF
Number of data records:       2
Date of last update    : 01/12/80
Field  Field Name  Type       Width    Dec
    1> LNAME       Character     10
    2> AGE         Character      2
    3  CITY        Character     10
    4  STATE       Character      2
    5  ADDRESS     Character     10
    6  NMEMO       Memo          10
** Total **                      45
```

**Example 2**—You can specify fields in unselected work areas using the ALIAS ->FIELDNAME designator.

```
SELECT 2
USE SALES
SELECT 3
SET FIELDS TO SALES->LNAME    && SET FIELDS to a field in area 2
```

Note that SET FIELDS TO affects commands such as BROWSE, CHANGE, COPY STRUCTURE, COPY TO, DISPLAY, EDIT, LIST, JOIN, SUM, and TOTAL.

## SPECIAL USE:

Use the ALIAS-> designator to include fields from related database files.

When combining fields from related files, avoid changing data unless you have a view of all fields from all files. If you change the key by which the files are related, the fields in your field list will become misaligned.

## VARIATIONS:

**dBASE IV:** You can SET read-only fields, calculated fields, and fields matching a wildcard <pattern>, in the form:

SET FIELDS TO [<field> [/R] / <calculated fieldname>]
    [,<field>[/R] / <calculated fieldname>...] /
    ALL [LIKE/EXCEPT <pattern>]

Read-only fields are ones you want to prevent the user from editing. Note that the slash (/) is a literal character you must enter with the R. To limit the field list to DEDUCTS, NAME, and PAY, while specifying PAY as read-only, use the command

```
SET FIELDS TO deducts, pay /R, name
```

A calculated field is the result of a valid dBASE expression. The <calculated fieldname> is a memory variable containing the expression. Note that the EDIT command doesn't immediately update the calculated field as you edit a record. BROWSE, however, updates calculated fields as soon as you move to a new field within a record.

**Example 3**—An invoice program in a towing company uses a calculated field MTOTAL to display the amount due. The program defines MTOTAL as the sum of MILES, PARTS, and LABOR.

```
USE invoice
SET FIELDS to miles, parts, labor, mtotal = miles + parts + labor, inv_num
DISPLAY
```

```
Record#    MILES     PARTS     LABOR             MTOTAL INV_NUM
      1    153.42    500.00    33.33             686.75 AABB
```

Calculated fields act like native database fields, as long as the database is open and the SET FIELDS definition is active. Because you can use any valid expression in a calculated field, you can go far beyond simple mathematics and do things such as include the time, date, diskspace, and record count as part of the fields list.

You can also have user defined functions in calculated fields. This lets you do complex computations without cluttering the SET FIELDS command. In the interactive mode, just include your user defined function in the calculated field, then SET PROCEDURE TO the program file containing your UDFs. In programs, simply add the user defined function to the end of a program file.

**Example 4**—The towing company from Example 3 expands its invoice to include over 15 items. To compute the invoice total efficiently, the programmer puts the formula in a user defined function.

```
USE invoice
SET FIELDS to miles, parts, labor, mtotal = TOWTOTAL(), inv_num
FUNCTION towtotal
*
subtotal = miles + parts + labor + pickup + insur + postage + ;
           handling + driver + hookup + overhed + expenses + tools + ;
           license + fuel + phone + oil
RETURN subtotal * .065     && Tax.
* End of TOWTOTAL
```

You can also define your field list using wildcard * and ? patterns. For example, you can SET a field list for ALL LIKE m*, ALL EXCEPT m*, or ALL LIKE P?P.

If you name your fields with some forethought about their grouping in lists, you can save program code by using wildcard characters as follows:

```
SET FIELDS TO ALL LIKE z*
```

or

```
SET FIELDS TO ALL EXCEPT r1?
```

## SEE ALSO:

Commands CLEAR FIELDS, SET FORMAT, SET RELATION, and SET SKIP.

# SET FILTER

## DIALECTS:

Clipper, dBASE III PLUS, dBASE IV, dBXL, FoxBASE+, and Quicksilver.

## SYNTAX:

SET FILTER TO [FILE <.QRY filename>/?] [<condition>]

## DEFINITION:

Makes visible only records for which the <condition> is true. The condition can be any valid expression.

SET FILTER acts only on the database file in the active work area. Therefore, FILTER conditions can exist independently in separate work areas.

Note that the filter is not activated until the record pointer moves. You may, therefore, want to issue a movement command such as GO TOP immediately after issuing SET FILTER.

Use SET FILTER TO by itself to turn the active filter off.

## RECOMMENDED USE:

SET FILTER offers a convenient way of selecting data; however, it is very slow on large files (thousands of records). If no matches exist, it examines every record.

SET FILTER is best suited to the interactive modes of dBASE III PLUS, dBASE IV, dBXL, and FoxBASE+.

In programs, use other commands such as COPY, LIST, or REPLACE. They all allow expressions and scopes that restrict the records to be processed.

**Example**—An insurance salesman maintains a list of clients in a database. When a client reaches age 22, the insurance rate decreases. Rather than scanning all records, the salesman uses SET FILTER to restrict the ones that appear.

```
. USE sales
. SET FILTER TO AGE > 22
. LIST
Record#  LNAME       AGE CITY        STATE
      3  Jones        23 Chicago     IL
     34  Smith        24 Ann Arbor   MI
     85  Paul         25 Sacramento  CA
```

Because certain insurance zones require a surcharge, the salesman adds a filter condition limiting records by CITY.

```
. SET FILTER TO AGE > 22 .AND. CITY = "Sacramento"
. GO TOP
. LIST
Record#  LNAME        AGE CITY       STATE
      5  Paul          25 Sacramento CA
```

Earlier in the week, the salesman had created a more complex FILTER criteria using CREATE QUERY. He stored it in a file called HIGHRISK.

```
. SET FILTER TO FILE highrisk
. GO TOP
```

## LIMITS/WARNINGS:

Note that you can still go directly to a hidden record using the GOTO <record number> command.

## VARIATIONS:

**Clipper:** Conditions may not be specified from QRY files. There is no CREATE/MODIFY QUERY.

**dBASE III PLUS, dBASE IV, dBXL:** You may create and save conditions with the interactive query processor CREATE/MODIFY QUERY, and then specify them as filter conditions. If a catalog is active (dBASE III PLUS and dBASE IV only), you can specify

```
SET FILTER TO FILE ?
```

and a list of available QRY files will appear.

**dBASE IV:** You cannot move the pointer to a hidden record using GOTO <record number>.

**FoxBASE+:** Conditions may not be specified from QRY files, since there is no CREATE/MODIFY QUERY.

## SEE ALSO:

Commands COPY, CREATE/MODIFY QUERY, LIST, REPLACE, and SET DELETED.

# SET FIXED

## DIALECTS:
Clipper, dBASE III PLUS, FoxBASE+, and Quicksilver.

## SYNTAX:
SET FIXED ON/OFF

## DEFINITION:
Determines whether to display the number of decimal places specified by the SET DECIMALS command.

With SET FIXED ON, the number of places follows SET DECIMALS. Places are either added or rounded to match the setting.

SET FIXED OFF displays numbers with their true number of places.

## DEFAULT:
OFF

## RECOMMENDED USE:
SET DECIMALS and SET FIXED control only how numbers are displayed. Internally, numbers retain their full values. Use SET DECIMALS and SET FIXED in screens and reports.

**Example**—A farm yield report shows tons of wheat in a year, and over ten years. To make the decimals consistent, the program uses SET DECIMALS and SET FIXED.

```
mtons = 453.045
mtotal = 54366.0348
SET DECIMALS TO 2
SET FIXED on
? mtons
453.05
? mtotal
54366.03
```

## VARIATIONS:
**Clipper:** You can use the logical expressions (.T.) or (.F.) to mean ON or OFF in the SET command. Enclose the logical value in parentheses.

**dBASE IV:** For compatibility, SET FIXED is recognized as a valid statement, but has no effect. The SET DECIMALS command alone changes and activates the DECIMALS setting. The default is 2 places (SET DECIMALS TO 2).

**dBXL:** SET FIXED has no effect in Version 1.2.

## SEE ALSO:

Command SET DECIMALS.

# SET FORMAT

## DIALECTS:

Clipper, dBASE III PLUS, dBASE IV, dBXL, FoxBASE+, and Quicksilver.

## SYNTAX:

SET FORMAT TO <FMT filename>/?

## DEFINITION:

Opens the specified format file and closes any open format file in the current work area.

A format file is a text file containing @...SAY...GETs. When you issue a command such as APPEND, CHANGE, EDIT, INSERT, or READ, the screen takes on the layout of the open format file. The previous screen is cleared.

To create multi-page entry screens, put READ commands in a format file wherever you want a page break. To page through the screens, use the PgUp and PgDn keys.

SET FORMAT TO or CLOSE FORMAT both close the format file in the selected work area.

Unless otherwise specified, SET FORMAT TO looks for a file with a FMT extension. If a dBASE III PLUS or dBASE IV catalog is active, SET FORMAT TO ? lists the available format files.

## RECOMMENDED USE:

SET FORMAT simplifies programming by letting you page easily through multiple screens. In the interactive mode, SET FORMAT lets you use custom data entry forms in commands such as EDIT and APPEND.

**Example 1**—A program that tracks impounded vehicles uses SET FORMAT to present multiple data entry screens. READ divides the format file into separate screens.

```
* VEHICLE.PRG
USE vehicles            && Contains vehicles stored on the lot.
SET FORMAT TO entry1    && Use format file ENTRY1.FMT.
EDIT                    && EDIT only available in dBASE III PLUS,
                        &&   dBASE IV, dBXL, and FoxBASE+.
```

```
* ENTRY1.FMT, 3 screen format file.
* Page 1
@ 1,1 SAY "Name: " GET name        && GET fields in the open database
@ 2,1 SAY "Address: " GET address
* <more @...SAYs>
READ
* Page 2
@ 1,1 SAY "Vehicle ID: " GET vin
@ 2,1 SAY "Color: "  GET color
* <more @...SAYs>
READ
* Page 3
@ 1,1 SAY "Make: " GET make
@ 2,1 SAY "Model: "  GET model
* <more @...SAYs>
READ
```

## VARIATIONS:

**Clipper:** Does not automatically clear the screen when a format file is activated. This lets you create windowing effects by overlaying screens. Format files may contain commands other than @...SAY...GETs and READs. For example, they may start with CLEAR.

Clipper does not support the CATALOG ? option of the SET FORMAT TO command.

**dBASE III PLUS:** Allows up to 32 screens in a format file.

**dBASE IV:** Allows up to 32 screens in a format file. You can use the CREATE/MODIFY screen program to create screen files (extension SCR). When you save the SCR file, dBASE generates a format file (extension FMT). When you SET FORMAT TO <FMT file>, or DO <FMT file> for the first time, dBASE IV compiles it with an extension of FMO, and executes it. Use MODIFY SCREEN when you want to change your format files, since it reads the SCR and FMT files together. dBASE III PLUS FMT files are compatible with dBASE IV.

**FoxBASE+:** Allows up to 128 screens in a format file. Use SET CLEAR OFF to stop FoxBASE+ from automatically clearing the screen when using format files. This lets you create windowing effects by overlaying screens. Note that SET CLEAR defaults to ON. FoxBASE+ does not support the ? option of the SET FORMAT TO command.

**Quicksilver:** Does not support the ? option (CATALOG lookup) of the SET FORMAT TO command.

## SEE ALSO:

Commands @...SAY...GET, CLOSE FORMAT, READ, and SET CLEAR.

# SET FUNCTION

## DIALECTS:

Clipper, dBASE III PLUS, dBASE IV, dBXL, FoxBASE+, and Quicksilver.

## SYNTAX:

SET FUNCTION <expN>/<expC> TO <exp>

## DEFINITION:

Programs the function keys (usually labeled "F1," "F2," etc.).

**<expN>** is the function key number. The FKMAX( ) function returns the number of programmable function keys.

**<expC>** is a function key label such as "F1", "F2", or "F3". You may use either a number or a label to specify a key. When using a label, be sure to enclose it in quotation marks, as in "F2". The unpronounceable FKLABEL( ) function returns the name of the specified function key.

**<exp>** refers to the program commands or values stored in the function key. You may include multiple commands by putting semicolons in-between. Each semicolon automatically inserts a carriage return (as if you had pressed the Enter key).

The expression stored in the function key must also be inside quotation marks. It is limited to 238 characters.

## DEFAULT:

dBASE III PLUS, dBASE IV, dBXL, and FoxBASE+ have preset function keys. To see the settings, type

```
.SET   <Enter>
```

An interactive menu will appear from which you must select the KEYS heading.

## RECOMMENDED USE:

Program function keys to execute common commands from the dot prompt or to repeat character strings or numbers during data entry.

**Example 1**—Store common commands in function keys for execution from the interactive mode.

```
.SET FUNCTION "F2" TO "LIST lname;"
```

Because function key labels vary among computers, use numbers when distributing applications.

**Example 2**—The marketing manager of a mailorder firm saves on typing by assigning common commands to function keys. For example, F3 clears the screen and opens the SALES database with an index.

```
.SET FUNCTION 3 TO "CLEAR;USE SALES INDEX SALESDEX;"
```

In this case, one keystroke replaces 33.

The functions FKMAX( ) and FKLABEL( ) are helpful in programming function keys by number. FKMAX( ) returns the number of available programmable function keys. FKLABEL( ) returns the name of a function key if passed its number.

## LIMITS/WARNINGS:

Numbers stored in <exp> will be evaluated as numeric even though they are specified in quotation marks. In fact, <exp> will give either a character or a numeric result, depending on circumstances.

Note that you cannot program the F1 key on an IBM PC using the SET FUNCTION command in dBASE III PLUS, dBXL, and FoxBASE+. F1 is reserved as a HELP key.

## VARIATIONS:

**Clipper:** Up to 39 function keys may be assigned. Besides F2 through F10 (F1 is reserved for HELP), you use SHIFT to get function keys 11 through 20 (e.g., F11 is SHIFT-F1). For function keys 21 through 30, press Ctrl (e.g., F21 is Ctrl-F1). For keys 31 through 40, press Alt (e.g., F31 is Alt-F1). Clipper accepts only function key numbers, not labels (such as "F2"). Note that function key strings may contain control characters. For example, to assign Ctrl-C to a function key (to issue a page down), use the command:

```
SET FUNCTION 4 to chr(3)
```

**dBASE IV:** You can program function keys F2 through F10, Shift-F1 through Shift-F9, and Ctrl-F1 through Ctrl-F10.

Specify these keys by number or name. F2 is function key 1, CTRL-F1 is function key 10, and SHIFT-F1 is function key 20.

F1, Shift-F10, and all Alt combinations are reserved. (You can program F1 with the ON KEY command, for example, ON KEY F1 <command>.)

To SET function key SHIFT-F3 to LIST NEXT 10, use the command:

```
SET FUNCTION SHIFT-F3 TO "LIST NEXT 10;"
```

or

```
SET FUNCTION 22 TO "LIST NEXT 10;"
```

The F11 and F12 keys on enhanced keyboards are not accessible through SET FUNCTION.

**dBXL:** Attempts to reset F1 are ignored. Attempts to set function keys beyond F10 cause a syntax error.

**FoxBASE+:** Trying to program the F1 key with the SET FUNCTION command causes a syntax error. A way around this limitation is to use the ON KEY command to designate F1 as a "hot key."

To redefine F1 (scan code 315), issue the command

```
ON KEY = 315 <command>
```

**Quicksilver:** Only supports the SET FUNCTION command when using the PC-DOS linker libraries. SET FUNCTION does not work with MS-DOS linker libraries. WordTech recommends using ESCape sequences from a DOS batch file or dBASE program to redefine function keys. ESCape sequences are hardware-dependent.

You may assign string values to the F1 key.

## SEE ALSO:

Commands HELP, ON KEY, SET, and SET KEY; functions FKLABEL( ) and FKMAX( ).

# SET GRAPHPRINT

## DIALECTS:

dBXL and Quicksilver only.

## SYNTAX:

SET GRAPHPRINT TO [[EPSONFX/HPLASERJET/
HPPLOTTER/IBM/OKIDATA][SIZE <expN1>]
[VERTICAL/HORIZONTAL] [ASPECT <expN2>]]

## DEFINITION:

Selects the graph printer and sets print options.

## OPTIONS:

You may specify any one of these printers:

| | |
|---|---|
| EPSONFX | Epson FX/LX dot matrix printer. |
| HPLASERJET | Hewlett-Packard Laserjet laser printer. |
| HPPLOTTER | Hewlett-Package Plotter (HPGL language) |
| IBM | IBM Graphics Printer, Epson MX dot matrix printers. |
| OKIDATA | Okidata dot matrix printers. |

IBM is the default.

SIZE <expN1> is the printed graph size. Sizes range from 0 (smallest) to 5 (largest). The default is printer dependent.

VERTICAL/HORIZONTAL orients the printed graph horizontally or vertically. The default is printer dependent.

ASPECT <expN2> is the ratio of horizontal dots to vertical dots in printed graphs. Because this ratio varies among printers, circles may appear as ovals. <expN2> is a decimal value greater than 0 and less than or equal to 1. The higher the value, the greater the vertical depth.

## RECOMMENDED USE:

Use SET GRAPHPRINT before printing graphs with the commands CREATE GRAPH, GRAPH FORM, MODIFY GRAPH, and RESTORE GRAPH.

**Example**—A pie chart shows a company's growth percentage. Database file GAINS contains five years' of quarterly data. SET GRAPHPRINT specifies an IBM printer with SIZE, VERTICAL, and ASPECT options.

```
SET GRAPHPRINT TO IBM VERTICAL SIZE 1 ASPECT .44
RESTORE GRAPH FROM gaingraf TO PRINT
```

## SPECIAL USE:

You can install the graph printer in dBXL's configuration file (CONFIG.XL) with the syntax

GRAPHPRINT=EPSONFX/IBM/OKIDATA/HPLASERJET/HPPLOTTER
[, <size>] [,VERTICAL/,HORIZONTAL] [,<aspect>]

## LIMITS/WARNINGS:

The ASPECT option can cause graph titles to overlap.

## VARIATIONS:

**Quicksilver:** You can also install printers with the INSTALL program.

SET GRAPHPRINT is not complete in Quicksilver 1.2 and is undocumented. Some forms of the command will compile; however, its effects are unpredictable.

## SEE ALSO:

Commands CREATE/MODIFY GRAPH, GRAPH FORM, and RESTORE GRAPH.

# SET HEADING

## DIALECTS:

dBASE III PLUS, dBASE IV, dBXL, and FoxBASE+.

## SYNTAX:

SET HEADING ON/OFF

## DEFINITION:

Controls the display of FIELD titles for the AVERAGE, DISPLAY, LIST, and SUM commands.

SET HEADING OFF to suppress FIELD titles.

## DEFAULT:

ON

## RECOMMENDED USE:

Use SET HEADING OFF to omit FIELD titles when you want to program your own.

**Example**—A theater management system lists work shifts each night. The program uses SET HEADING OFF to suppress field titles so custom titles can be displayed.

```
USE lateshift
SET HEADING OFF
? "Employee Name          Scheduled Hours "
DISPLAY ALL lname,shours FOR dateon = DATE()
```

```
Employee Name        Scheduled Hours
     1  Johnson              6-12
     5  Martinez             9-23
```

## VARIATIONS:

**Clipper, Quicksilver:** HEADING is always assumed to be OFF. To include field titles, you must program them explicitly.

## SEE ALSO:

Commands AVERAGE, DISPLAY, LIST, and SUM.

# SET HELP

## DIALECTS:
dBASE III PLUS and dBASE IV.

## SYNTAX:
SET HELP ON/OFF

## DEFINITION:
Controls whether the dBASE III PLUS message "Do you want some help?" or the dBASE IV message "Cancel, Edit, Help" appears when an incorrect command is entered in the interactive mode.

SET HELP does not affect the interactive help systems (F1 help) of dBASE III PLUS, dBASE IV, dBXL and FoxBASE+.

## DEFAULT:
ON. To change it (and get rid of the annoying message), set HELP=OFF in the CONFIG.DB file.

## RECOMMENDED USE:
When using dBASE III PLUS and dBASE IV, always SET HELP OFF (or change the setting in the CONFIG.DB file). The "Do you want some help?" and "Cancel, Edit, Help" prompts are redundant since HELP is available only through the F1 key.

## VARIATIONS:
**FoxBASE+:** SET HELP is allowed for compatibility with dBASE III PLUS, but has no effect.

## SEE ALSO:
Commands ASSIST and INTRO.

# SET HISTORY

## DIALECTS:

dBASE III PLUS, dBASE IV, dBXL, and FoxBASE+.

## SYNTAX:

SET HISTORY ON/OFF
SET HISTORY TO <expN>

## DEFINITION:

The HISTORY system saves and recalls commands executed from the interactive prompt. When you SET HISTORY ON, commands you type are saved in a HISTORY buffer. You can then display, edit, and reexecute them.

When you SET HISTORY OFF, no new commands are stored in the history buffer; however, old ones are still available.

SET HISTORY TO <expN> controls how many commands are saved in the HISTORY buffer. dBASE III PLUS, dBASE IV, dBXL, and FoxBASE+ default to 20.

## DEFAULT:

ON

## RECOMMENDED USE:

Use the up and down arrow keys on the numeric keypad to scroll through saved commands. You can execute the one on the command line by pressing the Enter key. Or you may first edit it and then execute it.

The command SET HISTORY TO determines how many commands are saved in the HISTORY buffer.

## VARIATIONS:

**dBXL:** If you repeat a command immediately, dBXL only puts it in the history buffer once. dBASE III PLUS, dBASE IV, and FoxBASE+ insert it multiple times.

dBXL lets you restore the HISTORY from previous sessions. When you include the statement SAVEHIST=ON in the configuration file (CONFIG.XL), dBXL creates a history log file DBXL.HIS in the current directory. You can specify a different directory at the DOS level with the command

SET HISTORY=\<path>\

**FoxBASE+:** When you SET HISTORY OFF, saved commands can no longer be edited and reexecuted using the arrow keys. LIST HISTORY and DISPLAY HISTORY still show the list of saved commands.

SET HISTORY TO controls only how many commands are displayed, not how many are actually stored. The HMEMORY parameter in the CONFIG.FX file controls the number stored.

## SEE ALSO:

Commands DISPLAY/LIST HISTORY and SET DOHISTORY.

# SET HOURS

## DIALECTS:
dBASE IV only.

## SYNTAX:
SET HOURS TO [12/24]

## DEFINITION:
Determines whether the clock displays in 12-hour or 24-hour time. 12- hour time shows hours, minutes, seconds, and am or pm. 24-hour time shows hours, minutes, and seconds.

The clock appears during full-screen operations such as CREATE and BROWSE, or all the time when you SET CLOCK ON.

SET HOURS does not affect the system time returned by the TIME( ) function.

## DEFAULT:
12. To return to 12-hour time, SET HOURS TO with no argument.

## RECOMMENDED USE:
Use SET HOURS to customize the clock display.

**Example**—Most conventional clocks display 12-hour time; however, some applications require 24-hour displays.

```
. SET HOURS TO 24
```

At 2:23:44 pm, the 24-hour clock displays

```
14:23:44
```

## SEE ALSO:
Command SET CLOCK; function TIME( ).

# SET INDEX TO

## DIALECTS:

Clipper, dBASE III PLUS, dBASE IV, dBXL, FoxBASE+, and Quicksilver.

## SYNTAX:

SET INDEX TO [<filename1>][,<filename2>]...[,<filename7>]

## DEFINITION:

Opens up to seven indexes associated with the active database file, where <filename> is the name of a existing index file. The command first closes all open indexes (in the same work area). SET INDEX TO without a file list, or CLOSE INDEX, closes all open index files in the current work area.

The index filename has a default extension of NDX.

SET INDEX TO ? lists available index files if a dBASE III PLUS or dBASE IV catalog is active.

The first file in the list, the *primary* index, determines the order in which records appear. Only it can be searched using the FIND and SEEK commands. However, other indexes are updated automatically when the associated key fields change. You can make any index the primary index by switching the file order in SET INDEX TO, or by using the command SET ORDER TO. SET ORDER TO is faster since it does not close and reopen the indexes.

## RECOMMENDED USE:

Use SET INDEX TO to activate indexes created by the INDEX command.

**Example**—A demographic application processes census data and generates useful reports. It uses SET INDEX TO with multiple index files to change the order of reports.

```
. USE census1
. SET INDEX TO lastdex,ssndex,agedex
. LIST
Record#  LASTNAME   AGE ZIP        SSN
      3  Anderson   59  99999      021224222
      2  Bellwood   50  01960      077772929
      1  Zorella    22  22222      122888929
```

In this example, LASTNAME is the primary index. You can change it by changing the order in the file list or by using SET ORDER TO.

## VARIATIONS:

**Clipper:** Index files have a default extension of NTX. To specify their filenames using macros, handle each one separately. For example:

```
maindex = "Name"
subdex  = "Age"
SET INDEX TO &maindex,&subdex
```

NTX files are not compatible with dBASE III PLUS or dBASE IV.

**Clipper, Summer 1987 and later:** You can use dBASE III PLUS/dBASE IV compatible indexes (NDX) by linking the NDX.OBJ file on the system disk to your application. dBASE III PLUS compatible indexes take slightly more disk space and update more slowly than the default indexes.

**dBASE IV:** The SET INDEX command takes the form

SET INDEX TO [<ndx or mdx filenames>
    [ORDER <ndx filename>/<mdx tag> [OF <mdx filename>]]]

You can specify index files (extension NDX) and multiple index files (MDX) on the same line. When you specify an NDX or MDX filename, dBASE IV first looks for an MDX file. If it doesn't find one, it looks for an NDX. If an MDX file and an NDX file have the same name, the NDX file will not be opened.

If an index file is first in the list, it becomes the controlling (master) index. If a multiple index file comes first, the database remains in natural order until you SET ORDER or use the SET INDEX ORDER clause.

The ORDER clause specifies which index or multiple index TAG controls the database's order. Use the OF <mdx filename> option if the controlling TAG is in a file other than the production MDX.

To SET INDEX TO two MDXs called MONTHMDX and AMTMDX, and an index file called PARTNO, use the command

```
SET INDEX TO monthmdx,amtmdx,partno ORDER nmonth OF amtmdx.mdx
```

The ORDER clause indicates that the TAG NMONTH in AMTMDX controls the index order.

The dBASE IV DELETE TAG command closes specific indexes by name. SET INDEX TO by itself and CLOSE INDEXES close all indexes.

You may open up to 10 index files per active database, and 47 TAGs per multiple index file. Multiple index files count as one open DOS file.

If you specify a key field when you first CREATE a database, dBASE IV automatically creates a production multiple index file with the same name as the database and an MDX extension. Whenever you USE the database, dBASE IV automatically opens the multiple index file.

**dBXL/Quicksilver:** SET INDEX TO first searches for index files in the directory specified by SET NDX. If you do not SET NDX, SET INDEX searches in the current directory. If it does not find the files there, it checks the paths defined by SET PATH.

**FoxBASE+:** Creates index files with an IDX extension. They are not compatible with dBASE III PLUS/dBASE IV NDX files.

SET INDEX TO first searches for an IDX file. If none exists, it then checks for an NDX extension. When it detects such a file, it automatically creates a compatible version with an IDX extension.

## SEE ALSO:

Commands CLOSE INDEX, COPY TAG, DELETE TAG, INDEX, REINDEX, SET ORDER, and USE.

# SET INSTRUCT

## DIALECTS:
dBASE IV only.

## SYNTAX:
SET INSTRUCT ON/OFF

## DEFINITION:
Controls the display of instruction boxes (summaries).

With SET INSTRUCT ON, when you issue a full-screen command, a summary of it appears for beginning users. The summary only appears the first time you use a command in a session.

The affected full-screen commands can be issued from the dot prompt or from the Control Center. They include APPEND, BROWSE, CHANGE/EDIT, CREATE, CREATE FORM, CREATE LABEL, CREATE QUERY, and CREATE REPORT.

SET INSTRUCT OFF turns off instruction boxes. You can also put INSTRUCT=OFF in CONFIG.DB.

## DEFAULT:
ON

## RECOMMENDED USE:
SET INSTRUCT ON is helpful for training beginning users.

## SEE ALSO:
Commands SET HELP and SET MENU; function SET( ).

# SET INTENSITY

## DIALECTS:

Clipper, dBASE III PLUS, dBASE IV, dBXL, FoxBASE+, and Quicksilver.

## SYNTAX:

SET INTENSITY ON/OFF

## DEFINITION:

Controls whether input fields appear in standard or enhanced video. Standard video means white characters on a black background. Enhanced, or reverse, video means black characters on a white background.

SET INTENSITY ON causes GETs and other full-screen input areas to appear in enhanced video.

SET INTENSITY OFF disables enhanced video.

Note that "Standard" and "Enhanced" have specific meanings when you use SET COLOR.

## DEFAULT:

ON

## RECOMMENDED USE:

Use SET INTENSITY OFF to omit reverse video from input fields during full-screen editing. You can mark the locations of input fields with delimiters by issuing SET DELIMITERS ON.

## VARIATIONS:

**Clipper:** You can use the logical expressions (.T.) or (.F.) to mean ON or OFF in the SET command. Enclose the logical value in parentheses.

## SEE ALSO:

Commands @...GET, SET COLOR, and SET DELIMITERS.

# SET KEY

## DIALECTS:

Clipper only.

## SYNTAX:

SET KEY <expN> TO [<filename>]

## DEFINITION:

Executes a program from any wait state when the user presses the specified key or key combination (Ctrl or Alt). The called program can be a PROCEDURE in an active procedure file.

<expN> represents the INKEY( ) value of the specified key. <filename> is the name of the program or PROCEDURE.

The wait state commands ACCEPT, INPUT, MENU TO, READ, and WAIT pause program execution.

*Note:* SET KEY always passes three parameters: the caller's name, the line number, and the name of the memory variable awaiting input (if there is one).

## RECOMMENDED USE:

SET KEY lets you run programs from any wait state with the press of a key. For example, you could execute a "pop-up" calculator or notepad. You can use the passed parameters to create context-sensitive subroutines based on the caller's name, line number, and GET memory variable.

**Example 1**—When entering invoice amounts in a legal office system, the secretary presses Ctrl-C to pop up a simple calculator. After adding, subtracting, multiplying, or dividing, the secretary presses "P" to paste the result into the pending GET. The SET KEY command in the calling program, INVOICE.PRG, executes CALC.PRG.

```
* INVOICE.PRG
CLEAR
SET KEY 3 TO calc     && Check for Ctrl-C.
@ 01,01 TO 06,60      && Draw box.
DO WHILE .t.
  ttot = 0.00
  @ 02,05 say "Enter amount, leave 0 to exit" GET ttot PICT "99999999.99"
```

```
  READ
  IF ttot = 0
    RETURN
  ENDIF
  @ 03,05 SAY STR(ttot,12,2)
ENDDO

* CALC.PRG
PARAMETERS x,y,z      && Must accept parameters even if they are not used.
SAVE SCREEN           && Save original screen image.
@ 0,0 CLEAR           && Issuing CLEAR alone would cancel any pending GETs.
INPUT "Amount 1: " TO amt1
sign = " "
DO WHILE sign # "-".AND.sign # "/".AND.sign # "+".AND.sign # "*"
  ACCEPT "Enter operator (+-/*): " TO sign
ENDDO
INPUT "Amount 2: " TO amt2
DO CASE
CASE sign = "-"
  mtotal = amt1 - amt2
CASE sign = "+"
  mtotal = amt1 + amt2
CASE sign = "/"
  mtotal = amt1 / amt2
CASE sign = "*"
  mtotal = amt1 * amt2
ENDCASE
? mtotal
WAIT "PRESS 'P' TO PASTE, ANY OTHER KEY TO RETURN w/o PASTE" TO action
IF UPPER(action) = "P"        && If user presses 'P', stuff
  KEYBOARD STR(mtotal,12,2)   &&  result in pending GET.
ENDIF
RESTORE SCREEN                && Restore original screen.
```

**Example 2**—The legal office system of Example 1 uses SET KEY to display lists of valid DEPT and ACCOUNT numbers. Here, the parameters are significant, as the lists are specific to the pending GET.

```
* POST.PRG
SET KEY 3 TO lookup   && Check for Ctrl-C.
CLEAR
DO WHILE .t.
  mdept = SPACE(4)
  maccount = SPACE(4)
  @ 04,01 SAY "Enter Department Number: " GET mdept
  @ 05,01 SAY "Enter Account Number: " GET maccount
  READ
  IF mdept = " "
    RETURN
  ENDIF
ENDDO
```

```
* LOOKUP.PRG
PARAMETERS prg,line,mvar
oldselct = SELECT()   && Store current work area in a memory variable.
SELECT 0              && Select first unused work area.
SAVE SCREEN
@ 0,0 CLEAR           && Use @...CLEAR instead of CLEAR to avoid
                      &&  clearing pending GETs.
DO CASE
  CASE UPPER(mvar) = "MDEPT"             && If you were editing MDEPT...
    ? "You were editing DEPARTMENT"      &&  display department codes.
    * <display department list>
  CASE UPPER(mvar) = "MACCOUNT"          && If you were editing MACCOUNT...
    ? "You were editing ACCOUNT"         &&  display account codes.
    * <display account list>
    * <more cases>
  ENDCASE
  WAIT
  RESTORE SCREEN
  SELECT oldselct                        && Return to original work area.
```

## LIMITS/WARNINGS:

**Note:** SET KEY always passes three parameters: the caller's name, the line number, and the name of the memory variable awaiting input (if there is one). Even if you do not use the parameters, you must declare them in the called procedure. Otherwise, an error condition will occur after several executions. Because the condition is not immediately apparent (either at compile time or at link-time), programs can fail unexpectedly.

Do not use CLEAR or READ in SET KEY subroutines because they deactivate GETs pending in the calling program. To clear the screen, use @ 0,0 CLEAR.

Note that if your subroutine moves the record pointer, you must restore its value before returning to the caller.

**Note:** Pressing F1 in Clipper executes a procedure or program called HELP. Like SET KEY, pressing F1 calls the HELP program with three parameters (caller's name, line number, and memory variable).

## SEE ALSO:

Commands @...SAY...GET

# SET LOCK

## DIALECTS:
dBASE IV only.

## SYNTAX:
SET LOCK ON/OFF

## DEFINITION:
Determines whether some commands initiate automatic file locking.

With SET LOCK ON, the commands AVERAGE, CALCULATE, COPY [STRUCTURE], COUNT, INDEX, JOIN, LABEL, REPORT, SORT, SUM, and TOTAL all lock the database file.

SET LOCK OFF disables the automatic locking feature, so that other users may access databases while these commands execute.

The affected commands generally do not change data, and therefore do not require locking. COPY, COPY STRUCTURE, INDEX, JOIN, TOTAL, and SORT have a data-writing phase when they create target files. The target files are considered to be in exclusive use for the duration of the command.

## DEFAULT:
ON

## RECOMMENDED USE:
Use SET LOCK OFF for greater concurrency. Be aware, however, that the commands affected by SET LOCK may produce inconsistent results if data changes during their execution. SET LOCK ON to guarantee consistent results.

**Example 1**—A sales report depends on current data. If it begins to SUM DAYSALES at 4:05 pm and ends at 4:06 pm, the programmer uses SET LOCK OFF to include all sales made within the minute. The consistency of the report does not matter.

**Example 2**—A closing sales and inventory report for five stores shows sales results as of 5:00 pm. Since all results must be consistent over time, the programmer issues SET LOCK ON.

## SEE ALSO:
Commands AVERAGE, CALCULATE, COPY [STRUCTURE], COUNT, INDEX, JOIN, LABEL, REPORT, SORT, SUM, and TOTAL.

# SET MARGIN

## DIALECTS:

Clipper, dBASE III PLUS, dBASE IV, dBXL, FoxBASE+, and Quicksilver.

## SYNTAX:

SET MARGIN TO <expN>

## DEFINITION:

Sets the left margin of the printer to column <expN>. Column numbers start with 0 at the far left.

SET MARGIN affects all printed output.

When using CREATE/MODIFY REPORT or CREATE/MODIFY LABEL, the SET MARGIN value is added to the LABEL or REPORT margin value.

## RECOMMENDED USE:

**Example**—Set the left margin to indent 25 spaces.

```
. SET MARGIN TO 25
```

## VARIATIONS:

**dBASE IV:** SET MARGIN is equivalent to the system variable _ploffset.

## SEE ALSO:

Commands @...SAY, LIST, SET DEVICE, SET PRINT, and SET PRINTER.

# SET MARK

## DIALECTS:
dBASE IV only.

## SYNTAX:
SET MARK TO [<expC>]

## DEFINITION:
Defines the character used to separate months, days, and years in date displays.

The specified character appears in date fields and memory variables.

The mark character remains in effect until you change it with another SET MARK, or with the SET DATE command.

SET MARK TO by itself returns date delimiters to the default (a slash in the U.S.). You can change the default in the CONFIG.DB file with the statement DATE=<date format>. See SET DATE for date formats.

## RECOMMENDED USE:
Use SET MARK to modify the date display when SET DATE does not provide the format you want.

**Example**—Joseph wants to display dates without delimiters. To do this, he uses SET MARK TO with a space.

```
. ? DATE()
02/03/89
. SET MARK TO " "
. ? DATE()
02 03 89
```

Dissatisfied, he changes the date delimiters to asterisks:

```
. SET MARK TO "*"
? DATE()
02*03*89
```

## SEE ALSO:
Commands SET CENTURY and SET DATE; functions CTOD( ), DATE( ), DMY( ), DTOC( ), and MDY( ).

# SET MEMOWIDTH

## DIALECTS:
dBASE III PLUS, dBASE IV, dBXL, and Quicksilver.

## SYNTAX:
SET MEMOWIDTH TO [<expN>]

## DEFINITION:
Controls the width of memo field output.

SET MEMOWIDTH TO alone restores the default MEMOWIDTH setting.

## DEFAULT:
50

## RECOMMENDED USE:
Use SET MEMOWIDTH when you produce memo field output with the commands DISPLAY, LIST, ?, ??, or REPORT FORM.

## LIMITS/WARNINGS:
The minimum MEMOWIDTH is 8.

## SEE ALSO:
Commands CREATE/MODIFY REPORT, DISPLAY, LIST, ?, and ??; functions MEMLINES( ) and MLINE( ).

# SET MENU

## DIALECTS:
dBASE III PLUS and FoxBASE+.

## SYNTAX:
SET MENU ON/OFF

## DEFINITION:
Determines whether a menu of cursor control keys appears during full-screen operations such as APPEND, BROWSE, and EDIT.

To toggle the MENU display, press the F1 key during full-screen operations.

## DEFAULT:
ON

## RECOMMENDED USE:
SET MENU ON is for novices using the interactive mode. SET MENU OFF in programs.

You can change the SET MENU default in the CONFIG file with the command

```
MENU=OFF
```

## VARIATIONS:
**dBASE IV:** SET MENU has no effect. Pressing F1 from BROWSE or EDIT displays information about the executing command.

## SEE ALSO:
Commands SET HELP and SET INSTRUCT.

# SET MESSAGE

## DIALECTS:

dBASE III PLUS, dBASE IV, dBXL, and FoxBASE+.

## SYNTAX:

SET MESSAGE TO [<expC>]

## DEFINITION:

Defines a string of up to 79 characters to be centered on line 24 of the screen. For it to display, the status bar must be on (SET STATUS ON).

SET MESSAGE TO by itself clears the message.

<expC> is any valid character expression. SET MESSAGE truncates strings longer than 79 characters, but does not generate an error.

## RECOMMENDED USE:

Use SET MESSAGE in the interactive mode to display system information, help messages, or reminders.

**Example 1**—You can use SET MESSAGE to display important system information such as remaining disk space. Note the use of character string constants, memory variables, and functions in the character expression.

```
* The DISKSPACE() function returns remaining disk space in bytes.
spaceleft = DISKSPACE()
* Convert diskspace frm numeric to character with STR() function,
* then perform a left trim (LTRIM) to strip leading blanks
str_left = LTRIM(STR(DISKSPACE()))
* CHR(16) and CHR(17) are left and right arrows.
SET MESSAGE TO chr(16) + "Remaining space: " + str_left + chr(17)
```

## LIMITS/WARNINGS:

Note that messages generated by the dBXL INTRO mode, the dBASE III PLUS Assistant, the BROWSE mode, and the dBASE IV Control Center overwrite user-defined messages.

## VARIATIONS:

**Clipper, FoxBASE+:** The form is

SET MESSAGE TO [<expN> [CENTER]]

<expN> is the row where MESSAGEs from @...PROMPT...MESSAGE command are to be displayed. They appear starting in column 0. (@...PROMPT...MESSAGE generates a reverse video "bounce bar" menu with optional MESSAGEs that change as the cursor bar moves). The CENTER (or CENTRE) option centers the message in Clipper only.

**Example 2**—Using SET MESSAGE TO [<expN>] with a "bounce bar" menu.

```
* Display the associated MESSAGEs on line 14 as the cursor bar
* moves between prompts
SET MESSAGE TO 14
@ 10,10 PROMPT "Backup Files" MESSAGE "Prepare two backup tapes"
@ 11,10 PROMPT "End Session"  MESSAGE "Close files, shut down system"
MENU TO response
```

In this example, when the cursor bar touches "Backup Files," the message "Prepare two backup tapes" appears on line 14. The message changes to "Close files, shut down system" when the bar moves to "End Session."

Note that SET MESSAGE TO 0 or SET MESSAGE TO by itself disables the display.

## SEE ALSO:

Commands @...PROMPT and SET STATUS; functions CHR( ) and DISKSPACE( ).

# SET MULTIUSER

## DIALECTS:
Quicksilver only.

## SYNTAX:
SET MULTIUSER ON/OFF

## DEFINITION:
Controls multiuser capabilities at the workstation level.

SET MULTIUSER OFF disables all multiuser commands and functions. All files are opened for exclusive use (single user only). FLOCK( ) and RLOCK( ) always return true .T.. ON NETERROR, SET AUTOLOCK, SET EXCLUSIVE, SET RETRY, UNLOCK, and USE EXCLUSIVE are ignored.

## DEFAULT:
ON

## RECOMMENDED USE:
SET MULTIUSER OFF to distribute a multiuser program for standalone use only. This lets resellers offer multiuser and single user versions without maintaining two sets of code.

You can also use SET MULTIUSER OFF to test multiuser applications in single user mode.

## LIMITS/WARNINGS:
SET MULTIUSER ON only in applications running under WordTech's Networker Plus multiuser software.

## SEE ALSO:
Command SET EXCLUSIVE.

# SET NDX

## DIALECTS:
dBXL and Quicksilver.

## SYNTAX:
SET NDX TO <path>

## DEFINITION:
Specifies which drive and directory contain index files. The <path> specification can include a drive designator and a path name terminated by a backslash.

## DEFAULT:
If you don't use SET NDX, Quicksilver and dBXL search for database files in the current directory and in ones specified by the SET PATH command.

## RECOMMENDED USE:
SET NDX and SET DBF let you store index files and database files in their own directories. This makes file storage more manageable. It also lets you address sets of database and index files by directory.

**Example**—A payroll program has index files in directory C:\PDEX and database files in C:\PFILES. The application uses SET DBF and SET NDX to find its files.

```
SET NDX TO C:\PDEX\
SET DBF TO C:\PFILES\
```

## LIMITS/WARNINGS:
Regardless of the NDX setting, DIR displays files in the current directory only.

## SEE ALSO:
Command SET DBF, SET DEFAULT, and SET PATH.

# SET NEAR

## DIALECTS:

dBASE IV only.

## SYNTAX:

SET NEAR ON/OFF

## DEFINITION:

Controls "closest match" SEEKing and FINDing. With SET NEAR ON, SEEKing or FINDing a nonexistent record moves the pointer to the one with the next higher key value than the search argument. FOUND( ) returns false (.F.).

If no record has a higher key value, the pointer moves to the End-of-File and FOUND( ) returns false (.F.).

SET NEAR respects the SET FILTER and SET DELETED settings when moving the record pointer.

## DEFAULT:

OFF

## RECOMMENDED USE:

SET NEAR ON is especially useful for processing records within ranges of values, when the exact limits may not be present. It is also useful for SEEKing values for which the exact spelling is unknown.

**Example**—A transaction report shows file updates beginning with 05/01/88. If no transactions occurred on that exact date (perhaps because it was a Sunday), the pointer normally moves to the End-of-File, and no records are processed. To overcome this problem, the programmer SETs NEAR ON. Even if the exact date is not found, processing continues with the next record.

```
SET NEAR ON
USE transacts INDEX transdex        && Indexed on DTOS(tdate)
startdate = CTOD("05/01/88")
enddate = CTOD("05/31/88")
SEEK DTOS(startdate)                && Even if STARTDATE is not FOUND,
DO WHILE tdate < enddate            &&   NEAR will move pointer to the
  SET PRINT on                      &&   next record.
```

```
  *< generate report>
  SET PRINT off
  SKIP
ENDDO
```

## LIMITS/WARNINGS:

SET RELATION disregards the NEAR setting.

## VARIATIONS:

**Clipper:** SET SOFTSEEK is equivalent to SET NEAR.

**dBASE III PLUS, dBXL, FoxBASE+ :** You can simulate SET NEAR ON in four steps:

1) APPEND a BLANK record to the database (be sure the index is active).
2) REPLACE the search argument into the new blank key field. This moves the new record to its correct index position.
3) DELETE the new record.
4) SKIP to the next record.

The pointer is now on the next higher record in the index. Unfortunately, you still have a deleted dummy record in your file which you should later remove by PACKing or reuse. You can hide it temporarily with SET DELETED ON.

## SEE ALSO:

Commands FIND, INDEX, SEEK, and SET SOFTSEEK.

# SET ODOMETER

## DIALECTS:

dBASE III PLUS, dBASE IV, dBXL, and FoxBASE+.

## SYNTAX:

SET ODOMETER TO <expN>

## DEFINITION:

Controls the update interval during execution of commands that display a record count. They include COPY, DELETE, and RECALL.

Because dBASE III PLUS and dBASE IV do not display a record count during indexing, SET ODOMETER does not apply to the INDEX command.

Note that a record counter only appears if you SET TALK ON.

## DEFAULT:

1

## RECOMMENDED USE:

SET ODOMETER relative to the size of the database files being processed. For example, use a large number (such as 100) when processing files of a thousand records or more. For files under 100 records, SET ODOMETER TO 10.

**Example**—A law clerk copies a file containing 30 records. She watches the record counter and notices that it jumps directly from 0 to 30. To make the display more meaningful, she uses SET ODOMETER TO 5, updating the counter every five records.

```
. SET ODOMETER TO 5
```

## VARIATIONS:

FoxBASE+ Applies to the INDEX command. Default is 100.

## SEE ALSO:

Commands COPY, DELETE, INDEX, RECALL, and SET TALK.

# SET OOPS

## DIALECTS:
dBXL only.

## SYNTAX:
SET OOPS TO [<expC1>][,<expC2>]]

## DEFINITION:
Redefines the silly "OOPS" error message.

dBXL's default error message consists of the word "OOPS:," and a brief explanation of the cause.

With SET OOPS, you can change "OOPS: " and display an additional comment at the end of the error message.

**<expC1>** is the expression that replaces "OOPS:". The error explanation that follows it is not affected.

**<expC2>** lets you specify a message to follow the error explanation.

**<expC1> and <expC2>** are limited to 15 characters each.

SET OOPS TO with no argument restores the ridiculous default.

## RECOMMENDED USE:
Use SET OOPS with a character string or function to provide more useful information in error messages.

**Example**—A spelling mistake causes a syntax error in a dBXL program, as follows:

```
DIPSLAY NEXT 10
OOPS: Unrecognized command verb:  DIPSLAY
```

To make the error message more useful, the programmer displays the available disk space and free memory.

```
SET OOPS TO STR(DISKSPACE(),9,0)+" ",  "   RAM:"+STR(MEMORY(),6,0)
```

The next time the error occurs, the following message appears:

```
DIPSLAY NEXT 10
8481008 Unrecognized command verb:  DIPSLAY   RAM: 129344
```

## SEE ALSO:
Command SET MESSAGE; functions DISKSPACE( ), MEMORY( ), and MESSAGE( ).

# SET ORDER

## DIALECTS:

Clipper, dBASE III PLUS, dBASE IV, dBXL, FoxBASE+, and Quicksilver.

## SYNTAX:

SET ORDER TO [<expN>]

## DEFINITION:

Designates a master index from the list of open index files. It does so without closing and re-opening indexes, thus executing faster than SET INDEX TO <filelist>.

<expN> is the index file's relative position in the index list. The list follows the SET INDEX and USE commands as in the following examples:

```
USE accounts INDEX acct,month,trans
SET INDEX TO acct,month,trans
```

ACCT, MONTH, and TRANS are index files 1, 2, and 3, respectively.

<expN> ranges from 0 to 7, depending on the number of files in the list. The primary index controls the order in which records appear. All other open indexes remain open.

SET ORDER TO 0, or SET ORDER TO alone, removes index control entirely, without actually closing the index files. Records appear in numerical order, and changes to the database file do not update the indexes.

A subsequent SET ORDER TO <expN> reinstates index control. If you add or change key fields after SETting ORDER TO 0, you must REINDEX the affected index files.

The ORDER( ) function returns the name of the primary index.

## RECOMMENDED USE:

Use SET ORDER TO [<expN>] to change the primary index, or to disable the index order (by omitting <expN>).

**Example**—An order entry program in a large department store tracks orders by item, date, and manufacturer. The program uses the main ORDERS file with an index file list. SET ORDER changes the primary index as required. ORDERS is indexed on ITEM, DATEORD, and MFG.

```
USE orders INDEX ITEM,DATEORD,MFG
```

In this line, ITEM is index 1 (the primary index), DATEORD is index 2, and MFG is index 3. When you LIST the database, note that the order is alphabetical by ITEM. ORDER(1) returns the primary index's name (ITEM).

```
. ? ORDER()
ITEM
. LIST
Record#  ITEM            MFG              DATEORD
      3  China plate     Rollings         02/17/88
      2  End table       SWC Corp.        10/04/87
      1  Hide-a-way bed  Int. Mattress    03/22/88
```

When you SET ORDER TO 2, the second index in the list (DATEORD) becomes the master.

When you SET ORDER TO 3, MFG becomes the primary index.

```
. LIST
Record#  ITEM            MFG              DATEORD
      1  Hide-a-way bed  Int. Mattress    03/22/88
      3  China plate     Rollings         02/17/88
      2  End table       SWC Corp.        10/04/87
```

SET ORDER TO 0 removes index control, but leaves the index files open. Records appear in numerical order.

## LIMITS/WARNINGS:

Because SET ORDER does not move the record pointer, a new order does not become active until you issue a command that does, such as FIND, GOTO, or LIST.

## VARIATIONS:

**Clipper, dBASE IV, FoxBASE+:** SET ORDER TO 0 does not prevent indexes from being updated when you add or change key fields in the database file. SET ORDER TO 0 simply deactivates the primary index. dBXL and Quicksilver follow dBASE III PLUS.

**dBASE IV:** SET ORDER TO <expN> does not work with multiple index files (extension MDX). Instead, use the command:

```
SET ORDER TO TAG <MDX tag> [OF <MDX filename>]
```

Use the OF <MDX filename> option when you have more than one multiple index file open and duplicate TAGs.

**Example**—A scheduling program in a university tracks research projects by number, starting date, and completion date. The program uses the PROJECTS file with a production multiple index file (called PROJECTS). SET ORDER changes the primary index as required. PROJECTS is indexed on three TAGs: PROJ_NUM, START, and COMPLETE.

```
. USE projects ORDER proj_num  && Production MDX activated automatically,
                               &&   and master index set to PROJ_NUM.
```

A DISPLAY STATUS shows the open database with PROJ_NUM as the master index TAG.

```
. DISPLAY STATUS
Currently Selected Database
Select area:  1, Database in Use: D:\DBASE\PROJECTS.DBF  Alias PROJECTS
Production     MDX file: D:\DBASE\PROJECTS.MDX
    Master Index TAG:      PROJ_NUM    Key: proj_num
           Index TAG:      START       Key: start
           Index TAG:      COMPLETE    Key: complete
```

When you SET ORDER TO TAG START, the second TAG index in the MDX becomes the master.

```
. DISPLAY STATUS
Currently Selected Database
Select area:  1, Database in Use: D:\DBASE\PROJECTS.DBF  Alias PROJECTS
Production     MDX file: D:\DBASE\PROJECTS.MDX
           Index TAG:      PROJ_NUM    Key: proj_num
    Master Index TAG:      START       Key: start
           Index TAG:      COMPLETE    Key: complete
```

The need to use TAGs rather than numbers is a minor inconvenience you can overcome with the MDX( ) and TAG( ) functions.

To SET the TAG order by number, use TAG( ) to store the TAG name in a variable. For readability, name the variable with the TAG number.

```
tag1 = TAG(1)
PROJ_NUM
```

Now, you can use TAG1 as an argument in the SET ORDER command, as follows:

```
SET ORDER TO &tag1
```

## SEE ALSO:

Commands INDEX, LIST, and SET INDEX; functions MDX( ), NDX( ), and TAG( ).

# SET PATH

## DIALECTS:
Clipper, dBASE III PLUS, dBASE IV, dBXL, FoxBASE+, and Quicksilver.

## SYNTAX:
SET PATH TO [<pathname>]

## DEFINITION:
Specifies MS-DOS directory trees where dBASE searches for files not located in the current directory. SET PATH TO by itself restores the default path (current directory).

The current directory is the one from which you started dBASE, or the one you change to using the MS-DOS CHDIR command. If you change disk drives with the SET DEFAULT command, the directory on the new drive is the current directory.

A pathname consists of a disk drive designator followed by a list of DOS directories separated by backslashes. The path list consists of a series of paths separated by commas or semicolons.

## DEFAULT:
Current directory

## RECOMMENDED USE:
Use SET PATH to specify directories (besides the default one) in which to search for files.

**Example**—An insurance agency maintains customer history records and claim reports in separate directories for better organization. The history records are in \CUSTHIST and the claims are in \CLAIMRPT. A single line in the program directs the application to search the proper directories:

```
SET PATH TO \CLAIMRPT,\CUSTHIST
```

To store the history records and claim reports on separate disks, include drive designators in the command:

```
SET PATH TO C:\CLAIMRPT, F:\CUSTHIST
```

Now your application can find claim reports on drive C and history records on drive F.

## LIMITS/WARNINGS:

*Note:* SET PATH affects only searches. It does not affect the DIRectory command. DIR only shows files in the current directory. Also, any files you create are always placed in the current directory unless you specify a disk drive or path. Many users find this inconvenient, especially when restoring MEM files from a directory specified by SET PATH. To SAVE the MEM file back where it came from, you must specify drive and directory explicitly. Avoid this problem by using the DOS Change Directory command (CD) from inside dBASE to move to your data drive. (dBXL and Quicksilver have their own CD command that works the same way.)

Let's assume that dBASE itself is in a directory called \DBMS. MEMory and data files are in \DATA. First run dBASE as in this example:

```
C>
C> CD \DBMS      <Enter>
C> DBASE         <Enter>
```

Then, from inside dBASE, issue the command

```
. RUN CD \DATA
```

\DATA becomes the current directory, even though it is not the one from which you started dBASE.

*Note:* SET PATH does not affect the DOS PATH command, or vice versa.

## VARIATIONS:

**Clipper:** You cannot use a semicolon to continue the SET PATH command on another line like other commands.

**dBXL, Quicksilver:** SET DBF or SET NDX limits searches to the current directory and the DBF and NDX directories for database and index files, respectively. dBXL and Quicksilver do not search directories specified by SET PATH. Without SET DBF or SET NDX, dBXL and Quicksilver search the current directory and the specified PATHs for all types of files.

**FoxBASE+:** Changing the PATH does not prevent programs loaded in memory from executing. Be sure to CLEAR PROGRAM to remove the currently loaded program from memory.

## SEE ALSO:

Commands CD, CLEAR PROGRAM, DIR, SET DBF, SET DEFAULT, and SET NDX.

# SET POINT

## DIALECTS:
dBASE IV only.

## SYNTAX:
SET POINT TO [<expC>]

## DEFINITION:
Changes the decimal point symbol to another symbol in all numeric output.

<expC> is any character.

You continue to specify decimal points in PICTURE templates, but they display as the new symbol.

SET POINT TO with no argument returns the decimal point to the default.

## RECOMMENDED USE:
Use SET POINT to customize numeric output for handling international funds or specialized units.

**Example**—A program tracks monetary exchanges. Some currencies use a comma instead of a decimal point. The programmer uses SET POINT to change the decimal point. Note that SET SEPARATOR changes the commas to periods.

```
SET SEPARATOR TO "."
SET POINT TO ","
mconvert = 673372.22
? mconvert PICTURE "$9,999,999.99"
$$$673.372,22
```

## SEE ALSO:
Commands @...SAY, SET CURRENCY, and SET SEPARATOR.

# SET PRECISION

## DIALECTS:
dBASE IV only.

## SYNTAX:
SET PRECISION TO [<expN>]

## DEFINITION:
Specifies the degree of numeric accuracy in operations using BCD (type N) data.

<expN> indicates the number of digits used internally in mathematical operations, ranging from 10 to 20.

## DEFAULT:
16

## RECOMMENDED USE:
Use SET PRECISION to increase numeric accuracy for scientific and engineering applications.

**Example**—Scientists plotting spacecraft trajectories increase the numeric precision to 20.

```
SET PRECISION TO 20
mdegrees = 38.487112489
```

Displaying memory shows the numeric value of MDEGREES:

```
    MDEGREES     priv    N          38.49    (38.48711248900000000)
```

## LIMITS/WARNINGS:
SET PRECISION does not affect the numeric display; SET DECIMALS does that job.

## SEE ALSO:
Command SET DECIMALS.

# SET PRINT

## DIALECTS:
Clipper, dBASE III PLUS, dBASE IV, dBXL, FoxBASE+, and Quicksilver.

## SYNTAX:
SET PRINT ON/OFF

## DEFINITION:
Directs all output, except @...SAYs, to the printer. Output also goes to the screen.

Use the command SET DEVICE TO PRINT to direct @...SAYs to the printer.

## DEFAULT:
OFF

## RECOMMENDED USE:
Most commands that display data on the screen allow the TO PRINT option. It has the same effect as SET PRINT ON, except that it applies only to the current command. Use SET PRINT ON to print the results of several commands. Use TO PRINT for single commands.

**Example 1**—An accounting program LISTs data on the printer. The program SETs PRINT ON, executes two LIST commands, then SETs PRINT OFF.

```
USE ar_main
SET PRINT on
LIST terms, past_due, clients
Record#  TERMS      PAST_DUE CLIENT
      1  NET30         53.00 ACME SOCKS
      2  NET30        464.00 MATSON LAW
      3  NET10       2982.30 ROBINSON
      4  COD         9292.99 JOHNSON
LIST ALL terms, past_due, clients FOR past_due > 3000
Record#  TERMS      PAST_DUE CLIENT
      4  COD         9292.99 JOHNSON
SET PRINT off
```

With the TO PRINT option, printing stops when output ends.

## VARIATIONS:
**Clipper:** You can use the logical expressions .T. or .F. to mean ON or OFF in the SET command. Enclose the logical value in parentheses.

**Clipper, FoxBASE+, and Quicksilver:** SET PRINT ON also sends print output to a file when you first SET PRINTER TO <filename>.

**dBASE IV:** SET PRINT ON also sends print output to a file when you first SET PRINTER TO FILE <filename>.

## SEE ALSO:

Commands LIST, SET DEVICE, and SET PRINTER.

# SET PRINTER

## DIALECTS:

Clipper, dBASE III PLUS, dBASE IV, dBXL, FoxBASE+, and Quicksilver.

## SYNTAX:

SET PRINTER TO [LPT1/LPT2/LPT3/COM1/COM2]

## DEFINITION:

Directs printed output to the specified DOS device. LPT1, LPT2, and LPT3 are parallel printer ports. COM1 and COM2 are serial communication ports.

Note that printing does not actually begin until you either SET PRINT ON, or SET DEVICE TO PRINT.

## DEFAULT:

LPT1 (PRN)

## RECOMMENDED USE:

Many PCs contain more than one kind of port. This gives you flexibility in choosing a printer (either serial or parallel), and it lets you connect more than one printer to a computer.

**Example 1**—A mail order company tracks telephone orders using dBASE. To keep from having to change forms, the operator enters orders on a computer attached to three printers, each with its own form.

Printer 1 prints packing slips. Printer 2 produces invoices. Printer 3, a laser printer, produces personalized letters. The order fulfillment program uses SET PRINTER TO to switch printers.

```
PROCEDURE ord_prt
* Prints three types of forms for order tracking program. Sends
* output to three different printers.
*
SET PRINTER TO lpt1     && LPT1 (parallel) connected to printer 1.
SET DEVICE TO print     && Direct output to a printer.
DO pack_prt             && Program PACK_PRT prints packing slips.
SET PRINTER TO lpt2     && LPT2 (parallel) connected to printer 2.
DO inv_prt              && Program INV_PRT prints invoices.
SET PRINTER TO com1     && COM1 (serial) connected to printer 3.
DO ltr_prt              && Program LTR_PRT produces form letters.
SET DEVICE TO screen    && Direct output to screen instead of printer.
```

## LIMITS/WARNINGS:

You can use the DOS MODE command to redirect output at the DOS level. For example, if your computer has no LPT2, you can redirect it to a serial port with the command

```
C> MODE LPT2:=COM1:
LPT2: redirected to COM1:
```

dBASE III PLUS then recognizes LPT2 as a valid device. When connecting your computer to serial printers, you must use the DOS MODE command to configure the serial port.

**Clipper, dBASE IV, dBXL, FoxBASE+, and Quicksilver:** SET PRINTER TO without an output device uses the default setting.

**dBASE III PLUS:** Your computer may freeze if you omit a device name. This condition may also damage open database files. To avoid it, be sure to specify only valid device names (check your typing!). dBASE III PLUS produces a syntax error if you specify a device not installed on your computer.

**dBASE IV:** Produces syntax errors if you specify a device not installed on your computer.

## VARIATIONS:

**Clipper:** You can specify a filename, instead of a DOS device, as a destination (e.g., SET PRINTER TO mfile). Clipper then directs all printer output to the file. Unless you specify an extension in the filename, Clipper assigns PRN. The filename may contain a disk drive designator and a full pathname. If you specify an existing file, it will be overwritten.

Clipper produces no error message or warning when you select a non-existent device—a tradeoff for allowing a filename as a device. Note that misspelling a device name, instead of producing an error message, will create a disk file with the incorrect name.

Clipper can send @...SAYs to a disk file, but only when you SET DEVICE TO PRINT.

**dBASE IV:** You can specify a filename, instead of a DOS device, as a print destination with the command

SET PRINTER TO FILE <filename>

The output file is formatted for the currently selected printer driver. You select printer drivers with the system variable _pdriver. For example, to change to the ASCII driver, issue the statement

```
_pdriver = "ASCII.PR2"
```

To change to an Epson LX-80, use the statement

```
_pdriver = "LX80.PR2"
```

Note that the specified driver must be in the default directory.

Formatted print output files have a PRT extension. If you specify ASCII.DPR as a printer driver, SET PRINTER TO FILE gives the output file a TXT extension.

After selecting a printer driver, you can then issue SET PRINTER TO FILE <filename>. Output will go to the specified file, formatted for the designated printer driver. You can then print the file from DOS with

COPY <filename.prt> <device>

You can direct print output to a network file server. On 3Com and IBM PC networks, use

SET PRINTER TO \\<computer name>\<printer name> = <destination>

<computer name> and <printer name> are the server and printer names assigned by the network.

<destination> is the DOS device (LPT1, LPT2, or LPT3) on the specified server.

**Example**—A file server FS1 has two shared printers, a Mannesmann Tally on LPT1 and an Epson FX-100 on LPT2. To select the Tally, an application issues the command

```
SET PRINTER TO \\FS1\TALLY=LPT1
```

On a Novell network, the SPOOL utility selects the printer. To switch to a shared network printer, issue

```
SET PRINTER TO \\SPOOLER/\\CAPTURE
```

(Note that SPOOLER and CAPTURE are synonyms).

On Novell, 3Com, and IBM PC networks, to flush the print spooler and return to the default local printer, issue

```
SET PRINTER TO <default>
```

If the default is a serial printer on COM2, issue

```
SET PRINTER TO COM2
```

**dBXL:** SET PRINTER TO <filename> not available. You can send @...SAYs to a disk file using SET DEVICE TO ALTERNATE and SET ALTERNATE ON.

**FoxBASE+:** You can send printer output to a disk file with the command

SET PRINTER TO <filename>

The output file has no assigned extension. Two more DOS device names, PRN and CON, are valid. PRN is a synonym for LPT1. CON refers to the console. SET PRINTER TO CON duplicates output on the screen.

You can send @...SAYs to a disk file, but only when you SET DEVICE TO PRINT.

**Quicksilver:** Lets you send printer output to a disk file; however, it does not allow pathnames in the destination filename. Nor does it overwrite an existing file of the same name. Instead, it appends the new output to the old file. To avoid this, ERASE the existing file before you SET DEVICE TO PRINT or SET PRINT ON.

Quicksilver can send @...SAYs to a disk file, but only when you SET DEVICE TO PRINT.

**Example 2**—A financial analyst wants to incorporate end-of-year reports in word processing documents. Using SET PRINTER TO <filename> and SET DEVICE TO PRINT sends formatted output to disk files. This works only in Clipper, FoxBASE+, and Quicksilver.

```
SET PRINTER TO eo_year   && File EO_YEAR is given a PRN extension in
                         &&  Clipper, none in FoxBASE or Quicksilver.
SET DEVICE TO print      && Begin sending @...SAY output to EO_YEAR
DO p_and_l               && Procedure P_AND_L prints profit and loss
                         &&  statement using @...SAYs.
SET DEVICE TO screen     && Resume sending @...SAY output to the screen.
SET PRINTER TO           && Reset PRINTER to the default (LPT1).
```

## SEE ALSO:

Commands @...SAY, ?, ???, SET DEVICE, and SET PRINT.

# SET PROCEDURE

## DIALECTS:

Clipper, dBASE III PLUS, dBASE IV, dBXL, FoxBASE+, and Quicksilver.

## SYNTAX:

SET PROCEDURE TO [<filename>]

## DEFINITION:

Opens a PROCEDURE file, loading the PROCEDUREs within it into memory. Only one procedure file may be opened at a time.

SET PROCEDURE TO by itself closes the open procedure file.

Procedures are executed like other programs, using the DO command.

When you issue DO with an open procedure file, dBASE first looks for the procedure to execute. If it doesn't find the procedure, it then checks for a program file (extension PRG). It then opens and reads the program, beginning execution.

Note that a program file and a procedure may have the same name. If so, dBASE executes the procedure unless you specify the program file with a disk drive designator or pathname.

## DEFAULT:

The procedure file name has a PRG extension by default.

## RECOMMENDED USE:

Put commonly used subroutines in PROCEDURE files. Because the PROCEDURE file is already open, DOing a procedure requires no file opening.

This can benefit data entry applications, especially when used for on-line validation routines and computations. During data entry, even slight delays can upset an operator's rhythm.

Also, PROCEDURES allow more levels of nested programs because more programs can be active. A procedure file containing many procedures counts as only one open file.

**Example**—A real estate management system consists of many program files and a procedure file containing 32 procedures. At the beginning of the main program, REALMAIN.PRG, the programmer includes the command to open the procedure file REALCALC.PRG. In REALCALC.PRG, procedure FUTURE computes future value based on TERM, PRINCIPAL, and INTEREST entered in REALMAIN.

```
* REALMAIN.PRG
SET PROCEDURE TO realcalc
STORE 0 to term,principal,interest
PUBLIC fval
@ 10,03 SAY "     Enter principal: " GET principal
@ 11,03 SAY "Enter term in months: " GET term
@ 12,03 SAY " Enter interest rate: " GET interest
READ
interest = interest / 12
DO future WITH principal,term,interest
? "Future value: " + TRANSFORM (fval,"$999,999,999.99")
* <more statements>

* REALCALC.PRG
*
PROCEDURE future
PARAMETERS principal,term,interest
fval = principal * (1 + interest / 100) ^ term
*
* <more procedures>
```

## VARIATIONS:

**Clipper:** Allows procedures anywhere in the compiled program without SET PROCEDURE TO. However, if a program file contains procedures and is not referenced by a DO <program name> elsewhere in the application, Clipper cannot find it at compile time. You must either use SET PROCEDURE TO<program name> to locate the procedures at compile time, or compile the procedure file separately, then link it.

There is no arbitrary limit on the number of procedure files. However, note that using procedure files offers no performance advantage. All programs and procedures ultimately reside in an executable file or in overlay files.

Procedure and program names must be unique.

**dBASE III PLUS, dBASE IV, and FoxBASE+:** A procedure file can open itself as shown here:

```
* MENU.PRG
SET PROCEDURE TO menu
DO proc1
PROCEDURE proc1
* <procedure statements>
PROCEDURE proc2
* <procedure 2 statements>
```

This lets you distribute an application as a single PRG file, without the need for a calling file to open it.

**dBASE IV:** All PROCEDUREs must end with a RETURN statement. You can put procedures in any program without a SET PROCEDURE command. Just put them at the end of the program file. Statements after a PROCEDURE...RETURN, except for other PROCEDUREs and FUNCTIONs, will never execute. A file can contain up to 1,170 procedures (limited by available memory).

For best performance and fewest object files, put as many procedures as possible in the main program file.

If a program file contains procedures and is not referenced by a DO <program name> elsewhere in the application, dBASE IV cannot find it. You must use SET PROCEDURE TO <program name> to locate the procedures at runtime.

You may DO a procedure in the current program file, or in the active PROCEDURE file. From a subroutine, you may also DO a procedure located in a calling program.

dBASE IV searches areas for the named procedure in the following order:

1. Currently executing object file (extension DBO)
2. An open procedure file using SET PROCEDURE TO
3. The other most recently opened calling object file
4. An object file with the same name as the procedure
5. A program file (extension PRG) with the same name as the procedure
6. An SQL program file (extension PRS) with the procedure name.

dBASE IV compiles program files before executing them.

*Warning:* dBASE IV will not execute a program on disk with the same name as an active procedure. The procedure always takes precedence.

**dBXL,Quicksilver:** The PROCEDURE statement must be the first command in the procedure file. This prevents procedure files from calling themselves as in dBASE III PLUS and FoxBASE+. Using procedures in Quicksilver has no performance advantage.

**FoxBASE+:** Using procedures offers a significant performance advantage. Fox Software offers a utility FOXBIND that puts programs in a single procedure file. It inserts the PROCEDURE <filename> declarations automatically.

*Warning:* FoxBASE+ has difficulty differentiating between procedures and program files with the same name.

To avoid this problem, 1) avoid duplicate names or 2) issue the CLEAR PROGRAM command before issuing another DO.

*Note:* In dBASE III PLUS (but not dBASE IV), a drive designator alone can differentiate between a procedure and a program file in a DO <filename> command. FoxBASE+ requires a pathname.

## SEE ALSO:

Commands COMPILE, DO, PARAMETERS, and PROCEDURE; function PROGRAM( ).

# SET PROMPT

## DIALECTS:
dBXL only.

## SYNTAX:
SET PROMPT TO [<expC>]

## DEFINITION:
Redefines the interactive prompt. It may display character strings and system information.

SET PROMPT TO alone resets the prompt to the default.

## RECOMMENDED USE:
Use SET PROMPT to provide system information to interactive users.

The prompt message may contain any of these system variables:

$a Active database alias
$b Vertical line (|)
$d System date
$f Active database name
$g Right angle bracket (>)
$h Backspace
$i Master index of active database
$n Default disk drive
$p Current directory of default drive
$s Space
$t System time
$v dBXL version number
$w Work area number of active database
$_ Carriage return/Line feed

**Example**—A researcher must use five open files when gathering data for a project. From the interactive mode, the researcher defines the prompt to provide information about the selected database.

```
SET PROMPT TO "> File: $a   Index: $i   Area: $w   Drive: $p $_>"
```

The prompt expression may also contain memory variables, internal functions, and other string operators. For example:

```
user = "John O'Toole"
space = DISKSPACE()
SET PROMPT TO "USER:"+user+" DISKSPACE:"+TRANSFORM(space,"99,999,999")+"$_>"
   USER:John O'Toole DISKSPACE:   5,519,560
   >
```

## SEE ALSO:
Command SET STATUS; functions DISKSPACE( ) and TRANSFORM( ).

# SET REFRESH

## DIALECTS:

dBASE IV only.

## SYNTAX:

SET REFRESH TO <expN>

## DEFINITION:

On a local area network, determines how often the screen is updated during BROWSE and EDIT to reflect changes made by other users. To use SET REFRESH, you must first use the CONVERT command to prepare databases for multiuser applications.

<expN> is the number of seconds between refreshes, in the range from 0 to 3,600 (one hour).

On a single-user system, SET REFRESH has no effect.

In the BROWSE mode, SET REFRESH updates all records except the current one.

In EDIT, SET REFRESH updates the current record, but only if it detects no keyboard input during the refresh interval.

## DEFAULT:

0

## RECOMMENDED USE:

Use SET REFRESH in applications with few transactions. It is quite distracting to watch data change on the screen during entry. (You can reduce the number of updates by increasing the refresh interval.) You can also use SET REFRESH in "read-only" screens where changes won't be a distraction.

When doing global transactions, take exclusive use of the file and make updates in batches. In general, SET REFRESH is useful in simple interactive "lookup" applications.

**Example**—An inventory application at a supermarket displays products in categories. The manager views the file in the BROWSE mode. To update it, she must first exit to a controlled data entry mode.

```
SET REFRESH TO 5
BROWSE NOEDIT NOAPPEND LOCK 1 FIELDS item,price,dept
SET REFRESH TO 0
```

## SPECIAL USE:

You can set the refresh rate in the CONFIG.DB file with

REFRESH = <expN>

## SEE ALSO:

Commands BROWSE, CONVERT, and EDIT; functions CHANGE( ) and LKSYS( ).

# SET RELATION

## DIALECTS:

Clipper, dBASE III PLUS, dBASE IV, dBXL, FoxBASE+, and Quicksilver.

## SYNTAX:

SET RELATION TO [<exp> / <expN> INTO <alias>]

## DEFINITION:

Links the currently selected database with another open database identified by its <alias>. SET RELATION links the files by a key index expression <exp> or by a numeric expression <expN> that evaluates to a record number.

When linked by a key expression, the child database must be indexed on it. When linked by a numeric expression (record number), indexes must not be used.

SET RELATION links two databases in a parent-child relationship. The active database is the parent, the INTO database is the child. When the parent's record pointer moves, the child's moves to the record matching the key expression. If no match is found, the child's pointer moves to the end-of-file, and the FOUND( ) function returns false (.F.).

dBASE III PLUS permits only one relation from one database into another. A parent database can have only one child. However, a child may have many parents. The biological analogy is a bit shaky here. You may also create a chain of relations, in which a child is itself a parent to another child.

SET RELATION TO also eliminates any previously set relation.

The RELATION does not take effect until you move the record pointer in the parent file.

## DEFAULT:

SET RELATION TO alone turns off the currently established RELATION.

## RECOMMENDED USE:

Use SET RELATION to reduce data redundancy and to simplify programming of multifile data entry screens and reports.

The key expression method of SETting RELATIONS is more flexible and reliable than the numeric expression (record number) method because record numbers are independent of the data. That is, a PACK or SORT changes record numbers, leaving the potential for errors.

If you must use a numeric key (for example, if there is not enough disk space for an index), control deletions and additions carefully. Record number relations work best when records match one-for-one.

**Example 1**—A mailing list database MAIL.DBF contains 100,000 records. Each consists of NAME, ADDRESS1, ADDRESS2, and ZIPCODE. Where are CITY and STATE? The program stores them in a related file called ZIPSTATE to conserve disk space and save data entry time.

The operator enters NAME, ADDRESS1, ADDRESS2, and ZIPCODE into MAIL.DBF. The program then searches ZIPSTATE using SEEK. If ZIPCODE is not found, the program prompts the operator to add the CITY and STATE. They are then available the next time the operator enters that ZIPCODE. As ZIPSTATE grows, less data entry is necessary. When generating reports or labels from MAIL, the relation points to the proper CITY/STATE record for a given ZIPCODE.

LABELGEN.PRG prints one-across labels using the database MAIL.DBF with a relation established into ZIPSTATE.

```
* LABELGEN.PRG
* ZIPCODE field is common to both databases
SELECT A    && Refer to relations by alias or work area letter.
USE mail
SELECT B
USE zipstate INDEX zipdex  && Indexed on ZIPCODE
SELECT A
SET RELATION TO zipcode INTO B
SET PRINT on
indent = 10          && Easy-to-change indent value.
DO WHILE .NOT. EOF()
   ? SPACE(indent) + name    ? SPACE(indent) + address1
   ? SPACE(indent) + address2
   ? SPACE(indent) + TRIM(B->city) + ", " + B->state + " " + zipcode
   ?
   ?
   SKIP
ENDDO
SET PRINT off
```

Note that LABELGEN.PRG extracts CITY and STATE directly from ZIPSTATE using the work area designator B->.

Assume that the space saved per record in MAIL equals the space wasted per record in ZIPSTATE. If MAIL grows to 150,000 records, but ZIPSTATE stops growing at 5,000, you save 145,000 CITY and STATE fields. If these fields are 22 bytes long, the total savings are 3,190,000 bytes. That is substantial, even in today's multi-megabyte world.

**Example 2**—A medical application stores histories and billing information in separate files related by patient number (PAT_NO). This avoids the duplication of billing information in each record. The billing file acts as parent. The following commands establish the relation:

```
SELECT A                     && Establish a work area and open
USE billing                  &&   the parent BILLING.DBF.
SELECT B                     && Change areas. Open child HISTORY.DBF, indexed
USE history INDEX pat_no     &&   on PAT_NO, a field common to both files.
SELECT A                     && Return to original work area.
* Set relation to the key expression (PAT_NO) in the child in work area B.
SET RELATION TO pat_no INTO history
```

With the relation established, moving the record pointer in BILLING causes the one in HISTORY to move to a record with the same PAT_NO.

**Example 3**—The same medical application as in Examples 1 and 2 stores insurance information in file INSURE. INSURE also contains a key field called PAT_NO (patient number). To relate INSURE to HISTORY and BILLING simultaneously requires a "chained" relation. Using BILLING as the parent, you could depict it as follows:

BILLING → HISTORY → INSURE

In the model, BILLING is the parent of HISTORY and HISTORY is the parent of INSURE. When the pointer moves in BILLING, the ones in HISTORY and INSURE follow. Of course, if there is no match in HISTORY, there can be no match in INSURE.

```
SELECT A                      && Establish a work area
USE billing                   &&   and open the parent BILLING.DBF.
SELECT B                      && Change areas.
USE history INDEX pat_no      && Open child HISTORY.DBF indexed on PAT_NO.
SELECT C                      && Change areas again and
USE insure INDEX pat_no2      &&    open INSURE with index PAT_NO2.
SELECT A
SET RELATION TO pat_no INTO history SELECT B
SET RELATION TO A->pat_no INTO insure
```

Note that the relation in work area B refers to a key expression in area A and a child database in area C. When the pointer in BILLING moves, the one in HISTORY moves to the corresponding record. When the record pointer in HISTORY moves, the one in INSURE moves to the corresponding record. You can set up to four indexed relations using this method (because you can have up to ten open files). Using record numbers and no indexes, you could set up to nine relations.

## VARIATIONS:

**Clipper:** You can specify multi-child relations in a single SET RELATION command using the syntax

SET RELATION TO [<exp> / <expN> INTO <alias> [,...8] ]

Up to 8 children may be related to a parent database file.

Clipper also has an ADDITIVE option that lets you add new relations in the current work area, using the form

SET RELATION [ADDITIVE] TO [<exp> / <expN> INTO <alias> [,...8]

**Example 4**—Example 2 also maintains a schedule database along with medical history and billing information. Using the schedule database, a doctor can view the billing and history files, plus look up the date of the patient's next visit. The following sequence establishes the relations.

```
SELECT A
USE billing
SELECT B
USE history INDEX pat_no
SELECT C
USE schedule INDEX pat_no2
SELECT D
USE transact INDEX pat_no3
SELECT A
SET RELATION TO pat_no INTO history, TO pat_no INTO schedule
```

An additional relation can be set in area A without releasing the previous relation:

```
SET RELATION ADDITIVE TO pat_no INTO transact
```

Moving the record pointer in BILLING causes the ones in HISTORY, SCHEDULE, and TRANSACT to move to records with the same PAT_NO.

Note that ADDITIVE comes after RELATION in Clipper.

**dBASE IV:** You can specify multi-child relations in a single SET RELATION command using

SET RELATION TO [<exp> / <expN> INTO <alias> [,...8] ]

You may relate up to 9 children to a parent database file.

You can also use the SET SKIP command to specify a one-to-many relationship from a parent record in one database to multiple records in another database. See SET SKIP for details.

**FoxBASE+**: The ADDITIVE option lets you set multiple relations. If you put ADDITIVE after SET RELATION, existing relations remain intact. We can establish ones like those in Example 4 as follows:

```
SELECT A
USE billing
SELECT B
USE history INDEX pat_no
SELECT C
USE schedule INDEX pat_no2
SELECT A
SET RELATION TO pat_no INTO history
SET RELATION TO pat_no INTO schedule ADDITIVE
```

Note that ADDITIVE comes at the very end in FoxBASE+.

**Quicksilver:** The default allows up to 10 open databases, six physically and up to four *virtually.* Although Quicksilver only opens six physically, it cleverly swaps additional files to make 10 appear to be open.

Unlike databases, relations must have their own physical buffer areas. The normal allowance is six relations, corresponding to the default number of *physical* buffer areas.

To increase the maximum number of relations to 10, re-install a large-memory linker library for a maximum of 10 physical buffer areas. To do this, run the install program using the linker libraries DB3PCL.LIB (included with Quicksilver) or DB3MSL.LIB (available separately from WordTech Systems).

## SEE ALSO:

Commands SELECT, SET INDEX, SET ORDER, SET SKIP, and USE.

# SET REPROCESS

## DIALECTS:

dBASE IV only.

## SYNTAX:

SET REPROCESS TO <expN>

## DEFINITION:

Determines how many times dBASE IV retries a record- or file-locking operation in multiuser applications.

The retry continues until the lock succeeds or the counter is exhausted. The counter (<expN>) ranges from -1 to 32,000. (Specifying -1 retries the lock indefinitely.)

After exhausting the reprocess counter, if the lock fails in a full- screen mode (BROWSE or EDIT), dBASE IV displays an error message that you can trap with the ON ERROR command.

In other contexts, RLOCK( ) and FLOCK( ) simply return false (.F.), making recovery the programmer's responsibility.

## DEFAULT:

0

## RECOMMENDED USE:

Always SET REPROCESS to as low a value as possible. If the system generates errors because files are inaccessible, raise the value in increments of 20 or 50 and test the results. The only way to find the best value is trial and error, since it depends on how well the application is designed. The best designed multiuser applications do not lock files and records longer than necessary to make the update.

**Example**—A real estate company uses dBASE IV on a local area network. During periods of heavy use, error messages report that other users have locked records and files. The programmer SETs REPROCESS TO 500 to give the FLOCK( ) and RLOCK( ) functions more time to succeed.

```
USE property
SET REPROCESS TO 500
* <SEEK appropriate record>.
IF RLOCK()
  REPLACE property WITH mprop, saleprice WITH msale
  UNLOCK
ELSE                  && If RLOCK() fails,
  DO recover          &&   do error-handling procedure.
ENDIF
```

## LIMITS/WARNINGS:

Avoid SET REPROCESS TO -1 if someone might leave a file locked indefinitely. If a user down the hall locks a file you want and leaves for lunch, SET REPROCESS TO -1 sends your computer to lunch as well.

## SEE ALSO:

Commands ON ERROR, SET AUTOLOCK, SET DELAY, SET LOCK, and SET REPROCESS; functions FLOCK( ), LOCK( ), and RLOCK( ).

# SET RETRACE

## DIALECTS:
dBXL and Quicksilver.

## SYNTAX:
SET RETRACE ON/OFF

## DEFINITION:
Controls the method of screen writing. Normally, it is continuous, creating a very fast display. On some terminals, however, this causes screen interference (snow). It depends on the type of color card and monitor. To eliminate snow, SET RETRACE ON, slowing the screen display.

## DEFAULT:
OFF

## RECOMMENDED USE:
If you use the PC-DOS Quicksilver libraries, you may encounter snow with a Color Graphics Adapter (CGA) or Enhanced Graphics Adapter (EGA). SET RETRACE ON will normally correct this problem.

dBXL's SETUP program lets you install dBXL with RETRACE ON or OFF. The SETUP program modifies the configuration file (CONFIG.XL), adding the statement RETRACE=<ON/OFF>. You can also install dBXL to use interrupt 10 for all screen displays. This lets you run on non-standard PCs and operating systems. If you install dBXL for interrupt 10 displays, SET RETRACE ON uses interrupt 10.

## LIMITS/WARNINGS:
Some older IBM PCs will not run Quicksilver-compiled programs without special installation because of the way Quicksilver writes to the screen. As older IBM PCs do not support horizontal retrace, SET RETRACE ON locks up the system. To correct this problem, use the Quicksilver INSTALL program to install Video Attributes and change the SET RETRACE command to use interrupt 10. Then put SET RETRACE ON in your program.

If you use the MS-DOS Quicksilver libraries, SET RETRACE has no effect. Quicksilver applications compiled for MS-DOS use the ANSI.SYS device driver to write to the screen.

*Note:* SET RETR means SET RETRY in Quicksilver, not SET RETRACE.

## VARIATIONS:

**FoxBASE+:** A command line option inhibits "snow" on non-IBM personal computers. To use it, enter

```
C> FOXPLUS -NOTIBM
```

from the DOS prompt. The NOTIBM switch is not available in FoxBASE+/386.

## SEE ALSO:

Command SET COLOR.

# SET RETRY

## DIALECTS:
Quicksilver only.

## SYNTAX:
SET RETRY TO [<expN>]

## DEFINITION:
Sets the number of times to RETRY a record lock (RLOCK( ) or LOCK( )), a file lock (FLOCK( )), or an automatic record or file lock (SET AUTOLOCK ON). RETRY also determines how many times Quicksilver tries to open a database file for exclusive use.

The attempts continue until the lock succeeds or the RETRY counter is exhausted. <expN> must be between 0 and 65535, inclusive.

If the lock fails, the program ends and control returns to DOS unless the ON ERROR or ON NETERROR command specifies a remedial action.

SET RETRY is similar to dBASE IV's SET REPROCESS command.

## DEFAULT:
10

SET RETRY TO alone restores the default setting.

## RECOMMENDED USE:
SET RETRY to a high number on networks with a high volume of transactions and many users. This reduces the chance of locking errors due to unavailable files or records.

**Example**—A commodity investment firm uses a Quicksilver program on a local area network. When many brokers enter orders simultaneously, network errors occur. Apparently, the RETRY default of 10 did not accommodate the heavy load of locking requests. To correct the problem, the programmer increases the number of retries to 200.

```
SET RETRY TO 200
```

## SEE ALSO:
Commands ON ERROR, SET AUTOLOCK, and SET REPROCESS.

# SET SAFETY

## DIALECTS:
dBASE III PLUS, dBASE IV, dBXL, and FoxBASE+.

## SYNTAX:
SET SAFETY ON/OFF

## DEFINITION:
Protects files from being destroyed by warning the user when an operation or command will overwrite one.

The dBASE III PLUS SAFETY prompt is:

```
<filename> already exists, overwrite it? (Y/N)
```

The dBASE IV SAFETY prompt is:

```
File already exists

Overwrite       Cancel
```

SET SAFETY OFF to disable the SAFETY feature.

## DEFAULT:
ON

## RECOMMENDED USE:
SET SAFETY OFF in programs since all operations that overwrite files are under the program's control.

Affected commands include COPY, CREATE, INDEX, JOIN, MODIFY STRUCTURE, SAVE, SORT, TOTAL, and ZAP.

## VARIATIONS:
**Clipper, Quicksilver:** Assume SET SAFETY OFF.

**FoxBASE+:** SAFETY does not protect files overwritten by the SET PRINTER command.

## SEE ALSO:
Command SET PRINTER.

# SET SCOREBOARD

## DIALECTS:

Clipper, dBASE III PLUS, dBASE IV, dBXL, FoxBASE+, and Quicksilver.

## SYNTAX:

SET SCOREBOARD ON/OFF

## DEFINITION:

Controls whether system messages appear on line 0 when STATUS is SET OFF.

With SET SCOREBOARD ON, messages appear on line 0. The messages include: "Del" (deleted record), "Ins" (INSERT mode on), "Num" (Num Lock on), and "Caps" (Caps Lock on). Valid range and valid date parameters also appear upon invalid input during data entry.

## DEFAULT:

ON

## RECOMMENDED USE:

SET SCOREBOARD OFF in programs when you want to use line 0 for custom menus, borders, or prompts.

## LIMITS/WARNINGS:

SET SCOREBOARD OFF turns line 0 messages off. It has no effect when the STATUS bar is active (SET STATUS ON).

*Warning:* Avoid using line 0 for menus and formats if you SET SCOREBOARD ON.

## VARIATIONS:

**Clipper:** Also controls MEMOEDIT( ) messages.

**dBASE IV:** Be sure to SET SCOREBOARD OFF when you use horizontal PAD menus on line 0.

## SEE ALSO:

Command SET STATUS.

# SET SEPARATOR

## DIALECTS:
dBASE IV only.

## SYNTAX:
SET SEPARATOR TO [<expC>]

## DEFINITION:
Specifies the numeric separator character in PICTURE template output.

You can change it from the default comma. <expC> is any character.

You continue to specify commas in PICTURE templates, but they display as the new symbol.

SET SEPARATOR TO with no argument restores the default comma.

SET SEPARATOR does not affect the decimal point. Use SET POINT instead.

## RECOMMENDED USE:
Use SET SEPARATOR in applications dealing with international funds or specialized units of measurement.

**Example**—A program converts dollars to pesos. The programmer uses SET SEPARATOR to change the numeric separator to a period, and SET POINT to change the decimal point to a comma.

```
SET SEPARATOR TO "."
SET POINT TO ","
mamount = 823372.22
? mamount PICTURE "$9,999,999.99"
$$$823.372,22
```

## SEE ALSO:
Commands @...SAY, SET CURRENCY, and SET POINT.

# SET SKIP

## DIALECTS:

dBASE IV only.

## SYNTAX:

SET SKIP TO [<alias1>[,<alias2>...]]

## DEFINITION:

Lets you define a one-to-many relation, in which a parent record may have multiple child records in a related file. You can then move the pointer among the child records, without moving the pointer in the single parent.

When issuing a command that uses a scope (such as LIST or DISPLAY), the parent record appears to repeat for each matching child record.

SET SKIP requires an active relation defined by SET RELATION.

<alias1>,<alias2>... is a list of open database file aliases linked by active relations. You can specify some or all of the open databases.

SET SKIP TO with no argument returns the relation to one-to-one.

## RECOMMENDED USE:

Use SET SKIP to create detail reports for a parent record.

**Example**—A doctor's office program has a PATIENT master file and a VISIT transaction file. The files are related by a common patient number, stored in PA_NUM and VIS_NUM. Each patient has multiple visits. With SET SKIP, the DISPLAY ALL command shows the parent record matching multiple child records. For example, patient Belair visited the doctor on 09/09/88, 07/11/87, and 06/13/87.

```
USE visit ORDER vis_num IN 2          && Child file.
USE patient ORDER pa_num IN 1         && Parent file.
SET RELATION TO pa_num INTO visit     && Relate by VIS_NUM (same as PA_NUM)
SET SKIP TO patient, visit            && SET SKIP to both files.
* Display all data using ALIAS->for clarity, although it is not
* necessary for displaying data from the selected work area.
DISPLAY ALL patient->name, patient->phone, visit->visdate, visit->condition
      2  Belair           503-555-2222   09/09/88       Checkup
      2  Belair           503-555-2222   07/11/87       Mumps
      2  Belair           503-555-2222   06/13/87       Headache
```

```
     3  Randall      888-555-8382   04/12/89      Flu
     3  Randall      888-555-8382   02/02/89      Hangnail
     3  Randall      888-555-8382   10/18/88      Sore throat
     1  Sanderson    619-555-1212   10/11/88      No problem
     1  Sanderson    619-555-1212   08/02/88      Rash
```

## SEE ALSO:

Commands DISPLAY ALL and SET RELATION.

# SET SOFTSEEK

## DIALECTS:

Clipper only.

## SYNTAX:

SET SOFTSEEK ON/OFF/(<expL>)

## DEFINITION:

Controls "closest match" SEEKing. With SET SOFTSEEK ON, SEEKing a nonexistent record moves the pointer to the record with the next higher key value than the search argument.

If no record has a higher key value, the pointer moves to the end-of-file and FOUND( ) returns false (.F.).

SET SOFTSEEK does not work with the FIND command.

## RECOMMENDED USE:

SET SOFTSEEK ON is especially useful for processing records within ranges of values, when the exact limits may not be present.

**Example**—A sales report shows transactions beginning with 02/02/88. If no transactions occurred on this date (perhaps because of the Groundhog Day Picnic), the pointer normally moves to the End-of-File, and no records are processed. To overcome this problem, the programmer SETs SOFTSEEK ON. Even if the exact date is not found, processing continues with the next available date.

```
USE transacts INDEX transdex        && Indexed on DTOS(tdate)
startdate = CTOD("02/01/88")
enddate = CTOD("02/29/88")
SEEK DTOS(startdate)                && Even if STARTDATE is not FOUND,
DO WHILE tdate < enddate            &&    SOFTSEEK will move pointer to
  SET PRINT on                      &&    next record.
  *<generate report>
  SET PRINT off
  SKIP
ENDDO
```

## LIMITS/WARNINGS:

SET RELATION ignores the SOFTSEEK setting.

## VARIATIONS:

**dBASE III PLUS, dBXL, FoxBASE+:** You can simulate SET SOFTSEEK ON in four steps:

1) APPEND a BLANK record to the database (be sure the index is active).
2) REPLACE the search argument into the new blank key field. This moves the new record to its correct index position.
3) DELETE the new record.
4) SKIP to the next record.

The pointer is now at the next higher record in the index. Unfortunately, you have a deleted dummy record in your file which you should later remove by PACKing or reuse. You can hide it temporarily with SET DELETED ON.

**dBASE IV:** The SET NEAR command controls closest match searching. SET NEAR works with SEEK or FIND.

## SEE ALSO:

Commands FIND, INDEX, SEEK, and SET NEAR.

# SET SPACE

## DIALECTS:
dBASE IV only.

## SYNTAX:
SET SPACE ON/OFF

## DEFINITION:
Determines whether expressions displayed with ? and ?? are separated by a space.

## DEFAULT:
ON

## RECOMMENDED USE:
Earlier versions of dBASE always put a space between expressions in a list printed with ? and ??. SET SPACE lets programmers omit the space for greater control over output. Spaces can be explicitly defined in the expression list.

**Example**—In a magazine subscription program, a programmer prints variables using ?. Although there are no spaces in the expression list, they appear between expressions.

```
? TRIM(subscribe),TRIM(address),TRIM(city)
Kalman 515 Main Street Boston
```

To omit the spaces, the programmer SETs SPACE OFF.

```
? TRIM(subscribe),TRIM(address),TRIM(city)
Kalman515 Main StreetBoston
```

To insert spaces in the expression list with complete control, the programmer can use the SPACE( ) function or literal spaces.

```
? TRIM(subscribe),SPACE(20),TRIM(address),"     ",TRIM(city)
Kalman                    515 Main Street     Boston
```

## SEE ALSO:
Command ?/??.

# SET SQL

## DIALECTS:
dBASE IV only.

## SYNTAX:
SET SQL ON/OFF

## DEFINITION:
Enables the Structured Query Language processing (SQL) mode from the interactive prompt.

SET SQL ON activates SQL, an alternate set of commands for creating, modifying, and querying databases.

When you SET SQL ON, dBASE IV recognizes SQL statements and a only a subset of traditional dBASE commands.

Programs that contain SQL must have a PRS extension. Such programs may not mix SQL and traditional dBASE data handling commands. Because dBASE IV recognizes the PRS extension, SET SQL ON is not necessary in programs.

## DEFAULT:
OFF

## RECOMMENDED USE:
dBASE IV has two languages for manipulating data: its own language and SQL embedded in a dBASE-language subset.

SQL is an industry-standard language for accessing and maintaining databases. Because it is standard, future versions of dBASE will be able to access data on mainframes and minicomputers, and on SQL-based database servers on local area networks.

Use SET SQL ON from the interactive prompt to enable the SQL mode.

You may not alternate between SET SQL ON and SET SQL OFF within a program.

## LIMITS/WARNINGS:
The dBASE IV Runtime Version does not execute SQL programs.

In PRS files (SQL programs), you may not use a semicolon as a line continuation character. The semicolon indicates the end of an SQL statement.

You may not use user defined functions in SQL mode.

SET SQL ON disables dBASE file-handling commands and functions. SQL commands replace them. The disabled commands and functions in dBASE IV Version 1.0 are:

ALIAS( )
APPEND [BLANK]
APPEND [FROM]
APPEND MEMO
ASSIST
AVERAGE
BOF( )
BROWSE
CALCULATE
CHANGE
CONTINUE
COPY MEMO
COPY STRUCTURE [EXTENDED]
COPY TO [ARRAY]
COUNT
CREATE [FROM
CREATE LABEL/REPORT/QUERY
CREATE TAG
DBF( )
DECLARE
DELETE
DELETED( )
DELETE FILE/TAG
DISPLAY
DISPLAY FILES/INDEXES/STRUCTURE/HISTORY
EDIT
EOF( )
EXPORT
FIELD( )
FIND
FLOCK( )
FOUND( )
GETENV( )
GO[TO]
IIF( )
IMPORT
INDEX
INSERT
JOIN
LABEL FORM
LIST FILES/INDEXES/STRUCTURE/HISTORY
LOCATE
LOOKUP( )
LIST
MEMOLINES( )
MLINE( )
MODIFY STRUCTURE
NDX( )
ORDER( )
PACK
RECALL
RECCOUNT( )
RECSIZE( )
REINDEX
REPLACE
REPORT FORM
RLOCK( )
SCAN...ENDSCAN
SEEK
SEEK( )
SELECT
SET BLOCKSIZE
SET CARRY
SET CATALOG
SET DELETED
SET DOHISTORY
SET ECHO
SET ESCAPE
SET EXCLUSIVE
SET FIELDS
SET FILTER
SET INDEX
SET MEMOWIDTH
SET NEAR
SET ORDER
SET SAFETY
SET SKIP
SET STEP
SET UNIQUE
SET VIEW
SKIP
SORT
SUM
TAG( )
TOTAL
UPDATE
ZAP

Note that the list of excluded commands and functions will change in future dBASE IV versions.

# SET STATUS

## DIALECTS:

dBASE III PLUS, dBASE IV, dBXL, and FoxBASE+.

## SYNTAX:

SET STATUS ON/OFF

## DEFINITION:

Controls the status bar displayed on line 22 of the screen. With SET STATUS ON, a bar appears across the bottom of the screen containing system information. It includes: current drive, active database file, current record, and total number of records. The STATUS line also indicates "Del" (deleted record), "Ins" (INSERT mode on), "Caps" (Caps Lock on), and "Num" (Num Lock on).

SET STATUS also controls display messages on line 24. With it ON, messages defined with the SET MESSAGE command appear there, as well as invalid RANGE and invalid DATE messages. SET STATUS OFF disables line 24 messages.

## DEFAULT:

ON, but you can change it by putting STATUS=OFF in the CONFIG file.

## RECOMMENDED USE:

Use SET STATUS OFF to disable the status bar when you run a program with custom screens. If your program addresses line 22 with STATUS ON, the status bar overwrites the output.

## LIMITS/WARNINGS:

**Note:** The status line always appears in ASSIST, CREATE/MODIFY REPORT, and BROWSE, regardless of the SET STATUS command.

## SEE ALSO:

Commands SET MESSAGE and SET PROMPT.

# SET STEP

## DIALECTS:

dBASE III PLUS, dBASE IV, dBXL, and FoxBASE+.

## SYNTAX:

SET STEP ON/OFF

## DEFINITION:

Pauses program execution after each statement to help in debugging.

With SET STEP ON, the prompt

```
Press SPACE to step, S to suspend, or Esc to cancel...
```

appears for each program line.

Pressing the space bar executes the next program line. All operations, except the screen display, work as usual. (The screen display may become difficult to read as the SET STEP prompt overwrites your screen output).

Pressing "S" suspends program execution. You can then do other operations and resume execution later by issuing the RESUME command.

Pressing the ESCape key CANCELs program execution, returning control to the interactive prompt.

## DEFAULT:

OFF

## RECOMMENDED USE:

SET STEP is a powerful debugging tool. During program suspension, you can manipulate files and create and inspect memory variables to determine the effects of program statements. You can also execute other programs and commands, including debugging commands such as SET DEBUG, SET ECHO, and SET TALK.

**Example 1**—A sales report program called SALESGEN.PRG generates erroneous results. Monthly sales total $24,000, yet the report shows only $16,000 among the three salespeople (MW, JM, and RC).

To debug the program, the programmer SETs STEP ON, then issues the command DO SALESGEN. When the program starts to print the results, she suspends execution. A LIST of the active database file shows:

```
  LIST
Record#       SALES CODE RDATE
      1    12000.00 MW   02/10/87
      3     4000.00 RC   02/14/87
```

She notices that record 2 does not appear. DISPLAY STATUS shows an active index called RDATE (reporting date) with a key of RDATE. She realizes that record 2 has a duplicate key and deduces that the index was created with UNIQUE inadvertently SET ON. The obvious solution is create a new index without UNIQUE. The file now looks like:

```
  LIST
Record#       SALES CODE RDATE
      1    12000.00 MW   02/10/87
      2     8000.00 JM   02/10/87
      3     4000.00 RC   02/14/87
```

The programmer then issues the RESUME command to continue program execution. This is a difficult error to spot, as it appears only when two salespeople report on the same day.

## VARIATIONS:

**Clipper:** Use DEBUG.OBJ, a debugging module you can link into your applications.

**dBASE IV:** Use DEBUG to activate the symbolic debugger. The debugger makes SET STEP unnecessary.

**Quicksilver:** Use the symbolic debugging tool dB Debugger.

## SEE ALSO:

Commands DEBUG, SET DEBUG, SET ECHO, SET TALK, SET TRAP, and SUSPEND.

# SET TALK

## DIALECTS:
dBASE III PLUS, dBASE IV, dBXL, and FoxBASE+.

## SYNTAX:
SET TALK ON/OFF

## DEFINITION:
Controls whether certain commands echo results on the screen during execution.

## DEFAULT:
ON

## RECOMMENDED USE:
With SET TALK ON, file handling commands (such as APPEND FROM, COPY TO, and INDEX) display record counters on the screen. Other commands such as AVERAGE and SUM show record counts and calculation totals. Memory variable assignments echo the STOREd values on the screen. (This is especially helpful for debugging because you can see values change).

SET TALK OFF turns off record counters, calculation totals, and memory variable assignments. It does not affect the SCOREBOARD or MESSAGE display.

To control the record counters displayed by the file handling commands (APPEND FROM, INDEX, etc.), use the SET ODOMETER command.

## LIMITS/WARNINGS:
Writing to the screen with SET TALK ON generally degrades program performance. For best performance, SET TALK OFF.

## VARIATIONS:
**Clipper, Quicksilver:** SET TALK is always assumed OFF.

## SEE ALSO:
Commands DEBUG, SET ECHO, SET ODOMETER, and SET STEP.

# SET TIME

## DIALECTS:

dBXL and Quicksilver.

## SYNTAX:

SET TIME TO <hh:mm:ss>

## DEFINITION:

Changes the system time to the specified value on the 24-hour clock. For example, 12:00:00 means 12 noon, and 18:00:00 is 6 p.m.

The TIME value is an unquoted string:

```
XL> SET TIME TO 05:05:30
XL> ? TIME()
05:06:20
```

Specifying a TIME value with a memory variable requires a macro:

```
XL> STORE "12:00:00" TO tstring
XL> SET TIME TO &tstring
XL> ? TIME()
12:01:02
```

## SEE ALSO:

Command SET CLOCK; functions DATE( ) and TIME( ).

# SET TITLE

## DIALECTS:
dBASE III PLUS and dBASE IV.

## SYNTAX:
SET TITLE ON/OFF

## DEFINITION:
Controls the dBASE III PLUS/dBASE IV file title prompt when a CATALOG is active.

With SET TITLE ON, dBASE III PLUS and dBASE IV ask for a title any time you create a new database file. dBASE then adds the title to the active catalog.

With SET TITLE OFF, the prompt does not appear and no file title is added. You may add one manually by EDITing or REPLACEing the TITLE field in the active catalog file located in work area 10.

## DEFAULT:
ON

## RECOMMENDED USE:
SET TITLE and SET CATALOG are designed primarily for use in the interactive mode.

## SPECIAL USE:
SETting CATALOG TO a nonexistent filename creates a new database file. This is the only way to create a database file under program control in dBASE III PLUS and dBASE IV. Some developers use this trick to supply programs to users as single program files. The program can then create other files using COPY STRUCTURE EXTENDED and CREATE FROM.

To create files in this way, you must first SET TITLE OFF and SET SAFETY OFF. Otherwise, the end user will be prompted unnecessarily for the CATALOG title.

## SEE ALSO:
Commands COPY STRUCTURE EXTENDED, CREATE FROM, SELECT, SET CATALOG, and SET SAFETY.

# SET TRAP

## DIALECTS:
dBASE IV only.

## SYNTAX:
SET TRAP ON/OFF

## DEFINITION:
Controls activation of the debugger when dBASE IV encounters a program error.

When you SET TRAP ON, an error stops execution and calls the debugger.

The ON ERROR command takes precedence over SET TRAP.

## DEFAULT:
OFF. Program errors produce an error message and prompt the user to Cancel, Ignore, or Suspend.

## RECOMMENDED USE:
Use SET TRAP ON during program development and testing. When an error occurs, you can set breakpoints, view variables, and execute the offending program line-by-line to locate the problem.

## SEE ALSO:
Commands DEBUG, SET DEBUG, SET DEVELOPMENT, SET ECHO, SET STEP, and SUSPEND.

# SET TYPEAHEAD

## DIALECTS:
Clipper, dBASE III PLUS, dBASE IV, dBXL, FoxBASE+, and Quicksilver.

## SYNTAX:
SET TYPEAHEAD TO <expN>

## DEFINITION:
Changes the size of the keyboard typeahead buffer. <expN> is the number of keystrokes; it must be an integer from 0 to 32,000 inclusive.

SET TYPEAHEAD TO 0 turns off the TYPEAHEAD buffer, and disables the INKEY( ) function and the ON KEY command.

SET TYPEAHEAD works only when you SET ESCAPE ON.

## DEFAULT:
20. In full-screen operations, such as EDIT, APPEND, or BROWSE, TYPEAHEAD only holds 20 characters.

## RECOMMENDED USE:
You may sometimes notice that you can type faster than a dBASE program can tolerate. You can often enter menu selections even before seeing the prompts if you have memorized the responses. The typeahead buffer holds keystrokes until the program can accept them.

**Example**—Occasionally, a program forces the user to read the on-screen prompts for warnings or instructions. In this example, SET TYPEAHEAD TO 0 disables the keyboard buffer for important messages:

```
CLEAR
SET TYPEAHEAD TO 0
WAIT "Press 'A' to archive or any other key to cancel" TO urgent
IF urgent = 'D'
  DO archive
ENDIF
```

## VARIATIONS:
**Clipper:** The largest value is 32,768. If you SET TYPEAHEAD TO 0, the Alt-C and Alt-D keys may not interrupt execution properly from a tight loop.

**dBXL:** The largest value is 129.

**FoxBASE+:** The largest value is 128.

## SEE ALSO:

Commands CLEAR TYPEAHEAD, KEYBOARD, and ON KEY; function INKEY( ).

# SET UDF

## DIALECTS:

dBXL and Quicksilver.

## SYNTAX:

SET UDF TO [<filename>] / ? / <pattern>]

## DEFINITION:

Opens the specified function file. If one is already open, SET UDF TO closes it before opening the next one.

SET UDF TO with no arguments closes an open function file.

SET UDF TO ? and SET UDF TO <pattern> display a menu of PRG files. ? shows all PRG files. <pattern> shows only ones matching the specified pattern. For example, to display all PRG files starting with "B," issue

```
SET UDF TO B*
```

## DEFAULT:

The file is assumed to have a PRG extension.

## RECOMMENDED USE:

SET UDF tells your application where to look for its user defined functions. Use SET UDF at the beginning of your application, or anytime you want to execute a user defined function in another UDF file. SET UDF TO also tells Quicksilver which UDF file to compile. This lets you use the -A option for automatic compilation.

**Example**—A dBXL reservation system uses 68 user defined functions. To circumvent the UDF file limit of 32 functions, the programmer uses SET UDF to change function files when necessary.

```
mvar = 10
SET UDF TO showfuncs   && UDF file contains display-oriented functions.
? SHOWPAGE(mvar1)      && User defined function shows page 10 of a report.
SET UDF TO de_funcs    && Switch to data entry user defined functions.
* <More statements>.
```

## SEE ALSO:

Commands FUNCTION and SET PROCEDURE.

# SET UNIQUE

## DIALECTS:
Clipper, dBASE III PLUS, dBASE IV, dBXL, FoxBASE+, and Quicksilver.

## SYNTAX:
SET UNIQUE ON/OFF

## DEFINITION:
Determines whether an index file will include records with duplicate keys. With SET UNIQUE ON, the INDEX command includes only the first record with a particular key value. SET UNIQUE ON is equivalent to INDEX ON <exp> TO <filename> UNIQUE.

SET UNIQUE is only relevant when an index file is created. An INDEX created with it ON remains UNIQUE, even when updated or REINDEXed.

With SET UNIQUE OFF, the INDEX command includes all records. Records with duplicate keys appear grouped together in numerical order.

## DEFAULT:
OFF

## RECOMMENDED USE:
Use SET UNIQUE to view only unique records or to purge duplicates from a file.

**Example 1**—A library system contains one record for each book. The librarian wants to produce an author index without duplicates.

```
USE booklist
LIST author
Record#  author
      1  Melville
      2  Howard
      3  Shakespeare
      4  Hooper
      5  Shakespeare
SET UNIQUE ON
INDEX ON author TO authindx
100% indexed          4 Records indexed
```

```
LIST author
Record#  author
      4  Hooper
      2  Howard
      1  Melville
      3  Shakespeare
```

The librarian could also use the INDEX command with the UNIQUE option:

```
INDEX ON author TO authindx UNIQUE
```

**Example 2**—Duplicate records in mailing lists cost extra postage, handling, and materials. SET UNIQUE ON offers a simple way to purge duplicates.

First, determine the significant key fields. In a typical mailing list, the first four letters of the LASTNAME, the ZIPcode, and the first three digits of the ADDRESS will suffice.

Next, INDEX on these fields either using the INDEX UNIQUE option or making sure UNIQUE is SET ON. Finally, COPY TO a temporary file. This file now contains only UNIQUE records.

```
USE maillist        && Use the mailing list file.
SET UNIQUE on       && Turn unique on.
* Create an index based on parts of the significant key fields.
* You may need to review the SUBSTR() function.
INDEX ON SUBSTR(lastname,1,4) + zip + SUBSTR(address,1,3) TO mailpurge
* Now only UNIQUE records appear in the INDEX.
* The temporary file will contain only records that appear in the INDEX.
COPY TO tempfile
USE
* TEMPFILE.DBF is now the master mailing list.
```

## VARIATIONS:

**Clipper:** In versions before Summer '87, SET UNIQUE affects all open indexes. It is not related to a specific index file. In the Summer '87 version, the UNIQUE attribute applies to an index file when it is created. For example, an index created with SET UNIQUE ON will remain unique regardless of the current UNIQUE setting. Also in Summer '87, you can use the logical expressions (.T.) or (.F.) to mean ON or OFF in the SET command. Enclose the logical value in parentheses.

## SEE ALSO:

Commands COPY, INDEX, LIST, and SET INDEX TO; functions INDEXKEY( ) and SUBSTR( ).

# SET USERHELP

## DIALECTS:

dBXL and Quicksilver.

## SYNTAX:

SET USERHELP ON/OFF

## DEFINITION:

Determines whether dBXL and Quicksilver display programmer-defined help messages when a user presses the F1 key during a READ.

The help messages are an option in the @...SAY command, as shown here:

```
@ 10,10 SAY "Enter Password: " GET psw ;
        HELP "If you forget your password, press ESC"
```

The F1 key displays the help message defined in the current @...SAY.

SET USERHELP ON/OFF works with SET USERHELP TO which defines the window where the help message appears.

## DEFAULT:

ON. If no help messages are specified, pressing the F1 key produces "No help available." To suppress that existentially discouraging message, SET USERHELP OFF.

## RECOMMENDED USE:

Use SET USERHELP ON/OFF to control the help option of the @...SAY command. In programs where you provide no HELP, SET USERHELP OFF.

## VARIATIONS:

**dBXL:** Redefining F1 with the ON KEY command turns off help messages, regardless of the USERHELP setting.

**Quicksilver:** Redefining F1 with the ON KEY or SET FUNCTION command turns off help messages unless you SET USERHELP.

## SEE ALSO:

Command @...SAY...HELP and SET USERHELP TO.

# SET USERHELP TO

## DIALECTS:
dBXL and Quicksilver.

## SYNTAX:
SET USERHELP TO [<WINDOW window name> / <window spec>]

## DEFINITION:
Defines a window in which to display help messages defined by the HELP option of @...SAY...GET.

The help messages appear when the user presses the F1 key, and SET USERHELP is ON.

SET USERHELP TO with no options restores the default user help window.

## DEFAULT:
Upper right corner of the screen (row 1, column 50 to row 8, column 78 with a one-character border).

## OPTIONS:
WINDOW <window name> is an existing window created by the WSET WINDOW command.

<window spec> is a complete window specification as follows:

```
<top row>,<left col>,<bot row>,<right col>
[CHARACTER <background char>]
[COLOR [<text],[[enhanced][,frame>]]
[FRAME <tl, t, tr, ls, rs, bl, b, br> / [DOUBLE]
```

See WSET WINDOW TO for details on specifying windows.

## RECOMMENDED USE:
Use SET USERHELP TO to position programmer-defined help messages on the screen. When the user presses the F1 key during a READ, the message appears in the specified window. When the user presses another key, the message disappears.

**Example**—A crowded editing screen does not leave much room for detailed explanations. Using the HELP option of the @...SAY...GET command, programmers can include custom help messages for each GET (See @...SAY...HELP). SET USERHELP TO incorporates dBXL and Quicksilver windowing to display the help message.

In this example, a service station management system includes custom help with each GET in an editing screen.

```
* GAS.PRG
CLEAR CHAR chr(177)
WSET WINDOW gashelp TO 1,1,4,50 DOUBLE
* Set userhelp to window GASHELP.
SET USERHELP TO WINDOW gashelp
* Open file and create variables with the same names as fields.
USE gasmaster AUTOMEM
@ 02,02 SAY "Enter pump reading: " GET  preading PICTURE "#####" ;
        HELP "5-digit number from dial 2"
@ 03,02 SAY "Enter gallons left: " GET gallons PICTURE "####" ;
        HELP "4-digit reading from dial 4"
READ
```

When the user presses F1, the associated HELP message appears in window GASHELP.

## SEE ALSO:

Commands @...SAY and WSET WINDOW.

# SET VIEW

## DIALECTS:
dBASE III PLUS, dBASE IV, and dBXL.

## SYNTAX:
SET VIEW TO <view filename>/? *dBASE III PLUS*
SET VIEW TO <query filename>/<view filename>/? *dBASE IV*

## DEFINITION:
### dBASE III PLUS and dBXL:
Opens a view file (extension VUE) created with CREATE/MODIFY VIEW or CREATE VIEW FROM ENVIRONMENT.

A view file contains a "snapshot" of the environment, including information about open database files, active relations, and active filters. SET VIEW TO <filename> opens the databases and activates relations specified in the view file. SET VIEW TO ? with an open catalog presents a menu of VUE files.

Specifically, a view contains all open database and index files and their work area numbers, the current work area number, all active relations, the active field list, the active filter, and the name of the open format file.

**Note:** SET VIEW TO updates an open catalog with the name of the VUE file, when SET CATALOG is ON. However, database files opened by SET VIEW TO are not added to the catalog.

### dBASE IV:
SET VIEW executes a query file (extension QBO or QBE) created by the CREATE/MODIFY QUERY/VIEW command or by the dBASE IV query-by-example program. SET VIEW also recognizes dBASE III PLUS view files (extension VUE).

dBASE IV searches for view or query files in this order:

1. Query object files (extension QBO).
2. Query source files (extension QBE).
3. dBASE III PLUS view files (extension VUE).

QBO and QBE files do not work with dBASE III PLUS.

## RECOMMENDED USE:
Use dBASE IV's SET VIEW to reestablish queries generated by the query-by-example program in the Control Center.

Use the dBASE III PLUS/dBXL SET VIEW to restore the working environment of a previous interactive session. This is convenient for experimenting with the dBASE interpreter or for recovering from interruptions. It is also good for keeping a copy of the environment in case of power problems or user errors.

**Example**—A real estate agent establishes filters and relations while using a database of investment properties. Her partner needs to use the computer briefly for another application. Before quitting dBASE, the agent can CREATE VIEW FROM ENVIRONMENT to preserve the open files and relationships.

```
. CREATE VIEW FROM ENVIRONMENT
Enter view file name: property

. CLOSE DATA
. CLEAR ALL
```

Upon returning to dBASE, the agent simply issues the command

```
. SET VIEW TO property
```

This restores all open files, relations, and filters. DISPLAY STATUS shows the environment just as she left it:

```
. DISPLAY STATUS
Currently Selected Database:
Select area:  1, Database in Use: C:PROPERTY.DBF   Alias: PROPERTY
Filter: CITY = "Houston"
Related into: PROPVALU
Relation: ZIPCODE

Select area:  2, Database in Use: C:PROPVALU.DBF   Alias: PROPVALU
Master index file:  C:ZIPEX.NDX  Key: ZIPCODE

Alternate file:
File search path:
Default disk drive: C: Print destination:  PRN:
Margin =      0
Current work area =    1
```

## VARIATIONS:

**dBXL:** SET VIEW TO <pattern> lets you restrict which files appear in the menu. For example, you can display all VUE files starting with "A" as follows:

```
SET VIEW TO A*
```

## SEE ALSO:

Commands CREATE/MODIFY VIEW/QUERY, CREATE VIEW FROM ENVIRONMENT, SET CATALOG, SET FIELDS, SET FILTER, SET INDEX, SET ORDER, and SET RELATION.

# SET WINDOW

## DIALECTS:

dBASE IV only.

## SYNTAX:

SET WINDOW OF MEMO TO <window name>

## DEFINITION:

Lets you specify a window to use when editing memo fields in operations such as APPEND, BROWSE, CHANGE, EDIT, and GET/READ.

When the user moves the cursor to a memo field and presses Ctrl-Home, the designated window opens.

The designated window must already be defined. If not, dBASE IV reports, "Window has not been defined."

The WINDOW option of the @...GET command overrides SET WINDOW OF MEMO.

## DEFAULT:

If you do not SET a WINDOW or use the WINDOW option of the @...GET command, memo editing uses the full screen.

## RECOMMENDED USE:

SET WINDOW OF MEMO works only with dBASE IV's editor. If you specify a different editor with the WP setting in CONFIG.DB (WP=<editor>), memo editing uses the full screen.

**Example**—A data entry program displays SAYs and GETs at the top of the screen. The program reserves the lower half of the screen for memo editing.

```
DEFINE WINDOW dataentry FROM 11,01 TO 23,50
SET WINDOW OF MEMO TO dataentry
* <Statements>.
*
@ 11,03 SAY "Your note: " GET notememo    && NOTEMEMO is a memo field.
*
READ
```

When the user moves the cursor to NOTEMEMO and presses Ctrl-Home, window DATAENTRY opens and editing begins.

## SEE ALSO:

Commands @...GET...WINDOW, ACTIVATE WINDOW, DEFINE WINDOW, and READ.

# SET WRAP

## DIALECTS:

Clipper only.

## SYNTAX:

SET WRAP ON/OFF/(<expL>)

## DEFINITION:

Controls whether the cursor bar in a light bar menu "wraps" from the last selection to the first, and back, when the user presses the appropriate cursor keys.

With SET WRAP ON and the cursor on the last selection, pressing the down or right arrow moves it to the first selection. With the cursor on the first selection, pressing the up or left arrow moves it to the last selection.

SET WRAP works only with @...PROMPT...MENU TO light bar menus.

## DEFAULT:

OFF. The cursor cannot normally move beyond the first and last selections.

## RECOMMENDED USE:

SET WRAP ON to make long light bar menus easier to use. This saves keystrokes in moving from one end of the menu to the other. SET WRAP does not affect light bar functions such as ADIR( ) and ACHOICE( ).

**Example**—A menu offers four report choices. With SET WRAP ON, the user can move the cursor bar from the first to the last selection with one keystroke.

```
SET WRAP ON
@ 05,01 PROMPT "1 across labels"
@ 06,01 PROMPT "2 across labels"
@ 07,01 PROMPT "4 across labels"
@ 08,01 PROMPT "6 across labels"
MENU TO which
DO CASE
  CASE which = 1
  * <more statements>
```

## SEE ALSO:

Commands @...PROMPT and MENU TO; functions ACHOICE( ) and ADIR( ).

# SHOW MENU/POPUP

## DIALECTS:

dBASE IV only.

## SYNTAX:

SHOW MENU <menu name> [PAD <pad name>] /
POPUP <popup name>

## DEFINITION:

Displays the specified menu or popup without activating it.

## OPTIONS:

If you specify PAD <pad name>, SHOW MENU displays the menu with the specified PAD highlighted.

## RECOMMENDED USE:

Use SHOW MENU/POPUP to display dummy menus and popups during program development. Also use them to display MENUs and POPUPs in user defined menuing routines. As the user defines the menu or popup, the routine can display the results immediately without interfering with program execution.

**Example**—A programmer lets users define menus with a program that prompts for PAD names and PROMPTs. The SHOW MENU command near the end simulates the menu as the user enters definitions. The program stores the menu definitions in array DEF[].

```
* UDM.PRG - Generates a MEM file containing a menu definition.
*
CLEAR
SET TALK OFF
SET SAFETY OFF
SET SCOREBOARD OFF
DECLARE def[6,3]                       && Array to hold menu definition.
mct = 1
DO WHILE mct <=6
  STORE SPACE(10) TO def[mct,1]  && Store default menu name.
  STORE SPACE(20) TO def[mct,2]  && Store default prompt name.
  STORE SPACE(55) TO def[mct,3]  && Store default command.
  mct = mct + 1
ENDDO
mname = SPACE(10)
@ 04,01 SAY "Menu name " GET mname VALID .NOT. " "$TRIM(mname)
```

```
READ                                && Get menu name.
DEFINE MENU &mname                  && Define menu with user defined name.
ctr = 1
DO WHILE ctr <= 6
* Get menu definitions, increase array counter for six possible PADs.
  @ 05,01 SAY "PAD Name  " GET def[ctr,1] VALID .NOT. " "$TRIM(def[ctr,1])
  @ 06,01 SAY "Prompt     " GET def[ctr,2]
  @ 07,01 SAY "Valid dBASE command" GET def[ctr,3]
  READ
  IF def[ctr,1] = " "               && If user leaves PAD blank, then RETURN.
    RETURN
  ENDIF
  * Define menu PADs and PROMPTs.
  DEFINE PAD &def[ctr,1] OF &mname PROMPT TRIM(def[ctr,2])
  SHOW MENU &mname                  && Use SHOW MENU to display menu prototype.
  ctr = ctr+1
ENDDO
SAVE ALL LIKE def* TO &mname   && Save array in a MEM file.
CLEAR ALL
RELEASE MENUS
* End of UDA.PRG
```

To decode menu definitions stored in an array, use the AMENU program that follows. AMENU asks for the MEM file name (the menu name), then activates the menu based on the stored values.

```
* AMENU.PRG
*
SET SCOREBOARD OFF
mname = SPACE(10)
@ 04,5 SAY "Enter name of menu to activate: " GET mname PICTURE "@!"
READ
RESTORE FROM &mname ADDITIVE   && Contains an array called def[x,3]
DEFINE MENU &mname
nuctr = 1
DO WHILE def[nuctr,1]<>  "  "
  DEFINE PAD &def[nuctr,1] OF &mname PROMPT TRIM(def[nuctr,2])
  ON SELECTION PAD &def[nuctr,1] OF &mname &def[nuctr,3]
  nuctr = nuctr + 1
ENDDO
ACTIVATE MENU &mname
```

## SEE ALSO:

Commands DEFINE MENU and DEFINE PAD.

# SKIP

## DIALECTS:

Clipper, dBASE III PLUS, dBASE IV, dBXL, FoxBASE+, and Quicksilver.

## SYNTAX:

SKIP [<expN>]

## DEFINITION:

Moves the record pointer in the active database file <expN> records.

The pointer will not move forward past the end-of-file (EOF) or backward past the beginning-of-file (BOF).

SKIP with no argument moves the pointer forward one record.

At the end-of-file, the EOF( ) function is true (.T.). The record number function RECNO( ) returns a value 1 greater than the last record number. Any further SKIPs forward do nothing except produce an error message.

With the record pointer at the first record, SKIP -1 moves it to the beginning-of-file. There the BOF( ) function is true (.T.). RECNO( ) returns the first record number. In an unindexed file, that number is always 1. In an indexed file, it could be anything because of the ordering by key values rather than record numbers.

At beginning-of-file, any further SKIPs backward do nothing except produce an error message.

**Example 1**—A library management system displays book summaries, one at a time. To "page" through the database, the user presses "F" to move forward or "B" to move backward.

```
DO WHILE .t.
  * <@...SAY...GETs>
  maction = "?"
  * Ask for user response. Force it to uppercase with "!" picture.
  @ 11,12 SAY "Skip (F)wd (B)wd (E)xit" GET maction PICTURE "!"
  READ
  DO CASE
    * Move forward only if user enters with "F" and not end-of-file.
    CASE maction = "F" .AND. .NOT. EOF()
      SKIP
    * Skip backward only if user enters "B" and not beginning-of-file.
    CASE maction = "B" .AND. .NOT. BOF()
      SKIP -1
```

```
    CASE maction = "E"       && Exit DO loop if user enters "E".
      CLEAR
      EXIT
  ENDCASE
ENDDO
```

## LIMITS/WARNINGS:

SKIP ignores records hidden by SET DELETED ON or SET FILTER TO <condition>.

## VARIATIONS:

**Clipper:** SKIP 0 writes the database file buffer to disk if its contents have changed. Normally, Clipper does not do this until the record pointer moves. SKIP 0 forces writing without moving the pointer. This avoids lost data in the event of power loss, user error, or program failure. SKIP 0 does not affect index files.

Unlike dBASE III PLUS, dBASE IV, dBXL, and FoxBASE+, Clipper produces no error messages if you try to SKIP beyond the beginning-or end-of-file. This is sensible since beginning- and end-of-file are easily detected with the EOF( ) and BOF( ) functions.

**Clipper, dBXL, Quicksilver:** To move the record pointer in an unselected work area, use the command

SKIP [<expN>] ALIAS <selection>

<selection> can be a work area number or letter, an ALIAS you assign when opening a file, or the actual filename.

For example, if the selected work area is 1, to SKIP 10 records in a file MAIL in area 2, use the command

```
SKIP 10 ALIAS 2
```

SKIP 10 ALIAS 2 is equivalent to:

```
SELECT 2
SKIP 10
SELECT 1
```

To use SKIP...ALIAS in dBXL and Quicksilver, you must have a file open in the current work area.

**dBASE IV:** You can move the record pointer in an unselected database using the command

SKIP [<expN>] IN <alias>

where <alias> is the database alias or filename.

**Quicksilver:** Leave a space before the minus sign when SKIPping backwards. Clipper, dBASE III PLUS, dBASE IV, dBXL, and FoxBASE+ all allow

```
SKIP-1
```

To prevent an error at compile time, Quicksilver requires

```
SKIP -1
```

Quicksilver does not produce error messages if you try to SKIP beyond the beginning- or end-of-file.

## SEE ALSO:

Command GO; functions BOF( ), EOF( ), and RECNO( ).

# SLEEP

## DIALECTS:

dBXL and Quicksilver.

## SYNTAX:

SLEEP <expN> / UNTIL "HH:MM:SS"

## DEFINITION:

Causes a program to pause <expN> seconds or until a specific time. With SET ESCAPE ON, pressing the ESCape key ends the pause and passes control to the next program line.

## OPTIONS:

UNTIL pauses the program until a time <expC1>, a 24-hour time string in the form "HH:MM:SS" (hours, minutes, and seconds). If the time you specify has already passed, SLEEP UNTIL does not pause.

## RECOMMENDED USE:

Use SLEEP instead of a DO WHILE loop to pause program execution. A DO WHILE pause requires four program lines, whereas SLEEP requires only one. Also, the timing of DO WHILE loops depends on the computer's speed. SLEEP measures real seconds on the clock.

"Real time" pauses can greatly enhance applications programs. You may have run programs in which screen messages and prompts rush by so fast you can't read them—the faster the computer, the faster the messages. As computers run even faster, such programs may become suitable only for speed readers.

**Example 1**—A programmer wants to add brief messages to a data entry screen. For example, when the operator encounters the End of File, the programmer wants to display a brief, but readable, message.

```
* <statements>
* Continue data entry or data editing until end-of-file.
IF .NOT. EOF()
  * <statements>
  SKIP              && Move to the next record.
ELSE
  ?? chr(7)
  @ 24,01 SAY "End of file. There are no more entries."
  SLEEP 3           && Wait three seconds.
  @ 24,00           && Clear message line.
ENDIF
```

**Example 2**—An inventory system uses three databases totaling over 15 megabytes in size. The programmer wants to reindex them, but wisely avoids doing so until other network users have gone home.

```
SLEEP UNTIL "22:00:00"        && Wait until 10 p.m.
USE inventl
INDEX ON partno TO invldex
USE invent2
INDEX ON partno TO inv2dex
USE invent3
INDEX ON descrip TO inv3dex
```

## LIMITS/WARNINGS:

The dBXL and Quicksilver manuals (Version 1.2b) document an additional option, UNTIL <expC1>,<expC2>, where <expC1> is the time and <expC2> is a date string in the form "MM/DD/YY" (month, day, year). This option does not work.

## VARIATIONS:

**Clipper, dBASE IV, FoxBASE+:** An optional numeric argument in the INKEY( ) function makes it pause in real seconds. For example,

```
? INKEY(40)
```

waits for forty seconds, or until you press a key. INKEY( ) also returns the ASCII version of the key pressed, for example

```
mkey = INKEY(40)      && If the user presses "u",the key value
? mkey                &&    is stored in variable MKEY.
117
```

INKEY(0) pauses until the user presses a key.

**dBASE III PLUS:** The following short procedure emulates the SLEEP command:

```
* SLEEP.PRG
PARAMETER seconds
PRIVATE timecount,matchtime,keypress STORE 0 to keypress,timecount
DO WHILE timecount < seconds .AND. keypress = 0
  STORE TIME() TO matchtime
  DO WHILE TIME() = matchtime
  ENDDO
  timecount = timecount + 1
  keypress = INKEY()
ENDDO
```

In a DO WHILE loop, SLEEP.PRG monitors the TIME( ) function until the clock ticks. Then the DO WHILE loop exits and the memory variable TIMECOUNT is increased by 1. When TIMECOUNT equals the number of seconds specified in the SECONDS parameter, SLEEP.PRG ends and the pause terminates. If you press a key while SLEEP is running, the INKEY( ) function stores the keystroke in memory variable KEYPRESS. At that point, the DO WHILE condition becomes false (KEYPRESS no longer is 0), and SLEEP terminates.

To include SLEEP.PRG in a program, use the command:

```
DO SLEEP WITH <expN>
```

where <expN> is the number of seconds. Unlike the SLEEP command, pressing the ESCape key interrupts the program's execution as expected.

## SEE ALSO:

Command DO WHILE; function TIME( ).

# SORT

## DIALECTS:

Clipper, dBASE III PLUS, dBASE IV, dBXL, FoxBASE+, and Quicksilver.

## SYNTAX:

SORT [<scope>] TO <filename> ON <field1> [/A] [/C] [/D]
[,<field2> [A/] [/C] [/D]...10] [ASCENDING/DESCENDING]
WHILE <condition>] [FOR <condition>]

## DEFINITION:

Copies the active database file to a new file, arranging records in alphabetical, chronological, or numerical order. The sort key consists of one or more character, numeric, or date fields. Data types may be mixed; the key cannot involve logical or memo fields.

SORTing on multiple fields first arranges the new database according to <field1>. Within <field1>, it orders records according to <field2>. Within <field2>, it orders records according to <field3>, etc. Put the most important SORT key first.

## DEFAULT:

Order is ascending ASCII.

SORT determines alphabetical and numerical order by ASCII rank. For example, ASCII "B" is 66, and ASCII "a" is 97. Hence "a" follows "B" in ascending SORTed order. This differs from a standard "telephone book" or "alphabetical" ordering.

The new database file has a default extension of DBF. SORT updates a catalog if one is active.

## OPTIONS:

/A, the default, SORTs in ascending order. /D SORTs in descending order. /C does not distinguish case. It may be combined with /A or /D. If you specify multiple key fields in the SORT command, each may have its own options. dBASE III PLUS, dBASE IV, and dBXL also allow the keywords ASCENDING and DESCENDING for /A and /D.

The ASCENDING and DESCENDING options affect all fields not already designated with the /A or /D options. ASCENDING or DESCENDING cannot go inside the field list. It must go at the beginning or end, as in these examples:

SORT DESCENDING ON <field1>/A, <field2>, <field3> TO <file>

or

SORT ON <field1>/A, <field2>, <field3> DESCENDING TO <file>

or

SORT ON <field1>/A, <field2>, <field3> TO <file> DESCENDING

To limit the number of records copied to the new file, SORT allows scope, WHILE, and FOR clauses. Also, SORT excludes deleted records from the new file if you SET DELETED ON. Likewise, it will not copy records hidden by an active filter.

## RECOMMENDED USE:

SORT works best for small databases because it requires temporary files up to three times the size of the original. It is also generally slower than indexing.

SORTing a database increases the speed of subsequent sequential processing. It is also useful for archiving large databases in SORTed order.

**Example 1**—A store manager must produce an inventory report containing tool bin codes between 4567 and 8999. Some bins hold several kinds of tools, so several tools have the same bin code. The manager wants to list the highest bin number first, with the tools sorted in ASCENDING order. (Note: BIN_CODE is a character field). Unsorted, the file TOOLMAIN looks like this:

```
USE toolmain
LIST bin_code,tool
Record#  bin_code tool
      1  4569     Lock-tite
      2  6000     Saw
      3  6001     Vice
      4  4568     Wrench
      5  4569     Broadhead
      6  4569     Phillips
      7  9010     Hammer
```

To produce the desired results, the manager issues the following SORT command:

```
SORT ON bin_code /D,tool /A TO tsort ;
        FOR bin_code > "4566" .AND. bin_code < "9000"
```

```
   6 record sort complete.
USE tsort
LIST bin_code,tool
Record#  bin_code tool
      1  6001     Vise
      2  6000     Saw
      3  4569     Broadhead
      4  4569     Lock-tite
      5  4569     Phillips
      6  4568     Wrench
```

SORT rearranged BIN_CODE in descending order, and TOOLs in ascending order within it. Note that the scope excluded record 7 since it was outside the specified range.

## LIMITS/WARNINGS:

**Clipper (Summer '87, file date 12-21-87):** The WHILE option causes intermittent errors and locks up the computer. To avoid this problem, use the FOR option in an indexed file with an approximate scope. Base your approximation on the probable number of matching records in the index.

For example, assume a database contains medical bills indexed on patient ID. The scope (NEXT 50) estimates the number of bills for the patient.

```
USE patient INDEX id                         && Indexed on patient ID.
m_id = "1582"
SEEK m_id                                    && SEEK first occurrence of ID.
SORT NEXT 50 ON invoice FOR id = m_id        && Estimate 50 patient invoices.
```

**Clipper and FoxBASE+:** Do not have a specified limit, except for the command line limit.

**dBASE III PLUS, dBASE IV, dBXL, and Quicksilver:** Allow up to 10 key SORT fields.

## VARIATIONS:

INDEX, the common alternative to SORT, orders records by creating a logical map of the database file. It does not physically alter the database file, nor does it create a new file. Instead, INDEX creates an INDEX file—a map that controls how records *appear* in the database file. Unlike SORT keys, INDEX keys can consist of any valid expression, including functions and string and numeric expressions.

**FoxBASE+:** The FIELDS <fieldlist> option lets you copy only specific fields to the new file. It goes at the end of the SORT command line:

FIELDS <fieldlist>

<fieldlist> may contain fields from the active database, plus fields from another open, unselected database using an alias prefix (->).

FoxBASE+ does not allow the ASCENDING and DESCENDING options.

**Example 2**—A prospect file has 30 fields. The sales representative needs a sorted list containing only NAME and PHONE for a calling program. The following command produces the report.

```
SORT ON name TO namesort FIELDS name,phone
```

Only the two fields, NAME and PHONE, appear in the sorted file NAMESORT.

**Quicksilver:** Allows only the following limited version of SORT in versions before 1.2:

SORT ON <field1>[+<field2>...] [DESCENDING] TO <filename>

Key fields must be concatenated with plus signs instead of commas. The only option is DESCENDING, and it must be spelled out. In addition, key fields must all be ordered the same way—either all ASCENDING (the default) or all DESCENDING. No scope, FOR, or WHILE clauses ate allowed. To work around the limited SORT command, use the INDEX and COPY commands. Quicksilver Version 1.2 corrects most of these limitations.

Quicksilver Version 1.2 does not allow the ASCENDING and DESCENDING options.

## SEE ALSO:

Commands COPY, INDEX, and SET FIELDS.

# STORE

## DIALECTS:
Clipper, dBASE III PLUS, dBASE IV, dBXL, FoxBASE+, and Quicksilver.

## SYNTAX:
STORE <exp> TO <memory variable list>

## DEFINITION:
Assigns values to memory variables. If a variable with the same name already exists, the new value replaces the old one. Otherwise, STORE creates a variable and gives it the value of <exp>.

<exp> can be any valid expression, including other memory variables or database field names. When you STORE a field name in a memory variable, the variable takes the value of the field's contents.

The number of memory variables in the list is restricted only by the 254-character command line limit.

The equal sign operator works like STORE except that it can only assign a value to one memory variable at a time.

## RECOMMENDED USE:
Use STORE to assign the same value to a list of memory variables. For single variables, use the equal sign operator. In dBASE III PLUS, dBXL, and FoxBASE+, = executes slightly faster than STORE. dBXL shows the greatest speed difference. Clipper, dBASE IV, and Quicksilver show no difference.

**Example**—A towing company invoicing program GETs user input in memory variables and computes totals. We use STORE to create a list of variables. The equal sign operator initializes a single variable, TOT_CHARGE, to the value of a numeric expression.

```
* Initialize multiple memory variables with STORE.
STORE 0 TO service,rate,towing,hours
* GET user input.
@ 01,01 SAY "Service: " GET service
@ 02,01 SAY "   Rate: " GET rate
@ 03,01 SAY " Towing: " GET towing
@ 04,01 SAY "  Hours: " GET hours
READ
* Initialize a single variable with the equal sign.
tot_charge = service + mileage + towing + (rate*hours)
? tot_charge       && Print total charge on the screen.
```

## LIMITS/WARNINGS:

**dBASE III PLUS:** Using STORE or the equal sign operator with REPLICATE( ) can lock up the computer when trying to create strings beyond the 254-character limit, as in the following:

```
mspace = SPACE(130)
mtest = REPLICATE(mspace,254)   && REPLICATE repeats MSPACE 254 times
                                &&   in an attempt to create a string.
```

This problem generally occurs when the string length computes to 33020 or more.

## VARIATIONS:

**dBXL, Quicksilver:** STORE AUTOMEM automatically assigns the contents of the current record's fields to memory variables. It gives the new memory variables the same names and data types as the corresponding fields. They can then be displayed for editing using @...SAY...GET. The memory variable indicator, m->, differentiates between memory variables and fields with the same names.

STORE <exp> TO <array name> initializes every element of an existing dBXL/Quicksilver array with the specified expression, as follows:

```
DIMENSION marray[2,2]
STORE SPACE(10) TO marray
```

**FoxBASE+:** STORE <exp> TO <array name> initializes every element of an existing array with the specified <exp>.

## SEE ALSO:

Commands ACCEPT, DIMENSION, PRIVATE, PUBLIC, READ, and REPLACE.

# SUM

## DIALECTS:
Clipper, dBASE III PLUS, dBASE IV, dBXL, FoxBASE+, and Quicksilver.

## SYNTAX:
SUM [<scope>] [<expression list>] [TO <memory variable list>]
  [FOR <condition>] [WHILE <condition>]

## DEFINITION:
Sums numeric fields, or expressions incorporating numeric fields, within the active database.

When TALK is SET ON, the results are displayed. With SET TALK OFF, the results are not displayed, and it is assumed you will store them in memory variables.

If the memory variables don't exist, SUM creates them.

If you SUM more than one expression, the first result goes into the first memory variable, the second goes into the second variable, and so on. This continues until there are no more results, or no more memory variables.

## DEFAULT:
SUM adds all numeric fields unless you provide an expression list. It adds all records unless you specify a <scope>, FOR, or WHILE clause.

## OPTIONS:
Scope, FOR, and WHILE options limit the SUM to selected records. <expression list> selects numeric records by field name, or by expressions containing field names.

## RECOMMENDED USE:
In both the interactive and program modes, SUM provides a way to process many records at a time quickly and easily. Use it as an alternative to complex programming that SKIPs through a file and increments counters.

SUM provides a powerful query capability that gives immediate results in the interactive mode. SUM adds numeric data items and, if you choose, stores the results in memory variables.

**Example**—A magazine management system tracks author pay (a miniscule amount in most cases!). To determine the total expenditure for contributing articles, the system SUMs the MONTHPAY and YTOD (year-to-date) fields for articles submitted in the current month. The SUM of MONTHPAY goes into variable MONTHTOT. YTOD goes into variable CUMULAT. The SUM includes only records for which the article is no older than 30 days (no earlier than 12/20/87).

```
. USE authors
. LIST
Record#  AUTHOR              MONTHPAY      YTOD ADATE    TITLE
      1  Foley                 450.00   2455.00 01/02/88 Roman Holiday
      2  Raffield              224.00   8721.22 12/22/87 Travels to China
      3  Hanson               1000.00   6877.22 12/27/87 Undersea Worlds
      4  Banyon                453.22   2378.33 10/10/87 '88 Nights

. ? DATE()
  01/20/88

. SUM ALL monthpay,ytod TO monthtot,cumulat FOR adate >= (date()-30)
     3 records summed
  monthpay        ytod
   1674.00    18053.44
. ? monthtot
     1674.00
. ? cumulat
    18053.44
```

The results can now be displayed or incorporated into reports.

The SUM list can include other kinds of expressions. For example, to roughly project the annual expenditures for articles, multiply the monthly total by 12.

```
. SUM monthpay*12 TO projpay
  4 records summed
    monthpay*12
        25526.64
```

## VARIATIONS:

**Clipper:** Because TALK is always assumed OFF, SUM requires a memory variable list.

**dBASE IV:** SUM creates floating point (type F) memory variables.

You can save SUM results in a one-dimensional array. The first result goes in the first array element, the second in the second element, and so on. If there are more array elements than results, the remaining elements are unchanged. If there are more results than array elements, the remaining results are not preserved.

**Example**—To produce a summary report, a property management program SUMs rents and other income. The results go into an array.

```
USE rents
DECLARE mresults[4]
SUM unit1, unit2, unit3, unit4 TO ARRAY mresults FOR month = 6
DISPLAY MEMORY
      User Memory Variables
MRESULTS     pub   A  [4]
   [1]       elem  N                    24  (24.00000000000000000)
   [2]       elem  N             246962.16  (246962.1600000000000)
   [3]       elem  N              10403.17  (10403.17000000000000)
   [4]       elem  N               6644.59  (6644.590000000000000)

 1 out of 500 memvars defined (and 4 array elements)
```

**dBXL:** Does not allow SCOPE before the expression list. The SCOPE must follow.

**Quicksilver:** Because TALK is always assumed OFF, SUM requires a memory variable list.

## SEE ALSO:

Commands AVERAGE, CALCULATE, COUNT, DECLARE, and TOTAL.

# SUSPEND

## DIALECTS:

dBASE III PLUS, dBASE IV, dBXL, and FoxBASE+.

## SYNTAX:

SUSPEND

## DEFINITION:

Pauses execution of a program, leaving memory variables and other environment attributes intact. SUSPEND is intended primarily for debugging.

SUSPEND returns to the interactive prompt, from which you can examine and create memory variables and manipulate files.

RESUME restarts a SUSPENDed program. Control passes to the next line.

## RECOMMENDED USE:

You can also invoke SUSPEND by selecting the SUSPEND option when you run a program with SET STEP ON, after a program error occurs, or after pressing ESCape during program execution if ESCAPE is SET ON. In all these situations, dBASE III PLUS, dBASE IV, dBXL, and FoxBASE+ prompt you to "Cancel, Ignore or Suspend."

When an error occurs, dBXL's FIX option lets you change and re-execute the program line that generated it.

Place SUSPEND at strategic points in your programs when they produce unexpected or confusing results. For example, put it in a report program that prints the wrong invoice number or other erroneous data. You can then examine the databases and memory variables, using DISPLAY STATUS and DISPLAY MEMORY, to determine whether values have been assigned incorrectly or the data has been corrupted.

**Example**—A receivables program draws data from two files and merges it into a single invoice. For an unknown reason, the report prints blank name and address fields.

ACCTNAME (work area 1) holds billing information. ACCTTRANS (work area 2) holds transaction records. The program moves to area 2, gets the account number, and SEEKs a matching number in area 1. Back in area 2, the program merges data from both files.

Because the program prints a blank invoice, the programmer puts a SUSPEND command after SEEK. When the program pauses, the programmer displays the account number and notices that it has no match in the ACCTNAME file. Because the SEEK cannot find a match, the ACCTNAME pointer moves to End of File.

```
SET DEVICE TO print
SELECT 1
USE acctname INDEX acctno
SELECT 2
USE accttrans
DO WHILE .NOT. EOF()
  CLEAR
  searchno = acctno
  SELECT 1
  SEEK searchno
  SUSPEND
  SELECT 2
  @ 02,01 SAY "Acct. #: " + acctno
  @ 05,10 SAY "Name............: " + acctname->name
  @ 06,10 SAY "Address.........: " + acctname->address
  @ 07,10 SAY "Transaction Date: " + dtoc(tdate) + " Amount: " + ;
              STR(tamount,7,2) + " Item: " + itemno
  @ 08,10 SAY "-----------------------------------------------------"
ENDDO
```

To correct the problem, the programmer modifies the program to check for a valid ACCTNAME before printing an invoice. (A prompt warns the user if there is an account number for a nonexistent ACCTNAME).

Once debugged, the program prints properly:

```
Acct. #: 5453
         Name............: Wolfen Communication
         Address.........: 2939 S. Main Street
         Transaction Date: 02/02/88 Amount: 2393.99 Item: 2233
         ""------------------------------------------------
```

## LIMITS/WARNINGS:

During SUSPEND, you cannot edit the open program file. You must first issue the CANCEL command. To edit a procedure file, you must first CLOSE PROCEDURE.

dBXL is the exception, since it lets you edit the executing command line with the FIX option.

## VARIATIONS:

**Clipper:** SUSPEND not available. Instead, link the DEBUG.OBJ module to your Clipper applications.

**dBASE IV:** If you SET TRAP ON, pressing ESCape runs the debugger.

**Quicksilver:** SUSPEND not available. Pressing the ESCape key lets you display, but not change, memory variables. For extensive debugging, include WordTech's dB Debugger module in your applications.

## SEE ALSO:

Commands CANCEL, DEBUG, DO, RESUME, SET DEBUG, SET ECHO, SET PROCEDURE, SET STEP, SET TALK, and SET TRAP.

# TEXT

## DIALECTS:
Clipper, dBASE III PLUS, dBASE IV, dBXL, FoxBASE+, and Quicksilver.

## SYNTAX:
TEXT
 [<character data>]
ENDTEXT

## DEFINITION:
Displays an unformatted block of text. Within it, no expressions or other commands are evaluated. Macros (&) are ignored.

TEXT output goes to the currently selected device (printer or screen).

## DEFAULT:
TEXT...ENDTEXT begins displaying on the next available line, starting with line 1. It will not display on line 0.

## RECOMMENDED USE:
TEXT...ENDTEXT provides a convenient way to include help or information messages in programs without using @...SAY or ? statements.

**Example**—In a hotel reservation system, a TEXT...ENDTEXT block presents information on report selections.

```
* <statements>
CLEAR
TEXT

                    Report Selection Descriptions

       1. % Occupancy:  Compares actual bookings with
                        hotel capacity by month and year
       2. Gross income: Totals and subtotals of all income
                        before expenses.
       3. Gross loss:   Computes expenses due to breakage,
                        vandalism, and bad debts.

ENDTEXT
```

## LIMITS/WARNINGS:

**dBASE III PLUS, dBXL:** Avoid starting text lines with CASE, DO CASE, ENDCASE, DO WHILE, ENDDO, IF, ELSE, or ENDIF. If you start a control structure immediately before a TEXT...ENDTEXT block, the interpreter searches for its terminator within the block. If the interpreter finds a corresponding command, the control structure becomes unbalanced and execution terminates. This problem is most common with IF...ELSE...ENDIF since IF and ELSE are commonly used words. No one is likely to use the word ENDDO for anything other than ending a DO WHILE.

In the following example, the interpreter assumes ELSE is a command, causing a syntax error on the next line:

```
mflag = .f.
IF mflag

  TEXT

    Please enter the customer's name and address, or
    else leave blank to exit.
    You can reenter this information later.

  ENDTEXT

ENDIF
```

## VARIATIONS:

**Clipper:** The options TO PRINT and TO FILE <filename> send TEXT blocks to the printer or to a file. They follow the TEXT statement on the same line.

## SEE ALSO:

Commands @...SAY, ?, and SET PRINT.

# TOTAL

## DIALECTS:

Clipper, dBASE III PLUS, dBASE IV, dBXL, FoxBASE+, and Quicksilver.

## SYNTAX:

TOTAL ON <key expression> TO <filename> [<scope>] [FIELDS <field list>]
    [WHILE <condition>] [FOR <condition>]

## DEFINITION:

Sums numeric fields for groups of records with the same keys, and sends the results to a summary database file.

The records to be summed must be either INDEXed or SORTed (grouped) on the key expression to be TOTALed.

TOTAL copies only one record to the summary file for each group of records with the same key. Numeric fields in the summary record contain totals for its group. Other fields contain the data from the first record in the group. The summary file has the same structure as the original database.

TOTAL updates an open dBASE III PLUS or dBASE IV catalog.

## DEFAULT:

All records TOTAL unless you specify a scope, FOR, or WHILE clause. All numeric fields TOTAL unless you specify a FIELD list.

## OPTIONS:

FIELDS <field list> specifies the numeric fields to TOTAL. It does not affect which fields are copied to the summary file.

Scope, WHILE, and FOR select records to TOTAL.

## RECOMMENDED USE:

The TOTAL command is really a subtotal command, as it produces totals for subgroups in a file.

**Example**—A sales application tracks amounts. The main transaction file is indexed on the salesperson's identification number ID. Using TOTAL, the program creates a summary file SALESTOT containing a total for each salesperson.

Notice that records in SALES are grouped by their key field ID. AMOUNT is the only numeric field.

```
USE sales
INDEX ON id TO idex
LIST
Record#  LNAME              ID   ITEM          AMOUNT
      1  Elliot             A900 Sofa          246.33
      6  Elliot             A900 Matress       234.22
      2  Petri              Z000 Sleeper       266.33
      4  Petri              Z000 Rocker       1092.44
      3  Wilander           X999 Table         888.00
      5  Wilander           X999 Desk          476.49
      7  Wilander           X999 Bed           209.92

TOTAL ON id TO salestot
     7 records totalled
     3 records generated
SELECT 2
USE salestot
LIST
Record#  LNAME              ID   ITEM          AMOUNT
      1  Elliot             A900 Sofa          480.55
      2  Petri              Z000 Sleeper      1358.77
      3  Wilander           X999 Table        1574.41
```

The summary file contains the total AMOUNT for each group, plus the data from the first record in each group.

## LIMITS/WARNINGS:

Totals in the summary file can exceed the field length and cause numeric overflow. Use MODIFY STRUCTURE to lengthen the fields in the original database to accommodate the largest possible number.

The FIELDS option only affects which numeric fields to TOTAL, not which ones to copy.

## VARIATIONS:

**Clipper:** If you do not use a FIELDS list, no fields will be totalled.

## SEE ALSO:

Commands AVERAGE, CALCULATE, COUNT, INDEX, and SUM.

# TYPE

## DIALECTS:

Clipper, dBASE III PLUS, dBASE IV, dBXL, FoxBASE+, and Quicksilver.

## SYNTAX:

TYPE <filename> [TO PRINT]

## DEFINITION:

Lists the contents of a text file. TYPE requires a full filename and extension.

If the file is not in the current directory, you must specify a drive and directory.

TYPEd files must contain only ASCII characters.

## OPTIONS:

TO PRINT directs output to the printer.

## RECOMMENDED USE:

In the interactive mode, use TYPE to view and print program files and ASCII documents. In programs, use it to display help text for end users. The text must not exceed a single screen, since the overflow will scroll out of view. The TYPE command generally doesn't provide enough control over text to be useful in programs. TEXT...ENDTEXT is an alternative way to display blocks of text, or store text in MEMO fields. TYPE is primarily for the interactive mode.

## LIMITS/WARNINGS:

You may not TYPE an open file, i.e., a program file may not TYPE itself. You cannot TYPE database, memory, or index files.

## VARIATIONS:

**Clipper:** TO PRINT not available. You can print or send TYPEd output to a file using DOS redirection:

```
TYPE <filename> > <filename>/PRN
```

**dBASE IV:** The TO FILE option sends TYPEd output to a text file as follows:

```
TYPE <filename> TO FILE <filename2>
```

Unless you specify otherwise, dBASE IV supplies a TXT extension.

The NUMBER option prints line numbers. For example:

TYPE <filename> NUMBER

The line numbers are helpful in debugging programs.

If you SET HEADING ON, dBASE IV also TYPEs the filename, the page number, and the system date on each TYPEd page.

## SEE ALSO:

Commands MODIFY COMMAND, SET HEADING, SET PRINT, and TEXT...ENDTEXT.

# UNLOCK

## DIALECTS:

Clipper, dBASE III PLUS, dBASE IV, FoxBASE+, and Quicksilver.

## SYNTAX:

UNLOCK [ALL]

## DEFINITION:

Multiuser command to release current record and file locks on the active database. The current lock is the last FLOCK( ), RLOCK( ), or LOCK( ) issued on the current database.

Records and files can be UNLOCKed only by the user who locked them.

UNLOCK does not affect files opened with USE <filename> EXCLUSIVE.

## OPTIONS:

UNLOCK ALL removes record and file locks from all open database files.

## RECOMMENDED USE:

One aim of multiuser programming is to keep files and records locked as briefly as possible. This lets users on a network share data more efficiently.

**Example**—You can only REPLACE a record if you lock either it or the file. To avoid inconveniencing other users, first lock the record with the RLOCK( ) function. Next, REPLACE the record. Finally, UNLOCK it as quickly as possible. (Notice that if the RLOCK( ) fails, an error trapping subroutine FAILLOCK executes).

```
IF RLOCK()
  REPLACE amount WITH 2345.33
  UNLOCK
ELSE
  DO faillock
ENDIF
```

## LIMITS/WARNINGS:

dBASE III PLUS: An UNLOCKed record remains locked to other users until you move the pointer. To correct this, issue GOTO RECNO( ) immediately after UNLOCK. This will reset the LOCK( )/RLOCK( ) status.

## VARIATIONS:

**dBASE IV:** You can UNLOCK a record or file in an unselected work area by using the IN <alias> option, as follows:

UNLOCK IN <alias>

## SEE ALSO:

Functions FLOCK( ), LOCK( ), and RLOCK( ).

# UPDATE

## DIALECTS:

Clipper, dBASE III PLUS, dBASE IV, dBXL, FoxBASE+, and Quicksilver.

## SYNTAX:

UPDATE ON <key field> FROM <alias> REPLACE <field1> WITH <exp1>
[,<field2> WITH <exp2>...] [RANDOM]

## DEFINITION:

Replaces fields in records of the current database with data from other databases.

The current database must be INDEXed or SORTed on the <key field>. Data is replaced for records with matching key fields.

The FROM database must also be INDEXed or SORTed unless you specify the RANDOM option.

The FROM database must be open in another work area.

Specifying field expressions from the unselected databases requires the ALIAS->FIELD syntax.

If the current file contains records with duplicate key fields, only the first record is UPDATEd.

## DEFAULT:

UPDATE affects all records in the active database. It ignores MEMO fields.

## OPTIONS:

You can UPDATE multiple fields with the "<field2> WITH <exp2>" option. The number of fields you can UPDATE is restricted by the command length limit.

RANDOM lets you UPDATE from an unindexed or unsorted database.

## RECOMMENDED USE:

Because it affects all records in the active database, use UPDATE for interval batch updates. For example, use it for daily, weekly, or monthly updates to databases such as inventories, client histories, or general ledgers. In this context, files you UPDATE FROM are transaction files.

**Example**—An accounting application consists of a general ledger file (GL) and a transaction file that tracks payables and receivables (AR_AP). GL is indexed on ACCT. AR_AP is unindexed.

At the end of each week, the program UPDATEs the year-to-date totals in GL from AR_AP.

```
USE gl
INDEX ON acct TO account
LIST acct,category,ytod
Record #  ACCT           CATEGORY              YTOD
       1   0001          PAYABLES          12000.00
       2   0002          RECEIVABLES       88500.00
       3   0003          PAYROLL           70000.50

SELECT 2
USE ar_ap
LIST acct,transacts
Record #  ACCT            TRANSACTS
       1  0002              4500.33
       2  0001               888.88

SELECT 1
UPDATE ON acct FROM ar_ap REPLACE ytod WITH ytod + ar_ap->transacts RANDOM
  2 records updated

LIST acct,category,ytod
Record #  ACCT           CATEGORY              YTOD
       1   0001          PAYABLES          12888.88
       2   0002          RECEIVABLES       93000.33
       3   0003          PAYROLL           70000.50
```

Because there is no matching record for ACCT 0003 in AR_AP, its YTOD does not change.

## LIMITS/WARNINGS:

On local area networks, you must USE the current file with the EXCLUSIVE option or lock it with FLOCK( ).

SET DELETED ON ignores deleted records in the source files, but deleted records in the target file are updated.

## SEE ALSO:

Commands COPY, JOIN, and TOTAL.

# UPSCROLL

## DIALECTS:
dBXL and Quicksilver.

## SYNTAX:
UPSCROLL <expN>

## DEFINITION:
Moves the current screen or window area up <expN> lines. Nothing happens if <expN> is negative or 0.

If you move the text off the screen or outside the window area, it will be erased.

## RECOMMENDED USE:
Use UPSCROLL with DOWNSCROLL to provide scrollable help screens or lookup windows.

**Example**—An invoicing application requires the entry of a customer account number for each invoice. If the operator forgets a number, he or she can look it up in a scrollable help window.

```
* HELPWIN.PRG
SET TALK OFF
WSET WINDOW acctlook TO 10,01,23,40     && Create window specification.
WSELECT 1                               && Select window area.
WUSE acctlook                           && Use acctlook window.
USE SALES
keypress = 0
? "Account number"              && List account numbers.
LIST accounts
DO WHILE keypress # 32          && DO WHILE user does not press space bar.
  keypress = INKEY()            && Store INKEY() to KEYPRESS variable.
  DO CASE
    CASE  KEYPRESS = 5          && If user presses up arrow,
      UPSCROLL 1                &&  scroll up 1.
    CASE KEYPRESS = 24          && If user presses down arrow,
      DOWNSCROLL 1              &&  scroll down 1.
  ENDCASE
ENDDO
```

## SEE ALSO:
Commands DOWNSCROLL, WSELECT, WSET WINDOW, and WUSE.

# USE

## DIALECTS:

Clipper, dBASE III PLUS, dBASE IV, dBXL, FoxBASE+, and Quicksilver.

## SYNTAX:

USE [[<filename>] [INDEX <index file list>] [ALIAS <alias name>]
[EXCLUSIVE]]

## DEFINITION:

Opens a database file in the current work area and moves the record pointer to the logical top of file. If the file is unindexed, the top is record 1. In an indexed file, the top is the record with the lowest key value.

Files may not be USEd in more than one work area at a time.

USE <filename> first closes the previously active database, format file, and index. It does not affect files in other work areas. USE alone simply closes the open files.

In dBASE III PLUS and dBASE IV, USE ? displays a list of cataloged database files when SET CATALOG is ON.

## DEFAULT:

USE assumes the database file has a DBF extension, unless you specify otherwise.

USE assumes the INDEX files have an NDX extension in dBASE III PLUS, dBXL, and Quicksilver, NDX or MDX in dBASE IV, NTX in Clipper, and IDX in FoxBASE+. (USE also recognizes NDX format in Clipper if you link the NDX.OBJ module with your application).

USE searches the current directory unless you specify a drive or path.

## OPTIONS:

INDEX opens up to seven index files in the current work area. It is the same as SET INDEX TO <index file list>. SET INDEX TO by itself and CLOSE INDEXES close indexes.

ALIAS assigns a name to the current work area. The default is the database file name. (You can also SELECT a work area by number or letter).

EXCLUSIVE prevents another network user from opening the file. It is accessible only to whoever opened it until he or she closes it.

## RECOMMENDED USE:

USE opens a database and indexes in the current work area. You can open several databases simultaneously in separate areas by changing areas and issuing more USEs.

**Example**—An environmental impact program stores data on the suitability of land for industrial use. The program compares a database of observations (OBSERVE) against a database of federal government specifications (FEDERAL) to assign a suitability grade.

The program opens FEDERAL in work area 1 and OBSERVE in area 2. It then examines OBSERVE and searches FEDERAL for matching keys using SEEK. Procedure GRADESUB computes a grade based on the TEST and QUOTIENT values. The DO WHILE loop repeats the analysis for every record in OBSERVE.

```
SELECT 1                          && Select work area 1 (the default).
USE federal INDEX dnsty,altud     && Open FEDERAL.DBF with two indexes.
SELECT 2                          && Select work area 2.
USE observe                       && Open OBSERVE.DBF
DO WHILE .NOT. EOF()              && Continue until end of FIELD.DBF.
  mtest = test                    && TEST is a field in OBSERVE.
  mcompare = quotient             && QUOTIENT is a field in OBSERVE.
  SELECT 1
  SEEK mtest                      && Search for value of TEST.
  DO gradesub WITH mcompare       && MCOMPARE is passed as a parameter
  SELECT 2                        &&  to procedure GRADESUB.
  SKIP                            && Move to next record in OBSERVE.
ENDDO
USE                               && Close files in current area (2).
SELECT 1
USE                               && Close files in area 1.
```

## VARIATIONS:

**dBASE IV:** You may open up to 10 index files per active database, and 47 TAGs per multiple index file. Multiple index files count as one open DOS file.

dBASE IV allows several options, in the form

USE [<database filename>] [IN <work area number>]
  [INDEX <NDX or MDX file list>
  [ORDER <NDX filename>/<tag> [OF <MDX filename>]]]
  [ALIAS <alias>] [EXCLUSIVE] [NOUPDATE]

You can use a database in an unselected work area with the IN option, where <work area number> is between 1 to 10.

You can specify index files (extension NDX) and multiple index files (MDX) on the same line. When you specify an NDX or MDX filename, dBASE IV first looks for an MDX file. If it doesn't find one, it looks for an NDX. If an MDX file and an NDX file have the same name, the NDX file will not be opened.

If an index file is first in the list, it becomes the controlling (master) index. If a multiple index file comes first, the database remains in natural order until you SET ORDER or invoke the USE command with an ORDER clause.

The ORDER clause specifies which index or multiple index TAG controls the database's order. Use the OF <mdx filename> option if the master TAG is in a file other than the production MDX.

To USE SALES.DBF with MDXs MONTHMDX and AMTMDX, and an index file PARTNO, issue the command

```
USE sales INDEX monthmdx,amtmdx,partno ORDER nmonth OF amtmdx
```

The ORDER clause indicates that the TAG NMONTH in AMTMDX controls the index order.

The DELETE TAG command closes individual indexes by name, whereas SET INDEX TO and CLOSE INDEXES close all open indexes.

The NOUPDATE clause opens the specified database for read-only use.

**dBXL, Quicksilver:** USE first searches for database and index files in the directory specified by SET DBF and SET NDX. If you do not SET DBF or SET NDX, USE searches in the current directory. If it does not find the files there, it checks the paths defined by SET PATH.

The AUTOMEM option creates a set of memory variables with the same names and data types as all non-memo fields in the database.

## SEE ALSO:

Commands CLEAR ALL, CLOSE DATABASES, DELETE TAG, INDEX, SET INDEX, and SET ORDER.

# WABANDON

## DIALECTS:
dBXL and Quicksilver.

## SYNTAX:
WABANDON [<area number> [TO <area number>]] / [ALL]

## DEFINITION:
De-selects window areas, returning control to area 0.

## OPTIONS:
<area number> specifies an area defined by the WSELECT command.

<area number> TO <area number> specifies a range of areas to de-select from lowest to highest.

ALL de-selects all areas.

## LIMITS/WARNINGS:
You may not WABANDON area 0.

## SEE ALSO:
Command WSET WINDOW.

# WAIT

## DIALECTS:

Clipper, dBASE III PLUS, dBASE IV, dBXL, FoxBASE+, and Quicksilver.

## SYNTAX:

WAIT [<prompt>] [TO <memory variable>]

## DEFINITION:

Pauses program execution until the user presses a key. WAIT displays the message "Press any key to continue.." on the next available line, starting in column 0.

## OPTIONS:

<prompt> replaces the default message. The new message must be delimited with double quotation marks, single quotation marks, or square brackets.

TO <memory variable> stores the pressed key in a character memory variable. If the variable does not already exist, WAIT creates it. If the user presses a non-printing character, such as the Enter key, the variable gets a null value.

## RECOMMENDED USE:

Use WAIT to pause between screen displays. It lets the user read program prompts, then press a key when ready to proceed.

**Example**—A help screen in an airline reservation system describes how to use a menu option. When the ticket agent finishes reading the screen, she presses a key to return to the menu.

```
TEXT
   Option 3 removes a passenger from the standby queue
   and advances all other waiting passengers.
ENDTEXT
WAIT
```

With the TO <memory variable> option, you can use WAIT to process user selections. The following example asks the user whether to print a report or display it on the screen. If the user presses Y or y, the report prints. Other keys have no effect.

```
WAIT "Send report to the printer? (Y/N) " TO response
IF response $ "Yy"
  SET PRINT on
ENDIF
```

## SPECIAL USES:

Sometimes, you may want to pause without displaying a message. Or you may want to display a message at a particular coordinate. To do this, use WAIT with a null string and supply a message:

```
@ 10,25 SAY "Press any key to continue"
WAIT ""
```

An alternative is the INKEY( ) function in Clipper, dBASE IV, and FoxBASE+. INKEY( ) with a numeric argument pauses for the specified number of seconds. For example, ? INKEY(10) pauses for 10 seconds. INKEY(0) pauses until the user presses a key. INKEY( ) also returns the ASCII version of the key.

Quicksilver's SLEEP command also pauses program execution for a specified length of time.

## SEE ALSO:

Commands ACCEPT and SLEEP; function INKEY( ).

# WCLOSE

## DIALECTS:
dBXL and Quicksilver.

## SYNTAX:
WCLOSE [[<area number> [TO <area number>]] / [ALL ]]

## DEFINITION:
Closes windows and displays the previous screen.

## OPTIONS:
WCLOSE by itself closes the current window and sets the selected area to 0.

WCLOSE <area number> closes the specified window. You may issue it from any other window; however, if you WCLOSE the active window, the selected area is set to 0.

WCLOSE <area number> TO <area number> specifies a range of windows to close. It must be specified from lowest area to highest. If you WCLOSE the active window, the selected area is set to 0.

## RECOMMENDED USE:
WCLOSE windows in the reverse of the order in which you opened them.

## LIMITS/WARNINGS:
You cannot WCLOSE area 0.

## SEE ALSO:
Command WSET WINDOW.

# WCOPY

## DIALECTS:
dBXL and Quicksilver.

## SYNTAX:
WCOPY TO <area number>

## DEFINITION:
Duplicates the current window and its frame in another window area.

If a window already exists in the target area, it is cleared.

## LIMITS/WARNINGS:
You cannot copy to area 0 or to the currently selected area.

## SEE ALSO:
Command WSET WINDOW.

# WDISPLAY

## DIALECTS:
dBXL and Quicksilver.

## SYNTAX:
WDISPLAY [[<area number> [TO <area number>]] / [ALL]]

## DEFINITION:
Clears the specified window(s) and re-displays the frames.

## OPTIONS:
<area number> is a window with the number from WSELECT.

<area number> TO <area number> clears and re-displays a range of windows specified from lowest number to highest.

ALL clears and re-displays all windows in all areas.

## SEE ALSO:
Command WSET WINDOW.

# WDISPLAY STATUS

## DIALECTS:
dBXL only.

## SYNTAX:
WDISPLAY STATUS

## DEFINITION:
Lists information about the current window settings. It lists the current window area number, the WSET FRAME setting, and all active window names and definitions.

## RECOMMENDED USE:
Use WDISPLAY STATUS to determine the current window settings. This is helpful during program design and debugging.

**Example**—While developing an accounting program, the programmer notices that lists are going to the wrong window. To trace the problem, the programmer uses WDISPLAY STATUS to show the current windows.

```
SUSPEND
. WDISPLAY STATUS
WDISPLAY STATUS
Current window area: 3
Frame: ON

Window name    Coordinates
MAIN          2,  2, 23, 20
SUB1          5, 10, 20, 49
SUB2         15, 15, 20, 79
```

## VARIATIONS:
**dBASE IV:** You can view window settings with the DISPLAY STATUS command.

**Quicksilver:** WDISPLAY STATUS compiles without error, but has no effect.

## SEE ALSO:
Commands DISPLAY STATUS, WSELECT, WSET WINDOW, and WUSE.

# WMOVE

## DIALECTS:

dBXL and Quicksilver.

## SYNTAX:

WMOVE TO <top row>[,<left col>]

## DEFINITION:

Moves the current window and restores the underlying screen.

On standard PCs, <top row> is a screen row from 0 to 23. <left col> is a screen column from 0 to 79.

## RECOMMENDED USE:

Specify <top row> and <left col> as one or two numbers. For example:

```
WMOVE TO 5,10
WMOVE TO 5
WMOVE TO ,10
```

## LIMITS/WARNINGS:

The window cannot extend beyond the screen's boundaries. Moving a window to a coordinate beyond the boundary produces an error.

## VARIATIONS:

**dBASE IV:** The MOVE WINDOW command is equivalent to WMOVE.

## SEE ALSO:

Commands MOVE WINDOW and WSET WINDOW.

# WRELEASE

## DIALECTS:
dBXL and Quicksilver.

## SYNTAX:
WRELEASE <name> / ALL

## DEFINITION:
Deletes a window, allowing a new one to be WSET. It does not affect the screen.

<name> refers to a window declared with WSET.

## RECOMMENDED USE:
dBXL and Quicksilver allow up to 99 active windows. Use WRELEASE to make room for more windows when you reach the limit.

## VARIATIONS:
dBASE IV: RELEASE WINDOWS is similar to WRELEASE.

## SEE ALSO:
Commands RELEASE WINDOWS, WSELECT, WSET WINDOW, and WUSE.

# WRESTORE

## DIALECTS:
dBXL and Quicksilver.

## SYNTAX:
WRESTORE [FROM <screen file>]

## DEFINITION:
Displays a window image from memory or from a file saved on disk with WSAVE.

WRESTORE by itself redisplays the image a window covered when it was opened. This temporarily covers, but does not deactivate the window.

## OPTIONS:
FROM <screen file> displays the image saved in a screen file. An SCN extension is the default. An open window in the current area is closed first.

## VARIATIONS:
**dBASE IV:** RESTORE WINDOWS is similar to WRESTORE.

## SEE ALSO:
Commands RESTORE WINDOWS and WSET WINDOW.

# WSAVE

## DIALECTS:
dBXL and Quicksilver.

## SYNTAX:
WSAVE [TO <screen file>]

## DEFINITION:
Saves the current window and its contents in a disk file or memory buffer.

WSAVE by itself saves in memory the window image in the selected area. When you close the window, the image reappears.

## OPTIONS:
WSAVE TO <screen file> saves the current window image in a disk file. <screen file> may be any valid filename. An SCN extension is the default.

The utility program BUILDWIN.EXE combines SCN files into a master file.

## VARIATIONS:
**dBASE IV:** SAVE WINDOW is similar to WSAVE.

## SEE ALSO:
Commands SAVE WINDOW, WSELECT, WSET WINDOW, and WUSE.

# WSELECT

## DIALECTS:
dBXL and Quicksilver.

## SYNTAX:
Selects the active window area.

To open a window, you must first WSELECT an area other than 0.

## DEFAULT:
If you do not open a window in the selected area, output goes to the entire screen.

## SEE ALSO:
Commands WSET WINDOW and WUSE WINDOW.

# WSET FRAME

## DIALECTS:
dBXL and Quicksilver.

## SYNTAX:
WSET FRAME ON/OFF

## DEFINITION:
Turns the window frame display ON or OFF.

WSET FRAME OFF suppresses window borders, or "frames." Active windows retain their set boundaries, but have no borders.

If you WSET FRAME OFF, frames will not appear when you WUSE or WDISPLAY a window.

## DEFAULT:
ON

## VARIATIONS:
**dBASE IV:** SET BORDER is similar to WSET FRAME.

## SEE ALSO:
Commands SET BORDER, WSELECT, WSET WINDOW, and WUSE.

# WSET SIZE

## DIALECTS:

dBXL and Quicksilver.

## SYNTAX:

WSET SIZE TO <top row>,<left col>,<bot row>,<right col>

## DEFINITION:

Changes the size of the current window, after first erasing it.

WSET SIZE uses four parameters representing points on the screen. <top row>,<left col> is the top left corner of the new text window. <bot row>,<right col> is the bottom right corner.

## LIMITS/WARNINGS:

Note that the coordinates give the corners of the text window, not the frame. The frame occupies an extra space.

## SPECIAL USES:

**dBXL and Quicksilver:** Windowing commands work on 132 column video boards. Your board should come with a setup utility for changing from 80 to 132 column mode. To use the 132 column mode, put the following commands at the beginning of your applications:

```
WSET FRAME OFF
WSELECT 0
RUN <setup utility>
WSET SIZE TO 0, 0, 24, 131
```

## LIMITS/WARNINGS:

If you specify a GET field that extends into the frame, dBXL may freeze, and you must reboot your computer.

## SEE ALSO:

Command WSET WINDOW.

# WSET TITLE

## DIALECTS:
dBXL and Quicksilver.

## SYNTAX:
WSET TITLE TO [<expC> [LEFT/CENTER/RIGHT]]

## DEFINITION:
Defines a character expression to display at the top of the active window's frame.

To display titles, WSET FRAME must be ON. Note that changes made with WSET TITLE do not appear until you issue WDISPLAY.

You may also set titles when you WUSE a window.

## DEFAULT:
WSET TITLE by itself centers <expC> (CENTER is unnecessary).

## OPTIONS:
WSET TITLE TO by itself erases an existing title and restores the original frame.

LEFT, RIGHT, and CENTER position the title.

## LIMITS/WARNINGS:
Defining a window title wider than the window causes an error.

## SEE ALSO:
Command WSET WINDOW.

# WSET WINDOW

## DIALECTS:
dBXL and Quicksilver.

## SYNTAX:
WSET WINDOW <name> TO <top row>,<left col>,<bot row>,<right col>
  [CHARACTER <background char>]
  [COLOR <text],[[enhanced][,frame>]]
  [FRAME <tl, t, tr, ls, rs, bl, b, br> / DOUBLE]

## DEFINITION:
Specifies a window for display with WUSE.

<name> must be a unique name of up to 10 characters. It may not contain an equal sign, ampersand, left parenthesis, or comma.

WSET WINDOW uses four parameters representing points on the screen. <top row>,<left col> is the top left corner of the text window. <bot row>,<right col> is the bottom right corner.

## OPTIONS:
CHARACTER defines a single character to fill the window's background.

COLOR lets you specify text, enhanced (GETs), and frame colors. SET COLOR TO can also specify colors, but only for text and enhanced modes. Only WSET WINDOW can set frame colors.

You can specify window and frame colors using standard color codes. Use a pair of codes separated by a slash to control foreground and background. You can also use the bright (+) and blinking (*) attributes for foreground colors. If you do not specify colors, the default is white on black (W/N).

FRAME lets you specify frame characters.

Choose characters in the format <tl, t, tr, ls, rs, bl, b, br>, where tl is top left, t is top edge, tr is top right, ls is the left side, rs is the right side, bl is bottom left, b is bottom, and br is bottom right. You may specify either literal characters individually enclosed in quotation marks, or extended ASCII characters (ASCII graphics) using the CHR( ) function. For example, to specify a frame with x's at the corners and horizontal and vertical lines at the top, bottom and sides, you would use the following specification:

```
WSET WIND small TO 12,23,20,56 FRAME "x","-","x","|","|","x","-","x"
```

This produces a window SMALL extending from coordinates 12,23 to 20,56. The frame would look like:

With no FRAME specification or DOUBLE option, the frame defaults to a single line.

Note that FRAME and DOUBLE are mutually exclusive.

## RECOMMENDED USE:

Use windows to display prompts, menus, and reports without disturbing the underlying text. They make it easy to create sophisticated user interfaces by letting you "layer," move, or resize screen objects.

**Example**—A mailorder firm tracks sales transactions by account number and item. All sales are made to existing clients whose names and account information are stored elsewhere in the system.

The two program modules open five windows. One is simply a background window. Another contains a welcoming message. The third is for data entry. A fourth is for "lookup." The fifth displays a user prompt.

DWIN.PRG first displays a welcoming message, and prompts the user to press the space bar to continue. A data entry window then appears. If the user leaves the ACCOUNT NUMBER field blank, LOOKUP.PRG displays the contents of a client/account number file. When the user finishes entering data, the message "Add Another?" appears. Pressing "Y" continues the program. Pressing "N" closes all windows and exits.

Create these two sample files to run DWIN.PRG:

```
ACCTDATA.DBF
Field  Field Name  Type       Length    Dec
    1  ACCT        Character       4
    2  ITEMNO      Character       4
    3  AMOUNT      Numeric         9      2

ACCTLOOK.DBF

Field  Field Name  Type       Length    Dec
    1  ACCTNO      Character       4
    2  NAME        Character      20
```

```
***********
* DWIN.PRG      Demonstrates dBXL's and Quicksilver's windowing.
SET SCOREBOARD off
SET TALK off
* Include SET HEADING off for dBXL only.
SET HEADING off        && Omits FIELD names from the DISPLAY command.
WSET FRAME on          && Display window frames.
WCLOSE all             && Be sure no window areas are open.
**** Set window names, coordinates, background CHARACTERs and FRAMEs.
* CHR(176) and CHR(178) are extended ASCII graphics characters.
WSET WINDOW backgrnd TO 1,1,24,78 CHARACTER CHR(176)
WSET WINDOW welcome  TO 5,10,18,70
WSET WINDOW acctadd  TO 2,2,12,40 ;
FRAME CHR(178),CHR(178),CHR(178),CHR(178),CHR(178),CHR(178),CHR(178),CHR(178)
WSET WINDOW lookup   TO 7,7,23,50
WSET WINDOW qmessage TO 9,20,12,37 CHARACTER "?"
WSELECT 1              && Select window area 1 and
WUSE backgrnd          &&   use BACKGRND window.
WSELECT 2              && Select window area 2 and use WELCOME window.
WUSE welcome
* Display TEXT message
TEXT

          WELCOME TO THE ACCOUNT MANAGEMENT SYSTEM
      This program module adds a new account transaction.
      If you forget a client's account number, leave the
      input field blank and press ENTER.

       Press SPACE BAR to continue.

ENDTEXT
WAIT ""                        && Pause without message (null string).
WCLOSE                         && Close current window area.
** Window and work area nos. match only to make it easy to associate them.
SELECT 3                       && Select work area 3.
USE acctdata AUTOMEM           && Use ACCTDATA. Create AUTOMEM variables.
WSELECT 3                        && Select window area 3.
WUSE acctadd TITLE " ADD A NEW ACCOUNT "     && Use window with a TITLE.
DO WHILE .t.
   WSELECT 3          && Always return to window area 3 at top of DO WHILE.
   SELECT 3
  * GET AUTOMEM variables with M-> to differentiate them from FIELDs.
  @ 03,03 SAY "   Enter item number: " GET m->itemno
  @ 04,03 SAY "        Enter amount: " GET m->amount
  @ 05,03 SAY "Enter account number: " GET m->acct PICTURE "####"
  @ 07,03 SAY " LEAVE ACCOUNT NUMBER BLANK "
  @ 08,03 SAY " FOR ACCOUNT LOOKUP TABLE.  "
  READ
  IF EMPTY(m->acct)          && If M->ACCT is empty,
    DO lookup                &&  DO LOOKUP program.
    LOOP                     && Return to top of DO WHILE.
  ENDIF
  APPEND AUTOMEM             && APPEND AUTOMEM variables.
```

```
  CLEAR AUTOMEM                 && Reset AUTOMEM variables to blank or 0.
  WSELECT 5                     && Select window area 5.
  WUSE qmessage                 && Display QMESSAGE window.
  lmove = 30                    && DO WHILE animates QMESSAGE window by
  DO WHILE lmove > 5            &&   decrementing WMOVE column coord.
    WMOVE TO 9,lmove            && LMOVE is the column coordinate.
    lmove = lmove - 1           && Subtract 1 from LMOVE until it equals 5.
  ENDDO
  WSET SIZE TO 9,05,14,60                && Enlarge window.
  WSET TITLE TO " ARE YOU SURE? "        && Set title within FRAME.
  WDISPLAY                               && Redisplay FRAME with title.
  response = .t.                         && Use logical variable for
  @ 01,08 CLEAR TO 03,25                 &&   user RESPONSE.
  @ 02,10 SAY " Add another?" GET response PICTURE "Y"
  READ
  IF .NOT. response             && If user chooses not to add another,
     WCLOSE ALL                 &&   close all window areas and
     RETURN                     &&   RETURN to calling level.
  ELSE
    WCLOSE                      && If user chooses to add another, close only
  ENDIF                         &&   area 5 and the QMESSAGE window.
ENDDO
* End of DWIN.PRG

************
* LOOKUP.PRG
* Called from DWIN.PRG
WSELECT 4
WUSE lookup TITLE " LOOK UP ACCOUNT NUMBERS "
SELECT 4
USE acctlook      && Use lookup database.
re_do = .t.
DO WHILE re_do    && Repeat DISPLAY as long as RE_DO is true.
  DISPLAY ALL TRIM(acctno) + " " + TRIM(name)
  * Display message at current row and column.
  ?
  @ ROW(),COL()+2 SAY "Redisplay? " GET re_do PICTURE "Y"
  READ
ENDDO
WRESTORE          && Restore screen image beneath LOOKUP window.
USE
* End of LOOKUP.PRG
```

## VARIATIONS:

**dBASE IV:** DEFINE WINDOW is similar to WSET WINDOW.

## SEE ALSO:

Commands DEFINE WINDOW, WCLOSE, WMOVE, WRESTORE, WSAVE, WSELECT, WSET FRAME, WSET TITLE, and WUSE.

# WSET WINFILE

## DIALECTS:
dBXL and Quicksilver.

## SYNTAX:
WSET WINFILE TO <filename>

## DEFINITION:
Opens a master screen file created by the WordTech BUILDWIN.EXE utility. The WRESTORE command can then retrieve WSAVEd screens by name.

If WRESTORE cannot find the specified screen in the open master file, it searches the current directory for an individual file with the same name.

## DEFAULT:
The master screen file has a WIN extension by default.

## SEE ALSO:
Commands WSAVE, WRESTORE, WSELECT, WSET WINDOW, and WUSE.

# WUSE

## DIALECTS:

dBXL and Quicksilver.

## SYNTAX:

WUSE [<window name>] [TITLE <string> [LEFT/CENTER/RIGHT]]

## DEFINITION:

Opens a window in the currently selected window area. If a window is already open, WUSE closes it before opening the new one.

You must define windows with the WSET WINDOW command before you can WUSE them.

## OPTIONS:

WUSE by itself closes the current window.

WUSE <window name> opens the specified window in the current area.

TITLE defines a character expression to display at the top of the frame. LEFT, CENTER, and RIGHT position the title; CENTER is the default. If the title is too long for the frame, it will be truncated.

To display titles, WSET FRAME must be ON.

## VARIATIONS:

**dBASE IV:** ACTIVATE WINDOW is similar to WUSE.

## SEE ALSO:

Commands ACTIVE WINDOW, WSELECT, WSET FRAME, WSET TITLE, and WSET WINDOW.

# ZAP

## DIALECTS:

Clipper, dBASE III PLUS, dBASE IV, dBXL, FoxBASE+, and Quicksilver.

## SYNTAX:

ZAP

## DEFINITION:

Removes all records from the active database. ZAP is equivalent to DELETE ALL followed by PACK, except that ZAP reclaims disk space used by memo fields.

ZAP executes much faster than the DELETE ALL/PACK combination because it does not have to look for DELETED records.

ZAP reindexes the open index files (with no records).

## RECOMMENDED USE:

Use ZAP to permanently remove records from a database file. ZAPped records cannot be RECALLed.

**Example**—A large inventory system maintains a transaction log in a database file. Every year, an archiving module copies the transaction log to a removable magnetic tape, then ZAPs the transaction log to start over.

```
USE tlog INDEX tdex,transdate
DO tapebak    && TAPEBAK subroutine makes archive tape.
ZAP
USE
```

## SEE ALSO:

Commands DELETE, RECALL, and PACK; function DELETED( ).

# SECTION 3

## dBASE® LANGUAGE FUNCTIONS

# &

## DIALECTS:
Clipper, dBASE III PLUS, dBASE IV, dBXL, FoxBASE+, and Quicksilver.

## SYNTAX:
&<memory variable>[.<expC>]
(Macro substitution function)

## DEFINITION:
The macro substitution function & replaces a character memory variable's name with its value. The value is treated as a literal, as if you had typed it instead of &<memory variable>. You can use the macro almost anywhere a literal can appear. Also, you can have several macros on one line.

The computer ignores ampersands (in character strings) that are not associated with valid memory variables. Two ampersands (&&) on a command line indicate a comment.

The legal uses of macros vary. For example, interpreters let you store entire commands in macros and execute them:

```
. STORE '? "Executing contents of MCOMMAND"' TO mcommand
. &mcommand
Executing contents of MCOMMAND
```

Clipper and Quicksilver do not allow this.

## OPTIONS:
Sometimes, spaces trail a substituted value. To remove them and concatenate the value with another character expression, put a period in-between. For example, the following commands build a filename ACCTMAIN by concatenating variable FILEDESC with the literal "MAIN".

```
STORE "acct" TO filedesc
USE &filedesc.main
```

The period is called the macro *terminator*. It does not appear in the resulting string.

## RECOMMENDED USE:

Programmers use macro substitution to write general purpose subroutines. It lets a routine do different tasks or use different data. Another use is to embed variables in character strings.

**Example 1**—Tired of writing new file-handling routines for each application, a programmer creates a generic version. The parameter FILEUSE designates which file to open. The macro (&) substitutes the parameter's value into the USE command.

```
* GENFILE.PRG
* Generic file handling program.
PARAMETERS fileuse
USE &fileuse
* <statements>
```

To execute GENFILE.PRG using the INVENTRY file, issue the command

```
DO genfile WITH "inventry"
```

**Example 2**—A program merges data with text to produce personalized notices. As it skips through the database file, it stores the field contents in memory variables. It then prints a confirmation using embedded macros.

```
name = "Ms. Joanna McNally"
apptdate = "March 3, 1987"

?
? "
? "&name,"
?
? "This is to confirm your appointment of &APPTDATE. If you"
? "cannot make it, please call our office as soon as possible."
```

The printed confirmation is:

```
Ms. Joanna McNally:

This is to confirm your appointment of March 3, 1987. If you
cannot make it, please call our office as soon as possible.
```

**Example 3**—To allow different search conditions, a report routine appears in a program repeatedly. An alternative is to specify the search condition with macro substitution.

For example, a typical literal condition in a DO WHILE statement might be:

```
DO WHILE lname = "St. James"
```

By adding the macro to the DO WHILE, the programmer needs only one routine:

```
* SERCHRPT.PRG
PARAMETERS condition
USE sales
DO WHILE &condition
  @ ROW(),COL()+10 SAY trim(fname)+ " " + lname
  SKIP
ENDDO
```

The program passes CONDITION to the report routine as a parameter:

```
DO serchrpt WITH "lname = 'St. James'"
```

**Example 4**—In dBASE III PLUS, dBASE IV, dBXL, and FoxBASE+, you can store commands in memory variables and execute them with a macro. This lets an application have its own command processor. The following program presents a custom prompt and accepts commands typed by the user. The macro function executes them as if they were typed at the interactive prompt. You can add validation to provide a custom interactive environment.

**Note:** You should add validation to prevent the user from entering commands that will corrupt the program environment, such as CLEAR, CLEAR MEMORY, or RELEASE.

To illustrate validation, this program fragment uses an IF statement to test input. If the user enters "USE payfile", the program ignores it and repeats the prompt, using the LOOP command to return to the top of the DO WHILE. The user can quit by typing "QUIT", "RETURN", or "EXIT".

```
DO WHILE .t.
  ACCEPT "Enter command-> " TO process
  IF UPPER(process) = "USE payfile"
    @ 01,01 SAY "You do not have clearance to look at PAYFILE"
    LOOP
  ENDIF
  * <more validation statements>
  &process          && Execute pseudo command processor.
ENDDO
```

## LIMITS/WARNINGS:

Macro may not exceed the system string/command length limits. For other LIMITS and WARNINGS, see *VARIATIONS*.

## VARIATIONS:

**Clipper:** Allows SET command switches in macros. For example, to SET BELL ON in Clipper, you could use:

```
switch = "ON"
SET BELL &switch
```

You can thus restore SET command switches from memory variables, MEM files, or databases. You can also change SET switches based on user input.

Unlike any other system, Clipper allows recursive macros.

**Clipper, Quicksilver:** Both compilers restrict commands and parts of commands in macros, but both allow command parameters. For example, the following macro is illegal.

```
pname = "DO submodule"
&pname
```

The legal usage is to put only the filename in the macro.

```
pname = "submodule"
DO &pname
```

Also, do not include keywords such as FOR and WHILE in macro expressions. The following usage is illegal because the expression includes FOR.

```
STORE "FOR lname = 'Smith'" TO condition
LIST lname &condition
```

Instead, separate the variable elements and leave the keyword as a literal as follows:

```
STORE "lname" TO field
STORE "lname = 'Smith'" TO condition
LIST &field FOR &condition
```

Both Clipper and Quicksilver restrict commas in macro expressions. Quicksilver prohibits them entirely. In Clipper, avoid putting comma-delimited INDEX file and FIELD lists in macros. Clipper allows commas in SET COLOR TO commands. Here is the correct way to specify an INDEX file list with macros:

```
ixfile1 = "statedex"
ixfile2 = "zipdex"
SET INDEX to &ixfile1,&ixfile2
```

Both compilers reevaluate a macro in a DO WHILE statement if its value changes.

**dBASE III PLUS, dBXL, FoxBASE+:** Macros in a DO WHILE statement are not reevaluated during iterations. Therefore, changes to the macro value within the loop do not affect the DO WHILE. Clipper, dBASE IV, and Quicksilver reevaluate the DO WHILE statement.

**dBASE IV:** Does not allow macros in user defined functions.

**Quicksilver:** Does not allow CCALL arguments, commands, or parts of commands in a macro. Macros may contain command parameters. Does not allow commas in macro expressions or macros in SET command switches.

### Macro comparison chart.

| | Clipper | III | IV | dBXL | Fox | QS |
|---|---|---|---|---|---|---|
| Recursion | ✓ | | | | | |
| DO WHILE reevaluation | ✓ | | ✓ | | | ✓ |
| Command execution | ✓ | ✓ | ✓ | ✓ | | |
| Keyword substitution | (limited) | ✓ | ✓ | ✓ | ✓ | |
| String substitution | ✓ | ✓ | ✓ | ✓ | ✓ | ✓ |
| Commas in macros | (limited) | ✓ | ✓ | ✓ | ✓ | |
| Macro in UDF | ✓ | n/a | | ✓ | ✓ | ✓ |

### Key:
III-dBASE III PLUS
IV-dBASE IV
Fox-FoxBASE+
QS-Quicksilver

## SEE ALSO:
Commands ?, DO, and DO WHILE.

# ABS( )

## DIALECTS:
Clipper, dBASE III PLUS, dBASE IV, dBXL, FoxBASE+, and Quicksilver.

## SYNTAX:
ABS(<expN>)

## RETURNS:
Numeric

## DEFINITION:
Returns the absolute value of a numeric expression. This is the value's magnitude, disregarding its sign.

## RECOMMENDED USE:
Use ABS( ) to compute absolute differences for statistical analysis.

**Example**—A statistical program computes the difference between the lowest and highest values in a market research survey. With the ABS( ) function, the program need not determine which number is higher.

```
stat1 =  -57
stat2 = 899
? abs(stat1-stat2)
956
stat1 = 899
stat2 = -57
? abs(stat1-stat2)
956
```

## SEE ALSO:
Functions FLOOR( ), INT( ), and ROUND( ).

# ACHOICE( )

## DIALECTS:

Clipper only.

## SYNTAX:

ACHOICE(<expN1>,<expN2>,<expN3>,<expN4>,<array1>[,<array2>
[,<expC>[,<expN5>[,<expN6>]]]])

## RETURNS:

Numeric

## DEFINITION:

Displays a fully-scrollable menu in a window, using an array for the selections. A light bar serves as the cursor. Menus may be nested.

ACHOICE( ) resembles the @...PROMPT...MENU TO command; however, MENU TO is not scrollable and is limited to 32 prompts per menu.

<expN1>,<expN2> is the top left window coordinate. <expN3>,<expN4> is the bottom right coordinate.

<array1> is an array of menu selections. They must be character strings.

<array2> is an array of logical elements (.T. or .F.) for each element in array 1. A true (.T.) element means that the corresponding element in <array1> can be selected. False (.F.) means that the element appears, but cannot be selected. You can make menu items either all selectable or all non-selectable, by using .T. or .F. as the argument.

<expC> is a user defined function executed in response to an invalid key. You must specify the function name in quotation marks, without parentheses or arguments. This feature lets you define your own keystroke handling routines. If you do not supply a user defined function, ACHOICE( ) offers a default mode.

<expN5> indicates the initial item to highlight when the menu is invoked.

<expN6> specifies the initial row position of the cursor relative to the window.

When a selection is made, ACHOICE( ) terminates the menu and returns the relative number of the chosen item (the subscript of the associated array element).

Cancelling the menu selection (with ESC) returns 0.

*Note:* You may omit ACHOICE( ) options from the end of the argument list (right to left). However, you may not omit ones from the middle.

ACHOICE( ) displays choices in the standard color. The selection cursor appears in enhanced color. Unavailable choices (.F. in <array2>) appear in the unselected color.

## MODES:

ACHOICE( ) has two modes: default and user defined function.

### DEFAULT MODE:

This easily implemented mode is a good choice if you are not experienced in writing user defined functions. If you do not specify a user defined function, ACHOICE( ) responds to keys as follows:

| **Key** | **Action** |
|---|---|
| Up Arrow | Up one selection |
| Down Arrow | Down one selection |
| Home | First selection |
| End | Last selection |
| PgUp | Up one page (relative to the window size) |
| PgDn | Down one page (relative to the window size) |
| Ctrl-PgDn | First selection |
| Ctrl-PgUp | Last selection |
| Enter | Make selection, return selection number (element) |
| ESCape | Cancel selection, return 0 |
| Left arrow | Cancel selection, return 0 |
| Right arrow | Cancel selection, return 0 |
| First letter | Select next element with first letter, return selection number (element) |

A simple ACHOICE( ) statement is:

```
mchoice = ACHOICE(01,02,05,15,master)
```

where 01,02 and 05,15 are the top left and bottom right coordinates respectively. MASTER is an array of menu selections.

## USER DEFINED FUNCTION MODE:

Specifying a user defined function in ACHOICE( ) shifts more responsibility to the programmer. Now ACHOICE( ) responds to fewer keys automatically. Specific actions depend on values passed between it and the user defined function.

ACHOICE( ) continues to handle the following keys:

| **Key** | **Action** |
|---|---|
| Up Arrow | Up one selection |
| Down Arrow | Down one selection |
| PgUp | Up one page (relative to the window size) |
| PgDn | down one page (relative to the window size) |
| Ctrl-PgDn | First selection |
| Ctrl-PgUp | Last selection |

Home, End, Enter, and Esc are invalid (keyboard exceptions).

Using the LASTKEY( ) function and parameters passed to the user defined function by ACHOICE( ), you can customize the response.

When the user presses an invalid key, ACHOICE( ) calls the user defined function, sending it three parameters: MODE, CURRENT ELEMENT in the array, and RELATIVE WINDOW POSITION. The MODE parameters are:

**ACHOICE( )** ——→ user defined function

| MODE | Description |
|---|---|
| 0 | Idle (no action) |
| 1 | Move cursor past top of list |
| 2 | Move cursor past end of list |
| 3 | Invalid key (keystroke exception) |
| 4 | No item selectable |

You must design the user defined function to evaluate these parameters, then return a value to ACHOICE( ). The values are:

**User defined function** ——→ ACHOICE( )

| **MODE** | **Description** |
|---|---|
| 0 | Cancel selection, return 0 |
| 1 | Make selection, return selection (element) number |
| 2 | Continue selection |
| 3 | Go to next selection, matching last key pressed |

## RECOMMENDED USE:

Use ACHOICE( ) to develop modifiable menu systems. You can store selections and actions in a database, then load them into arrays for display. To change a selection, you simply change the database, not the program. ACHOICE( ) itself is relatively easy to use; however, the array manipulation may be tricky.

**Example**—The main menu of an accounting system pops up in the top left corner of the screen. First, the program DECLAREs two arrays, MASTER and MACTION. MASTER holds the menu selection text. MACTION holds the corresponding subroutine names. The values are stored in MENU1.DBF. Its structure and contents are:

```
Structure for database: C:\GENLED\MENU1.DBF
Number of data records:       4
Date of last update   : 01/17/88
Field  Field Name  Type        Width    Dec
    1  MSELECT     Character      20
    3  ACTION      Character      10
** Total **                       31

. LIST mselect,action
Record#  mselect              action
      1  Payroll              SUB1
      2  End of Month         SUB2
      3  End of Year          SUB3
      4  Close Quarter        SUB4
```

The program opens MENU1.DBF and loads field MSELECT into array MASTER and field ACTION into array MACTION. In a DO WHILE loop, ACHOICE( ) displays MASTER. Memory variable MCHOICE contains the element number selected. If the return value is non-zero, the program executes the subroutine stored in the corresponding element in MACTION.

For example, if the user selects choice 1, "Payroll," the program issues the command DO SUB1.

```
DECLARE master[4], maction[4]
USE menu1
FOR ctr = 1 TO 4                  && Menu1 contains only four records.
  master[ctr] = mselect           && Load field MSELECT into array.
  maction[ctr] = action           && Load field ACTION into array.
  SKIP
NEXT
USE

* Set color to yellow on blue standard text, red on white
* enhanced text, blue border, brown on blue unselected text
```

```
SET COLOR TO gr+/b,r/w,b,,gr/b
DO WHILE .t.
  mchoice = ACHOICE(01,02,05,15,master)
  IF mchoice > 0
    subrout = maction[mchoice]
    DO &subrout
  ELSE
    RETURN
  ENDIF
ENDDO

PROCEDURE sub1          && Each procedure would have additional code.
@ 01,35 SAY "Post Payroll        "

PROCEDURE sub2
@ 01,35 SAY "End of Month Report"

PROCEDURE sub3
@ 01,35 SAY "End of Year Report "

PROCEDURE sub4
@ 01,35 SAY "Close Quarter       "
```

The user defined function mode can provide more control over key responses. Using the same data, the following program employs a user defined function AUDF to control menu response. To avoid repetition, the example does not contain the subroutine calls.

Note that in ACHOICE( ), .T. indicates that all elements are available for selection.

```
DECLARE master[4], maction [4]
USE menu1                  && Contains fields MSELECT and ACTION.
FOR ctr = 1 TO 4           && Menu1 contains only four records.
  master[ctr] = mselect    && Load selection field MSELECT into array.
  maction[ctr] = action    && Load character field ACTION into array.
  SKIP
NEXT

mchoice = ACHOICE(01,02,05,15,master,.t.,"audf")
* <From here, you can use MCHOICE to execute a subroutine

FUNCTION audf
PARAMETERS mode,celement,relpos
DO CASE
  CASE LASTKEY()=19 .OR. LASTKEY()=4   && Trap left or right arrow keys.
    RETURN 2                   && Continue selection process.
  CASE mode=3                  && If keystroke exception,
    RETURN 1                   &&   accept entry.
  CASE mode=1 .OR. mode=2      && If cursor goes past top or bottom
```

```
    ?? CHR(7)                   &&   of list, beep.
    RETURN 2                    && Continue selection process.
  OTHERWISE
    RETURN 2
ENDCASE
```

ACHOICE( ) is in EXTEND.LIB on the system disk.

## SEE ALSO:

Commands @...PROMPT...MENU TO, DECLARE, PARAMETERS, and SET COLOR; functions ADIR( ) and LASTKEY( ).

# ACCESS( )

## DIALECTS:

dBASE III PLUS and dBASE IV.

## SYNTAX:

ACCESS( )

## RETURNS:

Numeric

## DEFINITION:

Returns the access level of the last user to login through the dBASE III PLUS ADMINISTRATOR or dBASE IV PROTECT system.

ACCESS( ) always returns 0 in a single-user environment or if the user does not enter through the dBASE ADMINISTRATOR or PROTECT login screen.

To increase security, include a test for ACCESS( ) = 0 at the beginning of an application. If ACCESS( ) returns 0, the application is running on a single-user system or the user has bypassed the login screen.

## RECOMMENDED USE:

The dBASE III PLUS network administration program and the dBASE IV PROTECT program let you define access levels for system users. Users can then be restricted from files and parts of an application program, based on their clearances. Users with an ACCESS( ) level of 0 may not use encrypted files.

**Example**—Walter works in the sales department. His company uses an accounting system on a local area network for sales support. The system programmer must prevent Walter from accessing sensitive accounting data. To do so, he uses the ACCESS( ) function. He precedes certain program modules with an ACCESS( )-checking routine. Walter has access level 4. The security system keeps Walter from accessing salary records and sales projections for unannounced products.

```
* COMISIONS.PRG
* Program to access sales department commissions.
IF ACCESS() < 7
```

```
  ?
  ? "I'm sorry, you do not have clearance to proceed"
  WAIT "Press a key to return to previous menu"
  RETURN
ENDIF
* <more statements>
```

## VARIATIONS:

**dBASE IV:** If an unauthorized user tries to read or write an encrypted file, the error message "Unauthorized access level" appears. The user may still USE a file and issue file locks. To prevent unauthorized locks, the programmer can use ON ERROR and ERROR( ) to trap error 133 ("Unauthorized access level"), then USE or UNLOCK the file.

Note that dBASE IV will not display the login screen unless it finds the file DBSYSTEM.DB at startup. The file should be in the program directory.

## SEE ALSO:

Commands PROTECT and SET ENCRYPTION; functions NETNAME( ) and USER( ).

# ACOPY( )

## DIALECTS:

Clipper only.

## SYNTAX:

ACOPY(<array1>,<array2>[,<expN1>[,<expN2>[,<expN3>]]])

## RETURNS:

Nothing

## DEFINITION:

Copies elements from one array to another.

<array1> is the source and <array2> is the target.

<expN1> is the element in the source array from which to start copying (inclusive).

<expN2> is the number of elements to copy.

<expN3> is the element in the target array at which to start copying.

## RECOMMENDED USE:

**Example**—In an accounting application, an array AMENU contains ten menu selections. After the quarter is closed, some selections become invalid until another quarter passes (e.g., Close Quarter, Print Quarterly Report).

For the ACHOICE( ) function, a logical value in array AACTIVE designates that the corresponding element in AMENU is active. If the element is false (.F.), the menu selection is unavailable.

When the quarter closes, the program modifies the available menu options by changing the values in AACTIVE.

```
DECLARE amenu[10]
DECLARE aactive[10]
* <load arrays, make all elements of AACTIVE true (.T.).>
* <After running quarterly report, copy new values to AACTIVE.
* New array is CVALUES with some true elements and some false.>
DECLARE cvalues[10]
* <store values in CVALUES>
```

```
ACOPY(cvalues,aactive)    && Copies all values from CVALUES to AACTIVE.
ACHOICE(1,1,10,20,amenu,aactive)
```

ACOPY( ) is in EXTEND.LIB on the system disk.

## SEE ALSO:

Functions ACHOICE( ), ADEL( ), ADIR( ), AFIELDS( ), AFILL( ), AINS( ), ASCAN( ), ASEEK( ), and ASORT( ).

# ACOS( )

## DIALECTS:

dBASE IV only.

## SYNTAX:

ACOS(<expN>)

## RETURNS:

Floating point

## DEFINITION:

Computes the arccosine (inverse cosine) of <expN>, where <expN> is a value in the range -1.0 to +1.0.

ACOS( ) returns a floating point number (an angle in radians) in the range 0 to pi (3.14159).

The SET DECIMALS and SET PRECISION commands determine numeric accuracy.

Use DTOR( ) and RTOD( ) to convert degrees to radians and vice versa. A radian is approximately 57.3 degrees.

## RECOMMENDED USE:

Use ACOS( ) in engineering and scientific applications.

**Example**—An architectural engineering application expresses angles in radians. The cosine of angle A is 0.32. By taking its ACOS( ), the program determines A in radians to be .25.

```
m_acos = ACOS(.32)
         .25
```

## SEE ALSO:

Functions ASIN( ), ATAN( ), ATN2( ), COS( ), SIN( ), and TAN( ).

# ACTIVEWIN( )

## DIALECTS:
Quicksilver only.

## SYNTAX:
ACTIVEWIN( )

## RETURNS:
Logical

## DEFINITION:
Indicates whether a window is active in the currently selected area. True if a window is active in the current WSELECT area.

ACTIVEWIN( ) is the same as WACTIVE( ).

## SEE ALSO:
Commands WSELECT, WSET WINDOW, and WUSE; function WACTIVE( ).

# ADEL( )

## DIALECTS:

Clipper only.

## SYNTAX:

ADEL(<expC>,<expN>)

## RETURNS:

Nothing

## DEFINITION:

Deletes an array element. All succeeding elements move down one. <expC> is the array name. <expN> is the element to delete.

The last element in the array becomes undefined.

For example, assume a five-element array called TEST containing names for a lookup menu:

```
FOR ctr = 1 to 5
   ? test[ctr]
NEXT
Johnson
Barreda
Samuelson
Gillette
Wong
```

Using ADEL( ) to delete element two, "Barreda," moves all succeeding names down one. Element five becomes undefined.

```
ADEL(TEST,3)
FOR ctr = 1 to 4
   ? test[ctr]
NEXT
Johnson
Samuelson
Gillette
Wong
```

## RECOMMENDED USE:

Use ADEL( ) to remove values from an array containing a menu, lookup table, or pick list.

**Example**—An inventory system stores part numbers in an array. The numbers appear on the screen, allowing the user to delete them with a keystroke. The following program loads the array, GETs the part numbers, then lets the user scroll through the elements.

```
CLEAR
USE parts                         && Open PARTS database.
DECLARE parta[20]                 && Declare array PARTA.
FOR ctr = 1 TO 20
  parta[ctr] = partno             && Load data from records until
  SKIP                            &&   array is full.
NEXT

@ 10,01 SAY "Your choice => "
@ 11,01 SAY "Key control...PgUp, PgDn, delete with Ctrl-W, exit with ESC"
ctr = 1
DO WHILE .t.
  @ 10,18 GET parta[ctr]
  READ
  DO CASE
  * LASTKEY values: 18-PgUp, 3-PgDn, 13-Enter.
  CASE LASTKEY() = 18 .AND. ctr > 1          && Do not move past
                                             &&   first element.
    ctr = ctr - 1
  CASE LASTKEY() = 3.AND.ctr < LEN(parta)   && Do not move past
                                             &&   last element.
    ctr = ctr + 1
  CASE LASTKEY() = 23                        && Press Ctrl-W to
                                             &&   delete element.
    ADEL(parta,ctr)
  * move cases
  CASE LASTKEY() = 13
    mpart = parta[ctr]
    EXIT
  ENDCASE
ENDDO
```

ADEL( ) is in EXTEND.LIB on the system disk.

## LIMITS/WARNINGS:

Summer '87 version (file date 12-21-87, 2:00 a.m.): ADEL( ) cannot delete the last array element. To work around this problem, store a blank value (e.g., zero, a space, or a null string) in it.

## SEE ALSO:

Command DECLARE; functions ACHOICE( ), ADIR( ), AFILL( ), AINS( ), and ASCAN( ).

# ADIR( )

## DIALECTS:

Clipper only.

## SYNTAX:

ADIR(<expC1> [,<expC2>,[<expC3>,[<expC4>,[<expC5>,[<expC6>]]]]])

## RETURNS:

Numeric

## DEFINITION:

Returns the number of files in the current directory that match the skeleton specified in <expC1>, or fills a series of arrays with directory information.

Skeletons must be delimited, for example:

```
ADIR("*.*")
ADIR("*.DBF")
ADIR("?AR.DBF")
```

## OPTIONS:

The second expression, <expC2>, is an array in which to store the matching filenames. Elements are character type.

<expC3> is an array that holds the sizes of the matching files. Elements are numeric.

<expC4> is an array that holds the dates of the matching files. Elements are date type.

<expC5> is an array that holds the times of the matching files. Elements are character type.

<expC6> is an array that holds the DOS attributes of the matching files. Elements are character type. If you do not use this argument, ADIR( ) recognizes only Archive and Read Only files. (Archive files are normal DOS read/write files).

| **Attribute** | **Description** |
|---|---|
| A | Archive |
| D | Directory |
| H | Hidden |
| R | Read only |
| S | System |

To use arrays with ADIR( ), you must DECLARE one for each optional argument. Each array must have the same number of elements as files matching the skeleton.

Because ADIR( ) with no optional arguments returns the number of matching files, you can use it in a DECLARE statement as follows:

```
DECLARE array[ADIR("*.*")]
```

If you have several arrays, store the number of matches in a variable, then use it in each DECLARE. This is faster than repeating ADIR("*.*"):

```
mct = ADIR("*.*")
DECLARE mname[mct],msize[mct],mdate[mct],mtime[mct],mattrib[mct]
```

Then use ADIR( ) as follows:

```
ADIR("*.*",mname,msize,mdate,mtime,mattrib)
```

To get directory values for only selected arrays, use null arguments for the others, as follows:

```
mnull = ""
ADIR("*.*",mname,mnull,mdate,mnull,mattrib)
```

Arrays at the end of the list can simply be omitted.

## RECOMMENDED USE:

Use ADIR( ) to list available filenames or display directories.

**Example 1**—The user interface in an accounting system lets users choose database files to open from a list on the screen. ADIR( ) gathers the filenames into an array. Additional array handling techniques build the menu and selection mechanism.

```
CLEAR
DECLARE fhold[ADIR("*.*")]   && Create array with number of matching files.
```

```
ADIR("*.*", fhold)
@ 10,01 SAY "Your choice => "
@ 11,01 SAY "Key control...PgUp, PgDn, select with Enter, exit with ESC"
ctr = 1
DO WHILE .t.
  @ 10,20 GET fhold[ctr]
  READ
  DO CASE
    * LASTKEY values: 18 is PgUp, 3 is PgDn, 13 is Enter, 27 is ESC.
    * Do not move past first element.
    CASE LASTKEY() = 18 .AND. ctr > 1
      ctr = ctr -1
    *  Do not move past last element.
    CASE LASTKEY() = 3 .AND. ctr < LEN(fhold)
      ctr = ctr + 1
    CASE LASTKEY() = 13            && Press Enter to select file.
      mfile = fhold[ctr]           && MFILE is the chosen filename.
      EXIT
  ENDCASE
  @ 10,20 SAY SPACE(15)
ENDDO
```

**Example 2**—A file backup routine gathers directory information and makes backups based on specified times and dates. The program stores file information in arrays as follows:

```
mdbf = ADIR("*.dbf")
DECLARE mnames[mdbf],msize[mdbf],mdate[mdbf],mtime[mdbf]
ADIR("*.dbf",mnames,msize,mdate,mtime)
```

ADIR( ) is in EXTEND.LIB on the system disk.

## SEE ALSO:

Command DECLARE; functions ACHOICE( ), ADEL( ), AFILL( ), AINS( ), and ASCAN( ).

# AFIELDS( )

## DIALECTS:

Clipper only.

## SYNTAX:

AFIELDS([<array1>,[<array2>[,<array3>[,<array4>]]]])

## RETURNS:

Numeric

## DEFINITION:

Analyzes the active database file's structure and stores the fieldnames, field types, field lengths, and decimal lengths in arrays.

AFIELDS( ) also returns the smaller of the number of fields or the length of the shortest array used in its argument. For example, if you DECLARE MARRAY1[40], AFIELDS(marray1) returns 40. If you do not specify any parameters, AFIELDS( ) returns 0.

AFIELDS( ) stores fieldnames in <array1>, field types in <array2>, field lengths in <array3>, and decimal lengths in <array4>.

Fieldnames are character strings.

Field types are single characters as follows:

- C—Character
- D—Date
- L—Logical
- M—Memo
- N—Numeric

Field lengths and decimal lengths are numeric.

*Note:* To skip an array in the AFIELDS( ) list, use a null-valued variable in its place. For example, to use fieldnames and decimal lengths only, proceed as follows:

```
num = FCOUNT()
DECLARE mfield[num], mdec[num]
null = ""
null2 = ""
AFIELDS(mfield, null, null2, mdec)
```

## RECOMMENDED USE:

Use AFIELDS( ) to list database structures in user applications or utility programs.

**Example 1**—A personnel management system lets users choose fields from a list for inclusion in reports. The program first opens the database, then stores the field count (FCOUNT( )) in variable NUM. Four arrays (MFIELD, MTYPE, MWIDTH, and MDEC are declared to hold the file structure attributes. NUM, the field count, determines the number of elements in each array.

```
USE master
num = FCOUNT()
DECLARE mfield[num], mtype[num], mwidth[num], mdec[num]
AFIELDS(mfield, mtype, mwidth, mdec)
```

Once you have the structure information in arrays, you can manipulate it with other Clipper functions.

**Example 2**—A programmer writes a short program to display file structures. It prompts for the filename, then lists the fields and their attributes.

```
CLEAR
fname = SPACE(8)
@ 01,01 SAY "Enter filename without extension: " GET fname PICTURE "@"!
READ
fname = TRIM(fname)
IF .NOT. FILE("&fname..DBF")
  ? "File not found"
  RETURN
ENDIF
CLEAR
USE (fname)
num = FCOUNT()
DECLARE mfield[num],mtype[num],mwidth[num],mdec[num]
AFIELDS(mfield, mtype, mwidth, mdec)
FOR ct = 1 TO num
  * Note: SPACE(10-LEN(mfield[ct])) pads the fieldname string with
  * spaces to make it display in an even column.
  ? mfield[ct] + SPACE(10-LEN(mfield[ct])), mtype[ct], ;
        STR(mwidth[ct]), STR(mdec[ct])
  IF ct/23  = INT(ct/23)    && Execute on multiples of 23 (see INT().)
    ?
    WAIT "Press SPACE BAR to view more fields"
```

```
    @ ROW(),00                  && Clear WAIT message line.
  ENDIF
NEXT ct
WAIT "End of field list, press key to exit"
CLEAR
```

AFIELDS( ) is in EXTEND.LIB on the system disk.

## SEE ALSO:

Commands DECLARE and FOR...NEXT; functions ACHOICE( ), ACOPY( ), ADEL( ), AFILL( ), AINS( ), ASCAN( ), ASORT( ), and FCOUNT( ).

# AFILL( )

## DIALECTS:
Clipper only.

## SYNTAX:
AFILL(<expC>,<exp>[,<expN1> [,<expN2]])

## RETURNS:
Nothing

## DEFINITION:
Initializes an array <expC> with the value <exp>.

## DEFAULT:
AFILL( ) fills all elements.

## OPTIONS:
Optional numeric arguments specify a range from either <expN1> to the last element, or from <expN1> to <expN2>.

## RECOMMENDED USE:
Use AFILL( ) to assign default values to array elements.

**Example**—A shipping and mailing program initializes an array of rates with default zone charges of 5.00, 7.00, and 10.00 in selected ranges of elements.

```
CLEAR
DECLARE ratehold[10]            && Declare array RATEHOLD.
AFILL(ratehold,5.00,1,3)        && Fill elements 1, 2, and 3.
AFILL(ratehold,7.00,4,4)        && Fill elements 4, 5, 6, and 7.
AFILL(ratehold,10.00,8,3)       && Fill elements 8, 9, and 10.
```

This lets the programmer create a matrix of zones and zone charges. Another array contains the zones, with each element corresponding to an element in array RATEHOLD. When the user selects a zone, the program can look up the charge in RATEHOLD.

A display of RATEHOLD's contents shows the defaults:

```
FOR ctr = 1 TO 10
  ? ratehold[ctr]
NEXT
      5.00
      5.00
      5.00
      7.00
      7.00
      7.00
      7.00
     10.00
     10.00
     10.00
```

AFILL( ) is in EXTEND.LIB on the system disk.

## SEE ALSO:

Command DECLARE; functions ADEL( ), ADIR( ), AINS( ), and ASCAN( ).

# AINS( )

## DIALECTS:

Clipper only.

## SYNTAX:

AINS(<expC>,<expN>)

## RETURNS:

Nothing

## DEFINITION:

Inserts an "empty" (undefined) element into an array. <expC> is the array's name. <expN> is the element number.

The inserted element pushes everything after it up one position, eliminating the last element.

## RECOMMENDED USE:

Use AINS( ) to add a new value to an array. To avoid losing the last element, be sure to make the array large enough.

**Example**—A program scans a database file, storing customer account numbers in array PICK. When the clerk enters a new customer account, AINS( ) inserts the new number into the array.

The following program loads the array, GETs the new account number, then lets the user scroll through the array elements to pick an account number.

```
USE accounts INDEX acctdex        && Open accounts database.
DECLARE pick[23]                  && Declare array PICK.
FOR ctr = 1 TO 23
  pick[ctr] = acctno              && Load data from each record until
  SKIP                            &&   array is full.
  IF eof()                        && If end of file, end array loading.
   ctr = 23
  ENDIF
NEXT

macctno = SPACE(8)
@ 10,10 SAY "Enter new acct. number: " GET macctno PICTURE "########"
```

```
READ

AINS(pick,1)          && Insert new element 1.
pick[1] = macctno     && Replace new element with new account number.
ctr = 1
DO WHILE .t.
  @ 10,10 GET pick[ctr]
  READ
  DO CASE
    * LASTKEY values: 18 is PgUp, 3 is PgDn, 13 is Enter.
    CASE LASTKEY() = 18 .AND. ctr > 1       && Do not move past
                                            &&   first element.
      ctr = ctr - 1
    CASE LASTKEY() = 3 .AND. ctr < LEN(pick) && Do not move past
                                             &&   last element.
      ctr = ctr + 1
    CASE LASTKEY() = 13
      mpick = pick[ctr]
      EXIT
  ENDCASE
ENDDO
```

AFILL( ) is in EXTEND.LIB on the system disk.

## SEE ALSO:

Command DECLARE; functions ADEL( ), ADIR( ), AFILL( ), and ASCAN( ).

# ALIAS( )

## DIALECTS:

Clipper, dBASE IV, and FoxBASE+.

## SYNTAX:

ALIAS(<expN>)

## RETURNS:

Character string

## DEFINITION:

Returns the alias of an open database. <expN> is the work area number. The default (no parameter) is the alias of the currently selected database.

ALIAS( ) returns a null string when no database is open in the specified area.

## RECOMMENDED USE:

You can use ALIAS( ) to provide database information to the end user.

**Example**—A programmer writes a system utility that displays the names of all open files at the press of a key. The program first saves the screen image, then clears a block and draws a box. A counter in a DO WHILE loop increments both the selected area and the screen coordinate at which to display the filename.

```
@ 01,01 CLEAR TO 18,27          && Clear block on screen.
@ 01,01 TO 18,27 DOUBLE         && Draw double line border.
@ 02,05 SAY "***OPEN FILES***"  && Display header text.
@ 03,05 SAY "AREA  ALIAS"
increase = 1                    && Initialize counter to 1.
DO WHILE increase < 11          && Repeat DO WHILE 10 times.
  * At coordinate INCREASE+5,05 display the work area number
  *  and the name of the file open in the area.
  @ increase+5,05 SAY STR(increase,2,0) + "   " + ALIAS(increase)
  increase = increase + 1       && Add 1 to counter.
ENDDO
```

## SEE ALSO:

Function DBF( ).

# ALLTRIM( )

## DIALECTS:
Clipper only.

## SYNTAX:
ALLTRIM(<expC>)

## RETURNS:
Character

## DEFINITION:
Removes leading and trailing blanks from a character string.

ALLTRIM( ) is equivalent to LTRIM(TRIM(<expC>)).

## RECOMMENDED USE:
Use ALLTRIM( ) to format character strings in reports and on-screen forms.

ALLTRIM( ) is in EXTEND.LIB on the system disk.

## SEE ALSO:
Functions LTRIM( ) and TRIM( ).

# ALTD( )

## DIALECTS:
Clipper only.

## SYNTAX:
ALTD([<expN>])

## RETURNS:
Nothing

## DEFINITION:
Activates or disables Clipper's debugger. (To use it, you must link DEBUG.OBJ to your application.)

If used without an argument, ALTD( ) activates the debugger, preserving the current screen.

<expN> can have one of three values:

0—Pressing Alt-D has no effect.

1—Activates the debugger. After resuming program execution without the debugger, pressing Alt-D reactivates it.

2—Activates the debugger and immediately presents a view of active private variables.

ALTD( ) ignores invalid parameters.

## RECOMMENDED USE:
Use ALTD( ) to selectively activate or disable the debugger at different times or points in a program.

**Example 1**—A programmer links the debugger (DEBUG.OBJ) into all new applications. The debugger can then be activated or disabled using a command line parameter. If the user doesn't specify a parameter, the debugger is disabled. For security reasons, only the programmer need know that the debugger is available.

*Note:* Linking DEBUG.OBJ to your application inflates its size. After testing, relink your application without it.

```
* ACCOUNTS.PRG
PARAMETERS dbug      && Get command line parameter.
IF PCOUNT() = 0      && If no parameters are passed,
  dbug = 0           &&   disable the debugger.
ELSE
 dbug = VAL(dbug)
ENDIF
ALTD(dbug)
* <program statements>
```

With a program called ACCOUNTS, entering

**ACCOUNTS 0** or **ACCOUNTS**

disables the debugger.

Entering

**ACCOUNTS 1**

starts the application and immediately activates the debugger.

Entering

**ACCOUNTS 2**

starts the application and immediately presents the debugger's Private Variables screen.

## SEE ALSO:

Command SET ESCAPE; function SETCANCEL( ).

# AMPM( )

## DIALECTS:

Clipper only.

## SYNTAX:

AMPM(<expc>)

## RETURNS:

Character

## DEFINITION:

Converts a 24-hour time string in the form "HH:MM:SS" to its 12-hour equivalent, designating "am" or "pm".

For example, AMPM("13:12:22") returns the following:

```
1:12:22 pm
```

## RECOMMENDED USE:

Use AMPM( ) in reports or on-screen forms to display the 12-hour time. (The system time and default TIME( ) string is 24-hour time).

**Example**—A point of sale system displays the 12-hour time in the upper right corner of the main menu. Using INKEY( ), the clock ticks until the user presses a key.

```
* <@...SAY...GETs>
keypress = 0
DO WHILE keypress = 0
  @ 01,69 SAY AMPM(TIME())    && Display 12-hour time.
  interval = TIME()           && Save time in variable.
  keypress = INKEY()          && Check for KEYPRESS with INKEY()
  * Stay in DO WHILE until TIME()changes, updating screen each second.
  DO WHILE keypress=0 .AND. interval=TIME()
    keypress = INKEY()        && Check for KEYPRESS again.
  ENDDO
ENDDO
* <CASE structure to process user selections>
```

AMPM( ) is in EXTEND.LIB on the system disk.

## SEE ALSO:

Function TIME( ).

# ASC( )

## DIALECTS:

Clipper, dBASE III PLUS, dBASE IV, dBXL, FoxBASE+, and Quicksilver.

## SYNTAX:

ASC(<expC>)

## RETURNS:

Numeric

## DEFINITION:

Returns the ASCII value (0 through 127) of the leftmost character in <expC>.

For example, to return the ASCII value of "A", use:

```
? ASC("A")
65
```

The expression can also be a memory variable. This example returns the ASCII value of "R".

```
string = "Ronald"
? ASC(string)
82
```

ASC( ) is the inverse of the CHR( ) function.

## RECOMMENDED USE:

Use ASC( ) to manipulate character strings, as in encrypting passwords.

**Example**—For security, a program converts a password PSW into its ASCII equivalent using ASC( ).

PSW.PRG accepts PASS and stores its uppercase value in PSW. It then creates two variables, CTR and SCTR, which act as counters for the DO WHILE. The DO WHILE processes the PSW string once for each character it contains. The program then creates ASCODE, a character variable containing a number of spaces equal to twice the length of PSW.

The first line after the DO WHILE contains four functions: SUBSTR, ASC, STR, and STUFF. They execute from right to left. SUBSTR( ) evaluates PSW one character at a time, from left to right, starting at position CTR. As CTR increases,

ASC( ) converts each character to an ASCII value. STR( ) converts each numeric ASCII value into a character string of digits. STUFF( ) then inserts each ASCII value into the ASCODE string, building it from left to right as SCTR increases.

```
* PSW.PRG
* Accepts PSW, returns ASCODE. This could also be used like a
* Clipper, dBASE IV, FoxBASE+, or Quicksilver user defined function.
* FUNCTION psw      && Remove asterisk for Clipper, Quicksilver UDFs.
PARAMETERS pass
PRIVATE ascode,ctr,psw,sctr
psw = UPPER(pass)
STORE 1 TO ctr,sctr
ascode = SPACE(LEN(psw)*2)
DO WHILE ctr <= (LEN(psw))
  ascode = STUFF(ascode,sctr,2,STR(ASC(SUBSTR(psw,ctr,1)),2,0))
  ctr  = ctr + 1
  sctr = sctr + 2
ENDDO
* RETURN ascode     && Remove asterisk for user defined functions.
```

To convert the password "Samuel" using PSW.PRG as a procedure, enter:

```
. DO psw WITH "Samuel"
836577856976
```

To convert "Samuel" using PSW as a Clipper, dBASE IV, FoxBASE+, or Quicksilver user defined function, enter:

```
? psw("Samuel")
```

By examining ASCODE after each iteration of the DO WHILE, you can see the string being built from left to right. The letters that have been converted are at the right.

```
83              S
8365            SA
836577          SAM
83657785        SAMU
8365778569      SAMUE
836577856976    SAMUEL
```

You can reverse this process using CHR( ), the function that converts ASCII values to characters.

## SEE ALSO:

Functions CHR( ), IIF( ), LEN( ), and SUBSTR( ).

# ASCAN( )

## DIALECTS:
Clipper only.

## SYNTAX:
ASCAN(<expC>,<exp>[,<expN1> [,<expN2]])

## RETURNS:
Numeric

## DEFINITION:
Searches an array for an expression <exp>. If an element matches, ASCAN( ) returns its number. Otherwise, it returns zero.

By default, ASCAN( ) searches all elements. Two optional numeric arguments <expN1> and <expN2> contain the starting and ending elements in a range.

## RECOMMENDED USE:
Use ASCAN( ) to do quick array lookups.

**Example**—An array in a library application contains book reference numbers. It has 400 elements.

```
DECLARE bookref[400]
* <program code to load data into the array>

element = ASCAN(bookref,"A383AB.33")
? element
222
```

To search only elements 100 to 200, use the optional numeric arguments:

```
element = ASCAN(bookref,"ZZ3333",100,200)
? element
0
```

Reference number ZZ3333 was not found.

ASCAN( ) is in EXTEND.LIB on the system disk.

## SEE ALSO:
Command DECLARE; functions ACHOICE( ), ACOPY( ), ADEL( ), ADIR( ), AFILL( ), AINS( ), and ASORT( ).

# ASIN( )

## DIALECTS:
dBASE IV only.

## SYNTAX:
ASIN(<expN>)

## RETURNS:
Floating point

## DEFINITION:
Computes the arcsine (inverse sine) of <expN>.

<expN> is a number in the range -1.0 to 1.0.

ASIN( ) returns a floating point number (an angle in radians) in the range -1.57079 to 1.57079 (-pi/2 to pi/2) radians.

The SET DECIMALS and SET PRECISION commands determine numeric accuracy.

Use DTOR( ) and RTOD( ) to convert degrees to radians and vice versa. A radian is approximately 57.3 degrees.

## RECOMMENDED USE:
ASIN( ) is used in engineering and scientific applications.

**Example**—An architectural engineering application expresses angles in radians. The sine of angle A is 0.50. By taking its ASIN( ), the program determines A in radians to be .52.

```
m_asin = ASIN(.50)
               .52
```

## SEE ALSO:
Functions ACOS( ), ATAN( ), ATN2( ), COS( ), SIN( ), and TAN( ).

# ASORT( )

## DIALECTS:
Clipper only.

## SYNTAX:
ASORT(<array>,[,<expN1>[,<expN2>]])

## RETURNS:
Nothing

## DEFINITION:
Sorts an array in ascending order. All elements must be the same data type.

<array> is the array name. <expN1> is the element at which to begin sorting. <expN2> is the number of elements to sort.

## DEFAULT:
If you do not specify <expN1>, ASORT( ) begins with element 1. If you do not specify <expN2>, it sorts from <expN1> through the end of the array.

## RECOMMENDED USE:
Use ASORT( ) to present arrays in sorted order. This is useful when displaying lists, menu items, or reports.

**Example**—A file maintenance program displays sorted directory lists. The program first uses ADIR( ) to load directory information into array MDIR. ASORT( ) then sorts MDIR.

```
DECLARE mdir[ADIR("*.DBF")]
ADIR("*.DBF",mdir)
ASORT(mdir)
```

This sorts the entire MDIR array.

To sort MDIR from element 10 on, enter:

```
ASORT(mdir,10)
```

To sort from element 10 through element 14, enter

```
ASORT(mdir,10,5)
```

The sort includes the first element specified.

ASORT( ) is in EXTEND.LIB on the system disk.

## SEE ALSO:

Commands DECLARE and FOR...NEXT; functions ACHOICE( ), ACOPY( ), ADEL( ), AFILL( ), AINS( ), and ASCAN( ).

# AT( )

## DIALECTS:
Clipper, dBASE III PLUS, dBASE IV, dBXL, FoxBASE+, and Quicksilver.

## SYNTAX:
AT(<expC1>,<expC2>)

## RETURNS:
Numeric

## DEFINITION:
Searches for an occurrence of one character string within another and returns the position at which it starts. If <expC2> does not contain <expC1>, AT( ) returns 0.

<expC1> is called a *substring* of <expC2>.

## RECOMMENDED USE:
AT( ) searches for substrings.

**Example 1**—A bookkeeper searches a payroll file for information on employee Paula Weiss. He LOCATEs the record, then executes AT( ) to find the word "commission" in field PAYTYPE.

The bookkeeper specifies "commission" as AT's first parameter and the field name as the second:

```
. USE sales
. LOCATE FOR lname = "Weiss"
. ? AT("commission",PAYTYPE)
7
```

The word "commission" begins at the seventh position in the PAYTYPE field. Displaying the entire field shows that Paula Weiss also earns a salary.

```
. ? PAYTYPE
Earns commissions, plus salary
```

In more complex applications, other functions can use information provided by AT( ). Programmers commonly use it in applications requiring substring replacement via the STUFF function.

**Example 2**—A reporting program lets users define printer attributes within blocks of text. Using predefined delimiters, the user can specify where boldface blocks begin and end. To begin boldface, the user inserts a left arrow (<). To end it, he or she inserts a right arrow (>). The user may turn boldface on and off only once in a line.

The memory variables BOLDON and BOLDOFF contain printer control codes. FRM1 contains the first line of a report. (You could increment FRM<n> using macro substitution (&) within a DO WHILE loop to pass an entire report, a line at a time).

First, the AT( ) function searches FRM1 for a left delimiter (<). If it finds one (AT( ) greater than 0), STUFF inserts BOLDON at the AT( ) position and stores the resulting string in ILINE ("intermediate line").

The next line searches ILINE for a right delimiter (>). If it finds one, STUFF inserts BOLDOFF at the AT( ) position and stores the resulting string in PLINE ("print line").

If AT( ) does not find either delimiter, FRM1 is simply stored in PLINE and printed.

```
boldon =  CHR(27)+CHR(69)      && Epson LX/FX setup codes.
boldoff = CHR(27)+CHR(70)
frml = "This year's sales were <more than 25% higher> than last year's."

iline=IIF(AT("<",frml)>0,STUFF(frml,AT("<",frml),1,[&boldon]),frml)
pline=IIF(AT(">",iline)>0,STUFF(iline,AT(">",iline),1,[&boldoff]),iline)
SET PRINT on
? pline
?
SET PRINT off
```

When run, this program produces the following output:

This year's sales were **more than 25% higher** than last year's.

## SEE ALSO:

Functions IIF( ) and STUFF( ).

# ATAN( )

## DIALECTS:

dBASE IV only.

## SYNTAX:

ATAN(<expN>)

## RETURNS:

Floating point

## DEFINITION:

Computes the arctangent (inverse tangent) of <expN>, where <expN> is a floating point number.

ATAN( ) returns a floating point number (an angle in radians) in the range -1.57079 to 1.57079 (-pi/2 to pi/2) radians.

The SET DECIMALS and SET PRECISION commands determine the numeric accuracy displayed.

Use DTOR( ) and RTOD( ) to convert degrees to radians and vice versa. A radian is approximately 57.3 degrees.

## RECOMMENDED USE:

ATAN( ) is a trigonometric function used in engineering and scientific applications.

**Example**—An aircraft design program expresses angles in radians. The tangent of angle A is 2.5722. By taking its ATAN( ), the program determines A in radians to be 1.2000.

```
m_atan = ATAN(2.5722)
              1.2000
```

## SEE ALSO:

Functions ACOS( ), ASIN( ), ATN2( ), COS( ), SIN( ), and TAN( ).

# ATN2( )

## DIALECTS:

dBASE IV only.

## SYNTAX:

ATN2(<expN1>,<expN2>)

## RETURNS:

Floating point

## DEFINITION:

Computes the arctangent value from a known cosine and sine. ATN2( ) is equivalent to ATAN(sine/cosine).

ATN2( ) returns a floating point number in radians, in the range -3.14159 to +3.14159.

<expN1> is the cosine and <expN2> is the sine of an angle.

The SET DECIMALS command determines numeric accuracy displayed.

Use DTOR( ) and RTOD( ) to convert degrees to radians and vice versa. A radian is approximately 57.3 degrees.

## RECOMMENDED USE:

ATN2( ) is used in engineering and scientific applications. Use it instead of ATAN( ) to prevent divide by zero errors when using SIN( ) and COS( ) values directly.

**Example**—A scientist plotting a spacecraft's trajectory uses the arctangent in several computations. As the scientist plots a return trip, a trigonometric function causes an execution error:

```
SET DECIMALS TO 4
x = 2
y = PI()
? ATAN(COS(x)/SIN(y))
Execution error on ATAN()
```

Realizing that SIN(y) was 0, causing a "divide by zero" condition, the scientist replaces ATAN( ) with ATN2( ).

```
? ATN2(COS(x),SIN(y))
-1.5708
```

## SEE ALSO:

Functions ACOS( ), ASIN( ), ATAN( ), COS( ), SIN( ), and TAN( ).

# BAR( )

## DIALECTS:
dBASE IV only.

## SYNTAX:
BAR( )

## RETURNS:
Numeric

## DEFINITION:
Returns the number of the BAR or line selected from an active BAR or POPUP menu.

BAR( ) returns 0 if no menu is active.

## RECOMMENDED USE:
Use BAR( ) to get the user's menu selection. You can then execute a CASE or use the result in another function.

**Example**—A sales management program uses popup bar menus. When the user selects an item, the program uses the BAR( ) number to decide which CASE to execute. Each CASE executes a subroutine matching the menu selection.

```
DEFINE POPUP acct FROM 01,01 TO 15,50
DEFINE BAR 1 OF acct PROMPT "Browse Accounts"
DEFINE BAR 2 OF acct PROMPT "Edit Accounts"
DEFINE BAR 3 OF acct PROMPT "Delete Accounts"
ON SELECTION POPUP acct DO mcase    && Execute PROCEDURE mcase.
ACTIVATE POPUP acct

PROCEDURE mcase
mbar = BAR()                  && Store BAR() in a variable, instead
DO CASE                       &&   of using it in every CASE. This
  CASE mbar = 1               &&   improves execution speed since
    * <do browse program>     &&   it evaluates BAR() only once.
  CASE mbar = 2
    * <do edit program>
  CASE mbar = 3
    * <delete accounts program>
ENDCASE
```

This usage is comparable to the Clipper/FoxBASE+ @...PROMPT...MENU TO structure.

## LIMITS/WARNINGS:

BAR( ) is not valid from the dot prompt since no BAR or POPUP can be active.

## SEE ALSO:

Commands ACTIVATE POPUP, DEFINE BAR, and DEFINE POPUP; functions MENU( ), PAD( ), and PROMPT( ).

# BITSET( )

## DIALECTS:
dBXL and Quicksilver.

## SYNTAX:
BITSET(<expN1>,<expN2>)

## RETURNS:
Logical

## DEFINITION:
Determines whether the specified bit <expN2> in a number's (<expN1>) binary form is on. If so, BITSET( ) returns true.

BITSET( ) accepts a numeric argument and returns true (.T.) or false (.F.).

The binary form of a number consists of eight 0's and 1's (bits), where 0 means off and 1 means on.

<expN2> is a decimal integer between 0 and 7 inclusive. Bit 0 is the rightmost bit, bit 7 the leftmost.

## RECOMMENDED USE:
Use BITSET( ) to evaluate binary values returned by the IN( ) function when getting data from external devices (through a system port). Example devices are mouse interface cards, manufacturing control systems, or environmental monitors.

**Example**—Aaron Alarm Company installs alarms in warehouses. The company connects the alarms, through a system port, to PCs that monitor activity and bill customers accordingly. When an alarm sounds, a 2 (binary 00000010) is sent through input port 4. IN( ) reads the port. BITSET( ) checks the binary value and determines that bit 1 (second from the right) is on. After the alarm sounds and the log is updated, the OUT command clears the port.

```
DO WHILE .t.
  IF BITSET(IN(4),1)
    * ALARM SOUNDS
    DO alarmlog
    OUT 4,0
  ENDIF
ENDDO
```

## SEE ALSO:
Commands DOSINT and OUT; function IN( ).

# BOF( )

DIALECTS:
Clipper, dBASE III PLUS, dBASE IV, dBXL, FoxBASE+, and Quicksilver.

## SYNTAX:
BOF( )

## RETURNS:
Logical

## DEFINITION:
Returns logical .T. when the record pointer of the active database is at the beginning-of-file.

Beginning-of-file occurs when: 1) you try to move the pointer ahead of the first logical record in a file or 2) the file contains no records.

Even when BOF( ) is .T., you can access the first logical record in the file.

BOF( ) returns .F. when no database is in use. This can be misleading when debugging a program, since you might think that a database is open. To check, use DBF( ) to test the filename's length. If there is no open file, DBF( ) returns a null string (length 0).

```
IIF(LEN(DBF()) = 0,"NO FILE IN USE",DBF())
```

*Note:* Clipper's USED( ) function indicates whether a file is open. It returns true (.T.) if a file is in use.

## RECOMMENDED USE:
File handling routines that move through records in reverse order use BOF( ) to locate the lower boundary.

**Example**—A display program lets users move backward through records by pressing "B". The BOF( ) function monitors the lower boundary of the file.

```
* <Display, edit records, GET user response, F, B, or E>
DO CASE           && Begin CASE structure
  CASE maction = "B" .AND. .NOT. BOF()
    SKIP -1
  * <more cases>
```

## VARIATIONS:

**Clipper:** You can check an open file in another work area by using BOF( ) as the argument of the alias operator, as follows:

```
? <alias>->(BOF())
```

**dBASE IV:** You can check an open file in another work area by adding an alias name to BOF( ), in the form BOF([<expC>]).

**FoxBASE+:** You can check an open file in another work area by adding a numeric parameter to BOF( ), in the form BOF([<expN>]).

<expN> is the work area number.

## SEE ALSO:

Function EOF( ).

# CALL( )

## DIALECTS:

dBASE IV only.

## SYNTAX:

CALL("<module name>",<exp1>[,<exp2>,<exp3>,<exp4>,<exp5>,
<exp6>,<exp7>])

**Note:** The quotation marks around the module name are literals.

## RETURNS:

<exp1>'s type determines the return value's type.

## DEFINITION:

Executes a binary routine (extension.bin, and returns the first parameter's value. <module name> is a .bin routine already loaded into dBASE IV's bin table.

The CALL( ) function lets you execute BIN routines in places where you cannot use the CALL command. Typical examples are within the report generator, during data entry, and in commands such as SET FILTER and COUNT FOR.

You must first LOAD the routines into dBASE IV's BIN table.

## OPTIONS:

You may pass the routine up to seven parameters (<exp1>-<exp7>). One is mandatory for a return value. The BIN routine may modify the parameters.

## RECOMMENDED USE:

CALL( ) lets you use a BIN routine almost like a user defined function. A single line can replace a short program in dBASE III PLUS.

**Example 1**—A routine PROPER.BIN capitalizes the first letter of each word in field LNAME. In dBASE III PLUS, you must use the CALL command in a short program. The CALL( ) function does the same operation in one line.

```
* dBASE III PLUS example

GO TOP
```

```
DO WHILE .NOT. EOF()
  mlname=lname
  CALL proper WITH mlname
  REPLACE lname WITH mlname
  SKIP 1
ENDDO

* dBASE IV example

REPLACE ALL lname WITH CALL("proper",lname)
```

To REPLACE field LNAME2 while not altering LNAME, put parentheses around LNAME, thereby passing the *value* of the field instead of the field itself:

```
REPLACE ALL lname2 WITH CALL("proper",(lname))
```

## LIMITS/WARNINGS:

If you do not want the first parameter passed to be changed, enclose it in parentheses. This passes it by *value*, creating a temporary area for the return value as well.

dBASE IV can evaluate only seven expressions at one time. As the module's name is treated as an expression, CALL( ) can pass it only six literal expressions. Seven parameters (besides the name) may be passed, but at least one must be a field or memory variable.

## SEE ALSO:

Commands LOAD and CALL.

# CDOW( )

## DIALECTS:

Clipper, dBASE III PLUS, dBASE IV, dBXL, FoxBASE+, and Quicksilver.

## SYNTAX:

CDOW(<expD>)

## RETURNS:

Character string.

## DEFINITION:

Accepts the name of the day of the week (e.g., "Monday"). Accepts any date expression (memory variable, field, or function that returns a date). Sorry, despite the name, it does not display stock market averages.

## RECOMMENDED USE:

Use CDOW( ) to include days of the week in letters and reports.

**Example**—An accounting program produces a balance sheet with the day of the week printed at the top. CDOW( ) converts the date memory variable RDATE to the correct day.

```
rdate=CTOD('04/05/88')  && CTOD() converts characters to dates.
? "Report Day: " + CDOW(rdate)
* <report statements>
```

This part of the report would print as follows:

```
Report Day: Tuesday
```

In dBASE IV, you can replace CTOD( ) with curly braces as follows:

```
rdate={04/05/88}
```

## SEE ALSO:

Functions DAY( ) and DOW( ).

# CEIL( )

## DIALECTS:
dBXL and Quicksilver.

## SYNTAX:
CEIL(<expN>)

CEILING(<expN>) - dBASE IV only

## RETURNS:
Number

## DEFINITION:
Returns the smallest integer greater than or equal to its argument.

## RECOMMENDED USE:
CEIL( ) converts a number to the next higher integer. For example, it converts 1.01 to 2.00 as shown:

```
? CEIL(1.01)
2.00
```

CEIL( ) converts a negative number by truncating the fractional part:

```
? CEIL(-2.05)
-2.00
```

**Example**—A parking lot concession charges $3.00 for the first hour and $2 for each additional hour, or portion thereof. A program uses CEIL( ) to compute charges. A customer parks for 3.25 hours. He pays $3.00 for the first hour, plus $6.00 for the additional 2.25 hours.

```
parkhours = 3.25
IF parkhours > 1
  pay = 3.00 + (CEIL(parkhours-1) * 2.00)
ELSE
  pay = 3.00
ENDIF
? "Please pay: $" + STR(pay,5,2)
```

## SEE ALSO:
Functions FLOOR( ), INT( ), and ROUND( ).

# CENTER( )

## DIALECTS:
dBXL and Quicksilver.

## SYNTAX:
CENTER(<expC>,<expN>)

## RETURNS:
Character string.

## DEFINITION:
Centers <expC> within a line <expN> characters long by adding spaces at the beginning and end.

If the expression is longer than a line, CENTER( ) truncates it.

## RECOMMENDED USE:
CENTER( ) eliminates the need to count spaces to center text.

**Example**—The CENTER( ) function simplifies report formatting. A company annual report is printed with centered headings.

CENTER( ) centers "SenTech Corp. 1988 Annual Report" on a 65-character line:

```
@ ROW(),0 SAY CENTER("SenTech Corp. 1988 Annual Report",65)
@ ROW(),05 SAY "It was the best of times, it was the worst of times"
```

The heading prints as follows:

```
              SenTech Corp. 1988 Annual Report
     It was the best of times, it was the worst of times
```

## VARIATIONS:
**Clipper, dBASE IV:** You can simulate CENTER( ) with a brief user defined function that pads a string with spaces.

*Note:* The function is unnecessary with dBASE IV's @...SAY command, since it has PICTUREs, FUNCTIONs, and templates for aligning and centering text. See @...SAY for details.

The calling syntax is the same as the dBXL/Quicksilver CENTER( ). The function accepts two parameters, the string to center (STNG) and the length in which to center it (MLEN). Subtracting the length of STNG from MLEN and dividing by two produces the starting position of the centered string. STUFF( ) then inserts STNG into a blank string with length MLEN at the computed starting position.

If the string is too long, SUBSTR( ) truncates it. This differs slightly from the the dBXL/Quicksilver implementation which drops characters at the beginning and end. However, both implementations produce equally useless results if the input is invalid.

```
FUNCTION center
* Syntax: CENTER(<expC>,<expN>)
* Return <expC> centered in a line with a length <expN>.
PARAMETERS stng,mlen
*
RETURN SUBSTR(STUFF(SPACE(mlen),(mlen-(LEN(stng)))/2,len(stng),stng),1,mlen)
```

*Note:* STUFF( ) is in EXTEND.LIB on the Clipper system disk.

**dBASE III PLUS:** The lack of user defined functions means that you must center text by manipulating print coordinates. To center a string MSTRING on an 80-character line, subtract its length from the line length and divide by 2. Use the quotient as the column coordinate:

```
@ ROW(),(80-LEN(MSTRING))/2 SAY mstring
```

**FoxBASE+:** Because you cannot put a user defined function in an @...SAY statement, you must modify CENTER( ) to include the @...SAY.

```
* FCENTER.PRG
* Syntax: CENTER(<expN1>,<expN2>,<expC>,<expN3>). Prints <expC> centered
* in a line with length <expN3>, starting at coordinates <expN1,expN1>.
PARAMETERS c1,c2,stng,mlen
*
@ c1,c2 SAY ;
SUBSTR(STUFF(SPACE(mlen),(mlen-(LEN(stng)))/2,len(stng),stng),1,mlen)
RETURN ""
```

The following command centers text within 70 columns at line 5:

```
? FCENTER(5,0,"SenTech Corp. 1988 Annual Report",70)
```

## SEE ALSO:

Command @...SAY.

# CHANGE( )

## DIALECTS:
dBASE IV only.

## SYNTAX:
CHANGE( )

## RETURNS:
Logical

## DEFINITION:
Checks the current record to determine whether it has been changed since it was opened.

CHANGE( ) returns true (.T.) if the record has changed.

In preparing a multiuser application, you must first issue the CONVERT command to add a hidden field _DBASELOCK to the database structures. dBASE IV uses it to hold information about record and file locks. CHANGE( ) checks the first two bytes of _DBASELOCK to determine whether a record was CHANGEd. You can use the LKSYS( ) function to determine who has applied a lock, and the date and time it was applied.

## RECOMMENDED USE:
Use CHANGE( ) in multiuser applications that employ explicit locks. When you copy a record into memory variables for editing or viewing, another user may change the record before you copy the variables back. Since your changes are based on an old image of the record, they are probably invalid.

You can solve this problem by locking the record with RLOCK( ); however, it makes your record unavailable during editing. Alternatively, you can copy the record into memory variables and leave it unlocked during editing. In this way, the database file remains current. Before you copy the memory variables back into the record, use CHANGE( ) to determine whether it has changed. If it has, you can view the changes and determine whether yours are valid.

**Example**—An inventory program in an automobile parts store shows one muffler remaining in stock. The display is static, that is, it doesn't update automatically to reflect changes in quantity. When the clerk is ready to order, the program uses CHANGE( ) to check whether the record has changed. If the record changes, the program LOOPs, rereads the record, and redisplays it. If it hasn't changed, the program tries to lock it with RLOCK( ). If the lock fails, the program terminates. If the lock succeeds, the program checks QUANTITY to see if it can fill the order (this example assumes the quantity ordered is always 1). If the QUANTITY is sufficient, the program fills the order and subtracts 1 from QUANTITY. This process prevents two clerks from selling the same muffler at the same time.

```
Structure for database: D:\DBASE\PARTS.DBF
Number of data records:        2
Date of last update   : 08/14/88
Field  Field Name  Type         Width    Dec     Index
    1  PARTNO      Character        4                Y
    2  DESCRIP     Character       20                N
    3  QUANTITY    Numeric          3                N
** Total **                        28
```

(_DBASELOCK is hidden).

```
CLEAR
SET TALK OFF
SET REPROCESS TO 100            && Retry RLOCK() 100 times if necessary.
USE parts ORDER partdex
DO WHILE .t.
  CLEAR
  mpartno = SPACE(4)
  @ 10,10 SAY   "Part number:   " GET mpartno PICTURE "!!!!"
  READ
  SEEK mpartno
  mdescrip = descrip
  mqty = quantity
  @ 12,10 SAY "Description:   " + mdescrip
  @ 14,10 SAY "Quantity:      " + STR(mqty,3,0)
  morder = .f.
  @ 16,10 SAY "Do you want to order? " GET morder PICTURE "Y"
  READ
  IF .NOT. morder
    RETURN
  ENDIF
  IF CHANGE()        && If record has changed, display message and LOOP.
    WAIT "Item information has changed. Press a key to reenter."
    LOOP
  ENDIF
  IF .NOT. RLOCK()
     WAIT "Unable to lock record. Press a key to cancel this attempt. "
  ELSE
    IF quantity > 0
      REPLACE quantity WITH quantity - 1
```

```
      WAIT "Transaction complete. Press a key to continue."
      * <DO subroutines to print order, invoices, etc.>.
    ELSE
      WAIT "Insufficient quantity for order. Press a key to continue"
    ENDIF
  ENDIF
ENDDO
```

## LIMITS/WARNINGS:

You cannot view _DBASELOCK directly. Instead, you must use CHANGE( ) and LKSYS( ) to return its value.

## SEE ALSO:

Functions CHANGE( ), LKSYS( ), LOCK( ), and RLOCK( ).

# CHR( )

## DIALECTS:
Clipper, dBASE III PLUS, dBASE IV, dBXL, FoxBASE+, and Quicksilver.

## SYNTAX:
CHR(<expN>)

## RETURNS:
Character

## DEFINITION:
Converts a number to a character in the IBM Extended Character Set. <expN> is an integer between 1 and 255, inclusive.

CHR( ) is the inverse of ASC( ).

## RECOMMENDED USE:
CHR( ) lets you display and print non-keyboard characters. Examples of non-keyboard characters include:

```
* Ring the system bell.
? CHR(7)

* Eject a page. This has the same effect as EJECT.
SET PRINT on
? CHR(12)
```

Many printers use CHR( ) combinations to set attributes. For example, to put an Epson FX-85 in the elite mode, you would issue the commands:

```
SET PRINT on
? CHR(27) + CHR(77)
```

You can also use CHR( ) to simply display non-keyboard ASCII characters above decimal 127. They include foreign and graphics characters.

## LIMITS/WARNINGS:
You cannot send a null character CHR(0) to any device; however, some printers can interpret CHR(128) as CHR(0) by clearing bit 7.

## VARIATIONS:

CHR(0) has a length of 1 in Clipper and dBASE IV. It has a length of 0 in dBASE III PLUS, dBXL, FoxBASE+, and Quicksilver.

## SEE ALSO:

Function ASC( ).

# CMONTH( )

## DIALECTS:

Clipper, dBASE III PLUS, dBASE IV, dBXL, FoxBASE+, and Quicksilver.

## SYNTAX:

CMONTH(<expD>)

## RETURNS:

Character string

## DEFINITION:

Accepts a date expression (memory variable, field, or function that returns a date) and returns the name of the month (e.g., "July").

For example, to return the name of the current month, use the system date function DATE( ) as a parameter:

```
? CMONTH(DATE())
November
```

## RECOMMENDED USE:

Use CMONTH( ) to include the name of the month in letters and reports.

**Example**—A correspondence application prints business letters that require the date written out. CMONTH( ) prints the month, DAY( ) prints the day of the month. YEAR( ) prints the year. The STR( ) function converts the numeric DAY and YEAR values to character strings for concatenation with the CMONTH( ) string. Because the STR( ) function must accommodate a 2-digit number, a single-digit day of the month leaves a leading blank when converted to a string. LTRIM( ) strips the blank.

```
rd=CTOD('05/14/88')    && CTOD() converts characters to dates.
* rd = {05/14/88}      && dBASE IV syntax with date delimiters.
?
? CMONTH(rd) + " " + LTRIM(STR(DAY(rd),2,0)) + ", " + STR(YEAR(rd),4,0)
?
* <more letter>
```

This code fragment prints the date for 05/14/88 as:

```
May 14, 1988
```

## SEE ALSO:

Functions CDOW( ), CTOD( ), DATE( ), DOW( ), MONTH( ), and YEAR( ).

# COL( )

## DIALECTS:

Clipper, dBASE III PLUS, dBASE IV, dBXL, FoxBASE+, and Quicksilver.

## SYNTAX:

COL( )

## RETURNS:

Numeric

## DEFINITION:

Returns the column coordinate of the cursor's position. Coordinates range from 0 to 79 (left to right) on a standard screen.

For example, you can determine the cursor's position after displaying a string (in a program) as follows:

```
*
? "COL() returns the cursor's position"
?? COL()
35
```

## RECOMMENDED USE:

COL( ) lets you place screen output relative to the current cursor position. This is useful for designing screens with multiple @...SAY...GETs on a single line.

**Example**—A screen report generator displays several columns of data. It uses the COL( ) function to put space between them.

```
CLEAR
@ 5,COL() SAY "SSN: " GET ssn
@ 5,COL()+2 SAY "Employer: " GET employer
@ 5,COL()+2 SAY "No. of Dependents: " GET depends PICTURE "#"
```

This screen would appear as follows:

```
SSN:           Employer:                              No. of Dependents:
```

## SEE ALSO:

Functions FCOL( ), FROW( ), PCOL( ), PROW( ), and ROW( ).

# COMPLETED( )

## DIALECTS:
dBASE IV only.

## SYNTAX:
COMPLETED( )

## RETURNS:
Logical

## DEFINITION:
Indicates whether a transaction ended.

After you issue BEGIN TRANSACTION, COMPLETED( ) returns false (.F.) until you issue END TRANSACTION.

## DEFAULT:
False

## RECOMMENDED USE:
Use COMPLETED( ) to detect the end of a successful transaction.

**Example**—An accounting system updates a main ledger file and an invoice file. When the transaction is completed, COMPLETED( ) returns true.

```
ON error DO recvy
BEGIN TRANSACTION
  USE transact INDEX transdex
  REPLACE ALL commis WITH sales - (draw*pct)
END TRANSACTION
IF COMPLETED()
  @ 24,03 SAY "Transaction successfully completed"
ELSE
  @ 24,03 SAY "Transaction unsuccessful"
  ROLLBACK
ENDIF
```

## SEE ALSO:
Commands BEGIN TRANSACTION, END TRANSACTION, RESET, and ROLLBACK; functions ISMARKED( ) and ROLLBACK( ).

# COS( )

## DIALECTS:
dBASE IV only.

## SYNTAX:
COS(<expN>)

## RETURNS:
Floating point

## DEFINITION:
Computes the cosine of angle <expN> in radians.

The SET DECIMALS and SET PRECISION commands determine numeric accuracy.

Use DTOR( ) and RTOD( ) to convert degrees to radians and vice versa. A radian is approximately 57.3 degrees.

## RECOMMENDED USE:
COS( ) is a trigonometric function used in engineering and scientific applications.

**Example**—An architectural application expresses angles in radians. For example, if angle A is .3750 radians, its COS( ) is 0.9305.

```
mcos = COS(.3750)
 .9305
```

## SEE ALSO:
Functions ACOS( ), ASIN( ), ATAN( ), ATN2( ), SIN( ), and TAN( ).

# CTOD( )

## DIALECTS:
Clipper, dBASE III PLUS, dBASE IV, dBXL, FoxBASE+, and Quicksilver.

## SYNTAX:
CTOD(<expC>)

## RETURNS:
Date

## DEFINITION:
Converts a character expression to a date expression. <expC> is a literal character string or variable, by default in the form MM/DD/YY. (You can change forms with the SET DATE and SET CENTURY commands). CTOD( ) converts a blank character string into a blank date variable.

CTOD( ) is the inverse of DTOC( ) which converts date expressions to character.

## RECOMMENDED USE:
Clipper, dBASE III PLUS, dBXL, FoxBASE+, and Quicksilver do not let you create a date type string or variable by simply typing one. They derive all dates from date functions or date fields. dBASE IV, on the other hand, lets you use curly braces to indicate date type strings.

CTOD( ) creates date expressions from character string input. An example is

```
STORE CTOD("09/10/88") TO nextraise
```

Without CTOD( ), dBASE treats "09/10/88" as a character string.

**Example**—A furniture store invoicing program requires the user to enter both invoice and ship dates. The program then stores the dates in date fields in the database. To GET the invoice and ship dates in date type variables (to allow validation), initialize them with the CTOD( ) function.

```
* INV_GET.PRG
minv_date = CTOD("01/12/87")
mshp_date = CTOD("01/19/87")
* <initialize more variables>
@ 03,01 SAY "Enter invoice date: " GET minv_date
@ 04,01 SAY "Enter ship date: " GET mshp_date
```

```
* <more gets>
READ
```

Note that MSHP_DATE is initialized to be seven days later than MINV_DATE. This is the default time between invoicing and shipping.

## VARIATIONS:

**dBASE IV:** Curly braces act as date delimiters, letting you create date type variables and strings without CTOD( ). For example,

```
mshp_date = CTOD("01/19/87")
```

becomes

```
mshp_date = {01/19/87}
```

## SEE ALSO:

Commands SET DATE and SET CENTURY; functions DTOC( ) and DTOS( ).

# CURDIR( )

## DIALECTS:

Clipper only.

## SYNTAX:

CURDIR([<expC>])

## RETURNS:

Character

## DEFINITION:

Returns the name of the current DOS directory on a specified disk drive. CURDIR( ) returns a null string if the directory is the root.

CURDIR( ) also returns a null string if you specify an invalid drive or a drive that is not ready.

<expC> is the drive's letter. If you do not specify it, CURDIR( ) defaults to the current drive. As CURDIR( ) only looks at the first character of <expC>, you can put a colon or other text after the drive letter.

CURDIR( ) ignores the current DEFAULT and PATH settings.

## RECOMMENDED USE:

Use CURDIR( ) to verify the setup of disk drives and paths in application installation programs.

**Example**—A programmer develops financial programs for use in his company. He includes an installation procedure to verify that the user has created the necessary work directory.

```
*
IF .NOT. CURDIR() = "\STATS"      && Check the current directory.
   ?
   ? "Invalid directory. "
   ? "You must first make a directory (MD) on D: called \STATS"
   QUIT
ENDIF
```

The program also APPENDs data from network drives I and H. It first checks the names of the current directories on those drives.

```
? "Current directory on I: is " + CURDIR("I")
* Note that CURDIR() ignores characters after the drive letter.
? "Current directory on H: is " + CURDIR("H:")
 \S87
\M\DEPT\STATS
```

## SEE ALSO:

Commands SET DEFAULT and SET PATH.

# CURWIN( )

## DIALECTS:
Quicksilver only.

## SYNTAX:
CURWIN( )

## RETURNS:
Numeric

## DEFINITION:
Returns a value from 0 to 99 representing the currently selected window area.

To make windowing functions and commands consistent (all starting with W), Quicksilver version 1.1 replaced CURWIN( ) with WSELECT( ).

## SEE ALSO:
Commands WSELECT, WSET WINDOW, and WUSE; function WSELECT( ).

# DATE( )

## DIALECTS:
Clipper, dBASE III PLUS, dBASE IV, dBXL, FoxBASE+, and Quicksilver.

## SYNTAX:
DATE( )

## RETURNS:
Date

## DEFINITION:
Returns the system date. Unless you change formats with the SET CENTURY or SET DATE commands, DATE( ) uses the MM/DD/YY format.

The operating system controls the system date. No dBASE command can change it. You can change it from the MS-DOS prompt by typing DATE <enter>.

## RECOMMENDED USE:
In data entry, date input fields often default to the system date (i.e., "today's date"). This keeps operators from having to constantly reenter the same value. To get the default, initialize fields with the system date:

```
mdate = DATE()
@ 10,10 SAY "Enter today's date, or <enter> to accept: " GET mdate
```

Use DATE( ) to log transactions or updates to a database. For example, when a program generates invoices, REPLACE DATE( ) into a field reserved for the transaction date.

## LIMITS/WARNINGS:
Note that the SET DATE command changes only how the date is displayed. It does not change the system date itself.

## SEE ALSO:
Commands SET CENTURY and SET DATE; function TIME( ).

# DAY( )

## DIALECTS:
Clipper, dBASE III PLUS, dBASE IV, dBXL, FoxBASE+, and Quicksilver.

## SYNTAX:
DAY(<expD>)

## RETURNS:
Numeric

## DEFINITION:
Accepts a date expression and returns the day of the month as a number.

<expD> can be a memory variable, a field, or a function that returns a date.

For example, to return the DAY( ) of January 20, 1988, enter

```
. ? DAY(CTOD("01/20/88")
20
```

CTOD( ) converts "01/20/88" from character to date type.

## RECOMMENDED USE:
Use DAY( ) to display dates such as "September 15, 1987."

For a detailed example, see function CMONTH( ). Because DAY( ) returns a numeric value, it is also useful for computing days elapsed.

## SPECIAL NOTE:
dBASE IV lets you create a date literal without the CTOD( ) function. To do this, use braces around a date string, as follows:

```
{01/20/88}
```

To return the DAY( ) of January 20, 1988, enter

```
? DAY({01/20/88})
```

## SEE ALSO:
Functions CDOW( ), CMONTH( ), CTOD( ), DATE( ), DOW( ), and DTOC( ).

# DBEDIT( )

## DIALECTS:

Clipper only.

## SYNTAX:

DBEDIT([<expN1>[,<expN2>[,<expN3>[,<expN4>]]]]
[<array1>][,<expC>][,<array2>][,<array3>]
[,<array4>][,<array5>][,<array6>][,<array7>])

## RETURNS:

Nothing

## DEFINITION:

Allows full-screen, tabular editing of database records.

DBEDIT( ) supports all Clipper cursor movement keys. It accepts parameters for the size and position of the editing window. A parameter specifies a user defined function that controls the effects of keystrokes and cursor movements. A series of arrays holds PICTURE strings, column headings, line drawing characters, and column footers. Elements in the arrays correspond by number.

## OPTIONS:

### <expN1>...<expN4>

<expN1> is the top row of the editing window, <expN2> the leftmost column, <expN3> the bottom row, and <expN4> the rightmost column. The window must be at least three columns wide and four rows high. Fields wider than it are truncated.

### <array1>

An array of character elements containing field names or expressions. It may contain field names from multiple files. Specify ones from files in other work areas in the form "alias->field_name". All specified fields must exist (no error checking occurs). Fields specified without an alias designator are assumed to be in the current work area. Omitting <array1> defaults to all fields in the current work area.

**<expC>**
A user defined function that controls the effects of keystrokes and cursor movements. Specify the name inside quotation marks.

DBEDIT( ) passes two parameters to the user defined function: MODE and COUNTER. The function examines MODE and the value of LASTKEY( ), then returns a value to DBEDIT( ) indicating the action to take.

COUNTER indicates DBEDIT( )'s position in the array.

The MODEs sent from DBEDIT( ) to the user defined function are:

0 — DBEDIT( ) is idle, no keystrokes pending.

1 — The user tried to move the cursor past the beginning of file.

2 — The user tried to move the cursor past the end of file.

3 — The database file is empty.

4 — Value passed by LASTKEY( ).

The user defined function <expC> returns these values to DBEDIT( ):

0 — Quit DBEDIT( ).

1 — Continue DBEDIT (normal return).

2 — Refresh the screen and continue DBEDIT( ).

Use KEYBOARD in the user defined function to return keystrokes to DBEDIT( ). For example, to advance the cursor after editing or adding a field, use KEYBOARD CHR(4). To move the cursor back a space, use KEYBOARD CHR(13). (CHR(4) is Ctrl-E, CHR(13) is Ctrl-S).

**<array2>**
An array containing picture strings for formatting columns. Picture strings are templates or functions (see the @ command for descriptions). You can also specify a character expression instead of the array, displaying all columns with the same picture.

**<array3>**
An array containing column headings.

**<array4>**
An array of character elements for drawing the lines that separate headings from the field display area. You can specify a character expression instead for use in all heading lines.

**<array5>**
An array of character elements for drawing the lines that separate columns. You can specify a character expression instead for use in all column separators.

**<array6>**
An array of character elements for drawing the lines that separate footings from the field display area. You can specify a character expression instead for use in all footing separators.

**<array7>**
An array of character elements containing column footings. You can specify a character expression instead for use in all column footings.

*Note:* You may omit any DBEDIT( ) option (opting for the default) by substituting a dummy variable with a null value ("").

If you omit all options, DBEDIT( ) defaults to all fields in the current work area.

## RECOMMENDED USE:

Use DBEDIT( ) in programs to provide a simple way to edit records in tabular form.

**Example 1**—A programmer chooses the simplest form of DBEDIT( ). With no parameters, it defaults to all fields in the current work area.

```
USE mail
DBEDIT()
```

**Example 2**—As a convenience, the programmer of a mailing list system lets users edit records in a full-screen mode. Because the data is not sensitive, validation is not a major concern.

In this example, the calling program USEs the mail database. The programmer stores the field names in the FNAME array. The programmer then uses DBEDIT( ) with a complete array list to specify the window coordinates, pictures, headers, separator characters, and footers. The user defined function KEYCTRL controls cursor movement, based on the MODE and COUNTER parameters passed by DBEDIT( ).

```
CLEAR
USE mail
DECLARE fname[5],fpict[5],fheader[5],hedsep[5],colsep[5],footsep[5],;
        footer[5]
fname[1] = "NAME"          && Fields from MAIL.DBF
fname[2] = "ADDRESS"
fname[3] = "CITY"
fname[4] = "STATE"
fname[5] = "AMOUNT"
*
fpict[1] = "@!"            && Get valid pictures and functions.
fpict[2] = "@A"
fpict[3] = "@A"
fpict[4] = "!!"
fpict[5] = "999,999,999.99"
*
fheader[1] = "Cust. Name"  && Establish column headers.
fheader[2] = "Cust. Address"
fheader[3] = "City"
fheader[4] = "ST"
fheader[5] = "Amt"
*
hedsep[1] = CHR(205)       && Horizontal double line character
hedsep[2] = CHR(205)       &&   to separate header from column.
hedsep[3] = CHR(205)
hedsep[4] = CHR(196)       && Change to horizontal single line.
hedsep[5] = CHR(196)

colsep[1] = CHR(179)        && Vertical single line to separate columns.
colsep[2] = CHR(179)
colsep[3] = CHR(179)
colsep[4] = CHR(179)
colsep[5] = CHR(179)
*
footsep[1] = CHR(196)      && Horizontal single line to separate
footsep[2] = CHR(196)      &&   column from footer.
footsep[3] = CHR(196)
footsep[4] = CHR(196)
footsep[5] = "="
*
footer[1] = "Cust.Name"    && Establish column footers.
footer[2] = "Cust.Address"
footer[3] = "City"
footer[4] = "ST"
footer[5] = "Amt"
*
DBEDIT(2,0,23,60,fname,"keyctrl",fpict,fheader,hedsep,colsep,footsep,footer)
CLEAR
```

```
QUIT

FUNCTION keyctrl
PARAMETERS mode,counter
PRIVATE mfield
mfield = fname[counter]     && STORE current field in a memory variable.
DO CASE
  CASE mode = 0
    * User is not changing data. Display message and current record number.
    @ 1,50 SAY "Not editing RECORD: " + LTRIM(STR(RECNO()))
    RETURN(1)
  CASE mode = 1
    @ 1,50 SAY "Beginning of File           "
    RETURN(1)
  CASE mode = 2
    @ 1,50 SAY "End of File                 "
    RETURN(1)
  CASE mode = 3
    @ 1,50 SAY "No data in file. Add data? "
    * <routine to add data>
    RETURN(2)
  CASE LASTKEY() = 13
    mrow = ROW()
    mcol = COL()
    @ 1,50 SAY "    EDITING RECORD: " + LTRIM(STR(RECNO()))
    @ mrow, mcol GET &mfield   && Edit current record.
    READ
    KEYBOARD CHR(4)            && Move cursor by KEYBOARDing a character.
    RETURN(1)                  && Continue DBEDIT().
  CASE LASTKEY() = 27
    RETURN(0)                  && User pressed ESC key, quit.
  OTHERWISE
    RETURN(1)
ENDCASE
```

## LIMITS/WARNINGS:

Be sure to specify valid parameters, as DBEDIT does not check them.

DBEDIT( ) is in EXTEND.LIB on the system disk.

## SEE ALSO:

Commands @ (pictures and templates), BROWSE, and DECLARE; function MEMOEDIT( ).

# DBF( )

## DIALECTS:
Clipper, dBASE III PLUS, dBASE IV, dBXL, FoxBASE+, and Quicksilver.

## SYNTAX:
DBF( )

## RETURNS:
Numeric

## DEFINITION:
Returns the full filename of an open database file in the current work area.

For example, to determine the name of the open database in work area 2, enter the following:

```
. SELECT 2
. ? DBF()
C:sales.dbf
```

## DEFAULT:
Returns a null string if no database file is open in the selected work area.

## RECOMMENDED USE:
Use DBF( ) in the interactive mode to recall the open database file name. You could also use LIST or DISPLAY STATUS to list all open files.

## VARIATIONS:
**Clipper:** DBF( ) is in EXTEND.LIB on the system disk.

*Note:* Clipper's DBF( ) returns the ALIAS of the active database file.

**dBASE IV:** An optional form returns the filename of an open database file in an unselected work area. The alias name is a parameter as in

```
DBF(<expC>)
```

**FoxBASE+:** An optional form returns the filename of an open database file in an unselected work area. The area number is a parameter as in

```
DBF(<expN>)
```

## SEE ALSO:
Command DISPLAY STATUS; functions FIELD( ), NDX( ), RECCOUNT( ), and RECSIZE( ).

# DBFILTER( )

## DIALECTS:
Clipper only.

## SYNTAX:
DBFILTER( )

## RETURNS:
Character

## DEFINITION:
Returns the active filter expression as a character string. Returns a null value if no filter is active.

## DEFAULT:
Returns the expression from the current work area unless you specify an alias in the form

```
ALIAS->(DBFILTER())
```

## RECOMMENDED USE:
Use DBFILTER( ) during debugging to test filter activity or to provide users with filter status information. Also use it to save and restore filter settings.

**Example 1**—A personnel system lets users choose "views" of the data based on filters selected from a menu. To remind users of the selected filter, the program displays DBFILTER( ) in a status line at the bottom of the screen.

```
SELECT 1
USE employs
SET FILTER TO grade = "1B" .AND. salary > 20000
SELECT 2
USE managers
SET FILTER TO grade = "2C"
* <program code>
*
@ 22,03 SAY "FILTER SETTINGS:"
@ 23,03 SAY "Managers.dbf: " + DBFILTER()           && Current work area
@ 24,03 SAY "Employs.dbf : " + employs->(DBFILTER()) && Other work area
```

The status line appears as follows:

```
FILTER SETTINGS:
Managers.dbf: grade="2C"
Employs.dbf : grade="1B".AND.salary>20000
```

**Example 2**—The personnel system from Example 1 lets users SET filters from a menu, then saves the setting in a database file for later restoration. The user need not redefine the filter at the start of the next session.

```
STORE ALIAS() to m_alias
STORE DBFILTER() to m_filter
SELECT 0                    && Select first unopened work area.
USE viewfile
REPLACE f_alias with m_alias, f_filter with m_filter
USE viewfile
m_alias = f_alias
m_filter = f_filter
SELECT 1

USE (m_alias)               && The parentheses around M_ALIAS act like a
SET FILTER TO &m_filter     &&   macro, passing the variable by reference.
```

## SEE ALSO:

Commands CREATE VIEW, SET FILTER, and SET VIEW; functions DBRELATION( ) and DBRSELECT( ).

# DBRELATION( )

## DIALECTS:
Clipper only.

## SYNTAX:
DBRELATION(<expN>)

## RETURNS:
Character

## DEFINITION:
Returns the relation expression from the current work area as a character string.

<expN> is the relative position of an expression in a list. (Because Clipper allows multiple relations from a file, you must specify which expression you want to return).

DBRELATION( ) returns a null string if no RELATION is SET.

## RECOMMENDED USE:
DBRELATION( ) lets you save and restore RELATION settings. Used with DBRSELECT( ) and ALIAS( ), it lets you store the current settings in memory variables, REPLACE them in a field, or SAVE them in a MEM file. Upon returning to a program, you can restore them.

**Example**—A sales tracking system lets users define complex relationships and filters from a menu. Users can save the settings in a database and restore them for the next session.

```
SELECT 1
USE sales INDEX sales
SELECT 2
USE inventry INDEX inventry
SELECT 3
USE history INDEX history
SELECT 1
SET RELATION TO code INTO inventry,;
             TO code INTO history

m_alias=ALIAS()           && Returns SALES.
```

```
m_relate=DBRELATION(2)      && Returns CODE.
m_select=ALIAS(DBRSELECT(2))       && Returns HISTORY.
```

To later restore the second relation, the program uses the sequence:

```
USE (m_alias)
SET RELATION TO &m_relate INTO &m_select
```

## SEE ALSO:

Functions DBFILTER( ) and DBRSELECT( ).

# DBRSELECT( )

## DIALECTS:

Clipper only.

## SYNTAX:

DBRSELECT(<expN>)

## RETURNS:

Numeric

## DEFINITION:

Returns the work area number of the target database (the INTO database) specified in a SET RELATION command. If no relation is active, DBRSELECT( ) returns 0.

<expN> is the relative position of a relation statement in a list. (Because Clipper allows multiple relations from a file, you must specify which one you want).

## RECOMMENDED USE:

Use DBRSELECT( ) with DBRELATION( ) and ALIAS( ) to store relation settings in memory variables. You can thus save them in a database or MEM file and restore them later.

**Example**—An inventory program saves complex relationships and filters in a database, simulating a dBASE III PLUS VUE file.

```
* Note: Using the same name for indexes and database files
* makes it easier to specify index names without having
* to derive them from the environment.
SELECT 1
USE invent INDEX invent
SELECT 2
USE source INDEX source
SELECT 3
USE sales INDEX sales
SELECT 1
SET RELATION TO code INTO source, TO code INTO sales
m_relate=DBRELATION(2)      && Returns CODE.
m_alias=ALIAS()             && Returns INVENT.
* DBRSELECT() returns the work area number of the target database
```

```
*   specified in RELATION 2. You can determine the database name from
*   the number by using it as the argument in the ALIAS() function.
*
m_area=DBRSELECT(2)          && Returns 3 (work area 3)
m_select=ALIAS(m_area)       && ALIAS(3) returns SALES.
```

To later restore the second relation, the program uses the statements:

```
* USE invent INDEX invent
USE (m_alias) INDEX (m_alias)
* SET RELATION TO code INTO sales
SET RELATION TO &m_relate INTO &m_select
```

## SEE ALSO:

Commands SET RELATION; functions DBFILTER( ) and DBRELATION( ).

# DELETED( )

## DIALECTS:
Clipper, dBASE III PLUS, dBASE IV, dBXL, FoxBASE+, and Quicksilver.

## SYNTAX:
DELETED( )

## RETURNS:
Logical

## DEFINITION:
Indicates whether the current record is marked for deletion. If so, DELETED( ) returns true (.T.).

DELETED( ) returns false (.F.) if the record is not deleted or if no database is active.

## RECOMMENDED USE:
Use DELETED( ) in file maintenance programs that DELETE and RECALL records.

**Example**—A roofing company uses a program to track work assignments. Each assignment has its own record. If the customer cancels the work order, the operator DELETEs the record.

For auditing purposes, all work orders stay in the database. When printing reports at the end of the month, the program includes only records that are NOT deleted.

```
SUM subtotal FOR .NOT. DELETED() TO sub1
```

Note that you can hide DELETED( ) records with the SET DELETED ON command.

At the end of each month before PACKing the work assignment file, the system supervisor copies all deleted records to an archive. She issues the commands:

```
. COPY TO cancels FOR DELETED()
10 records copied
. PACK
    88 records
```

## VARIATIONS:

**Clipper:** You can check for a DELETED( ) record in an unselected work area by specifying the DELETED( ) expression as the argument of the alias operator, as follows:

```
? <alias>->(DELETED())
```

**dBASE IV:** You can check for a DELETED( ) record in an unselected work area by specifying the alias name as an argument of the DELETED( ) function, as in:

```
? DELETED(<expC>)
```

**FoxBASE+:** An optional form applies to an unselected work area. The area number is a parameter as in:

```
? DELETED(<expN>)
```

## SEE ALSO:

Commands DELETE, PACK, RECALL, SET DELETED, and ZAP.

# DESCEND

## DIALECTS:
Clipper, dBXL, and Quicksilver.

## SYNTAX:
DESCEND *(Clipper)*
DESCEND(<expC>) *(dBXL/Quicksilver)*

## RETURNS:
Character

## DEFINITION:
Subtracts the ASCII value of each character in <expC> from 255, the highest ASCII value. This lets you create indexes in descending order.

## RECOMMENDED USE:
Use DESCEND( ) to create indexes in descending alphabetical order, reverse chronological order, or reverse numeric order.

To use DESCEND( ) on numeric or date fields, first convert them to character strings using the DTOC( ) and STR( ) functions.

**Example**—A magazine subscription system produces reports that list subscribers by expiration date and by last name. The program uses DESCEND( ) to index the file appropriately (earliest expiration date first).

Note that the DTOS( ) function converts a date variable to a character variable in the YYYYMMDD format.

```
USE sublist
. LIST
Record#  SUBSCRIBER                  MAGSLEFT EXPIRES
      1  Wiegands                          25 04/10/88
      2  Davidson                           9 04/10/88
      3  Girard                            10 10/10/89

. INDEX ON DESCEND(DTOS(expires)) TO exp_dex
. LIST
Record#  SUBSCRIBER                  MAGSLEFT EXPIRES
      3  Girard                            10 10/10/89
```

```
      1  Wiegands                    25 04/10/88
      2  Davidson                     9 04/10/88

. INDEX ON DESCEND(subscriber) TO sub_dex
. LIST
Record#  SUBSCRIBER            MAGSLEFT EXPIRES
      1  Wiegands                    25 04/10/88
      3  Girard                      10 10/10/89
      2  Davidson                     9 04/10/88
```

To SEEK a value indexed with DESCEND( ), use it in the expression as in the following example:

```
SEEK DESCEND(DTOS(expires))
```

## VARIATIONS:

**Clipper:** DESCEND( ) does not require an expression of character type. It returns the data type of its argument. For example, to INDEX on a date field in descending order, use it as follows:

```
INDEX ON DESCEND(date_fld) TO dat_fld
```

To SEEK a date indexed in descending order, issue the command

```
SEEK DESCEND(date_fld)
```

**dBASE III PLUS, dBASE IV, and FoxBASE+:** You can create reverse numeric indexes by indexing on the negated key field as in:

```
INDEX ON -scount TO countdex
```

## SEE ALSO:

Commands INDEX; functions ASC( ), DTOS( ), and STR( ).

# DIFFERENCE( )

## DIALECTS:
dBASE IV only.

## SYNTAX:
DIFFERENCE(<expC1>, <expC2>)

## RETURNS:
Numeric

## DEFINITION:
Indicates the difference between the SOUNDEX( ) values of two character expressions.

The returned value ranges from 0 to 4. Matching expressions return 4. Expressions with no matching characters return 0.

## RECOMMENDED USE:
Use DIFFERENCE( ) to do searches with varying degrees of exactness.

**Example**—A contact database contains 10,000 names. When looking up names, the operator can indicate the degree of certainty in the spelling. Obviously, it is high for "Jones" and low for "Kistiakowsky." For example, when looking up "Jamison," the operator indicates that only three characters must match in the SOUNDEX( ) value of the name.

```
LIST contact FOR DIFFERENCE(contact,"Jamison") > 3
```

Jameson, Jaymison, and Jamieson will also do.

## LIMITS/WARNINGS:
DIFFERENCE is not very reliable in practice. For example, two completely different expressions return a value of 2 because their lengths are the same:

```
? DIFFERENCE("xyz","abc")
2
```

## SEE ALSO:
Function SOUNDEX( ).

# DISKSPACE( )

## DIALECTS:
Clipper, dBASE III PLUS, dBASE IV, dBXL, FoxBASE+, and Quicksilver.

## SYNTAX:
DISKSPACE( )

## RETURNS:
Numeric

## DEFINITION:
Returns the number of available bytes on the current disk drive.

## RECOMMENDED USE:
Use DISKSPACE( ) to determine whether a disk has enough room for operations such as SORT, INDEX, or COPY. A command that creates an output file will fail if there is not enough disk space. Note that all systems handle Disk Full errors poorly, creating the potential for damaged or lost data.

**Example**—A department store program sorts databases and copies them. Every time it executes SORT or COPY, a subroutine compares the file size with the disk space available. It computes file size as the number of records times the record size, plus the size of the database file header. If the file size exceeds one half the disk space, an error subroutine prompts the user to select an alternate course of action.

You can determine the size of the header with the formula

32 x <field count> + 35

To determine the field count, use FIELD( ) in a DO WHILE loop to test each field name. FCOUNT counts each field, until FIELD( ) returns a null string.

```
fcount = 1                          && Start with FIELD 1.
DO WHILE LEN(FIELD(fcount)) > 0     && Continue until length is null.
  fcount = fcount + 1               && Increment counter.
ENDDO
fcount = fcount - 1                 && FCOUNT cannot start at 0, so
                                    &&   adjust final total.
```

```
header = (32 * fcount) + 35                      && Compute header size.
totsize = recsize() * reccount() + header        && Compute total file size.
IF totsize > DISKSPACE()/2
  * <error routine>
ENDIF
```

Note that Clipper has a field count function FCOUNT( ) that can replace the DO WHILE LEN(FIELD(fcount)) structure. Clipper also has a HEADER( ) function that returns the header size.

## VARIATIONS:

**Clipper:** You can specify a numeric argument in DISKSPACE( ) for checking another disk drive. DISKSPACE(1) checks the space on drive A, DISKSPACE(2) checks drive B, and DISKSPACE(3) checks drive C. Warning: If you specify an invalid drive, DISKSPACE( ) produces erroneous results.

DISKSPACE( ) is in EXTEND.LIB on the system disk.

## SEE ALSO:

Functions HEADER( ), RECCOUNT( ), and RECSIZE( ).

# DMY( )

## DIALECTS:
dBASE IV only.

## SYNTAX:
DMY(<expD>)

## RETURNS:
Character

## DEFINITION:
Converts a date expression to a DD Month YY format. If you SET CENTURY ON, the result is DD Month YYYY.

DD appears without a leading zero if it is only one digit. The month is spelled out.

## RECOMMENDED USE:
Use DMY( ) to report dates in the European conventional format.

**Example**—A daily report displays the date at the top in DMY format.

```
mdate = DATE()
@ 04,01 SAY DMY(mdate)
```

It prints as:

```
18 June 88
```

With SET CENTURY ON, the date prints as:

```
18 June 1988
```

## SEE ALSO:
Commands SET CENTURY and SET DATE; functions CDOW( ), CMONTH( ), DATE( ), DOW( ), MDY( ), and MONTH( ).

# DOSERROR( )

## DIALECTS:
Clipper only.

## SYNTAX:
DOSERROR( )

## RETURNS:
Numeric

## DEFINITION:
Returns the number of the latest DOS error when a file open command or RUN command fails. The numbers have the following meanings:

1 Invalid function number
2 File not found
3 Path not found
4 Too many files open
5 Access denied (file already open)
6 Invalid handle
7 Memory control blocks corrupted
8 Insufficient memory
9 Invalid memory block address
10 Invalid environment
11 Invalid format
12 Invalid access code
13 Invalid data
14 Undefined
15 Invalid drive specified
16 Tried to remove current directory
17 Not same device
18 No more files
19 Disk write-protected, cannot write
20 Unknown unit
21 Drive not ready
22 Unknown command
23 Data error (CRC failure)
24 Bad request structure length
25 Seek error
26 Unknown media type
27 Sector not found
28 No more paper in printer
29 Write fault
30 Read fault
36 Sharing buffer overlow
37-49 Undefined
50 Network request not supported
51 Remote computer not listening
52 Duplicate name on network
53 Network name not found
54 Network busy
55 Network device no longer exists
56 Network BIOS command limit exceeded
57 Network adapter hardware error
58 Incorrect response from network
59 Unexpected network error
60 Incompatible remote adapter
61 Print queue full
62 Not enough space for print file
63 Print file deleted
64 Network name deleted
65 Network access denied
66 Network device type incorrect
67 Network name not found
68 Network name limit exceeded
69 Network BIOS session limit exceeded
70 Temporarily paused
71 Network request not accepted
72 Print or disk redirection paused
73-79 Undefined
80 File already exists
81 Reserved
82 Cannot make directory entry
83 Fail on INT 24H

31 General failure
32 File sharing violation
33 Lock violation
34 Invalid disk change
35 File Control Block unavailable
84 Too many redirections
85 Duplicate redirection
86 Invalid password
87 Invalid parameter
88 Network device fault

## RECOMMENDED USE:

When a file open error or a RUN error occurs, Clipper automatically calls the user defined functions OPEN_ERROR( ) or MISC_ERROR( ), respectively. Use DOSERROR( ) in the functions to report and recover from errors.

**Example**—A programmer specifies a file that doesn't exist. When the error occurs, Clipper calls the OPEN_ERROR( ) user defined function with five parameters: NAME, LINE, INFO, MODEL, and _1. NAME is the procedures name, LINE is the line number, and INFO is a description of the error. _1 is additional information passed to the function, in this case the offending filename. The actual error number comes from DOSERROR( ). When the error occurs, Clipper calls OPEN_ERROR( ). It displays the error information in a double-line box. The user can press 'R' to retry the operation that caused the error, or any other key to terminate the program.

```
* MAIN.PRG
USE msalez                                 && File does not exist.
* <More statements>.
*
FUNCTION open_error
PARAMETERS name, line, info, model, _1     && Parameters passed by
                                           &&   Clipper automatically.
SET DEVICE TO SCREEN                       && Make sure output goes
                                           &&   to screen.
SAVE SCREEN
@ 08,07 CLEAR TO 15,55
@ 09,08 TO 15,54 DOUBLE
@ 10,10 SAY "Procedure " + M->name + " line number " + LTRIM(STR(M->line))
@ 11,10 SAY "Description " + M->info + " " + M->_1
@ 12,10 SAY "DOS error number " + " (" + LTRIM(STR(DOSERROR())) + ")"
@ 14,10 SAY "Press 'R' to retry, any other key to quit"
INKEY(0)
IF .NOT. CHR(LASTKEY()) $ "rR"
  @ 14,10 SAY "EXITING PROGRAM DUE TO OPEN ERROR"
  QUIT
ENDIF
RESTORE SCREEN
RETURN .T.
```

## SEE ALSO:

Command RUN; functions FERROR( ) and FOPEN( ).

# DOW( )

## DIALECTS:

Clipper, dBASE III PLUS, dBASE IV, dBXL, FoxBASE+, and Quicksilver.

## SYNTAX:

DOW(<expD>)

## RETURNS:

Numeric

## DEFINITION:

Returns the number of the day of the week, ranging from 1 to 7. Sunday is day 1.

## RECOMMENDED USE:

Use DOW( ) for day-related computations.

**Example**—A restaurant system maintains a traffic log to project the amount of food to prepare each day. The traffic projection is a relative numeric factor. Every morning, the manager reads the projection and plans the menu accordingly.

The weekly projection consists of 7 records with two fields each, F_FACTOR and MDAY. F_FACTOR is the food factor. MDAY is the day of the week. The program LOCATEs the record for the current day of the week. It first stores DOW( ) in variable SDAY. This makes it easier to use the current day of the week in several subsequent computations.

```
sday = DOW(DATE())
? sday
2

LOCATE FOR mday = sday
? f_factor
2.7
* <More computations>.
```

## VARIATIONS:

In dBASE IV you can create a date literal without CTOD( ). To do this, use braces to delimit a date string, as follows:

```
{01/20/88}
```

To return the DOW( ) of January 20, 1988, enter

```
? DOW({01/20/88})
```

## SEE ALSO:

Functions CDOW, CMONTH( ), CTOD( ), DATE( ), DAY( ), DTOC( ), and MONTH( ).

# DTOC( )

## DIALECTS:
Clipper, dBASE III PLUS, dBASE IV, dBXL, FoxBASE+, and Quicksilver.

## SYNTAX:
DTOC(<expD>)

## RETURNS:
Character

## DEFINITION:
Converts a date expression to a character expression. <expD> can be a date memory variable or a function that returns a date.

DTOC( ) is the inverse of the CTOD( ) function that converts character expressions to date.

## RECOMMENDED USE:
You must convert expressions of different data types to a common type before concatenating them. Use DTOC( ) to convert dates to character strings.

**Example**—The installment loan department of Banco Nacional issues late payment reminders. The program that generates them prints the system date as a character string:

```
@ 04,10 SAY "**BANCO NACIONAL Friendly Reminder**"
@ 05,10 SAY "Reminder date: " + DTOC(DATE())
* <more @...SAY statements>
```

The next line displays a response date stored in a date field RDATE:

```
@ 06,10 SAY "Please respond by: " + DTOC(rdate)
```

The actual reminder looks like:

```
**BANCO NACIONAL Friendly Reminder**
Reminder date:  02/24/88
Please respond by:  03/01/88
```

Later versions refer to friendly collection agencies and to the sad fates of friends who didn't pay their bills.

## SEE ALSO:
Functions CDOW( ), CTOD( ), and DATE( ).

# DTOR( )

## DIALECTS:
dBASE IV only.

## SYNTAX:
DTOR(<expN>)

## RETURNS:
Numeric

## DEFINITION:
Converts degrees to radians.

<expN> is the angle in degrees.

The conversion formula is

$$N \times 1.745329 \times 10^2$$

where N is the angle in degrees.

## RECOMMENDED USE:
DTOR( ) is used in engineering and scientific applications.

**Example**—In determining the sine of an angle, a scientist converts degrees to radians.

```
msin = SIN(DTOR(40))
  0.64
```

## SEE ALSO:
Command SET DECIMALS; functions ACOS( ), ATAN( ), ATN2( ), COS( ), RTOD( ), and SIN( ).

# DTOS( )

## DIALECTS:
Clipper, dBASE IV, dBXL, and Quicksilver.

## SYNTAX:
DTOS(<expD>)

## RETURNS:
Character

## DEFINITION:
Accepts a date expression and returns a character string in the format YYYYMMDD, for example, DTOS of "02/17/89" is "19890217."

## RECOMMENDED USE:
The format of DTOS( ) is independent of the system date format determined by the SET DATE TO or SET CENTURY commands. Normally, files indexed on date field keys depend on the system date format. If that format changes (e.g., because of SET DATE AMERICAN or SET DATE ANSI), the index updates do not work the same way. DTOS( ) provides a consistent index key.

**Examples**—Fastmail Software, Inc. takes telephone orders for software products and fulfills them in the order received. The order program indexes sales by date.

```
USE orders
INDEX ON DTOS(orderdate) TO ordqueue
Indexing TO C:\TEXT\ORDQUEUE.NDX...
100% indexed.        5 Records indexed.
LIST orderdate
Record#  ORDERDATE
      4  03/09/77
      2  02/24/78
      1  02/20/79
      5  03/19/86
      3  05/01/88
```

Of course, the person who phoned in an order in March 1977 may be getting a bit anxious. He may not even want dBASE I for his Altair anymore.

## SEE ALSO:
Command INDEX, SET CENTURY, and SET DATE; functions CTOD( ) and DESCEND( ).

# EMPTY( )

## DIALECTS:
Clipper, dBXL, and Quicksilver.

## SYNTAX:
EMPTY(<exp>)

## RETURNS:
Logical

## DEFINITION:
Returns true (.T.) if the specified expression contains no data. EMPTY( ) accepts data of all types. <exp> may be a field, memory variable, or literal expression.

EMPTY( )'s operation depends on the expression's data type. EMPTY( ) returns .T. when:

- a character expression contains all spaces;
- a numeric expression evaluates to 0;
- a logical expression evaluates to false;
- a date expression evaluates to " / / ";
- a memo field is blank.

## RECOMMENDED USE:
Use EMPTY( ) to validate input during data entry, or to limit global operations to records containing valid data.

**Example 1**—A common design technique lets users exit a menu by leaving an input area blank. In this example, when the user presses the space bar, program control returns to the previous level.

```
response = "?"
@ 10,10 SAY "Enter your selection A-M"
@ 11,10 SAY "or press SPACE BAR to exit" GET response PICTURE "!"
READ
IF EMPTY(response)
  RETURN
ENDIF
```

**Example 2**—Fashion Year magazine has a program to analyze the cost of articles. The managing editor requests a report on the average (miniscule) payment to authors. Because the database contains names of authors who receive no pay (they may be staff writers for public relations agencies), the zero values will distort the AVERAGE. EMPTY( ) limits the average to non-zero fields. MONTHPAY is a numeric field containing the payment amount.

```
. AVERAGE monthpay FOR .NOT. EMPTY(monthpay)
4 Records averaged.
MONTHPAY
  531.80
```

## VARIATIONS:

You can simulate EMPTY( ) with a dBASE IV or FoxBASE+ user defined function as follows:

```
PARAMETERS x

mtype = TYPE("x")
DO CASE
  CASE mtype = "C"
    retval = (LEN(TRIM(x))=0)
  CASE mtype = "N" .OR. mtype = "F"
    retval = (x=0)
  CASE mtype = "L"
    retval = x
  CASE mtype = "D"
    retval = ("  "$DTOC(x))
ENDCASE

RETURN retval
```

## LIMITS/WARNINGS

Use EMPTY( ) carefully, since zero-valued and blank fields often represent legitimate data. (Some relational DBMS's have a null data type that lets you specify a field as null, or "not applicable").

If you need to treat zero-valued and blank fields as legitimate data, but also have records you want to exclude from certain operations, add a logical field to your database called EXCLUDE. Set it to .T. in records you want to ignore. In the Fashion magazine example, you would use the syntax

```
. AVERAGE monthpay FOR .NOT. exclude
4 Records averaged.
```

```
MONTHPAY
531.80
```

The logical field can be set by the user or by the program, depending on a condition.

## SEE ALSO:

Command AVERAGE; functions IIF( ) and LEN( ).

# EOF( )

## DIALECTS:

Clipper, dBASE III PLUS, dBASE IV, dBXL, FoxBASE+, and Quicksilver.

## SYNTAX:

EOF( )

## RETURNS:

Logical

## DEFINITION:

Returns true (.T.) when the record pointer in the active database is at the end-of-file.

End-of-file occurs when: 1) you try to move the record pointer beyond the last logical record in a database file, or 2) a file contains no records.

EOF( ) returns false if no database is in use. This can be misleading when debugging a program, since you might think that a database is open. To determine whether one is, use DBF( ) to test the filename's length. If there is no open file, DBF( ) returns a null string (length 0).

```
IIF (LEN(DBF()) = 0,"NO FILE IN USE",DBF())
```

## RECOMMENDED USE:

File handling routines that move through records use EOF( ) to locate the upper boundary.

**Example**—An editing program lets users view records by pressing "F" to move forward a record at a time. The EOF( ) function detects the end-of-file. CASE MACTION executes the SKIP command as long as EOF( ) is false.

```
* <Display, edit records, GET user response>
*
* Move forward if user enters "F" and NOT end-of-file.
CASE maction = "F" .AND. .NOT. EOF()
  SKIP
```

## VARIATIONS:

**Clipper:** You can check an open file in another work area by using EOF( ) as the alias operator's argument, as follows:

```
? <alias>->(EOF( ))
```

**dBASE IV:** You can check an open file in another work area by adding a character parameter, in the form EOF(<expC>). <expC> is the alias name of the unselected database.

**FoxBASE+:** You can check an open file in another work area by making the area number a parameter, in the form EOF(<expN>).

## SEE ALSO:

Functions ALIAS( ) and BOF( ).

# ERROR( )

## DIALECTS:
dBASE III PLUS, dBASE IV, dBXL, FoxBASE+, and Quicksilver.

## SYNTAX:
ERROR( )

## RETURNS:
Numeric

## DEFINITION:
Returns the number of the last error condition when the ON ERROR command is active. The ERROR( ) number has a corresponding description you can return with the MESSAGE( ) function.

*Note:* The RETURN and RETRY commands reset the ERROR( ) number and the MESSAGE( ). Error numbers are specific to each dBASE implementation.

## DEFAULT:
Returns 0 if no error condition exists.

## RECOMMENDED USE:
Use ERROR( ) to identify error conditions and describe or initiate corrective action.

**Example**—A program in a government office tracks materials requisitions. An error-trapping procedure identifies system errors and takes action.

It tests for such common errors as FILE ALREADY OPEN and FILE NOT FOUND. If the program tries to open an already opened file, it SUSPENDs operation to let the supervisor close the file and perform repairs. If a file cannot be found, the program CANCELs.

```
DO CASE
CASE ERROR() = 1    && dBASE III PLUS error code (file not found).
  CANCEL
CASE ERROR() = 3    && File already open.
  SUSPEND
```

```
  * <more cases>
ENDCASE
? message()        && Message function describes error condition.
```

## VARIATIONS:

**Clipper:** Use FERROR( ) to return file errors and DOSERROR( ) for DOS errors.

## SEE ALSO:

Commands ON ERROR, RETRY, RETURN, and SUSPEND; functions DOSERROR( ), FERROR( ), MESSAGE( ), and PROGRAM( ).

# ERRORLEVEL( )

## DIALECTS:

Clipper only.

## SYNTAX:

ERRORLEVEL([<expN>])

## RETURNS:

Numeric

## DEFINITION:

Both returns and sets the DOS error level.

ERRORLEVEL( ) with no argument returns the current DOS error level setting. The optional <expN> sets the level to a number between 0 and 255, inclusive.

## RECOMMENDED USE:

Use ERRORLEVEL( ) with the SWITCH.EXE utility to control the execution of chained application programs. In such programs, one application exits to the operating system before the next one begins, as if they were being executed from a batch file. By examining the DOS error level, the SWITCH utility can execute a designated program.

**Example**—A retail management system tracks sales and inventory. The system includes modules for point of sale, file maintenance, and telecommunications (to send data back to the main office). Before exiting from point of sale, the system sets the error level according to the user's choice.

```
* Get user response: 1 for point of sale, 2 for file maintenance,
* 3 for telecommunications.
@ 05,01 PROMPT "Point of Sale"
@ 06,01 PROMPT "File Maintenance"
@ 07,01 PROMPT "Telecommunications"
MENU TO action
ERRORLEVEL(action)
QUIT
```

You then run SWITCH with the syntax

SWITCH <main> <p1> <p2> ... <p9>

where <main> is the caller and <p1> through <p9> are subprograms corresponding to error levels. If you set error level to 2, program p2 executes.

## LIMITS/WARNINGS:

You may not use the RUN command to SET other DOS environment variables. Because RUN loads a second copy of COMMAND.COM (MS/PC-DOS), variables SET with RUN are released when the RUN is complete.

## SEE ALSO:

Command QUIT; function GETENV( ).

# EXP( )

## DIALECTS:

Clipper, dBASE III PLUS, dBASE IV, dBXL, FoxBASE+, and Quicksilver.

## SYNTAX:

EXP(<expN>)

## RETURNS:

Numeric

## DEFINITION:

Returns the value of e raised to the power <expN>.

e, the base of natural logarithms, is approximately 2.71828.

## DEFAULT:

EXP( )'s result has a minimum of two decimal places. You may increase precision with the SET DECIMALS command.

## RECOMMENDED USE:

Mathematicians, scientists, and engineers often use EXP( ) in formulas.

**Example**—To store the value of e to the fifth power in a variable MEXP, use the statement

```
mexp = EXP(5)
```

A test of MEXP's value shows:

```
? mexp
    148.41
```

## SEE ALSO:

Functions LOG( ) and LOG10( ).

# FCLOSE( )

## DIALECTS:

Clipper only.

## SYNTAX:

FCLOSE(<expN>)

## RETURNS:

Logical

## DEFINITION:

Closes a DOS file and saves it on disk. <expN> is the numeric file handle returned by FCREATE( ) or FOPEN( ).

If the closure fails, FCLOSE( ) returns false (.F.).

## RECOMMENDED USE:

Use FCLOSE( ) to save a file and release its handle. Failure to FCLOSE( ) a file could lead to lost data if Clipper exits improperly.

**Example**—After editing a text file in a real estate system, the programmer FCLOSEs it before proceeding to the next operation. FCLOSE is the last step.

```
tempvar = space(250)                && Initialize buffer variable.
mhandle = FOPEN("TOWNHS.4SL",2)     && Open TOWNHS.4SL file.
FREAD(mhandle,@tempvar,250)         && Read text into memory variable.
FSEEK(mhandle,0)                    && Set pointer to beginning of file.
mbuf = HARDCR(MEMOEDIT(tempvar))   && Edit memory variable with MEMOEDIT( ).
FWRITE(mhandle,mbuf)                && Write result back to file.
FCLOSE(mhandle)                     && Close file, release handle, save data.
```

## LIMITS/WARNINGS:

FCLOSE( ) is for advanced programmers who understand how DOS handles files.

FCLOSE( ) is in EXTEND.LIB on the system disk.

## SEE ALSO:

Functions FCREATE( ), FERROR( ), FOPEN( ), FREAD( ), FREADSTR( ), FSEEK( ), and FWRITE( ).

# FCOL( )

## DIALECTS:
dBXL and Quicksilver.

## SYNTAX:
FCOL( )

## RETURNS:
Numeric

## DEFINITION:
Returns the column coordinate in an open output file.

You must first select the output file with SET ALTERNATE TO.

## DEFAULT:
Returns 0 if no ALTERNATE file is open.

## RECOMMENDED USE:
FCOL( ) lets you send output to an ALTERNATE file at a position relative to the current column position. This is useful for formatting disk file output.

**Example**—A report generator prints several columns of data. It uses the FCOL( ) function to put space between the columns.

```
CLEAR
@ 5,FCOL() SAY "SSN: "            "
@ 5,FCOL()+2 SAY "Employer:                   "
@ 5,FCOL()+2 SAY "No. of Dependents:    "
```

The screen would appear as follows:

```
SSN:            Employer:                          No. of Dependents:
```

## SEE ALSO:
Functions COL( ), POW( ), PCOL( ), PROW( ), and ROW( ).

# FCOUNT( )

## DIALECTS:

Clipper and FoxBASE+.

## SYNTAX:

FCOUNT( )

## RETURNS:

Numeric

## DEFINITION:

Returns the number of fields in the active database file.

## DEFAULT:

Returns 0 if no database file is open in the current directory.

## RECOMMENDED USE:

Clipper lacks DISPLAY STRUCTURE. So you must use functions such as AFIELDS( ), FCOUNT( ), FIELDNAME( ), LEN( ), and TYPE( ) to display file structure information.

FCOUNT( ) also lets you access database fields without knowing their names in advance. You can thus write general purpose programs that analyze structures and adapt to them.

**Example**—A general purpose Clipper application lets you view and edit database files without knowing their structures in advance. The program stores a single record in an array with FCOUNT( ) elements. FIELD( ) gets the field name based on its relative number in the file.

```
PARAMETER filename
* Filename entered by user or passed from a program as a PARAMETER.
USE (filename)
* FCOUNT() is the number of fields/array elements to initialize.
DECLARE showfile[FCOUNT()]
* CTR increases until it reaches FCOUNT().
FOR ctr = 1 TO FCOUNT()
  * Variable CONTENTS holds the name of each field as CTR increases.
  contents = FIELD(ctr)
  * Store each field in an element in array SHOWFILE.
  showfile[ctr] = &contents
NEXT ctr    && Increment CTR.
```

The program produces an array SHOWFILE with FCOUNT( ) elements. You can display or edit it with similar routines. For example, you could use the program below to EDIT it for the current field.

```
FOR ctr = 1 to FCOUNT()
  @ ctr,1 GET showfile[ctr]
NEXT ctr
READ
```

*Note:* To use these routines with FoxBASE+, replace FOR...NEXT with DO WHILE and increment CTR inside the loop. Use DIMENSION instead of DECLARE. Change USE(filename) to USE &filenames.

## VARIATIONS:

**dBASE III PLUS, dBASE IV, dBXL, Quicksilver:** You can simulate FCOUNT( ) with a short routine that evaluates field lengths. When the field length is 0, the counter stops.

```
ctr = 1
DO WHILE LEN(FIELD(ctr))>0
  ctr = ctr + 1
ENDDO
? ctr - 1
```

**FoxBASE+:** You can check the field count of an open file in another work area by using its number as a parameter in the form FCOUNT([<expN>]).

## SEE ALSO:

Commands DECLARE, DIMENSION, and FOR...NEXT; functions AFIELDS( ) and FIELD( ).

# FCREATE( )

## DIALECTS:
Clipper only.

## SYNTAX:
FCREATE(<expC>[,<expN>])

## RETURNS:
Numeric

## DEFINITION:
Creates a new DOS file or overwrites an existing file and returns a numeric file handle. File handles are between 0 and 65,535, inclusive. If FCREATE( ) cannot create a file, it returns -1.

The file remains open until you either close it with FCLOSE( ) or exit the application normally.

<expC> is the filename and path. <expN> is one of the following DOS file attributes:

0—Normal (read/write)

1—Read only

2—Hidden (not visible in directory searches)

4—System (not visible in directory searches)

FCREATE( ) gives the new file a DOS open mode of 2 (read/write). This differs from a file attribute; see FOPEN( ) for a list of DOS open modes.

Because all DOS file operations require a handle, be sure to store it in a memory variable when you open the file.

## DEFAULT:
If you omit the path, FCREATE( ) defaults to the current directory. If you omit the <expN> option, FCREATE( ) defaults to an attribute of 0 (normal).

## RECOMMENDED USE:

FCREATE( ) is for advanced programmers who understand DOS files. Use it with FCLOSE( ), FERROR( ), FOPEN( ), FREAD( ), FREADSTR( ), and FSEEK( ) to read and write foreign (non-dBASE) data structures and text file formats. Applications include exchanging data with remote systems and importing data from gathering devices.

**Example**—Because FCREATE( ) does not conflict with open database files and work areas, programmers may opt for direct DOS file manipulation.

For example, a statistical program could analyze a database file and write the results in a format recognizable by a plotting device.

```
fhandle = FCREATE("stat.out",0)
IF fhandle = -1
  @ 23,01 SAY "Unable to create file"
ENDIF
```

## LIMITS/WARNINGS:

If you do not specify a path in the filename argument, FCREATE( ) writes to the current directory, ignoring the DEFAULT and PATH settings.

FCREATE( ) is in EXTEND.LIB on the system disk.

## SEE ALSO:

Functions FCLOSE( ), FERROR( ), FOPEN( ), FREAD( ), FREADSTR( ), FSEEK( ), and FWRITE( ).

# FERROR( )

## DIALECTS:
Clipper only.

## SYNTAX:
FERROR( )

## RETURNS:
Numeric

## DEFINITION:
Returns the last DOS error after you use a DOS file function. If no error occurred, FERROR( ) returns 0.

## RECOMMENDED USE:
FERROR( ) is for advanced programmers who understand how DOS handles files.

Use FERROR( ) after low level file operations such as FCLOSE( ), FCREATE( ), FOPEN( ), FREAD( )), FREADSTR( ), FSEEK( ), and FWRITE( ). FERROR( ) traps errors such as those caused by trying to write to a read-only file, or by closing a nonexistent file. If FERROR( ) returns a non-zero value, you may elect to retry the operation or abandon it.

**Example 1**—After executing the DOS file handling commands FOPEN( ) and FREAD( ), a program issues FCLOSE( ) to close the file. Unfortunately, the file handle has been overwritten by another command using the same memory variable name. Trying to close the file with an invalid file handle causes an error.

```
* FHANDLE is invalid file handle.
IF .NOT. FCLOSE(fhandle)
  ? "Unable to close file. Error #: ", FERROR()
ENDIF
```

In this case, FERROR( ) returns 6.

**Example 2**—A subroutine tries to open a nonexistent text file. FERROR( ) returns 2 and the subroutine RETURNs to the calling program.

```
fname = "medical.txt"
fhandle = FOPEN("&fname",2)
IF FERROR() # 0
  @ 23,01 SAY "Unable to open" + &name
  RETURN
ENDIF
```

FERROR( ) is in EXTEND.LIB on the system disk.

## SEE ALSO:

Functions DOSERROR( ), FCLOSE( ), FCREATE( ), FOPEN( ), FREAD( ), FREADSTR( ), FSEEK( ), and FWRITE( ).

# FIELD( )

## DIALECTS:
Clipper, dBASE III PLUS, dBASE IV, dBXL, FoxBASE+, and Quicksilver.

## SYNTAX:
FIELD(<expN>)

## RETURNS:
Character

## DEFINITION:
Returns the name of the specified field in the active database. <expN> is the field's relative number.

FIELD( ) returns fieldnames in uppercase letters.

## DEFAULT:
Returns a null string if no database is open in the selected work area or if the field number is invalid.

## RECOMMENDED USE:
Use FIELD( ) to access field contents by number. This is useful in general purpose programs that do not know the database structures in advance.

**Example**—A general purpose dBASE III PLUS program processes files without knowing their structures in advance. The program stores a single record in a number of memory variables equal to the number of fields.

First, the program counts the fields by searching through them until it finds one with a zero length. The field count is stored in variable FCOUNT.

Then the program stores the fields in the memory variables MFIELDn, where n is the field number. Once initialized, these variables can be displayed and edited.

```
* A database must be in use.
fctr = 1
DO WHILE LEN(FIELD(fctr)) > 0     && Increment FIELD().
  fctr = fctr+1
ENDDO
```

```
fcount = fctr-1
ctr = 1                          && CTR increases until it reaches FCOUNT.
DO WHILE ctr <= fcount
  contents = FIELD(ctr)          && CONTENTS holds name of each field.
  sctr = LTRIM(STR(ctr,3,0))     && Store field contents in variables
  mfield&sctr = &contents        &&  MFIELD1-MFIELD(fcount).
  ctr = ctr + 1                  && Increment CTR.
ENDDO
```

You can REPLACE fields similarly.

## VARIATIONS:

**Clipper:** FIELDNAME( ) is a synonym for FIELD( ).

**dBASE IV:** You may designate a field from an open file in any work area by adding a character parameter, in the form FIELD(<expN>,<expC>). <expN> is the field number; <expC> is the ALIAS of the specified database.

**FoxBASE+:** FIELD( ) will work on open files in other work areas if you use the area number as a second parameter, in the form FIELD(<expN1>)[,<expN2>].

## SPECIAL USE:

FIELD( ) lets you treat database files much like arrays, since you need only an "element" number rather than a name.

## SEE ALSO:

Functions DBF( ), FCOUNT( ), NDX( ), RECCOUNT( ), and RECSIZE( ).

# FIELDNAME( )

## DIALECTS:
Clipper only.

## SYNTAX:
FIELDNAME(<expN>)

## RETURNS:
Character

## DEFINITION:
Same as FIELD( ).

# FILE( )

## DIALECTS:
Clipper, dBASE III PLUS, dBASE IV, dBXL, FoxBASE+, and Quicksilver.

## SYNTAX:
FILE(<expC>)

## RETURNS:
Logical

## DEFINITION:
Determines whether a file exists. If so, FILE( ) returns true (.T.).

<expC> must be a valid filename, including the extension. To specify a file not in the default directory, you must either SET PATH TO the drive and directory, or include a drive and path name in FILE( ).

FILE( ) ignores case.

## RECOMMENDED USE:
Use FILE( ) to check the existence of database and index files before opening them. This prevents program errors when a file has inadvertently been erased.

**Example**—A file maintenance module of a loan tracking program checks initially whether index files exist. If not, it recreates them automatically.

```
* CHEKFILE.PRG
IF .NOT. FILE("amain.ndx")
  INDEX ON loancode TO amain
ENDIF
IF .NOT. FILE("namedex.ndx")
  INDEX ON reg_lname TO namedex
ENDIF
IF .NOT. FILE("acctdex.ndx")
  INDEX ON acct TO acctdex
ENDIF
```

## LIMITS/WARNINGS:
**dBASE III PLUS:** Reports the existence of a file in the current directory if it exists anywhere in the operating system's search path. FILE( ) reports true regardless of the SET PATH TO command. To avoid this problem, always

specify the full drive and path. Clipper, dBASE IV, dBXL, FoxBASE+, and Quicksilver do not exhibit this problem.

**dBASE III PLUS and dBASE IV:** FILE( ) uses a DOS file handle. If the maximum number of files are open (including databases, programs, and dBASE III PLUS itself), FILE( ) returns false even when the file exists.

## SEE ALSO:

Commands SET DEFAULT and SET PATH.

# FIXED( )

## DIALECTS:

dBASE IV only.

## SYNTAX:

Converts F type data (IEEE 754 long real floating point) to N type (fixed point, binary coded decimal).

For greater precision in numeric comparisons, dBASE IV allows both floating point (type F) and fixed point (type N) numeric data.

## RECOMMENDED USE:

Mixing types N and F in an equation always produces a result of type F.

Use FIXED( ) when the result must be type N.

**Example**—The results of trignometric functions are always of type F. To produce fixed point results, an application uses FIXED( ).

```
mresult = FIXED(ACOS(1))+ 3.55
? mresult
       3.55
```

A check of MRESULT shows that it is type N.

```
? TYPE("mresult")
N
```

## SEE ALSO:

Function FLOAT( ).

# FKLABEL( )

## DIALECTS:

Clipper, dBASE III PLUS, dBASE IV, dBXL, FoxBASE+, and Quicksilver.

## SYNTAX:

FKLABEL(<expN>)

## RETURNS:

Character

## DEFINITION:

Returns the name of the first valid programmable function key. <expN> is the key's relative number. Note: Do not pronounce this function's name in mixed company!

On keyboards with no HELP key, FKLABEL(1) refers to function key 2. Such keyboards reserve function key 1 for HELP, making it non-programmable.

## RECOMMENDED USE:

The markings on programmable function keys vary among computer makes and models. To make programs run on a variety of computers, use FKLABEL( ) to program function keys. It assures that your programs do not try to assign values to invalid keys.

**Example**—A programmer developing point-of-sale applications simplifies the user interface by programming function keys to execute menu selections. Because the programs run on a variety of computers, she defines function keys using FKLABEL( ).

```
SET FUNCTION FKLABEL(1) TO "DO endofyear;"
SET FUNCTION FKLABEL(2) TO "DO closqrtr;"
SET FUNCTION FKLABEL(3) TO "DO backup;"
```

## VARIATIONS:

**Clipper:** FKLABEL( ) is in EXTEND.LIB on the system disk.

**dBASE IV:** You may assign values to up to 28 keys (9 function keys, 10 Ctrl-<function> keys, and 9 Shift-<function> keys). SHIFT-F10 is reserved for the macro menu.

## SEE ALSO:

Command SET FUNCTION; function FKMAX( ).

# FKMAX( )

## DIALECTS:

Clipper, dBASE III PLUS, dBASE IV, dBXL, FoxBASE+, and Quicksilver.

## SYNTAX:

FKMAX( )

## RETURNS:

Numeric

## DEFINITION:

Returns the number of programmable function keys on the keyboard.

## RECOMMENDED USE:

The markings on programmable function keys varies among computer makes and models. To make programs run on a variety of computers, use FKMAX( ) and FKLABEL( ) to adapt to different keyboards. FKLABEL( ) returns the names of programmable function keys.

**Example**—A commercial medical office program uses function keys to simplify menu selections. To take advantage of all available keys, the program must first count them with FKMAX( ).

The next program stores function key assignments in a database SETKEYS containing a field KEYDEF. A DO WHILE repeats the SET FUNCTION command until it reaches the maximum number of function keys FKMAX( ) or the end of the SETKEYS file.

```
USE setkeys
ctr = 1
DO WHILE ctr <= FKMAX() .AND. .NOT. EOF()
  SET FUNCTION FKLABEL(ctr) TO keydef
  SKIP
  ctr = ctr + 1
ENDDO
USE
```

## VARIATIONS:

**Clipper:** FKMAX( ) is in EXTEND.LIB on the system disk. It works correctly only on IBM PC/XT/AT and compatible computers.

## SEE ALSO:

Command SET FUNCTION; function FKLABEL( ).

# FLOAT( )

## DIALECTS:
dBASE IV only.

## SYNTAX:
FLOAT(<expN>)

## RETURNS:
Floating point numeric

## DEFINITION:
Converts N type data (fixed point, binary coded decimal) to F type (real, long IEEE 754 floating point).

For greater precision in numeric comparisons, dBASE IV allows both floating point (type F) and fixed point (type N) numeric data types.

## RECOMMENDED USE:
Floating point numbers have greater precision than fixed point numbers and are independent of dBASE IV's SET PRECISION statement. SET DECIMALS affects how the numbers are displayed, but not their internal precision. Use floating point numbers in scientific applications requiring high numeric precision.

**Example**—All constants default to type N. Use FLOAT( ) to change them to type F before storing them in variables.

```
SET DECIMALS TO 4
mradian = FLOAT(1.533E+02)
? mradian
       153.3000
```

A check of MRADIAN shows that it is type F.

```
? TYPE("mradian")
F
```

## SEE ALSO:
Function FIXED( ).

# FLOCK( )

## DIALECTS:

Clipper, dBASE III PLUS, dBASE IV, FoxBASE+, and Quicksilver.

## SYNTAX:

FLOCK( )

## RETURNS:

Logical

## DEFINITION:

Tries to lock a database file, returning true (.T.) if successful.

If FLOCK( ) succeeds, the file stays locked until the user who locked it either issues the UNLOCK command or closes it (with CLEAR ALL, CLOSE DATABASES, QUIT, or USE.

FLOCK( ) prevents multiple users on local area networks or multiuser computers from simultaneously changing data in a file.

## RECOMMENDED USE:

In the multiuser environment, updates that affect multiple records generally require the file to be locked or opened with the USE EXCLUSIVE option. This prevents such operations from altering records being accessed by other users.

**Example**—Jack in accounting must run a closing report that totals monthly sales. To prevent Jill in sales from updating the file during the report process, Jack locks it. This is the real reason why Jill was not sad when "Jack fell down and broke his crown."

Because FLOCK( ) only tries to lock a file once, the programmer puts it in a loop so it repeats if unsuccessful. FLOCK( ) can only succeed if no other user has already locked the file or a record in it. The programmer hopes the file will become available within the time it takes to execute the DO WHILE 300 times. If not, he abandons the attempt. (If Jack suffers his famous head injury with the file locked, the programmer certainly does not want to keep poor Jill waiting forever.)

```
USE acctmain
DO WHILE .NOT. FLOCK() .AND. ctr < 300
  ctr = ctr + 1
ENDDO
```

## VARIATIONS:

**Clipper:** FLOCK( ) releases a locked file. You may issue it on any open file, regardless of work area, by specifying an alias, as follows:

```
ALIAS->(FLOCK( ))
```

**Clipper, dBASE IV, FoxBASE+:** FLOCK( ) lets others read, but not update the locked file. USE...EXCLUSIVE is the only command that stops others from reading a file.

**dBASE III PLUS, Quicksilver:** FLOCK( ) prevents others from either reading or updating a locked file.

**dBASE IV:** You may issue an FLOCK( ) on any open file, regardless of work area, by specifying an ALIAS as an argument in the form:

```
FLOCK(<expC>)
```

**Quicksilver:** With SET AUTOLOCK ON, certain commands lock files automatically.

## SEE ALSO:

Commands SET AUTOCLOCK ON, SET EXCLUSIVE, SET REPROCESS, SET RETRY, and USE...EXCLUSIVE; functions LOCK( ) and RLOCK( ).

# FLOOR( )

## DIALECTS:
dBASE IV, dBXL, and Quicksilver.

## SYNTAX:
FLOOR(<expN>)

## RETURNS:
Numeric

## DEFINITION:
Returns the largest integer less than or equal to its argument. FLOOR( ) leaves decimal zeroes to the number of places specified by SET DECIMALS.

If its argument is negative, FLOOR( ) returns the next smaller integer.

FLOOR( ) with a positive argument works like INT( ), except that INT( ) discards the decimals.

## RECOMMENDED USE:
FLOOR( ) is often used in engineering, financial, and scientific applications. For example, to evaluate the FLOOR( ) of 126.33, enter:

```
? FLOOR(126.33)
126.00
```

To evaluate the FLOOR( ) of -88.88, enter:

```
? FLOOR(-88.88)
-89.00
```

## SEE ALSO:
Functions CEIL( ), INT( ), and ROUND( ).

# FOPEN( )

## DIALECTS:

Clipper only.

## SYNTAX:

FOPEN(<expC>[,<expN>])

## RETURNS:

Numeric

## DEFINITION:

Opens a DOS file and returns its handle. File handles are numbers between zero and 65,535 inclusive. FOPEN( ) returns -1 if an error occurs while opening the file.

The file remains open until you either close it with FCLOSE( ) or exit the application normally.

<expC> is the filename and path. <expN> is one of the following DOS open modes:

0—Read only

1—Write only

2—Read/write

Because all DOS file operations require a handle, be sure to store it in a memory variable when you open the file.

## DEFAULT:

If you do not specify a path, FOPEN( ) defaults to the current directory. If you do not specify a DOS file mode, 0 is the default.

## RECOMMENDED USE:

FOPEN( ) is for advanced programmers who understand DOS files. Use it with FCLOSE( ), FCREATE( ), FERROR( ), FREAD( ), FREADSTR( ), and FSEEK( ) to read and write foreign (non-dBASE) data structures and text file formats. Applications include exchanging data with remote systems and importing data from gathering devices.

**Example**—A law office system manages formatted client data and free form text (contracts and correspondence). Documents are created with word processors and manipulated by Clipper's DOS file functions. FOPEN( ) opens the file and returns the name of the file handle. If it succeeds, FERROR( ) returns 0.

```
fname = "johnson.ltr"
fhandle = fopen("&fname",2)
IF ferror() # 0
  @ 23,01 SAY "Unable to open" + fname
  RETURN
ENDIF
```

## LIMITS/WARNINGS:

If you do not specify a path in the filename argument, FOPEN( ) searches the current directory, ignoring the DEFAULT and PATH settings. Also, remember to close open files.

FCREATE( ) is in EXTEND.LIB on the system disk.

## SEE ALSO:

Functions FCLOSE( ), FCREATE( ), FERROR( ), FREAD( ), FREADSTR( ), FSEEK( ), and FWRITE( ).

# FOUND( )

## DIALECTS:
Clipper, dBASE III PLUS, dBASE IV, dBXL, FoxBASE+, and Quicksilver.

## SYNTAX:
FOUND( )

## RETURNS:
Logical

## DEFINITION:
Returns true (.T.) in the currently selected work area when CONTINUE, FIND, LOCATE, or SEEK finds a matching record.

If true, FOUND( ) remains true until you move the record pointer with something other than another successful CONTINUE, FIND, LOCATE, or SEEK.

FOUND( ) also returns a meaningful value in the work area of a file related by SET RELATION. When the record pointer moves in the parent file, and a matching record is found in the related file, FOUND( ) returns true (.T.).

## DEFAULT:
FOUND( ) always returns false (.F.) unless you issue a successful CONTINUE, FIND, LOCATE, or SEEK command.

## RECOMMENDED USE:
**Example**—A theater membership program maintains a member file. A member can call to renew an annual subscription, requiring the program to find the record. Because the file is indexed on last names, the program issues a SEEK. FOUND( ) indicates whether the name is in the database. If SEEK finds the name, the program displays the record. If SEEK fails, the program displays a warning message.

```
mlname = SPACE()
SEEK TRIM(mlname)
IF FOUND()
  @ 10,10 SAY "    Name: " + TRIM(forename) + " " + surname
  @ 11,10 SAY "Address: " + address
```

```
  * <more @..SAYs>
ELSE
  alte = .f.
  @ 10,10 SAY "Member not found"
  @ 11,10 SAY "Try an alternate spelling? (Y/N)" GET alte PICTURE "Y"
  READ
ENDIF
```

## VARIATIONS:

**dBASE IV:** An optional form operates on work areas other than the current one. To use it, add an alias name to FOUND( ), in the form FOUND(<expC>).

**FoxBASE+:** An optional form operates on work areas other than the current one. To use it, add the area number in the form FOUND(<expN>).

## LIMITS/WARNINGS:

FOUND( ) is unreliable in dBASE III PLUS and FoxBASE+ (but not in dBASE IV). It sometimes returns incorrect values. Instead, use EOF( ) to check the success of FIND and SEEK. Use an IF statement to check the success of a LOCATE. For example, assuming condition = "lname = 'Smith'":

```
LOCATE FOR &condition
IF &condition
  * <match found>
ELSE
  * <match not found>
ENDIF
```

## SEE ALSO:

Commands CONTINUE, FIND, LOCATE, and SEEK.

# FREAD( )

## DIALECTS:

Clipper only.

## SYNTAX:

FREAD(<expN1>,@<memvarC>,<expN2>)

## RETURNS:

Numeric

## DEFINITION:

Reads characters in an open file into a character memory variable and returns the number of bytes read. It returns 0 if the operation fails. FREAD( ) begins reading at the current file pointer position.

<expN1> refers to the numeric file handle returned by FOPEN( ) or FCREATE( ).

<memvarC> is the existing character memory variable in which to store data read from the file. (The required @ symbol indicates that the variable is passed by reference).

<expN2> specifies how many bytes to read into the memory variable. In a successful read, FREAD( ) returns <expN2>.

## RECOMMENDED USE:

Use FREAD( ) to gather data from text files.

**Example**—A medical office application stores notes in text files labeled with unique filenames. FREAD( ) saves the notes in a memory variable which can then be edited with MEMOEDIT( ).

```
* Text editing routine.
block = space(500)                  && Initialize buffer variable.
mhandle = FOPEN("sam911.med",2)     && Open SAM911.MED
FREAD(mhandle,@block,500)           && Read text into memory variable.
FSEEK(mhandle,0)                    && Set pointer to beginning of file.
mbuf = HARDCR(MEMOEDIT(block))      && Edit memory variable with MEMOEDIT().
FWRITE(mhandle,mbuf)                && Write result back into file.
```

## LIMITS/WARNINGS:

FREAD( ) is for advanced programmers who understand DOS files.

FREAD( ) is in EXTEND.LIB on the system disk.

## SEE ALSO:

Command PARAMETERS; functions FCLOSE( ), FERROR( ), FOPEN( ), FREADSTR( ), FSEEK( ), and FWRITE( ).

# FREADSTR( )

## DIALECTS:

Clipper only.

## SYNTAX:

FREADSTR(<expN1>,<expN2>)

## RETURNS:

Character string

## DEFINITION:

Reads/returns characters in an open file. You can store the result in a memory variable.

<expN1> is the numeric file handle returned by FOPEN( ) or FCREATE( ).

<expN2> specifies how many bytes to read from the current DOS file pointer position. The argument can be positive or negative. FREADSTR( ) ends if it encounters a null character (ASCII 0), indicating an error or the end of file.

READSTR( ) can accommodate strings up to 64K bytes long.

## RECOMMENDED USE:

Use FREADSTR( ) to gather data from text files. Use FERROR( ) to determine whether the read succeeded.

**Example**—An educational program stores student observations in text files. FREADSTR( ) captures the information in a memory variable that you can store in a database file.

```
observe = space(150)              && Initialize buffer variable.
mhandle = FOPEN("labwork.txt",2)  && Open LABWORK.TXT
mbuf = FREADSTR(mhandle,150)      && Read text into memory variable.
IF FERROR() # 0
  @ 23,01 SAY "Reading text file, press a key to return"
  WAIT ""
ENDIF
mbuf1 = SUBSTR(mhandle,1,75)      && Manipulate string with standard
mbuf2 = SUBSTR(mhandle,75,75)     &&   SUBSTR() function.
REPLACE lab1 WITH mbuf1,lab2 with mbuf2
```

## LIMITS/WARNINGS:

FREADSTR( ) is for advanced programmers who understand DOS files.

Do not abbreviate this function as Clipper will confuse it with FREAD( ).

FREADSTR( ) is in EXTEND.LIB on the system disk.

## SEE ALSO:

Functions FCLOSE( ), FERROR( ), FOPEN( ), FREAD( ), FSEEK( ), and FWRITE( ).

# FROW( )

## DIALECTS:
dBXL and Quicksilver.

## SYNTAX:
FROW( )

## RETURNS:
Numeric

## DEFINITION:
Returns the row coordinate in an open output file.

You must first select the output file with SET ALTERNATE TO and SET DEVICE TO ALTERNATE.

## DEFAULT:
0 if no ALTERNATE file is open.

## RECOMMENDED USE:
FROW( ) lets you send output to an ALTERNATE file at a position relative to the current row. This is useful for building documents from data with varying numbers of items. You can also use FROW( ) in generalized routines. By using relative row coordinates, you can design a single report for several applications.

**Example**—A financial analysis program creates a document containing the results of several computations. The user selects which computations to do, and the program presents the results in a disk file as a single report. Because the number of elements in the report varies, each module uses relative positioning. For example, a growth projection report first skips a line, then prints its results:

```
* ANALYSIS.PRG
SET ALTERNATE TO ratechrt
SET DEVICE TO alternate
SET ALTERNATE on
* <report selection menu>
DO ratesys          && One selection is RATESYS.
* RATESYS.PRG
```

```
USE rates
@ FROW()+1,01 SAY "MONTH------GROWTH RATE----ACCELERATION OF GROWTH"
@ FROW()+1,01 SAY "------------------------------------------------"
monthctr=1
DO WHILE monthctr <= 12 .and. .not. EOF()
  @ FROW()+1,01 SAY pmonth+SPACE(8)+STR(rate,5,2)+SPACE(8)+STR(acc,5,2)
  SKIP
  monthctr = monthctr + 1
ENDDO
```

## SEE ALSO:

Commands SET ALTERNATE and SET DEVICE; functions COL( ), FCOL( ), and PCOL( ).

# FSEEK( )

## DIALECTS:
Clipper only.

## SYNTAX:
FSEEK(<expN1>,<expN2>[,<expN3>])

## RETURNS:
Numeric

## DEFINITION:
Moves the DOS file pointer.

<expN1> is the numeric file handle returned by FCREATE( ) or FOPEN( ).

<expN2> is the number of characters away from the beginning of file, end of file, or current position as selected by <expN3>. <expN2> may be positive or negative.

<expN3> selects the origin in an open file using the following codes:

0 Beginning of file

1 Current pointer position

2 End of file

Note that FREAD( ) and FWRITE( ) also move the file pointer.

## DEFAULT:
0, beginning of file, if you do not specify a file position.

## RECOMMENDED USE:
FSEEK( ) gives you byte-level control over file writes and reads since FREAD( ) and FWRITE( ) begin at the current file pointer position.

**Example**—A real estate application stores property information in text files. FREAD( ) captures data in a memory variable that you can edit with MEMOEDIT( ). FSEEK( ) moves the pointer back to the beginning of file so the next FWRITE overwrites the data, instead of appending it.

```
tempvar = space(250)                  && Initialize buffer variable.
mhandle = FOPEN("CONDO1.4SL",2)       && Open CONDO1.4SL file.
FREAD(mhandle,@tempvar,250)           && Read text into memory variable.
FSEEK(mhandle,0)                      && Set pointer to beginning of file.
mbuf = HARDCR(MEMOEDIT(tempvar))      && Edit memory variable with MEMOEDIT().
FWRITE(mhandle,mbuf)                  && Write result back to file.
```

## LIMITS/WARNINGS:

FSEEK( ) is for advanced programmers who understand how DOS handles files.

FSEEK( ) is in EXTEND.LIB on the system disk.

## SEE ALSO:

Functions FCLOSE( ), FCREATE( ), FERROR( ), FOPEN( ), FREAD( ), FREADSTR( ), and FWRITE( ).

# FV( )

## DIALECTS:

dBASE IV only.

## SYNTAX:

FV(<expN1>,<expN2>,<expN3>)

## RETURNS:

Numeric

## DEFINITION:

Computes the future value of regular deposits yielding a fixed interest rate for a number of periods.

Future value is the total deposit plus the generated interest.

<expN1> is the payment amount. It can be positive or negative.

<expN2> is the decimal interest rate compounded once per period. It must be positive. Note that while interest rates are usually expressed as annual figures, most fixed rate accounts compound monthly, so divide your rate by 12.

<expN3> is the number of periods.

## RECOMMENDED USE:

Use FV( ) to project earnings from fixed rate investments.

**Example**—A savings plan calls for monthly $100 deposits that earn 7.5 percent compounded monthly. After one year, the account is worth $1242.12.

```
payment = 100
rate = .075/12
periods = 12
mworth = FV(payment,rate,periods)
    1242.12
```

## SEE ALSO:

Command CALCULATE.

# FWRITE( )

## DIALECTS:

Clipper only.

## SYNTAX:

FWRITE(<expN1>,<memvarC>[,<expN2>])

## RETURNS:

Numeric

## DEFINITION:

Writes a memory variable to an open DOS file and returns the number of bytes written. Writing begins at the current file pointer position (see FSEEK( )).

If the write does not succeed, FWRITE( ) returns 0.

<expN1> is the numeric file handle returned by FOPEN( ) or FCREATE( ).

<expC> is an existing character memory variable containing the string to write.

<expN2> is the number of bytes to write from the memory variable. If you omit it, FWRITE( ) writes the entire variable. FWRITE( ) returns the value <expN2> after a successful write.

## RECOMMENDED USE:

Use FWRITE( ) to store data in text files.

**Example**—A statistical analysis program puts data in text files for an external graphics package. The program scans a database file in a loop, writing data into the open file.

```
USE stats
fhandle = FCREATE("temp.txt",0)
DO WHILE .not. EOF()
  mstat = stat
  FWRITE(fhandle,mstat)
  SKIP
ENDDO
```

Printing TEMP.TXT shows the STAT fields from each record concatenated in a string without line breaks. In each execution of the loop, the file pointer moves to the end of a written string.

## LIMITS/WARNINGS:

FWRITE( ) is for advanced programmers who understand how DOS handles files.

FWRITE( ) is in EXTEND.LIB on the system disk.

## SEE ALSO:

Functions FCLOSE( ), FCREATE( ), FERROR( ), FOPEN( ), FREAD( ), FREADSTR( ), and FSEEK( ).

# GETE

## DIALECTS:
Clipper only.

## SYNTAX:
GETE<expC>

## RETURNS:
Character

## DEFINITION:
Returns the contents of a DOS environmental variable. <expC> is a variable such as COMSPEC, PATH and USER. GETE is the same as GETENV in other dialects. GETE is in EXTEND.LIB on the system disk.

## SEE ALSO:
Function GETENV( ).

# GETENV( )

## DIALECTS:
dBASE III PLUS, dBASE IV, dBXL, FoxBASE+, and Quicksilver.

## SYNTAX:
GETENV(<expC>)

## RETURNS:
Character

## DEFINITION:
Returns the contents of a DOS environmental variable. <expC> is a variable such as COMSPEC, PATH, or USER.

DOS environmental variables are like dBASE memory variables. They are defined at the operating system level with the DOS SET command. See your DOS manual for more information.

GETENV( ) returns a null string if it does not find <expC>.

## RECOMMENDED USE:
Use GETENV( ) to incorporate operating system information into your applications.

**Example**—A publishing conglomerate uses several multiuser database applications on a local area network. To identify users, the system supervisor includes a SET statement in the batch file of each workstation. The DOS statement

```
SET USER="PAULA"
```

creates a DOS environmental variable USER containing the value "PAULA." Now, when Paula begins working with a database application on the network, GETENV( ) takes her name from USER and stores it in the user log.

```
m_user = GETENV("USER")
USE userlog EXCLUSIVE
APPEND BLANK
REPLACE username WITH m_user
REPLACE timein WITH TIME()
USE
```

## LIMITS/WARNINGS:

When assigning environmental variables, do not put spaces between the variable name and the equal sign, or between the equal sign and the assigned value. Doing so will cause GETENV( ) to return a null value.

You cannot SET DOS environment variables with the RUN command.

## VARIATIONS:

**Clipper:** Use GETE( ) instead of GETENV( ).

## SEE ALSO:

Command SET ERRORLEVEL; functions DISKSPACE( ), GETE, and OS( ).

# HARDCR( )

## DIALECTS:

Clipper only.

## SYNTAX:

HARDCR(<expC>)

## RETURNS:

Character

## DEFINITION:

Replaces all soft carriage returns [CHR(141)] in <expC> with hard carriage returns [CHR(13)].

HARDCR( ) is in EXTEND.LIB on the system disk.

## RECOMMENDED USE:

Clipper's MEMOEDIT( ) function has automatic word wrap that stores memo field text with soft carriage returns. This causes a problem when displaying memo fields without MEMOEDIT( ). The text appears scrambled. HARDCR( ) corrects the problem.

**Example**—A library application stores magazine abstracts in Clipper memo fields. During data entry, MEMOEDIT( ) controls text input, leaving soft carriage returns at the end of every line.

To generate reports that include the memo field ABSTRACT, the programmer uses HARDCR( ) with the memo field name as the parameter.

```
* <@...SAYs>
? HARDCR(abstract)
TITLE: ELEMENTARY MATHEMATICAL ANALYSIS

A full-year course for secondary school juniors or seniors,
or for college freshmen
```

To actually change the carriage returns in the memo field from soft to hard, the programmer later REPLACEs the field with its own HARDCR( ) version.

```
REPLACE abstract WITH HARDCR(abstract)
```

## SEE ALSO:

Functions MEMOEDIT( ), MEMOTRAN( ), and MEMOWRITE( ).

# HEADER( )

## DIALECTS:
Clipper only.

## SYNTAX:
HEADER( )

## RETURNS:
Numeric

## DEFINITION:
Returns the size (in bytes) of the active database file's header. Returns 0 if no database is active.

## RECOMMENDED USE:
Use HEADER( ) with DISKSPACE( ) and RECSIZE( ) to determine whether a disk has enough room for operations such as SORT, INDEX, or COPY.

**Example**—A subroutine makes floppy disk backups of database files. Before doing so, it compares the file size with the available disk space. The subroutine computes file size as the number of records times the record size, plus the size of the database file header.

```
totsize = RECSIZE()*RECCOUNT() + HEADER()   && Compute total file size.
IF totsize > DISKSPACE(1)                   && The 1 means A: in Clipper.
  * <error routine>
ELSE
  * <copy routine>
ENDIF
```

## VARIATIONS:
You can also determine the header size with the formula

32 x <field count> + 35

For example, to find the header size in FoxBASE+, issue the command

header = 32 x FCOUNT( ) + 35

Because dBASE III PLUS, dBASE IV, dBXL, and Quicksilver lack a FCOUNT( ) (field count) function, issue the commands

```
IF LEN(TRIM(FIELD(1))) = 0
  RETURN
ENDIF
fcount = 1
DO WHILE LEN(TRIM(FIELD(fcount))) > 0
  fcount = fcount + 1
ENDDO
 header = 32 * fcount + 35
```

HEADER( ) is in EXTEND.LIB on the system disk.

## SEE ALSO:

Functions DISKSPACE( ), RECCOUNT( ), and RECSIZE( ).

# HTOI( )

## DIALECTS:
dBXL and Quicksilver.

## SYNTAX:
HTOI(<expC>)

## RETURNS:
Numeric

## DEFINITION:
Returns the decimal value of its hexadecimal argument.

Specify the argument as a character string of numbers.

## RECOMMENDED USE:
Use HTOI( ) to convert hexadecimal numbers to decimal.

Programmers traditionally refer to DOS function calls by hexadecimal value. Because dBXL and Quicksilver do not recognize literal hexademical numbers, use HTOI( ) to specify them as arguments. Affected commands and functions include DOSINT, IN( ), and OUT.

**Example**—A program uses DOSINT to determine the valid disk drives. DOSINT uses DOS functions 19h and 0Eh, specified in hexadecimal and converted to decimal in the HTOI( ) function.

```
* <More statements>.
*
doscall   = HTOI("21")
cur_disk  = HTOI("1900")          && AX=1900h = current disk DOS call.
sel_drive = HTOI("0E00")          && AX=0e00h = select drive DOS call.
axreg = cur_disk
DOSINT doscall,axreg              && call DOS (get current drive)
init_drive = MOD(axreg,abyte)     && MOD() masks off AH value,
*                                 && saves current drive from AL
* <More statements>.
```

See command DOSINT for the complete valid drive program. (VALDRIVE.PRG).

## SEE ALSO:
Commands DOSINT and OUT; functions ITOH( ) and IN( ).

# IF( )

## DIALECTS:
Clipper only.

## SYNTAX:
IF(<expL>,<exp1>,<exp2>)

## RETURNS:
Character, date, logical, or numeric

## DEFINITION:
Synonym for IIF( ).

# IIF( )

## DIALECTS:
Clipper, dBASE III PLUS, dBASE IV, dBXL, FoxBASE+, and Quicksilver.

## SYNTAX:
IIF(<expL>,<exp1>,<exp2>)

## RETURNS:
Character, date, logical, or numeric

## DEFINITION:
Evaluates the logical expression <expL>. If it is true, IIF( ) returns <exp1>. Otherwise, it returns <exp2>.

<exp1> and <exp2> may be character, date, logical, or numeric expressions, as long as they are both the same type. The returned expression also has that type.

IIF( ) simulates IF...ELSE...ENDIF on a single line.

## RECOMMENDED USE:
For faster execution, use IIF( ) instead of IF..ELSE..ENDIF statements with just two alternatives.

You can also use IIF( ) in most expressions, such as index expressions, @...SAYs, REPORT FORMs, and label formats.

**Example 1**—A data editing routine in a medical office program displays a message for DELETED records. Initially, the programmer used IF...ELSE...ENDIF to display the message as follows:

```
IF DELETED()
  @ 01,50 SAY "DELETED"
ELSE
  @ 01,50 SAY "       "
ENDIF
```

If the record is deleted, the program displays "DELETED" in the top right-hand corner of the screen. Otherwise, the program prints spaces there to overwrite previous "DELETED" messages.

To speed execution, the programmer converts the IF...ELSE...ENDIF to IIF( ) as follows:

```
@ 01,50 SAY IIF(DELETED(),"DELETED","        ")
```

**Example 2**—The president of Rapid Corp. asks for a telephone directory from his data processing department. He wants it printed in alphabetical order, keyed on LASTNAME for easy reference.

Because some LASTNAME fields are empty, the programmer uses IIF( ) to include COMPANY in the alphabetic order. A LIST of the file shows eight records, including three without LASTNAMEs:

```
USE clients
LIST lastname,company
Record#  LASTNAME   COMPANY
     1  Johnson
     2  Adams
     3  Briggs
     4  Zarzuela
     5  Simone
     6             Harrison Products
     7             Marseilles Communications
     8             Zanfir Products
```

When LASTNAME is empty, IIF( ) designates COMPANY as the key field.

IIF( ) first determines whether LASTNAME is empty. If so, it returns COMPANY. If not, it returns LASTNAME.

```
INDEX on IIF(lastname = "    ",company,lastname) TO subdex
```

The resulting index shows LASTNAME and COMPANY in the same alphabetical order:

```
Record#  LASTNAME   COMPANY
     2  Adams
     3  Briggs
     6             Harrison Products
     1  Johnson
     7             Marseilles Communications
     5  Simone
     8             Zanfir Products
     4  Zarzuela
```

## SPECIAL USES:

You can use IIF( ) to index on logical keys by substituting 1's and 0's for true and false values, as follows:

```
INDEX ON IIF(<expL>,"1","0")
```

This produces an index based on the logical field, yet the actual key is of character type. See INDEX for an example.

## VARIATIONS:

**Clipper:** <expl> and <exp2> can be different data types. Also, the expression that does not execute may contain an error without causing a runtime problem. IF( ) is a synonym for IIF( ).

## SEE ALSO:

Commands CASE, DO CASE, ELSEIF, IF, and INDEX.

# IN( )

## DIALECTS:
dBXL and Quicksilver.

## SYNTAX:
IN(<expN>)

## RETURNS:
Numeric

## DEFINITION:
Returns a number from a system input port, used to get data from a device other than the keyboard.

<expN> is the port number. Port numbers vary with computer model.

## RECOMMENDED USE:
Use IN( ) to connect dBXL to external devices such as mouse interface cards, cash registers, and custom devices. Use BITSET( ) to test the binary value IN( ) returns.

**Example**—A monitoring device controls an automated assembly line. When a malfunction occurs, the device sends a 3 (binary 00000011) through the PC's input port 5. IN( ) reads port 5. BITSET( ) checks the binary value and determines that bit 0 (the rightmost bit) is on. A telecommunications program then calls the supervisor via modem to report the malfunction.

```
DO WHILE .t.
  IF BITSET(IN(5),0)
    DO call_super
    OUT 5,0
  ENDIF
ENDDO
```

## SEE ALSO:
Command OUT; function BITSET( ).

# INDEXEXT

## DIALECTS:
Clipper only.

## SYNTAX:
INDEXEXT( )

## RETURNS:
Character

## DEFINITION:
Returns "NTX" for Clipper's default index structure, or "NDX" if you link your application with NDX.OBJ.

## RECOMMENDED USE:
Clipper (Summer '87) supports two index structures. By linking NDX.OBJ with an application, programmers can override Clipper's default (NTX) indexes, substituting dBASE III PLUS- and dBASE IV-compatible (NDX) indexes.

To maintain source code portability, independent of the index structure, use INDEXEXT( ) when specifying index filenames in a program.

**Example**—A finance company stores account information on a computer. When the program starts in the morning, it uses the FILE( ) function to ensure that the necessary indexes exist. The programmer uses INDEXEXT( ) to specify the index extension.

```
CLEAR
IF .NOT. FILE("ACCT." + INDEXEXT())
  resp = " "
  @ 23,03 SAY "ACCT." + INDEXEXT() + " NOT FOUND. "
  @ 24,03 SAY "Rebuild it now? " GET resp PICT "!" VALID "YN"$resp
  READ
  IF resp = "Y"
    * <rebuild index file>
  ELSE
    * <alternate program>
  ENDIF
ENDIF
```

## SEE ALSO:
Command INDEX; functions FILE( ), INDEXKEY( ), and INDEXORD( ).

# INDEXKEY( )

## DIALECTS:

Clipper only.

## SYNTAX:

INDEXKEY(<expN>)

## RETURNS:

Character

## DEFINITION:

Returns the key expression of an active index. <expN> is the position of the index in the commands

USE <database> [INDEX [<index1>] [,<index2>] [,<index3>]... [,<index7>]]

and

SET INDEX TO [<index1>] [,<index2>] [,<index3>]...[,<index7>]

If the specified index does not exist, INDEXKEY( ) returns a null string.

In addition to its relative position in the list, you can refer to the master index (the controlling index) as number 0. (For example, you can change the master index using the SET ORDER command without affecting the original index numbers).

## RECOMMENDED USE:

Use INDEXKEY( ) in user applications to display index expressions, or in system utility programs to maintain index files. INDEXKEY( ) is also helpful in debugging.

**Example 1**—A program opens a database file with two indexes. If the index files become corrupted or are not updated, the user can choose to rebuild them using the key returned by INDEXKEY( ).

```
USE master INDEX acctdex, maindex
* <More statements>
yesindex = .f.
@ 11,01 SAY "Do you want to reindex?" GET yesindex PICTURE "Y"
```

```
READ
IF yesindex
  key1 = INDEXKEY(1)          && Returns UPPER(ACCT).
  key2 = INDEXKEY(2)          && Returns MAIN.
  USE master
  INDEX ON &key1 TO acctdex   && INDEX ON UPPER(ACCT) TO acctdex
  INDEX ON &key2 TO maindex   && INDEX ON MAIN TO MAINDEX
ENDIF
```

**Example 2**—To debug a complex banking application, a programmer displays INDEXKEY( ) when opening an index. If a search fails, or an index becomes corrupted, INDEXKEY( ) helps trace the problem.

```
USE assets INDEX massets,liabilities
? "  PRIMARY KEY: " + INDEXKEY(0)
? "SECONDARY KEY: " + INDEXKEY(1)
  PRIMARY KEY: mtotal
SECONDARY KEY: expense
```

## VARIATIONS:

**dBASE IV:** See function KEY( ) for equivalent.

**FoxBASE+:** See function SYS(14) for equivalent.

## SEE ALSO:

Commands SET INDEX TO, SET ORDER TO, and USE; functions INDEXEXT( ), INDEXORD( ), KEY( ), and SYS( ).

# INDEXORD( )

## DIALECTS:

Clipper only.

## SYNTAX:

INDEXORD( )

## RETURNS:

Numeric

## DEFINITION:

Returns the relative position in the index list of the master index.

If there is no controlling index (ORDER is SET to 0), or if no index is open, INDEXORD( ) returns 0.

## RECOMMENDED USE:

Use INDEXORD( ) to save and restore index settings.

**Example**—An auto parts inventory database has three open indexes. When a user wants to search the database, the main program module calls a subroutine that changes the index order depending on the user's request. To maintain a modular design, the subroutine restores the original master index before returning to the main program.

```
* MAIN.PRG
*
USE parts INDEX partno,descrip,vehicle
SET ORDER TO 3          && VEHICLE is the master index.
* <user selects search>
DO searcher
* SEARCHER.PRG
*
morder = INDEXORD()     && MORDER is 3 on entry to SEARCHER.PRG
* <user selects new order-by part number (PARTNO)>
SET ORDER TO 1
* <search code>
* <before returning to MAIN.PRG, restore original order>
SET ORDER TO morder
RETURN
```

## SEE ALSO:

Commands INDEX, SET INDEX, and SET ORDER; functions INDEXEXT( ), INDEXKEY( ), and ORDER( ).

# INKEY( )

## DIALECTS:

Clipper, dBASE III PLUS, dBASE IV, dBXL, FoxBASE+, and Quicksilver.

## SYNTAX:

INKEY( )

## RETURNS:

Numeric

## DEFINITION:

Returns an integer, between 1 and 255, that represents the ASCII value of the last key the user pressed.

If there is more than one character in the typeahead buffer, INKEY( ) returns the first one.

SET TYPEAHEAD TO 0 disables INKEY( ).

Note that many INKEY( ) values for Ctrl-key and Alt-key combinations are system specific. The following list summarizes the values:

### Clipper

| | | |
|---|---|---|
| F1 | 28 | |
| F2 to F10 | -1 to -9 | |
| Ctrl-F1 to Ctrl-F10 | -20 to -29 | |
| Ctrl-A to Ctrl-Z | 1 to 26 | (Ctrl-S has no effect) |
| Alt-F1 to Alt-F10 | -30 to -39 | |
| Alt-1 to Alt-0 | 376 to 385 | |

| | | | | | | | |
|---|---|---|---|---|---|---|---|
| Alt- - | 386 | Alt-Y | 277 | Alt-D | 288 | Alt-Z | 300 |
| Alt-+ | 387 | Alt-U | 278 | Alt-F | 289 | Alt-X | 301 |
| Alt-Q | 272 | Alt-I | 279 | Alt-G | 290 | Alt-C | 302 |
| Alt-W | 273 | Alt-O | 280 | Alt-H | 291 | Alt-V | 303 |
| Alt-E | 274 | Alt-P | 281 | Alt-J | 292 | Alt-B | 304 |
| Alt-R | 275 | Alt-A | 286 | Alt-K | 293 | Alt-N | 305 |
| Alt-T | 276 | Alt-S | 287 | Alt-L | 294 | Alt-M | 306 |

## dBASE III PLUS

| | | |
|---|---|---|
| F1 | 28 | |
| F2 to F10 | -1 to -9 | (return -64 with TYPEAHEAD SET TO 1) |
| Ctrl-F1 to Ctrl-F10 | 94 to 103 | |
| Ctrl-A to Ctrl-Z | 1 to 26 | (Ctrl-S should return 19, but does not work reliably) |
| Alt-F1 to Alt-F10 | 104 to 113 | |
| Alt-0 to Alt-F9 | 31 | |

| | | | | | | | |
|---|---|---|---|---|---|---|---|
| Alt-Q | 16 | Alt-I | 23 | Alt-G | 34 | Alt-C | 46 |
| Alt-W | 17 | Alt-O | 24 | Alt-H | 35 | Alt-V | 47 |
| Alt-E | 18 | Alt-P | 25 | Alt-J | 36 | Alt-B | 48 |
| Alt-R | 19 | Alt-A | 30 | Alt-K | 37 | Alt-N | 49 |
| Alt-T | 20 | Alt-S | 31 | Alt-L | 38 | Alt-M | 50 |
| Alt-Y | 21 | Alt-D | 32 | Alt-Z | 44 | | |
| Alt-U | 22 | Alt-F | 33 | Alt-X | 45 | | |

## dBASE IV

| | | |
|---|---|---|
| F1 | 28 | |
| F2 to F10 | -1 to -9 | |
| Ctrl-F1 to Ctrl-F10 | -10 to -19 | |
| Ctrl-A to Ctrl-Z | 1 to 26 | |
| Shift-A to Shift-Z | 65 to 90 | |
| Shift-F1 to Shift F9 | -20 to -28 | Shift-F10 reserved for macro menu |
| Alt-F1 to Alt-F10 | 0 | Alt-keys reserved for macro execution |
| Alt-0 | -452 | |
| Alt-1 to Alt-9 | -451 to -443 | |
| Alt-A to Alt-Z | -435 to -410 | |
| 0 to 9 | 48 to 57 | |

## dBXL

| | | |
|---|---|---|
| F1 | 28 | |
| F2 to F10 | -1 to -9 | |
| Ctrl-A to Ctrl-Z | 1 to 26 | (Ctrl-S has no effect) |
| Ctrl-F1 to Ctrl-F10 | 94 to 103 | |
| Alt-F1 to Alt-F10 | 104 to 113 | |
| Alt-0 to Alt-9 | 31 | |
| Alt-- and Alt-_ | 31 | (Alt-hyphen and Alt-underscore) |
| Alt-+ and Alt-= | 156 | |

| | | | |
|---|---|---|---|
| Alt-A | 30 | Alt-N | 49 |
| Alt-B | 48 | Alt-O | 24 |
| Alt-C | 46 | Alt-P | 25 |

| | | | |
|---|---|---|---|
| Alt-D | 32 | Alt-Q | 16 |
| Alt-E | 18 | Alt-R | 19 |
| Alt-F | 33 | Alt-S | 31 |
| Alt-G | 34 | Alt-T | 20 |
| Alt-H | 35 | Alt-U | 22 |
| Alt-I | 23 | Alt-V | 47 |
| Alt-J | 36 | Alt-W | 17 |
| Alt-K | 37 | Alt-X | 45 |
| Alt-L | 38 | Alt-Y | 21 |
| Alt-M | 50 | Alt-Z | 44 |

## FoxBASE+

| | | |
|---|---|---|
| F1 | 28 | |
| F2 to F10 | -1 to -9 | |
| Ctrl-F1 to Ctrl-F10 | 94 to 103 | |
| Ctrl-A to Ctrl-Z | 1 to 26 | (Ctrl-H is 127) |
| Alt-F1 to Alt-F10 | 104 to 113 | |
| Alt-0 | 19 | |
| Alt-1 to Alt-9 | 120 to 128 | |

| | | | | | | | |
|---|---|---|---|---|---|---|---|
| Alt-Q | 16 | Alt-I | 23 | Alt-G | 34 | Alt-C | 46 |
| Alt-W | 17 | Alt-O | 24 | Alt-H | 35 | Alt-V | 47 |
| Alt-E | 18 | Alt-P | 25 | Alt-J | 36 | Alt-B | 48 |
| Alt-R | 19 | Alt-A | 30 | Alt-K | 37 | Alt-N | 49 |
| Alt-T | 20 | Alt-S | 31 | Alt-L | 38 | Alt-M | 50 |
| Alt-Y | 21 | Alt-D | 32 | Alt-Z | 44 | | |
| Alt-U | 22 | Alt-F | 33 | Alt-X | 45 | | |

## Quicksilver

| | | |
|---|---|---|
| F1 | 28 | |
| F2 to F10 | -1 to -9 | |
| Ctrl-F1 to Ctrl-F10 | 94 to 103 | |
| Ctrl-A to Ctrl-Z | 1 to 26 | (Ctrl-H is 127, Ctrl-S has no effect) |
| Alt-F1 to Alt-F10 | 104 to 113 | |
| Alt-0 to Alt-9 | 31 | |

| | | | | | | | |
|---|---|---|---|---|---|---|---|
| Alt-Q | 16 | Alt-I | 23 | Alt-G | 34 | Alt-C | 46 |
| Alt-W | 17 | Alt-O | 24 | Alt-H | 35 | Alt-V | 47 |
| Alt-E | 18 | Alt-P | 25 | Alt-J | 36 | Alt-B | 48 |
| Alt-R | 19 | Alt-A | 30 | Alt-K | 37 | Alt-N | 49 |

| | | | | | | | |
|---|---|---|---|---|---|---|---|
| Alt-T | 20 | Alt-S | 31 | Alt-L | 38 | Alt-M | 50 |
| Alt-Y | 21 | Alt-D | 32 | Alt-Z | 44 | | |
| Alt-U | 22 | Alt-F | 33 | Alt-X | 45 | | |

Because INKEY( ) returns a value for almost any key pressed, it lets you use non-printing keys such as the arrows, PgUp, and PgDn. These keys have the following equivalents:

| SPECIAL KEYS | ASCII VALUES | EQUIVALENT KEYS |
|---|---|---|
| Home | 1 | Ctrl-A |
| Ctrl-Right arrow | 2 | Ctrl-B |
| PgDn | 3 | Ctrl-C |
| Right arrow | 4 | Ctrl-D |
| Up arrow | 5 | Ctrl-E |
| End | 6 | Ctrl-F |
| Del | 7 | Ctrl-G |
| PgUp | 18 | Ctrl-R |
| Left arrow | 19 | Ctrl-S |
| Ins | 22 | Ctrl-V |
| Ctrl-End | 23 | Ctrl-W |
| Down arrow | 24 | Ctrl-X |
| Ctrl-Left arrow | 26 | Ctrl-Z |
| Ctrl-Home | 29 | Ctrl-] |
| Ctrl-PgDn | 30 | Ctrl-^ |
| Ctrl-PgUp | 31 | Ctrl-_ |

## DEFAULT:

If no key is pressed, INKEY( ) returns 0.

## RECOMMENDED USE:

INKEY( ) can get user responses without pausing program execution as with a READ, ACCEPT, or WAIT.

**Example 1**—In the midst of printing, a mailing label jams the platen. Names and addresses continue to print; however, they overwrite since the labels are not advancing.

The print program allows the user to press "C" to force a stop. To do this, it uses INKEY( ) within a DO WHILE loop to check for a key press. Because it does not pause execution, INKEY( ) does not interfere with label printing.

```
SET PRINT ON
DO WHILE .NOT. EOF() .AND. INKEY() # 67
  ?
  ? NAME
  ? COMPANY
  ? ADDRESS
  ? TRIM(CITY) + ", " + STATE + " " + ZIP
  ?
  SKIP                    && Move to next record.
ENDDO
SET PRINT OFF             && Upon exiting DO WHILE, SET PRINT OFF.
```

**Example 2**—A record editing program in a project management system uses INKEY( ) to get single character responses to prompts. This lets the programmer get user responses without conflicting with pending GETs (a READ statement would activate them).

```
* <@...SAY...GETs>                          && Display GETs.
@ 23,01 SAY "Edit this record? (Y/N)"       && Issue prompt.
act = 0                                     && Initialize ACT.
DO WHILE act # 89 .AND. act # 78            && Continue DO WHILE until
  act = INKEY()                             &&   user presses Y or N.
ENDDO
IF CHR(act) = "Y"                           && Convert ASCII value
  READ                                      &&   back to original character.
ELSE                                        && If user enters Y, READ pending
  CLEAR GETS                                &&   GETs; otherwise, CLEAR them.
ENDIF
```

**Example 3**—A menu system in a stock market analysis program uses arrow keys to move a highlighted cursor. INKEY( ) gets the user's response.

```
* <cursor movement routine>
action = 0
DO WHILE action = 0
  action = INKEY()
ENDDO
DO CASE
  CASE action = 4
    * pressed right arrow
  CASE action = 19
    * pressed left arrow
  CASE action = 5
    * pressed up arrow
  CASE action = 24
    * pressed down arrow
ENDCASE
```

**Example 4**—A car rental agency uses a program to track vehicle maintenance. For convenience, each menu displays a clock based on the system time. The clock ticks until the user presses a key.

```
* <@...SAY...GETs>
keypress = 0
DO WHILE keypress = 0
  @ 24,70 SAY TIME()          && Display time.
  interval = TIME()           && Store time in variable.
  keypress = INKEY()          && Check for KEYPRESS with INKEY()
  * Stay in DO WHILE until TIME() changes, updating screen once per second.
  DO WHILE keypress=0 .AND. interval=TIME()
    keypress = INKEY()        && Check for KEYPRESS again.
  ENDDO
ENDDO
* <CASE structure to process user selections>
```

## LIMITS/WARNINGS:

**dBASE III PLUS:** When you SET TYPEAHEAD TO 1, INKEY( ) may erroneously return -64 when you press a function key from F2 through F10.

## VARIATIONS:

**Clipper, dBASE IV, FoxBASE+:** An optional argument in the form

```
INKEY(<expN>)
```

pauses program execution for the number of seconds given by <expN>. The pause is in "real-time" seconds, independent of the computer's processing speed. If the user presses a key during a pause, INKEY( ) returns its value.

INKEY(0) pauses program execution until the user presses a key.

The dBXL/Quicksilver SLEEP( ) function also pauses program execution in "real" seconds.

## SEE ALSO:

Commands ON KEY and SET TYPEAHEAD; functions CHR( ), LASTKEY( ), READKEY( ), SINKEY( ), and SLEEP( ).

# INT( )

## DIALECTS:

Clipper, dBASE III PLUS, dBASE IV, dBXL, FoxBASE+, and Quicksilver.

## SYNTAX:

INT(<expN>)

## RETURNS:

Numeric

## DEFINITION:

Returns the largest integer that does not exceed its argument. (INT( ) discards the decimal point and all digits to its right).

INT( ) is like FLOOR( ), except that its result is an integer rather than a decimal number.

## RECOMMENDED USE:

The primary use of INT( ) is to select every "Nth" record from a database.

**Example**—The manager of a list rental agency receives an order for a list consisting of every eighth name. Nth record selections are a common way to sample names without using the entire list. The list manager uses INT( ) to select the names using the equation

```
RECNO()/8 = INT(RECNO()/8)
```

The equation is true when record number is divisible by 8. You can use it in any command that accepts a FOR condition.

The selection commands create a temporary file as follows:

```
USE dblists
COPY TO TEMP FOR (RECNO()/8 = INT(RECNO()/8))
```

DBLISTS contains 10,000 records. A listing of TEMP shows 1250 records—one of every eight in DBLISTS.

## SEE ALSO:

Functions CEIL( ), FLOOR( ), and ROUND( ).

# ISALPHA( )

## DIALECTS:

Clipper, dBASE III PLUS, dBASE IV, dBXL, FoxBASE+, and Quicksilver.

## SYNTAX:

ISALPHA(<expC>)

## RETURNS:

Logical

## DEFINITION:

Returns true if the first character in its argument is a letter.

## RECOMMENDED USE:

Use ISALPHA( ) to validate filenames, since they may not start with a number. Also use it in routines that manipulate character strings, doing tasks such as mid-string character replacements. Such routines include password encryption and name capitalization.

**Example 1**—A sales program prompts the user to enter a filename in which to save summary data. After the user responds, ISALPHA( ) tests the first character to make sure it is not a number.

```
mname = SPACE(8)
DO WHILE .NOT. ISALPHA(mname)
  @ 10,10 SAY "Enter filename: " GET mname
  READ
ENDDO
SAVE ALL LIKE res* TO &mname
```

Using a VALID clause, you can reduce the number of lines (not available in dBASE III PLUS).

```
mname = SPACE(8)
@ 10,10 SAY "Enter filename: " GET mname VALID ISALPHA(mname)
READ
```

**Example 2**—To conserve fields in very large applications, some programmers use single fields for multiple data items. For example, a character field PART with a length of 30 may contain both a part description and a part number as follows:

```
PART
Screwdriver9383754
Wrench8384777
```

You can find the part number by checking ISALPHA( ) of each character in the field as follows:

```
ctr = 1
DO WHILE ISALPHA(SUBSTR(part,ctr,1))
  ctr = ctr + 1
ENDDO
```

When ISALPHA returns false to indicate the first digit, the DO WHILE terminates with CTR pointing to the digit. The part number is the rest of the field, which we can obtain with

```
partnum = TRIM(SUBSTR(part,ctr,30-ctr))
```

## VARIATIONS:

**Clipper:** ISALPHA( ) is in EXTEND.LIB on the system disk.

## SEE ALSO:

Functions ISLOWER( ) and ISUPPER( ).

# ISCOLOR( )

## DIALECTS:
Clipper, dBASE III PLUS, dBASE IV, dBXL, FoxBASE+, and Quicksilver.

## SYNTAX:
ISCOLOR( )

## RETURNS:
Logical

## DEFINITION:
Returns true on computers with a color graphics card.

## RECOMMENDED USE:
ISCOLOR( ) lets you write programs for both color and monochrome displays. Use it to specify video attributes or colors depending on the type of display.

**Example**—The Real Time Real Estate program can use a color display. To differentiate between color and monochrome displays, the programmer includes ISCOLOR( ) at the beginning of the program when setting colors.

```
* REALT.PRG
* <set up environment>
IF ISCOLOR()                  && If ISCOLOR() is true,
  SET COLOR TO BG+/N,R/W      &&   set colors to CYAN on BLACK
ENDIF                         &&   with RED on WHITE input fields
                              &&   and no border.
```

In this example, if ISCOLOR( ) is false, the default video settings apply.

## LIMITS/WARNINGS:
Some graphics cards emulate color on a monochrome screen by displaying shades to represent different colors. (These cards, sometimes called *composite cards*, are found in many portable computers, and in Compaq and AT&T monochrome computers.) Although ISCOLOR( ) returns true for composite cards, some color combinations may be unreadable due to a lack of contrast.

## VARIATIONS:
**Clipper:** ISCOLOUR( ) is an alternate spelling.

## SEE ALSO:
Command SET COLOR; function SETCOLOR( ).

# ISLOWER( )

## DIALECTS:
Clipper, dBASE III PLUS, dBASE IV, dBXL, FoxBASE+, and Quicksilver.

## SYNTAX:
ISLOWER(<expC>)

## RETURNS:
Logical

## DEFINITION:
Returns true if the first character in its argument is a lowercase letter. Any other character returns false.

## RECOMMENDED USE:
Use ISLOWER( ) when manipulating strings in reports or in routines that convert data from upper to lowercase.

**Example**—A telemarketing company rents lists from several sources. One such list (in a database) contains the fields CONTACT, ADDRESS, CITY, STATE, and ZIPCODE. CONTACT may hold a proper name, a title, or a comment. The program must differentiate among these items to print them correctly.

The program uses ISLOWER( ) to distinguish the items by capitalization. Titles are in all uppercase, and proper names are in upper and lower case. Comments begin with lowercase.

ISLOWER( ) checks the first and second characters of the CONTACT field. If the first character is uppercase and the second lower, the program assumes it has found a proper name. If the first character is lowercase, the program assumes a comment. If the first and second characters are uppercase, the program assumes a title.

```
IF ISLOWER(contact)  && Check first character of CONTACT. If lower,
  comment = contact  &&   assume the field contains a comment.
ELSE
  IF ISLOWER(SUBSTR(contact,2,1))  && Check second character. If lower,
    proper = contact               &&   assume proper name.
  ELSE
```

```
    title = contact                    && If upper, assume title.
  ENDIF
ENDIF
```

## VARIATIONS:

**Clipper:** ISLOWER( ) is in EXTEND.LIB on the system disk.

## SEE ALSO:

Functions ISALPHA( ), ISUPPER( ), LOWER( ), and UPPER( ).

# ISMARKED( )

## DIALECTS:
dBASE IV only.

## SYNTAX:
ISMARKED([<expC>])

## RETURNS:
Logical

## DEFINITION:
Indicates whether a database is in a state of change.

After BEGINning TRANSACTION, dBASE IV puts a marker, called the integrity flag, in the file header when the file is in a state of change. If ISMARKED( ) detects the marker, it returns true (.T.).

## DEFAULTS:
Unless you specify an optional alias, ISMARKED( ) checks the database in the current work area.

ISMARKED( ) returns false (.F.) if issued with no file in use.

## RECOMMENDED USE:
Use it after restarting a program that was interrupted by an error or power failure to determine whether a database is in a state of change. If ISMARKED( ) is true, a transaction has begun. Also, use ISMARKED( ) in a multiuser environment to determine whether another user has begun a transaction.

**Example**—A power loss during a transaction leaves ISMARKED( ) set true. Upon reentry into the program, it will return .T., warning that the file may be corrupted. The program can then recover by RETURNing or by resetting the marker with the RESET command. Resetting the marker accepts possibly bad data.

```
USE accounts EXCLUSIVE
IF ISMARKED()
  mreset = .f.
```

```
  @ 24,03 SAY "Database file " + DBF() + " is in a state of change. "+;
        "Do you wish to RESET it?" GET mreset PICTURE "Y"
  IF mreset
    RESET       && Requires EXCLUSIVE use of the file.
  ELSE
    RETURN
  ENDIF
ENDIF
```

## SEE ALSO:

Commands BEGIN TRANSACTION, END TRANSACTION, RESET, and ROLLBACK; functions COMPLETED( ) and ROLLBACK( ).

# ISPRINTER( )

## DIALECTS:
Clipper only.

## SYNTAX:
ISPRINTER( )

## RETURNS:
Logical

## DEFINITION:
Indicates whether the current parallel printer port is ready. It returns true (.T.) if the port is ready and the printer is online, or false (.F.) if the port is not ready or the printer is off-line.

Similar to dBASE IV's PRINTSTATUS( ), FoxBASE+'s SYS(13), and dBXL's and Quicksilver's PRINTER( ).

## RECOMMENDED USE:
Use ISPRINTER( ) before printing to check the printer's status.

**Example**—Before printing a balance sheet, ISPRINTER( ) checks the printer's status. The programmer puts ISPRINTER( ) in a user defined function called CHKPRINT( ) that returns true (.T.) if the printer is online, and false if not.

```
* CHKPRINT
FUNCTION chkprint
*
PRIVATE pkey,success
pkey = 0
SET DEVICE TO SCREEN              && Make sure printer is not already on.
DO WHILE pkey # 27  .AND. .NOT. ISPRINTER()
  @ 01,01 SAY "Printer not ready. "+;
              "Press ESC to cancel, or any other key to retry"
  pkey = INKEY(0)
ENDDO
IF pkey # 27
  SET DEVICE TO PRINT
ENDIF
RETURN (pkey # 27)
```

The caller uses CHKPRINT( ) to determine whether to print as follows:

```
IF CHKPRINT()    DO acct_rpt
ELSE
  * DO <recovery procedure>
ENDIF
```

## SEE ALSO:

Functions PRINTSTATUS( ), PRINTER( ), and SYS(13).

# ISUPPER( )

## DIALECTS:
Clipper, dBASE III PLUS, dBASE IV, dBXL, FoxBASE+, and Quicksilver.

## SYNTAX:
ISUPPER(<expC>)

## RETURNS:
Logical

## DEFINITION:
Returns true if the first character in its argument is an uppercase letter. Any other character returns false.

## RECOMMENDED USE:
Use ISUPPER( ) in routines that manipulate strings, such as capitalization or encoding programs. It is similar to ISLOWER( ).

## VARIATIONS:
**Clipper:** ISUPPER( ) is in EXTEND.LIB on the system disk.

## SEE ALSO:
Functions ISALPHA( ), ISLOWER( ), LOWER( ), and UPPER( ).

# ITOH( )

## DIALECTS:

dBXL and Quicksilver.

## SYNTAX:

ITOH(<expN1>[,<expN2>])

## RETURNS:

Character

## DEFINITION:

Accepts a number <expN1> and returns its hexadecimal value as a character string.

## OPTIONS:

<expN2> is the length of the string returned by ITOH( ), padded with leading zeroes if necessary.

## RECOMMENDED USE:

ITOH( ) converts decimal numbers to hexadecimal. Use it with functions and commands that use hexadecimal arguments or return decimal values. Such functions and commands include HTOI( ) (hexadecimal to decimal), DOSINT, IN( ), and OUT.

See command DOSINT for detailed examples.

## SEE ALSO:

Commands DOSINT and OUT; functions HTOI( ) and IN( ).

# KEY( )

## DIALECTS:
dBASE IV only.

## SYNTAX:
KEY([<mdx filename>,]<expN>[,<alias>])

## RETURNS:
Character

## DEFINITION:
Returns the key expression of an active index. <expN> is the position of the index in the commands:

USE <database> [INDEX [<index1>] [,<index2>] [,<index3>]... [,<index7>]]

and

SET INDEX TO [<index1>] [,<index2>] [,<index3>]... [,<index7]

If the specified index does not exist, KEY( ) returns a null string.

## OPTIONS:
### <mdx filename>
You can use KEY( ) to determine the position of an index TAG within a multiple index.

The original order in which you add indexes (TAGs) to the MDX file determines their positions. <expN> is the TAG number.

You can specify the MDX of an unselected database by supplying its ALIAS as a KEY( ) argument.

## RECOMMENDED USE:
Use KEY( ) to display index expressions in applications, or to maintain index files in system utility programs. It is also helpful in debugging.

**Example 1**—A utility program opens a database file, then prompts the programmer to specify index filenames from the directory list. The user can then choose to rebuild the indexes using the key returned by KEY( ).

```
SELECT 1
* <User selects ACCTDEX and MAINDEX>.
USE master INDEX acctdex, maindex
* <use other files in different work areas>
SELECT 2
yesindex = .f.
@ 11,01 SAY "Do you want to reindex?" GET yesindex PICTURE "Y"
READ
IF yesindex
  * Use ALIAS since current work area is 2 and files are in 1.
  key1 = KEY(1,"master")        && Returns UPPER(ACCT)
  key2 = KEY(2,"master")        && Returns MAIN
  ndx1 = NDX(1,"master")        && Returns ACCTDEX
  ndx2 = NDX(2,"master")        && Returns MAINDEX
  SELECT 1
  USE master
  INDEX ON &key1 TO &ndx1
  INDEX ON &key2 TO &ndx2
ENDIF
```

**Example 2**—To debug a complex banking application, a programmer displays index keys when opening an MDX file. If a search fails, or an index becomes corrupted, KEY( ) helps trace the problem. This is similar to DISPLAYing STATUS.

```
* Note that the MDX name goes before the tag number.
USE assets ALIAS trans                && Automatically opens ASSETS.MDX.
ctr=1                                 &&   since it is a production MDX.
DO WHILE "" # KEY("ASSETS",ctr)       && Do while result not null.
  * The TAG() function returns the TAG name.
  ? STR(ctr,2,0) + ". Tag: " + TAG(ctr) + ",  Key: " + KEY("ASSETS",ctr)
  ctr = ctr + 1
ENDDO
```

The report shows a list of TAG names and key expressions:

```
1. Tag: NAME,  Key: substr(name,1,10)
2. Tag: STATE,  Key: state
3. Tag: SALESTOT,  Key: total
4. Tag: MATCH,  Key: substr(state,1,2)+substr(zip,1,4)
5. Tag: CITY,  Key: substr(city,1,4)
```

## VARIATIONS:

**Clipper:** See function INDEXKEY( ) for equivalent.

**FoxBASE+:** See function SYS(14) for equivalent.

## SEE ALSO:

Commands SET INDEX TO, SET ORDER TO, and USE; functions INDEXEXT( ), INDEXKEY( ), INDEXORD( ), SYS( ), and TAG( ).

# LASTKEY( )

## DIALECTS:
Clipper and dBASE IV.

## SYNTAX:
LASTKEY( )

## RETURNS:
Numeric

## DEFINITION:
Returns the ASCII version of the last key pressed.

## DEFAULT:
If no key was pressed, LASTKEY( ) returns 0.

## RECOMMENDED USE:
Use LASTKEY( ) after a READ to determine how it was completed. With LASTKEY( ), you can designate different actions for different keys pressed.

**Example**—A data entry program lets users abandon changes to active GETs by pressing Ctrl-Q or ESC. LASTKEY( ) checks which key terminated the read. If it is not Ctrl-Q or ESC, the program REPLACEs the database fields with the GET variables.

```
ctrlq = 17
m_esc = 27
* <initialize variables>
@ 02,01 SAY "Enter account number: " GET macct
@ 03,01 SAY "Enter invoice number: " GET minv
@ 04,01 SAY "Enter invoice total : " GET mtot
@ 05,01 SAY "Enter sales tax     : " GET mtax
READ
IF LASTKEY() = ctrlq .OR. LASTKEY() = m_esc   && Ctrl-Q or ESC
  @ 07,01 SAY "Are you sure you want to abandon changes? (Y/N) "
  WAIT "" TO sure
  IF sure $ "Yy"
    RETURN
  ENDIF
ENDIF
REPLACE acct with macct,inv with minv,tot with mtot,tax with mtax
```

## SEE ALSO:
Function READKEY( ).

# LASTREC( )

## DIALECTS:
Clipper only.

## SYNTAX:
LASTREC( )

## RETURNS:
Numeric

## DEFINITION:
Returns the number of records in the active database. Same as RECCOUNT( ).

## SEE ALSO:
Function RECCOUNT( ).

# LEFT( )

## DIALECTS:

Clipper, dBASE III PLUS, dBASE IV, dBXL, FoxBASE+, and Quicksilver.

## SYNTAX:

LEFT(<expC>,<expN>)

## RETURNS:

Character

## DEFINITION:

Returns a number of characters specified by <expN> from a string <expC>, starting with the leftmost character.

If <expN> is 0 or negative, LEFT( ) returns a null string.

LEFT( ) is the same as SUBSTR(<expC>,1,<expN>).

## RECOMMENDED USE:

Use LEFT( ) in string handling routines such as password encryption, upper/lower case conversion, and match coding. Also use LEFT to truncate data to fit in reports.

**Example 1**—When creating columnar reports from a database file, it is not always possible to include entire fields. When fields exceed the length of the paper, they wrap to the next line. To avoid this, truncate them using LEFT( ).

In this example, LNAME and FNAME are both 25 characters long. To fit them on one line with COMMENT, you must abbreviate them to ten characters each with LEFT( ).

```
SET PRINT on
DO WHILE .NOT. EOF()
  ? LEFT(lname,10) + " " + LEFT(fname,10) + LEFT(comment,40)
  SKIP
ENDDO
```

**Example 2**—A magazine subscription service uses match codes to identify subscribers. The first five characters of the code are the subscriber's Zip Code.

The next five are the first five characters of the subscriber's last name. The next four are the first four letters or digits of the street address. The last four characters indicate expiration date.

Using LEFT( ) and SUBSTR( ), a program divides the code into its components.

```
match   = "83222RONSO22340988"
mzip    = LEFT(match,5)
mlast   = SUBSTR(match,6,5)
mstreet = SUBSTR(match,11,4)
mexpire = SUBSTR(match,14,4)
? "Zip: " + mzip + " Last: " + mlast + " Street: " + mstreet + ;
  " Expiration: " + mexpire
   Zip: 83222 Last: RONSO Street: 2234 Expiration: 0988
```

## VARIATIONS:

**Clipper:** LEFT( ) is in EXTEND.LIB on the system disk.

**dBASE IV:** You can specify a memo field as the first argument in LEFT( ).

## SEE ALSO:

Functions STUFF( ) and SUBSTR( ).

# LEN( )

## DIALECTS:

Clipper, dBASE III PLUS, dBASE IV, dBXL, FoxBASE+, and Quicksilver.

## SYNTAX:

LEN(<expC>)

## RETURNS:

Numeric

## DEFINITION:

Returns the number of characters in the string <expC>.

## RECOMMENDED USE:

The versatile LEN( ) function has uses in many string handling routines. For example, you can use it to determine if a character expression contains data or to center text on the screen.

Sophisticated string handling routines often use LEN( ) to control processing within a DO WHILE loop. For an example, see function ASC( ).

**Example 1**—A mailing program uses dBXL's EMPTY( ) function to determine whether a string is blank. EMPTY( ) returns true if the specified string contains no data. The program presents blank input fields for each new record. The user can fill them in, or leave them blank to exit. If the user leaves the first field blank, EMPTY( ) returns true and data entry ends.

To convert this program to dBASE III PLUS or FoxBASE+ (neither has an EMPTY( ) function), the programmer uses LEN( ). First, TRIM( ) removes all trailing blanks. Because empty fields are all blanks, if the LEN( ) of the TRIM of the field is 0, the field is empty.

```
@ 01,01 SAY "Surname: " GET mlast  && Memory variable MLAST
* <@...SAY...GETs>                 &&   holds last name.
READ
IF LEN(TRIM(mlast))=0        && If LENgth of TRIM of MLAST equals 0,
  EXIT                       &&   EXIT DO WHILE and proceed to next
ELSE                         &&   statement; if MLAST contains data,
  LOOP                       &&   go to top of DO WHILE and resume
ENDIF                        &&   data entry.
```

**Example 2**—In FoxBASE+ and dBASE III PLUS, you can center text on the screen using LEN( ). First subtract the length of the string from the screen length (80), then divide by 2.

```
mstring = "JPD Software Accounting"
@ ROW(),(80-LEN(mstring))/2 SAY mstring
```

The text, "JPD Software Accounting" appears centered on the screen in the current ROW( ).

**Example 3**—A dBASE III PLUS data entry program creates sets of memory variables for adding and editing records. Like the dBXL and Quicksilver AUTOMEM option, this program creates memory variables with the same names as their corresponding fields. It uses LEN( ) to initialize the memory variables to the same lengths as the matching fields.

First, the program sets CTR to 1. The DO WHILE repeats as long as the LEN( ) of the field name is not zero. The names of the fields change as CTR increases (INFIELD holds each field name temporarily).

TYPE( ) determines whether the field is Character, Numeric, Logical, or Date. If character, the program STOREs enough spaces in the variable to give it the field's length. If numeric, the memory variable is given the value 0. If logical, the variable is made false. The system date is stored in a date variable.

```
ctr = 1
DO WHILE LEN(FIELD(ctr)) > 0        && DO WHILE the FIELD is not null.
  infield = FIELD(ctr)              && Put field name in INFIELD.
  DO CASE
    CASE TYPE(FIELD(ctr)) = "C"                 && If char. type, store
      STORE SPACE(LEN(FIELD(ctr))) TO &infield  &&   spaces in variable.
    CASE TYPE(FIELD(ctr)) = "N"                 && If numeric, store
       STORE 0 TO &infield                      &&   0 in variable.
    CASE TYPE(FIELD(ctr)) = "L"                 && If logical, store
      STORE .F. TO &infield                     &&   .F. in variable.
    CASE TYPE(FIELD(ctr)) = "D"                 && If date, store system
      STORE DATE() to &infield                  &&   date in variable.
  ENDCASE
  ctr = ctr + 1                                 && Increment field
                                                &&   counter.
ENDDO
```

## SPECIAL USE:

**Clipper:** LEN( ) can also return the number of elements in an array. Use the array's name as an argument as follows:

```
DECLARE tarray[10]
? LEN(tarray)
10
```

**dBASE IV:** LEN( ) applies to memo fields.

## SEE ALSO:

Command DECLARE; functions ASC( ), AT( ), and TRIM( ).

# LIKE( )

## DIALECTS:
dBASE IV only.

## SYNTAX:
LIKE(<expC1>,<expC2>)

## RETURNS:
Logical

## DEFINITION:
Compares a character string containing wildcard symbols with another character string. LIKE( ) returns true (.T.) if the strings match.

<expC1> is a character string containing the wildcard symbols ? or *. The question mark represents a single character, and the asterisk stands for multiple characters. You can put the wildcard characters anywhere in the string, any number of times.

<expC2> can be a literal, a memory variable, or field.

The LIKE( ) function is case sensitive.

Pattern matching follows these conventions:

| | |
|---|---|
| At the end of a string: | ? LIKE("David *","David Kalman") |
| At the beginning of a string: | ? LIKE("* Kalman","David Kalman") |
| Anywhere in a string: | ? LIKE("*ris Jo*","Chris Johnson") |
| A single character: | ? LIKE("David ?alman","David Kalman") |

## RECOMMENDED USE:
Use LIKE( ) to query the database when you don't know the exact spelling. In databases containing ID numbers, you can use LIKE( ) to classify groups of records.

**Example**—An automobile mechanic keeps a database of clients. The clerk remembers that Robert Aronsen's Volkswagen is due for an oil change, but can't remember how to spell "Aronsen."

```
USE clients
LIST ALL fname,lname FOR LIKE("Ar*",lname)
Record#   fname          lname
      5   Sally          Arbol
     11   Randall        Arnold
     22   Mitch          Aronson
     38   Robert         Aronsen
     52   Randy          Argent
```

A quick look shows that records 22 and 38 contain "Aronson" or "Aronsen."

**Example**—An inventory database contains construction materials for homes and for swimming pools. The second two characters of the part number always indicate the type of material, "HO" for "home" and "SP" for swimming pool. Using these codes, the LIKE( ) function provides a handy way to request sets of records.

```
LIST ALL partno, descrip FOR LIKE("??HO*",partno)
Record#   partno        descrip
      9   15HOA838      frame joint
     99   19HOB83       reinforcement girder
    122   45HO66AB      dry wall
    333   12HO7         plaster
```

## SEE ALSO:

Command LIST; functions DIFFERENCE( ) and SOUNDEX( ).

# LINENO( )

## DIALECTS:
dBASE IV only.

## SYNTAX:
LINENO( )

## RETURNS:
Numeric

## DEFINITION:
Returns the relative line number of the executing program. It counts from the top of the file, including comments and continuation lines.

## RECOMMENDED USE:
Use LINENO( ) in the interactive debugger to set execution breakpoints.

You can also use it to return the current line number after you SUSPEND program execution.

**Example**—When debugging a bibliography application, the programmer sets breakpoints in the debugger's Breakpoint Window. Specifying LINENO( ) = 6 makes the program pause at line 6.

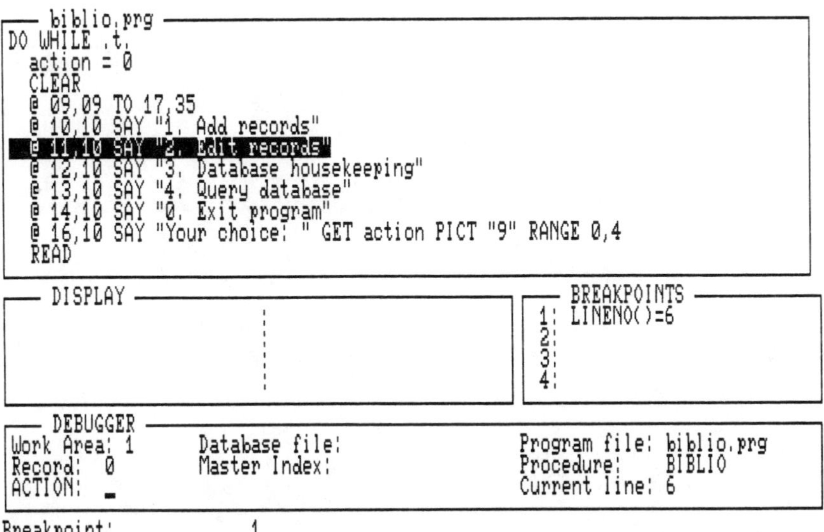

## LIMITS/WARNINGS:

LINENO( ) counts from the top of the program file instead of from the top of the executing procedure as you might expect.

## SEE ALSO:

Command DEBUG; function PROGRAM( ).

# LKSYS( )

## DIALECTS:

dBASE IV only.

## SYNTAX:

LKSYS(<expN>)

## DEFINITION:

Returns information about a locked file or the current record.

LKSYS(3) returns the time the lock was applied.

LKSYS(4) returns the date the lock was applied.

LKSYS(5) returns the name of the user who applied the lock.

LKSYS( ) works only with databases prepared with the CONVERT command. CONVERT adds a hidden field _DBASELOCK that holds the information returned by LKSYS( ) and the CHANGE( ) function. When you are viewing your data, _DBASELOCK is invisible. It is visible when you DISPLAY or MODIFY STRUCTURE.

## RECOMMENDED USE:

Use LKSYS( ) in multiuser applications to display information about the holder of record and file locks. If John in accounting locks a record or file, then goes for a three-martini lunch, everyone on the network knows who to blame.

```
IF .NOT. FLOCK()
  @ 22,01 SAY "File not available."
  @ 23,01 SAY LKSYS(5)+" locked the file at "+LKSYS(3)+" on "+LKSYS(4)
ENDIF
```

## LIMITS/WARNINGS:

LKSYS( ) checks only the current record.

The CONVERT command takes a numeric argument between 8 and 24 indicating the length of the hidden _DBASELOCK field. If you want to return the full information using LKSYS( ), be sure to specify a length of 24 in CONVERT. Otherwise, the information will be truncated. Note that _DBASELOCK occupies space in the database like any other field.

## SEE ALSO:

Commands CONVERT, SET REFRESH, and UNLOCK; functions CHANGE( ), FLOCK( ), LOCK( ), and RLOCK( ).

# LOCK( )

## DIALECTS:

Clipper, dBASE III PLUS, dBASE IV, FoxBASE+, and Quicksilver.

## SYNTAX:

LOCK( )

## RETURNS:

Logical

## DEFINITION:

Tries to lock the current record. If successful, it returns true (.T.). The record can then be changed only by whoever locked it.

LOCK( ) is the same as RLOCK( ).

If LOCK( ) succeeds, the record stays locked until whoever locked it either issues the UNLOCK command, or closes the file (with CLEAR ALL, CLOSE DATABASES, QUIT, or USE).

LOCK( ) prevents multiple users from accessing the same database record simultaneously.

## RECOMMENDED USE:

LOCK( ) and RLOCK( ) protect the integrity of data, that is, they allow changes only in a controlled way.

**Example 1**—A clerk in an automobile parts warehouse receives a telephone order for two generators. She enters the part code into the computer. The display shows 14 in stock. She enters a quantity of two. At the same time, another clerk is also viewing the generator record. He tries to order all 14 generators. Because the first clerk has accessed and locked the record, the second clerk must wait until the first transaction is finished before proceeding. Otherwise, they might have sold more generators than were actually in stock.

```
USE carparts INDEX partdex
DO WHILE .t.
  * <SEEK part_num>
  ctr = 0
```

```
  DO WHILE .NOT. LOCK() .AND. ctr < 100
    ctr = ctr + 1
  ENDDO
  IF .NOT. LOCK()
    @ 24,02 SAY "Record unavailable. Press any key to reenter part num."
    WAIT ""
    LOOP
  ELSE
    mpart = partnum
    mdesc = descrip
    mqty  = qty
    @ 02,02 SAY "Part number: " GET mpart
    @ 03,02 SAY "Description: " GET mdesc
    @ 04,02 SAY "Quantity:    " GET mqty
    READ
  ENDIF
ENDDO
```

## VARIATIONS:

**Clipper:** Issuing another LOCK( ) or RLOCK( ) releases a previous LOCK( ) or RLOCK( ). Clipper only prevents other users from changing a locked record. All users may still read it.

Locking a record does not lock its child records in a relation.

**dBASE III PLUS:** LOCK( ) and RLOCK( ) prevent both read and write access by other users.

Locking a record does not lock its child records in a relation.

After you UNLOCK a record, it still remains locked to other users until you move the pointer. To avoid problems, issue GOTO RECNO( ) immediately after UNLOCK. This will reset the LOCK( )/RLOCK( ) status.

**dBASE IV:** Locking the parent record in a relation automatically locks the child records.

LOCK( ) and RLOCK( ) only prevent other users from updating a locked record. All users may still read it.

You can lock multiple records in a file with a single LOCK( ) function. The full syntax is

LOCK([<expC list>] [,<alias>])

<expC> is a list of record numbers in a string. The <alias> is the alias name of a database file open in any work area. Omitting the record number arguments locks only the current record. Omitting the alias argument locks only records in the currently selected database file.

dBASE IV locks individual records automatically when you issue commands such as REPLACE and EDIT. This makes LOCK( ) unnecessary in many instances. Therefore, LOCK( ) is best used when REPLACEing data in multiple records as part of a transaction. For example, to lock records 7 and 8 in a real estate database, you would issue:

```
timeout = 0
DO WHILE .NOT. LOCK("7,8","REAL") .AND. timeout < 100
  timeout = timeout + 1
ENDDO
```

dBASE IV permits a maximum of 50 simultaneous locks.

**FoxBASE+:** Locking a record does not lock its child records in a relation.

LOCK( ) and RLOCK( ) automatically re-read the current record to assure that you have the latest version of the data.

LOCK( ) and RLOCK( ) only prevents other users from updating a locked record. All users may still read it.

Certain FoxBASE+ commands automatically lock the current record. They include DELETE, RECALL, and REPLACE with a scope of NEXT 1 or RECORD <n>. They also include DELETE and RECALL with no scope, and GATHER. APPEND BLANK locks the record being appended and the file header. To prevent errors when two users APPEND BLANK simultaneously, either lock the file with FLOCK( ), or trap the error and RETRY until the APPEND BLANK succeeds:

```
ON ERROR DO apptry
USE prospects
APPEND BLANK
ON ERROR
PROCEDURE apptry
IF ERROR() = 108       && FoxBASE+ "File in use" error
  RETRY
ENDIF
```

**Quicksilver:** LOCK( ) and RLOCK( ) prevent other users from updating a record. With SET AUTOLOCK ON, the REPLACE command locks the record automatically.

Locking a record does not lock its child records in a relation.

## SEE ALSO:

Command UNLOCK; functions ERROR( ) and FLOCK( ).

# LOG( )

## DIALECTS:
Clipper, dBASE III PLUS, dBASE IV, dBXL, FoxBASE+, and Quicksilver.

## SYNTAX:
LOG(<expN>)

## RETURNS:
Numeric

## DEFINITION:
Returns the natural logarithm of its argument. Natural logarithms have a base of e. LOG( ) returns x in the equation

$e^x$ = <expN>

e is approximately 2.71828.

<expN> must be greater than 0.

## RECOMMENDED USE:
LOG( ) is used in scientific formulas describing chemical, electrical, and physical properties.

**Example**—An equation determining electrical resistance uses the natural logarithm of the starting voltage divided by the ending voltage.

```
volt = 112
voltend = 105
voltlog = LOG(volt/voltend)
.06
```

## SEE ALSO:
Functions EXP( ) and LOG10( ).

# LOG10( )

## DIALECTS:

dBASE IV, dBXL, and Quicksilver.

## SYNTAX:

LOG10(<expN>)

## RETURNS:

Numeric (dBXL, Quicksilver)

Floating point numeric (dBASE IV)

## DEFINITION:

Returns the logarithm to base 10 of its argument (the common logarithm). LOG10(<expN>) returns y in the equation

$$\langle expN \rangle = 10^{Y}$$

or

$$LOG10(x) = y$$

The argument must be positive.

## RECOMMENDED USE:

The common logarithm is used to solve exponential equations. To find LOG10( ) of 2.411, enter:

```
? log10(2.411)
 0.382
```

## SEE ALSO:

Functions EXP( ) and LOG( ).

# LOOKUP( )

## DIALECTS:

dBASE IV only.

## SYNTAX:

LOOKUP(<return exp>, <search exp>, <field>)

## RETURNS:

Programmer defined

## DEFINITION:

Searches for a record matching <search exp>. It looks for <search exp> in the specified <field>.

If it finds a match, LOOKUP( ) returns <return exp> from the matching record and moves the pointer to it. Otherwise, LOOKUP( ) moves the pointer to the end-of-file. It also returns a blank string, zero, a blank date, or false (.F.), depending on the type of <return exp>.

LOOKUP( ) is a "smart" function. If you have an open index file or mdx TAG, it will do an indexed search (a SEEK). If there is no index available, LOOKUP( ) does a sequential search (a LOCATE).

### <return exp>

The expression to return from a matching record. It typically is a field, or a calculation derived from a field.

### <search exp>

The expression you want to find.

### <field>

The field in which to search.

## DEFAULTS:

Searches the database in the current work area. You can search one in an unselected work area by using the ALIAS-> specifier with the return expression and the <field> name.

## RECOMMENDED USE:

Use LOOKUP( ) to find data in an unselected database file (indexed or not) and return a single value from it.

**Example**—A data entry operator enters a student registration number. LOOKUP( ) searches the MASTER student list, and returns the student's last name for verification. Using the ALIAS, this is done without disturbing the database files in the selected work area.

```
USE master ORDER st_id IN 5
DO WHILE .t.
  student = SPACE(4)
  @ 10,10 SAY "Enter identification: " GET student PICTURE "@!"
  READ
  IF student = "    "
    EXIT
  ENDIF
  choice = LOOKUP(MASTER->st_lname, student, MASTER->st_id)
  @ 11,00
  @ 11,10 SAY choice
ENDDO
```

To return multiple values, use the SEEK( ) function instead. SEEK( ) itself does not return data; however, it indicates whether data was found (true or false), and moves the pointer to the found record. For example, using LOOKUP( ) to return multiple data items creates inconsistent, repetitive code. If LOOKUP( ) doesn't find the expression you specified, it stores empty fields in the target variables.

```
mlname = LOOKUP(MASTER->lname,student,MASTER->id)   && Return last name.
mcity  = MASTER->city                               && Return city.
mstate = MASTER->city                               && Return state.
IF EOF()                   && If LOOKUP() failed,
   * <statements>.         &&   retry search, set variables to defaults,
   *                       &&   or cancel.
   *
ENDIF
```

SEEK( ) is more logical, and gives you more control.

```
IF SEEK(student,"MASTER")  && If SEEK doesn't find the STUDENT, then
  mlname  = MASTER->lname  &&   the following statements never execute.
  mcity   = MASTER->city
  mstate  = MASTER->state
ELSE
  * <statements>.          && If SEEK is false, do alternative statements.
ENDIF
```

## LIMITS/WARNINGS:

Searching for compound (multiple field) index key values does not work. Because <field> is a single fieldname, use single field index keys for reliable searches.

LOOKUP( ) cannot return multiple values from the found record.

## SEE ALSO:

Commands LOCATE and SEEK; functions EOF( ), FOUND( ), and SEEK( ).

# LOWER( )

## DIALECTS:
Clipper, dBASE III PLUS, dBASE IV, dBXL, FoxBASE+, and Quicksilver.

## SYNTAX:
LOWER(<expC>)

## RETURNS:
Character

## DEFINITION:
Converts all uppercase letters in a character expression to lowercase.

LOWER( ) does not affect non-alphabetic characters.

## RECOMMENDED USE:
Because dBASE is case-sensitive, convert character strings to either uppercase or lowercase when evaluating them. This assures that the program evaluates them consistently.
**Example**—A user prompt in an accounting program requests a "Y" or "N" response. Because the program uses WAIT TO to get the response, there is no way to force either upper or lower case entry. Thus, the program must disregard case. To do this, it uses LOWER( ) when evaluating the string.

```
WAIT "Continue with end of month posting? (Y/N)" TO action
IF LOWER(action) = "y"
  DO eompost
ENDIF
```

The UPPER( ) function will also do the job.

## SEE ALSO:
Functions ISUPPER( ), ISLOWER( ), and UPPER( ).

# LTRIM( )

## DIALECTS:
Clipper, dBASE III PLUS, dBASE IV, dBXL, FoxBASE+, and Quicksilver.

## SYNTAX:
LTRIM(<expC>)

## RETURNS:
Character

## DEFINITION:
Removes leading blanks from <expC>.

## RECOMMENDED USE:
When using the STR( ) function to convert a number to a string, you must specify the total number of digits, including the decimal point and signs. If the number is shorter than the specified length, STR( ) adds leading blanks. LTRIM( ) removes them.

**Example**—A report program prints the date on each page. The STR( ) function converts the numeric DAY to a character string; however, when DAY( ) is a single digit, STR( ) leaves a leading blank which LTRIM( ) removes.

```
rd=CTOD('05/01/88')    && CTOD( ) converts characters to dates.
?
? CMONTH(rd) + " " + LTRIM(STR(DAY(rd),2,0)) + ", " + STR(YEAR(rd),4,0)
?
* <more report>
```

This code fragment prints the date 05/01/88 as

```
May 1, 1988
```

## SEE ALSO:
Functions ALLTRIM( ), STR( ), and TRIM( ).

# LUPDATE( )

## DIALECTS:

Clipper, dBASE III PLUS, dBASE IV, dBXL, FoxBASE+, and Quicksilver.

## SYNTAX:

LUPDATE( )

## RETURNS:

Date

## DEFINITION:

Returns the date on which the active database was last changed. LUPDATE( ) uses the system date.

LUPDATE( ) returns a blank date if no file is in use.

## RECOMMENDED USE:

Use LUPDATE( ) to verify database transactions and avoid repetitions. It is also useful for identifying recently changed files that should be archived.

**Example**—Newton Corp. updates a master archive at the end of each day. Before appending new records from the main transaction files, the program checks LUPDATE( ) for each file and compares it to a value stored in a transaction log file. If the values are the same, the program skips the file.

```
SELECT 1
USE log INDEX filename     && Open transaction log indexed on filename.
SELECT 2
USE archive                && Open main archive file.
SELECT 3
USE sales2                 && Open transaction file SALES2.
mlupdate = LUPDATE()       && Store LUPDATE() to mlupdate.
USE                        && Close transaction file SALES2.
SELECT 1
SEEK "sales2"              && SEEK filename in LOG.
IF mlupdate # dupdate      && If the dates are not the same,
  SELECT 2                 &&   return to ARCHIVE and
  APPEND from sales2       &&   append records from SALES2.
ELSE
  ? "Moving to next file"
ENDIF
* <Repeat process for each file, or make filenames variable and
*  execute within a DO WHILE>.
```

## VARIATIONS:

**Clipper:** LUPDATE( ) is in EXTEND.LIB on the system disk.

**dBASE IV:** You can apply LUPDATE( ) to an unselected database by using an alias as the argument, in the form

```
LUPDATE(<expC>)
```

## SEE ALSO:

Functions DBF( ), FIELD( ), NDX( ), RECCOUNT( ), RECSIZE( ), and TAG( ).

# MAX( )

## DIALECTS:
Clipper, dBASE III PLUS, dBASE IV, dBXL, FoxBASE+, and Quicksilver.

## SYNTAX:
MAX(<expN1>,<expN2>)

## RETURNS:
Numeric

## DEFINITION:
Returns the larger of two numeric expressions.

## RECOMMENDED USE:
MAX( ) compares any two valid numeric expressions, including numeric fields, and returns the larger. However, it cannot return the maximum value of a field throughout a database.

**Example**—A job placement agency signs a service contract for maintaining its mainframe and personal computers. The contract stipulates payment of an $850 per month retainer, or $85 per hour, whichever is higher.

A billing program generates the monthly total using MAX( ) to determine the proper charge. When HOURNUM exceeds 10, SERVICE equals HOURNUM times 85. Otherwise, SERVICE equals 850.

```
* <GET number of hours, parts, etc.>
service = MAX(850,HOURNUM*85)
```

## VARIATIONS:
**Clipper, FoxBASE+:** MAX( ) also returns the later of two dates.

**dBASE IV:** MAX( ) also returns the later of two dates. It differs from the MAX( ) option of the CALCULATE command which returns the maximum value from groups of records.

## SEE ALSO:
Command CALCULATE; function MIN( ).

# MDX( )

## DIALECTS:
dBASE IV only.

## SYNTAX:
MDX(<expN>[,<alias>])

## RETURNS:
Character

## DEFINITION:
Returns the name of an open MDX (multiple index) file.

<expN> is the number indicating the position of the MDX file within the file list of USE and SET INDEX TO.

SET ORDER TO does not affect MDX( ).

If you specify a nonexistent index file, MDX( ) returns a null string.

## OPTIONS:
To find the name of an active MDX file in an unselected work area, supply the ALIAS name as the second argument.

## RECOMMENDED USE:
Use MDX( ) to display the active MDX files during development and debugging. This is helpful when using index-dependent commands such as SET RELATION and SEEK.

**Example**—While debugging a sales tracking system, a programmer includes a procedure SHOWMDX to display the names of active MDX files. At key breakpoints, the programmer includes the command DO SHOWMDX.

```
* SHOWMDX.PRG
? DBF()          && Show active database filename.
ctr = 1
* Do while MDX(ctr) doesn't return a null value.
DO WHILE "" # MDX(ctr)
  ? "MDX FILE " + STR(ctr,1,0) + ": " + MDX(ctr)
  ctr = ctr + 1
ENDDO
```

To find the name of an MDX file in an unselected area, use the alias as an MDX( ) argument. For example, MDX(2,"SALES") returns the name of the second MDX associated with the SALES database.

## SEE ALSO:

Commands INDEX and SET INDEX TO; functions DBF( ), NDX( ), and TAG( ).

# MDY( )

## DIALECTS:
dBASE IV only.

## SYNTAX:
MDY(<expD>)

## RETURNS:
Character

## DEFINITION:
Converts a date expression to a Month DD, YY format. If you SET CENTURY ON, the result is Month DD, YYYY.

DD appears without a leading zero if it has only one digit. Month is spelled out. A comma appears after the day.

## RECOMMENDED USE:
Use MDY( ) to report dates in a readable format.

**Example**—A monthly report displays the date in the top left corner in MDY format.

```
mtoday = DATE()
@ 04,01 SAY MDY(mtoday)
```

It prints as

```
September 5, 88
```

With SET CENTURY ON, the date prints as

```
September 5, 1988
```

## SEE ALSO:
Commands SET CENTURY and SET DATE; functions CDOW( ), CMONTH( ), DATE( ), DOW( ), DMY( ), and MONTH( ).

# MEMLINES( )

## DIALECTS:
dBASE IV only.

## SYNTAX:
MEMLINES(<expC>)

## RETURNS:
Numeric

## DEFINITION:
Counts the number of word-wrapped lines that a memo field fills when formatted.

The SET MEMOWIDTH command sets the memo's width.

<expC> is the memo field name.

## RECOMMENDED USE:
Use MEMLINES( ) to compute page breaks when including free form text in formatted reports. It works with MLINE( ) to control text formatting.

**Example**—A legal application includes case abstracts in memo field ACASE. To print the text on a form 15 lines long, MEMLINES( ) measures its formatted length, and MLINE( ) extracts and prints lines.

```
USE abstract
SET DEVICE TO PRINT
SET MEMOWIDTH TO 20
tlen = MEMLINES(acase)          && Measure text formatted to 20 characters.
mline = 1                       && Start counter for memo line (MLINE).
pline = 1                       && Start counter for print line (PLINE).
DO WHILE mline <= tlen          && PLINE increases from 1 to MEMLINES().
  extract = MLINE(acase,mline)  && Function MLINE extracts line from memo.
  @ pline,01 SAY extract
  mline = mline + 1         && Increase MLINE by 1 until out of lines.
  pline = pline + 1         && Increase PLINE by 1 until
  IF pline = 15             &&   it reaches 15, then
    EJECT                   &&   EJECT and reset PLINE to 1.
    pline = 1               &&   (It actually prints only 14 lines.)
    ENDIF
ENDDO
EJECT
SET DEVICE TO screen
```

## LIMITS/WARNINGS:

The name MEMLINES( ) is easy to confuse with Clipper's MEMOLINE( ), which does a different function. MEMLINES( ) is equivalent to Clipper's MLCOUNT( ).

## SEE ALSO:

Functions HARDCR( ), MEMOEDIT( ), MEMOREAD( ), MEMOTRAN( ), MEMOWRIT( ), MLCOUNT( ), and MLINE( ).

# MEMOEDIT( )

## DIALECTS:

Clipper only.

## SYNTAX:

MEMOEDIT(<expC1>,[<expN1>,<expN2>,<expN3>,<expN4>]
[,<expL1>][,<expC2>] [,<expN5>][,<expN6>][,<expN7>]
[,<expN8>])[,<expN9>][,<expN10>])

## RETURNS:

Character

## DEFINITION:

Opens a window for editing character strings or memo fields. MEMOEDIT( ) provides full cursor movement commands and automatic word wrap. If you modify the memo or string, it returns the modified string. If you make no changes, it returns the original string.

<expC1> is the name of a memo field, or a string memory variable. Using optional numeric arguments and a user defined function, you can control the cursor and customize MEMOEDIT( )'s response to key inputs.

## OPTIONS:

The optional numeric expressions <expN1>, <expN2>, <expN3>, and <expN4> are the coordinates of the editing window. <expN1>,<expN2> is the top left position. <expN3>,<expN4> is the bottom right. If you do not specify coordinates, MEMOEDIT( ) uses the entire screen.

<expL> specifies whether the user can change a memo field. If it is true, the user can update the memo (update mode); if it is false, he or she can only examine the memo (browse mode).

<expC2> is a user defined function that executes when the user presses a key not recognized by MEMOEDIT( ) (a key exception). Key exceptions include Function, Ctrl, and Alt combinations. See *User defined function* below for more information.

<expN5> sets the line length. If it exceeds the width of the editing window, the line scrolls horizontally.

<expN6> sets the width of tab characters. If you specify it, MEMOEDIT( ) inserts hard tab characters (09H) when you press the Tab key. If you do not specify <expN6>, MEMOEDIT( ) inserts four spaces when you press Tab.

<expN7> is the initial line position of the cursor within the memo.

<expN8> is the initial column position of the cursor within the memo.

<expN9> is the initial row to place the cursor relative to the window position. The default is zero.

<expN10> is the initial column to place the cursor relative to the window position. The default is zero.

*Note:* To skip an argument (choosing the default), pass a dummy variable with a null value in its position.

## USER DEFINED FUNCTION:

In response to a key exception, MEMOEDIT( ) executes the user defined function specified in <expC2>, automatically passing it three parameters: MODE, LINE, and COLUMN.

MODE tells the user defined function about the state of MEMOEDIT( ). The MODEs are:

| Mode | Description |
|---|---|
| 0 | Idle, no key to process. |
| 1 | User enters key exception without changing memo |
| 2 | User enters key exception, changing memo |
| 3 | Startup |

LINE and COLUMN relay the cursor position. LINE begins at 1, and COLUMN begins at 0.

### MODE 0

MODE 0 indicates that there is no key exception to process. The function can ignore MODE 0, or use it simply to track the cursor's position and display the line and column numbers (using the LINE and COLUMN parameters).

## MODE 1

MODE 1 indicates that the user has pressed a key exception without changing the memo.

## MODE 2

MODE 2 indicates that the user has pressed a key exception, but has changed the memo.

## MODE 3

MODE 3, the startup mode, indicates that the user has just invoked MEMOEDIT( ). When it detects MODE 3, the user defined function can configure MEMOEDIT( )'s insert, scroll, or word wrap toggles by RETURNing the appropriate codes.

MEMOEDIT( ) continues to call the function with MODE 0 until it RETURNs 0. MEMOEDIT( ) then presents the memo or character string for editing.

The codes RETURNed to MEMOEDIT( ) from the function are based on Clipper's INKEY( ) values.

MEMOEDIT( ) User Function Return Codes

| Value | Action |
|---|---|
| 0 | Take default action |
| 1 | Move to top of editing window |
| 2 | Reform text (Ctrl-B) |
| 3 | Move down one page |
| 4 | Move right one space |
| 5 | Move up one line |
| 7 | Delete one character |
| 18 | Move up one page |
| 19 | Move left one space |
| 22 | Toggle insert mode |
| 23 | Save and exit |
| 24 | Move down one line |
| 29 | Move to top of memo |
| 30 | Move to bottom of memo |
| 32 | Ignore or disable the current key |
| 33 | Insert the control key into the text as data |
| 34 | Toggle word wrap |
| 35 | Toggle vertical text scrolling |
| 100 | Move right one word |
| 101 | Move to bottom right of window |

You can use LASTKEY( ) in the user defined function to redefine key combinations. For example, you could define Alt-F2 to open a lookup window during data entry.

You can also assign the function keys to move the cursor, or save or abandon an edited memo or character string.

Note that you cannot redefine or ignore keys normally used to control MEMOEDIT( ). They include cursor keys, the Enter key, backspace, Tab, Del, and other character keys.

## MEMOEDIT( ) Editing Features

### Text Reformatting

MEMOEDIT( ) follows the WordStar(tm) convention for reformatting text (Ctrl-B). Press Ctrl-B or RETURN 2 from the user defined function. Reformatting ends with the next hard carriage return or the end of the memo, whichever comes first.

### Text Scrolling

By default, MEMOEDIT( ) scrolls the text vertically when the user presses the up and down arrow keys. The cursor stays on the same line. RETURNing 35 from the user defined function turns the scrolling off, instead letting the cursor move from line to line.

### Word Wrap

MEMOEDIT( )'s word wrap defaults to ON. You can turn it off by RETURNing 34 from the user defined function.

With word wrap on, a word that does not fit on a line moves to the next one. MEMOEDIT( ) inserts a soft carriage return/line feed at the break. With word wrap off, the line scrolls horizontally for its defined width (the width of the window by default). To move to the next line, the user must press Enter to insert a hard carriage return/line feed.

See HARDCR( ) and MEMOTRAN( ) for information on formatting memos with soft carriage returns.

### Control Keys

Cursor movement keys generally mimic WordStar™ conventions.

| | |
|---|---|
| Ctrl-A or Ctrl-Left arrow | Move left one word |
| Ctrl-B | Reformat memo (word wrap) |
| Ctrl-D or right arrow | Move right one space |
| Ctrl-E or up arrow | Move up one line |
| Ctrl-F or Ctrl-Right arrow | Move right one word |
| Ctrl-S or left arrow | Move left one space |
| Ctrl-T | Delete word to the right |
| Ctrl-X or down arrow | Move down one line |
| Ctrl-W | Finish editing and save changes |
| Ctrl-Y | Delete current line |
| ESC | Cancel editing without saving changes |
| Home | Beginning of current line |
| End | End of current line |
| Ctrl-Home | Top of current window |
| Ctrl-End | Bottom of current window |
| PgUp | Move up one page |
| PgDn | Move down one page |
| Ctrl-PgUp | Top of memo |
| Ctrl-PgDn | End of memo |

## RECOMMENDED USE:

Use MEMOEDIT( ) to change or display memo fields. It is also useful for editing long character memory variables. Clipper limits the length of character strings to 64K. So you can store an entire memo field in a memory variable, then manipulate it like a character variable.

**Example 1**—A scientific application stores laboratory observations of cell cultures in a Clipper memo field. The field is called OBSERVE, and each record pertains to a different petri dish. To edit a memo field, the biologist selects "E" from the menu.

```
DO CASE
  * <user enters "E">
  CASE action = "E"
    SAVE SCREEN
    REPLACE observe WITH MEMOEDIT(observe,02,02,18,50,.T.)
    * <more cases>
ENDCASE
RESTORE SCREEN
```

The program first saves the current screen with SAVE SCREEN. Then it issues MEMOEDIT( ) in a REPLACE statement, indicating that changes to the memo will be saved. The top left corner of the editing window is at coordinate 2,2, and the bottom left corner is at 18,50. After the user finishes editing the memo, RESTORE SCREEN redisplays the previous screen.

**Example 2**—In the application from Example 1, a program module lets scientists review the observations. MEMOEDIT( ) displays memo field OBSERVE, but the .F. parameter prevents them from making changes.

```
MEMOEDIT(observe,02,02,18,50,.F.)
```

**Example 3**—When adding new memos to a database, the scientific application from Examples 1 and 2 first stores text in a memory variable. When the user finishes editing, the memory variable is REPLACEd into the memo field. This keeps the database file open no longer than is necessary to do the REPLACE, protecting data from power failures and program errors.

In this example, MOBSERVE is a character memory variable. The user defined function MCONTROL assesses the parameters MODE, LINE, and COLUMN. At startup (MODE 3), MCONTROL activates the insert mode (KEYBOARD CHR(22)), and turns word wrap and scrolling off.

Since only one expression can be RETURNed at a time, the program uses the logical variables FIRST and SECOND to determine how many times MCONTROL has been called. Because MODE 3 (startup) repeats until it detects a RETURN of 0, MCONTROL can RETURN a different value each time it is called, even if the MODE doesn't change.

```
CLEAR PUBLIC first      && Set flag to count number of times
                        &&   MEMOEDIT calls the UDF.
first = .t.
@ 01,01 TO 19,51
* Window goes from 02,02 to 18,50, the udf is MCONTROL.
* The line length is 79 (it scrolls beyond the window). The tab
* setting is 4 spaces, and the initial cursor position is 5,5.
mosbserve = " "
mobserve = MEMOEDIT(mobserve,02,02,18,50,.T.,"mcontrol",79,4,5,5)
USE results INDEX dishdex
GOTO 10
REPLACE observe WITH mobserve
USE
RELEASE first,second

FUNCTION mcontrol
PARAMETERS mode,line,column
@ 24,30 SAY "<PRESS F2 TO ABANDON, F3 TO SAVE>"
DO CASE
  CASE mode = 0
   @ 24,01 SAY "COORD: " + STR(line,3,0) + "," + STR(column,2,0)
  CASE mode = 3
```

```
    * Use variable "flag" FIRST to count the number of calls to the UDF.
    * This lets you do multiple RETURNs for the same MODE.
    KEYBOARD CHR(22)      && Toggle insert mode ON.
    IF first              && First is flag set in calling program.
      first = .f.         && Make FIRST false, so it won't execute again.
      PUBLIC second
      second = .t.
      RETURN 34           && Turn WORD WRAP OFF.
    ELSEIF second
      second = .f.
      RETURN 35           && Turn SCROLLING OFF.
    ENDIF
  CASE mode = 1 .or. mode = 2
    IF LASTKEY() = -1       && Abandon memo if user presses F2.
      KEYBOARD CHR(27)
    ELSEIF LASTKEY() = -2 && Save memo if user presses F3.
      KEYBOARD CHR(23)
    ENDIF
ENDCASE
RETURN 0
```

## LIMITS/WARNINGS:

MEMOEDIT's word wrap inserts soft carriage returns. To convert them to hard returns for display, use the HARDCR( ) function.

MEMOEDIT( ) is in EXTEND.LIB on the system disk.

## SEE ALSO:

Functions HARDCR( ), MEMOLINE( ), MEMOREAD( ), MEMOTRAN( ), MEMOWRIT( ), and MLCOUNT( ).

# MEMOLINE( )

## DIALECTS:
Clipper only.

## SYNTAX:
MEMOLINE(<expC>,<expN1>,<expN2>)

## RETURNS:
Character

## DEFINITION:
Formats a line of text from a memo field or character expression.

<expC> is the memo field name or character expression from which to extract the line. In character expressions, lines are strings delimited by carriage return/line feeds.

<expN1> is the length of the formatted line. If you choose a memo field line longer than the formatted line you specify, MEMOLINE( ) wraps extra words to the next line. If the memo field line is shorter, MEMOLINE( ) pads the string with blanks.

<expN2> is the line number to format. If it is invalid, MLINE( ) returns a null string.

MEMOLINE( ) is similar to dBASE IV's MLINE( ) function.

## RECOMMENDED USE:
Use MEMOLINE( ) to produce reports using free form text input.

**Example**—A patient's hospital record includes formatted data and free form text. To print the text, MEMOLINE( ) extracts and formats lines from memo field PATIENT.

```
USE p_records
SET DEVICE TO PRINT
FOR lcount = 1 TO 60
  extract = MEMOLINE(patient,55,lcount)
  IF extract == ""      && == is like SET EXACT ON for this comparison.
```

```
    EJECT                  && If EXTRACT is null, then EJECT and EXIT.
    EXIT
  ENDIF
  @ lcount,01 SAY extract
NEXT
SET DEVICE TO screen
```

## LIMITS/WARNINGS:

MEMOLINE( ) is in EXTEND.LIB on the system disk.

MEMOLINE( ) is easy to confuse with dBASE IV's MEMLINES( ) function. It is functionally equivalent to dBASE IV's MLINE( ) function.

## SEE ALSO:

Functions HARDCR( ), MEMLINES( ), MEMOEDIT( ), MEMOREAD( ), MEMOTRAN( ), MEMOWRIT( ), and MLINE( ).

# MEMOREAD( )

## DIALECTS:
Clipper only.

## SYNTAX:
MEMOREAD(<filename>)

## RETURNS:
Character

## DEFINITION:
Reads a text file from disk. You can then store it in a memory variable, REPLACE it into a memo field, or edit it with MEMOEDIT( ).

You must specify a full <filename>, including the extension.

## RECOMMENDED USE:
MEMOREAD( ) lets you import entire text files into programs. This is useful for managing documents produced by word processors.

**Example**—A scientific application stores laboratory observations of cell cultures in a Clipper memo field. The memo field is OBSERVE, and each record in the database pertains to a different petri dish. Some scientists in the field record observations using a text editor. MEMOREAD( ) later imports their findings into memo field OBSERVE.

```
* <Routine to go to correct record>.
REPLACE observe WITH MEMOREAD("FIELD.TXT")
```

## LIMITS/WARNINGS:
Text files must be in ASCII format.

MEMOREAD( ) is in EXTEND.LIB on the system disk.

## SEE ALSO:
Command REPLACE; function MEMOEDIT( ).

# MEMORY( )

## DIALECTS:

Clipper, dBASE IV, dBXL, and Quicksilver.

## SYNTAX:

MEMORY(0) (Clipper, dBASE IV)
MEMORY( ) (dBASE IV, dBXL, Quicksilver)

## RETURNS:

Numeric

## DEFINITION:

Returns the amount of available memory.

Clipper and dBASE IV return K bytes, dBXL and Quicksilver return bytes.

## RECOMMENDED USE:

Use MEMORY( ) during program development to determine how much memory a compiled application requires. MEMORY( ) is also useful for checking whether your computer has enough free memory to RUN external DOS commands or programs.

**Example 1**—A programmer wants to give end users access to an external text editor from within a dBASE IV application. Because the amount of free memory can vary, MEMORY( ) tests how much is available before running the editor. (The text editor requires 50K).

```
IF MEMORY() > 50
  RUN qedit
ELSE
  ? "Insufficient memory to run editor"
ENDIF
```

**Example 2**—While developing a dBXL/Quicksilver program, a programmer uses MEMORY( ) to display the available memory and the amount taken by the program.

```
availmem = MEMORY()
totmem   = 655360
usedmem  = totmem - availmem
```

```
? "Available memory " + STR(availmem,8,0)
? "Memory used " + STR(usedmem,8,0)
```

The same example in Clipper requires slightly different syntax. The memory function must have a 0 parameter, and the number of bytes must be multiplied by 1024.

```
availmem = MEMORY(0) * 1024
totmem   = 655360
usedmem  = totmem - availmem
? "Available memory " + STR(availmem,8,0)
? "Memory used " + STR(usedmem,8,0)
```

In dBASE IV, MEMORY( ) does not require an argument.

## VARIATIONS:

**dBASE IV:** MEMORY( ) produces the same results with no argument and with an argument of 0.

**FoxBASE+:** The SYS(12) function returns the available memory in bytes.

## SEE ALSO:

Function SYS(12).

# MEMOTRAN( )

## DIALECTS:

Clipper only.

## SYNTAX:

MEMOTRAN(<expC>[,<expC2>][,<expC3>])

## RETURNS:

Character

## DEFINITION:

Replaces the carriage return/line feed characters in a character expression (usually a memo field) with other characters as follows:

- Hard carriage returns (CHR(13) + CHR(10)) convert to semicolons.
- Soft carriage returns produced by automatic word wrap (CHR(141) + CHR(10)) convert to spaces.

## OPTIONS:

MEMOTRAN( ) lets you define replacement characters for hard and soft carriage returns. <expC2> replaces hard carriage returns, <expC3> replaces soft carriage returns.

## RECOMMENDED USE:

MEMOTRAN( ) lets you format text for use with an external editor by removing incompatible end-of-line characters. MEMOTRAN( ) also lets you alter or remove the formatting of memo fields.

**Example**—A law office program stores case notes in memo fields. Very often, an attorney must include the notes in a word processing document. Before exporting the text to the word processor, MEMOTRAN( ) replaces all hard carriage returns with tildes (~) and all soft carriage returns with spaces. This lets the secretary reformat the text without end-of-line commands in the wrong places.

```
USE caseload
* <CASENOTE is a MEMO field>
REPLACE casenote WITH MEMOTRAN(casenote,"~"," ")
```

MEMOTRAN( ) is in EXTEND.LIB on the system disk.

## SEE ALSO:

Functions MEMOEDIT( ), MEMOREAD( ), and MEMOWRIT( ).

# MEMOWRIT( )

## DIALECTS:

Clipper only.

## SYNTAX:

MEMOWRIT(<filename>,<expC>)

## RETURNS:

Logical

## DEFINITION:

Writes a character string to a disk file. If the write succeeds, MEMOWRIT( ) returns true (.T.).

## RECOMMENDED USE:

MEMOWRIT( ) lets you export memo fields or other character strings to text files for use with a word processor.

**Example**—A high school teacher tracks the progress of his students with Clipper memo fields. The non-memo fields hold statistics, whereas the memo fields hold observations and recommendations. When the teacher produces progress reports, he exports the text for word processing, using MEMOWRIT( ). (He first uses MEMOTRAN( ) to remove the hard and soft carriage returns).

```
USE class
* <STUDENTS is a memo field>
* Remove hard and soft carriage returns with MEMOTRAN().
REPLACE students WITH MEMOTRAN(students," "," ")
* STU_NUM is a student number the program uses as a filename.
valchk = MEMOWRIT("&stu_num.doc",students)
@ 24,03 SAY IIF(valchk,"Writing &stu_num","Unable to write &stu_num")
```

If the write succeeds, memory variable VALCHK is true and the message "Writing <filename>" appears. If false, the message "Unable to write <filename>" appears.

MEMOWRIT( ) is in EXTEND.LIB on the system disk.

## SEE ALSO:

Functions MEMOEDIT( ), MEMOREAD( ), and MEMOTRAN( ).

# MENU( )

## DIALECTS:
dBASE IV only.

## SYNTAX:
MENU( )

## RETURNS:
Character

## DEFINITION:
Returns the name of the most recently activated menu. The menu must still be active.

MENU( ) returns the menu name in uppercase characters.

If no menu is active, MENU( ) returns a null string.

## RECOMMENDED USE:
Use MENU( ) during debugging to display the name of the active menu. Also, by returning the name, you can design subroutines that do different operations depending on the calling menu.

**Example 1**—In debugging a menu system, a programmer puts MENU( ) at the top of every procedure. When a procedure executes, it displays the name of the calling menu.

```
DEFINE MENU planner
DEFINE PAD sel1 OF planner PROMPT "Project sales 10 months"
DEFINE PAD sel2 OF planner PROMPT "Plot sales 10 months"
ON SELECTION PAD sel1 OF planner DO fproject
ON SELECTION PAD sel2 OF planner DO fplot
ACTIVATE MENU planner
*
* <more menus>.

PROCEDURE fproject
? MENU()              && Returns "PLANNER".
* <statements>.
*
* End of procedure
```

**Example 2**—An application has a HELP prompt in every menu. Choosing HELP executes a procedure MHELP that displays information about the available menu selections. The MHELP procedure gets the calling menu's name from MENU( ) and uses it like a parameter.

```
* MAIN.PRG—Main application program
*
* Define a window to contain help text, activated in MHELP.
DEFINE WINDOW helpwind FROM 16,01 TO 23,70 PANEL
*
CLEAR
SET TALK OFF
DEFINE MENU master                                    && Main menu.
DEFINE PAD sel1 OF master PROMPT "File Maintenance"
DEFINE PAD sel2 OF master PROMPT "Record Updates"
DEFINE PAD sel3 OF master PROMPT "Get HELP about this menu"
ON SELECTION PAD sel1 OF master DO fmaint
ON SELECTION PAD sel1 OF master DO recup
ON SELECTION PAD sel3 OF master DO mhelp
ACTIVATE MENU master

PROCEDURE mhelp
*
ACTIVATE WINDOW helpwind
menuname = MENU()
DO CASE
  CASE menuname = "MASTER"
    @ 01,02 SAY "This is the main menu. From it, you can select"
    @ 02,02 SAY "other menus. File Maintenance lets you reindex"
    @ 03,02 SAY "database files. Record Updates lets you edit and"
    @ 04,02 SAY "add customer records."
  * UTILITY is another menu in the calling program.
  CASE menuname = "UTILITY"
    @ 01,02 SAY "This is the Utility menu. From it, you can backup"
    @ 02,02 SAY "your databases or purge duplicate records"
  * <More cases>.
  *
ENDCASE
WAIT ""
DEACTIVATE WINDOW helpwind
RETURN
```

## SEE ALSO:

Commands ACTIVATE MENU, DEFINE MENU, IF, ON SELECTION PAD, and PROCEDURE.

# MESSAGE( )

## DIALECTS:
dBASE III PLUS, dBASE IV, dBXL, FoxBASE+, and Quicksilver.

## SYNTAX:
MESSAGE( )

## RETURNS:
Character

## DEFINITION:
When ON ERROR is active, MESSAGE( ) returns a description of the last error condition.

RETURN and RETRY clear MESSAGE( ).

If no message exists, or if ON ERROR is inactive, MESSAGE( ) returns a null string.

Note that messages and error numbers are specific to each dBASE-compatible system.

## RECOMMENDED USE:
Use MESSAGE( ) with ERROR( ) to trap and report errors. They can help you specify corrective actions or display error information.

**Example**—A program tracks merchandise for a a department store. Within it, an error-trapping procedure identifies system errors and responds to them.

The error-trapping program tests for common errors, such as FILE ALREADY OPEN and FILE NOT FOUND. If the program tries to open an already-opened file, the program SUSPENDs operations to let the supervisor close the file and do other repairs. If a file cannot be found, the program CANCELs.

```
ON ERROR DO errtrap
USE acquires            && File inadvertently erased.
PROCEDURE errtrap
@ 24,03 SAY MESSAGE()   && Message function describes error condition.
DO CASE
```

```
  CASE ERROR() = 1      && dBASE III PLUS error code (file not found).
    CANCEL
  CASE ERROR() = 3      && File already open.
    SUSPEND
    * <more cases>
ENDCASE
```

## VARIATIONS:

**FoxBASE+:** Using MESSAGE(1) returns the program line that caused the error. This is useful for debugging and for documenting program errors. For example, you could create an error-trapping procedure that saves, in a database, error messages and the program lines that caused them.

## SEE ALSO:

Commands ON ERROR, RETRY, RETURN, and SUSPEND; functions DOSERROR( ), ERROR( ), and FERROR( ).

# MIN( )

## DIALECTS:
Clipper, dBASE III PLUS, dBASE IV, dBXL, FoxBASE+, and Quicksilver.

## SYNTAX:
MIN(<expN1>,<expN2>)

## RETURNS:
Numeric

## DEFINITION:
Returns the smaller of its numeric arguments.

## RECOMMENDED USE:
MIN( ) compares any two valid numeric expressions, including numeric fields, and returns the smaller. However, it cannot return the minimum value of a field throughout a database.

**Example**—Members of a health club pay $10 for each class they attend up to seven per month. Any beyond seven are free.

The membership program tracks classes attended, and charges members the MIN( ) of either $70 or the number of classes times $10.

```
dues = MIN(70,classes*10)

* <GET number of hours>
service = MAX(850,hournum*85)
```

## VARIATIONS:
**Clipper, FoxBASE+:** MIN( ) also returns the earlier of two date expressions.

**dBASE IV:** The MIN( ) option of the CALCULATE command lets you compute the minimum value across multiple fields in a database.

## SEE ALSO:
Command CALCULATE; function MAX( ).

# MLCOUNT( )

## DIALECTS:
Clipper only.

## SYNTAX:
MLCOUNT(<expC>[,<expN1>][,<expN2>][,<expL>)

## RETURNS:
Numeric

## DEFINITION:
Counts the number of word-wrapped lines that a character expression or memo field fills when formatted.

<expC> is the memo field name or character expression to count. (Note that "lines" are strings delimited by carriage return/line feeds).

<expN1> is the number of characters per line.

<expN2> is the size of embedded tab characters. It defaults to four. If you specify it to be larger than <expN1>, it defaults to one less than <expN1>.

The logical expression <expL> toggles word wrap. The default is on (.T.).

## RECOMMENDED USE:
Use MLCOUNT( ) to place page breaks when including free form text in formatted reports. MLCOUNT( ) works with MEMOLINE( ) to control text formatting.

**Example**—A library application includes book abstracts in a memo field ABOOK. To print the text, MLCOUNT( ) measures the formatted length of the text, and MEMOLINE( ) extracts and prints lines.

```
USE sales
SET DEVICE TO PRINT
* Count 40-character lines. The "" (null) holds the places
*  of unused optional arguments.
tlen = MLCOUNT(abook,40,"",.F.)
pline = 1                         && Start counter for print line (PLINE)
FOR mline = 1 TO tlen             && MLINE increases from 1 to MLCOUNT()
```

```
  extract = MEMOLINE(abook,40,mline)
  @ pline,01 SAY extract
  pline = pline + 1          && Increase print line by 1 until
  IF pline = 20              &&   it reaches 20, then
    EJECT                    &&   EJECT and reset print line (PLINE)
    pline = 1                &&   to 1.
    ENDIF
NEXT
SET DEVICE TO screen
```

## LIMITS/WARNINGS:

MLCOUNT( ) is in EXTEND.LIB on the system disk.

## SEE ALSO:

Functions HARDCR( ), MEMLINES( ), MEMOEDIT( ), MEMOREAD( ), MEMOTRAN( ), and MEMOWRIT( ).

# MLINE( )

## DIALECTS:

dBASE IV only.

## SYNTAX:

MLINE(<expC>,<expN>)

## RETURNS:

Character

## DEFINITION:

Returns a specific line of text from a memo field. The SET MEMOWIDTH command determines the line width.

<expC> is the memo field from which to extract the line.

<expN> is the line number to return. If you specify an invalid number, MLINE( ) returns a null string.

## RECOMMENDED USE:

Use MLINE( ) to produce reports using free form text input.

**Example**—A student's academic record includes formatted data and free form text. To print the text, MLINE( ) extracts lines from memo field STUDENT.

```
USE s_records
SET DEVICE TO PRINT
SET MEMOWIDTH TO 55
FOR lcount = 1 TO 60
  extract = MLINE(student,lcount)
  IF extract == ""       && == is like SET EXACT ON for this comparison.
    EJECT                && If EXTRACT is null, then EJECT and EXIT.
    EXIT
  ENDIF
  @ lcount,01 SAY extract
NEXT
SET DEVICE TO screen
```

## VARIATIONS:

**Clipper:** MEMOLINE( ) is equivalent.

## SEE ALSO:

Functions HARDCR( ), MEMOEDIT( ), MEMLINE( ), MEMOLINE( ), MEMOREAD( ), MEMOTRAN( ), and MEMOWRIT( ).

# MOD( )

## DIALECTS:

Clipper, dBASE III PLUS, dBASE IV, dBXL, FoxBASE+, and Quicksilver.

## SYNTAX:

MOD(<expN1>,<expN2>)

## RETURNS:

Numeric

## DEFINITION:

Returns the modulus, the remainder from dividing <expN1> by <expN2>.

The formula is

<expN1> - FLOOR(<expN1>/<expN2>) x <expN2>

where <expN1> and <expN2> are numeric expressions.
*Note:* FLOOR( ), a dBASE IV/dBXL/Quicksilver function, returns the largest integer less than or equal to its argument.

## RECOMMENDED USE:

Use MOD( ) in base number conversions, such as minutes to hours and inches to yards.

**Example 1**—An aeronautical application converts total inches into feet and inches when tracking trajectories. Instead of reporting 34,522 inches, the program reports the following:

```
totinch = 34522
feet = INT(totinch/12)
inches = MOD(totinch,12)
? "FEET: " + LTRIM(STR(feet,6,0)) + "  INCHES: " + LTRIM(STR(inches,6,0))
  FEET: 2876  INCHES: 10
```

MOD( ) limits INCHES to the range 0 to 11.

## VARIATIONS:

**Clipper:** MOD( ) is in EXTEND.LIB on the system disk. Clipper also has a modulus operator %, as in <expN1> % <expN2>.

**FoxBASE+:** MOD( ) appears to be derived from a different internal formula:

INT(<expN1> - <expN2> x INT(<expN1> / <expN2>))

**Clipper, dBASE III PLUS, dBXL, Quicksilver:** When <expN2> is zero, MOD( ) returns <expN1> (in Clipper, you must first link the error-handler ALTERROR.OBJ). Otherwise, it returns a "division by 0" error. Clipper versions before Summer '87 return 0. FoxBASE+ produces a "division by 0" error.

The FoxBASE+ result ("Division by 0" error) is technically correct, but requires greater care by the programmer.

## MOD( ) VARIATIONS

| dBASE III PLUS/ dBXL | Clipper Summer 1987 | FoxBASE+ | dBASE IV |
|---|---|---|---|
| MOD( 3, 0) = 3 | 3% 0 = 3 | MOD( 3 0) = error | MOD( 3 0) = error |
| MOD( 3,-2) = -1 | 3% -2 = -1.00 | MOD( 3,-2) = 1.00 | MOD( 3,-2) = -1 |
| MOD(-3, 2) = 1 | -3% 2 = 1.00 | MOD(-3, 2) = -1.00 | MOD(-3 2) = 1 |
| MOD(-3, 0) = -3 | -3% 0 = -3 | MOD(-3, 0) = error | MOD( 3, 0) = error |
| MOD(-1, 3) = 2 | -1% 3 = 2.00 | MOD(-1, 3) = -1.00 | MOD(-1 3) = 2 |
| MOD(-2, 3) = 1 | -2% 3 = 1.00 | MOD(-2, 3) = -2.00 | MOD(-2 3) = 1 |
| MOD( 2,-3) = -1 | 2% -3 = -1.00 | MOD( 2,-3) = 2.00 | MOD( 2,-3) = -1 |
| MOD( 1,-3) = -2 | 1% -3 = -2.00 | MOD( 1,-3) = 1.00 | MOD( 1,-3) = -2 |

Quicksilver returns erroneous results for all negative values of <expN2>:

| Quicksilver |
|---|
| MOD( 3, 0) = 3 |
| MOD( 3,-2) = error |
| MOD(-3, 2) = 1 |
| MOD(-3, 0) = -3 |
| MOD(-1, 3) = 2 |
| MOD(-2, 3) = 1 |
| MOD( 2,-3) = error |
| MOD( 1,-3) = error |

## LIMITS/WARNINGS:

Algorithms based on MOD( ) must be tested for each dBASE environment. Your results are almost certain to vary.

## SEE ALSO:

Functions FLOOR( ) and INT( ).

# MONTH ( )

## DIALECTS:

Clipper, dBASE III PLUS, dBASE IV, dBXL, FoxBASE+, and Quicksilver.

## SYNTAX:

MONTH(<expD>)

## RETURNS:

Numeric

## DEFINITION:

Returns a number from 1 to 12 representing the month in the date expression <expD>.

<expD> may be any expression that returns a date, including a memory variable, a field, or a function.

## RECOMMENDED USE:

Use MONTH( ) in computations that depend on calendar months such as payment schedules and end-of-month reports.

**Example 1**—A property management program computes monthly rents for tenants of a large apartment complex. The landlord schedules a 10 percent rent increase starting in March. The program derives MONTH( ) from the system date to determine when to implement the increase.

```
IF MONTH(DATE()) >= 3
  STORE rent * 1.1 TO rent
ENDIF
```

**Example 2**—A the end of the year, a payroll program produces a summary report for each month. The program lists the taxable and non-taxable income for employees for the MONTH( ) derived from date field PAYDATE.

```
SET PRINT on
ctr = 1
DO WHILE ctr <=12
  LIST taxable,nontax FOR MONTH(paydate) = ctr
  ctr = ctr + 1
ENDDO
SET PRINT off
```

## SEE ALSO:

Functions CMONTH( ), DAY( ), and YEAR( ).

# NDX( )

## DIALECTS:
dBASE III PLUS, dBASE IV, dBXL, FoxBASE+, and Quicksilver.

## SYNTAX:
NDX(<expN>)

## RETURNS:
Character

## DEFINITION:
Returns the name of an open index file.

<expN> is a number from 1 to 7 indicating the position of the index file in the file list of SET INDEX TO and USE.

SET ORDER TO does not affect NDX( ).

The first index file in the list (the primary index) is number 1.

If you specify a nonexistent index file, NDX( ) returns a null string.

## RECOMMENDED USE:
Use NDX( ) to display the active index files during development and debugging. This is helpful when using index-dependent commands such as SET RELATION and SEEK.

You can also use NDX( ) to handle open index files without knowing their names.

**Example**—While debugging an inventory management system, a programmer includes a simple procedure SHOWDEX to display the names of open index files. At key breakpoints, the programmer includes the command DO SHOWDEX.

```
* SHOWDEX.PRG
? DBF()          && Show active database filename.
ctr = 1
* If length of the index name is 0 (null), stop counting.
DO WHILE LEN(NDX(ctr)) > 0
  ? "INDEX " + STR(ctr,1,0) + ": " + NDX(ctr)
  ctr = ctr + 1
  IF ctr = 8
    EXIT
  ENDIF
ENDDO
```

## VARIATIONS:

**dBASE IV:** Allows an alias name as an argument for checking an unselected database file. The full syntax is

NDX(<expN>,<alias>)

To check the name of index 2 in a file REAL.DBF (in an unselected work area), specify NDX( ) as follows:

```
? NDX(2,"REAL")
```

If the alias does not exist, dBASE IV reports "ALIAS name not found."

**FoxBASE+:** The numeric range of <expN> extends to 8, and NDX(8) always returns a null string. This lets programmers determine the last valid index by testing for the null string rather than for both a null string and an invalid index number (ctr = 8 in the example).

## SEE ALSO:

Commands INDEX and SET INDEX TO; functions ALIAS( ), DBF( ), and MDX( ).

# NETERR( )

## DIALECTS:

Clipper only.

## SYNTAX:

NETERR( )

## RETURNS:

Logical

## DEFINITION:

Returns true (.T.) if APPEND BLANK, USE, or USE...EXCLUSIVE fails during multiuser operation.

NETERR( ) returns true if you try to USE a file that is already in exclusive use or locked by another user, if you try to APPEND BLANK at the same time as another user, or if you try to APPEND BLANK when another user has locked the file.

## RECOMMENDED USE:

Use NETERR( ) to program retries of failed USE or APPEND BLANK attempts. If NETERR( ) is false (.F.), you can stop retrying.

**Example**—Because APPEND BLANK changes data in the file header (the record count), it requires momentary exclusive access to the file. If the file is not available, you can retry APPEND BLANK until NETERR( ) returns false.

```
FOR ctr = 1 to 200      && Retry 200 times if necessary.
  APPEND BLANK
  IF NETERR()           && If NETERR() is true,
    INKEY(1)            &&  pause one second.
  ELSE
    ctr = 200           && If NETERR() is false, exit FOR/NEXT.
  ENDIF
NEXT
```

## SEE ALSO:

Commands APPEND BLANK and USE...EXCLUSIVE; functions ERROR( ), FLOCK( ), INKEY( ), and RLOCK( ).

# NETNAME( )

## DIALECTS:

Clipper only.

## SYNTAX:

NETNAME( )

## RETURNS:

Character

## DEFINITION:

Returns the computer workstation identification as set in the IBM PC Local Area Network.

The identification name is a string fifteen characters long. If it was not set, NETNAME( ) returns a null string.

## RECOMMENDED USE:

Use NETNAME( ) to monitor which workstations have logged onto a network application.

**Example**—The network administrator in a defense plant monitors multiuser applications on the local area network. When a network user executes a Clipper application, a subroutine updates a log file indicating the date, time, and NETNAME( ).

```
ctr = 1                  && Initialize retry counter if USE EXCLUSIVE fails.
DO WHILE ctr < 50        && Retry USE EXCLUSIVE 50 times if necessary.
  USE log EXCLUSIVE      && Use log file exclusively.
  INKEY(2)               && Pause 2 seconds between retries.
  ctr = ctr + 1          && Increment counter.
ENDDO
IF NETERR()              && If USE EXCLUSIVE fails...
  DO nerror              &&   do error subroutine.
ENDIF
APPEND BLANK             && Add record containing date, time, and name.
REPLACE logdate WITH DATE(), logtime WITH TIME(), netname WITH NETNAME()
```

## LIMITS/WARNINGS:

NETNAME( ) works only on the IBM PC Local Area Network.

## SEE ALSO:

Functions OS( ) and SYS(0).

# NETWORK( )

## DIALECTS:
dBASE IV only.

## SYNTAX:
NETWORK( )

## RETURNS:
Logical

## DEFINITION:
Returns true (.T.) when dBASE IV is running on a local area network.

## RECOMMENDED USE:
Use NETWORK( ) to determine whether to execute network-specific commands and functions. You can use it to branch in an IF...ENDIF structure.

**Example**—When running on a network, an application maintains a user log on the server. However, if it is running on a single user system, it skips the user login routines.

```
IF NETWORK()
  * <Do user login routines>
ENDIF
```

## SEE ALSO:
Functions NETNAME( ) and USER( ).

# NEXTKEY( )

## DIALECTS:

Clipper only.

## SYNTAX:

NEXTKEY( )

## RETURNS:

Numeric

## DEFINITION:

Returns the ASCII version of the next keystroke without clearing the keyboard buffer. If no key is pressed, NEXTKEY( ) returns 0. The ASCII values are the ones returned by INKEY( ) and LASTKEY( ) (see INKEY( ) for a complete list).

The ASCII values range from -39 to 386. NEXTKEY( ) recognizes all key combinations, including ones involving function keys, Ctrl, and Alt.

## RECOMMENDED USE:

Use NEXTKEY( ) to get user input without clearing the keyboard buffer. This lets you pass the pressed key to a subroutine or menu that will use it.

**Example**—NEXTKEY( ) solves the problem of calling help from an INKEY( ) loop. Normally, pressing F1 from a wait state (ACCEPT, READ, or WAIT) calls a program HELP.PRG. Since INKEY( ) is not a wait state, pressing F1 to call help does not work. (INKEY( ) is often used to do other processing, such as displaying the time, while awaiting input.)

The problem is that INKEY( ) removes the key from the buffer. In Clipper versions before Summer '87, you can use the KEYBOARD command to reenter the pressed key. In Summer '87, NEXTKEY( ) preserves the keypress. The WAIT near the bottom of the loop provides the conduit for calling help.

```
* MAIN.PRG—Lookup program displays information during data entry.
*
SET PROC TO HELP          && Included so HELP.PRG will compile without
SET CURSOR OFF            &&  a direct reference (without a DO).
CLEAR
@ 10,18 SAY "(C)ustomer IDs"
```

```
@ 11,18 SAY "(A)ccount Numbers"
@ 12,18 SAY "(E)xit" DO WHILE .t.
  nkey = 0
  DO WHILE nkey = 0
    @ 01,60 SAY AMPM(time())   && Display the 12-hour clock.
    nkey = NEXTKEY()           && Get next key pressed and store in NKEY.
  ENDDO
  DO CASE
    CASE nkey = ASC("C")
      * <DO customer id subroutine>
    CASE nkey = ASC("A")
      * <DO account number subroutine>
    CASE nkey = ASC("E")
      SET CURSOR ON
      EXIT
  ENDCASE
  SET CONSOLE OFF    && Disable screen to prevent keys from appearing.
  WAIT               && WAIT processes F1 key and clears keyboard buffer.
  SET CONSOLE ON
ENDDO

* HELP.PRG
PARAMETERS x,y,z     && Required parameters passed by F1
SAVE SCREEN
CLEAR
@ 10,10 say "This is help text"
INKEY(0)             && Pause until a key is pressed (non-WAIT state).
RESTORE SCREEN
KEYBOARD CHR(13)     && Keyboard CARRIAGE RETURN to clear pending WAIT.
```

NEXTKEY( ) is in EXTEND.LIB on the system disk.

## LIMITS/WARNINGS:

In a DO WHILE loop, you must clear the keyboard buffer before getting the next key. Otherwise, NEXTKEY( ) will repeatedly "stuff" itself with the same key.

## SEE ALSO:

Command KEYBOARD; function INKEY( ).

# ORDER( )

## DIALECTS:

dBASE IV only.

## SYNTAX:

ORDER([<alias>]/<work area number>)

## RETURNS:

Character

## DEFINITION:

Returns the name of the controlling MDX (multiple index file) tag or index file. If you do not specify an alias or work area number, ORDER( ) operates on the current work area.

ORDER( ) returns the index name or TAG in uppercase without an extension.

If no index or TAG is active, ORDER( ) returns a null string.

## OPTIONS:

The <alias> or <work area number> lets you specify a file in an unselected work area.

## RECOMMENDED USE:

Use ORDER( ) to identify the controlling index to the user or for debugging purposes.

**Example 1**—An inventory application has a main file INVENT and four indexes. The user can define which one controls the order. For testing purposes, the program displays the ORDER( ).

```
? ORDER("INVENT")
PARTNO
```

To specify the database by its work area number, the program uses the following syntax:

```
? ORDER(1)
PARTNO
```

You can omit <alias> and <argument> if you are checking a database in the current work area.

You can also use ORDER( ) to manipulate indexes without knowing their names.

**Example 2**—A generic reporting module for a sales application relies on a previous program to open databases and indexes. It then uses ORDER( ) to save the controlling index name. When finished reporting, it restores the original order.

```
old_order = ORDER()
* <Do reporting operations.>
SET ORDER TO TAG (old_order)
```

## SEE ALSO:

Commands INDEX, SET INDEX, and SET ORDER; functions INDEXORD( ), KEY( ), MDX, NDX( ), and TAG( ).

# OS( )

## DIALECTS:
Clipper, dBASE III PLUS, dBASE IV, dBXL, FoxBASE+, and Quicksilver.

## SYNTAX:
OS( )

## RETURNS:
Character

## DEFINITION:
Returns the name and version number of the computer's operating system.

## RECOMMENDED USE:
Use OS( ) when writing programs for both MS-DOS and UNIX, or to take advantage of features in particular versions of an operating system.

**Example**—To handle the different disk directory structures of DOS and UNIX, a programmer uses OS( ) to determine which file path program to execute.

```
IF "DOS" $ OS()         && If "DOS" is in the OS string,
  DO DOSpath            &&   DO DOS file path program.
ELSE                    && If not DOS, then
  DO UNIXpath           &&   DO UNIX file program.
ENDIF
```

## VARIATIONS:
**Clipper:** OS( ) is a user defined function in EXAMPLEP.PRG on the system disk. It is also linked into EXTEND.LIB on the system disk. It always returns a constant "MS/PC-DOS", regardless of the operating system. Nantucket includes it for compatibility with dBASE III PLUS.

## SEE ALSO:
Functions GETENV( ) and VERSION( ).

# PAD( )

## DIALECTS:
dBASE IV only.

## SYNTAX:
PAD( )

## RETURNS:
Character

## DEFINITION:
Returns the uppercase name of the most recently selected PAD in an active menu. PADs are selections specified in the DEFINE PAD command.

If no menu is active, PAD( ) returns a null string.

## RECOMMENDED USE:
Use PAD( ) to display the name of the selected pad during debugging.

**Example**—The top menu in an inventory program has four pads. To debug the menu system, the programmer uses the PAD( ) function in every procedure to display the name of the selected pad.

```
* INVENT.PRG—Main application program
DEFINE MENU topmenu
DEFINE PAD sel1 OF topmenu PROMPT "File Maintenance"
DEFINE PAD sel2 OF topmenu PROMPT "Record Updates"
DEFINE PAD sel3 OF topmenu PROMPT "Summary Report"
DEFINE PAD sel4 OF topmenu PROMPT "Inventory Report"
ON SELECTION PAD sel1 OF topmenu DO fmaint
ON SELECTION PAD sel2 OF topmenu DO rupdate
ON SELECTION PAD sel3 OF topmenu DO sumrept
ON SELECTION PAD sel4 OF topmenu DO invrept
ACTIVATE MENU topmenu

PROCEDURE fmaint
? PAD()              && Returns "SEL1"

PROCEDURE rupdate
? PAD()              && Returns "SEL2"
```

```
PROCEDURE sumrept
? PAD()             && Returns "SEL3"

PROCEDURE invrept
? PAD()             && Returns "SEL4"
```

## LIMITS/WARNINGS:

PAD( ) is not valid from the dot prompt, since there can be no active menu.

## SEE ALSO:

Commands @...PROMPT, DEFINE BAR, DEFINE MENU, DEFINE PAD, DEFINE POPUP, MENU TO, ON PAD, and ON SELECTION PAD; functions MENU( ) and POPUP( ).

# PAYMENT( )

## DIALECTS:
dBASE IV only.

## SYNTAX:
PAYMENT(<expN1>,<expN2>,<expN3>)

## RETURNS:
Numeric

## DEFINITION:
Computes the periodic payment needed to pay off the principal and interest of a loan.

<expN1> is a principal balance; it may be negative.

<expN2> is the constant interest rate *per period.* For example, you would express an 18 percent annual interest rate as .18/12 or 0.015.

<expN3> is the number of payments. Fractional payments are rounded automatically.

## RECOMMENDED USE:
PAYMENT( ) is useful in many financial applications, ranging from real estate to banking.

**Example**—Dave's new car cost $9,000...until he added the automatic transmission, cruise control, and air conditioning options, bringing the total to $10,500. With $1,000 for a down payment, he financed $9,500 for 60 months at an annual interest rate of 13.75 percent (.1375 in decimal). Using PAYMENT( ), we can calculate his monthly payment with:

```
SET DECIMALS TO 2
mtotal = PAYMENT(9500,.1375/12,60)
? mtotal
219.82
```

*Note:* Because interest is computed annually, divide by 12 to get the rate per period.

## SEE ALSO:
Command CALCULATE; functions FV( ) (future value), and PV( ) (present value).

# PCOL( )

## DIALECTS:

Clipper, dBASE III PLUS, dBASE IV, dBXL, FoxBASE+, and Quicksilver.

## SYNTAX:

PCOL( )

## RETURNS:

Numeric

## DEFINITION:

Returns the printer's current column coordinate relative to the SET MARGIN command. SET MARGIN defaults to 0.

For example, you can determine the printer's position after printing a string (in a program):

```
?? PCOL()
35
```

The printer must be on to use PCOL( ).

## RECOMMENDED USE:

PCOL( ) lets you send output to the printer at a coordinate relative to the current position. This is useful for printing reports that display multiple @...SAY...GETs on a single line.

**Example**—A report generator prints several columns of data. It uses the PCOL( ) function to separate them.

```
CLEAR
@ 5,PCOL() SAY "SSN: " +  ssn
@ 5,PCOL()+2 SAY "Employer: " + employer
@ 5,PCOL()+2 SAY "No. of Dependents: " + depends
```

Typical output would be:

```
SSN: 010-22-99XX  Employer: Acme Publishing  No. of Dependents:  2
```

If you SET MARGIN TO 10, printing starts at column 10; however, PCOL( ) still returns 0 as the starting position.

## VARIATIONS:

**dBASE IV:** The _ploffset system variable is equivalent to SET MARGIN. It defaults to 0.

**FoxBASE+:** You need not turn on the printer to use PCOL( ) if you redirect output using the command SET PRINTER TO <filename>.

## SEE ALSO:

Command SET MARGIN; functions COL( ), FCOL( ), FROW( ), PROW( ), and ROW( ).

# PCOUNT( )

## DIALECTS:
Clipper only.

## SYNTAX:
PCOUNT( )

## RETURNS:
Numeric

## DEFINITION:
Returns the number of parameters passed to a procedure or user defined function.

## RECOMMENDED USE:
PCOUNT( ) lets programs pass an unknown number of parameters. If a program expects parameters, and none is passed, it can prompt the user to supply them. Some general purpose subroutines may also allow a variable number of parameters.

Example—A telephone contact system accepts names to search for on the DOS command line. The program expects a name and a data file as PARAMETERs. If the user does not supply them, the program asks for them.

```
* CONTACT.PRG
PARAMETERS name,file
IF PCOUNT() = 0
  ACCEPT "Enter name:  " TO name
  ACCEPT "Enter file:  "  TO file
ENDIF
IF PCOUNT() = 1
  ACCEPT "Enter file:  " TO file
ENDIF
USE (file) INDEX (file)
SEEK name
```

## SEE ALSO:
Commands DO and PARAMETERS.

# PI( )

## DIALECTS:
dBASE IV only.

## SYNTAX:
PI( )

## RETURNS:
Floating point

## DEFINITION:
Returns 3.14159265358979311 6, the approximate ratio of the circumference of a circle to its diameter (represented by the Greek letter pi). Pi is a non-repeating irrational number.

## RECOMMENDED USE:
Use PI( ) in scientific applications involving circles, spheres, cones, or other curves.

**Example**—A farmer wants to compute the volume of a cylindrical grain silo. The formula is (pi × radius squared × height). Given a radius of 25 feet, and a height of 125 feet, she determines the volume to be 245436.93 cubic feet.

```
volume = PI() * 25^2 * 125
? volume
245436.93
```

## SEE ALSO:
Functions ACOS( ), ASIN( ), ATAN( ), ATN2, COS( ), SIN( ), and TAN( ).

# POPUP( )

## DIALECTS:

dBASE IV only.

## SYNTAX:

POPUP( )

## RETURNS:

Character

## DEFINITION:

Returns the uppercase name of the active popup menu.

If none is active, POPUP( ) returns a null string.

## RECOMMENDED USE:

Use POPUP( ) during debugging to display the name of the active popup menu. Also, by returning the name, you can design subroutines that do different operations depending on the caller.

**Example 1**—In debugging a menu system, a programmer puts POPUP( ) at the top of every procedure. When a procedure executes, it displays the name of the calling menu.

```
DEFINE POPUP banks FROM 01,01 TO 10,30
DEFINE BAR 1 OF students PROMPT "List Savings and Loans"
DEFINE BAR 2 OF students PROMPT "Geographic Focus"
* <Define more bars>.
ON SELECTION POPUP students DO mbanks
ACTIVATE POPUP students

PROCEDURE mbanks
mbar = BAR()
? POPUP()              && Returns BANKS.
DO CASE
  CASE mbar = 1
    DO savings
  CASE mbar = 2
    DO geofocus
  * <More CASES>.
ENDCASE
*
* End of procedure.
```

**Example 2**—An academic management program lets administrators track students through a four-year curriculum. A procedure containing a CASE structure is called by two different POPUPs. To determine the calling POPUP, the procedure uses the POPUP( ) function.

```
DEFINE POPUP students FROM 01,01 TO 10,30
DEFINE BAR 1 OF students PROMPT "Update G.P.A."
DEFINE BAR 2 OF students PROMPT "Change Student Status"
DEFINE BAR 3 OF students PROMPT "File Maintenance"
ON SELECTION POPUP students DO mcase
ACTIVATE POPUP students
DEFINE POPUP fmaint FROM 11,01 TO 20,30
* <Define more bar statements>.
*

PROCEDURE mcase
mbar = BAR()
mpop = POPUP()              && Get name of calling popup.
DO CASE
  CASE mbar = 1 .AND. mpop = "STUDENTS"
    * <Update G.P.A. subroutine>.
  CASE mbar = 2 .AND. mpop = "STUDENTS"
    * <Change Student Status subroutine>.
  CASE mbar = 3 .AND. mpop = "STUDENTS"
    * <File maintenance>.
  CASE mbar = 1 .AND. mpop = "FMAINT"
    *
  CASE mbar = 2 .AND. mpop = "FMAINT"
    *
ENDCASE
```

## SEE ALSO:

Commands ACTIVATE POPUP, DEACTIVATE, and DEFINE POPUP; functions BAR( ), MENU( ), PAD( ), and PROMPT( ).

# PRINTER( )

## DIALECTS:
dBXL and Quicksilver.

## SYNTAX:
PRINTER(<expC>)

## RETURNS:
Logical

## DEFINITION:
Returns true (.T.) if the device specified in the argument is READY. The valid devices have port names LPT1, LPT2, LPT3, COM1, and COM2.

If the printer is disconnected or off line, PRINTER( ) returns false (.F.).

## DEFAULT:
PRINTER( ) returns true (.T.) if you use an invalid port name. So check your spelling.

## RECOMMENDED USE:
Use PRINTER( ) to test printer readiness when changing ports with the SET PRINTER command.

**Example**—A shipping program prints invoices, packing slips, and labels. To avoid changing forms, the program prints each on a different printer. When changing ports, it uses PRINTER( ) to check status. The program alerts the clerk if the printer is off line.

After changing printers, the program initializes a memory variable RDYPRINT with a value of true (.T.). Inside a DO WHILE loop, PRINTER( ) tests the specified printer. If it returns false, RDYPRINT becomes false and the DO WHILE repeats. The WAIT command pauses execution to let the clerk put the printer back on line or cancel the print job.

```
SET PRINTER TO LPT2
rdyprint = .t.
DO WHILE rdyprint
```

```
  IF PRINTER("LPT2")
    rdyprint = .t.
    DO labels     && If printer is ready, print labels.
  ELSE
    rdyprint = .f.
    ?? CHR(7)     && If not ready, alert shipping clerk with beep/message.
    WAIT "LPT2 OFFLINE. Type 'C' to cancel, "+;
         "or any other key to retry" TO response
    IF response $ "cC"
      EXIT
    ENDIF
  ENDIF
ENDDO
```

## LIMITS/WARNINGS:

PRINTER( ) may not work properly on computers that are not 100 percent IBM PC-compatible.

## SEE ALSO:

Function ISPRINTER( ), PRINTSTATUS( ), and SYS(13).

# PRINTSTATUS( )

## DIALECTS:
dBASE IV only.

## SYNTAX:
PRINTSTATUS( )

## RETURNS:
Logical

## DEFINITION:
Indicates whether the current parallel printer port is ready. PRINTSTATUS( ) returns true (.T.) if the port is ready and the printer is online, and false (.F.) otherwise.

Similar to Clipper's ISPRINTER( ), FoxBASE+'s SYS(13), and Quicksilver's PRINTER( ). Unfortunately, this function has no standard name.

## RECOMMENDED USE:
Use PRINTSTATUS( ) before printing reports to check the printer's status.

**Example**—Before printing a sales summary, PRINTSTATUS( ) checks the printer. The programmer puts PRINTSTATUS( ) in a user defined function CHKPRINT( ) that both checks the status and SETs DEVICE TO PRINT.

```
* CHKPRINT
FUNCTION chkprint
*
PRIVATE pkey,success
SET DEVICE TO SCREEN            && Make sure printer is not already on.
pkey = 0
DO WHILE pkey # 27.AND.(.NOT. PRINTSTATUS())
  @ 01,01 SAY "Printer not ready. "+;
              "Press ESC to cancel, or any other key to retry"
  pkey = INKEY(0)
ENDDO
IF pkey # 27
  SET DEVICE TO PRINT
ENDIF
RETURN = (pkey # 27)
```

The calling program uses CHKPRINT( ) to determine whether to print as follows:

```
IF CHKPRINT()
  DO acct_rpt
ELSE
  * DO <recovery procedure>
ENDIF
```

## SEE ALSO:

Function PRINTER( ), PRINTSTATUS( ), and SYS(13).

# PROCLINE( ); PROCNAME( )

## DIALECTS:

Clipper only.

## SYNTAX:

PROCLINE( )
PROCNAME( )

## RETURNS:

PROCLINE( )—Numeric
PROCNAME( )—Character

## DEFINITION:

PROCLINE( ) returns the number of the currently executing program line. PROCNAME( ) returns the name of the currently executing procedure.

## RECOMMENDED USE:

Use PROCLINE( ) and PROCNAME( ) during program development to display information about the currently executing program.

**Example**—A programmer uses PROCLINE( ) and PROCNAME( ) to trace program flow when using SET KEY procedures. When control passes to a procedure, its name appears. At specified breakpoints, the programmer uses PROCLINE( ) to trace the execution of individual lines.

```
SET KEY 21 TO calc      && Execute calc.prg when user presses Ctrl-U.
* <more statements>


* CALC.PRG
* Compute sales tax for sales items.
PARAMETERS name,line,memvar   && Accept required SET KEY parameters.
? PROCNAME()                  && Display procedure name.
* <more statements>
? "Now executing: "+STR(PROCLINE(),3,0)  && Convert PROCLINE to string.
```

## VARIATIONS:

**dBASE IV:** PROCLINE( ) resembles dBASE IV's LINENO( ) function. PROCNAME( ) resembles dBASE IV's PROGRAM( ) function.

**FoxBASE+:** PROCNAME( ) resembles FoxBASE+'s SYS(16) function. SYS(16) returns the program name, and also lets you trace back multiple execution levels.

## SEE ALSO:

Command SET KEY; functions PROGRAM( ) and SYS(16).

# PROGRAM( )

## DIALECTS:

dBASE IV only.

## SYNTAX:

PROGRAM( )

## RETURNS:

Character

## DEFINITION:

Returns the name of the currently executing function, procedure, or program.

PROGRAM( ) returns an uppercase name without an extension.

If no program is running, it returns a null string.

## RECOMMENDED USE:

Use PROGRAM( ) to determine which program or procedure caused an error. After SUSPENDing program execution, use PROGRAM( ) from the dot prompt to return the program's name. You can also use it in the debugger's display or breakpoint window, or within a program to display the names of functions as they execute.

**Example 1**—An inventory management system consisting of 10 modules stops in the middle of an input screen. The display seems to freeze, leaving no alternative but to reboot. The programmer suspects that the user defined function CHKPRINT( ) is causing the problem. To debug the program, he runs the debugger and uses PROGRAM( ) as a breakpoint condition to isolate the suspect function. In the breakpoint window, he enters

```
PROGRAM() = "CHKPRINT" .AND. LINENO()=5
```

This tells the debugger to stop at line 5 of CHKPRINT. From there, the programmer can step through the function, watching it execute.

**Example 2**—To stop execution when a particular subprogram begins executing, use PROGRAM( ) in the breakpoint window as shown:

```
── r_add.prg ─────────────────────────────────────────────
* R_ADD.PRG
CLEAR
mpart = SPACE(4)
mdesc = SPACE(25)
msource = SPACE(25)
@ 10,10 SAY "Part... "  GET mpart
@ 11,10 SAY "Desc... "  GET mdesc
@ 12,10 SAY "Source. "  GET msource
READ
*

── DISPLAY ──────────────────────        ── BREAKPOINTS ──────────
                                          1: PROGRAM()="R_ADD"
                                          2:
                                          3:
                                          4:

── DEBUGGER ──────────────────────────────────────────────
Work Area: 1     Database file:        Program file: r_add.prg
Record:  0       Master Index:         Procedure:    R_ADD
ACTION:  _                             Current line: 2
Breakpoint:          1
```

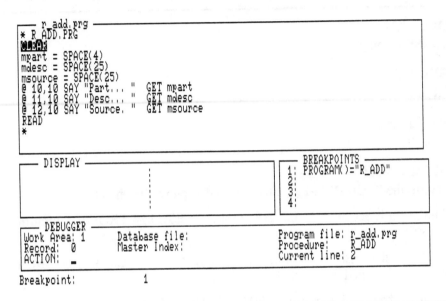

When subprogram R_ADD begins executing, PROGRAM( ) returns "R_ADD" and the breakpoint expression is true.

**Example 3**—You can also use program() in an ON ERROR command, to identify the location of an error. The following statement eases debugging by indicating the program in which the error occurred and the line number.

```
ON ERROR ? "Executing program: " + PROGRAM() + ;
 "  Error occured on line: " + STR(lineno(),5,0)
```

## VARIATIONS:

**Clipper:** PROGRAM( ) is similar to Clipper's PROCNAME( ) function.

**FoxBASE+:** PROGRAM( ) is similar to SYS(16). SYS(16) returns the program name, and also lets you trace back multiple execution levels.

## SEE ALSO:

Commands DEBUG, ON ERROR, SET TRAP, and SUSPEND; functions ERROR( ), LINENO( ), MESSAGE( ), PROCNAME( ), and SYS(16).

# PROMPT( )

## DIALECTS:

dBASE IV only.

## SYNTAX:

PROMPT( )

## RETURNS:

Character

## DEFINITION:

Returns the PROMPT string of the selected popup or bar menu.

If no menu is active, or if the user presses the ESC key, PROMPT( ) returns a null string.

If you use the FIELD option of the DEFINE POPUP command, PROMPT( ) returns the selected field's contents.

If you use the FILES option of DEFINE POPUP, PROMPT( ) returns the selected filename in uppercase, including its extension and path.

If you use the STRUCTURE option, PROMPT( ) returns the name of the selected field in uppercase.

## RECOMMENDED USE:

Use PROMPT( ) to pass FIELD, FILES, or STRUCTURE data from a pick list to a subroutine.

**Example**—A sales program lets the user select a database from a POPUP list. When the selection is made, the ON SELECTION command executes PROCEDURE MFILES. In the procedure, the PROMPT( ) function returns the selected filename as the argument of a USE command.

```
DEFINE POPUP showfiles FROM 01,01 TO 10,30 PROMPT FILES LIKE *.DBF
ON SELECTION POPUP showfiles DO mfiles
ACTIVATE POPUP showfiles
PROCEDURE mfiles
USE (PROMPT())              && Puts the selected file into use.
RETURN
```

## SEE ALSO:

Commands DEFINE POPUP, ON SELECTION PAD, and ON SELECTION POPUP; functions BAR( ) and POPUP( ).

# PROPER( )

## DIALECTS:

dBXL and Quicksilver.

## SYNTAX:

PROPER(<expC>)

## RETURNS:

Character

## DEFINITION:

Converts <expC> to upper and lower case, capitalizing the first character and any character after a space or punctuation mark. PROPER( ) converts all other characters to lowercase.

To convert "david m. kalman" to upper and lower case, you would use PROPER( ) as follows:

```
? PROPER("david m. kalman")
David M. Kalman
```

PROPER( ) correctly capitalizes names with apostrophes, hyphens, and most titles:

```
? PROPER("dr. david m. kalman, jr.")
  Dr. David M. Kalman, Jr.

? PROPER("david m. kalman-nugent")
  David M. Kalman-Nugent

? PROPER("DAVID M. O'LEARY")
  David M. O'Leary
```

Names with internal capital letters but no special punctuation (such as MacDonald and LeVine), and some titles do not convert properly:

```
? PROPER("david m. kalman, iii")
  David M. Kalman, Iii

? PROPER("david m. macdonald")
  David M. Macdonald
```

## DEFINITION:

Use PROPER( ) to display proper names in the correct case.

**Example**—For ease of data entry, a mailing program stores data in all uppercase. When producing reports, the program uses PROPER( ) to convert names to upper and lower case.

```
?
?
? mdate
?
? PROPER(mname)
? maddress
? TRIM(mcity)+ " " + mstate + mzip
?
```

## SEE ALSO:

Functions LOWER( ) and UPPER( ).

# PROW( )

## DIALECTS:
Clipper, dBASE III PLUS, dBASE IV, dBXL, FoxBASE+, and Quicksilver.

## SYNTAX:
PROW( )

## RETURNS:
Numeric

## DEFINITION:
Returns the printer's current row position.

EJECT sets PROW( ) to 0.

## RECOMMENDED USE:
Use PROW( ) to print at a row relative to its predecessor. This is helpful when formatting reports and printing non-standard forms.

**Example 1**—A bus ticketing application prints tickets on continuous paper, ten rows apart.

```
USE ticket
SET DEVICE TO PRINT
DO WHILE .NOT. EOF()
  @ PROW()+10,01 SAY "Passenger's Name: " + pname
  @ PROW(),01 SAY    "Destination     : " + pdest
  * <more ticket information>
  SKIP
ENDDO
```

**Example 2**—A stock market report lists weekly advances and declines. When the printer row position exceeds 59, the program EJECTs a page.

```
USE stocks
DO WHILE .NOT. EOF()
  ? sname + "  High: " + STR(high,8,2) + "  Low: " + STR(low,8,2)
  IF PROW() > 59
    EJECT
  ENDIF
  SKIP
ENDDO
```

## SPECIAL USES:

In all systems except Clipper, a dollar sign in an @...SAY statement indicates the current row or column. For example, to print a name on the current row, use the command

```
@ $,02 SAY "Name " + sname
```

## LIMITS/WARNINGS:

PROW( ) does not allow a negative offset.

## SEE ALSO:

Commands EJECT, SET DEVICE TO, and SET PRINTER; functions COL( ), FCOL( ), FROW( ), PCOL( ), and ROW( ).

# PV( )

## DIALECTS:
dBASE IV only.

## SYNTAX:
PV(<expN1>,<expN2>,<expN3>)

## RETURNS:
Numeric

## DEFINITION:
Computes the present value of equal periodic payments, invested at a constant interest rate. The value returned is the part applied to the principal.

<expN1> is a positive or negative payment amount that includes principal and interest.

<expN2> is the constant interest rate **per period**, expressed as a decimal value. For example, you would express an 18 percent annual interest rate compounded monthly as .18/12, or .015.

<expN3> is the number of payments. Fractional values are rounded automatically.

## RECOMMENDED USE:
PV( ) is useful in financial applications such as banking and real estate.

**Example**—Joan makes a $500 monthly payment for her mortgage at the fixed annual rate of 11.5 percent compounded monthly. After five years (60 payments), she wants to know how much she has paid on the principal (i.e., the present value).

```
SET DECIMALS TO 2
mtotal = PV(500,.115/12,60)
? mtotal
22734.91
```

To determine the interest paid, Joan subtracts the present value ($22734.91) from her total payments ($500 × 60 or $30,000), yielding $7265.09.

## SEE ALSO:
Command CALCULATE; function FV( ) (future value).

# RAND( )

## DIALECTS:

dBASE IV only.

## SYNTAX:

RAND([<expN>])

## RETURNS:

Numeric

## DEFINITION:

Returns a random number in the range 0 through 1 inclusive.

Numbers generated by RAND( ) are not truly random. Instead, they are produced by a formula based on a *seed* value. The same seed always produces the same sequence of "random" numbers.

## OPTIONS:

<expN> is the seed (may be positive or negative).

If the seed is negative, RAND( ) derives the actual seed from the system clock.

## DEFAULT:

If you do not supply a seed the first time you issue RAND( ), dBASE supplies a default of 100001. You can restore the default by issuing RAND(100001).

## RECOMMENDED USE:

For maximum randomness, seed RAND( ) from the system clock by making its argument negative. Avoid seeding RAND( ) with a constant unless you want to repeat a sequence of numbers.

**Example**—A student testing program uses RAND( ) to select the order in which questions are posed. The program INDEXes the questions on the string value of RAND( ), plus one character of the CATEGORY field.

```
USE test
INDEX ON STR(RAND(-1),4,2)+SUBSTR(category,1,1) TO t_order
```

Using -1 as an argument makes RAND( ) derive its seed from the system clock. The order of the questions will differ for every generation of the index.

# RAT( )

## DIALECTS:

Clipper only. Other systems lack this sophisticated-sounding command.

## SYNTAX:

RAT(<expC1>,<expC2>)

## RETURNS:

Numeric

## DEFINITION:

Searches for the last (rightmost) occurrence of one character string <expC1> within another <expC2> and returns the position at which it starts. If <expC2> does not contain <expC1>, RAT( ) returns 0.

<expC1> is called a *substring* of <expC2>.

RAT( ) is similar to AT( ), except that AT( ) searches for the first occurrence of <expC1> instead of the last.

## RECOMMENDED USE:

Use RAT( ) in string manipulation routines to find and extract substrings.

**Example**—The contents of field NAME are in the form LASTNAME, FIRSTNAME. For printing, the form must be converted to FIRSTNAME LASTNAME. First, RAT( ) finds the last comma in the field, providing a base for the SUBSTRING( ) function. SUBSTR( ) is then used to transpose the sections.

```
USE customers
DO WHILE .NOT. EOF()
  pos = RAT(",",name)      && POS is the location of the last comma.
  new = TRIM(SUBSTR(name,pos+1,30-pos+1))+" "+LTRIM(SUBSTR(name,1,pos-1))
  REPLACE name WITH new
  SKIP
ENDDO
```

Before the conversion, the names appear as follows:

```
      LIST name
     Record#  NAME
           1  Holden, Susan
           2  Kalman, David M.
           3  Randall, III, Byron
```

Afterward, the names are:

```
LIST name
Record#  NAME
      1   Susan Holden
      2   David M. Kalman
      3   Byron Randall,III
```

RAT( ) is in EXTEND.LIB on the system disk.

## SEE ALSO:

Functions AT( ) and SUBSTR( ).

# READEXIT( )

## DIALECTS:
Clipper only.

## SYNTAX:
READEXIT([<expL>])

## RETURNS:
Logical

## DEFINITION:
Controls whether the "up arrow" and "down arrow" keys exit a READ.

An argument of true (.T.) allows exits, false (.F.) prevents them.

READEXIT( ) with no parameter returns the current setting. This lets you save the value for later restoration.

If you set READEXIT(.T.), READKEY( ) returns 0 when you exit a GET with an up or down arrow.

## DEFAULT:
False

## RECOMMENDED USE:
READEXIT( ) provides compatibility with dBASE III PLUS and dBASE IV which allow you to exit a READ with the up or down arrow keys.

**Example**—A corporate office uses both Clipper and dBASE III PLUS and dBASE IV applications. For consistency in data entry forms, the Clipper applications use READEXIT( ).

```
* ENTRY.PRG
* Housekeeping.
CLEAR ALL
SET SCORE OFF
READEXIT(.T.)
* <more commands>
```

In some parts of a program, exiting with the arrow keys might not be desirable. A good example of this is when you use several character fields to simulate a memo. Users often use the arrow keys to navigate through text, making it possible to exit a read inadvertently.

To prevent such exits, specify

```
READEXIT(.F.)
```

## SEE ALSO:

Command READ; function READINSERT( ).

# READINSERT( )

## DIALECTS:
Clipper only.

## SYNTAX:
READINSERT([<expL>])

## RETURNS:
Logical

## DEFINITION:
Controls the insert mode setting for READ and MEMOEDIT( ). True (.T.) turns insert on. False (.F.) turns it off.

If you do not specify an argument, READINSERT( ) returns the current setting (.T. or .F.).

If you specify an argument, READINSERT( ) returns the previous setting.

## DEFAULT:
False

## RECOMMENDED USE:
Use READINSERT( ) during data entry, especially in memos, to activate the insert mode as if the user had pressed the Ins key.

Example—A legal office system uses MEMOEDIT( ) to enter client data. To reduce the risk of overwriting data, the program activates the insert mode. First, it saves the previous setting for later restoration.

```
minsert = READINSERT(.T.)          && Activate insert mode and
                                   &&  save previous setting.
MEMOEDIT(client,5,10,20,69,.T.)
READINSERT(minsert)                && Restore last setting.
```

## SEE ALSO:
Command READ; functions MEMOEDIT( ) and READEXIT( ).

# READKEY( )

### DIALECTS:

Clipper, dBASE III PLUS, dBASE IV, dBXL, FoxBASE+, and Quicksilver.

### SYNTAX:

READKEY( )

### RETURNS:

Numeric

### DEFINITION:

Returns an integer value referring to the key pressed to exit the latest full-screen editing command.

The full-screen editing commands include APPEND, BROWSE, CHANGE, CREATE, EDIT, INSERT, MODIFY, and READ.

Each key pressed returns one of two possible codes. If the user did not change the data, READKEY( ) returns a number from 0 to 36. Otherwise, it returns from 256 to 292. The change value is 256 larger than the no change value. dBASE III PLUS, dBASE IV, dBXL, Quicksilver, and FoxBASE+ READKEY( ) values are:

| | | **READKEY( ) returns:** | |
|---|---|---|---|
| **Key pressed** | **Description** | **without change** | **with change** |
| Ctrl-H<br>Ctrl-S<br>Backspace<br>Left arrow | Left one space | 250 | 256 |
| Ctrl-D<br>Ctrl-L<br>Right arrow | Right one space | 1 | 257 |
| Ctrl-A<br>Home | Left one word | 2 | 258 |
| Ctrl-F<br>End | Right one word | 3 | 259 |
| Ctrl-E<br>Ctrl-K<br>Up arrow | Back one field | 4 | 260 |
| Ctrl-J<br>Ctrl-X<br>Down arrow | Forward one field | 5 | 261 |

| Key pressed | Description | READKEY( ) returns: without change | with change |
|---|---|---|---|
| Ctrl-R | Back one screen | 6 | 262 |
| PgUp | | | |
| Ctrl-C | Forward one screen | 7 | 263 |
| PgDn | | | |
| Ctrl-Q | Exit, abandon changes | 12 | 12 |
| Esc | | | |
| Ctrl-W | Exit, save changes | 270 | 270 |
| Ctrl-M | Return | 15 | 271 |
| Enter key | | | |
| Ctrl-Home | Menu display toggle | 33 | 289 |
| Ctrl-PgUp | | 34 | 290 |
| Ctrl-PgDn | | 35 | 291 |
| F1 * | HELP key | 36 | 292 |

*(dBXL/Quicksilver do not exit on F1. They branch to user help.)

Clipper values differ.

## RECOMMENDED USE:

Use READKEY( ) to specify an action after the user exits a full-screen editing command. Such actions often include:

1) data validation;

2) another full-screen editing command to give the "panning" effect of moving from screen to screen;

3) REPLACEing data into a data file;

4) branch to another procedure.

**Example**—To allow greater error-checking and data validation in an invoicing application, a programmer simulates the EDIT command in programs (EDIT does not allow PICTUREs, templates, range checking, or other validation).

Using READKEY( ), the programmer controls the movement of the record pointer based on how the user exits the READ. Pressing PgUp or Ctrl-R causes a SKIP -1. Pressing PgDn or Ctrl-C causes a SKIP.

```
USE invoicel
DO WHILE .t.
  mhours = hours
  mrate = rate
  mservice = service
  @ 00,01 SAY recno()
  @ 01,01 SAY "Number of hours: " GET mhours RANGE 1,40
  @ 02,01 SAY "Hourly rate     : " GET mrate RANGE 1,300
  @ 03,01 SAY "Service charge  : " GET mservice
```

```
  READ
  mread = READKEY()     && Store READKEY() in memory variable so we
                        &&   don't lose its value during the next READ.
  IF mread > 255        && If the data was changed,
    msave = "?"         &&   ask user whether to save it.
    @ 05,01 SAY "Save changes? (Y/N) " GET msave PICTURE "!"
    READ
    IF msave = "Y"      && If user responds "Y", replace data into fields.
      REPLACE hours WITH mhours,rate WITH mrate,service WITH mservice
    ENDIF
  ENDIF
  IF (mread = 6 .OR. mread = 262) .AND. (RECNO() > 1)  && If PgUp or Ctrl-R,
    SKIP - 1                                           &&   skip backwards.
  ENDIF
  IF (mread = 7 .OR. mread = 263) .AND. ;
     (RECNO() < RECCOUNT())                            && Skip forward.
    SKIP
  ENDIF
ENDDO
```

## SPECIAL USE:

You can use READKEY( ) to simulate the Clipper/FoxBASE+ UPDATED( ) function. To determine whether data was changed in the previous full-screen operation, use the statement

```
? READKEY() >= 256
```

It returns true (.T.) if data was changed.

## VARIATIONS:

**Clipper:** READKEY( ) is in EXTEND.LIB on the system disk. READKEY( ) return values differ from those in dBASE III PLUS and dBASE IV. Use the UPDATED( ) function to determine whether the user changed data.

### Exit Codes

| Exit Key: | Clipper: |
|---|---|
| Backspace | Does not exit |
| Ctrl-D, Ctrl-L | Does not exit |
| Left arrow | Does not exit |
| Right arrow | Does not exit |
| Up arrow | Does not exit |
| Down arrow | Does not exit |
| PgUp | 6 |
| PgDn | 7 |
| Esc | 12 (Esc only) |
| Ctrl-Q | Does not exit |

### Exit Codes (cont'd)

Ctrl-W . . . . . . . . . . . . 14
Ctrl-End . . . . .Does not exit
Any character
typed beyond . . . . . . . .271
the field's end
Enter key . . . . . . . . . . 15
Ctrl-Home . . .Does not exit
Ctrl-PgUp . . . .Does not exit
Ctrl-PgDn . . . .Does not exit
F1 . . . . . . . . .Does not exit

If you change the contents of the field, Clipper adds 256 to the READKEY( ) value.

If you set READEXIT(.T.), Clipper lets you exit a field with an up or down arrow. In this case, READEXIT( ) returns 0, regardless of whether data was changed.

## SEE ALSO:

Commands ON KEY and READ; functions LASTKEY( ) and UPDATED( ).

# READVAR( )

## DIALECTS:
Clipper only.

Same as dBASE IV VARREAD( ).

## SYNTAX:
READVAR( )

## RETURNS:
Character

## DEFINITION:
Returns the name of the memory variable or field in the current GET or PROMPT.

If none is active, READVAR( ) returns a null string.

## RECOMMENDED USE:
Use READVAR( ) in user defined functions that return a value to the current READ, or do data validation on a field basis. READVAR( ) is also useful for creating custom help systems based on the current GET or PROMPT variable.

**Example**—A hotel reservation system checks the number of available rooms when a reservation is made. The VALID clause activates the user defined function AVAIL( ), using the requested number of rooms as an argument. READVAR( ) identifies the GET variable to validate. AVAIL( ) then compares the number of rooms requested to the number available in the log file RESERVES. If the clerk requests fewer rooms than are available, the system fulfills the request and AVAIL( ) returns true (.T.). Otherwise, AVAIL( ) returns false (.T.) and displays a warning.

```
* HOTEL.PRG
STORE 0 TO singles,doubles
@ 10,10 SAY "Number of single rooms to reserve: " ;
        GET singles VALID AVAIL(singles)
@ 11,10 SAY "Number of double rooms to reserve: " ;
        GET doubles VALID AVAIL(doubles)
READ
```

```
FUNCTION avail
PARAMETERS num
USE reserves                          && RESERVES is a log
DO CASE                               &&   indicating rooms available.
  CASE READVAR() = "SINGLES"
    ok = (srooms>num)                 && Check SROOMS.
    @ 24,03 SAY IIF(ok,SPACE(26),"Only "+LTRIM(STR(srooms))+;
             " rooms available")
  CASE READVAR() = "DOUBLES"
    ok = (drooms>num)                 && Check DROOMS.
    @ 24,03 SAY IIF(ok,SPACE(26),"Only " +LTRIM(STR(drooms))+;
             " rooms available")
ENDCASE
RETURN ok
```

## SEE ALSO:

Commands APPEND, DEFINE WINDOW, EDIT, READ, and SET KEY.

# RECCOUNT( )

## DIALECTS:
Clipper, dBASE III PLUS, dBASE IV, dBXL, FoxBASE+, and Quicksilver.

## SYNTAX:
RECCOUNT( )

## RETURNS:
Numeric

## DEFINITION:
Returns the total number of records in the active database file. It includes records hidden by active filters or SET DELETED ON.

To determine RECCOUNT( ) for the active database, use the command

```
? RECCOUNT()
244
```

## DEFAULT:
Zero if no file is active in the current work area.

## RECOMMENDED USE:
Use it with DISKSPACE( ) and RECSIZE( ) to determine whether a disk has enough room for operations such as SORT, INDEX, and COPY. A command that creates an output file will fail if there is not enough disk space.

For a detailed example, see function RECSIZE( ).

## VARIATIONS:
**Clipper:** Same as LASTREC( ).

**dBASE IV:** You can specify an unselected work area by using its ALIAS as a parameter, in the form

RECCOUNT(<expC>)

**FoxBASE+:** You can specify an unselected work area by using its number as a parameter, in the form

RECCOUNT(<expN>)

## SEE ALSO:
Functions DBF( ), DISKSPACE( ), FCOUNT( ), HEADER( ), LASTREC( ), and RECSIZE( ).

# RECNO( )

## DIALECTS:
Clipper, dBASE III PLUS, dBASE IV, dBXL, FoxBASE+, and Quicksilver.

## SYNTAX:
RECNO( )

## RETURNS:
Numeric

## DEFINITION:
Returns the current record number.

If the database is empty, RECNO( ) returns 1. It returns 0 if no database is open.

If the record pointer moves ahead of the first record (BOF( ) = .T.), RECNO( ) returns 1.

If the record pointer moves past the last record (EOF( ) = .T.), RECCOUNT( ) returns one more than than the total number of records.

## RECOMMENDED USE:
Use RECNO( ) to save the position of the current record in a memory variable. This lets you close the current file, operate on other files, and then return to where you left off.

RECNO( ) is also useful for displaying the current record number so users know their position in a file.

**Example 1**—An editing screen in a mailing list management program displays the record number at the top.

```
@ 01,05 SAY "Record number: " + STR(RECNO(),3,0)
@ 04,05 SAY "    Name: " GET name
@ 05,05 SAY "Company: " GET company
@ 06,05 SAY "Address: " GET address
@ 07,05 SAY "    City: " GET city
@ 08,05 SAY "   State: " GET state
READ
```

**Example 2**—A video store application uses several files, each with several indexes. The files include rental transactions, sales transactions, inventory, and memberships. To keep the application within the system limits for open files, some operations temporarily close a database, saving its current record number in a memory variable. When other operations are complete, the program re-opens the original file and moves the record pointer to the original record.

```
USE sales INDEX acct,paysh,vidrent
* <user selects lookup in another file>
marker = RECNO()                    && Store record number in MARKER.
USE                                 && Close SALES.
* <do other operations>
USE sales INDEX acct,paysh,vidrent  && Return to original file
GOTO marker                         &&   and original record.
```

## VARIATIONS:

**dBASE IV:** You can specify an unselected work area by using its ALIAS as a parameter, in the form

RECNO(<expC>)

**FoxBASE+:** You can specify an unselected work area by using its number as a parameter, in the form

RECNO(<expN>)

## SEE ALSO:

Functions LASTREC( ) and RECCOUNT( ).

# RECSIZE( )

## DIALECTS:

Clipper, dBASE III PLUS, dBASE IV, dBXL, FoxBASE+, and Quicksilver.

## SYNTAX:

RECSIZE( )

## RETURNS:

Numeric

## DEFINITION:

Returns the record size in the current database file.

## DEFAULT:

0 if no file is in USE.

## RECOMMENDED USE:

Use RECSIZE( ) with DISKSPACE( ) and RECCOUNT( ) to determine whether a disk has enough room for operations such as COPY, INDEX, and SORT. A command that creates an output file will fail if there is not enough disk space.

**Example**—An advertising program sorts databases and copies them. Before a SORT or COPY, a procedure compares the file size with DISKSPACE( ). The subroutine computes file size as RECCOUNT( ) times RECSIZE( ), plus the size of the database file header. If the file size exceeds one half the DISKSPACE( ), an error routine prompts the user to select an alternative action.

You can determine the size of the header with the formula

32 x <field count> + 35

To determine the field count, use FIELD( ) in a DO WHILE loop to test each field name. FCOUNT counts each field, until FIELD( ) returns a null string.

```
fcount = 1                        && Start with FIELD 1.
DO WHILE LEN(FIELD(fcount)) > 0   && Continue until FIELD returns null.
  fcount = fcount + 1             && Increment counter.
ENDDO
```

```
fcount = fcount - 1                 && FCOUNT cannot start at 0, so
                                    &&   adjust final total.
header = (32 * fcount) + 35         && Compute header size.
totsize = recsize() * reccount() + header   && Compute total file size.
IF totsize > DISKSPACE()/2
  * <error routine>
ENDIF
```

Note that Clipper has a field count function FCOUNT( ).

## VARIATIONS:

**Clipper:** RECSIZE( ) is in EXTEND.LIB on the system disk.

**dBASE IV:** You can specify an open database in an unselected work area by using its ALIAS as an argument, in the form

RECSIZE(<expC>)

**FoxBASE+:** You can specify an open database in an unselected work area by using its work area number as an argument, in the form

RECSIZE(<expN>)

## SEE ALSO:

Functions DISKSPACE( ), FCOUNT( ), and RECCOUNT( ).

# REPLICATE( )

## DIALECTS:

Clipper, dBASE III PLUS, dBASE IV, dBXL, FoxBASE+, and Quicksilver.

## SYNTAX:

REPLICATE(<expC>,<expN>)

## RETURNS:

Character

## DEFINITION:

Repeats a character string <expC> a number of times specified by an integer <expN>. (REPLICATE ignores fractions.)

The total length of the resulting character string must not exceed 254.

## RECOMMENDED USE:

Use REPLICATE( ) to produce menu frames by repeating regular or extended ASCII characters. You can also use it to generate crude bar graphs.

**Example**—Placing frames around menus and prompts can make the screen more attractive and easier to read. REPLICATE( ) lets you create long character strings efficiently for this purpose.

In this example, REPLICATE( ) creates horizontal lines of dollar signs for the top and bottom parts of the menu frame.

```
@ 02,02 REPLICATE("$",25)
@ 03,02 "$"
@ 03,27 "$"
@ 04,02 "$"
@ 04,27 "$"
@ 05,02 REPLICATE("$",25)
@ 04,04 SAY "TOTAL: " + STR(total,7,2)
```

The frame appears as follows:

```
$$$$$$$$$$$$$$$$$$$$$$$$$$$
$                         $
$ TOTAL:  888.22          $
$$$$$$$$$$$$$$$$$$$$$$$$$$$
```

## LIMITS/WARNINGS:

dBASE III PLUS: Using STORE or the equal sign operator with REPLICATE( ) can lock up the computer when trying to create strings beyond the 254-character limit, as in the following:

```
mspace = SPACE(130)
mtest = REPLICATE(mspace,254)   && REPLICATE repeats MSPACE 254 times
                                &&   in an attempt to create a string.
```

This problem generally occurs when the string length computes to 33020 or more.

## SEE ALSO:

Commands @...TO and STORE; function SPACE( ).

# RESTSCREEN( )

## DIALECTS:
Clipper only.

## SYNTAX:
RESTSCREEN(<expN1,expN2>, <expN3,expN4>, <expC>)

## RETURNS:
Nothing

## DEFINITION:
Restores a screen saved by the SAVESCREEN( ) function.

<expN1,expN2> is the top left coordinate of the screen, <expN3,expN4> is the bottom right coordinate. <expC> is the character variable containing the screen.

## RECOMMENDED USE:
Use RESTSCREEN( ) with SAVESCREEN( ) to manipulate partial screen images. They are useful for creating multi-layered user interfaces in which menus, help windows, and dialog boxes pop up on the screen. For simple applications, the SAVE SCREEN and RESTORE SCREEN commands are easier to use; however, they work only with entire screens. If you want multiple layers with the ability to move objects, use RESTSCREEN( ) and SAVESCREEN( ).

**Example**—In an accounting application, a user presses F1 to call help. The program saves a designated region of the screen, then overlays the help message there. Afterward, the program restores the original region.

```
* GLEDGER.PRG
CLEAR
* <user presses F1 in the READ to execute HELP.PRG>
macctno = space(10)
* <more SAYs and GETs>
*
@ 04,10 SAY "Enter ID: " GET macctno
READ
*
* HELP.PRG
PARAMETERS x,y,z     && Parameters sent automatically.
*
```

```
m_basel = SAVESCREEN(1,1,15,40)    && Save screen region.
@ 01,01 TO 06,39
@ 02,02 SAY "======DATA ENTRY HELP========"
@ 03,02 SAY "Enter client's account number"
@ 04,02 SAY "from the range 2222-3323, then"
@ 05,02 SAY "return to menu 2 and press 'C'"
WAIT ""
* <statements>...
RESTSCREEN(1,1,15,40,m_basel)
*
```

## LIMITS/WARNINGS:

Be sure to restore screens in regions the same size as the ones from which you saved them. You may change locations, but the size must stay the same.

Do not use the RESTORE SCREEN command to restore SAVESCREEN( ) regions.

The ANSI.OBJ screen driver does not support RESTSCREEN( ).

RESTSCREEN( ) is in EXTEND.LIB on the system disk.

## SEE ALSO:

Commands RESTORE SCREEN and SAVE SCREEN; function SAVESCREEN( ).

# RIGHT( )

## DIALECTS:

Clipper, dBASE III PLUS, dBASE IV, dBXL, FoxBASE+, and Quicksilver.

## SYNTAX:

RIGHT(<expC>,<expN>)

## RETURNS:

Character

## DEFINITION:

Returns <expN> characters of a character expression <expC>, counting from right to left.

If <expN> is negative or zero, RIGHT( ) returns a null string.

## RECOMMENDED USE:

Use RIGHT( ) to extract data from the right side of a string.

Example—A programmer uses DOS directory information within dBASE applications to determine which files to back up. First, the programmer RUNs the DOS DIR command with the redirection (>) option. The option saves the directory listing in an ASCII file. Then, using APPEND FROM...SDF, the programmer imports the ASCII file into a database file containing one 80-character field LINE.

Each record contains a single directory entry. A typical entry is

```
15  EQUIP    PRG      1398   3-14-87  10:41p
```

The program uses RIGHT( ) to extract the time of the last update (information that is not available through dBASE directly).

```
lup_time = RIGHT(TRIM(line),6)
? lup_time
10:41p
```

## VARIATIONS:

**Clipper:** RIGHT( ) is in EXTEND.LIB on the system disk. It can take a memo field as an argument.

**dBASE IV:** RIGHT( ) can take a memo field as an argument.

## SEE ALSO:

Functions AT( ), LEFT( ), LTRIM( ), RTRIM( ), STUFF( ), SUBSTR( ), and TRIM( ).

# RLOCK( )

## DIALECTS:
Clipper, dBASE III PLUS, dBASE IV, FoxBASE+, and Quicksilver.

## SYNTAX:
RLOCK( )

## RETURNS:
Logical

## DEFINITION:
Tries to lock the current record. Same as function LOCK( ).

## SEE ALSO:
Functions FLOCK( ) and LOCK( ).

# ROLLBACK( )

## DIALECTS:
dBASE IV only.

## SYNTAX:
ROLLBACK( )

## RETURNS:
Logical

## DEFINITION:
Indicates whether the last ROLLBACK succeeded. If so, ROLLBACK( ) returns true (.T.).

## DEFAULT:
True

## RECOMMENDED USE:
dBASE IV's transaction processing features let you ROLLBACK, or undo, a transaction. However, under some conditions, a ROLLBACK will fail.

Use ROLLBACK( ) after issuing the ROLLBACK command. If the ROLLBACK fails (ROLLBACK( ) returns false), use RESET to reset the file's integrity tag or restore from backups.

**Example**—A power loss during a transaction leaves the integrity tag set to true. Upon restarting the program, ISMARKED( ) returns .T., warning that the file may be corrupted. The program can then try to recover by issuing ROLLBACK. If the ROLLBACK fails, ROLLBACK( ) returns false and the program issues the RESET command to reset the integrity tag.

```
USE accounts EXCLUSIVE
IF ISMARKED()
  ROLLBACK
  IF .NOT. ROLLBACK()
    RESET
  ENDIF
ENDIF
```

## SEE ALSO:
Commands BEGIN TRANSACTION, END TRANSACTION, RESET, and ROLLBACK; functions COMPLETED( ) and ISMARKED( ).

# ROUND( )

## DIALECTS:

Clipper, dBASE III PLUS, dBASE IV, dBXL, FoxBASE+, and Quicksilver.

## SYNTAX:

ROUND(<expN1>,<expN2>)

## RETURNS:

Numeric

## DEFINITION:

Returns <expN1> rounded to <expN2> decimals.

ROUND( ) returns a rounded whole number if <expN2> is negative.

## RECOMMENDED USE:

Use ROUND( ) to specify the numeric accuracy of computations.

**Example**—A commodity trading program computes prices to thousandths of dollars. For example, wheat might trade at 1.246 dollars per bushel. When computing totals, however, the program ROUNDs prices to the nearest cent.

```
cost = 2546 * 1.246    && 2546 bushels times 1.246.
? cost
 3172.316

? ROUND(cost,2)
 3172.32
```

## LIMITS/WARNINGS:

**Clipper:** Versions before Summer '87 round both positive and negative numbers incorrectly. For example, ROUND(3.5,0) produces 3 instead of 4 and ROUND(-11.5,0) produces -11 instead of -12. Do not use ROUND( ) in Clipper versions before Summer '87.

**dBASE III PLUS:** Numbers in the range 4096.355 through 5242.355 round improperly. ROUND(4096.355,2) produces 4096.35, incorrectly rounding down. ROUND( ) should return 4096.36.

**dBASE III PLUS, dBASE IV:** Negative numbers are rounded improperly. For example, rounding -11.5 with 0 decimal places should produce -12. dBASE III PLUS and dBASE IV produce -11.

To work around the problem in dBASE IV, take the absolute value of the number before rounding, and multiply by its SIGN( ) as follows:

```
mnum = -11.5
? ROUND(ABS(mnum),0) * SIGN(mnum)
-12
```

As dBASE III PLUS doesn't have a SIGN function, you must determine the sign using IIF as follows:

```
mnum = -11.5
? ROUND(ABS(mnum),0) * IIF(mnum<0,-1,1)
-12
```

Note that the SET DECIMALS command rounds correctly despite the errors in the ROUND( ) function. For example:

```
SET DECIMALS TO 0
* SET FIXED ON  && Used in dBASE III PLUS, but not dBASE IV.
mnum = -11.5
? mnum
-12
```

## SEE ALSO:

Functions CEILING( ), FLOOR( ), INT( ), MOD( ), STR( ), and VAL( ); command SET DECIMALS.

# ROW( )

## DIALECTS:

Clipper, dBASE III PLUS, dBASE IV, dBXL, FoxBASE+, and Quicksilver.

## SYNTAX:

ROW( )

## RETURNS:

Numeric

## DEFINITION:

Returns the vertical coordinate of the cursor's position. Coordinates range from 0 (top) to 24 (bottom) on a standard screen.

## RECOMMENDED USE:

ROW( ) lets you place output on the screen relative to the current cursor position. This is useful for displaying @...SAYs and GETs from general purpose subroutines. You do not need to know the exact cursor position.

**Example**—A procedure centers text on the screen, using a parameter to pass data. Because the procedure does not know the current position, it uses the ROW( ) function to place the text.

```
* CENTER.PRG
PARAMETERS mstring
@ ROW(),(80-LEN(mstring))/2 SAY mstring
```

To call CENTER.PRG, you would issue the command

```
string = "You pressed an incorrect key, try again"  && Sample message.
DO CENTER WITH string
```

## SEE ALSO:

Functions COL( ), FCOL( ), FROW( ), PCOL( ), and PROW( ).

# RTOD( )

## DIALECTS:
dBASE IV only.

## SYNTAX:
RTOD(<expN>)

## RETURNS:
Numeric

## DEFINITION:
Converts radians to degrees.

<expN> is the angle in radians.

The conversion formula is

```
N x 57.3
```

where N is the angle in radians. (57.3 is 180/pi).

## RECOMMENDED USE:
RTOD( ) is used in engineering and scientific applications.

**Example**—To plot a graph, a scientist converts 0.2618 radians to degrees. The result is 15.

```
mdegrees = RTOD(0.2618)
  15.00
```

## SEE ALSO:
Functions ACOS( ), ATAN( ), ATN2( ), COS( ), DTOR( ), SIN( ), and TAN( ); command SET DECIMALS.

# RTRIM( )

## DIALECTS:
Clipper, dBASE III PLUS, dBASE IV, dBXL, FoxBASE+, and Quicksilver.

## SYNTAX:
RTRIM(<expC>)

## RETURNS:
Character

## DEFINITION:
Removes spaces from the end of a character string. RTRIM( ) is the same as TRIM( ).

## SEE ALSO:
Functions LEFT( ), LTRIM( ), RIGHT( ), STUFF( ), and TRIM( ).

# SAVESCREEN( )

## DIALECTS:

Clipper only.

## SYNTAX:

SAVESCREEN(<expN1,expN2>, <expN3,expN4>)

## RETURNS:

Character

## DEFINITION:

Saves a region of the screen in a character memory variable for later restoration with RESTSCREEN( ).

<expN1,expN2> is the top left coordinate of the region to save.

<expN3,expN4> is the bottom right coordinate.

## RECOMMENDED USE:

Use RESTSCREEN( ) with SAVESCREEN( ) to manipulate partial screen images. They are useful for creating multi-layered user interfaces in which menus, help windows, and dialog boxes pop up on the screen. For simple applications, the SAVE SCREEN and RESTORE SCREEN commands are easier to use; however, they work only with entire screens. If you want multiple layers with the ability to move objects, use RESTSCREEN( ) and SAVESCREEN( ).

**Example 1**—An inventory application lets the user select from a "pulldown" box created with ACHOICE( ). Before displaying the box, the program saves the screen region.

```
* MENU.PRG
DECLARE main[10]      && Declare array for ACHOICE().
USE action            && Database file action contains menu choices.
FOR i = 1 to 10       && Count from 1 to 10.
  main[i] = item      && Store item in array element.
  SKIP                && Skip to next record.
NEXT

m_base1 = SAVESCREEN(1,1,15,40)       && Save screen region.
@ 01,01 CLEAR TO 15,40                && Clear region.
```

```
@ 01,01  TO 15,40                     && Show double line border.
mchoice = ACHOICE(02,02,14,39,main)   && Display menu in window with
*                                     &&   coordinates one less
* <statements/subroutines>            &&   than region and border.
RESTSCREEN(1,1,15,40,m_base1)         && Restore original screen.
*
```

## LIMITS/WARNINGS:

SAVESCREEN( ) saves up to 4000 byte screens.

Be sure to restore a screen in a region the same size as the one from which it was saved. You may change locations, but the size must stay the same.

Do not use RESTORE SCREEN to restore SAVESCREEN( ) regions.

The ANSI.OBJ screen driver does not support SAVESCREEN( ).

SAVESCREEN( ) is in EXTEND.LIB on the system disk.

## SEE ALSO:

Commands RESTORE SCREEN and SAVE SCREEN; function RESTSCREEN( ).

# SECONDS( )

## DIALECTS:
Clipper only.

## SYNTAX:
SECONDS( )

## RETURNS:
Numeric

## DEFINITION:
Returns the system time as a number of seconds since midnight.

SECONDS( ) returns a number ranging from 0 to 86399 (23 hours, 59 minutes, and 59 seconds).

## RECOMMENDED USE:
Use SECONDS( ) to simplify time computations and create indexes based on time-ordered events.

**Example**—A scheduling program keeps appointments in a career counseling office. The schedule is indexed on appointment time, which is stored internally as SECONDS( ). To minimize conversions, when a customer makes an appointment, the program stores both TIME( ) and SECONDS( ) in the database file.

```
USE appts INDEX apptsecs
appt = TIME()
@ 02,02 SAY "Enter time: " GET appt PICTURE "99:99:99"
READ
REPLACE apptime WITH appt
REPLACE apptsecs WITH SECONDS()
LIST apptsecs
Record#  APPTSECS
      6  74750
      4  78769
      7  78820
      1  87650
      3  87658
      2  89087
      5  92794
```

## VARIATIONS:
**FoxBASE+:** Use the function SYS(2) to return seconds elapsed since midnight.

## SEE ALSO:
Functions SYS(2) and TIME( ).

# SEEK( )

## DIALECTS:
dBASE IV only.

## SYNTAX:
SEEK(<exp>[,<alias>])

## RETURNS:
Logical

## DEFINITION:
Searches a database file using its primary index, returning true (.T.) if the search succeeds or false (.F.) if it fails.

The SEEK( ) expression <exp> is a numeric or character expression matching the key expression of the primary index.

If the SEEK( ) succeeds, the record pointer moves to the matching record. Otherwise, it moves to the end of file.

SEEK( ) combines the command SEEK and the function FOUND( ).

## DEFAULT:
SEEK( ) searches the database in the current work area.

## OPTIONS:
You can specify an unselected work area by using its alias as the second SEEK( ) argument. Be sure that the unselected database has an open index.

## RECOMMENDED USE:
You can use SEEK( ) to replace the combination of the SEEK command and FOUND( ). This simplifies code and makes it more readable. It is also easier to type. A better use of SEEK( ), and probably the reason why it exists, is in a VALID clause of @...SAY...GET. This lets you easily validate user input against a "lookup" database.

**Example**—A programmer creates a lookup database to verify company codes. When the user enters a code, SEEK( ) searches for it in the database. If it is found, SEEK( ) returns true (.T.) to the VALID statement and the user may proceed. If the SEEK( ) fails, the ERROR clause prompts the user to reenter the value.

```
SELECT 1
USE main
SELECT 2
USE lookup INDEX codedex
SELECT 1
* <Data entry code.>
mcode = SPACE(4)
@ 10,01 SAY "Enter company code: " GET mcode VALID SEEK(mcode,"LOOKUP") ;
                    ERROR "Code not found, please reenter "
READ
```

## VARIATIONS:

You can simulate SEEK( ) with a Clipper, dBXL, FoxBASE+, or Quicksilver user defined function:

```
FUNCTION useek        && Make a PROCEDURE in FoxBASE+.
PARAMETERS mexp,malias

oldalias = STR(SELECT())
SELECT &malias        && In Clipper, you can use parentheses around MALIAS
SEEK mexp             &&   instead of the macro (&).
isfound = FOUND()     && Save the FOUND() value after a SEEK since a
SELECT &oldalias      &&   subsequent change in work areas will reset it.
RETURN isfound
```

Be sure to pass both parameters to the user defined function. For example, to SEEK a code of "ABCD" in file CODES, issue USEEK( ) as follows:

```
? USEEK("ABCD","CODES")
```

You can also use USEEK with numeric expressions.

## SEE ALSO:

Commands @...SAY...GET, FIND, FUNCTION, SEEK, and SELECT; functions FOUND( ), LOOKUP( ), and SELECT( ).

# SELECT( )

## DIALECTS:
Clipper, dBASE IV, dBXL, FoxBASE+, and Quicksilver.

## SYNTAX:
SELECT( )

## RETURNS:
Numeric

## DEFINITION:
Returns the number of the currently selected work area.

Work area numbers range from 1 to 10.

## RECOMMENDED USE:
Use SELECT( ) to indicate the current work area number while debugging applications. Also use it to store the number before running a subroutine that changes areas. Upon RETURNing from the subroutine, you can then re-SELECT the original work area with a CASE statement.

**Example 1**—While debugging an accounting system, the programmer displays the SELECT( ) area at the top of every program module. This helps detect errors.

```
* AR_RPT.PRG
? "Current work area:" + STR(SELECT(),2,0)
* <more statements>
```

If, for example, the current work area is 5, the following message appears:

```
     Current work area: 5
```

**Example 2**—The accounting system from Example 1 includes a procedure that opens a database file and displays a "lookup" list. When the user presses a key, the program stores the current work area number in memory variable OLD_AREA. The lookup procedure changes areas, leaving the previous one intact. Upon completion, it returns to the original area.

```
* LOOKUP.PRG
SELECT 2
old_area = STR(SELECT())      && Store work area in OLD_AREA.
SELECT 8                      && Select new work area.
* <lookup operations>
SELECT &old_area
RETURN                        && Return to caller.
```

## VARIATIONS:

**Clipper:** Work area numbers range from 0 to 254. SELECT( ) also accepts an alias as an argument, returning its work area number or zero if it does not exist. The alias can be in an unselected work area. For example, SELECT("ACCT") returns the work area number of the alias ACCT.

**dBASE IV:** SELECT( ) returns the highest unused work area number. This allows you to select an unused work area with:

```
SELECT SELECT()
```

## LIMITS/WARNINGS:

dBASE IV's SELECT( ) differs from the Clipper, dBXL, FoxBASE+, and Quicksilver SELECT( ). See *Variations* above.

## SEE ALSO:

Command SELECT; functions ALIAS( ) and WSELECT( ).

# SET( )

## DIALECTS:

dBASE IV only.

## SYNTAX:

SET(<cxpC>)

## RETURNS:

Character/Numeric

## DEFINITION:

Returns the current setting of SET ON and SET TO options.

<expC> is the command keyword, such as BELL, CARRY, or ECHO. SET( ) accepts four character abbreviations.

SET( ) returns the data type appropriate to the SETting, for example, SET("BELL") returns "ON" or "OFF" (character type), whereas SET("DECIMALS") returns a number.

## RECOMMENDED USE:

Use SET( ) to inform the user of the current settings, for example:

```
? SET("BELL")
OFF
```

You can then let the user change the SETting.

SET( ) also lets you save and restore SETtings. This is helpful for creating generic program modules that do not conflict.

**Example**—A generic file maintenance program can be called from an inventory application. To preserve the settings established by the application, the maintenance program saves them with SET( ).

```
* Save SETtings (shown with sample values).
mbell = SET("BELL")          && BELL was SET ON.
mescape = SET("ESCAPE")      && ESCAPE was SET OFF.
mexact = SET("EXACT")        && EXACT was SET OFF.
mdeleted = SET("DELETED")    && DELETED was SET OFF.
```

```
*
* <Do other modules, then return to caller>.
*
* Restore previous SETtings.
SET BELL &mbell
SET ESCAPE &mescape
SET EXACT &mexact
SET DELETED &mdeleted
```

## LIMITS/WARNINGS:

SET( ) does not recognize the DEVICE keyword.

## SEE ALSO:

Commands DISPLAY STATUS and SET; function SELECT( ).

# SETCANCEL( )

## DIALECTS:
Clipper only.

## SYNTAX:
SETCANCEL([<expL>])

## RETURNS:
Logical

## DEFINITION:
Enables or disables the runtime termination key Alt-C.

SETCANCEL( ) works like SET ESCAPE, except that it returns a value you can save and restore.

An argument of true (.T.) lets you press Alt-C to stop program execution. An argument of false (.F.) disables Alt-C.

SETCANCEL( ) with no argument returns the current setting (.T. or .F.). With an argument, it returns the previous setting.

## RECOMMENDED USE:
Use SETCANCEL( ) to prevent users from ending program execution abnormally, short of pulling the plug or flipping the switch. This reduces the risk of damage to data files.

**Example**—Before posting transactions to the main database, SETCANCEL(.F.) disables the Alt-C key combination.

```
oldcancel = SETCANCEL(.F.)  && Disable Alt-C and save previous setting.
* <update files>
SETCANCEL(oldcancel)        && Restore previous setting.
```

## SEE ALSO:
Command SET ESCAPE; function ALTD( ).

# SETCOLOR( )

## DIALECTS:
Clipper only.

## SYNTAX:
SETCOLOR([<expC>])

## RETURNS:
Character

## DEFINITION:
Returns the current color setting and optionally sets new colors.

The argument <expC> is a valid color specification string. Valid specifications consist of standard, enhanced, border, background, and unselected color settings.

See command SET COLOR TO for a color table and a description of color specifications.

When you specify <expC>, SETCOLOR( ) changes the colors. The new colors take effect with the next screen display command.

SETCOLOR( ) with no argument returns the color value for the current screen. With an argument, it returns the colors before the new ones go into effect.

## RECOMMENDED USE:
SETCOLOR( ) supersedes the SET COLOR TO command since it lets you save and restore color settings from the environment. This makes it especially useful in modular programming since you can change colors in subroutines, then restore the original settings.

**Example 1**—A programmer maintains a library of common subroutines and user defined functions to speed program development. To prevent conflicts, subroutines save the current colors before activating new ones. Before the RETURN, SETCOLOR( ) restores the original colors. The following function accepts a filename and a fieldname as parameters. It then displays the specified field in a bounce bar menu. The original color value is stored in variable OLDCOLOR. Just before the function RETURNs, SETCOLOR( ) restores OLDCOLOR.

```
FUNCTION windosel
PARAMETERS mdbf,mfield
PRIVATE oldcolor,mrec,mchoice,pt1,pt2,pt3,pt4,ctr
*
oldcolor = SETCOLOR("GR+/B,R/W,R,,GR")    && Save prior color setting.
USE (mdbf)
mrec=RECCOUNT()
pt1 = 1
pt2 = 1
pt3 = 5
pt4 = LEN(&mfield)+3
DECLARE master[mrec]    && Array has same number of elements as records.
FOR ctr=1 TO mrec
  master[ctr]=&mfield
  SKIP
NEXT
@ pt1,pt2 TO pt3,pt4
mchoice=ACHOICE(pt1+1,pt2+1,pt3-1,pt4-1,master)
SETCOLOR(oldcolor)          && Restore original setting.
RETURN mchoice
```

**Example 2**—A programmer includes a field in a database specifically for setting colors. To prevent reprogramming, the field can simply be edited to change the colors of the application.

```
USE msystem
mcolor=TRIM(fcolor) && FCOLOR is a character field in the database.
                    &&   with a value of "GR+/B,R/W,B"
SETCOLOR(mcolor)    && Sets color to value stored in mcolor,
                    &&   in this case, yellow on blue standard,
                    &&   red on white enhanced, and a blue border.
active=SETCOLOR()   && Store current color setting in variable ACTIVE.
```

A display of variable ACTIVE shows the current color string, including defaults not even specified in field FCOLOR:

```
? active
GR+/B,R/W,B,N,R/W
```

## LIMITS/WARNINGS:

Unlike the SET COLOR TO command, SETCOLOR( ) without a parameter does not restore the color to its default, "W/N,I/N,N,N,I/N".

You cannot use numeric color specifications with SETCOLOR( ). It allows only letters.

SETCOLOR( ) is in EXTEND.LIB on the system disk.

## SEE ALSO:

Command SET COLOR TO.

# SETPRC( )

## DIALECTS:

Clipper only.

## SYNTAX:

SETPRC(<expN>,<expN2>)

## DEFINITION:

Changes the printer row and column coordinates (PROW( ) and PCOL( )) to the specified values, without moving the print head.

<expN> is the row; <expN2> is the column.

## RECOMMENDED USE:

Normally, printing at a coordinate less then a previous coordinate causes the printer to eject a page. With SETPRC( ), you can set the logical printer coordinate to the top of the page, without moving the print head or ejecting a page.

**Example**—Printing on non-standard sized forms usually requires the use of printer-specific codes to set the page length or top-of-form. With SETPRC( ) as an alternative, you can print a form, reset the logical top-of-form, then resume printing. This method works uniformly on all printers.

The following example prints a 22-line invoice on a 25-line form, then resets PROW( ) and PCOL( ) to 0,0. Without any EJECTs, invoices print on consecutive 25-line forms.

```
USE inv_data
SET DEVICE TO PRINT
DO WHILE .NOT. EOF()
  * <Print 22 line invoice>
  @ 01,01 SAY "Hourly           : " + STR(hourly,8,2)
  @ 02,01 SAY "Number of Hours: " + STR(numhours,5,0)
  @ 03,01 SAY "Second Person   : " + STR(second,8,2)
  @ 04,01 SAY "Mileage         : " + STR(miles,8,2)
  * <more @...SAYS>
  @ 23,01 SAY "Please pay —> " + STR(total,8,2)
  SETPRC(0,0)              && Set page to top-of-form.
  SKIP
ENDDO
SET DEVICE TO SCREEN
```

## SEE ALSO:

Functions PCOL( ) and PROW( ).

# SIGN( )

## DIALECTS:
dBASE IV only.

## SYNTAX:
SIGN(<expN>)

## RETURNS:
Numeric

## DEFINITION:
Indicates whether a number is negative, positive, or zero.

<expN> is any numeric expression.

## RECOMMENDED USE:
Use SIGN( ) in computations to keep track of signs while dealing with absolute values.

**Example**—An accounts payable/receivable system tracks cash flow. In computing the absolute difference between debits and credits for a graph, the programmer first saves the original SIGNs of both variables (they could be negative if they represent bad debts or uncollected payables).

```
credit = 2212
debit = -877
signdeb = SIGN(debit)      && sdebit now is -1.
signcred = SIGN(credit)    && scredit now is 1.
```

After doing the computations, the programmer restores the original signs:

```
credit = (credit * signcred)
debit = (debit * signdeb)
```

## VARIATIONS:
You can simulate SIGN( ) with a Clipper, dBXL, FoxBASE+, or Quicksilver user defined function.

```
FUNCTION sign       && Use a PROCEDURE for FoxBASE+
PARAMETERS expN
RETURN IIF(expN#0, IIF(expN>0,1,-1), 0)
```

Call the SIGN( ) user defined function as you would in dBASE IV.

## SPECIAL USE:

Because rounding with no decimal places doesn't work properly with some negative numbers, you must use SIGN( ) to ensure correct results. For example, rounding -9.5 to 0 decimal places should produce -10. dBASE IV produces -9.

To solve the problem, take the absolute value of the number before rounding, and multiply it by its SIGN( ) as follows:

```
mnum = -9.5
? ROUND(ABS(mnum),0) * SIGN(mnum)
-10
```

## SEE ALSO:

Functions ABS( ) and ROUND( ).

# SIN( )

## DIALECTS:
dBASE IV only.

## SYNTAX:
SIN(<expN>)

## RETURNS:
Floating point

## DEFINITION:
Computes the sine of an angle, where <expN> is its size in radians.

SIN( ) returns a floating point number in the range -1.0 to +1.0.

Use DTOR( ) and RTOD( ) to convert degrees to radians and vice versa. A radian is approximately 57.3 degrees.

The SET DECIMALS and SET PRECISION commands determine numeric accuracy.

## RECOMMENDED USE:
SIN( ) is a trigonometric function used in engineering and scientific applications.

**Example**—An aerospace application for determining rocket trajectories expresses angles in radians. Angle B is 4.2 radians; its SIN( ) is -0.87.

```
msin = SIN(4.2)
?msin
-0.87
```

## SEE ALSO:
Functions ACOS( ), ASIN( ), ATAN( ), ATN2( ), COS( ), DTOR( ), PI( ), RTOD( ), and TAN( ).

# SINKEY( )

## DIALECTS:

Quicksilver only.

## SYNTAX:

SINKEY( )

## RETURNS:

Numeric

## DEFINITION:

Checks the keyboard for a pressed key. Returns the character value if the user presses a key while the command is executing.

SINKEY( ) is like INKEY( ), except that INKEY( ) returns an ASCII value. Despite its name, SINKEY is neither immoral nor disgusting.

If the user presses a single character key, SINKEY( ) returns it. If the user presses a Ctrl, Function, or cursor key, SINKEY( ) returns two characters. The first is always the blank character hexadecimal FF (CHR(12)). The second character is as follows:

| Key pressed | Second character returned | Key pressed | Second character returned | Key pressed | Second character returned |
|---|---|---|---|---|---|
| F1 | ; | Ctrl-F9 | f | Shift-F3 | V |
| F2 | < | Ctrl-F10 | g | Shift-F4 | W |
| F3 | = | Ctrl- ← | s | Shift-F5 | X |
| F4 | > | Ctrl- → | t | Shift-F6 | Y |
| F5 | ? | Ctrl- ↑ | N/A | Shift-F7 | Z |
| F6 | @ | Ctrl- ↓ | N/A | Shift-F8 | [ |
| F7 | A | Alt-F1 | h | Shift-F9 | \ |
| F8 | B | Alt-F2 | i | Shift-F10 | ] |
| F9 | C | Alt-F3 | j | Shift- ← | N/A |
| F10 | D | Alt-F4 | k | Shift- → | N/A |
| ← | K | Alt-F5 | l | Shift- ↑ | N/A |
| → | M | Alt-F6 | m | Shift- ↓ | N/A |
| ↑ | H | Alt-F7 | n | | |
| ↓ | P | Alt-F8 | o | | |

| | | | |
|---|---|---|---|
| Ctrl-F1 | ^ | Alt-F9 | p |
| Ctrl-F2 | _ | Alt-F10 | q |
| Ctrl-F3 | ` | Alt- ← | N/A |
| Ctrl-F4 | a | Alt- → | N/A |
| Ctrl-F5 | b | Alt- ↑ | N/A |
| Ctrl-F6 | c | Alt- ↓ | N/A |
| Ctrl-F7 | d | Shift-F1 | T |
| Ctrl-F8 | e | Shift-F2 | U |

## RECOMMENDED USE:

Use SINKEY( ) to get user input without pausing program execution. Because it returns the actual key pressed (whereas INKEY( ) returns an ASCII value), use it rather than INKEY( ) to increase program readability.

**Example 1**—During printing, a mailing label jams the platen. Names and addresses continue to print; however, they overwrite as the labels cannot advance.

The print program allows the end user to press "C" to force a stop. To do this, the program uses SINKEY( ) inside a DO WHILE loop, checking for a press of a key. Because it does not pause execution, SINKEY( ) does not interfere with label printing.

```
CLEAR TYPEAHEAD
SET PRINT ON
keypress = ""
* DO WHILE KEYPRESS is not "C" or "c" (and not end of file).
DO WHILE .NOT. EOF() .AND. .NOT. keypress $ "cC"
  ?
  ? NAME
  ? COMPANY
  ? ADDRESS
  ? TRIM(CITY) + ", " + STATE + " " + ZIP
  ?
  SKIP                     && Move to next record.
  keypress = SINKEY()      && Store SINKEY() value in KEYPRESS.
ENDDO
SET PRINT OFF              && Upon exiting DO WHILE, SET PRINT OFF.
```

**Example 2**—The main menu of an order entry system displays a clock using the system time. The clock ticks until the user presses a key. SINKEY( ) stores the key value in memory variable KEYPRESS. When the length of KEYPRESS exceeds one (when any key is pressed), execution of the DO WHILE ends and the clock stops.

```
CLEAR TYPEAHEAD
* <@...SAY...GETs>
keypress = ""
```

```
DO WHILE LEN(keypress) < 1
  @ 24,70 SAY TIME()            && Display time.
  interval = TIME()             && Store time in variable.
  keypress = SINKEY()           && Check for KEYPRESS with SINKEY()
  * Stay in DO WHILE until TIME() changes, updating screen a maximum
  *   of once per second.
  DO WHILE LEN(keypress) < 1 .AND. interval = TIME()
    keypress = SINKEY()         && Check for KEYPRESS again.
  ENDDO
ENDDO * <CASE structure to process user selections>
```

## LIMITS/WARNINGS:

SINKEY( ) only checks the keyboard momentarily, rather than repeating until a key is pressed.

SINKEY( ) does not detect the ESCape key.

SINKEY( ) is hardware specific and may not work on machines with non-standard character sets.

Avoid using SINKEY( ) in the condition of a DO WHILE or CASE statement. (Previous CASEs will remove the first character from the keyboard buffer).

## VARIATIONS:

**Clipper, FoxBASE+:** You can simulate SINKEY( ) with a user defined function that returns the CHR( ) of an INKEY( ) value.

*Clipper:*

```
FUNCTION SINKEY
*
* Accepts keyboard input and returns its character value.
RETURN CHR(INKEY())
```

*FoxBASE+:*

```
* SINKEY.PRG
*
* Accepts keyboard input and returns its character value.
RETURN CHR(INKEY())
```

## SEE ALSO:

Commands CLEAR KEY and SET TYPEAHEAD; functions CHR( ) and INKEY( ).

# SOUNDEX( )

## DIALECTS:
Clipper, dBASE IV, dBXL, and Quicksilver.

## SYNTAX:
SOUNDEX(<expC>)

## RETURNS:
Character

## DEFINITION:
Converts <expC> to a four-character, phonetically equivalent, SOUNDEX string. Similar, but not necessarily identical, character strings may have the same SOUNDEX( ) values.

SOUNDEX( ) generally disregards differences in vowels.

For example, the following names all have the same SOUNDEX( ) value:

```
? SOUNDEX("Peoples")
P142
? SOUNDEX("Peeples")
P142
? SOUNDEX("Peples")
P142
```

Completely different strings produce different SOUNDEX( ) values:

```
? SOUNDEX("Maryanne")
M650
? SOUNDEX("George")
G620
```

SOUNDEX( ) is not case-sensitive.

## RECOMMENDED USE:
Use SOUNDEX( ) in applications that search for key values when the exact spelling is not known. When you index files on SOUNDEX( ) values, you can use FIND or SEEK to find records with SOUNDEX( ) keys.

**Example**—A credit information service searches for customer histories. The main database file is indexed on the SOUNDEX( ) value of the CUSTOMER last name. This lets the operator find matching records when the spelling is not exact.

To set up the database, the programmer issues the following commands:

```
USE customers
INDEX ON SOUNDEX(lastname) TO custdex
```

To search the database, the program GETs the search value and SEEKs its SOUNDEX( ) equivalent.

```
search = SPACE(15)
@ 10,10 SAY "Enter name to search: " GET search
READ
SEEK SOUNDEX(search)
```

## LIMITS/WARNINGS:

SOUNDEX( ) keys are rarely unique, so you will often have to search through many records before finding the correct one. To avoid this inconvenience, first search for exact keys, then switch to SOUNDEX( ) only if necessary.

SOUNDEX( ) values can vary slightly among the systems. To minimize differences, avoid any punctuation in SOUNDEXed fields. Also, to run applications on different systems, create a generic re-SOUNDEX( ) routine to INDEX or REPLACE SOUNDEX fields, if necessary.

## VARIATIONS:

**Clipper:** SOUNDEX( ) is in EXTEND.LIB on the system disk.

## SEE ALSO:

Commands INDEX and SEEK; functions DIFFERENCE( ) and LIKE( ).

# SPACE( )

## DIALECTS:
Clipper, dBASE III PLUS, dBASE IV, dBXL, FoxBASE+, and Quicksilver.

## SYNTAX:
SPACE(<expN>)

## RETURNS:
Character

## DEFINITION:
Creates a character string containing <expN> spaces.

## RECOMMENDED USE:
Use SPACE( ) to initialize character memory variables.

**Example**—The editing routine in a truck management program keeps data in memory variables until the user indicates he or she has finished editing. The programmer uses SPACE( ) to initialize each character memory variable.

```
SET DELIMITERS on
mroute = SPACE(30)
mdriver = SPACE(25)
mlicense = SPACE(15)
@ 01,01 SAY "  Enter route " GET mroute
@ 02,01 SAY " Enter driver " GET mdriver
@ 03,01 SAY "Enter license " GET mlicense
READ
```

When this program runs, each GET assumes the length of its particular memory variable:

```
   Enter route :                              :
  Enter driver :                         :
 Enter license :               :
```

## SEE ALSO:
Function REPLICATE( ).

# SQRT( )

## DIALECTS:

Clipper, dBASE III PLUS, dBASE IV, dBXL, FoxBASE+, and Quicksilver.

## SYNTAX:

SQRT(<expN>)

## RETURNS:

Numeric

## DEFINITION:

Returns the square root of its argument, which must be a positive number.

The returned value has the same number of decimal places as <expN>, or the number defined by the SET DECIMALS command, whichever is larger.

## RECOMMENDED USE:

**Example**—An architectural application uses SQRT( ) in formulas to determine the amount of materials required for geometrical designs. To determine the area of an equilateral triangle with sides of 300 inches, use the formula

$$A = \frac{s^2 \times \sqrt{3}}{4}$$

where $s$ is the length of a side.

In dBASE, this evaluates as follows:

```
SET DECIMALS TO 2
area = (300^2) * SQRT(3) / 4
? area
    38971.14
```

## SEE ALSO:

Command SET DECIMALS; functions ABS( ) and INT( ).

# STR( )

## DIALECTS:
Clipper, dBASE III PLUS, dBASE IV, dBXL, FoxBASE+, and Quicksilver.

## SYNTAX:
STR(<expN>[,<length>[,<decimals>]])

## RETURNS:
Character

## DEFINITION:
Converts <expN> to a character string.

<expN> is a numeric expression. <length> is the total number of characters created by STR( ), including decimals, the decimal point, and a sign. <decimals> gives the number of decimal places to include in the string.

If you specify a <length> less than the number of digits left of the decimal point, STR( ) returns asterisks (numeric overflow).

If you specify fewer <decimals> than in the original number, STR( ) truncates the output.

If you specify a <length> greater than the number of digits left of the decimal point, STR( ) pads the output with leading blanks.

STR( ) is the inverse of VAL( ).

## DEFAULT:
If you do not specify <length> or <decimals>, STR( ) returns 10 digits. If you specify only <length> and not <decimals>, STR( ) truncates to the nearest integer.

You must specify a <length> to specify <decimals>.

## RECOMMENDED USE:
Use STR( ) to include numbers in character expressions such as @...SAYs and filenames.

**Example 1**—The invoicing program at a local newspaper reminds readers how many issues remain in their subscriptions. The program stores the number in the memory variable ISSUES. The reporting program merges ISSUES with character text using STR( ).

```
issues = 21
@ 09,01 SAY "Renew Today!"
@ 10,01 SAY "You have only " + STR(issues,2,0) + " issues remaining!"
```

The following appears at the top of the renewal notice:

```
Renew Today!
You have only 21 issues remaining!
```

**Example 2**—A report lists stock market data in several formats. Subroutines STOCK1 through STOCK10 create the listings and store the results in text files TEMP1.TXT through TEMP10.TXT. The STR( ) function converts the counter CTR to character type to concatenate it with both the output filename and the subroutine name. LTRIM( ) removes leading blanks. The resulting string is stored in variable STR_CTR. The macro (&) function then evaluates STR_CTR as a literal string.

```
USE stockdata
ctr = 1
DO WHILE ctr < 10
  str_ctr = LTRIM(STR(ctr,1,0))    && Store string of CTR in STR_CTR.
  SET ALTERNATE TO temp&str_ctr    && Create numbered text file.
  SET ALTERNATE ON
  DO stock&str_ctr                 && DO numbered subroutine.
  ctr = ctr + 1                    && Increment CTR by one.
ENDDO
SET ALTERNATE ON                   && Close last text file.
```

## SEE ALSO:

Functions SUBSTR( ) and VAL( ).

# STRTRAN( )

## DIALECTS:

Clipper only.

## SYNTAX:

STRTRAN(<expC1>,<expC2>[,<expC3>][,<expN1>][,<expN2>])

## RETURNS:

Character

## DEFINITION:

Searches for occurrences of one string within another (substrings), and replaces them with a third string.

<expC1> is the string to search. <expC2> is the substring to find.

## OPTIONS:

<expC3> is the replacement string. If you omit it, STRTRAN( ) deletes all matches.

<expN1> is the first match to replace. If you omit it, replacements begin with the first match.

<expN2> designates the number of matches to replace. If you omit it, STRTRAN( ) replaces all matches.

## RECOMMENDED USE:

STRTRAN( ) is useful in many string routines, including simple data encryption, memo field handling, and general database housekeeping.

**Example 1**—Joan creates text reports using Clipper memo fields. To speed data entry, she employs several abbreviations that she later replaces using STRTRAN( ). Examples are "DV", meaning "Dear Valued Customer:", and "TY", meaning "Thank you for your business!" To prevent incorrect replacements, Joan puts a bracket ([) ahead of all abbreviations.

Joan's most recent memo before translation:

```
[DV

Our annual clearance sale begins on Nov. 3. Don't miss it.
Hours will be 9 a.m. to 8 p.m. All items up to 50% off.
 <more text>

[TY
```

After translation, it reads

```
Dear Valued Customer:

Our annual clearance sale begins on Nov. 3. Don't miss it.
Hours will be 9 a.m. to 8 p.m. All items up to 50% off.
  <more text>

Thank you for your business!
```

In the program, MEMOEDIT( ) lets Joan create or change a memo. Before printing the report, STRTRAN( ) searches for her abbreviations and replaces them with predefined character strings. Abbreviations and their strings could also be stored in a file, then loaded into memory variables or arrays for easier program modification.

```
USE names
REPLACE newmemo WITH MEMOEDIT(newmemo)
temp = STRTRAN(newmemo,"[TY","Thank you for your business!")
temp = STRTRAN(temp,"[DV","Dear Valued Customer:")
* <more STRTRAN()s>
*
REPLACE newmemo WITH temp
```

**Example 2**—Because data can come from many sources (electronic networks, mailing list brokers, and data entry services), it is not always in a form we like. Names or titles may be misspelled or capitalized incorrectly. Strange delimiters (usually those used by other database systems) appear in unlikely places. STRTRAN( ) can help put your database in order.

For example, your data entry operators put an asterisk in a CTYSTATE field after the state when you only want one after the city, as follows:

```
Peabody* MA*01960
```

To correct the problem throughout the file, issue the following command:

```
REPLACE ALL ctystate WITH STRTRAN(ctystate,"*"," ",2)
```

Note that <expC2> is an asterisk. <expC3> is a space. <expN1> is 2, indicating that the replacement begins with the second occurrence. The function omits <expN2>.

## VARIATIONS:

You can simulate STRTRAN( ) by making the following program into a dBASE IV, dBXL, FoxBASE+, or Quicksilver user defined function.

The first three parameters are the same as in the Clipper version. The fourth, <expN>, indicates how many replacements to make, rather than the starting number as in Clipper.

```
* STRTRAN.PRG
* Function syntax: STRTRAN(<expC1>,<expC2>,<expC3>,<expN>)
* Returns: character
PROCEDURE strtran
PARAMETERS str1,str2,str3,expN      && Note: no error checking to increase
PRIVATE pos,rstr,slen,npos,nlen     &&    execution speed.
*
pos = AT(str2,str1)                 && Get position of first occurrence.
rstr = str1                         && Create string work variable.
slen = LEN(str2)                    && Get length of substring to find.
npos = pos                          && Create position work variable.
i = 1                               && Start counter.
DO WHILE pos > 0 .AND. i < expN + 1   && If > 0, POS points to next match.
  rstr = STUFF(rstr,npos,slen,str3)   && Insert replacement string.
  mlen = len(rstr)                    && Compute new string length.
  nlen = npos + slen + 1              && Compute new starting position.

  * New starting position is where replacement string ends plus
  *   the number of characters already searched. SUBSTR() must
  *   not look beyond end of string, so that must also be computed.

  pos=IIF(nlen<mlen,AT(str2,SUBSTR(rstr,nlen,mlen-npos-1)),0)
  npos = pos + slen + npos          && Compute new starting position.
  i = i + 1                         && Increase counter.
ENDDO
RETURN rstr
```

## SEE ALSO:

Command PARAMETERS; functions AT( ) and SUBSTR( ).

# STUFF( )

## DIALECTS:

Clipper, dBASE III PLUS, dBASE IV, dBXL, FoxBASE+, and Quicksilver.

## SYNTAX:

STUFF(<expC1>,<expN1>,<expN2>,<expC2>)

## RETURNS:

Character

## DEFINITION:

Replaces part of character string <expC1> with character string <expC2>.

<expN1> is the position at which to start replacing. <expN2> is the number of characters to replace.

If <expN2> is 0, STUFF( ) does not replace any characters. Instead, it inserts <expC2> into <expC1> starting at <expN1>.

If <expC2> is null, STUFF( ) removes the number of characters from <expC1> given by <expN2>.

## RECOMMENDED USE:

STUFF( ) lets you easily rearrange character strings and insert new values.

**Example 1**—The customer account number for a monthly book club contains several significant pieces of information including: customer name, status (paid or trial), address, and expiration. A typical account number would be "KALMAN4675010689". The last four characters indicate the expiration date. The eleventh and twelfth characters, "01", indicates the account is on a "trial" basis ("02" would indicate "paid"). When the account is paid, the STUFF( ) function replaces the "01" with "02."

```
account = "KALMAN4675010689"
account = STUFF(account,11,2,"02")
? account
KALMAN4675020689
```

**Example 2**—A user defined function (Clipper, dBASE IV, or FoxBASE+) centers text within a specified number of spaces for display. Parameter STNG is the character string. MLEN is the length in which to center it. STUFF( ) inserts STNG into a blank string, SPACE(mlen), at a position derived by subtracting one half STNG's length from the total length MLEN.

```
* FUNCTION center              && Clipper syntax.
PROCEDURE center               && FoxBASE+ syntax.
* Syntax: CENTER(<expC>,<expN>)
*
PARAMETERS stng,mlen
RETURN STUFF(SPACE(mlen),(mlen-(LEN(stng)))/2,LEN(stng),stng)
```

To use function CENTER in a FoxBASE+ report, store the CENTER( ) of a string in a memory variable, then SAY it.

```
text = "Press any key to continue"
ctext = CENTER(text,40)
@ 10,01 SAY ctext
```

In Clipper, you can use CENTER( ) in the @...SAY command directly.

```
@ 10,01 SAY CENTER(text,40)
```

dBXL and Quicksilver already have a CENTER( ) function.

## VARIATIONS:

**Clipper:** STUFF( ) is in EXTEND.LIB on the system disk.

**dBASE IV:** STUFF( ) allows a memo field as an argument.

## SEE ALSO:

Functions IIF( ) and SUBSTR( ).

# SUBSTR( )

## DIALECTS:

Clipper, dBASE III PLUS, dBASE IV, dBXL, FoxBASE+, and Quicksilver.

## SYNTAX:

SUBSTR(<expC>,<expN1>,[<expN2>])

## RETURNS:

Character

## DEFINITION:

Extracts a string from within string <expC>, starting at position <expN1> and continuing for <expN2> characters.

The extracted string is called a *substring*.

## DEFAULT:

If you omit <expN2>, SUBSTR( ) extracts through the end of <expC>.

## RECOMMENDED USE:

Use SUBSTR( ) to evaluate and manipulate strings.

**Example 1**—When printing a columnar report, the titles do not always fit. Using SUBSTR( ), you can split a title and print it in pieces.

```
mtitle = "Incremental growth of profits"
@ 01,01 SAY SUBSTR(mtitle,1,11)
@ 02,01 SAY SUBSTR(mtitle,12,11)
@ 03,01 SAY SUBSTR(mtitle,23)
```

```
Incremental
growth of
profits
```

**Example 2**—An account code identifies customers of a mail order company. The first five characters are the Zip Code. The next five are the first five characters of the first name. The next four are the first four letters of the last name. The last four are the date of the last order.

Using SUBSTR( ), the program breaks the code into its components.

```
acct    = "92222GERALBROW0988"
mzip    = SUBSTR(acct,1,5)
mfirst  = SUBSTR(acct,6,5)
mlast   = SUBSTR(acct,11,4)
lastord = SUBSTR(acct,14,4)
? "Zip: " + mzip + " First: " + mfirst + " Last: " + mlast + ;
         " Last order: " + lastord
Zip: 92222 First: GERAL Last: BROW Last order: 0988
```

## VARIATIONS:

**Clipper:** You can begin SUBSTR( ) from the right side of the string by specifying a negative starting position <expN1>. For example, to extract the last four digits from a vehicle identification number, use SUBSTR( ) as follows:

```
mvin = "2444848563AAX"
? SUBSTR(mvin,-1,4)
3AAX
```

**dBASE IV:** SUBSTR( ) allows a memo field as an argument.

## SEE ALSO:

Functions LEFT( ), RAT( ), RIGHT( ), STR( ), STRTRAN( ), and STUFF( ).

# SYS( )

## DIALECTS:

FoxBASE+ only.

## SYNTAX:

SYS(<expN>,[options])

## RETURNS:

Character

## DEFINITION:

Returns system information.

## RECOMMENDED USE:

Use SYS( ) functions to incorporate system information in FoxBASE+ applications. Because they return the SETtings of system attributes (such as DEVICE, TALK, and PRINT), you can use them to restore settings after recovery from error conditions.

### SYS(0)

Returns the machine name and number on a local area network. In single user systems, it returns 1.

### SYS(1)

Returns the system date as a Julian day number. Fox Software provides it to maintain compatibility with the original dBASE II-compatible FoxBASE.

On 11/11/87, SYS(1) returns

```
. ? SYS(1)
2447111
```

### SYS(2)

Returns the number of seconds elapsed since midnight. Use it to "time-stamp" file updates, or to do elapsed time computations. For example, the time elapsed between the start and end of a subroutine would be the ending time minus the starting time.

```
start = SYS(2)
* <do subroutine>
end = SYS(2)

? (VAL(end) - VAL(start))/3600
6.0233
```

Divide seconds by 3600 to return hours.

Note that START and END must occur within the same day on the system clock. Nightowls beware!

See function SECONDS( ).

### SYS(3)

Returns a unique name you can use for temporary files. The filename changes each time you use SYS(3), preventing you from overwriting files.

```
tempname = SYS(3)
COPY ALL sales TO &tempname
? tempname
04393B07
```

Be sure to save SYS(3) in a memory variable; otherwise, your program will not "know" the temporary filename and will be unable to delete the file.

### SYS(5)

Returns the current default disk drive specified by the command SET DEFAULT (A:, C:, etc.). See command SET DEFAULT.

### SYS(6)

Returns the current print device specified by the command SET PRINT TO <PRN:/filename>. See command SET PRINT TO.

### SYS(7[,w])

Returns the name of the current format file. Option <w> refers to a work area number. If you do not specify one, SYS(7) defaults to the current area. SYS(7[,w]) returns a null character when no format file is active.

### SYS(9)

Returns the FoxBASE+ serial number. Use it to match your professional Fox-BASE+ application with a specific copy of FoxBASE+. If you are a FoxBASE+

dealer, this may inhibit unauthorized duplication of both the application and FoxBASE+. See function VERSION( ).

### SYS(10,d)

Converts a Julian day number d to a character string in the date format MM/DD/YY. Fox Software provides it to maintain compatibility with the original dBASE II-compatible FoxBASE.

### SYS(11,s)

Converts a date or character string in MM/DD/YY format to a Julian day number. Fox Software provides it to maintain compatibility with the original dBASE II-compatible FoxBASE.

### SYS(12)

Returns the amount of free memory. Use it to test the amount of memory before running external programs. For example, if you want to RUN an external program that requires 256K of memory, first use SYS(12) to determine whether enough memory is available. FoxBASE+ will normally trap insufficient memory errors; however, SYS(12) can insulate the end user from alarming error messages.

```
IF VAL(SYS(12)) > 256000
   RUN WS
ELSE
   MODI COMM
ENDIF
```

### SYS(13)

Returns the state of the printer. If it is not ready, SYS(13) returns "OFFLINE." If it is ready, SYS(13) returns "READY." Use SYS(13) to check the printer status before issuing SET PRINT ON or SET DEVICE TO PRINT. It returns "READY" if you specify a file as the PRINT device.

```
IF SYS(13) = "OFFLINE"
  @ 10,10 SAY "PRINTER NOT READY. "
  * <user options>
ELSE
  SET PRINT ON
  * <print report>
  SET PRINT OFF
ENDIF
```

### SYS(14,n[,w])

Returns the key expression for index file <n>, where <n> is the index number (its position in the index list) from 1 to 7. <w> is a work area other than the current one. If you do not specify <w>, SYS(14) defaults to the current area. If no index exists for the number <n> you specify, SYS(14) returns a null character.

### SYS(15,t,s)

Translates characters with diacritical marks in string <s> into characters without diacritical marks found in table <t>. Fox Software provides SYS(15) and the table EUROPEAN.MEM so European users can create correct indexes. (Indexing on fields containing diacritical marks does not usually produce a correct order).

To index on a field SURNAME that contains characters with accents and other diacritical marks, use SYS(15) as follows:

```
INDEX ON SYS(15,european,surname) TO namedex
```

### SYS(16[,<expN>])

Returns the name of an executing program. The option <expN> is the number of levels of DO nesting to trace. It can range from 0 to N, where N is the total number of DOs executed. An argument of 0 or 1 returns the name of the master program. If you omit the argument, SYS(16) returns the name of the currently executing program. If <expN> exceeds the number of available nesting levels, SYS(16) returns a null.

The following program displays program names at all levels of execution.

```
level = 1
DO WHILE SYS(16,level) # ""
  ? SYS(16,level)
  level = level + 1
ENDDO
```

### SYS(17)

Returns the name of the processor (e.g., 8088, 80286, or 80386).

### SYS(100)

Returns the current CONSOLE setting (ON/OFF). See command SET CONSOLE; function SYS(103).

**SYS(101)**
Returns the current DEVICE setting (PRINT/SCREEN).

**SYS(102)**
Returns the PRINT setting (ON/OFF).

**SYS(103)**
Returns the TALK setting (ON/OFF).

Use SYS(100) through SYS(103) to restore system attributes after error recovery. When branching with the ON ERROR command, save the previous settings at the beginning of the error-handling subroutine.

```
ON ERROR DO errhandle
* <error condition>
* ERRHANDLE.PRG
mtalk = SYS(103)
mdevice = SYS(101)
mprint = SYS(102)
mconsole = SYS(100)
* <error handling routine>
SET TALK &mtalk
SET DEVICE TO &mdevice
SET PRINT &mprint
SET CONSOLE &mconsole
```

## SEE ALSO:

Commands INDEX, SET CONSOLE, SET DATE, SET DEFAULT, SET DEVICE, SET PRINT, SET PRINTER, and SET TALK; functions MEMORY( ), NETNAME( ), OS( ), PROCNAME( ), and SET( ).

# TAG( )

## DIALECTS:
dBASE IV only.

## SYNTAX:
TAG([<.mdx name>,]<expN>[,<alias>])

## RETURNS:
Character

## DEFINITION:
Returns the name of the specified multiple index (MDX) file TAG or index (NDX) filename. <expN> is the TAG's number in the MDX file or the index's position in the INDEX list.

The TAG's number is determined by the order in which it was created. The index's number depends on its position in the list defined by the USE...INDEX or SET INDEX TO commands.

If there is no open index, TAG( ) returns a null string.

## OPTIONS:
<mdx name> is the name of an open MDX file in the current work area.

You can specify a database in an unselected work area by using its <alias> as a TAG( ) argument.

You can specify only one option (<alias> or <mdx filename>) at a time.

## RECOMMENDED USE:
Use TAG( ) to refer to MDX tags by number instead of name. This lets you treat TAGs as variables rather than constants.

**Example**—A file maintenance program uses a specified file, then displays the available TAGs in the associated MDX file.

```
PROCEDURE showtag
PARAMETERS filename
USE (filename)
```

```
ctr = 1
DO WHILE "" # TRIM(TAG(ctr))
  ? TAG(ctr)
  ctr = ctr + 1
ENDDO
```

The command produces the following result when applied to a sales tracking database:

```
DO showtag WITH "CLIENTS"
LNAME
FNAME
COMPANY
ZIPDEX
```

Within the DO WHILE...ENDDO structure, the program could also STORE the TAG names in an array or in memory variables. Users could then be prompted to select available TAGs from a menu.

## SEE ALSO:

Command INDEX; functions DBF( ), INDEXKEY( ), INDEXORD( ), NDX( ), and ORDER( ).

# TAN( )

## DIALECTS:

dBASE IV only.

## SYNTAX:

TAN(<expN>)

## RETURNS:

Floating point

## DEFINITION:

Computes the tangent of an angle.

<expN> is the angle in radians.

The SET DECIMALS command determines the numeric accuracy of the result.

Use DTOR( ) and RTOD( ) to convert degrees to radians and vice versa. A radian is approximately 57.3 degrees.

## RECOMMENDED USE:

TAN( ) is a trigonometric function used in engineering and scientific applications.

**Example**—A structural engineering application expresses angles in radians. Angle A is 3.344 radians. Its TAN( ) is 0.21.

```
SET DECIMALS TO 2
mtan = TAN(3.344)
?mtan
0.21
```

## SEE ALSO:

Functions ACOS( ), ASIN( ), ATAN( ), ATN2( ), COS( ), and SIN( ).

# TIME( )

## DIALECTS:
Clipper, dBASE III PLUS, dBASE IV, dBXL, FoxBASE+, and Quicksilver.

## SYNTAX:
TIME( )

## RETURNS:
Character

## DEFINITION:
Returns the system time as a character string in the form HH:MM:SS.

Because TIME( ) returns a string, you must convert it to numeric to do computations.

## RECOMMENDED USE:
Use TIME( ) to "stamp" records with the time of their last update (assuming you set the system time correctly). Also use it to do elapsed time computations.

**Example 1**—Whenever an operator updates data in a medical program, the TIME( ) and DATE( ) are stored in the associated record.

```
* <@...SAY...GETs>
REPLACE patient WITH mpatient,acct WITH macct,insured WITH minsured
REPLACE up_time WITH TIME(), up_date WITH DATE()

LIST patient,up_time,up_date

Record#  PATIENT          UP_TIME    UP_DATE
      1  Aaron            10:23:16   05/22/87
      2  Bellamy          11:45:17   08/07/87
      3  D'Amico          15:38:17   09/20/87
      4  Faulk            08:10:46   04/30/87
      5  Gillette         16:44:37   10/01/87
      6  Glazier          22:34:66   06/13/87
      7  Goldberg         19:16:36   06/24/87
```

**Example 2**—To calculate the difference between times, you must convert the character TIME( ) to numeric. To do so, use the VAL( ) function. The following procedure uses VAL( ) to split the time string into its components. It then multiplies hours times 3600 and minutes times 60. The total number of seconds stored in ELAP is the elapsed time.

```
* ELAPSE.PRG
* Displays seconds elapsed between a beginning and ending TIME().
beg = TIME()
* <Do operations>
end = TIME()
elap=((VAL(end)*3600)+(VAL(SUBSTR(end,4,2))*60)+(VAL(RIGHT(end,2))))-;
     ((VAL(beg)*3600)+(VAL(SUBSTR(beg,4,2))*60)+(VAL(RIGHT(beg,2))))
? "Elapsed time: " + STR(elap,8,0)
```

With a BEGinning time of 00:13:03 and an ENDing time of 00:22:52, the elapsed time is 589 seconds.

## VARIATIONS:

**Clipper:** The SECONDS( ) function returns the time as numeric seconds (and hundredths of seconds) since midnight. This simplifies elapsed time computations. Clipper provides a user defined function ELAPTIME( ) that returns a time string showing elapsed time. It is in EXTEND.LIB on the system disk.

**FoxBASE+:** TIME(1) returns the time string with hundredths of seconds:

```
? TIME(1)
08:15:21.33
```

SYS(2) returns seconds since midnight. This simplifies elapsed time computations.

## SEE ALSO:

Command SET TIME; functions SECONDS( ) and SYS(2).

# TONE( )

## DIALECTS:
Clipper only.

## SYNTAX:
TONE(<expN1>,<expN2>)

## RETURNS:
Nothing

## DEFINITION:
Sends a tone through the computer's speaker with a specified frequency and duration.

<expN1> is the frequency in cycles per second (Hertz). Audible frequencies range from 20 to approximately 17000—higher if you have canine hearing.

<expN2> is the duration in eighteenths of a second.

TONE( ) truncates decimals for both arguments.

## RECOMMENDED USE:
Use TONE( ) to inform the user about a program's status.

**Example**—Warning "buzzers" inform users about system errors. Steady, low-pitched beeps confirm that a process is continuing as expected. Brief tones rising in pitch can encourage users when they take an appropriate action or announce the end of a process.

```
*REWARD.PRG-Positive feedback.
FOR ctr = 50 TO 100 STEP 10
  TONE(ctr^2,1)
NEXT

*MINOR.PRG-Minor warning such as out of paper.
FOR ctr = 1 TO 10
  TONE(40,10)
  TONE(50,20)
NEXT
```

```
*MAJOR.PRG—Major warning, just shy of reactor meltdown.
FOR ctr = 1 TO 20
  TONE(5000,3)
  TONE(2000,5)
NEXT
```

TONE( ) is in EXTEND.LIB on the system disk. Its assembly language source code is in EXAMPLEA.ASM.

## SEE ALSO:

Command SET BELL; function CHR( ) (? CHR(7)).

# TRANSFORM( )

## DIALECTS:

Clipper, dBASE III PLUS, dBASE IV, dBXL, FoxBASE+, and Quicksilver.

## SYNTAX:

TRANSFORM(<exp>,<expC>)

## RETURNS:

Character

## DEFINITION:

Formats a numeric or character expression according to the PICTURE format in <expC>.

TRANSFORM( ) always returns a character expression.

A PICTURE consists of a TEMPLATE or FUNCTION. See @...SAY...GET for a detailed explanation of PICTUREs.

## RECOMMENDED USE:

PICTUREs are usually associated with @...SAY statements. With TRANSFORM( ), you can use them to format and display expressions with the commands ?, ??, DISPLAY, and LIST. TRANSFORM( ) also lets you format output in LABEL and REPORT forms.

**Example**—An inventory application produces LIST-oriented reports (as opposed to page-formatted reports). By using TRANSFORM( ), the programmer formats numbers and strings with all the functions and templates in @...SAY PICTUREs.

For example, TRANSFORM( ) displays AMOUNTs in the SALES file with leading dollar signs and commas instead of spaces.

```
USE SALES
LIST TRANSFORM(amount,"$9,999.99")
Record #  TRANSFORM(amount,"$9,999.99")
      1  $1,728.00
      2  $2,197.00
      3  $2,744.00
```

To display AMOUNTS with CR if positive, and DB if negative, the programmer uses TRANSFORM with the @C and @X functions.

```
LIST TRANSFORM(AMOUNT,"@C@X 9,999.99")
Record#  TRANSFORM(AMOUNT,"@C@X 9,999.99")
      1   1,728.00 CR
      2   2,197.00 CR
      3   2,744.00 DB
      4   3,375.00 CR
      5   4,096.00 CR
```

TRANSFORM also formats character and date strings in similar reports. For example, an inventory report goes to the main office in London. When listing dates, the programmer specifies European format (DD/MM/YY) with TRANSFORM( ).

```
LIST amount, TRANSFORM(saledate,"@E")
 Record#     AMOUNT TRANSFORM(saledate,"@E")
       1    1331.00 07/08/86
       2    1728.00 18/08/87
       3    2197.00 29/08/87
       4   -2744.00 09/09/88
```

At the end of the report, SUM TO saves the sum of AMOUNT in MAMOUNT. The ? then displays the total, formatted with TRANSFORM.

```
SUM amount TO mamount
? TRANSFORM(mamount,"@C@X *9,999,999.99")
****13,927.00 CR
```

## SEE ALSO:

Command @...SAY for a complete list of PICTUREs and FUNCTIONs. See also commands DISPLAY and LIST.

# TRIM( )/RTRIM( )

## DIALECTS:

Clipper, dBASE III PLUS, dBASE IV, dBXL, FoxBASE+, and Quicksilver.

## SYNTAX:

TRIM(<expC>)

## RETURNS:

Character

## DEFINITION:

Removes spaces from the end of a character string.

The TRIM( ) of an empty character string is a null string (zero length).

RTRIM( ) is a synonym for TRIM( ).

## RECOMMENDED USE:

**Example 1**—A project management system contains a field FORENAME with a length of 20. It accommodates the longest known first name. However, most names have fewer characters, leaving spaces at the end. When printing a name, you must use TRIM( ) to remove the extra spaces.

```
? TRIM(forename) + " " + lastname
```

**Example 2**—The input screen of a general ledger system lets users leave the first field blank to exit to a menu. When the user exits the GET, the LEN( ) and TRIM( ) functions test its memory variable. If the length of its TRIM( ) is zero, the field is blank.

```
mlname = 20
@ 10,10 SAY "Enter last name (or leave blank to exit): " GET mlname
READ
IF LEN(TRIM(mlname))=0
  CLEAR
  RETURN
ENDIF
```

## VARIATIONS:

**Clipper:** ALLTRIM( ) removes both leading and trailing blanks.

## SEE ALSO:

Functions ALLTRIM( ), STUFF( ), and SUBSTR( ).

# TYPE( )

## DIALECTS:
Clipper, dBASE III PLUS, dBASE IV, dBXL, FoxBASE+, and Quicksilver.

## SYNTAX:
TYPE(<expC>)

## RETURNS:
Character

## DEFINITION:
Returns the data type of the contents of <expC>. The type is a single uppercase letter, given by:

| | |
|---|---|
| C | Character |
| D | Date |
| L | Logical |
| M | Memo |
| N | Numeric |
| U | Undefined |

To test a literal string or expression (not in a memory variable), enclose it in quotation marks in the TYPE( ) argument (you must test data of all types in character expression form).

You must also enclose memory variables in quotation marks unless they contain the name of another memory variable.

## RECOMMENDED USE:
Use TYPE( ) to determine if a memory variable exists. Also use it when manipulating data of unknown types, as in general purpose file handling subroutines.

TYPE( ) can also validate an expression. It returns "U" if the expression is undefined.

**Example 1**—A sales contact application contains a "quick lookup" feature. The salesperson can execute the program with one of two command line parameters, LASTNAME or DOLLAR volume. Depending on the data TYPE( ), the program decides which index to search.

```
PARAMETERS searchkey
USE sales
IF TYPE("searchkey") = "N"
  SET INDEX TO vol_dex
ELSE
  SET INDEX TO name_dex
ENDIF
SEEK searchkey
```

**Example 2**—A database report program analyzes the structure of any file and SUMs all numeric fields. It stores the SUM results in memory variables with names corresponding to the field numbers. The program uses the SUM results to analyze and report the data.

The program processes each field in a DO WHILE structure. It continues as long as the length of the fieldname is non-zero. The TYPE( ) function then tests each field. If it returns "N," the program SUMs the field and stores the result in a memory variable numbered with the field number.

```
PARAMETERS filename
USE &filename                        && USE file passed as a parameter.
fieldnum = 1                         && Initialize field counter.
DO WHILE LEN(FIELD(fieldnum)) # 0    && DO WHILE the field is valid.
  fname = FIELD(fieldnum)            && Store field name in FNAME.
  IF TYPE(fname) = "N"               && If field is numeric,
    string = LTRIM(STR(fieldnum))    &&   convert FIELDNUM to a string,
    SUM &fname TO f_sum&string       &&   SUM to f_sum1, f_sum2, f_sum3, ...
  ENDIF
  fieldnum = fieldnum + 1            && Increment field counter.
ENDDO
```

## VARIATIONS:

**Clipper:** "A" indicates an array reference. Reference to an array element returns its type. Also note that type "U" can indicate an undefined variable, an undefined array reference, a user defined function, or an immediate if expression. Type "UE" indicates a syntax error. Type "UI" indicates an invalid function name.

When evaluating an IIF( ) statement, TYPE( ) tests the evaluated (true) expression. If it is invalid, TYPE( ) returns "UE".

## SEE ALSO:

Command PARAMETERS; function FIELD( ).

# UPDATED( )

## DIALECTS:
Clipper and FoxBASE+.

## SYNTAX:
UPDATED( )

## RETURNS:
Logical

## DEFINITION:
Indicates whether data was changed during the last READ.

UPDATED( ) returns true (.T.) if the data changes.

## RECOMMENDED USE:
Use UPDATED( ) after a READ to determine whether data was changed. If not, you do not need to issue REPLACE commands.

**Example**—A data entry program checks whether the user changed data in the active GETs. If UPDATED( ) returns .T., the program REPLACEs the database fields with the contents of the GET variables. Otherwise, the program skips the GETs.

```
* <initialize variables>
@ 02,01 SAY "Enter account number: " GET macct
@ 03,01 SAY "Enter invoice number: " GET minv
@ 04,01 SAY "Enter invoice total : " GET mtot
@ 05,01 SAY "Enter sales tax     : " GET mtax
READ
IF UPDATED()
  REPLACE acct WITH macct,inv WITH minv,tot WITH mtot,tax WITH mtax
ENDIF
```

## VARIATIONS:
**dBASE III PLUS, dBASE IV, dBXL, Quicksilver:** READKEY( ) returns a value of 256 or more if data was changed in the previous full screen operation. You can simulate UPDATED( ) with the statement

```
? READKEY() >= 256
```

If the statement returns true (.T.), data was changed.

## SEE ALSO:
Functions CHANGED( ), LASTKEY( ), and READKEY( ).

# UPPER( )

## DIALECTS:

Clipper, dBASE III PLUS, dBASE IV, dBXL, FoxBASE+, and Quicksilver.

## SYNTAX:

UPPER(<expC>)

## RETURNS:

Character

## DEFINITION:

Converts all lowercase letters in <expC> to uppercase.

UPPER( ) does not affect characters other than lowercase letters.

## RECOMMENDED USE:

Because dBASE expressions are case sensitive, convert character strings to either uppercase or lowercase when evaluating them. This assures consistency.

**Example**—A user prompt in an accounting program requests a "Y" or "N" response. Because the program uses WAIT TO to get the response, there is no way to force either upper or lower case entry. Thus, the program must disregard case. To do this, it evaluates the UPPER( ) value of the string.

```
WAIT "Continue with end of month posting? (Y/N)" TO action
IF UPPER(action) = "Y"
  DO eompost
ENDIF
```

UPPER( ) is often used in index key expressions to simplify searches. You can then SEEK the UPPER( ) value of a search expression, disregarding case.

## SEE ALSO:

Functions ISUPPER( ), ISLOWER( ), and LOWER( ).

# USED( )

## DIALECTS:
Clipper only.

## SYNTAX:
USED( )

## RETURNS:
Logical

## DEFINITION:
Returns true (.T.) if a database file is open in the current work area. Otherwise, it returns false (.F.).

## RECOMMENDED USE:
Issue USED( ) in multiuser environments to determine if the previous USE command succeeded. If another user has exclusive use, USED( ) returns false (.F.). Note that NETERR( ) returns true (.T.).

```
SET EXCLUSIVE OFF
FOR ctr = 1 to 500
  USE accounts
  IF USED()  && USE succeeds
    EXIT
  ELSE
    @ 24,01 SAY "Retrying " + STR(ctr,1,3) + " out of 500 times"
  ENDIF
NEXT
```

## LIMITS/WARNINGS:
Although USED( ) can help you navigate through work areas when looking for an unoccupied one, SELECT(0) is more direct.

## VARIATIONS:
**dBASE III PLUS, dBASE IV, dBXL, FoxBASE+, Quicksilver:** You can tell if a database file is open by testing the return value of the DBF( ) function as follows:

```
mused = LEN(TRIM(DBF()))>0
```

If the LENgth of the TRIM of the DBF is zero, no file is in use. MUSED then is (.F.).

## SEE ALSO:
Commands SELECT and USE; function NETERR( ).

# USER( )

## DIALECTS:
dBASE IV only.

## SYNTAX:
USER( )

## RETURNS:
Character

## DEFINITION:
Returns the current user's name if the PROTECT system is active. If the system is not PROTECTed, USER( ) returns "" (a null string).

## RECOMMENDED USE:
Use USER( ) to create custom security systems in applications.

**Example**—A multiuser accounting program limits access to different modules by checking the USER( ) name. A database file contains valid users for specific modules.

```
* MODULE PAYROLL
USE pass INDEX passdex
SEEK USER()   && USER() is "DAVIDK".
IF .NOT. FOUND()
  CLEAR
  ?
  ? "I'm sorry, you do not have access privileges to this module."
  ? "Please see the system administrator for more information."
  WAIT
  CLEAR
  RETURN
ENDIF
```

## SEE ALSO:
Command PROTECT; functions ACCESS( ) and NETWORK( ).

# USERNO( )

## DIALECTS:
Quicksilver only.

## SYNTAX:
USERNO( )

## RETURNS:
Numeric

## DEFINITION:
Returns the number of the current workstation on a local area network.

The Networker Plus module automatically assigns each station (running a Quicksilver application) a unique identification number. The number remains in effect until the user exits the application.

Numbers are not necessarily assigned in sequence. If there are ten stations, and user 8 exits, the next user to log on becomes user 8.

Multiuser dBXL users and interactive Networker Plus Dialog users are also assigned user numbers.

## DEFAULT:
In a single-user mode, USERNO( ) returns 0.

## RECOMMENDED USE:
Use USERNO( ) in filenames to prevent different Quicksilver programs on a local area network from creating files with identical names.

**Example**—A sales application creates temporary files during report writing. First, it stores the string version of USERNO( ) in STATION. The program opens PROSPECTS, then copies all records for SALARY greater than $50,000. If USERNO( ) is 3, the resulting file is called PRIME3.DBF.

```
station = STR(USERNO(),1,0)
USE prospects INDEX lname
COPY TO prime&station FOR salary > 50000
```

## LIMITS/WARNINGS:

Because USERNO( ) is specific to Quicksilver, it does not protect files from being overwritten by other dBASE-compatible applications. A better solution is to define unique DOS variables in the AUTOEXEC files of each work station, then use the GETENV( ) function to identify the workstation.

## SEE ALSO:

Function GETENV( ).

# VAL( )

## DIALECTS:
Clipper, dBASE III PLUS, dBASE IV, dBXL, FoxBASE+, and Quicksilver.

## SYNTAX:
VAL(<expC>)

## RETURNS:
Numeric

## DEFINITION:
Converts character expressions to numeric.

VAL( ) processes only the digits to the left of the first non-numeric character in <expC>, ignoring leading blanks.

Moving from left to right, VAL( ) terminates when it encounters a non- digit.

If the first non-blank character is not a digit, VAL( ) returns 0.

The SET DECIMALS command controls how VAL( ) displays decimals.

VAL( ) is the inverse of STR( ).

## RECOMMENDED USE:
To do computations on numbers stored as character strings, or on functions that return numbers in character form, you must first convert them to numerics with VAL( ).

**Example**—A medical research program tracks how long it takes drugs to dissolve. The program uses the TIME( ) function to mark the start time. Because TIME( ) returns a character string, it is difficult to compute time differences. To simplify computations, the program uses VAL( ) to convert TIME( ) into the number of seconds since midnight.

```
mtime = TIME()               && As an example, TIME() = 17:21:34
* Use SUBSTR() to extract HH, MM, and SS characters.
hours = SUBSTR(mtime,1,2)
minutes = SUBSTR(mtime,4,2)
seconds = SUBSTR(mtime,7,2)
* Multiple hours x secs. per hour, minutes x secs. per minute,
*   then add seconds for total seconds since midnight.
? (VAL(hours) * 3600) + (VAL(minutes) * 60) + VAL(seconds)
62494
```

## SEE ALSO:
Functions STR( ), SUBSTR( ), and TIME( ).

# VARREAD( )

## DIALECTS:
dBASE IV only.

## SYNTAX:
VARREAD( )

## RETURNS:
Character

## DEFINITION:
Returns the name of the memory variable or field in the current GET or PROMPT.

If no GET or PROMPT is active, VARREAD( ) returns a null string.

*Note:* VARREAD( ) was renamed from READVAR( ) to avoid conflicting with READKEY( ) when abbreviated. See READVAR( ) for an example.

## VARIATIONS:
**Clipper:** READVAR( ) does the same task.

## SEE ALSO:
Commands APPEND, DEFINE WINDOW, EDIT, READ, and SET KEY; function READVAR( ).

# VERSION( )

## DIALECTS:

Clipper, dBASE III PLUS, dBASE IV, dBXL, FoxBASE+, and Quicksilver.

## SYNTAX:

VERSION( )

## RETURNS:

Character

## DEFINITION:

Returns the name and version number of the compiler or interpreter in use.

## RECOMMENDED USE:

Use VERSION( ) to identify which system is in use. This lets you implement version specific commands without re-coding.

**Example**—A commercial hotel reservation system runs under Clipper, dBASE III PLUS, dBASE IV, FoxBASE+, or Quicksilver. The programmer uses VERSION( ) to optimize the method of getting user responses. If VERSION( ) contains "Fox" or "Clip," the program uses bounce bar menus (see MENU TO). If VERSION( ) contains "Quick," the program uses windows. Otherwise, it uses standard menu routines.

```
DO CASE
  CASE "Fox" $ VERSION() .or. "Clip" $ VERSION( )
    DO mbounce
  CASE "Quick" $ VERSION()
    DO mwindow
  CASE "dBASE IV" $ VERSION()
  OTHERWISE
    DO mstandrd
ENDCASE
```

## VARIATIONS:

**Clipper:** VERSION( ) is in EXTEND.LIB on the system disk.

**dBASE III PLUS, dBASE IV:** VERSION(1) returns Ashton-Tate's internal revision number and the date the dBASE program was created. Normally, the dBASE III PLUS VERSION( ) returns

```
. ? VERSION()
dBASE III PLUS  Version 1.1
```

Adding a 1 to the function changes the output to:

```
. ? VERSION(1)
dBASE III PLUS Version 2.0x100 (02/28/87)
```

**FoxBASE+:** VERSION(1) returns Fox Software's internal revision number and the date the FoxBASE+ program was created. Normally, VERSION( ) returns

```
. ? VERSION()
FoxBASE+ Rev 2.00
```

VERSION(1) returns

```
. ? VERSION(1)
FoxBASE+ Rev 2.00 [01-July-87]  Serial # XXXXXXXXX
```

## SEE ALSO:

Command PUBLIC; Appendix 2, "Sensing the Environment."

# WACTIVE( )

## DIALECTS:

dBXL and Quicksilver.

## SYNTAX:

WACTIVE( )

## RETURNS:

Logical

## DEFINITION:

Indicates whether a window is active in the currently selected area.

When WACTIVE( ) evaluates true, a window is active in the current WSELECT area.

To make windowing commands and functions consistent (all starting with W), WACTIVE( ) replaced ACTIVEWIN( ) in Quicksilver Version 1.1.

## RECOMMENDED USE:

A general purpose windowing subroutine must avoid areas with active windows. WACTIVE( ) determines whether a window is active.

**Example**—A general purpose windowing routine pops up lists of disk files when the user presses a particular key. To avoid conflict with other applications, the routine checks whether a window is active in the selected area. If WACTIVE( ) detects a window, it increases the WAREA counter and checks successive areas until it finds an unoccupied one.

```
WSET WINDOW nuscreen TO 1,1,18,30
warea = 0
DO WHILE WACTIVE()
  warea = warea + 1
  WSELECT warea
ENDDO
WUSE nuscreen
```

## SEE ALSO:

Commands WSELECT and WUSE; function WACTIVE.

# WORD( )

## DIALECTS:
Clipper only.

## SYNTAX:
WORD(<expN>)

## RETURNS:
Nothing

## DEFINITION:
Converts numeric parameters from Clipper's internal format (type DOUBLE) to integers (type INT) to pass them to C subroutines with the CALL command.

<expN> is a numeric value ranging from -32,767 to 32,767.

## RECOMMENDED USE:
Without WORD( ), numeric parameters are passed in IEEE 754 floating point format (8 byte floating point representation with a 53 bit characteristic and an 11 bit exponent biased by 1023). This causes longer subroutines since each one must convert DOUBLEs to INTs.

**Example**—A graphics subroutine plots data on a bar graph. Data is passed using WORD( ).

```
yaxis = 44
CALL c_bar WITH WORD(yaxis)
```

## SEE ALSO:
Command [C]CALL.

# WSELECT( )

## DIALECTS:

dBXL and Quicksilver.

## SYNTAX:

WSELECT( )

## RETURNS:

Numeric

## DEFINITION:

Returns the number of the currently selected window area. Area numbers range from 0 to 99.

## RECOMMENDED USE:

Use WSELECT( ) with WACTIVE( ) to avoid conflicts between windowing subroutines. You can also use WSELECT( ) with WSET TITLE TO to display the currently selected window area within the window frame.

**Example**—A general purpose routine creates a window that lists valid account numbers when the user presses a key. To avoid conflict with the existing application, the routine checks for an active window in the selected area. If WACTIVE( ) detects a window, it increases the WAREA counter and re-checks successive areas until it finds an unoccupied one. When it succeeds, WSET TITLE TO displays the WSELECT( ) area number in the window frame. This routine avoids WSELECTing area 0. It also assumes that at least one of the 99 window areas is available. You could add error trapping code to prevent the routine from failing due to lack of available window areas.

```
WSET WINDOW lscreen TO 1,1,18,40
warea = 1
DO WHILE WACTIVE()
  warea = warea + 1
  WSELECT warea
ENDDO
WUSE lscreen
WSET TITLE TO "WINDOW AREA: " + STR(WSELECT(),2,0)
WDISPLAY
```

## SEE ALSO:

Commands WDISPLAY, WSELECT, WSET, and WUSE; function WACTIVE( ).

# YEAR( )

## DIALECTS:
Clipper, dBASE III PLUS, dBASE IV, dBXL, FoxBASE+, and Quicksilver.

## SYNTAX:
YEAR(<expD>)

## RETURNS:
Numeric

## DEFINITION:
Returns a four-digit year from the specified date expression.

## RECOMMENDED USE:
Use YEAR( ) to compute years elapsed, or to simply display the year in its four-digit form.

**Example**—An insurance program computes an applicant's age by subtracting his or her birthdate from the current date.

```
today = YEAR(DATE())
? today
1988
previous = CTOD("09/21/62")
elapsed = YEAR(today) - YEAR(previous)
? elapsed
26
```

## SEE ALSO:
Functions DAY( ) and MONTH( ).

# APPENDIX 1

## CLIPPER SUMMER '87 RESERVED WORDS

Do not use the following words in Clipper programs. Those preceded by asterisks may not even be used in abbreviated form.

*BATCH
*BEGINAREA
CODE
DATA
*DEBUG
*ENDAREA
ERRORLEVEL
INDEXEXT
INDEXORD
*FILE
*HEIGHT
*LIBRARY
*LOWERCASE
*MAP
NETERR
*NOBELL
*OUTPUT
PROCFILE
READEXIT
READINSERT
*SEARCH
*SECTION
SETPRC
SUMMER87
SYSTEM
*UPPERCASE
*VERBOSE
*WIDTH
*WORKFILE

# APPENDIX 2

## SENSING THE ENVIRONMENT

As noted throughout this book, the commands and functions of the dBASE dialects vary. For example, dBXL and Quicksilver provide the PROPER() function for capitalizing names. The other systems offer no equivalent. Where equivalent commands and functions exist, variations in usage and syntax can produce unexpected results.

A difficulty arises when you want to use more than one system. For example, you may prefer to develop programs using an interpreter such as dBASE III PLUS, dBASE IV, dBXL, or FoxBASE+. But you may eventually want to compile the programs with Clipper or Quicksilver. Because the commands and functions differ, you face time-consuming conversions unless you plan carefully.

To write programs that work with more than one system, consider these approaches:

1) Use only common commands and functions (a subset).
2) Detect the system in use and conditionally execute specific commands and functions.

The advantages of the first approach are maximum portability and simplified maintenance. Your programming constructs tend to be simpler. The disadvantages include lower productivity and slower running programs. System-specific enhancements often improve productivity and increase execution speed.

The advantage of the second approach is optimized performance. The disadvantages include an increase in application size (because of alternative sequences) and increased difficulty of maintenance. As system versions change, upgrading a program with multiple sets of program instructions can be tricky.

If you use only a subset of dBASE commands and functions, your programs will probably not need to detect which compatible system is running. However, if you optimize performance by using system-specific commands and functions, you need a way to tell one system from another. The VERSION() function, special memory variables, and special comment notation can let you easily determine which system is in use.

## Clipper, FoxBASE+, Quicksilver

### Special Variables

When you declare a memory variable PUBLIC, its initial value is normally false (.F.). Clipper, FoxBASE+, and Quicksilver all have special variables that initialize to true (.T.) when you declare them PUBLIC. Your program can use them to differentiate systems.

Clipper provides the variable CLIPPER. Declaring PUBLIC CLIPPER gives it a value of true (.T.). You can then define conditional structures that execute commands depending on CLIPPER's value.

The same holds in FoxBASE+, except that the variable's name is FOX. PUBLIC FOX initializes it with a value of true (.T.).

Because Quicksilver has two operating modes, d-code and optimized native code, it provides two special variables, XQUICKS and XNATIVE. XNATIVE refers to the native code optimizer.

If you declare a public variable XQUICKS, it will always be initialized to .T. in a Quicksilver-compiled application. The variable XNATIVE will only be initialized to .T. if the application is running in optimized native code.

## Quicksilver

### Comment Notation

Special notation (*\ and &&\) make program statements "invisible" to all dBASE-compatible systems except Quicksilver and dBXL.

For example, the statements

```
*\ ? BITSET(3,0)
&&\ DOSINT mvar
```

are treated as program comments (NOTE) in Clipper, dBASE III PLUS, dBASE IV, and FoxBASE+. dBXL and Quicksilver recognize them as valid commands and execute them accordingly.

**Note:** To treat *\ and &&\ as standard NOTEs in dBXL, put the statement COMMENT=OFF in the CONFIG.XL file. In Quicksilver, use the -\ compiler switch.

Normally, Quicksilver cannot compile unsupported commands such as EDIT and BROWSE, even if they are "hidden" by the special memory variables XQUICKS or XNATIVE. However, the *QSOFF and *QSON switches let you compile and run applications despite the presence of unsupported commands. All text between *QSOFF and *QSON is ignored, for example

```
*QSOFF
BROWSE
*QSON
```

lets you include the BROWSE statement in a Quicksilver program.

Other systems treat *QSOFF and *QSON like program comments.

## dBASE III PLUS/dBASE IV/dBXL

### VERSION( ) Function

dBASE III PLUS, dBASE IV, and dBXL lack special identifying memory variables. However, the VERSION( ) function lets you simulate this feature.

The following code uses the $ operator to determine whether the string returned by VERSION( ) contains "dBASE III PLUS," "dBASE IV," or "dBXL." If it contains "dBASE III PLUS," the code creates a PUBLIC memory variable DBASE3 and makes it true (.T.). If VERSION( ) returns "dBXL," the code creates a PUBLIC memory variable DBXL and makes it true. The dBASE IV version creates a PUBLIC memory variable DBASE4 and makes it true.

```
DO CASE
CASE "dBASE III PLUS" $ VERSION()
  PUBLIC dbase3
  dbase3 = .t.
CASE "dBXL" $ VERSION()
  PUBLIC dbxl
  dbxl = .t.
CASE "dBASE IV" $ VERSION()
  PUBLIC dbase4
  dbase4 = .t.
ENDCASE
```

At any point thereafter, you can run dBASE III PLUS-, dBASE IV-, or dBXL-specific commands by testing the PUBLIC variables.

**Example 1**—To include a FoxBASE+-specific function in a dBASE III PLUS program, declare PUBLIC FOX. Then test FOX to determine which system is running. If FOX is true, use the FoxBASE+ SYS(3) function to create a temporary filename. If it is false, explicitly create a temporary file name.

```
* UPDATE.PRG
* <statements>
USE acctmain
PUBLIC FOX
IF FOX              && If TRUE, use SYS(3) to create a temporary filename.
  tname = SYS(3)
  COPY TO &tname FOR acctno = "1252"
  LIST acctno
  DELETE FILE &tname..DBF
ELSE
  COPY TO templ FOR acctno = "1252"
  LIST acctno
  DELETE FILE templ.dbf
ENDIF
```

**Example 2**—The Quicksilver XNATIVE variable differentiates between d-code mode and optimized mode. For example, the CCALL command is available only in the optimized mode. You can text XNATIVE to determine whether CCALL is currently available.

```
IF XNATIVE
  CCALL SUMADDON WITH memvar
ELSE
  LOAD SUMADDON
  CALL SUMADDON WITH memvar
  * Use the LOAD/CALL scheme instead.
ENDIF
```

**Example 3**—Clipper, FoxBASE+, and Quicksilver all try to compile unsupported commands, even if they are "hidden" by a special memory variable (CLIPPER/FOX/XQUICKS). Clipper and FoxBASE+ generate error messages, but do produce programs that run. Quicksilver compiles only trivial unsupported commands (such as SET TALK), but refuses to compile commands such as BROWSE and EDIT. To compile these commands in Quicksilver, you must use the *QSOFF and *QSON switches to hide them.

```
PUBLIC xquicks,clipper
IF xquicks .OR. clipper
  DO browprog
ELSE
  *QSOFF
  BROWSE
  *QSON
ENDIF
```

## SEE ALSO:

Command PUBLIC; function VERSION(); Appendix 4: Quicksilver/dBXL Environment Variables.

# APPENDIX 3

## SCAN CODES/ASCII CHART

### ASCII Characters

| LSD | MSD | 0<br>000 | 1<br>001 | 2<br>010 | 3<br>011 | 4<br>100 | 5<br>101 | 6<br>110 | 7<br>111 |
|---|---|---|---|---|---|---|---|---|---|
| 0 | 0000 | NUL | DLE | SP | 0 | @ | P | ` | p |
| 1 | 0001 | SOH | DC1 | ! | 1 | A | Q | a | q |
| 2 | 0010 | STX | DC2 | " | 2 | B | R | b | r |
| 3 | 0011 | ETX | DC3 | # | 3 | C | S | c | s |
| 4 | 0100 | EOT | DC4 | $ | 4 | D | T | d | t |
| 5 | 0101 | ENQ | NAK | % | 5 | E | U | e | u |
| 6 | 0110 | ACK | SYN | & | 6 | F | V | f | v |
| 7 | 0111 | BEL | ETB | ' | 7 | G | W | g | w |
| 8 | 1000 | BS | CAN | ( | 8 | H | X | h | x |
| 9 | 1001 | HT | EM | ) | 9 | I | Y | i | y |
| A | 1010 | LF | SUB | * | : | J | Z | j | z |
| B | 1011 | VT | ESC | + | ; | K | [ | k | { |
| C | 1100 | FF | FS | , | < | L | \ | l | \| |
| D | 1101 | CR | GS | – | = | M | ] | m | } |
| E | 1110 | SO | RS | . | > | N | ^ | n | ~ |
| F | 1111 | SI | US | / | ? | O | _ | o | DEL |

### Auxiliary Byte Values for the Special Keys and Combinations on the IBM Standard PC Keyboard

| Value (Hex) | Key | Value (Hex) | Key |
|---|---|---|---|
| 0F | Shift-Tab | 14 | Alt-T |
| 10 | Alt-Q | 15 | Alt-Y |
| 11 | Alt-W | 16 | Alt-U |
| 12 | Alt-E | 17 | Alt-I |
| 13 | Alt-R | 18 | Alt-O |

| Value (Hex) | Key | Value (Hex) | Key |
|---|---|---|---|
| 19 | Alt-P | 57 | Shift-F4 |
| 1E | Alt-A | 58 | Shift-F5 |
| 1F | Alt-S | 59 | Shift-F6 |
| 20 | Alt-D | 5A | Shift-F7 |
| 21 | Alt-F | 5B | Shift-F8 |
| 22 | Alt-G | 5C | Shift-F9 |
| 23 | Alt-H | 5D | Shift-F10 |
| 24 | Alt-J | 5E | Ctrl-F1 |
| 25 | Alt-K | 5F | Ctrl-F2 |
| 26 | Alt-L | 60 | Ctrl-F3 |
| 2C | Alt-Z | 61 | Ctrl-F4 |
| 2D | Alt-X | 62 | Ctrl-F5 |
| 2E | Alt-C | 63 | Ctrl-F6 |
| 2F | Alt-V | 64 | Ctrl-F7 |
| 30 | Alt-B | 65 | Ctrl-F8 |
| 31 | Alt-N | 66 | Ctrl-F9 |
| 32 | Alt-M | 67 | Ctrl-F10 |
| 3B | F1 | 68 | Alt-F1 |
| 3C | F2 | 69 | Alt-F2 |
| 3D | F3 | 6A | Alt-F3 |
| 3E | F4 | 6B | Alt-F4 |
| 3F | F5 | 6C | Alt-F5 |
| 40 | F6 | 6D | Alt-F6 |
| 41 | F7 | 6E | Alt-F7 |
| 42 | F8 | 6F | Alt-F8 |
| 43 | F9 | 70 | Alt-F9 |
| 44 | F10 | 71 | Alt-F10 |
| 47 | Home | 72 | Ctrl-PrtSc |
| 48 | Up arrow | 73 | Ctrl-Left arrow |
| 49 | PgUp | 74 | Ctrl-Right arrow |
| 4B | Left arrow | 75 | Ctrl-End |
| 4D | Right arrow | 76 | Ctrl-PgDn |
| 4F | End | 77 | Ctrl-Home |
| 50 | Down arrow | 78 | Alt-1 |
| 51 | PgDn | 79 | Alt-2 |
| 52 | Insert | 7A | Alt-3 |
| 53 | Delete | 7B | Alt-4 |
| 54 | Shift-F1 | 7C | Alt-5 |
| 55 | Shift-F2 | 7D | Alt-6 |
| 56 | Shift-F3 | 7E | Alt-7 |

| Value (Hex) | Key | Value (Hex) | Key |
|---|---|---|---|
| 7F | Alt-8 | 82 | Alt-Hyphen |
| 80 | Alt-9 | 83 | Alt-= |
| 81 | Alt-0 | 84 | Ctrl-PgUp |

## Keyboard Scan Codes for the Standard IBM PC Keyboard

| Value (Hex) | Key | Value (Hex) | Key |
|---|---|---|---|
| 1 | Esc | 21 | F |
| 2 | 1 | 22 | G |
| 3 | 2 | 23 | H |
| 4 | 3 | 24 | J |
| 5 | 4 | 25 | K |
| 6 | 5 | 26 | L |
| 7 | 6 | 27 | ; |
| 8 | 7 | 28 | ’ |
| 9 | 8 | 29 | ‘ |
| A | 9 | 2A | Left Shift |
| B | 0 | 2B | / |
| C | - | 2C | Z |
| D | = | 2D | X |
| E | Backspace | 2E | C |
| F | Tab | 2F | V |
| 10 | Q | 30 | B |
| 11 | W | 31 | N |
| 12 | E | 32 | M |
| 13 | R | 33 | , |
| 14 | T | 34 | . |
| 15 | Y | 35 | / |
| 16 | U | 36 | Right Shift |
| 17 | I | 37 | ° (PrtSc) |
| 18 | O | 38 | Alt |
| 19 | P | 39 | Space Bar |
| 1A | [ | 3A | Caps Lock |
| 1B | ] | 3B | F1 |
| 1C | Enter | 3C | F2 |
| 1D | Ctrl | 3D | F3 |
| 1E | A | 3E | F4 |
| 1F | S | 3F | F5 |
| 20 | D | 40 | F6 |

| Value (Hex) | Key | Value (Hex) | Key |
|---|---|---|---|
| 41 | F7 | 4B | Left Arrow |
| 42 | F8 | 4C | Blank key (on pad) |
| 43 | F9 | 4D | Right Arrow |
| 44 | F10 | 4E | + (on numeric pad) |
| 45 | Num Lock | 4F | End |
| 46 | Scroll Lock | 50 | Down Arrow |
| 47 | Home | 51 | PgDn |
| 48 | Up Arrow | 52 | Ins |
| 49 | PgUp | 53 | Del |
| 4A | - (on numeric pad) | | |

## Character Codes for the IBM PC Video Display

| Value (Hex) | Character | Value (Hex) | Character |
|---|---|---|---|
| 00 | (null) | 17 | ↨ |
| 01 | ☺ | 18 | ↑ |
| 02 | ● | 19 | ↓ |
| 03 | ♥ | 1A | → |
| 04 | ♦ | 1B | ← |
| 05 | ♣ | 1C | (cursor right) |
| 06 | ♠ | 1D | (cursor left) |
| 07 | (beep) | 1E | (cursor up) |
| 08 | (backspace) | 1F | (cursor down) |
| 09 | (tab) | 20 | (space) |
| 0A | (line feed) | 21 | ! |
| 0B | (home) | 22 | " |
| 0C | (form feed) | 23 | # |
| 0D | (carriage return) | 24 | $ |
| 0E | ♫ | 25 | % |
| 0F | ☼ | 26 | & |
| 10 | ► | 27 | ' |
| 11 | ◄ | 28 | ( |
| 12 | ↕ | 29 | ) |
| 13 | !! | 2A | * |
| 14 | ¶ | 2B | + |
| 15 | § | 2C | , |
| 16 | ▬ | 2D | - |

| Value (Hex) | Character | Value (Hex) | Character |
|---|---|---|---|
| 2E | . | 53 | S |
| 2F | / | 54 | T |
| 30 | 0 | 55 | U |
| 31 | 1 | 56 | V |
| 32 | 2 | 57 | W |
| 33 | 3 | 58 | X |
| 34 | 4 | 59 | Y |
| 35 | 5 | 5A | Z |
| 36 | 6 | 5B | [ |
| 37 | 7 | 5C | \ |
| 38 | 8 | 5D | ] |
| 39 | 9 | 5E | ^ |
| 3A | : | 5F | — |
| 3B | ; | 60 | ' |
| 3C | < | 61 | a |
| 3D | = | 62 | b |
| 3E | > | 63 | c |
| 3F | ? | 64 | d |
| 40 | @ | 65 | e |
| 41 | A | 66 | f |
| 42 | B | 67 | g |
| 43 | C | 68 | h |
| 44 | D | 69 | i |
| 45 | E | 6A | j |
| 46 | F | 6B | k |
| 47 | G | 6C | l |
| 48 | H | 6D | m |
| 49 | I | 6E | n |
| 4A | J | 6F | o |
| 4B | K | 70 | p |
| 4C | L | 71 | q |
| 4D | M | 72 | r |
| 4E | N | 73 | s |
| 4F | O | 74 | t |
| 50 | P | 75 | u |
| 51 | Q | 76 | v |
| 52 | R | 77 | w |

| Value (Hex) | Character | Value (Hex) | Character |
|---|---|---|---|
| 78 | x | 9C | £ |
| 79 | y | 9D | ¥ |
| 7A | z | 9E | Pt |
| 7B | { | 9F | ƒ |
| 7C | ¦ | A0 | á |
| 7D | } | A1 | í |
| 7E | ~ | A2 | ó |
| 7F | ⌂ | A3 | ú |
| 80 | Ç | A4 | ñ |
| 81 | ü | A5 | Ñ |
| 82 | é | A6 | ª |
| 83 | â | A7 | º |
| 84 | ä | A8 | ¿ |
| 85 | à | A9 | ⌐ |
| 86 | å | AA | ¬ |
| 87 | ç | AB | ½ |
| 88 | ê | AC | ¼ |
| 89 | ë | AD | ¡ |
| 8A | è | AE | « |
| 8B | ï | AF | » |
| 8C | î | B0 | ░ |
| 8D | ì | B1 | ▒ |
| 8E | Ä | B2 | ▓ |
| 8F | Å | B3 | │ |
| 90 | É | B4 | ┤ |
| 91 | æ | B5 | ╡ |
| 92 | Æ | B6 | ╢ |
| 93 | ô | B7 | ╖ |
| 94 | ö | B8 | ╕ |
| 95 | ò | B9 | ╣ |
| 96 | û | BA | ║ |
| 97 | ù | BB | ╗ |
| 98 | ÿ | BC | ╝ |
| 99 | Ö | BD | ╜ |
| 9A | Ü | BE | ╛ |
| 9B | ¢ | BF | ┐ |

| Value (Hex) | Character | Value (Hex) | Character |
|---|---|---|---|
| C0 | └ | E0 | α |
| C1 | ┴ | E1 | β |
| C2 | ┬ | E2 | Γ |
| C3 | ├ | E3 | π |
| C4 | ─ | E4 | Σ |
| C5 | ┼ | E5 | σ |
| C6 | ╞ | E6 | μ |
| C7 | ╟ | E7 | τ |
| C8 | ╚ | E8 | Φ |
| C9 | ╔ | E9 | Θ |
| CA | ╩ | EA | Ω |
| CB | ╦ | EB | δ |
| CC | ╠ | EC | ∞ |
| CD | ═ | ED | Ø |
| CE | ╬ | EE | ε |
| CF | ╧ | EF | ∩ |
| D0 | ╨ | F0 | ≡ |
| D1 | ╤ | F1 | ± |
| D2 | ╥ | F2 | ≥ |
| D3 | ╙ | F3 | ≤ |
| D4 | ╘ | F4 | ⌠ |
| D5 | ╒ | F5 | ⌡ |
| D6 | ╓ | F6 | ÷ |
| D7 | ╫ | F7 | ≈ |
| D8 | ╪ | F8 | ° |
| D9 | ┘ | F9 | • |
| DA | ┌ | FA | · |
| DB | █ | FB | √ |
| DC | ▄ | FC | $^{n}$ |
| DD | ▌ | FD | $^{2}$ |
| DE | ▐ | FE | ■ |
| DF | ▀ | FF | (blank 'FF') |

# APPENDIX 4

## QUICKSILVER/dBXL ENVIRONMENT VARIABLES

### DESCRIPTION:

At runtime, Quicksilver automatically creates seven public memory variables, and dBXL creates four. They provide information about the computer on which your application is running, and about parameters passed to the application from the operating system command line.

Environment variables are created only when you start up the application. They are not updated during program execution.

| dBXL | NAME | DATA TYPE | RETURNS |
|---|---|---|---|
| ✓ | XARGC | Numeric | number of command-line arguments |
| | XARG00 | Character | program name (command-line argument). |
| ✓ | XCOLOR | Logical | TRUE if the system has a color monitor |
| ✓ | XCURRDIR | Character | current default directory |
| ✓ | XDRIVE | Character | current default drive |
| | XPRINTBUSY | Logical | TRUE if the printer is "busy" |
| | XPRINTON | Logical | TRUE if the printer is on (on/off) |

In Quicksilver programs, XARG00 always contains the compiled program's name. dBXL creates XARG00 only if you specify a program name on the command line, as follows:

```
C> DBXL <program name>
```

XARG00 is the name of a program (PRG) file if you specify one.

Besides the variables listed above, dBXL and Quicksilver create up to thirty others, named XARG01 through XARG30, that contain arguments passed on the command line. This is similar to the C method of passing command-line arguments.

As of Version 1.1, dBXL does not support XPRINTON or XPRINTBUSY.

You can release environment variables just like "regular" memory variables, thereby freeing memory. To release all Quicksilver environment variables, use

RELEASE ALL LIKE X*

Of course, be sure that you have no other variable names starting with X. To use environment variables later, save them in a MEM file with the command

SAVE ALL LIKE X* TO ENVIRON

Later in the program you can reload them with

RESTORE FROM ENVIRON ADDITIVE

## RECOMMENDED USE:

**XARGC/XARGn:** The XARG environment variables let the application use data supplied on the DOS command line without a PARAMETERS statement.

XARGC is the total number of arguments passed. It lets the program process command line arguments by number without having to error-check ranges.

**Example 1**—Program menus that help novices can hinder experienced users. Command line arguments allow experienced users to bypass them. To run a credit search program CSEARCH, a novice simply types its name at the DOS prompt. A menu appears, and the user makes the desired selections. An expert user enters the program name, along with command line arguments that specify name, identification number, and address.

From the DOS prompt, the user types

```
C> CSEARCH "Robertson" "ROB33" "29 S. Main St."
```

The program first checks for the correct number of parameters. If it does not find them, it presents the menu. Otherwise, it uses the parameters to call a subroutine.

```
IF xargc = 4
  DO namefind WITH xarg01,xarg02,xarg03
ELSE
  DO menu
ENDIF
```

**Example 2**—A brief subroutine inventories Quicksilver environment variables and reports their meanings. Use it during program development and debugging to validate parameters and system attributes.

```
CLEAR
@ 6,12 SAY "Startup default disk drive is: " + xdrive
@ 7,12 SAY "Startup default directory is: "  + xcurrdir
@ 8,12 SAY "Printer was " + IIF(xprinton,"on","off") +;
```

```
          "at startup and was " + IIF(xprintbusy,"","not ") + "busy"
@ 9,12 SAY "You have a color monitor " +;
          IIF(ISCOLOR(),"","but it is inactive")
@ 10,12 SAY "Name of this program is: " + xarg00
er of command-line arguments was: " + LTRIM(STR(xargc-1))
IF xargc < 2          && XARG00 counts as one argument.
  @ 12,12 SAY "There were no command-line arguments"
ELSE
  @ 12,12 SAY "The command-line arguments were:"
  commandln = ""
  FOR argc = 1 TO (xargc - 1)
    cargc = "0" + LTRIM(STR(argc))
    cargc = "XARG" + cargc
    commandln = commandln + " " + &cargc.
    NEXT argc
    @ 15,12 SAY commandln
    ?
ENDIF
WAIT
```

**XCOLOR/XPRINTBUSY/XPRINTON:** Avoid using them. The ISCOLOR() and PRINTER() functions provide more reliable information for determining monitor type and printer,

**XCURRDIR/XDRIVE:** Use XCURRDIR and XDRIVE when you change default drives and directories and later want to return to the originals.

**Example 3**—A program stores transaction and archive data on different drives and directories. System data such as passwords and user logs remain in the default directory. At various times, the program changes defaults. Because the original values remain in XCURRDIR and XDRIVE, the program can easily return to them.

```
SET DEFAULT TO E:
SET DBF TO \transacts
DO transact
SET DEFAULT TO xdrive
SET DBF TO xcurrdir
```

## LIMITS/WARNINGS:

**XCOLOR:** XCOLOR is not the same as the ISCOLOR() function. In Quicksilver, XCOLOR is TRUE (.T.) if a color monitor is connected to the system, regardless of whether it is active (as in a system with two monitors). To test whether the active monitor is color, use the ISCOLOR() function.

In dBXL Version 1.1, XCOLOR returns the same values as ISCOLOR().

**XPRINTON/XPRINTBUSY:** The printer status variables only reflect conditions at startup. Furthermore, on some machines XPRINTON may be initialized as .F. if the printer is offline, even if it is turned on. WordTech recommends using Quicksilver's PRINTER() function to check printer status.

**dBXL:** Note that for dBXL to create environmental variables, you must include the line

```
XVARS=ON
```

in the configuration file CONFIG.XL.

See commands PUBLIC and SET PRINTER; functions ISCOLOR(), PRINTER(), and SYS(13).

# APPENDIX 5

## dBASE IV SYSTEM VARIABLE SUMMARY

**_alignment = "<left/center/right>"**

*Default:* LEFT

*Example:* ALIGNMENT = "LEFT"

Controls text alignment when _WRAP is true (.T.).

**_box = <.t./.f.>**

*Default:* .T.

*Example:* _BOX = .t.

When true (.T.), prints the box specified with the DEFINE BOX command.

**_indent = <expN>**

*Range:* 0-254

*Default:* 0

*Example:* _indent = 20

Indents text <expN> spaces when _WRAP is true (.T.). You can set the indent for each ? command. (_INDENT + _LMARGIN) may not exceed the _RMARGIN setting. _INDENT is also added to the _PLOFFSET setting.

**_lmargin = <expN>**

*Range:* 0-254

*Default:* 0

*Example:* _lmargin = 30

Sets the left margin when _WRAP is true (.T.). The left margin is the column where unindented text begins printing. _LMARGIN is added to the page left offset (_PLOFFSET).

**_padvance = "<formfeed/linefeeds"**

*Default:* "FORMFEED"

*Example:* _padvance = "FORMFEED"

Specifies how the printer advances paper when an EJECT is issued or when a report reaches the maximum page length (_PLENGTH). FORMFEED advances the paper one page as defined by the printer's internal setting. In a PRINTJOB, the LINEFEEDS option subtracts _PLINENO from _PLENGTH to determine the number of lines to advance to the top of the next form. EJECT outside a printjob advances the paper by calculating the current line number and subtracting it from _PLENGTH as follows: (_PLENGTH - MOD(PROW(),_PLENGTH)).

**_pageno = <expN>**

*Range:* 1-32,767

*Default:* 1

*Example:* _pageno = 9 && Set page number to 9.

Returns the current page number, or assigns a new one. Use it to print page numbers during printjobs. _PAGENO increases by 1 when a page ejects. When setting _PAGENO, be sure it falls between the current beginning page (_PBPAGE) and ending page (_PEPAGE); otherwise, nothing will print.

**_pbpage = <expN>**

*Range:* 1-32,767

*Default:* 1

*Example:* _pbpage = 5

Determines the beginning page for a printjob. May not exceed the ending page (_PEPAGE). No printing occurs if _PAGENO is less than _PBPAGE; however, non-printing pages scroll internally. Printing begins with _PAGENO equal to _PBPAGE.

**_pcolno = <expN>**

*Range:* 0 to 255 when _WRAP is false (.F.), or 0 to _RMARGIN when _WRAP is true (.T.).

*Example:* _pcolno = 34 && Set print column to 34.

Moves the printhead to column <expN>, or returns the current column position. Works only in printjobs. The printer need not be on.

**_pcopies = <expN>**

*Default:* 1

*Range:* 1-32,767

*Example:* _pcopies = 10

Determines how many copies to print in a printjob. Use it before the PRINTJOB command.

**_pdriver = "<printer driver name>"**

*Default:* Assigned during installation or by PDRIVER in CONFIG.DB.

*Example:* _pdriver = "LX80" && Install Epson LX-80 printer.

Activates the specified printer driver (extension PR2), or returns the current driver. _PDRIVER looks in the current directory on the current drive unless you specify otherwise.

**_pecode = <expC>**

*Range:* Limited to 255 bytes.

*Default:* Null

*Example:* _pecode = "{27}E" && Epson emphasized mode.

Sends a string of printer control codes upon ENDPRINT. Use _PECODE to change print characteristics or reset them when PRINTJOB ends. See the command ??? for a list of control code specifiers. You must have the correct printer driver installed with _PDRIVER.

**_peject = "<before/after/both/none>"**

*Default:* NONE

*Example:* _peject = "BEFORE"

Determines when a page ejects relative to a PRINTJOB. BEFORE ejects before printing the first page. AFTER ejects after printing the last page. BOTH ejects before and after. NONE omits the page eject.

**_pepage = <expN>**

*Range:* 1-32,767

*Default:* 32,767

*Example:* _pepage = 8

Determines the ending page for a PRINTJOB. May not be less than the beginning page (_PBPAGE). No printing occurs if _PAGENO is greater than _PEPAGE.

**_pform = "<print form filename>"**
*Default:* Null

*Example:* _PFORM = "REPORT"

Activates a print form file. When you create a report with the report generator (CREATE/MODIFY REPORT), you can optionally save the system variable settings in a print form file. You can then use the file with other reports created externally. Print form files have a default extension of PRF.

**_plength = <expN>**
*Range:* 1 to 32,767

*Default:* 66

*Example:* _plength = 50 && Set page length of 50

Changes the page length setting, or returns its value. The page length is the total number of lines per page, including headers and footers.

**_plineno = <expN>**
*Range:* 0 to (_plength -1)

*Default:* 0

*Example:* _plineno = 10 && Set line number to 10

Sets the printer line number, or returns its value. Stays in effect regardless of whether the printer is on or off.

**_ploffset = <expN>**
*Range:* 0 to 254

*Default:* 0

*Example:* _ploffset = 5

Offset from the left edge of the paper. <expN> is the number of columns to offset. _LMARGIN is relative to _PLOFFSET. _PLOFFSET is equivalent to the SET MARGIN command.

**_ppitch = " /default/elite/pica"**
*Default:* "DEFAULT"

*Example:* _ppitch = "ELITE"

Changes the printer pitch. _PPITCH depends on the installation of the correct printer driver with _PDRIVER. If you change the pitch with a control code or with a printer DIP switch, _PPITCH may not match the actual output until you issue another _PPITCH statement.

**_pquality = <.t./.f.>**

*Default:* .F.

*Example:* _pquality = .t.

Toggles draft or letter quality printer output. _PQUALITY depends on the installation of the correct printer driver with _PDRIVER. If you change the quality with a control code or with a printer DIP switch, _PQUALITY may not match the actual output until you issue another _PQUALITY statement.

**_pscode = <expC>**

*Range:* Limited to 255 bytes

*Default:* Null

*Example:* _pscode = "{ESC}4" && Select Epson italic mode.

Specifies the printer setup codes issued when the PRINTJOB command executes. You can reset the printer at the end of a printjob with _PECODE.

**_pspacing = <1/2/3>**

*Default:* 1

*Example:* _pspacing = 2

Controls line spacing for screen, printer, and disk file output.

**_pwait = <.t./.f.>**

*Default:* .F.

*Example:* _pwait = .t.

Pauses printing after each page when true (.T.). This lets you use sheet fed paper. Pauses occur with each EJECT, or when the current line number reaches the page length (_PLENGTH). For printjobs, use _PWAIT before the PRINTJOB command.

**_rmargin = <expN>**

*Range:* 1 to 255

*Default:* 80

*Example:* _rmargin = 60

Sets the right margin. Must exceed (_LMARGIN + _INDENT). Works only when _WRAP = .T.

**_tabs = [<1,N2,N3,...>]**

*Default:* Null

*Example:* _tabs = "10,25,30"

Sets tab stops in the program/memo editor. The numbers N1, N2, N3... must be in ascending order.

**_wrap = <.t./.f.>**

*Default:* .F.

*Example:* _wrap = .t.

Toggles word wrapping on and off. When true, wraps ?/?? output between _LMARGIN and _RMARGIN. Breaks lines between words or numbers.

# APPENDIX 6

## COMMANDS AND FUNCTIONS OMITTED FROM THIS EDITION

### CLIPPER

EXTEND system assembly language interface functions

EXTEND system C interface functions

Functions added or documented too late to include:

BIN2I()
BIN2L()
BIN2W()
I2BIN()
L2BIN()

EXTEND.LIB functions without direct equivalents in other systems:

ACCEPTAT()
CURRENCY()
DAYS()
DIM2()
DUP_CHK()
ELAPTIME()
LENNUM()
SECS()
STRZERO()
TSTRING()
VALIDTIME()

### dBASE IV

SQL commands

### dBXL/QUICKSILVER DIAMOND RELEASE (1.2)

NetworkerPlus multiuser/multitasking/messaging commands and functions:

DIALOG
EXECUTE()
FLAG()
MSGQUEUE()
NEXECUTE
NFLAG

NHALT
NRECSCR
NRESET
NSENDMSG
NSENDTSK
NSET MSGBELL
NSET MSGQUEUE
NSET TASKQUEUE
NSET SNOOP
NSLEEP
NWHO
NWHOAMI
ON NETERROR
RECEIVE()
RRECEIVE
SEND MESSAGE
SEND SCREEN
SEND TASK
SENSERANGE
SET FLAG
SET MSGBELL
SET MSGQUEUE
SET MSGWIN
SET SENSERANGE
SET SNOOP ON
SET TASKQUE
USERNAME()
USERCOUNT()
WHOHASIT()
WHOAMI()
WHOSENTIT()

# dBASE LANGUAGE GLOSSARY

**APPLICATION**—A group of integrated programs and database files designed to do a particular job, such as accounting, point of sale, or client management.

**COMMAND**—A statement, either in a program or issued from a prompt, that initiates an action.

**COMPILER**—A program that translates programs from a form understandable by humans into one executable by computers. For maximum efficiency, a compiler translates an entire program in advance of execution. Examples of compiled languages are C, COBOL, and dBASE (using Clipper, dBASE IV, or Quicksilver).

Strictly speaking, compilers produce "machine code" which a computer can execute directly. Through popular usage, "compiler" also refers to programs that produce intermediate code requiring further translation at runtime.

See also INTERPRETER.

**CONDITION**—An optional command clause that restricts the processing of records.

The two conditional clauses are:

```
WHILE <expL>
FOR <expL>
```

WHILE conditions process records consecutively, within the active scope, until the logical expression <expL> becomes false. WHILE terminates even if other non-consecutive records satisfy <expL>.

FOR conditions evaluate all records within the active scope, ignoring those that do not satisfy <expL>. Processing continues until the end-of-file.

<expL> is sometimes called <condition>.

**COORDINATES**—The paired numbers representing points on the screen or on a printed report. The coordinates are R and C, where R is a vertical *row* position and C is a horizontal *column* position (left to right). Addressable rows on standard PC screens range from 0 (top) to 24 (bottom). Columns range from 0 (far left) to 79 (far right). In printed reports, the ranges are limited to the actual page size. The R and C coordinates are designated as <coord>.

**DATABASE FILE**—A table containing information labeled by field name and record number. dBASE data files have the extension DBF. A collection of database files is called a *database*.

See also FIELD and RECORD.

**FIELD**—A storage space in a database file for a single data item. The structure defines each field's size and type. Sequential sets of fields are called *records*.

Fields are sometimes called *columns*.

See also RECORD.

**FUNCTION**—A command-like keyword that evaluates a number, string, or logical condition, and returns a value in its place. Functions consist of a name followed by parentheses. The parentheses may contain arguments.

Functions are evaluated like expressions. You may use one anywhere a constant may appear, as long as it returns the proper data type.

In Clipper, you can begin a command line with a function. This lets you execute functions much like commands, a benefit most noticeable with user defined functions.

See also USER DEFINED FUNCTION.

**INDEX**—A table of pointers that orders a database file according to a key expression. When the index is activated, the database file appears in the defined order, although it is not reordered physically as in a SORT. Index extensions vary:

*Clipper:* NTX (or NDX when you link NDX.OBJ)

*dBASE III PLUS, dBXL, and Quicksilver:* NDX

*dBASE IV:* NDX (or MDX for multiple index files)

*FoxBASE+:* IDX

See also command INDEX.

**INTERPRETER**—A program that translates programs from a form understandable by humans into one executable by computers. An interpreter translates and executes programs one line at a time. The most popular interpreter is the Microsoft (or GW) BASIC that comes with most PC's. Examples of dBASE interpreters include dBASE III PLUS, dBXL, and FoxBASE+.

See also COMPILER.

**KEYWORD**—A function, command, or command option. Keywords are not case-sensitive. They may be abbreviated to four characters.

dBASE does not generally reserve keywords, but their use in other contexts, such as in memory variable names, is confusing and therefore inadvisable. Clipper (Summer '87 version) does reserve words that confuse either the compiler or linker when used out of context. See Appendix 1 for a list.

See also COMMAND and FUNCTION; Appendix 1: Clipper Summer '87 Reserved Words.

**LINKER**—A program that creates an executable program (EXE extension), letting you specify object modules (OBJ), runtime libraries (LIB), and memory allocation. Linkers include Microsoft LINK, Borland's TLINK, and Phoenix Technologies' PLINK86.

Linkers are also called *linkage (link) editors.*

**MACRO**—In dBASE, the use of a memory variable's value as if it had been typed directly. This requires the & operator. For example, you could store the scope "NEXT 10" in memory variable SEARCH, then use it in a command such as

```
LIST &SEARCH
```

In general, a "macro" is a series of commands that can be executed with a single reference. For example, a keyboard macro program assigns a series of commands to a single key.

**MEMORY VARIABLE**—A temporary holding place for data. Memory variables are created explicitly by the commands PUBLIC, PRIVATE, and STORE, and by the equal sign operator. Other commands, such as ACCEPT,

INPUT, and SUM, create them automatically to hold results. The AUTOMEM feature in dBXL and Quicksilver also creates memory variables.

A memory variable takes on the data type of the value stored in it. Types include logical, character, date, and numeric. FoxBASE+ and Clipper also have array and screen data types. There is no memo data type for variables.

Memory variables are accessible in the program in which they are given a value, and in all subprograms it calls.

PRIVATE specifically limits the scope of memory variables to the current program and its subprograms. This prevents name conflicts between subprograms (particularly library programs) and their callers.

PUBLIC makes memory variables accessible throughout an application unless a PRIVATE declaration masks them in a subprogram. See also the commands PRIVATE, PUBLIC, RELEASE, and STORE.

**PROGRAM**—A list of commands that initiates a series of actions. The commands are stored in an ASCII text file, and they execute sequentially. Programs may be interpreted or compiled.

Uncompiled dBASE programs generally have a PRG extension, the default. If you use a different extension, you must specify it explicitly when issuing the DO <program name> command.

Groups of related programs form an application.

See also COMPILER and INTERPRETER.

**RECORD**—A sequential grouping of fields in a database file. APPENDing a record adds a complete set of fields to the file and increases the record counter by one.

Records are sometimes called *rows*.

See also FIELD.

**RECORD POINTER**—A mechanism that indicates the current record in an open database file. The pointer is not visible. Instead, you know where it is from the current record number. You can access the current record's fields by name.

Pointers in multiple open files are independent, although you can link them using the SET RELATION command. When no relation is set, moving the pointer in an open file does not affect other pointers.

When you open a database file, the pointer starts at record 1. If you open a database file as an index, the pointer starts at the record with the lowest key value.

If the pointer is at the first record, SKIP -1 moves it to the beginning-of-file (BOF). At BOF, the BOF() function evaluates TRUE (.T.). The RECNO() function returns the first record number. In an unindexed file, that number is always 1. In an indexed file, it is arbitrary because of the ordering by key values rather than record numbers.

When the pointer is at the end-of-file, the EOF() function evaluates TRUE (.T.). RECNO() returns a value one greater than the last record number. If a file has no records, EOF() and BOF() are TRUE (.T.), and RECNO() returns 1.

Commands such as APPEND, GOTO, LIST, and SKIP move the pointer.

**SCOPE**—A clause you can add to many commands to specify a range of records to process. Commands that allow scopes include AVERAGE, COPY, DELETE, DISPLAY, LIST, RECALL, SORT, and SUM.

Scopes are:

ALL
NEXT <expN>
RECORD <expN>
REST*

(*REST is not available in Clipper versions before Summer '87. Substitute the condition WHILE .T.)

ALL specifies all records. NEXT <expN> counts records starting with the current one to the End of File. RECORD <expN> specifies a particlar record. REST means all records from the current one to the end-of-file.

Scopes usually ignore records hidden by SET DELETED ON and SET FILTER TO. However, NEXT <expN> always includes the current record, even if it is hidden. If, for example, the record pointer rests at a hidden record, LIST NEXT 5 shows the current record, then the NEXT four visible records, if any.

RECORD <expN> also accesses hidden records by moving directly to the specified record number.

*Note:* In dBASE IV NEXT and RECORD <expN> ignore all records hidden by SET FILTER

ALL and REST move the record pointer consecutively through the file, stopping at the End of File.

**TAG**—The name of an index within a dBASE IV multiple index file.

**WORK AREA**—A logical division of the computer's memory into independent zones. Each one can hold an open database file and its related index files. Simultaneous open files reside in separate areas.

10 is the current standard for the number of work areas. The SELECT command can reference areas by number, letter (A-J), or ALIAS. For example, to choose area 2 containing the open file ACCOUNTS, you could issue any of the following commands:

```
SELECT 2
SELECT B
SELECT accounts
```

Work area 1 is the default. The open database file in the current area is called the *active database.*

To access data in other areas, you must specify field names using the work area letter (A-J) or alias name in the form LETTER->FIELDNAME or ALIAS->FIELDNAME.

Most commands and functions affect only the active file. For example, SKIP moves its pointer forward one record. It does not affect any other file unless you first set a RELATION. Some commands have options for processing data in unselected work areas.

**USER DEFINED FUNCTION (UDF)**—A function written by the application programmer for use in Clipper, dBASE IV, dBXL, FoxBASE+, or Quicksilver. Clipper and Quicksilver allow UDFs written in the dBASE language, C, and assembly language. FoxBASE+, dBASE IV, and dBXL allow only dBASE language UDFs. You can use UDFs just about anywhere you can use an internal function.

See also command FUNCTION.

# Reader Comments
# The dBASE® Handbook

This book has been edited, the edited material reviewed, and the program matter tested and checked for accuracy; but bugs find their way into books as well as software. Please take a few minutes and tell us if you have found any errors, and give us your general comments regarding the quality of this book. Your time and attention will help us improve this and future products.

Did you find any mistakes? (If so, where?)________________________________

______________________________________________________________

______________________________________________________________

Is this book complete? (If not, what should be added?)____________________

______________________________________________________________

______________________________________________________________

What do you like about this book?____________________________________

______________________________________________________________

______________________________________________________________

What do you not like about this book?_________________________________

______________________________________________________________

______________________________________________________________

What other books would you like to see developed?______________________

______________________________________________________________

______________________________________________________________

Other comments:_________________________________________________

______________________________________________________________

______________________________________________________________

If you would like to be notified of new editions of this book and/or other books that may be of interest to you, please complete the following:

Name:__________________________________________________________

Address:________________________________________________________

City/State/Zip:___________________________________________________

Mail to:

Microtrend™ Books
Slawson Communications, Inc.
165 Vallecitos de Oro
San Marcos, CA 92069-1436